Rethinking
the Penal State

In this book based on his 2024 Adorno Lectures, Loïc Wacquant combines social theory, comparative history, and structural ethnography to probe criminal punishment as a core function of the state. Extending Pierre Bourdieu's signal concepts of bureaucratic field and symbolic power, Wacquant resolves the opposition between rationalist theories of penality running from Jeremy Bentham to Karl Marx and emotionalist theories descending from Immanuel Kant to Émile Durkheim to capture the constitutive *duality of punishment*, at once material and symbolic, an instrument of class control and a means of communicating values, endlessly oscillating between reformation and retribution.

By rolling out the police, court, prison, and their bureaucratic tentacles, the penal state curates crime, contains moral disorders, manages urban marginality, and effectively draws the boundaries of citizenship. Its day-to-day deployment also signals sovereignty and serves to manufacture political legitimacy in the eyes of the general population. But the penal Leviathan is a *bifurcated state* which captures nearly exclusively dispossessed and dishonored categories by targeting their tainted neighborhoods: it is everywhere a class-splitting and a race-making institution based on the stubborn differentiation of dignified "paper penality" and degrading "street penality." The structural osmosis between districts of urban dereliction and the carceral institution on both sides of the Atlantic is such that we cannot understand the penal state without understanding the dual city and vice versa.

To flesh out penal power as strategic action, Wacquant takes us deep inside a criminal court in California where we discover that the prosecutor who negotiates guilty pleas is the human spear of the state. In his daily tussles with defense attorneys and the sentencing judge, he calibrates and drives the concrete infliction of physical and psychic force upon bodies deemed out of order. Getting inside the machinery of criminal justice shows that punishment must be positioned at the epicenter of the political sociology of statecraft, group-making, and place-making in the metropolis as well as brought to the forefront of civic debate, rather than abandoned to the periodic panic-peddling of electoral politics. Instead of chasing the chimera of abolition, we should muster the intellectual resources needed to reclaim the vexed duality of "law and order" for a progressive politics. This requires articulating a *radical penal minimalism* suited to reconciling punishment and democratic citizenship.

Elegantly formulated and crisply argued, this book will be of interest to social scientists, criminologists, and jurists as well as to scholars across the disciplines looking for novel ways to envisage the state, the law, punishment, the city, and inequality.

Loïc Wacquant is Professor of Sociology at the University of California, Berkeley, and Researcher at the Centre Européen de Sociologie et de Science Politique, Paris. His books are translated into twenty languages and include *The Invention of the "Underclass"* (2022), *Bourdieu in the City* (2023), and *Racial Domination* (2024), all published by Polity.

RETHINKING
THE PENAL STATE

Loïc Wacquant

polity

First published in 2026 by Polity Press Ltd.

Polity Press Ltd.
65 Bridge Street
Cambridge CB2 1UR, UK

Polity Press Ltd.
111 River Street
Hoboken, NJ 07030, USA

ISBN-13: 978-1-5095-7303-5
ISBN-13: 978-1-5095-7304-2 (pb)

A catalogue record for this book is available from the British Library.

Library of Congress Control Number: 2025947890

Typeset in 10.5 on 12pt Plantin MT Pro
by Cheshire Typesetting Ltd, Cuddington, Cheshire
Printed and bound in Great Britain by Ashford Colour Ltd

Cover image: The 2006 carceral riots of Franco de Rocha
Photo © Paulo Leibert/Agência Estado
Epigraph from Michel Foucault, *La Société punitive* (1974) © EHESS/Seuil/Gallimard, 2013 and 2023. Used with permission.

The publisher has used its best endeavours to ensure that the URLs for external websites referred to in this book are correct and active at the time of going to press. However, the publisher has no responsibility for the websites and can make no guarantee that a site will remain live or that the content is or will remain appropriate.

Every effort has been made to trace all copyright holders, but if any have been overlooked the publisher will be pleased to include any necessary credits in any subsequent reprint or edition.

For further information on Polity, visit our website:
politybooks.com

À mes nièces et mes neveux,
vifs et aimants,
en leur souhaitant une belle vie

Contents

Contents

Contents

Tables, Figures and Photos

Tables

Figures

Photos

About the Cover Image

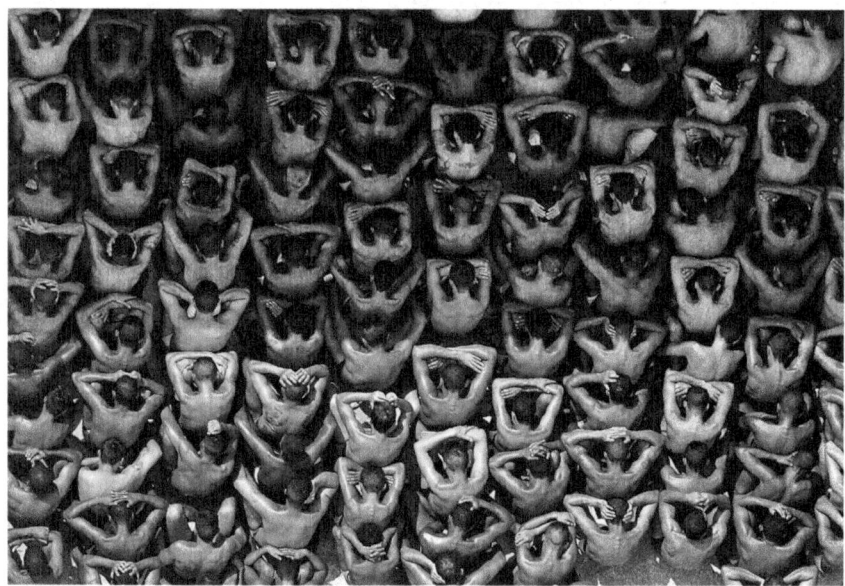

Packed inmates stripped to their underwear sit prostrate in the prison yard under the fierce watch of the military "shock units" called in to put down the carceral riot at Franco de Rocha, Greater São Paulo, in May of 2006. The riot was one in a wave of coordinated attacks around the state orchestrated by the criminal mega-gang Primeiro Comando da Capital (PCC) against law-enforcement institutions in retaliation for the transfer of their leaders to high-security penitentiaries and to demonstrate their de facto *control of penal facilities. The attacks included coordinated revolts in 83 prisons, with*

widespread destruction and hostage-taking, the targeted killings of police, and the firebombing of city buses and public buildings as well as hundreds of assaults on police stations, courts, fire departments, hospitals, schools, and banks, causing some 170 deaths and generating a climate of chaos and terror for five days. According to human rights agencies, over 500 people, most of them poor young men of color from the urban periphery, were later killed in police retaliation, upwards of 100 victims of summary executions. (For an analysis of the rise of the PCC and its role in organizing this direct challenge to the penal state, read Bruno Paes Manso and Camila Nunes Dias, A Guerra. A Ascensão do PCC e o Mundo do Crime no Brasil, São Paulo, Todavia, 2018).

This episode captures both the brutal power of the penal state and direct defiance of the same, triggering the seemingly uncontrolled but actually targeted resort to force, legitimate or not. It ties together penality, marginality, and dangerosity. And it reminds us of what citizens in advanced societies take for granted: that violence is under control, the streets are peaceful and one can go about one's business without fearing for life and limb, and that the Leviathan acts in accordance with legal standards and rules. Except in the stigmatized neighborhoods of relegation of the postindustrial metropolis.

© *Photo by Paulo Leibert/Agência Estado.*

[Sociology] can teach us to treat historical institutions – whatever they may be – with respect, but without fetishism, by making us aware of what is both necessary and provisional in them, their force of resistance and their infinite variability.

—Émile Durkheim, *Les Règles de la méthode sociologique* (1895)

A Genealogical Sketch

A brief and selective genealogy of this book is in order for readers interested in its origins and arc. Writing a tome on the penal state in 2024–5 is closing an analytic circle I began tracing back in 1996 when I first broached the concept in an article entitled "De l'État charitable à l'État pénal. Notes sur le traitement politique de la misère en Amérique" ("From charitable state to penal state: notes on the political treatment of poverty in America"). Viewing this question through European lenses, it was self-evident to me that the shift in poverty policy from support to discipline during the 1990s was a matter of the Leviathan. The article was published in an obscure journal, *Regards sociologiques*, but was soon translated into German, Italian, and Portuguese, reprinted in an anthology appropriately titled *Der Leviathan in unserer Zeit*, and then followed by a series of op-eds on the topic published in France, Germany, Spain, and Brazil. This was an early sign that the topic was one that could grab an audience and cross disciplinary boundaries as well as national borders. There was more to the analytic story than a rehash of US exceptionalism propelled by the racialized moral panic of the "underclass."

In 1998, I edited a thematic issue of *Actes de la recherche en sciences sociales* (the journal founded and directed by Pierre Bourdieu) entitled "From Social State to Penal State" with invited contributions from Nils Christie, the trio of Katherine Beckett, Bruce Western and a juvenile David Harding, David Garland and Dario Melossi – not a bad casting in hindsight. Again, Scandinavia, the US, the UK, Italy, and France: an international venture was needed to not get trapped by one or another national doxa on punishment. I published two articles in this issue: "L'ascension de l'État pénal en Amérique" and "La tentation pénale en Europe."

This early work has two existential roots. The first is French: when I was a student in economics at École des HEC and sociology at the University of Paris, Nanterre, in the early 1980s, I taught a weekly class at the Fleury-Mérogis prison south of Paris under the aegis of GENEPI (a national student group for prison education). I had somehow picked up and read with fascination the French translation of a book by the psychotherapist Dennie Briggs entitled *Fermer les prisons* (the English original is *In Place of Prison: A Report on California's New Correctional Alternatives*, 1975), an early call for decarceration and reparation that seemed to me both sensible, obvious, and urgent. This is what got me interested in teaching behind bars.

2

The second root is American, or Chicagoan to be more precise: Ashante, my ring buddy and sparring partner from my days in the Woodlawn boxing gym on the city's South Side (1988–91), had spent a decade in prison when I met him and he became my key informant on carceral society and culture. After the gym closed, he found himself sucked back into the street economy and I found myself sucked into trying to extricate him from the iron clutches of the penal state – I would periodically bail him out of jail and pay for his attorney to minimize his prison time. It was in that boxing gym that the hypothesis that urban marginality and penality are joined at the hip incubated. It was during the following decade scuffling with the carceral dragon from the outside that the idea of a shift from welfare to prisonfare morphed from hunch to thesis.

In 1999, I published *Les Prisons de la misère* (appropriately dedicated to Ashante) which introduced the notion of *État pénal* into the French public debate and the circles of prison activists (Observatoire International des Prisons, Ban public, Ligue des Droits de l'Homme, etc.). The book takes its readers on a whirlwind tour of the global diffusion of "zero tolerance" policing and assorted law-and-order nostrums made in the USA, encapsulated by the absurdist slogan "prison works." That diffusion, tristely, explains the international success of the book which was soon translated in twenty languages. I had thought of my studies of punishment as a temporary detour in my scientific trajectory; I was proven wrong. A flood of invitations to write and speak about the penal state kept me going. I visited and lectured in jails and prisons on three continents. Jump to 2009: *Punishing the Poor* charts the growth and deployment of America's gargantuan punishment apparatus and theorizes penalization as a component of neoliberal statecraft. I was struck, at the time, that scholars of neoliberalism as a global revolution from above had entirely missed the carceral boom that everywhere accompanied economic deregulation and social welfare retrenchment.

Two more milestones were what Robert Merton calls "oral publications." In 2006, I co-organized with Bruce Western a mini-conference on "Probing the penal state" at Berkeley with an illustrious cast of established scholars and a rambunctious phalanx of doctoral researchers, at which I presented rough notes on "What Is the Penal State and Why It Matters." It was premature; I still had not figured out the beast. I knew I needed a robust theory of the state to start from, but I did not have one at hand. In 2009, I gave the British Journal of Sociology Lecture under the title "Bringing the Penal State Back In." To my eternal regret, I missed the rigid deadline set by the journal to deliver my paper for publication, which was to be discussed by Nicola Lacey, David Garland, and Saskia Sassen (to whom I present my late apologies). For that lecture, I had assembled a wealth of historical materials on the invention of the penal prison in early modern Europe that, duly reworked, have found their way into chapter 2 of the present book. My hunch then and now was that we can understand penality in the late twentieth century by returning to the late sixteenth century when the workhouse was devised and deployed. Transformations of capitalism, urban marginality, and penality walk hand in hand, although not through some magic "correspondence," but through struggles internal and external to the Leviathan. So I have been on the tracks of the penal state for a good long while, an institution that is both familiar and still intimidating after all these years.

The story could have stopped there. But, in 2013, I taught an undergraduate seminar SOC 190: "Punishment and Confinement in Modern Society," which included a class field project called Penoak "designed to draw a portrait of Penal Oakland, that is, producing data on the police, courts, jail, and probation/parole in the city in contrast to social, educational, medical, and housing services to discern how punishment concretely impinges on urban society" (as the description on the syllabus put it). It was an exercise in applied sociology, a straightforward rolling out of the model developed in *Punishing the Poor*. Long story short, that project was a total flop but it pointed me toward the personification of the penal state in the prosecutor and the public defender duking it out daily in the county courthouse under the stern gaze of the judge.

So, in March of 2014, I resolved to confront abstract theory with concrete history-in-the-making by turning to the field to reconstruct

3

my understanding of the penal state from the ground up. Pivoting to ethnography created a salutary cultural shock and a mental maelstrom. To sum up: nothing was like what I expected, nothing was like what I was reading on the topic. So I kept burrowing my way into the local judicial scene for some three years, producing mounds of luxuriant empirical materials on "The Social Life of the County Criminal Court," a tiny portion of which found its way into chapter 3. The court and its wings turned out to be the nuclear reactor of the penal state, or, to borrow a favorite expression of judges, "where the sausage is made."

Theory, history, ethnography: the present book allows me to indulge in my three intellectual loves. These three perspectives on penality are animated by the conviction that each needs and benefits from the others. Theory guides the reading of history and the implementation of ethnography. History defamiliarizes the ethnographic present and opens wide the theoretical lens. Ethnography suggests new theoretical lines and supplies nourishment for querying history. When I was invited to give the 2024 Adorno Lectures, I knew immediately what they would be about and how they would unfold.

Overture

On Punishment, the State and Citizenship

"There is no crueler tyranny than that which is exercised in the shadow of the law and with the colors of justice."
Montesquieu, *Considérations sur les causes de la grandeur des romains et de leur décadence* (1734)

In this book, based on the three Adorno Lectures I delivered in Frankfurt in November of 2024, I elaborate and deploy the concept of penal state by drawing in turn on social theory, comparative history, and structural ethnography. I construct an abstract notion inspired by Pierre Bourdieu's theory of fields and symbolic power and I argue for its centrality in the study of citizenship, public policy, and urban inequality in the twenty-first century.[1] I am particularly interested in capturing how the building of the neoliberal Leviathan, with its enlarged and aggressive punishment apparatus, impacts the formation and fate of the "precariat" – the precarious fractions of the postindustrial proletariat entrapped in the neighborhoods of relegation of the dualizing metropolis which are its privileged target. But I contend that the relevance of penality as core state capacity goes far beyond the populations processed by the police, courts, and prison: it stamps physical, social, and symbolic space at large.

In advanced society, penal power works to define core social categories, starting with the citizen as anchor of the democratic nation-state. Invading the underbelly of the city, it contains disorders and

[1] See, in particular, Pierre Bourdieu, *Langage et pouvoir symbolique* (2001), and idem, *Microcosmes. Théorie des champs* (2022b).

validates the exclusion of its most marginal elements. Deployed in the criminal court, it incarnates itself in the daily work of organizational creatures – prosecutor, defense attorney, judge – tasked with tagging bodies out of order and thereby contains danger and pollution. At any one moment, penal power is both the product, the instrument, and the stake of social struggles over the definition and the delivery of this most elusive yet cherished virtue and public good that is "justice."[2]

The criminal as anti-citizen

This is because *the criminal and the citizen are co-constructed* in materiality and discourse, starting with the law as an ensemble of realized categories. Historians have documented that, by defining the offender and how to treat him, the state defines the citizen by way of contraposition. Thus, in his sweeping account of changes in penal legislation in England between 1830 and 1914, *Reconstructing the Criminal* (1994), Martin Joel Wiener demonstrates how the reevaluation of the criminal in English law and culture remade the figure of the full-fledged member of the national community and how the new vision of the citizen, in turn, shaped that of the felon.[3] In *Policing Paris: The Origins of Modern Immigration Control between the Wars* (2006), Clifford Rosenberg shows that the Paris and later national police of France were transformed during the interwar years in reaction to an obsessive concern over immigrant criminality and possible Bolshevik terrorist acts. The police became the first institution to enforce distinctions of citizenship and national origins.[4] This is not a European peculiarity: the same notion is propounded by historians of crime, punishment, and politics in Latin America, such as Thomas Holloway in *Policing Rio de Janeiro* (1993), Robert M. Buffington in *Criminal and Citizen in Modern Mexico* (2000), and Pablo Picatto in *City of Suspects: Crime in Mexico City, 1900–1931* (2001).[5]

[2] An excellent anthology of classical and contemporary texts is Magali Bessone (ed.), *La Justice* (2000).

[3] Martin Joel Wiener, *Reconstructing the Criminal: Culture, Law, and Policy in England, 1830–1914* (1994).

[4] Clifford D. Rosenberg, *Policing Paris: The Origins of Modern Immigration Control between the Wars* (2006).

[5] Thomas Holloway, *Policing Rio de Janeiro: Repression and Resistance in a Nineteenth-Century City* (1993); Robert M. Buffington, *Criminal and Citizen in Modern Mexico* (2000); Pablo Picatto, *City of Suspects: Crime in Mexico City, 1900–1931* (2001). The

In *Punishment and Political Order*, the political theorist Keally McBride argues convincingly that "punishment is where the ideals of a polity come to be dramatically situated in close proximity with the realities of governance" and that criminal sanctions serve to articulate "liberal principles such as responsibility and personhood."[6] But she stops short of making the link with citizenship as a central institution of liberal modernity. Citizenship is not just a legal status carrying a bundle of rights and obligations setting a plane of equality; it is also a source of identity, an anchor of social ties, and a basis for formal belonging to a political community. I submit that, in advanced society, the citizen is defined by two boundaries, an *external* boundary governed by nationality statutes that differentiates her from the foreigner, and an *internal* boundary drawn by criminal law and social welfare regulations that separates her from persons deemed to have violated the civic covenant and its moral rules by dint of their deviant conduct and whose membership has therefore been amputated, suspended, or terminated.[7]

A major surprise upon scouring the literature on citizenship is the absence of sustained consideration of the *truncated civic status of criminal defendants and convicts*. Two major anthologies on the topic contain no discussion of the question despite its recurrence in advanced societies.[8] There exists a vast body of publications on second-tier citizenship and on the "empty promise" of equality among citizens, that is, the gap between ideal and real standards, but the main characters in that story are women and ethnic-national minorities. In her influential tome on *Semi-Citizenship in Democratic Politics*, the political scientist Elizabeth Cohen forges the concept to illumine the condition of persons who hold some, but not all, of the rights constitutive

distinction between citizen and criminal has long been central across the continent, as documented by Ricardo D. Salvatore et al., *Crime and Punishment in Latin America: Law and Society since Late Colonial Times* (2001). It is expressed nowadays in the ordinary opposition between *gente* and *marginais* in Brazil and *gente* and *pibes chorros* in Argentina.

[6] Keally McBride, *Punishment and Political Order* (2007), pp. 10 and 13.

[7] On the external boundary, the classic work is Rogers Brubaker, *Citizenship and Nationhood in France and Germany* (1992). The internal boundary is spanned by Kaaryn S. Gustafson, *Cheating Welfare: Public Assistance and the Criminalization of Poverty* (2011); Amy E. Lerman and Vesla M. Weaver, *Arresting Citizenship: The Democratic Consequences of American Crime Control* (2014); and Vincent Dubois, *Contrôler les assistés. Genèses et usages d'un mot d'ordre* (2021).

[8] Sian Lazar (ed.), *The Anthropology of Citizenship: A Reader* (2013); Ayelet Shachar et al. (eds.), *The Oxford Handbook of Citizenship* (2017).

of a democratic citizenry. Migrants, children, and disabled persons are the three main categories that are "neither full citizens nor non-citizens." Cohen presents a dizzying array of historical examples, but offenders do not figure among them. The police, criminal court, jail, and prison appear nowhere in her book.[9] Similarly, in her recent panoramic dissection of "Citizenship Studies: Policy Causes and Consequences" published in *Annual Review of Political Science*, Sara Wallace Goodman omits penal institutions and policies altogether.[10]

Theoretical studies of citizenship tackle criminal conviction as an obstacle to political participation and a bar to naturalization,[11] never as *negative bureaucratic and symbolic capital* with detrimental ramifications across the gamut of institutions and social relations as well as marker of a spoiled identity. This is all the more remarkable considering that the concept of citizenship – famously defined by Hannah Arendt as "the right to have rights" – has undergone continuous semantic expansion and analytic proliferation over the past two decades. Beyond the hallowed trilogy introduced in 1949 by T.H. Marshall, with its successive layering of civil, political, and social rights,[12] scholars have spawned a suite of new dimensions of citizenship: sexual, ecological, cultural, ethical, etc. They have multiplied the "sites (bodies, courts, borders, networks, media)," the "scales (cities, empires, nations, states, federations, leagues)," and "the acts (voting, volunteering, blogging, protesting, resisting, and organizing)" through which subjects seize on and act out citizenship.[13] But they have failed to theorize how the penal state recalibrates membership in a radical manner for those it captures and processes. For members

[9] Elizabeth F. Cohen, *Semi-Citizenship in Democratic Politics* (2009). Offenders are mentioned only thrice, in reference to administrative decisions that hamper the "mobility of convicted criminals" (p. 120); "rules regarding the employability and movement of people with contagious diseases or criminal records" (p. 124); and Hannah Arendt's characterization of stateless persons as being more marginal than criminals (p. 190), a revealing formulation she does not elaborate on. Crime and punishment are also mentioned *in transitu* when tackling how juvenile justice takes into account the semi-citizen status of children (p. 190).

[10] Sara Wallace Goodman, "Citizenship Studies: Policy Causes and Consequences" (2023). A partial exception is Charles R. Epp et al., *Pulled Over: How Police Stops Define Race and Citizenship* (2014), but it fails to engage citizenship theory as such in spite of its implacable empirical demonstration.

[11] Milena Tripkovic, *Punishment and Citizenship: A Theory of Criminal Disenfranchisement* (2019).

[12] T.H. Marshall, *Citizenship and Social Class* (1949).

[13] Engin F. Isin, "Citizenship in Flux: The Figure of the Activist Citizen" (2009), p. 368.

of the urban precariat who are its main clientele, the concept of *penal citizenship* as bundle of dishonor, liabilities, and prohibitions is indispensable to make sense of their shrunken status and problematic presence in the body politic. This is manifested in the criminal record which functions in the manner of a *negative passport* restricting its bearer's peregrinations across symbolic, social, and physical space. It is not happenstance if most advanced societies bar foreign applicants who have committed crimes from citizenship.

Students of punishment, for their part, have carefully enumerated the diminished rights and augmented obligations triggered by a criminal conviction – centering on the United States, where the collateral consequences of conviction are uniquely broad and severe.[14] But their focus has been on the convict himself as a sort of self-standing *sub-citizen* stuck on a penal island, missing how his legal figure traces the social and symbolic silhouette of the worthy, deserving, full-fledged member of the civic community by contrast. They have taken citizenship for granted as an institutional given instead of realizing that the citizen and the felon are what the German historian Reinhart Koselleck calls "counter-concepts" (*Gegenbegriffe*), an asymmetrical binary in which one term is endowed with superior moral value and the other simultaneously debased.[15] Reuben Miller and Forrest Stuart fall into this *substantivist* trap – as opposed to adopting a *relational* perspective – when they insist that "carceral citizenship" constitutes "an alternate legal reality" of its own instead of spotlighting the many-sided contrasts between the citizen and the criminal as a single socio-symbolic structure.[16] More crucially still, scholars of penality have not theorized the fact that both are *conjoint state categories* resulting from acts of legitimate nomination, positive and negative, that inscribe the notion, not just in the law, but also in subjectivity (habitus) and in social space (distributions of capital).[17] The *stigma* of the convict and the *aura* of the citizen are the two sides of the same institutional coin

9

[14] David S. Kirk and Sara Wakefield, "Collateral Consequences of Punishment: A Critical Review and Path Forward" (2018).

[15] Reinhart Koselleck, *Futures Past: On the Semantics of Historical Time* ([1979] 2004).

[16] Reuben Jonathan Miller and Forrest Stuart, "Carceral Citizenship: Race, Rights and Responsibility in the Age of Mass Supervision" (2017). Logically, the concept should be *penal*, and not carceral, citizenship given that most offenders are everywhere given non-custodial sentences such as fines, restitution, community service, or probation.

[17] Pierre Bourdieu, "Esprits d'État. Genèse et structure du champ bureaucratique" (1993a). I discuss this view of the state as the "central bank of symbolic capital" and fount of consequential classification in chapter 1, *infra*, pp. 106–10.

and a sociological account of punishment must imperatively attend to its contested minting by the Leviathan.

It suffices to pay attention to the many modalities and corollaries of penality to realize that it is *a boundary-drawing, category-forging, and identity-making force* crucial to the production of citizenship by the active designation and differential treatment of those deemed to be failed parties to the civic compact.[18] Traveling overseas and back in time, we discover that the antagonistic twinning of citizen and criminal was reactivated in the European colonies, where punishment was vital to statecraft and to the enforcement of the caste division between citizen and subject as the foundation of imperial order, as shown by Isabelle Merle and Adrian Muckle in their deft dissection of the punishment regime of *indigénat* in French overseas possessions.[19] Closer to home, in both the United States and the European Union, the penal apparatus is being reinforced and flung to handle irregular migration; closed detention centers are mushrooming and deportation is being ramped up; a chauvinistic politics of surveilled mobility establishes a direct link between domestic order and the securing of national borders, thus redrawing the material and symbolic boundaries of membership.[20] In colonial societies as in the contemporary metropole, moreover, the association of punishment with racialized ethnicity cements the vision of the criminal as a dark-skinned agent of dissent and disorder in need of stern discipline and firm castigation, climaxing with incarceration as a form of internal expulsion and quarantine.

Next, I contend that the *penal state is a distinctively urban institution*. It is designed and rolled out in the city to corral and control the problem populations that coalesce in its underbelly and to patrol the

---

[18] This is missed by the legal scholar Markus Dubber when he writes, surprisingly, that, while "the concept of citizenship can play a useful role in a descriptive account of penal practice," it nonetheless "contributes nothing to a normative theory of criminal law, however, being either empty, as a proxy for personhood, or pernicious, as a proxy for insiderhood." Markus D. Dubber, "Citizenship and Penal Law" (2010), p. 190.

[19] Isabelle Merle and Adrian Muckle, *L'Indigénat. Genèses dans l'empire français, pratiques en Nouvelle-Calédonie* (2019). I dissect this regime in chapter 2, pp. 208–15.

[20] Marie-Claire Caloz-Tschopp, *Les Étrangers aux frontières de l'Europe et le spectre des camps* (2004); Sonia Paone, *Città in frantumi. Sicurezza, emergenza e produzione dello spazio* (2008); Katja Franko Aas and Mary Bosworth (eds.), *The Borders of Punishment: Migration, Citizenship, and Social Exclusion* (2013); Vanessa Barker, *Nordic Nationalism and Penal Order: Walling the Welfare State* (2017); Fabian Georgi, *Grenzen und Bewegungsfreiheit: Eine kritische Einführung* (2025).

territories they inhabit.[21] This was true at the end of the sixteenth century when the workhouse prison was invented in response to the wave of vagrants and beggars flooding the growing cities of northern Europe with the rise of mercantile capitalism. It was verified after the mid-nineteenth century on both sides of the Atlantic where the urban bourgeoisie grew fearful of the "dangerous classes" migrating and consolidating in industrial centers.[22] It was confirmed at the end of the twentieth century as the prison boomed conjointly with visible and disruptive poverty on the streets of major cities, incarnated by the itinerant homeless and the pressing panhandler spawning public sentiments of physical insecurity and moral impropriety as well as by the episodic rioting of youths from the periphery fueled by abrasive relationships with the police.[23] This means that students of inequality and marginality in the metropolis cannot continue to ignore the penal state as they have studiously done since the birth of urban sociology a century ago.[24]

[21] Foucault discerned this association but did nothing with it: "I believe that the integration of the city into the central mechanisms of power, or rather, the inversion that made the city the primary problem, even before the problem of territory, is a phenomenon, a characteristic reversal of what happened between the seventeenth and the early nineteenth centuries. A problem to which one had to respond with new power mechanisms, the form of which is undoubtedly to be found in what I call security mechanisms. Basically, we had to reconcile the fact of the city with the legitimacy of sovereignty." Michel Foucault, *Sécurité, territoire, population. Cours au Collège de France, 1977–1978* (2004), p. 66.

[22] See, respectively, Bronisław Geremek, *La Potence ou la pitié. L'Europe et les pauvres du Moyen Âge à nos jours* ([1978] 1987); Louis Chevalier, *Classes laborieuses et classes dangereuses à Paris pendant la première moitié du XIXᵉ siècle* (1958); Gareth Stedman Jones, *Outcast London: A Study in the Relationship Between Classes in Victorian Society* (1971); Eric H. Monkkonen, *The Dangerous Class: Crime and Poverty in Columbus, Ohio, 1860–1885* (1975); and Richard J. Evans, *Tales from the German Underworld: Crime and Punishment in the Nineteenth Century* (1998).

[23] On street derelicts, see Philippe Bourgois and Jeff Schonberg, *Righteous Dopefiend* (2009); Daniel Cefaï and Édouard Gardella, *L'Urgence sociale en action. Ethnographie du Samu social de Paris* (2011); and Jürgen von Mahs, *Down and Out in Los Angeles and Berlin: The Sociospatial Exclusion of Homeless People* (2013). On urban riots in Western Europe, read Margit Mayer et al. (eds.), *Urban Uprisings: Challenging Neoliberal Urbanism in Europe* (2016), and Julien Talpin, *La Colère des quartiers. Enquête socio-historique à Roubaix* (2024). The long and continuing tradition of singling out the "disreputable poor" for special treatment by the state is recapitulated by David Matza, "Poverty and Disrepute" (1961).

[24] Astonishingly, the words criminal court, prosecutor, jail, and prison appear not a single time in the 700 pages of *The Oxford Handbook of Urban Politics* edited by Karen Mossberger et al. (2015).

The state as curator of crime

The "crime and punishment" diptych is historically constitutive of the discipline of criminology and serves as anchor for the doxic understanding of penality in both the academic and public debate. According to this viewpoint, public authority merely *responds* to offending behavior which arises and varies independently from culture and politics. Criminal justice is a technical appendage of government whose deployment tracks the physiognomy and frequency of crime. This is the *positivist* and *depoliticized* vision of penality which, paradoxically, "disappears" the very state it serves (1). This position is untenable: the same behavior is deemed criminal or not at different epochs and in different societies (think of homosexuality); sanctions for a given crime vary similarly across time and space (theft is sanctioned by amputation here and by fines there); levels and trends of punishment do not track levels of crime across time and across countries (compare the US with Canada over the past half-century).

The rival approach is *constructivist* and *politicized*: it stresses the variability of definitions of crime and the arbitrary nature of punishment as products of power relations. In its more radical variant, it considers the need for "law and order" as a social fiction and the corresponding clamor for penal repression as the spawn of false consciousness (2). This position is equally untenable: crime is not just a figment of the collective imagination; however defined, it does happen. It disrupts people's lives; it causes pain and anxiety which courses through the social body and feeds a legitimate demand for the intervention of the penal Leviathan, especially in the nether regions of social and physical space.

These two viewpoints, the positivist and the constructivist, are allied enemies in the sense that each needs and reinforces the other in its specific blindness. The positivist criminologist cannot comprehend the politics of classification; the constructivist sociologist is reticent to acknowledge the materiality of offending. Beyond their antagonism, they share the same static and mechanical vision of the state which ignores its internal differentiation and the struggles that animate it. Together, they occlude the *double truth of crime* as material conduct that violates criminal statutes and triggers punishment *regardless of its etiology* and as an ensemble of symbolic representations and bureaucratic practices that express and displace social ills and moral tensions associated with crime (3).

Instead of entering into questions of quiddity, causality, and intensity, let me propose a different formulation of that vexed dyad: *the state curates crime* in the sense that it selects, appropriates, arranges, and exhibits it for order maintenance, bureaucratic expediency, civic instruction, and political profit – much like a museum curator manages its collections and organizes artistic displays for the viewing pleasure and cultural education of its visitors. *Selects and appropriates*: the Leviathan picks and chooses what behavior is deemed criminal as well as what criminal behavior is detected, denounced, and diligently pursued by its penal wing (as opposed to its social and medical wings). A classic illustration is the long-standing leniency toward corporate crime versus the growing severity toward low-level street crime on both shores of the Atlantic (4). Another is the persistent indifference to sexual crimes committed within the privacy of the family, as with spousal rape and incest, which the state declined to own until very recently, and even then, only gingerly (5). *Arranges and exhibits*: the state deploys its expertise, puts together policy packages, formulates rules of implementation and showcases its action as a crime-fighting agency. Curating crime entails establishing a narrative and engaging with an audience to meet its expectations of order and satiate its appetite for moral tales (6).

But, in advanced society, the state is not a despotic apparatus floating up in historical ether. While it enjoys a measure of autonomy, it is embedded in *social space*, which is inhabited by myriad agents who escape its direct control or challenge its day-to-day operations. It is also contained within the *field of power*, where it vies for supremacy with the holders of other forms of capital (economic, political, journalistic, juridical, scientific, etc.) (7). The penal Leviathan thus cannot mechanically impose its interests and will; it must respond to challenges and claims from a range of actors (politicians, journalists, judicial experts, academics, activists, and the electorate at large) who support, contest, and otherwise shape its agencies and policies, asking alternately for more punishment (e.g., sex offenders), less punishment (e.g., drug consumers) or different punishment (e.g., juvenile and corporate delinquency). To evoke again the metaphor of the museum, the curator is also given artworks she is forced to acquire, display, and narrate (8).

So much to say, to make matters clear, that crime is very real, that its nature and variations matter, and that it must be integrated into a comprehensive sociology of the penal state. Not because it *determines* punishment but inasmuch as it constitutes the *raw materials* that

13

the Leviathan excavates, refines and molds in accordance with its own imperatives and in response to the demands and claims promulgated by agents battling over safety, morality, and justice within the bureaucratic, juridical, political, journalistic, and academic fields.

1. David Matza puts it thus: "Among their most notable accomplishments, the criminological positivists succeeded in what would seem the impossible. They separated the study of crime from the workings and theory of the state." David Matza, *Becoming Deviant* (1969), p. 143.
2. A mild version of this argument is Joseph R. Gusfield, *The Culture of Public Problems: Drinking-Driving and the Symbolic Order* (1981). A virulent one is Avi Boukli and Justin Kotzé (eds.), *Zemiology: Reconnecting Crime and Social Harm* (2018). For a reflection on its dangers, read Stanley Cohen, "Crime and Politics: Spot the Difference" (1996).
3. I extend here the mode of reasoning of Pierre Bourdieu in his discussion of the "double truth of work" in *Méditations pascaliennes* (1998).
4. John Hagan, *Who Are the Criminals? The Politics of Crime Policy from the Age of Roosevelt to the Age of Reagan* (2010); Pierre Lascoumes and Carla Nagels, *Sociologie des élites délinquantes. De la criminalité en col blanc à la corruption politique* (2014).
5. Kersti Yllö and M. Gabriela Torres (eds.), *Marital Rape: Consent, Marriage, and Social Change in Global Context* (2016); Léonore Le Caisne, *Un Inceste ordinaire. Et pourtant tout le monde savait* (2014).
6. Lois Presser and Sweinung Sandberg (eds.), *Narrative Criminology: Understanding Stories of Crime* (2015). Bruce Western treats trends in crime as a "context rather than cause" of carceral expansion for the period 1980–2001. But context evokes a static factor and an automatic effect when the state, political elites, and the media actively and continually shape and paint that "context." Bruce Western, *Punishment and Inequality in America* (2006), pp. 48–9.
7. Pierre Bourdieu, "Champ du pouvoir et division du travail de domination" (2011). I discuss the nesting of the penal state inside the bureaucratic field and the latter's nesting inside the field of power and social space in chapter 1, *infra*, pp. 90–2, 100–2.
8. I thank David Garland for challenging the metaphor of the museum curator and pushing me to elaborate it. For an illustration of the myriad agents shaping penal policy in the US case, see Vanessa Barker, *The Politics of Imprisonment: How the Democratic Process Shapes the Way America Punishes Offenders* (2009); Philip Goodman et al., *Breaking the Pendulum: The Long Struggle over Criminal Justice* (2017); and Heather Schoenfeld, *Building the Prison State: Race and the Politics of Mass Incarceration* (2018).

14

The many faces and functions of penality

By rolling out the police, court, prison and their bureaucratic tentacles, I will argue, the penal state curates crime, contains sociomoral disorders, manages urban marginality, and effectively draws the boundaries of civic membership. Its day-to-day deployment signals sovereignty on the domestic front and serves to manufacture legitimacy in the eyes of the broad citizenry, for whom enforcing safety and order on the street remains the most elemental and the most tangible mission of government. But the penal state is a *bifurcated state* which captures in its net nearly exclusively deprived and defamed populations by targeting their neighborhoods: it is everywhere a class-splitting and race-making institution based on the stubborn differentiation of principled "paper penality" and arbitrary "street penality." The social and cultural meshing between the carceral institution and districts of dereliction on both sides of the Atlantic cements that bifurcation. Punishment must therefore be placed at the epicenter of the political sociology of statecraft, group-making and place-making in the metropolis as well as brought to the forefront of civic debate, rather than abandoned to the periodic panic-peddling of electoral politics. I endeavor to demonstrate these propositions in three steps corresponding to three chapters.

15

1. Penality as core state capacity and negative sociodicy

The first chapter takes a social-theoretical approach. I start with the *puzzle of a mutual ignorance*: with precious few exceptions (among them Thomas Hobbes), theorists of the state, past and present, have neglected punishment while theorists of punishment, past and present, have neglected the state.[25] I bring these two theoretical strands together to argue that penality is a *core state capacity* – an indispensable institutionalized means of public action – and that you cannot grasp the one without grasping the other. Pacifying social space and installing a functioning triad of police, court, and prison are a *sine qua non* of modern state-building and democratic citizenship, as

[25] Two illustrious examples suffice here: Bob Jessop, *The State: Past, Present, Future* (2015), who does not engage punishment, and David Garland, *Punishment and Modern Society: A Study in Social Theory* (1990), who does not engage the state. Hobbes's disputed views on penality are discussed by Alan Norrie, "Thomas Hobbes and the Philosophy of Punishment" (1984).

demonstrated in hyperbolic form by colonial rule and, *a contrario*, by the predicament of failing states.[26]

I selectively canvas theories of punishment (from Émile Durkheim to Georg Rusche to Michel Foucault) and theories of the state (from Max Weber and Michael Mann to James Scott and Pierre Bourdieu). I show that the opposition between rationalist and emotionalist theories of punishment propounded by the Marxists and the Durkheimians, respectively, is mirrored by the opposition between Jeremy Bentham's consequentialist philosophy and Immanuel Kant's deontological philosophy of punishment mandating reformation and retribution, respectively. I resolve this opposition by spotlighting the *division of penal labor* and the *constitutive duality of criminal sanction*, at once material and symbolic, an instrument of class control and a means of broadcasting community values, endlessly swinging between rehabilitation (future-oriented and centered on the offender) and just desert (past-oriented and centered on the offense).

I elaborate a robust analytic concept of the penal state as a specialized *sector of the bureaucratic field* – in Bourdieu's sense of the term[27] – entrusted with interpreting and enforcing criminal statutes, thus putting the law to work to foster social and moral order. Like the state itself, this sector is a *site of polarized struggles*. It is animated by a structural tension between the (masculine) Right hand of discipline and the (feminine) Left hand of protection as well as riven by patterned struggles over the very definition of "justice" oscillating between reformation and retribution. This oscillation is founded on the fact that, in liberal democratic regimes, heirs to the Enlightenment, the penal state contains within itself both the dark and the bright side of modernity when it comes to penality: Kantian just desert to sanction violations of the sanctity of the person and private property, Benthamite rehabilitation to reckon with the personhood of the offender.[28] Breaking decisively with the political-economic approach, I reach beyond materialist perspectives to stress the symbolic purpose

---

[26] Sylvie Thénault, *Violence ordinaire dans l'Algérie coloniale. Camps, internements, assignations à résidence* (2012); Zaryab Iqbal and Harvey Starr, *State Failure in the Modern World* (2015).

[27] Bourdieu, "Esprits d'État. Genèse et structure du champ bureaucratique."

[28] This oscillation is founded in the polarized *structure* of the penal state and is not a mere product of partisan battles over punitive policy as argued by Philip Goodman et al. in *Breaking the Pendulum: The Long Struggle over Criminal Justice* (2017). The metaphor of "plate tectonics" they use obscures the hard-wired architecture of the penal state *qua* state as mapped out in chapter 1, *infra*, pp. 99–106.

of criminal punishment as *public disgrace*:[29] to brighten the boundaries of citizenship and to legitimize the social and moral dereliction of marginal categories in the double order of class and status. Properly conceived, penality is a form of *negative sociodicy*, a state-sponsored, secular "theodicy of misfortune" in Max Weber's sense of the term.

I conclude this chapter by spotlighting three structural properties of the penal state: it is polarized by the tension between punitive autonomy and protective heteronomy; it is Janus-faced in that it simultaneously delivers a public good for the citizenry (safety on the streets, morality in the home, and the defense of property) and a private bad for the criminal (physical and psychic pain), which implies that its legitimacy is constitutively compromised; and it is bifurcated by class, ethnicity, and place. This bifurcation is not an incidental but a structural property of the penal Leviathan, which challenges conventional approaches to criminal justice and raises vexing questions of organizational reform, policy change, and civic equity – which I tackle in the book's conclusion.

17

2. Marginality, ethnicity, territory

The second chapter turns to social history and comparative sociology to resolve another puzzle: the stunning *return of the prison* to the institutional and political forefront of advanced societies at century's close when, for three decades after World War II, it had been deemed moribund and obsolete, fated to wither away. Probing this comeback reveals that, since its invention in the late sixteenth century and into the early twenty-first century, the prison has been integral to statecraft. Change the state and penality changes. This is no different in the age of triumphant neoliberalism, which has entailed the strengthening of the "penal fist" of the Leviathan to complement and fortify the "invisible hand" of market deregulation.[30]

---

[29] For insightful reflections on its obverse, see Julian Pitt-Rivers, "The Place of Grace in Anthropology" (2011). Here Foucault unknowingly repeats Durkheim's position point by point (as I will show *infra*, p. 48): "Infamy is a perfect punishment since it is the immediate and spontaneous reaction of society itself; it varies with each society; it is graduated according to the harmfulness of each crime ... It is strictly adequate to the principles of penality" (*Sécurité, population, territoire*, pp. 260–1).
[30] Loïc Wacquant, *Punishing the Poor: The Neoliberal Government of Social Insecurity* (2009b); idem, "Three Steps to a Historical Anthropology of Actually Existing Neoliberalism" (2012b).

The social history of the prison delivers a clear lesson: everywhere the carceral institution has always targeted *doubly subordinated categories* in the order of class (the poor) and status (the outsider, local, ethnonational, or ethnoracial). How is that possible? What are the *mechanisms through which this selectivity* is achieved in formally democratic societies based on isonomia?[31] How does it perpetuate itself? I compare the differential policing and disproportionate incarceration of blacks in the United States and of postcolonial migrants and refugees in Western Europe to answer these questions by focusing on space as a prism of state action.

I build on Markus Dubber's duality of *Rechtsstaat* and *Polizeistaat*[32] to introduce a distinction between dignified "paper penality," aimed at the bourgeoisie, and degrading "street penality," aimed at the precariat, to argue that it is by *targeting territory* where street penality is implemented that the state trains and captures primarily destitute and disparaged categories. With the return of the prison and the entrenchment of novel forms of urban marginality in the neoliberal era, the carceral archipelago and districts of dereliction in the metropolis have become linked by a relationship of *structural osmosis*. This institutional interlock explains that the priority clientele of penal institutions everywhere – and not just in the United States – are poor young men from stigmatized ethnic categories and territories. In every advanced society, punishment is racialized and racializing because criminal sanction and race are two germane forms of state-sponsored *infamia* – a term used by ancient Romans to designate juridical exclusion from citizenship.[33] This is true even in the most humane and light-footed penal systems such as those of Nordic countries where, remarkably, the ethnoracial slant of policing and incarceration is particularly pronounced.

This demonstrates that the penal state is a *distinctively urban institution*: it was born with and for the metropolis – a brute fact routinely overlooked by sociologists of punishment and historians of the city. Since the middle of the nineteenth century, it has fed on the latter's

---

[31] A genealogy of this core Western legal category is John Lombardini, "Isonomia and the Public Sphere in Democratic Athens" (2013). Its mental ecology is sketched by Jean-Pierre Vernant, *Les Origines de la pensée grecque* (1962).

[32] Markus D. Dubber, *The Dual Penal State: The Crisis of Criminal Law in Comparative-Historical Perspective* (2018).

[33] Sarah Bond, "Altering Infamy: Status, Violence, and Civic Exclusion in Late Antiquity" (2014). For a full treatment of race as public dishonor, see Loïc Wacquant, *Racial Domination* (2024b), pp. 84–91.

underbelly and it has in turn solidified its distinctive society, culture, and public image.[34] Transformations of urban marginality are tightly bound with transformations of penality, so much so that we can, by anticipation, discern in the makeup of the carceral population the visage of the new urban precariat in the making.

I close this chapter by taking a historical detour to consider the deployment of state punishment in the colonies as a chief means of controlling population and territory as well as to run the imperial economy and secure the caste society. *Colonial penality is exacerbated, suffusive and multifunctional.* Raw violence and racial rule lie at its very core. It rides on special crimes, special punishment, and special agencies to administer it that contravene the legal standards of the metropole. As an extreme case stripping the Leviathan down to its essentials, the penal regime of the colony confirms that punishment is a crucial vector of statecraft and consists at bottom in the forceful corralling of bodies out of order. I use this historical outlier to throw light on the logics and limits of the penalization of poverty in the badlands of the postindustrial city where law enforcement is likewise intensified, racialized, and inflected in violation of common legal rules and civic values. Moreover, as in the colony, the very excess of punishment that the state inflicts in neighborhoods of relegation undermines its legitimacy in the eyes of their residents and thereby feeds the very disorders the state claims to stamp out.[35] This is a textbook demonstration of the *iatrogenic logic of penalization*: in the absence of strict sociolegal safeguards, it aggravates the very problems it is supposed to solve.

3. Penal power incarnate: a day in the life of a prosecutor

The third chapter draws on immersive ethnography to take the reader to the point of production of punishment. Penal power is not just a paper abstraction suited to theoretical construction and philosophical disquisition. It resides in the concrete infliction of physical and psychic force upon bodies deemed misplaced in the physical, social, and

[34] Dominique Kalifa, *Les Bas-fonds. Histoire d'un imaginaire* (2013).

[35] Durkheim pointed out long ago that the excess of punishment undermines punishment and the sanctions must be carefully calibrated lest they fail to evoke the "moral shame" that normally accompanies them. Émile Durkheim, *L'Éducation morale* (1925), pp. 165–6. For an empirical demonstration in the case of the US, see Christopher Muller and Daniel Schrage, "Mass Imprisonment and Trust in the Law" (2014).

symbolic grid of the city through the mediation of the authoritative words and deeds of *penal agents of flesh and blood*:[36] police, prosecutors, judges, private and public defense attorneys, court clerks and bailiffs, prison wardens and guards, and probation and parole officers, as well as third-sector outfits running correctional services and court-mandated programs. I demonstrate this by delving deep into the everyday activities, organizational reasoning, and professional strategies of a pivotal prosecutor at work "dealing cases" in a California county criminal court I observed from within for some three years.

Moving from structure to action, penal input (the police) and output (the prison) to penal throughput (the court), and from a top-down vision – a necessary moment of analysis – to a bottom-up perspective enables us to capture the situated reasoning and tactical conduct of the prosecutor as operant driver of judicial negotiation and sanction. To capture penality in the making, it proves essential to shift from the public stage to the closed wings of the courthouse where deals are hammered out, which requires breaking with a long lineage of interactionist research anchored by the concept of "courtroom workgroup."[37] For the judicial behavior visible in "open court" pertains to bureaucratic routine and institutional ceremonial. It merely rubber stamps and enters into the official record decisions that have been haggled over and agreed upon backstage.

The negotiation of guilty pleas, the main tool for criminal adjudication in the United States (increasingly imported or imitated around the world),[38] is driven by the position of attorneys in the local judicial field riven by a daily *tussle over the purpose and priority of justice*, castigate or protect, negotiate or litigate, assert morality or safeguard legality, prioritize the deviant act or recognize the deviating social trajectory beyond the courthouse. I show that this polarization, which mirrors the duality of retributivist and consequentialist philosophies of punishment outlined in chapter 1, organizes not just the opposi-

---

[36] On the carnal conception of the social agent, see Loïc Wacquant, "For a Sociology of Flesh and Blood" (2015). For an illustration, read the analysis of policing as emotional bodywork by Stephanie Schmidt, *Affekt und Polizei. Eine Ethnografie der Wut in der exekutiven Gewaltarbeit* (2022).

[37] The concept was coined by James Eisenstein and Herbert Jacob in their classic *Felony Justice: An Organizational Analysis of Criminal Courts* (1977). It is central to field studies of the criminal court, as evidenced by Lisa Flower and Sarah Klosterkamp (eds.), *Courtroom Ethnography: Exploring Contemporary Approaches, Fieldwork and Challenges* (2023).

[38] Máximo Langer, "Plea Bargaining, Conviction Without Trial, and the Global Administratization of Criminal Convictions" (2021).

tion between prosecutors and public defenders but also the internal architecture of each of their offices.

Getting into "the trenches" of negotiated justice reveals that, far from wielding *absolute* discretion as conventional legal scholarship would have it,[39] the prosecutor's latitude is *bounded* by a series of concentric circles of constraints and facilitations imposed by her social and symbolic embeddedness in a team, office, and courthouse with their distinctive histories and manifested by the collective expectations that restrain and channel penal action. What I call *judicial tagging*, the operation whereby a prosecutorial profile is fabricated and affixed onto the defendant, is not an individual activity driven by the personal whims of the prosecutor but an ongoing collective achievement produced by relations of material and symbolic power between prosecutor, defense attorney, and judge, as well as among each of these professions.

From within the innards of the court, I sound a note of caution about the contested role of race and class in the determination of prosecutorial strategy and outcome. Race is not the solid and unidirectional variable it appears to be from afar and its effects are not what race-centric scholars and activists would expect. But advocates of *racial theology in punishment studies* are never hindered by their inability to produce robust data from within penal institutions and by evidence contrary to their dogma since they proceed through *petitio principii* validated by the racial yearning of their readers. By contrast, class discrimination in judicial treatment is both prevalent and hypervisible, and yet accepted as a matter of course. But to fully measure its impact, it is necessary to differentiate between the three class fractions composing the urban proletariat – the solid working class, the shifting precariat, and the street drifters – and to avoid the confusion created by the reigning "disparity talk."

I close the book by reuniting ethnography, history, and theory to stress the centrality of punishment in the *definition and defense of civic membership* in advanced societies. The delivery of legitimate material and symbolic violence by the penal state draws the boundary between "friends" and "enemies" (in the language of Carl Schmitt), those who respect the social and moral order and those who infringe upon it, and serves to render legible and set apart the human carriers of pollution and danger (in the language of Mary Douglas).[40] Along

21

[39] Angela J. Davis, *Arbitrary Justice: The Power of the American Prosecutor* (2007).
[40] Carl Schmitt, *The Concept of the Political* ([1932] 2008); Mary Douglas, *Purity and Danger: An Analysis of Concepts of Pollution and Taboo* (1966).

with the welfare recipient and the foreign immigrant, two categories with which it overlaps closely in the public imagination, the convict draws out the figure of the *anti-citizen* surrounded by a sulfurous halo created by collective emotions of scorn and fear.

Finally, I point out the sociological naiveté and political implausibility of abolitionism, a politics of punishment that has recently become *de rigueur* in some academic and activist circles in the United States. Penality can no more be eliminated than crime can. Instead, I defend what I call *radical penal minimalism*, a position that recognizes both the need for the penal state and the need to transform it profoundly to drastically reduce its footprint and make it the treatment of last resort for the social ills of the city. The legendary Norwegian criminologist Nils Christie, one of the founders of modern prison abolitionism, wrote a provocative book smartly entitled *A Suitable Amount of Crime* reflecting on his lifelong quest for the meaning of crime, arguing that it is a shallow, fluid, and fungible category unbounded but by culture and politics.[41] One way to encapsulate the conclusion of the present tome is to propose that, insofar as societies come to resolve the historical task of determining *a suitable amount of punishment*, the latter can and should be minimized to the extreme.

A historicist-analytical approach

Before we set out on this intellectual voyage, a warning: this book is an exercise in *historicist-analytical sociology*, a mode of reasoning that seeks to (i) clearly define its concepts and terminology; (ii) sharply distinguish folk from analytical categories; (iii) disaggregate phenomena into their constituent parts; (iv) uncover the mechanisms that produce, reproduce, or transform these phenomena; and (v) take seriously the temporal dimension, recognize historical discontinuities, and strive to recover lost historical possibilities.[42] This means

---

[41] "Since crime does not exist as a stable entity, the crime concept is suited to all sorts of control purposes. It is like a sponge. The term can absorb a lot of acts – and people – when external circumstances make that useful. But it can also be brought to reduce its content, whenever suitable with those with a hand on the sponge. This understanding opens up new questions. It opens up for discussion when enough is enough. It paves the way for what is a suitable amount of crime." Nils Christie, *A Suitable Amount of Crime* (2004), p. 6.

[42] I try to exemplify this approach in my book *Jim Crow. Le terrorisme de caste en Amérique* (2024a), especially pp. 19–26 and 145–59. This epistemic approach is my

that I approach the authors I discuss in the first chapter, not as a political philosopher, but as a sociologist seeking resources for fashioning a robust analytical framework. My attitude is that of a *conceptual scavenger*. It means also that, in the second chapter, I provide, not a thorough panorama, but a selective reading of the literature on incarceration and inequality aimed at spotlighting the class and ethnoracial slant of penality and at building a bridge between the study of punishment and the study of the city. In the third chapter, I push aside the standard literature on "negotiated justice" to pull apart plea bargaining as process and product so as to flesh out the graduated exercise of penal power from the ground up.

I strive to adopt and keep this historicist-analytical posture to the hilt. Thus I will come to my concluding position – affirming the necessity of the penal state, advocating for radical penal minimalism, calling for a progressive rethinking of "law and order" rather than its knee-jerk denunciation – *reluctantly* and *against* my ingrained philosophical inclinations and prior political wishes. But I am a social scientist, not a philosopher, which means that I have to square the malleable world of ideas with hard social facts, past and present, and balance idealism and realism to yield what Pierre Bourdieu calls "rational utopianism."[43] I have to think structurally of institutional (imp)possibilities and (im)probabilities taking into account comparative history. For that I use counterfactual reasoning, involving what Max Weber calls "objective possibility" (*objektive Möglichkeit*) and "adequate causation" (*adäquate Verursachung*)[44] but projected forward, into a hypothetical future, rather than backward to illuminate trajectories past.

23

adaptation and extension of the principles formulated by Peter Hedström and Peter Bearman (eds.), *The Oxford Handbook of Analytical Sociology* (2009), to which I add the historical dimension by drawing on Max Weber's essays on method, especially *The Methodology of the Social Sciences* (1949).

[43] "A good use of sociology as a tool for transforming the social world would be to define the limits of what can be done and then to go as far as possible beyond those limits with the tiniest chance of success." Pierre Bourdieu (with Roger Chartier), *Le Sociologue et l'historien* ([1988] 2011), pp. 53–4.

[44] Weber, *The Methodology of the Social Sciences*, pp. 164–75.

Mapping penality across the Atlantic

My analysis *selectively* tracks down structural similarities and functional parallels between the United States and Western Europe, with a focus on France, to better specify the modalities of penalization as state policy. These include germane adaptations and borrowings by the continental counties, such as zero-tolerance policing, the militarization of law enforcement, youth curfews, mandatory minimum sentences, automatic recidivism statutes, and guilty plea procedures (1). But similarity is not replication and even less identity.

I am emphatically *not* arguing that Europe is in the throes of sweeping "Americanization" or that it follows the US trajectory with a lag of one to two decades. First, the notion of *Americanization itself is incoherent* and confusing: that country harbors 50 states and some 3,100 counties each with its own justice policy, such that national trends hide wide local variations – Vermont looks like Sweden and Mississippi is worse than Russia.

Second, *the scale and virulence of penalization remain vastly different* on the two sides of the Atlantic, with the United States standing as an extreme outlier on just about every indicator (2). Its recent drop notwithstanding, the rate of incarceration in the US is five to twelve times greater than in member countries of the European Union; 56 percent of American convicts serve sentences exceeding ten years as against 14 percent in Europe; some 56,000 are doing life without the possibility of parole compared to a few hundred in Europe; more than 30,000 are housed in "supermax" facilities compared to an estimated couple of thousands on the other side of the Atlantic. Probation is deployed *en masse* (covering 4.2 million at its peak in 2008) as a means of surveillance and sanction, not as a springboard for social reintegration. The collateral consequences of criminal conviction are sweeping and dire (they curtail access to employment, housing, welfare, education, parenting, and voting); and individual criminal justice records are public, broadly diffused through the internet and accessible to employers, realtors, and other commercial operators to discriminate based on judicial status. Such data are kept under strict control and are accessible only by judicial authorities in the main countries of the EU. Finally, the wide diffusion of guns and the extraordinary levels of concentrated lethal violence in the US shape urban policing and, by extension, contaminate the entire penal chain even as it concerns a small percentage of all offenders (3).

Europe does not follow in the footsteps of the US but there is a *European road to the penalization of urban marginality*, and inside of it, distinct Mediterranean, continental, and Scandinavian paths (4). First, punitive containment in the Old World is effected primarily by the "front-end" of the penal chain, the police, rather than the "back-end" of the prison as in the US, due mostly to the ability of magistrates to resist the punitive push and the limited carceral capacity. Second, in the main European countries, the activation of the penal wing of the state has been accompanied, not by the wholesale retraction but by the resilience and even selective extension of the social safety net for the most vulnerable populations, albeit with a disciplinary inflection. In other words, the penalization and socialization of urban marginality have been combined rather than the former replacing the latter. Third, and most crucially, the deeply engrained notion of human rights in legislation, political culture, and among justice professionals has limited recourse to incarceration (5). But crossing the Atlantic will reveal that *the mechanisms of penalization are the same*: the targeting of doubly marginalized categories, the differential policing of territory, the deployment of fast-track adjudication, the incarceration of social derelicts falling through the social safety net, and the interlock between the neighborhood and the prison.

25

1. Loïc Wacquant, *Prisons of Poverty* (2009a).
2. For compact characterizations of the US as "penal outlier," see Kevin R. Reitz (ed.), *American Exceptionalism in Crime and Punishment* (2017), and David Garland, *Law and Order Leviathan: America's Extraordinary Regime of Policing and Punishment* (2025). Michael Campbell makes a convincing plea for considering punishment in the US at the subnational level in "Varieties of Mass Incarceration: What We Learn From State Histories" (2018).
3. There are an estimated 390 million firearms in circulation in the country (120 firearms per 100 residents, six times the rate for France), which directly affects crime, policing, and prosecution. The American homicide rate was roughly ten times European rates at its peak and more than 70 times greater in the poor segregated neighborhoods of the dual metropolis. The police in the United States kill upwards of 1,000 people every year compared to fewer than 200 in all of Europe. On the "violence-centric" culture of American police officers and departments, read the chilling ethnography of Michael Sierra-Arévalo, *The Danger Imperative: Violence, Death, and the Soul of Policing* (2024).
4. Loïc Wacquant, *Punishing the Poor: The Neoliberal Government of Social Insecurity* (2009b) and idem, "The Wedding of Workfare and Prisonfare in the 21st Century" (2012a). On European variants, see, respectively, Ignacio González Sánchez, *Neoliberalismo y castigo* (2021); Bernd Maelicke and Stefan Suhling (eds.), *Das Gefängnis auf dem Prüfstand: Zustand und Zukunft des Strafvollzugs*

(2017); and Thomas Ugelvik and Jane Dullum (eds.), *Penal Exceptionalism? Nordic Prison Policy and Practice* (2011).

5. Sonja Snacken, "Human Dignity and Prisoners' Rights in Europe" (2021). For the contrast with the US, see Jonathan Simon, "For a Human Rights Approach to Reforming the American Penal State" (2019).

Clarifications on vocabulary: (i) I will refer to the precarious fractions of the proletariat – in the technical sense of sellers of labor power – generically as the *precariat*, comprised of the chronically unemployed and wage earners stuck in casual, low-pay, part-time, intermittent, or otherwise insecure employment; (ii) I will refer to the middle and upper classes conjointly as the *bourgeoisie* in the sense of holders of economic and cultural capital that can be transmitted and converted into expanded life chances; (iii) I will refer to the impoverished and stigmatized districts, commonly perceived as redoubts of vice and violence, situated at the bottom of the system of places that make up a metropolis, as *neighborhoods of relegation*; (iv) by black *hyperghetto* I will mean the historical remnants of the communal ghetto of the Fordist-industrial era (1917–68) after its implosion, a sociospatial formation doubly segregated by race and class, stripped of its institutional buffer and devoid of economic function in the metropolis; (v) I will use the term *ethnicity* to designate a social principle of vision and division based on claims to collective honor and encompassing race (as naturalized and disguised ethnicity), religion, region, and nation. Ethnic division will refer primarily to the black/white opposition in the United States and to the national/immigrant (of postcolonial, non-Western, or refugee origin) cleavage in Western Europe.

As concerns justice activities and institutions, (vi) I will call *penal triad* the troika of police, court, and prison which, with some variations, constitutes the administrative core of criminal justice in advanced societies. A more comprehensive roster of punishment agents varies by country and includes jail and juvenile facilities, halfway houses and reentry establishments, night prisons, detention centers for irregular migrants, court-mandated programs, probation, parole, administrators of judicial databases, and the gamut of public, commercial, and nonprofit professionals involved in delivering criminal sanctions by delegation. (vii) I will use the term *punishment*, seemingly self-evident, to designate, not just the execution of state sanctions after adjudication, but the full chain of criminal capture and management, including the police and the court. The reason is

26

simple: though they are not tasked with sanctioning convicts, both of these institutions mete out species of punishment of their own – imposed on the guilty and the innocent alike. In their daily action, the police inflict material force (e.g., a stop-and-frisk check, an arrest) and symbolic force (manifested in the fear, anger, and humiliation entailed in an identity check or an interrogation). As for the court, its routine functioning similarly imposes physical, psychic, administrative, economic, and emotional costs upon the people it processes and their loved ones. (viii) In the court, I deploy the adjective "judicial" to cover the joint activities of the triangle formed by the prosecutor, the defense attorney (public and private), and the judge, and not the latter alone, because all three are engaged in a daily struggle to seize and wield the authority to define and deliver "justice."

27

Finally, at the cost of disappointing readers looking for a politicized "intervention," let me make clear that the purpose of this book is not to denounce or castigate the penal state – as is the case in most social studies of punishment – but to articulate a concept, deploy it in history, and validate it empirically.[45] This validation can *then* serve as basis for institutional critique and civic action depending on one's personal ethics and politics. I will tackle in conclusion the question of abolition, an approach to penality premised, precisely, on the principled condemnation of the penal state *ex principio*. This principle leads abolitionists to make grievous errors of institutional analysis, militant tactics, and political strategy, errors that could have been avoided by starting off with a cool head and a sober heart. It makes them blind to the sociologically grounded alternative to both the penal status quo and abolition: radical penal minimalism.

Social scientists are not moralists: their mission is to describe, interpret and explain social phenomena, uncover the mechanisms that sustain them and thereby discover counterfactuals that forge a path toward plausible historical alternatives.[46] Not to judge an institution but to dissect it and make sure to pursue their investigation wherever it takes them, with no prejudices, no blinders, and no reservations as to what they may discover, even – I would indeed say *especially* – when this challenges their most cherished moral commitments and political proclivities. Although my friendly critique of abolitionism

[45] That was the critique of my two earlier books on the topic, *Punishing the Poor* (2009b) and *Prisons of Poverty* (2009a), by the comparative criminologist David Nelken, "Denouncing the Penal State" (2010).
[46] Geoffrey Hawthorn, *Plausible Worlds: Possibility and Understanding in History and the Social Sciences* (1993).

is Durkheimian, centered as it is on the structural-functional indispensability of the penal state in advanced society, when it comes to the vexed relationship between science and politics, I am doggedly Weberian.[47] For, when sociology does its job well, it does not need to raise its voice in indignation: simple enunciation inevitably turns into denunciation every time it constructs objects inimical to human dignity and antithetical to democratic ideals.

28

[47] Max Weber, *Le Savant et le politique, une nouvelle traduction* ([1917, 1919] 2003).

1

Penality as Core State Capacity and Negative Sociodicy

Public ministers are also all those that have authority from the sovereign to procure the execution of judgements given; to publish the sovereigns commands; to suppress tumults; to apprehend and imprison malefactors; and other acts tending to the conservation of the peace. For every act they do by such authority is the act of the Commonwealth; and their service answerable to that of the hands in a body natural.

Thomas Hobbes, *Leviathan* (1651)

In 1933, a brilliant young scholar by the name of Georg Rusche, trained in the philosophy of law, economics, and social science at Göttingen, published an article in the second issue of the *Zeitschrift für Sozialforschung,* the journal just launched by the Institut für Sozialforschung that was then the institutional home of the Francfort School of Marxism.[1] The short article, running all of 15 pages, was entitled "Arbeitsmarkt und Strafvollzug." It laid out the lineaments of a book commissioned by the institute as part of its intellectual agenda to expand the parameters of Marxist analysis to encompass and critique all the major institutions of bourgeois society. The book, which would appear six years later in the United States, co-signed with the legal scholar Otto Kirchheimer, as *Punishment and Social Structure* (1939), argues that there exists a one-to-one correspondence between the mode of production and the mode of punishment across eight centuries of Western history.[2]

[1] Dario Melossi, "Georg Rusche: A Biographical Essay" (1980).
[2] The English translations of the article and book are Georg Rusche, "Labor Market

The 1933 article and the 1939 book fell into immediate oblivion due to the coming to power of the Nazis, the subsequent exile of the Frankfurt School and the outbreak of World War II, only to be rediscovered in the 1970s in the United States and Europe and promptly canonized as "*the* Marxist" approach to punishment.[3] One could argue that, in actuality, it is more Weberian than Marxist, since it recognizes the role of religion, fiscal capacity, and even sexuality in the formation of penal policy. But it is certainly *historical and materialist* and so it spawned a strand of inquiry known as the "political economy of punishment" whose favorite topic is the relation between the labor market and incarceration.[4] For this lineage, punishment is a rational response by capitalists to the challenges of labor, in terms of abundance, discipline, and militancy – an instrument of class control whose use is ramped up during the depressive cycles of the economy which devalue labor and cause social unrest. The penal state is one of many tools in the hands of the "executive committee of the ruling class," in Karl Marx's famed expression.

Punishment and social structure revisited

But Rusche was not the first to pose the question of the connection between penality and social structure. In his discussion of crime and the law in *De la division du travail social* in 1893 and in his formulation of the "Two Laws of Penal Evolution," a long article published in 1899 in *L'Année sociologique*, the founder of French sociology Émile Durkheim had proposed that punishment is a revelator of the state of social solidarity and its application a means of revivifying the latter.[5]

and Penal Sanction: Thoughts on the Sociology of Criminal Justice" ([1933] 1978), and Georg Rusche and Otto Kirchheimer, *Punishment and Social Structure* ([1939] 2005). The book was published by Columbia University Press because, to flee Nazism, the Institut für Sozialforschung had relocated in New York and become affiliated with Columbia University. It opened on a foreword by Thorsten Sellin, America's most eminent student of penality at the time, and a prefatory note by Max Horkheimer, the director of the institute.

[3] The book was republished in 1968 in the United States, translated into German in 1972, Spanish in 1974, Italian in 1978, Portuguese in 1990, and French in 1994. In every country it was hailed as paradigmatically Marxist.

[4] For a broad overview of this approach, see Dario Melossi et al. (eds.), *The Political Economy of Punishment Today: Visions, Debates and Challenges* (2017).

[5] Émile Durkheim, *De la division du travail social* ([1893] 1990); idem, "Deux lois de l'évolution pénale" ([1899] 1969).

Penal sanctions stoke and direct collective emotions toward the offenders whose misbehavior accentuates the boundaries between insiders and outsiders, members of the community and those who violate its norms and desecrate its values. These two texts uncover the communicative function of punishment and initiated a vein of research that stresses the ritualized, ceremonial, and phatic nature of criminal sanction, in short, the *symbolic* dimension of penality. The distinctive focus of this Durkheimian strand of studies of punishment is on the collective beliefs and representations (in the twofold sense of psychology and theater) that both feed on and stage criminal sanctions grasped as cultural performances. Punishment is an irrational response to violations by derelict members which serves to reaffirm the shared rules bounding the collectivity. The penal state is a structurally benevolent contraption that coordinates societal needs and deploys sanctions to mark difference and produce social cohesion.

31

It is conventional, in studies of penality, to oppose these two approaches, the materialist and the symbolic, descended from Marx (after Bentham) and Durkheim (after Kant) respectively.[6] They paint two pictures of criminal justice that are mutually hostile and seemingly irreconcilable, and they ask their reader to take sides. In my book *Punishing the Poor*, I make one simple but decisive move: I join rather than oppose these two paradigms.[7] The rationale for rejecting this opposition is that, in advanced societies, punishment is a complex, multilayered, and versatile institution such that it can *simultaneously or alternately* obey a rational logic in one sector and an emotional logic in another; reinforce class control *and* draw community boundaries; respond to changes in the economy *and* react to the diffusion of status anxiety; effect the control of labor *and* assuage collective sentiments; and drive the pursuit of interest *and* obey the pull of identity.[8]

[6] Two books emblematic of this fierce antagonism are Alessandro De Giorgi, *Re-Thinking the Political Economy of Punishment: Perspectives on Post-Fordism and Penal Politics* (2006), and Philip Smith, *Punishment and Culture* (2008).

[7] Loïc Wacquant, *Punishing the Poor: The Neoliberal Government of Social Insecurity* (2009b). This approach aims to bring together the material and the symbolic dimensions of social reality and causation under a single theoretical canopy. It differs from David Garland's call for a principled analytical pluralism that "explores penality from a number of different angles in an effort to construct a composite picture of the phenomenon" by playing different theoretical interpretations off against each other (*Punishment and Modern Society: A Study in Social Theory*, 1990, p. 278–9).

[8] David Garland urges us to see punishment as "a complex social institution," as something "akin to Mauss's idea of a 'total social fact', which on its surface appears to be self-contained, but which in fact intrudes into many of the basic spheres of social

Zoom to the mid-1970s and you find Michel Foucault summarily dismissing Durkheim in two lines and one footnote – a philosopher of Foucault's rank could not possibly lower himself to engage the work of a mere sociologist – and heaping praise upon "the great book" of Rusche and Kirchheimer – read in English since it had not yet appeared in French translation – in *Surveiller et punir* (1975). For Foucault, however, punishment changes not in keeping with modes of production but through rupture as the modality of power shifts abruptly between 1760 and 1840 from the centralized, top-down power of the sovereign to the bottom-out diffusion of disciplines "throughout the thickness of the social body." These disciplines aim to "make bodies docile and useful" for the emerging capitalist economy but the ramification of "the carceral" transcends economic rationality. "Biopower" and "power-knowledge" combine to fabricate a "disciplinary individual" shaped by the "great rise of the apparatuses of normalization and the whole gamut of effects they wield through the establishment of new objectivities."[9] I mention *Discipline and Punish* here because it is far and away the single most influential book in the study of the prison in the global academy and yet it is written *against* the idea of the penal state.

In this tome and in the lecture course at the Collège de France on "the punitive society" that preceded it, penality assumes the form of a "microphysics of power" operating beyond and behind the state, which is but a fictional figurehead.[10] Later, in his lecture course on *Sécurité, territoire, population*, Foucault proposes that three modalities of power coexist: sovereignty, disciplines, and governmentality. But the latter concept serves to dissolve the notion of the state to replace it with practices, strategies, and technologies deployed for the "conduct of conduct."

Foucault complains at length about "over-valuing the problem of the State ... But the State, no more today than in the course of its history, has had this unity, this individuality, this rigorous functionality and, I would even say, this importance. After all, the State is perhaps no more than a composite reality and a mythologized abstraction whose importance is much smaller than we think. Perhaps it is. What is important for our

life ... At once an element of social organization, an aspect of social relations, and an ingredient of individual psychology, penality runs like a connecting thread through all the layers of social structure, connecting the general with the particular, the center with its periphery" (*Punishment and Modern Society*, p. 288).

[9] Michel Foucault, *Surveiller et punir. Naissance de la prison* (1975), p. 313.

[10] Michel Foucault, *La Société punitive. Cours au Collège de France, 1972–1973* (2013).

modernity, that is, for our actuality, is not the 'statification' of society, it is what I would rather call the 'governmentalization of the State.'[11] So much to say that, paradoxically, Foucault has done more than any other scholar to popularize the study of the prison and, at the same time, to pulverize and disappear the penal state.

In the three chapters that compose this book, I propose to mate the materialist (Benthamite, rationalist, control-oriented, and centered on class) and the symbolic (Kantian, emotionalist, communicative, and community-forming) approaches to criminal sanction to elaborate a robust concept of the *penal state* rooted in Pierre Bourdieu's theory of fields and symbolic power; to specify its structure and differential deployment across social and physical space through what I call "paper penality" and "street penality"; and to reveal how it operates at ground level in the everyday reality of a criminal court as seen through the deeds of a prosecutor negotiating guilty pleas.

In this first chapter, my starting point is *perplexity at a reciprocal ignorance*: contemporary theorists of the state routinely overlook penal institutions while theorists of punishment stay mum about the state as a distinctive organization of power. To remedy this hiatus, I explicate the views of penality propounded by Émile Durkheim, Georg Rusche, and Michel Foucault. I relate them to the duality of reformation and retribution as two opposed philosophies of penal sanction, the one mundane and rational in Bentham's sense, the other sacred and moral in Kant's sense. I then consider the conceptions of the state found in the writings of Max Weber, Michael Mann, James Scott, and Pierre Bourdieu.

I draw selectively on their work to argue that penality – understood in an expansive mode as the categories, institutions, practices, and representations centered on the production, diffusion, and enforcement of criminal statutes – is a *core capacity of the modern state*. It serves not so much to deter and sanction crime as to *manage marginality* in the city, *stage sovereignty* and *signal legitimacy*. Its agencies penetrate the nether regions of social and physical space and make legible their residents, which they proceed to paint in the colors of danger and dissolution – from the "*Lumpenproletariat*" and the "residuum" to the "submerged tenth" and the "underclass."[12] It follows that

---

[11] Michel Foucault, *Sécurité, territoire, population. Cours au Collège de France, 1977–1978* (2004), p. 112.

[12] Loïc Wacquant, *The Invention of the "Underclass": A Study in the Politics of Knowledge* (2022), pp. 15–26. For a parallel historical study of figures of urban danger and

conceptions of the state are wanting when they forget punishment as a bureaucratic function and political mission while theories of punishment are lax and lacking when they fail to root its delivery in the architecture of the Leviathan. In particular, it is critical to link social policy, carried out by the Left (protective) hand of the state, to penal policy, rolled out by the Right (punitive) hand of the state, for the two work in tandem to manage disruptive poverty in the metropolis. Likewise, studies of urban marginality fail gravely when they omit the pivotal role of the police, which patrols districts of dereliction, and the jail, which feeds on and nourishes the disorders visited upon their population. The city is key to the development of the penal state and penality is central to the establishment of the urban order, real or imagined.

The puzzle of reciprocal ignorance

It is inherently difficult to capture an intellectual silence and document an absence in scholarship. It is always possible to find one author or one passage in a text that seems to refute the thesis that something is amiss. So the strategy I adopted to demonstrate that theorists of the state have overlooked punishment while theorists of punishment have ignored the state is to focus on panoramic books and synthetic articles, taking stock of major pronouncements on both sides.

1. The absence of penality in theories of the state

First, let me document the *conspicuous absence of penality* in contemporary theories of the state by canvassing recent panoramas on the Leviathan. In a chapter devoted to the genealogy and anatomy of "The Modern State" in an influential *Handbook of Political Theory*, the political philosopher Christopher Morris argues that the modern use of the term signals a new conception of the polity in which "geography acquires a new significance, the territorialization of political obligation."[13] When he catalogues "the institutions through which

---

dissolution in Brazil, read Michel Misse, *Malandros, marginais e vagabundos. A acumulação social da violência no Rio de Janeiro* (2023).

[13] Christopher W. Morris, "The Modern State" (2004, p. 197). See also, idem, *An Essay on the Modern State* (1998).

the state acts," he lists in passing "the government, the judiciary, the bureaucracy [and] the police" but says no more. Indeed, he questions the notion that the threat or use of force is central to the state, arguing that the latter's power rests on authority, consent, and legitimacy equated with legality. He asserts that "there does not seem to be a conceptual connection between states and coercion," overlooking the historical link between them as well as its modern concretization in the penal apparatus.[14] Morris notes that territoriality implies the tracing of borders, a dividing line between an inside and an outside marking the boundary of sovereignty. But he does not consider *internal borders* between the different regions of social and physical space within a given society – those very borders that the penal state is entrusted with patrolling.

In a compact and provocative synthesis, the sociologist Matthias Vom Hau organizes a vast array of writings on state theory into four intellectual traditions: class-analytic (Poulantzas, Jessop, Offe, Przeworski), liberal (Dahl, Levi, Hechter, Tyler), neo-Weberian (Mygdal, Tilly, Mann, Evans, Wimmer), and cultural (Foucault, Mitchell, Adams, Steinmetz).[15] He extracts from a selection of key authors in each of these traditions their root concepts, views of state–society relations, roster of state capacities, and the foundations of consent. The discussion of state capacities in the four lineages contains but four words on penal institutions. Thus, in the class-analytic lineage, state capacity includes the ability "to control borders, *enact law and order*, enforce contracts, collect taxes, and supply public goods from their relations to distinct social classes and from the legacies of past class struggles."[16] But criminal justice institutions are not considered core state capacities. The ability and, indeed, responsibility of the Leviathan to stipulate and enforce criminal law appears nowhere. Similarly, the panoramic review of theories and issues in the study of the state gathered by Colin Hay and British colleagues in political science is typical in that it contains not one line on penality.[17] The book canvasses pluralism, elitism, Marxism, public choice, institutionalism, feminism, green theory, poststructuralism: none of these

35

---

[14] Norbert Elias, *The Civilizing Process: Sociogenetic and Psychogenetic Investigations* ([1939] 2000); Charles Tilly, *Coercion, Capital, and European States, AD 990–1990* (1993).
[15] Matthias Vom Hau, "State Theory" (2015). Of these seventeen authors, only two, Tom Tyler and Michel Foucault, tackle punishment.
[16] Ibid., p. 133, my italics.
[17] Colin Hay et al. (eds.), *The State: Theories and Issues* (2022).

theories have anything to say on state punishment. Issues examined include the shift from government to governance, transformations of sovereignty and community, changes in statehood, and the redrawing of the public/private boundary. Interestingly, all these issues are relevant to the transformations of the penal state in advanced society over the past half-century but, again, the latter is nowhere to be found.

The stunning resurgence of the prison in nearly all advanced societies after the mid-1970s (discussed later in the second chapter) is completely missed by the *Oxford Handbook of the Transformation of the State* (2015), which reports on the work of a multidisciplinary team of distinguished scholars from 11 countries led by the Bremen policy scholar Stephan Leibfried. Among the topics receiving a full chapter under the "Crucial issues" rubric, we find the overhaul of the welfare state, gender equality, the regulatory state and migration, but not a word on criminal justice despite its stunning growth and explosive political sensitivity over the past half-century as evidenced by the international spread of "penal populism."[18]

The multidisciplinary volume edited by Kimberly Morgan and Ann Shola Orloff, taking stock of advances in theory and research on the state in the half-century after the publication of the path-breaking 1985 book, *Bringing the State Back In*, promises to "theorize political authority and social control," but, remarkably, it omits criminal control and marginality management altogether.[19] The title of the book, *The Many Hands of the State*, extends Pierre Bourdieu's metaphor of the Right hand and Left hand of the state (about which more later, *infra*, pp. 99–106), purporting to draw attention to the core functions of the state. But the Right hand of the state is conspicuously missing from the book, and with it the penal institution. In their chapter on "The Civil Rights State," Desmond King and Robert Lieberman do note that "the United States has developed a vast, punitive, and decidedly race-laden 'carceral state' that has imprisoned and disenfranchised a large and disproportionate share of young black men, with disastrous consequences for racial equality in economic opportunity and political empowerment," but they draw no theoretical

---

[18] Stephan Leibfried et al. (eds.), *The Oxford Handbook of Transformations of the State* (2015); Julian V. Roberts et al., *Penal Populism and Public Opinion: Lessons from Five Countries* (2002); Denis Salas, *La Volonté de punir. Essai sur le populisme pénal* (2005).
[19] Kimberly J. Morgan and Ann Shola Orloff (eds.), *The Many Hands of the State: Theorizing Political Authority and Social Control* (2017); Dietrich Rueschemeyer et al. (eds.), *Bringing the State Back In* (1985).

implication from this development.[20] As for Christian Davenport, he manages to discuss the role of the state in the "performance of order" and in subjugating population without a single mention of the police, court, and prison.[21]

In the chapter entitled "Rethinking the State" opening the broad-ranging volume on *The Dynamics of States: The Formation and Crises of State Domination* (2016) around the globe, the political scientists Joel Mygdal and Karl Schlichte propose that "a pervasive, transformative crisis of the state has occurred in recent decades, forcing a reevaluation of existing conceptual models" when applied to Asia, Africa, and Latin America.[22] But the book devotes all of two lines to the partial privatization of police and prison and does not reflect on the ramifying mutations of the triad police–court–prison on these three continents, including the spectacular spread of police violence and the stunning growth of incarceration in all of Latin America since the return of formal democracy.[23]

Finally, in a deep book canvassing the "past, present and future" of the state, Bob Jessop, its most prolific contemporary theorist, fails to make room for the police, criminal court, and prison as organizational capacities of the Leviathan. The penal triad appears nowhere in his thoroughgoing historical discussion and schematization. In a table summing up the "cumulative genesis of the modern state," he lists in passing the army and police as the "power basis" and force as the "political steering mechanism" of the "absolute or security state" of the early modern era from the fifteenth to seventeenth century. But these notions vanish afterwards in the "constitutional," "social (welfare)" and even, surprisingly, in the "supervision state" of the twentieth and twenty-first centuries. The word punishment appears thrice in brief discussions of Nietzsche, Poulantzas, and dictatorship as if penality was irrelevant to the establishment of political rule and social order in liberal democratic societies.[24]

37

---

[20] Desmond King and Robert C. Lieberman, "The Civil Rights State: How the American State Develops Itself" (2017), p. 194.

[21] Christian Davenport, "Performing Order: An Examination of the Seemingly Impossible Task of Subjugating Large Numbers of People, Everywhere, All the Time" (2017).

[22] Joel S. Mygdal and Klaus Schlichte, "Rethinking the State" (2016), p. 2.

[23] Between 1992 and 2016, the incarceration rate measured by the number of inmates per 100,000 residents jumped from 74 to 349 in Brazil, 100 to 306 in Uruguay, 69 to 257 in Peru, 78 to 243 in Colombia, 154 to 242 in Chile, and 62 to 200 in Argentina.

[24] Bob Jessop, *The State: Past, Present, Future* (2015), pp. 30, 15, 229, 23.

The vanishing of penality in the Marxist theory of the state

Two illustrious Marxist scholars gave pride of place to the penal triad in their theories of the state in the late 1960s. The British political theorist Ralph Miliband adopted this approach in an instant classic, *The State in Capitalist Society*, published on the morrow of the 1968 protests. He began with an ostensive definition of key state institutions as "the government, the administration, the military and the police, the judicial branch, sub-central government and parliamentary assemblies" (1). A couple of years later, the French Marxist philosopher Louis Althusser echoed him in a famous essay on "Ideology and Ideological State Apparatuses." Althusser distinguished a relatively unified "repressive state apparatus," comprising "the army, the police, the courts, the prisons, etc.," from diverse, relatively autonomous, "ideological state apparatuses" such as the family, education, the media, and organized religion (2). The former operate through physical violence and legal constraint while the latter work via persuasion. But neither Miliband nor Althusser developed the penal side of their theories of the state and punishment subsequently dropped out of the Marxist agenda altogether. It is conspicuously absent from Bob Jessop's panoramic review and reconstruction of theories of *The State: Past, Present, Future* from the 1960s to 2015 (3).

Reflecting back on the Marxist lineage, one thinks of Lenin's explication and extension of Friedrich Engels's view of state power as materialized by "special bodies of armed men having prisons, etc., at their command" (4). It characteristically took penality for granted and therefore not in need of theoretical or political analysis. Another silence on punishment is particularly strident and puzzling: that of Antonio Gramsci, who spent over a decade behind bars and yet wrote not a line about the prison as a core institution of the state in his posthumously published *Prison Notebooks* (4). One can only speculate about what a neo-Gramscian theory of the penal Leviathan as producer of hegemony would be, but it would no doubt converge with the argument I make later in this chapter about penality as negative sociodicy "normalizing" the social misfortune of the precariat and supporting the moral order of society.

1. Ralph Miliband, *The State in Capitalist Society* (1969), p. 54.
2. Louis Althusser, *Pour Marx* (1971).

3. Bob Jessop, *The State: Past, Present, Future* (2015).
4. V.I. Lenin, *The State and Revolution* ([1917] 2024), chapter 1, Section 4.
5. Antonio Gramsci, *Prison Notebooks* (1992–2007).

One last manifestation of the puzzle of the blindness of students of the state for punishment, the most puzzling of them all: the world's most distinguished student of punishment, David Garland, took a detour from his usual intellectual agenda to write an elegant and erudite primer entitled *The Welfare State: A Very Short Introduction* (2014a). In it, he retraces the birth, development, and endurance of the social wing of the Leviathan but, strikingly, he has nothing to say about its penal wing. It is as if the two sides of the state did not communicate with each other, developed separately and functioned in silos such that you can understand welfare (in its expansive meaning of protection from unemployment, poverty, illness, and old age) and state formation more broadly without bringing penality into the analytic equation. This is all the more striking considering that Garland's first book, published 30 years earlier, was precisely a landmark historical sociology of the invention of "penal welfarism" in England and Wales during the first third of the twentieth century that demonstrated that "'the penal' and 'the social' cannot be conceived of as separate and exclusive realms, since the two are interpenetrating and interdependent."[25]

2. The absence of the state in theories of penality

Now let me document the *conspicuous absence of the state* in contemporary works on penality. Two signal exceptions are the writings of the Canadian legal scholar Markus Dubber and the Scottish sociologist and criminologist David Garland, which I will discuss later.

The intellectual current that has done the most to question the textual and internalist approach to the law, the "law and society" paradigm, creates by its very designation the impression that there exists a direct relation between the law and society that is not mediated by the history, structure, and policies of the state, including in domains beyond criminal law and its administration. Work in this vein typically takes for granted and invisibilizes the state. Thus Kitty Calavita's widely read *Invitation to Law and Society* (2016) eschews all discussion

---

[25] David Garland, *Punishment and Welfare: A History of Penal Strategies* (1985), p. 291.

of the Leviathan.[26] This is in part due to the doxic assumption made by US scholars that their country has a "weak state" when, precisely, the penal wing of American government at all levels is hypertrophied, deeply penetrative, and immensely noxious.[27]

The excellent *Sage Handbook of Punishment and Society*, edited by Jonathan Simon and Richard Sparks (2012) and mapping out this fast-expanding arena of research, contains but a few lines on the state and the concept rates just a handful of mentions in the detailed index.[28] The book scans seven theoretical approaches to penality, only one of which, that building on Norbert Elias's work, makes room for the role of the Leviathan. But even that chapter spotlights the cultural, cognitive, and libidinal dimensions of the "civilizing process" and gives short shrift to the monopolization of force and the law by the state – it is dispatched in two lines.[29] Similarly, David Garland's thorough review of work produced in this intellectual stream to mark the twentieth anniversary of the journal *Punishment & Society* notes "considerable intellectual progress" with "improvement in theory and method" and draws a catalog of topics and middle-range theories. These include "basic questions about the normative foundations of punishment; the communicative functions of punishment; the forms of punishment; the nature of penal power; and penal control's relation to social control."[30] What goes missing is the structure, history, and policies of the penal state *qua* state both theoretically and historically in light of its neoliberal remaking, including the ballooning of prison everywhere after the mid-1970s. This is surprising since Garland himself devoted his 2012 Sutherland Lecture before the American Society of Criminology to specifying a concept of the penal state, to which I return later.[31]

Even students of punishment who explicitly theorize carceral growth in advanced society fail to bring the state as such into the penal equation.

---

[26] Kitty Calavita, *Invitation to Law and Society: An Introduction to the Study of Real Law* (2016).

[27] For a convincing refutation of this national myth enshrined by conventional social science, read William J. Novak, "The Myth of the 'Weak' American State" (2008).

[28] Jonathan Simon and Richard Sparks (eds.), *The Sage Handbook of Punishment and Society* (2013).

[29] John Pratt, "Punishment and the Civilizing Process" (2013).

[30] David Garland, "Theoretical Advances and Problems in the Sociology of Punishment" (2018), p. 17.

[31] David Garland, "Penality and the Penal State" (2013a). See my discussion *infra*, pp. 115–17.

The legal scholar Nicola Lacey comes close to doing so in her comparative study, *The Prisoners' Dilemma: Political Economy and Punishment in Contemporary Democracies*.[32] She contrasts postindustrial nations based on the combination of modes of economic regulation and electoral systems coalescing into two regimes, neoliberal and neo-corporatist. Her causal model of punitiveness versus tolerance also takes into account the power of the executive, the weight of intermediate groups and cultural attitudes. She does acknowledge the role of the state on the social welfare front but stops short of delving into its penal wing.

Similarly, Michael Campbell and Heather Schoenfeld develop a provocative multivariate model of penal transformation in the United States during the closing three decades of the twentieth century at the level of the federated states. They focus on the weight of politics, the interplay between the national and local levels of policy-making and the strategies of interest groups such as police unions, prosecutors' associations, and crime victims' groups, but they do not draw a structural map allowing us to situate these actors in and about the bureaucratic field.[33] Indeed, the latter notion does not figure in their account, which centers on the dyad of the "penal field" and the "political field," which they variously (mis)characterize as "overlapping," "merged," and "converging." They miss the topological moment at the core of Pierre Bourdieu's concept of field, which they deploy as a rhetorical device to organize their rich historical narrative rather than as an analytic construct to elaborate an architectured picture of the penal state properly so-called. Their focus on "micro-level interactions" reveals that their concept is closer to the "organizational field" of Paul DiMaggio and Woody Powell than to Bourdieu's *champ* which requires, as a first step, situating the field in question inside the field of power.[34]

The political scientist Marie Gottschalk deploys the category of "carceral state" to diagnose America's run-up to hyperincarceration in her impressive book *Caught* (2016). Under her pen, the term "encompasses

41

---

[32] Nicola Lacey, *The Prisoners' Dilemma: Political Economy and Punishment in Contemporary Democracies* (2008).

[33] Michael C. Campbell and Heather Schoenfeld, "The Transformation of America's Penal Order: A Historicized Political Sociology of Punishment" (2013). This model is further refined in Heather Schoenfeld, *Building the Prison State: Race and the Politics of Mass Incarceration* (2018).

[34] Paul J. DiMaggio and Walter W. Powell, "The Iron Cage Revisited: Institutional Isomorphism and Collective Rationality in Organizational Fields" (1983). Campbell and Schoenfeld do not engage Bourdieu's work. They rely instead on Joshua Page's account of field theory (who in turn relies on my reading of Bourdieu but misses the topological moment), which is the source of their interactionist misinterpretation of the concept. I return to this point in my discussion of Page, *infra*, pp. 99–161.

not only the country's vast archipelago of jails and prisons but also the growing range of penal punishments and controls that lie in the never-never land between prison and full citizenship, from probation and parole to immigrant detention, felon disenfranchisement, and extensive lifetime restrictions on sex offenders."[35] But the carceral state (or its synonym the "prison state") is a descriptive and not an analytic category which isolates the systemic output of incarceration from the input of the police and the throughput of the court, thus gravely truncating the penal apparatus. The prison is located at the tail end of the chain of punishment; it does not control the flow and shape the profile of the population it confines: it is a *dependent and reactive institution* and not a governing one – except in the restricted sense of governing inmates. The "carceral state" is a misnomer.[36]

The rich thematic issue of *Theoretical Criminology* devoted to "the state of the state" in 2017 promises to remedy the inattention of students of punishment to the Leviathan. The articles gathered by Vanessa Barker and Lisa Miller "examine the role of the state as a driver of penal order and how, in turn, penal order shapes the character and contours of the state." They cover a broad array of penal sites and countries, including "unequal policing in Latin America, vigilante justice in South Africa, border control in Northern Europe, contested state sovereignty in Southern Europe, the high murder rates of black women, the fractured nature of penal reform in Michigan, and the mass surveillance of former inmates in the USA." But the different papers rest on discrepant and tacit understandings of the Leviathan and they fail to engage state theory as such. They raise the question, "How should the state be defined, vis-à-vis criminal justice and punishment?,"[37] but they do not answer it conclusively. In the end, the whole is less than the sum of the parts and the reader is left wanting for a closing article that would articulate a coherent concept of the penal state.

In that same issue of *Theoretical Criminology*, Ashley Rubin and Michelle Phelps's stimulating paper charts the growing use of "penal

[35] Marie Gottschalk, *Caught: The Prison State and the Lockdown of American Politics* (2016), p. 1.

[36] The same conceptual confusion constricts some of the contributions gathered by Kelly Lytle Hernández et al. in the stimulative thematic issue of the *Journal of American History* devoted to "Historians and the Carceral State" (2015).

[37] Vanessa Barker and Lisa L. Miller, "Introduction to the Special Issue on the State of the State" (2017), p. 418.

state" and "carceral state" in the literature on punishment and society, which confirms how – on my reading – the term has been employed as a rhetorical placeholder or, in its more careful usages, defined in extension (via enumeration) instead of intension (specifying necessary and sufficient properties). They propose to "fracture the penal state" to bring attention to state actors in various degrees of "conflict." But they forget to expound a robust construct of the state, which is a logical prerequisite for articulating a concept of penal state, and they confuse the penal *state* proper with the penal *field* (a distinction I elaborate later in this chapter, see *infra*, pp. 96–8), while exaggerating the degree of dispersion and incoherence of the former – because their theorization is based only on the US case. The virtue of Pierre Bourdieu's concept of field is precisely to allow us to hold together the unity of *the* penal state as an analytical construct while mapping its varied internal structure as a dynamic system of objective positions and correlative strategies, rather than a "*messy amalgamation* of political, legal, and bureaucratic actors all with their own interests and perspectives."[38]

43

Finally, just three of 25 chapters in the comprehensive *Sage Handbook of Criminological Theory* make *oblique references* to the state, and then only to argue that it has "withered away" and needs to be displaced or effaced from the analysis of punishment.[39] The neo-Foucauldian advocate of risk theory Pat O'Malley argues for replacing the state with a more differentiated and diffuse sense of control captured by the category of governmentality.[40] The chapter by Katja Franko Aas on "Global Criminology" discusses "the introduction of market solutions in the field of punishment and social control" and trumpets the need to "decenter the state in a global age." She confidently asserts that, "if traditionally the issues of security and justice were the main prerogative of the state, the neoliberal styles of governance, on the other hand, encourage individuals, institutions and local communities to take active responsibility for managing their crime problems, in line with other risks and uncertainties."[41] Michael Cavadino echoes this position in his chapter on changes in penology when he asserts that "managerial crime prevention and harm reduc-

---

[38] Ashley Rubin and Michelle S. Phelps, "Fracturing the Penal State: State Actors and the Role of Conflict in Penal Change" (2017), p. 423, my italics.
[39] Eugene McLaughlin and Tim Newburn (eds.), *The Sage Handbook of Criminological Theory* (2010).
[40] Pat O'Malley, "Governmental Criminology" (2010), pp. 319, 321, 323, 326.
[41] Katja Franko Aas, "Global Criminology" (2010), p. 435.

tion approaches [place] responsibility on citizens rather than the state to guard themselves against crime."[42]

I realize full well that this is not a fashionable theoretical position, but I wish to *reassert the centrality of the state in the production of social order, the delivery of public safety and the management of urban marginality* – a key focus of governmental action ever since the birth of the modern police and the penal prison.[43] Individual practices, group strategies, and diffuse organizational mechanisms feeding Foucauldian "governmentality" are always deployed in the long shadow of the state. Objectively: the state provides the infrastructure which permits other institutions to develop and it channels their operations in myriad ways, positive and negative. Subjectively: the state inculcates the cognitive categories guiding agents in their everyday world and sets the horizon of collective expectations that motivate them.[44]

Moreover, in contemporary society, governmentality is a modality of power deeply inflected by class and ethnicity. It corresponds faithfully to the experience of punishment of the middle and upper classes, a principled "paper penalty" made of the courteous deployment of legal texts, the urbane formalities of judicial procedures shepherded by a mannerly private attorney, and soft-edged procedures of control applying out of custody with due respect of fundamental rights.[45] But it does not capture the raw experience of the residents of neighborhoods of relegation, where arbitrary "street penalty" takes the form of the constant harassment, overt racial scorn, and routine brutality of the police, diffident relations with a rushed public defender, chaotic court hearings and the omnipresent threat of incarceration, starting with remand custody.[46] To put it crudely, in the dual metropolis,

---

[42] Michael Cavadino, "Penology" (2010), p. 455.

[43] Eric H. Monkkonen, "History of Urban Police" (1992); Pieter Spierenburg, "Four Centuries of Prison History: Punishment, Suffering, the Body, and Power" (1996).

[44] "In our societies, the state makes a decisive contribution to the production and reproduction of the instruments of construction of social reality. As an organizational structure and agency regulating practices, it constantly exerts a formative action on durable dispositions, through all the physical and mental constraints and disciplines that it uniformly imposes on all agents." Pierre Bourdieu, "Esprit d'État. Genèse et structure du champ bureaucratique" (1993a), p. 59.

[45] Matthew Clair, *Privilege and Punishment: How Race and Class Matter in Criminal Court* (2020); Julien Larregue, *Au Coeur de l'Etat pénal. Les avocats de la défense sous contrainte* (2026).

[46] Didier Fassin, *La Force de l'ordre. Une anthropologie de la police des quartiers* (2011a); Victor M. Rios, *Punished: Policing the Lives of Black and Latino Boys* (2011).

44

the bourgeoisie gets governmentality while the precariat gets the penal state – or, worse, gets both.

At minimum, the state must be *perceived* as enforcing the law and producing public safety and tranquility on the street, for that is the key to the prosaic projection of sovereignty in the city. In districts of urban dereliction, in particular, the state is central to the *simultaneous production and disruption* of social order, and these neighborhoods are the primary target of punishment (as I will show in the second chapter). As for the other actors brought into the security loop – individuals, households, or firms – they extend, but do not replace or displace, the power of the Leviathan. Private operators take part in punishment via precisely stipulated and revocable delegation; they do not challenge the state's monopoly but affirm it by operating strictly within its ambit. Civil society outfits such as crime victims' associations also orient themselves toward, and make claims on, the state, reinforcing its prerogatives even as they decry its failings. In short, *penality is both the duty and the perquisite of the state.* So I now turn to the social theorist who can help us elaborate this proposition.

But, before I do, let me interject the reason for what I have called the "puzzle of mutual ignorance." Why is it that theorists of the state have been disinterested in punishment? The answer is that the Leviathan is a noble, "high," and "pure" scientific object whereas penality, as a response to crime, is an ignoble, "lowly," and "dirty" topic. This, in turn, is an expression of the respective social status of the figures running the state (elected politicians, high civil servants) for the benefit of the citizenry and of the personnel running the justice apparatus (police, court attorneys, and prison guards) for the detriment of criminals.[47] As for students of penality, they were long trapped inside the "crime-and-punishment" box explored by the low-prestige, empiricist, and technical discipline of criminology. The coalescing subfield of "punishment and society" animated by the eponymous journal over the past two decades has been research-driven and has favored theories of the "middle range."[48] As a result, it has failed to draw the full implications of the conceptual distinction between state and society.

45

[47] This symbolic division also explains the long blindness of American social scientists to the carceral explosion staring them in the face, as shown by Marie Gottschalk, "Hiding in Plain Sight: American Politics and the Carceral State" (2008).
[48] Garland, "Theoretical Advances and Problems in the Sociology of Punishment."

Durkheim, Rusche, and Foucault on penality: Passion, labor, disciplines

Three thinkers set out fruitful principles, craft powerful concepts, and put forth substantive theses about punishment that help us elaborate a rigorous social theory of the penal state: Émile Durkheim, Georg Rusche, and Michel Foucault. I discuss them *in seriatim*.

1. Durkheim on passion as *"the soul of penality"*

Émile Durkheim is the first sociologist to give us essential tools for thinking about penality and its social springs. His foundational theory of punishment flows from his revolutionary definition of crime as an act that "offends strong and definite states of the collective conscience," a definition that inverts conventional causality: "We must not say that an action shocks the common conscience because it is criminal, but rather that it is criminal because it shocks the common conscience. We do not reprove it because it is a crime, but it is a crime because we reprove it."[49] Even in the simplest social formations, there will always be some actions that deviate from normative expectations and trigger indignation. It follows that crime is "normal" and not pathological, an "integral part of all healthy societies."[50]

Punishment is, accordingly, the normal reaction of the collectivity to violations of its sanctified rules of conduct. In precapitalist societies, this reaction is expressed and directed by the heads of kinship, tribal, religious, or political groupings; in complex societies, its delivery is entrusted to the state and, within the state, to special organs tasked with justice. Its form may diversify, but its function is invariant: punishment is a "passionate reaction" of "graduated intensity" whereby society avenges "the outrage to morality" and "maintains social cohesion intact."

46

---

[49] Émile Durkheim, *De la division du travail social* ([1893] 1990), pp. 47, 48. This is a proto-constructivist concept of crime that anticipates constructivism by a half-century (if we date the latter from the neo-Husserlian phenomenology of Alfred Schutz).

[50] "Whether it is *useful or not*, crime, in any case, is normal because it is tied to the fundamental conditions of all social life. It is this way because there cannot be a society in which individuals do not diverge more or less from the collective type." Émile Durkheim, "Crime et santé mentale" (1895), p. 176. This does not obviate the fact that the intensity and frequency of crime can become excessive and thus pathological for a given societal type.

The nature of punishment has not been changed in its essentials. All that we can say is that the need for vengeance is better directed today than in the past. The spirit of foresight which has been awakened no longer leaves the field so free for the blind action of passion. It restrains it within certain limits; it opposes absurd violence and wanton ravaging. Being more enlightened, it spills out less randomly. We no longer see it, to satisfy itself anyway, turn against the innocent. But it nevertheless remains *the soul of penality*. We can thus say that punishment consists in a *passionate reaction of graduated intensity*, . . . which society exercises, through the agency of a constituted body, upon those of its members who have violated certain rules of conduct.[51]

That punishment, thus defined as "socially organized sanction," is "an act of vengeance," however euphemized, does not mean that its main target is the offender. In another stunning inversion, Durkheim proposes that "punishment is above all *designed to act upon law-abiding folks (honnêtes gens)*. For, since it serves to heal wounds inflicted upon collective sentiments, it can only fulfill this role where such sentiments exist and insofar as they are active."[52] *Contra* the rational approach rooted in Jeremy Bentham's utilitarianism in the tow of Cesare Beccaria, for which criminal sanction aims to fashion future behavior through deterrence and rehabilitation, the author of *Suicide* insists that

47

> the essential function of punishment is not to make the culprit expiate his fault by making him suffer, or to intimidate possible imitators by means of threats, but to *reassure those consciences which the violation of the rule can and must necessarily disturb* in their faith – even as they fail to realize it – and to show them that this faith continues to be justified.[53]

So much to say, in yet another striking statement, that punishment is a *communicative device*, "a notation, a language through which the public conscience of society . . . expresses the sentiment that the reproved act inspires among its members."[54] Punishment reaffirms normative principles by singling out those who violate them for opprobrium. In his 1902 lecture course at the Sorbonne published posthumously as *L'Éducation morale*, Durkheim discusses the principles and techniques of "academic penality," that is, the economy of

[51] Durkheim, *De la division du travail social*, pp. 57 and 64, my italics.
[52] Ibid., p. 77, my italics.
[53] Émile Durkheim, *L'Éducation morale* (1925), p. 26, my italics.
[54] Ibid., p. 147.

punishment designed to instill in pupils the spirit of discipline, the attachment to the group and the autonomy of will that constitute morality. He stresses how punishment creates outcasts:

> To punish is to reprove, it is to blame. Thus, at all times, the main form of punishment has been to blacklist the guilty party, to hold him at a distance, to isolate him, to create a vacuum around him, to separate him from law-abiding folks.[55]

Since "penal reaction" varies in accordance with the "vivacity of the offended sentiment" and the "severity of the offense committed," punishment naturally gravitates toward proportionality:

> The proportionality that is observed everywhere between crime and punishment is therefore established with mechanical spontaneity, without the need for scholarly supputations to calculate it. What determines the gradation of crimes is also what determines the gradation of punishments; the two scales cannot, therefore, fail to correspond, and this correspondence, while necessary, is also useful.[56]

This homeostatic mechanism can be shown to work over the grand sweep of history. Surveying the evolution of penality from ancient to modern times, Durkheim formulates "two laws of penal evolution." The quantitative law states that criminal sanctions become less severe across the centuries; the qualitative law reports that "deprivation of liberty and of liberty alone tends increasingly to become the normal type of repression" in complex societies. In another stroke of sociological genius, Durkheim shows that the sacralization of the individual which leads us to punish those who attack others also causes us to moderate their punishment.

> What tempers the *collective anger which is the soul of punishment* is the sympathy that we feel for any man who suffers, the horror which any destructive violence evokes in us. Now it is the same sympathy and the same horror which set off this same anger. The very cause that sets into motion the repressive apparatus tends to stop it. It is the same mental state which goads us to punish and to moderate punishment.[57]

[55] Ibid.
[56] Durkheim, *De la division du travail social*, p. 68.
[57] Émile Durkheim, "Deux lois de l'évolution pénale" ([1899] 1969), p. 268, my italics. Elsewhere Durkheim confirms: "The collective sentiment offended by the crime is also offended by the sanction. In this way, a kind of compensation is established that

But penality can lag behind the new cultural and moral sensibilities that crystallize at a given epoch. Indeed, this was the case for European societies at the time of Durkheim's writing, when he speaks of

> the state of crisis in which criminal law finds itself among all civilized peoples. We have reached the point where the penal institutions of the past have either disappeared or else survive only by force of habit, but without others being born that better respond to the new aspirations of the moral conscience.[58]

It is the role of the state as an "organ of reflection," a coordinating agency of supra-individual intelligence, to "concentrate on the law" to restore its organic relation to the current collective conscience, and to "organize the moral life of the country" so as to foster "equality and thus justice."[59] By derivation, this applies to the criminal justice apparatus as a structurally benevolent agency that serves the needs of the society construed as a unified whole.

For the founder of French sociology, then, penality is a phatic agency operating in the expressive or symbolic register; it involves an emotive action propelled by bursts of "collective sentiments" which brighten the boundaries of a community whose solidarity it thereby reinforces. Collective meaning, shared rituals, public ceremonies, expressions of feelings, and assertions of morality, the marking of social boundaries: these are the staples of the Durkheimian sociology of penality.[60] The limitations of Durkheim's model of punishment are the direct obverse of its strengths: it lacks a material grounding and dismisses too quickly the effects of criminal sanction on the conduct of various categories of offenders and would-be offenders. It treats society as an integrated totality rather than a system of relations of power and thus overlooks the stratification of the functions of punishment along the twofold order of class and status. It presupposes

49

prevents the punishment from growing as the intensity of blame does." Durkheim, "Crime et santé mentale," p. 175.

[58] Durkheim, "Deux lois de l'évolution pénale," p. 273.

[59] Émile Durkheim, "L'État" ([1900] 1975), p. 177.

[60] Exemplary illustrations of the Durkheimian paradigm include Frank Tannenbaum, *Crime and the Community* (1938); Kai Erikson, *Wayward Puritan: A Study in the Sociology of Deviance* (1966); Hans Boutellier, *Crime and Morality: Significance of Criminal Justice in Post-Modern Culture* (2000); Smith, *Punishment and Culture*; and David Garland, *Peculiar Institution: America's Death Penalty in an Age of Abolition* (2010).

an agreement on moral values and standards of conduct and thus ignores the politics of sanction:[61] the struggles to define criminality and to decide what type of offense to prioritize and what arm of the state will be tasked with responding to it, social, medical, or penal, and, if penal, what philosophy of punishment to apply. Finally, Durkheim's model assumes a historical continuity of the *longue durée* in penal transformation which makes it ill-equipped to capture medium-term oscillations and short-term bursts of punitiveness and the variable disconnect between the reality and the perception of criminal insecurity.[62]

2. Rusche on labor and "the mode of punishment"

The materialist approach to the law initiated by Marx and Engels and famously elaborated by Georg Rusche and Otto Kirchheimer in *Punishment and Social Structure* (1939) is in every respect diametrically opposed to the Durkheimian approach. For the Marxists and their allies in the lineage of radical criminology, punishment is a rational instrument of class control. It is propelled, not by passion but by interest, and it fosters not solidarity but exploitation. Such are the lessons drawn from a historical sociology of punishment in Western Europe over eight centuries uncovering a stubborn "correspondence" between the mode of production and the mode of punishment.[63] Penality is quintessentially a class institution, as demonstrated by three propositions.

Karl Marx on the theft of wood in the Rhineland

As editor of the *Rheinische Zeitung*, the young Karl Marx, then aged 24, wrote a series of five articles dissecting the debates on the criminalization of the collection of fallen wood by poor peasants in the

---

[61] Stuart A. Scheingold, *The Politics of Law and Order: Street Crime and Public Policy* (1984); John Hagan, *Who are the Criminals? The Politics of Crime Policy from the Age of Roosevelt to the Age of Reagan* (2010).

[62] Goodman et al., *Breaking the Pendulum*; Laurent Bonelli, *La France a peur. Une histoire sociale de "l'insécurité"* (2010).

[63] "Every system of production tends to discover punishments which correspond to its productive relationships." Georg Rusche and Otto Kirchheimer, *Punishment and Social Structure* ([1939] 2005), p. 5.

Moselle region that can be read as an adumbration of his later views on penality, property, and labor (1). State authorities and the forest owners conspired to revoke the customary right to gather dead wood and debated the option to jail wood collectors as common offenders, to force them to pay fines or to make them work for the landlord maintaining communal roads (2). Penalization thus effected the destruction of the commons and turned forced labor into free labor for the benefit of the private owner. Criminality emerges as the result of relations of class power and penality as a state instrument to foster the interests of the propertied (3). These two propositions are the pillars of the Marxist approach to punishment.

1. Karl Marx, "Debates on the Law on Thefts of Wood" ([1842] 2017). The articles were provocative. They caused the Prussian authorities to close down the journal and forced Marx to go into exile in Paris, never to return to Germany.
2. The economic and legal contexts of Marx's intervention are reconstructed by Peter Linebaugh, "Karl Marx, the Theft of Wood, and Working Class Composition: A Contribution to the Current Debate" (1976).
3. On the relevance of these texts to current struggles over the commons, read Daniel Bensaïd, *Les Dépossédés. Karl Marx, les voleurs de bois et le droit des pauvres* (2007).

First, according to Rusche, crime is a direct consequence of economic oppression and material deprivation. This is a straightforward Marxist position formulated earlier by Friedrich Engels, for whom the destitution and demoralization of the worker caught in the capitalist "social war" turns him "into a criminal – as inevitably as water turns into steam at boiling point."[64] While it is true that offenses are committed by people across the social structure, it is equally "clear that criminal law and the daily work of the criminal courts are directed almost exclusively against those people whose class background, poverty, neglected education, or demoralization led them to crime."[65] But there is more: we cannot reduce punishment to an institutional response to offending:

[64] Friedrich Engels, *The Condition of the Working Class in England* ([1845] 1987), p. 149. A thorough catalog of Marx and Engels's dispersed pronouncements on punishment can be found in James Parisot, "Marx and Engels on Prisons and Capitalism" (2025).
[65] Georg Rusche, "Labor Market and Penal Sanction: Thoughts on the Sociology of Criminal Justice" ([1933] 1978), p. 11.

The bond, transparent or not, that is supposed to exist between crime and punishment . . . must be broken. Punishment is neither a simple consequence of crime, nor the reverse side of crime, nor a mere means which is determined by the end to be achieved. Punishment must be understood as a social phenomenon freed from both its juristic concept and its social ends.[66]

Second, to fulfill their deterrent function, "sanctions must appear even worse than the strata's present living conditions" – an application of the principle of "less eligibility" formulated by Jeremy Bentham in his utilitarian view of welfare policy. If inmates are treated better behind bars than the poorest of the poor on the outside, wouldn't the latter take to crime in order to improve their lot and receive "three meals and a cot" for free? This principle presuming individual rationality constrains the possibilities for penal reform and puts a cap on the improvement of the condition of convicts.[67]

Third, the historical analysis of penality must imperatively supplement economic analysis. Then it will disclose that "every system of production tends to discover punishments which correspond to its productive relationships." For that, it must escape the chronicle of jurists ("meticulous collectors of curiosities") and forsake the evolutionary tale of a gradual transition from past cruelty to contemporary humanitarianism to focus on "the relationship between criminal law and economics, the history of class struggle."[68] The transformation of penal practices across the centuries reveals that punishment has varied in keeping with the scarcity or abundance of labor: when workers are rare and thus valuable, society moves away from corporeal punishment (or extermination) to incarceration. This is the materialist counter to the idealist explanation of the long-term transformation of penality offered by Durkheim a half-century earlier.

Rusche distinguishes four historical stages in the long trend of punishment: (i) in the early medieval period, a system of fines and penance corresponds to a thinly populated peasant economy in which labor is scarce and crimes against property infrequent; (ii) in the late Middle Ages, whipping, mutilation, and killing spread in response to social upheavals and class polarization caused by the emergence of

[66] Ibid., p. 11. This passage is repeated nearly identically in *Punishment and Social Structure*, p. 5.

[67] A provocative revisit of this dilemma is François Bonnet, *The Upper Limit: How Low-Wage Work Defines Punishment and Welfare* (2019).

[68] Rusche, "Labor Market and Penal Sanction," p. 13.

capitalist production spawning rampant theft and robbery by hordes of beggars, unrest, and revolts culminating in peasant wars; (iii) in the modern era after 1600, with the expansion of trade and markets, labor becomes scarce again, its condition improves and punishment shifts from the gallows to the prison, proving the "fatal dependency" of criminal sanction on economic factors – humanitarianism triumphs because it is "absolutely profitable";[69] (iv) at the turn of the eighteenth century, the industrial revolution replaces workers with machines and a new "reserve army of labor" coalesces; punishment becomes harsher as houses of correction turn into virtual chambers of torture; solitary confinement arises as a "punitive device which could arouse fear even in the hungry and act as a deterrent for people who did not know how to stay alive."[70]

53

Rusche is fully aware of the analytic limitations of Marxism when it comes to accounting for penal policy:

> The dependency of crime and crime control on economic and historical conditions does not, however, provide a full explanation ... The penal system and the ritual of criminal procedure are shaped by various forces, including religious and sexual phenomena.[71]

Punishment and Social Structure also singles out a major determinant of the form and intensity of punishment: the fiscal capacity of the state. But, within these limits, "economic-historical analysis" will allow us to bring to light essential mechanisms. In a neglected passage of "Arbeitsmarkt und Strafvollzug," Rusche asserts that the materialist approach "has not sufficiently consider[ed] the impact of the *sense of honor and fear of disgrace* associated with punishment."[72] The German legal scholar continues with this passage that echoes Durkheim's stress on the psychosocial effects of criminal sanction and Weber's concern with their legitimacy:

> The solidity of the social structure does in no way depend only on the strength of external measures of coercion which are supposed to guarantee the continuation of society. The great majority of people has to be *psychically willing* to accommodate to the existing society, to *regard the state as their state, the law as their law*. But, according to experience,

[69] Ibid., p. 14.
[70] Ibid., p. 15.
[71] Ibid., p. 11.
[72] Ibid., p. 11, my italics.

there are classes for whom this adjustment and identification break down.[73]

Nonetheless, Rusche and Kirchheimer make the state of the labor market the pivotal factor affecting punishment as do the authors who have situated their work in the Marxist stream.[74] But, in late capitalist societies, employment conditions are not determined solely by the sheer scarcity or abundance of laborers, as the two German scholars claim. Rather, they are set conjointly by a host of intermeshed institutions, including state policies, education, household formation, gender relations, immigration, and so on. Consider how unionization and state regulation of the economy impact the parameters of employment. Nonetheless, against liberal idealism, Rusche and Kirchheimer affirm the primacy of material factors and make a strong claim for the economic roots and functions of punishment, well summed up in this striking formulation of Friedrich Engels: "It has been shown that there has been a constant relationship between the number of arrests and the annual consumption of bales of cotton."[75] For the Marxist lineage, the penal state is a class institution by virtue of its target, its calibration, and its evolution.

The flaws of Rusche and Kirchheimer's theory of punishment are evident. They grant scant autonomy to the state and, inside the state, to the penal apparatus, despite their last-ditch efforts to encompass punishment under the Nazis (a chapter written by Kirchheimer alone and tacked on to the book without Rusche's knowledge), a spectacular instance of autonomization if there ever was one.[76] They faintly recognize but then vastly underestimate the role of symbolic divisions in the production of penal law and in the targeting of offenders. The notion of "correspondence" between mode of production and mode of punishment is crude and historically untenable: consider the wide

---

[73] Ibid., p. 11.

[74] Exemplary studies include Thorsten Sellin, *Slavery and the Penal System* (1976); Richard Quinney, *Critique of the Legal Order: Crime Control in Capitalist Society* (1974); Steven Spitzer, "Toward a Marxian Theory of Deviance" (1975); E.P. Thompson, *Whigs and Hunters: The Origin of the Black Act* (1975); Dario Melossi and Massimo Pavarini, *The Prison and the Factory: Origins of the Penitentiary System* (1981); Peter Linebaugh, *The London Hanged: Crime and Civil Society in the Eighteenth Century* (2001); and De Giorgi, *Re-Thinking the Political Economy of Punishment*.

[75] Engels, *The Condition of the Working Class in England*, p. 26.

[76] Rusche and Kirchheimer, *Punishment and Social Structure*, chapter 11. A deep dive into Nazi penality is Nikolaus Wachsmann, *Hitler's Prisons: Legal Terror in Nazi Germany* (2015).

variety of kinds and intensity of punishment across capitalist societies, such as the United States and Norway or England and Germany
today, as well as the abrupt and rapid reversals in penal trends in any
given country, as with the Netherlands between 1990 and 2010 or
Finland from 1970 to 2000. These short-term variations, unrelated
to changing labor market conditions, seem to contradict the "severity
hypothesis" according to which the scarcity of labor moderates punishment.[77] Finally, Rusche and Kirchheimer strive to escape from the
Marxist straitjacket when they mention state taxation, religion, and
sexuality as factors formative of punishment, but they fail to relate
them clearly to the economic forces they prioritize. They fall into the
usual trap of functionalism, namely, the failure to specify mechanisms
linking production and punishment.[78]

Remarkably, *Punishment and Social Structure* was reviewed in *The Economic
Journal* in March of 1940 by none other than T.H. Marshall a decade
before the latter put the institution of citizenship on the map of social science with his iconic tome on *Citizenship and Social Class* (1949). Marshall
notes that "the problem studied is important and extremely difficult to
handle, and it is treated from an unfamiliar angle."[79] He praises the erudition of Rusche and Kirchheimer and the boldness of their inquiry. But he
also finds that they "try to press their point too far and to make everything
fit in too neatly" with their theoretical model even as he expresses "gratitude for what has been achieved." In the nineteenth century, "the simple
correlation between penal methods and economic systems breaks down."
As for "the thesis that penal methods have no visible effect on crime rates,"
it is "probably true" but the data adduced "are rather violently tortured to
give it extra support."

3. Foucault on the "disciplinary society"

The writings and lectures of Foucault on punishment are protean,
diffuse, and unsystematic. The French philosopher changes concepts and positions often and abruptly, from the lecture course at the

[77] Michael Cavadino and James Dignan, *Penal Systems: A Comparative Approach*
(2005); Lacey, *The Prisoners' Dilemma: Political Economy and Punishment in
Contemporary Democracies*.
[78] A remedy for this flaw is Christopher Muller and Daniel Schrage, "The Political
Economy of Incarceration in the Cotton South, 1910–1925" (2021).
[79] T.H. Marshall, "Review of Rusche and Kirchheimer, *Punishment and Social
Structure*" (1940), pp. 126–7.

55

Collège de France on *La Société punitive* (1974), in which he hews close to a standard materialist account of penality that one might characterize as neo-Ruschian; to *Surveiller et punir* (1975), in which he gives pride of place to the notions of "discipline" and "power-knowledge"; to the lecture course on *Sécurité, population, territoire* (1978), in which these are replaced by the "triangle sovereignty–discipline–security" and reframed with the concept of "governmentality." For the sake of clarity, and considering its global impact, I focus on the Foucault of *Surveiller et punir*, from which I extract four propositions.

First proposition and first surprise, Foucault does not set out to write a history of the prison – contrary to the subtitle and academic reputation of the book – but uses the birth of the prison as a springboard to sketch "a correlative history of the modern soul and of a new power to judge: a genealogy of the present scientifico-judicial complex upon which the power to punish rests."[80] *Contra* continuist accounts that portray the gradual evolution of penality in Western modernity as driven by the rise of humanitarian ideals, Foucault stresses historical discontinuity and material forces.[81] Between 1760 and 1840, an abrupt shift took place in European societies from the centralized, negative, political-juridical power of the sovereign to the diffuse, positive, biopower of disciplines.[82] This caesura takes the form of a *sudden penal transition* from spectacular torture targeting the body to invisible incarceration targeting the soul; from the macrophysics of power held by the state to the microphysics of "the carceral" spreading throughout society capillary-style; from the terror instilled by the discrete acts of the absolute ruler to the "training" of individuals effected by the continual and graduated application of myriad disciplines. The lesson here is that

---

[80] Foucault, *Surveiller et punir*, p. 30.

[81] Here Foucault dismisses Durkheim: if we follow the latter's view, "we risk positing as the principle of punitive mitigation processes of individualization which are rather the effects of new tactics of power" (*Surveiller et punir*, p. 31).

[82] The concept of biopower, referring to techniques that fructify persons and populations, is elaborated by Foucault in the first volume of his *Histoire de la sexualité* (1976). But it first appears in print in the summary of his 1971 lecture course at the Collège de France and it is lurking, unnamed, in his account of the impact of the carceral form. Michel Foucault, *Théories et institutions pénales. Cours au Collège de France 1971–1972* (2021).

penal systems must be replaced within a definite "political economy" of the body and its forces, of their utility and their docility, of their distribution and their submission.[83]

The second proposition concerns the disciplines, that is, techniques of distribution and control of activities that rely on "hierarchical surveillance," "normalizing sanction," and "examination."[84] Their task is to *make bodies useful and docile*, two properties that dynamically reinforce each other. Many disciplinary procedures have a long history with roots in convents, armies, and factories. But, in the eighteenth century, they become "general formulas for domination" that spread across myriad institutions where they spawn bodies of specialized knowledge that in turn reinforce power (thus the compound concept *"pouvoir-savoir"*): the school gives birth to pedagogy, the clinic to medicine, the asylum to psychiatry, the barracks to military strategy, the factory workshop to industrial engineering, and the prison to criminology. The "gradual extension of apparatuses of discipline" and their "multiplication throughout the social body" ushers in "the disciplinary society."[85]

57

Third proposition: the paradigmatic concretization of disciplinary power is Jeremy Bentham's Panopticon, a circular prison house which submits inmates to the constant gaze of an invisible guard situated at its center and thereby impels them to constantly conform their behaviors to institutional expectations. The Panopticon can be applied indifferently to workshops, schools, and prisons "every time we are dealing with a multiplicity of individuals to whom one must impose a task or a conduct." It is "an intensifier of power at the same time as a multiplier of production."[86] Its dissemination transports the carceral form outside the penitentiary; as a result, judicial penality recedes: "The carceral circles widen and the prison form slowly attenuates before disappearing." Foucault writes:

[83] Foucault, *Surveiller et punir*, p. 33. Foucault uses two terms: *dressage* and *dressement*. The French *dressage* is stronger than the English translation "training": it can also be translated as taming, as one does an animal to which one teaches obedience, skills, and tricks. As for *dressement*, it evokes *redressement*, the act of setting something straight. Facilities for juvenile detention in France used to be called *maisons de redressement*.

[84] Regrettably, Foucault ignores Max Weber's germane concept of discipline, defined in *Economy and Society* ([1920] 1978, p. 53) as "the probability that by virtue of habituation a command will receive prompt and automatic obedience in stereotyped forms, on the part of a given group of persons."

[85] Foucault, *Surveiller et punir*, p. 212.

[86] Ibid., p. 242.

The judges of normality are present everywhere. We are in the society of the teacher-judge, the doctor-judge, the educator-judge, the "social worker"-judge. They all foster the reign of the universality of the normative ... In the midst of all these tightening mechanisms of normalization, the specificity of the prison and its role as a seal lose their raison d'être.[87]

Lastly, the prison separates out different forms of illegalities and fosters the crystallization of a new social type: "the delinquent as pathological subject." Its failure to rehabilitate him is only apparent, for the couple police–prison makes his delinquency "manipulable"; it succeeds in diverting public attention from the illegalisms of the bourgeoisie.

Punishments are not intended to suppress offenses, but rather to distinguish them, to distribute them, to use them; they not only render docile those who are ready to transgress the laws, but they tend to make transgression of the laws part of a general tactic of subjugations. Penality, then, would be a manner of managing these illegalisms, to draw the limits of tolerance, to give room to some, to put pressure on others ... If we speak of class justice, it is not just that the law itself or the way it is applied serves the interests of a class, it is because the whole differential management of illegalisms through the agency of penality is part of these mechanisms of domination.[88]

Foucault is a shapeshifting writer and an elusive thinker who worked self-consciously at not being pinned down – as expressed in this famous passage of *L'Archéologie du savoir*: "Do not ask who I am and do not ask me to remain the same: this is the ethics of state bureaucracy which governs our identity papers. Let it leave us free when it comes to writing."[89] He explicitly disavows elaborating an overarching theory of punishment, claiming instead to propound only local analyses. But, in fact, he deploys *several such theories* in the course of his analysis of the generalization of carceral penality at the close of the eighteenth century. *Surveiller et punir* reveals him to be a materialist, like Rusche, but he gives pride of place to discourses and collective representations, like Durkheim. Yet it is most illuminating to

---

[87] Ibid., pp. 311, 313.
[88] Ibid., p. 286. "Delinquency, solidified by a penal system centered on prisons, represents a diversion of illegalism to the circuits of illicit profit and illicit power of the dominant class."
[89] Michel Foucault, *L'Archéologie du savoir* (1969), p. 28.

read him as a closet Weberian (who does not know he is one: Foucault never engaged the author of *Wirtschaft und Gesellschaft*). Like Weber, he is concerned with the cultural uniqueness of the West; he unravels multi-sited processes of rationalization; and he sees modern institutions primarily as stifling the inherent profusion of human desires (or pleasures).

Foucault on what Durkheim did not say about the disciplines

In his 1972–3 lecture course on "The Punitive Society" at the Collège de France, preparatory to the writing of *Surveiller et punir*, for the first and only time in all of his writings, Foucault engages Émile Durkheim. But, surprise, not Durkheim the theorist of penality (in *De la division du travail social* and "The Two Laws of Penal Evolution"), but Durkheim the theorist of anomie in *Le Suicide* (1). Foucault proposes that, as it shifts from sovereignty to discipline, power "abandons the sumptuosity of visible rituals" to assume "the insidious, quotidian, habitual form of the norm, and this is how it hides as power and presents itself as society" (2). The role of the seventeenth-century ceremony is taken up by "what we call the collective conscience" that Durkheim "makes the object of sociology."

Foucault continues: for the author of *Suicide*, "what characterizes the social as such," as distinct from the political and the economic, is "nothing other than the system of disciplines." It seems that he gives credit to Durkheim and enrolls him into his own theoretical model, but here is the catch: "Society, said Durkheim, is the system of disciplines; but what he did not say is that this system must be liable to an analysis within the strategies specific to a system of power" (3). In other words, for Foucault, the social is a mask as power disguises itself as society. For Durkheim, it is the opposite: power is secreted by society as the supra-individual entity endowed with force which forges and controls individuals. After this confrontation, there remains a question for Foucault, unanswered: what is the material substrate of disciplinary power, if any, or does it exists of its own volition and momentum?

1. Émile Durkheim, *Le Suicide. Étude sociologique* ([1897] 1990). Durkheim uses "anomie" (literally the absence of law, *nomos*) to describe the disruption of normative systems that weakens, nay erases, standards of conduct and valuation,

and releases our desires from their collective guardrails. Anomie takes many forms, among them economic, conjugal, and sexual. In his famous typology of suicide, anomie (normative confusion or effacement) stands opposed to fatalism (normative implacability) in the order of cultural *regulation* as egoism stands opposed to altruism in the order of social *integration*.
2. Michel Foucault, *La Société punitive. Cours au Collège de France, 1972–1973* (2013), p. 243.
3. Ibid.

A close reading of *Surveiller et punir* reveals that Foucault proposes not one but three models of the rise and spread of the prison. The first is an economic variant of a standard Marxist story: the rise of capitalism changes the physiognomy of crime which in turn provokes changes in penality that benefit the bourgeoisie. The second is a demographic explanation in the mold of the Annales school: the growth in population, accompanied by the increase in wealth and scaling up of groups, changes the volume and profile of criminality, which yields a new politics of punishment. The third is Weberian: the irruption of "biopower" provokes the multiplication and extension of disciplinary devices which culminate in panopticism as a matrix of subjugation and subjectivation – an apparatus strongly reminiscent of Max Weber's "iron cage" (*stahlhartes Gehäuse*).[90] But this all makes *Surveiller et punir* a strangely self-refuting book: of what use is the prison when "disciplinary coercion" already impregnates the gamut of institutions, schools, hospitals, asylums, barracks, and workshops and has fabricated a "disciplinary individual"? It is revealing in this regard that the penitentiary makes its first full-fledged appearance in the book only on page 268. Who, indeed, needs "judicial penality" in the kingdom of the "infra-penality" of disciplines?

Foucault gets much of his history and sociology of punishment factually wrong;[91] he garbles chronology; he conflates penal discourses

[90] Max Weber, *The Protestant Ethic and the Spirit of Capitalism* ([1904–1905] 1930), p. 181.
[91] Empirical and theoretical critiques of *Surveiller et punir* include Michelle Perrot (ed.), *L'Impossible prison. Recherches sur le système pénitentiaire au XIXe siècle* (1980); John Pratt, "'This is Not a Prison': Foucault, The Panopticon and Pentonville" (1993); Neil Brenner, "Foucault's New Functionalism" (1994); Jan Ellen Goldstein (ed.), *Foucault and the Writing of History* (1994); Gérard Noiriel, *Sur la "crise" de l'histoire* (1996); Karl von Schriltz, "Foucault on the Prison: Torturing History to Punish Capitalism" (1999); C. Fred Alford, "What Would It Matter if Everything Foucault Said About Prison Were Wrong?" (2000); Pieter Spierenburg, "Punishment, Power, and History: Foucault and Elias" (2004). For a more sanguine appreciation, read

and penal practices, assuming that the blueprints by thinkers and programs by policy-makers capture the real delivery of punishment.[92] He correlatively ignores actually existing penitentiary regimes and the factors behind their wide variations. He offers no coherent explanation for the sudden mutation of power from sovereign to disciplinary that has thrust the prison to the institutional forefront. He waffles in his characterization of "the carceral," using in turn the dispersed images of the archipelago, continuum, network, pyramid, mesh, circles, and lattice. Later, in his lecture courses at the Collège de France extending *Surveiller et punir*, the French philosopher jumps from concept to concept without clear justification and abandons the notion of disciplinary society and individual altogether. As quickly as it appeared, the prison vanishes from both his intellectual horizon and theorizing about Western modernity.

61

But, along the way, Foucault puts forth two important ideas that I want to retain and fructify. First, the prison is a *dividing institution*; it creates salient social cleavages, marks out a distinct population, the delinquents, and creates *a new social type, the incorrigible criminal*, which enters into the public imagination – an imagination fastened on the city's underbelly and the festering threats it harbors.

> The *delinquent is to be distinguished from the offender* by the fact that it is not so much his act as his life that is relevant in characterizing him. The penitentiary operation, if it is to be a genuine re-education, must total-ize the existence of the delinquent, making the prison a sort of artificial and coercive theatre in which it will be reexamined end to end. *The legal punishment bears upon an act, the punitive technique on a life*; it falls to this punitive technique, therefore, to reconstitute all the sordid details of a life in the form of knowledge, to fill in the gaps of that knowledge and to act upon it by a practice of compulsion.[93]

Jonathan Simon, "Punishment and the Political Technologies of the Body" (2013), and David Garland, "What is a 'History of the Present'? On Foucault's Genealogies and their Critical Preconditions" (2014b).

[92] For one, Bentham's blueprint for the Panopticon was never implemented – a development Foucault concedes but without drawing its consequences. The architectural design was copied but the social mechanism of automatic surveillance never worked. See Smith, *Punishment and Culture*, chapter 4, for a fuller discussion which shows that, far from functioning as the fulcrum of a new form of disciplinary individuation, Bentham's contraption was a classic utilitarian vehicle for "deterrence, less eligibility, and cultural pressures for self-sufficiency" (p. 102).

[93] Foucault, *Surveiller et punir*, p. 255, my italics.

In his lecture course on "the punitive society," Foucault goes one step further and speaks of a veritable "civil war," a war "of the rich against the poor" in the course of which the criminal becomes "a social enemy."[94] Next, penal power, like all power, is not just repressive but also *productive*: it generates new social relations, institutions, bodies of knowledge, and subjectivities. The notion is formulated thus in the last paragraph of *Surveiller et punir*:

> The notions of institutions of repression, rejection, exclusion, marginalization, are not adequate to describe, at the very centre of the carceral city, the formation of the insidious leniencies, unavowable petty cruelties, small acts of cunning, calculated procedures, techniques, "sciences" that permit in the end the fabrication of the disciplinary individual.[95]

This means that the imprint of the penal state on society goes far beyond those directly and indirectly touched by the police, court, and prison. On this count, Durkheim, Rusche, and Foucault vary on the specifics but agree on the weight and shaping power of criminal justice on the social body.

Reformation versus retribution: Meshing philosophies of punishment

To sum up, the political-economic (Marxist) and the solidaristic-communicative (Durkheimian) approaches to punishment anchor rival paradigms through a series of homological oppositions captured in table 1. Foucault falls somewhere in between: he is a materialist and focuses on the body but he also accords pride of place to discourses and representations, as with the bodies of knowledge that accrete around forms of power. Weber can also be located in this intermediate theoretical position. There is, moreover, a homology between the duality of the Marxist/materialist/rationalist and the Durkheimian/symbolic/emotionalist *theories* of punishment and the duality of utilitarian and retributivist *philosophies* of penality descended from Jeremy

---

[94] Michel Foucault, *La Société punitive*, p. 15. Civil war is "the permanent state from which one can and must understand a certain number of tactics of struggle, of which penality is a privileged example."

[95] Foucault, *Surveiller et punir*, p. 315. This proposition is further elaborated by Foucault in *Power/Knowledge: Selected Interviews and Other Writings, 1972–1977* (1980).

Table 1
Marx versus Durkheim:
two social theories of penality.

MARX(IST)	DURKHEIM
material	symbolic
rational	emotional
instrumental	expressive
interest	passion
control	communication
exploiting labor	drawing boundary
class	community
ensure domination	vivify solidarity
profane	sacred

Bentham and Immanuel Kant, respectively.[96] Let me consider these paired dichotomies.

For the Marxists and other rationalists, penality is a material agency serving class interests and geared primarily to the control of labor; it is an instrument of class domination connecting economy and society and stamping profane reality. This approach is informed by utilitarianism as descended from Jeremy Bentham in that it treats both the criminal and the penal state as rational agents seeking to maximize utility and efficiency. By contrast, for the Durkheimians and assorted emotionalists, punishment is a symbolic agency expressing the passion of the community whose boundaries it brightens and solidarity it rekindles. It draws on, and in turn feeds, the sense of the sacred that enshrouds shared values. It situates itself in the lineage of Kantian penality based on deontological principles, starting with the categorical imperative and the principle of proportionality (*jus talionis*) which the penal state must uphold. These theoretical oppositions are thus replicated at the level of philosophies of punishment by the antinomy between consequentialism (another name for utilitarianism) and retributivism (one variant of which is just desert).[97]

---

[96] Tony Draper, "An Introduction to Jeremy Bentham's Theory of Punishment" (2002); Nelson Potter, "Kant on Punishment" (2009).

[97] A compact explication of these two visions is Didier Fassin, "Punishment" (2018). An extended discussion is David Boonin, *The Problem of Punishment* (2008), chapters 2 and 3, who argues that neither the consequentialist nor the retributivist philosophy

Philosophers from Aristotle and Aquinas, Hobbes and Montesquieu, to Kant and Bentham have offered luminous reflections on the purposes, justifications, and calibration of punishment. Novelists from Victor Hugo and Fiodor Dostoyevsky to Franz Kafka and Ernest Gaines have likewise contributed to the long train of rumination on penal sanction, its social meanings, and its existential ramifications. Together these authors craft accounts of criminal sanction that capture its multilayered character and run in myriad directions. The views of contemporary legal theorists and penologists are decidedly flatter and narrower. It is customary for them to distinguish between five practical rationales of punishment: deterrence, rehabilitation, incapacitation, retribution, and restoration – to which some analysts and activists have recently added the vague category of "transformation."[98] I propose to collapse these rationales into the *polar opposition between reformation (or rehabilitation) and retribution (or just desert)* as the two philosophies corresponding to the rationalist and emotionalist theories of punishment, respectively, and suited, as we shall see later, to the Left hand and Right hand of the penal state. I canvas the oppositions between rational consequentialism and emotional retributivism (summarized in table 2) and argue that we must overcome their dualism on paper because both are involved in the daily workings of the justice apparatus by virtue of the division of judicial labor across types of offenses in the court.[99]

provides a valid moral warrant for the state to exercise penal power and proposes to substitute victim restitution for punishment.

[98] A meticulous examination of philosophical justifications for criminal sanction is Zachary Hopkins and Antony Duff, "Legal Punishment" (2021). Three excellent selections of texts on classical and contemporary debates in the philosophy and social theory of punishment are Antony Duff and David Garland (eds.), *A Reader on Punishment* (1994); Michael Tonry (ed.), *Why Punish? How Much? A Reader on Punishment* (2010); and Jesper Ryberg (ed.), *The Oxford Handbook of the Philosophy of Punishment* (2024).

[99] This is not to say that this opposition has not been bridged by theorists of penality. In *State Punishment: Political Principles and Community Values* (1988), Nicola Lacey divides philosophies of criminal sanction into "backward-looking justifications" (retributive theory) and "forward-looking justifications," broken down into general deterrence, individual deterrence, rehabilitation, social protection, grievance-satisfaction and the maintenance of respect for the legal system, and reparation and restitution. She also spotlights "mixed theories of punishment," including H.L.A. Hart's hybrid theory (justifying punishment on utilitarian grounds and its distribution on retributivist grounds) and weak retributivism for which "offences give the state a right to punish, but not a duty to do so" (p. 53).

Table 2
Bentham versus Kant:
two philosophies of punishment.

BENTHAM *rationalist* **reformation** **(consequentialist)**	**KANT** *emotionalist* **retribution** **(just desert)**
prospective	retrospective
offender-centered	offense-centered
tailored penalty	uniform penalty
chance of recidivism	seriousness of crime
indeterminate sentencing	determinate sentencing
high social variation	no social variation
discrimination	hyper-punitiveness

Reformation is a prospective or consequentialist philosophy based on an expansive "social" reading of criminality for which the defendant is not just a rational actor responding to legal incentives, but a malleable, situated social being and punishment a flexible tool for shaping and even improving future behavior so as to reduce recidivism. It is anchored by a *heteronomous* reading of penal law in the sense that it makes ample room for extra-juridical concerns such as the personal profile of the defendant and the social environment that will help her avoid reoffending or not.[100] It is the philosophy of punishment fostered by the Left hand of the state, the hand that protects. It stands in an elective affinity with the rationalist theory of punishment running from Beccaria to Bentham to Georg Rusche.

By contrast, *retribution* is, as a retrospective philosophy of punishment, based on a restrictive, strictly "legal" reading of criminality; it expresses an *autonomous* vision of penal law as a closed discursive universe which should not be adulterated by extra-juridical considerations and concerns. It focuses not on the future conduct of the offender but on his past actions. It is the philosophy of punishment

[100] "The premise from which Bentham started was that no two people are the same, no two crimes are the same, and it is the duty of the law to accommodate such variables before inflicting pain, in the name of the state." Draper, "An Introduction to Jeremy Bentham's Theory of Punishment," p. 2. On the opposition between the internalist and externalist reading of the law, see Pierre Bourdieu, "La force du droit. Éléments pour une sociologie du champ juridique" (1986).

suited to the Right hand of the state, the hand that disciplines. It stands in an elective affinity with the emotionalist theory of penality running from Kant to Durkheim to contemporary neo-Durkheimians such as Hans Boutellier and David Garland. Let me consider each in turn before pointing to their *de facto* reconciliation in day-to-day judicial practice.

Jeremy Bentham versus Immanuel Kant on the purpose of punishment

On account of Foucault's famous interpretation, Jeremy Bentham's views on punishment have been incorrectly reduced to the Panopticon and the attendant themes of regimentation, surveillance, and control (1). But they are in fact much richer than this distorted picture lets on – indeed foundational to contemporary penality. Building on Cesare Beccaria's rationalist *Dei delitti e delle pene* (1764), the father of modern utilitarianism develops a *consequentialist* theory for which criminal sanction should minimize pain and maximize social utility.

Punishment is "an evil" since it inflicts a pain (of four types: physical, political, moral, and religious), but it is justified by its effect on the offender and the broader society, whose greater good it should aim to secure (2). Eschewing vengeance, it should be minimized while being sufficient to effect deterrence, incapacitation, and rehabilitation: deterrence to prevent individuals from committing crimes in the first place; incapacitation to "disable" the offender (that is, "preventing further mischief"); "reform" to preclude him reiterating his offense in the future. Sanctions should be scaled to achieve this triple purpose as does the prison when it is rationally designed and run. When they fail to do so and cause further harm without social benefits, as the death penalty does, they should be banned. Bentham's concern for quantification in response to varied amounts of mischief caused by crimes led him to support in turn corporal punishment in his early work, incarceration in his middle work, and non-afflictive sanctions such as fines and banishment in his late work. I propose that materialist theories of punishment, exemplified by those of Marxian and Marxist thinkers, present an internal affinity with Bentham's teleological conception. Both are rationalist and instrumental.

Immanuel Kant's position is diametrically opposed to Bentham's. His approach is *deontological*, meaning that it evaluates an action not by its consequences but by its conformity to a moral rule treated as an absolute. It anchors a *retributivist* conception of punishment whose strong version is *jus talionis*, an eye for an eye, although Kant allowed for the modulation of this biblical principle (3). Whereas consequentialism looks forward at future conduct and societal welfare, retributivism looks backward at the offense, isolates it, and gauges its seriousness so as to make the punishment "fit the crime." This is because, for Kant, the offender is endowed with reason and the moral capacity to make choices, and he has chosen to violate criminal law. He therefore deserves to be punished and punishment should be commensurate with his blameworthiness. "The law concerning punishment is a categorical imperative, and woe to him who rummages around the winding paths of a theory of happiness looking for some advantage to be gained by releasing the criminal from punishment or by reducing the amount of it" (4). Criminal sanction is not an instrument of public governance deployed to protect the social contract but a moral obligation upheld by the state. This is why Kant favored a broad use of the death penalty but opposed torture executions on the ground that even "a vicious person" deserves respect in his quality as a person: the criminal is not a sub-human, no matter how grave his offense (5).

I submit that symbolic theories of punishment, as exemplified by Émile Durkheim's (who was a dyed-in-the-wool Kantian) and his epigones, are derived from, or germane to, Kant's conception based on ethical duty as promulgated in a cultural community. Both are expressive and emotionalist in that they give a central role to moral indignation. The Marxian view of punishment thus stands opposed to the Durkheimian outlook as Bentham is opposed to Kant.

Yet instrumental rationality and moral reason together do not exhaust possible visions of penality. A third position, which escapes this duality, is staked out by Friedrich Nietzsche who rejects normative theory in favor of a *genealogical approach* focused on how punishment emerges in history and actually operates in contemporary society. In his reflections *On the Genealogy of Morals* (1887), the notion of justice emerges as a thin rationalization of domination and hides the "will to power" (*der Wille zur Macht*). What motivates punishment is the luxurious pleasure to make the offender suffer, not for some ulterior motive, but for its own sake; it assuages ressentiment and gratifies the human instinct to assert superiority (6). Consistent with his vitalist philosophy, Nietzsche is content with deconstructing punishments while rejecting claims to both rationality and morality.

1. Michel Foucault presents Bentham's Panopticon as the materialization of a new insidious and all-encompassing regime of disciplinary penality in *Surveiller et punir. Naissance de la prison* (1975), pp. 200ff.
2. This theory is elaborated in *An Introduction to the Principles of Moral and Legislation* (1789, chapter 13) and a bushel of dispersed texts. For a clear and compact summation, see Tony Draper, "An Introduction to Jeremy Bentham's Theory of Punishment" (2002).
3. Kant's view on punishment are sketched in a few pages on "The Doctrine of Right" contained in the *Groundwork of the Metaphysics of Morals* (1785). An authoritative interpretation is Nelson Potter, "Kant on Punishment" (2009), who shows that Kant's thinking on punishment was much more subtle than generally recognized and includes non-retributive elements.
4. Immanuel Kant, "The Penal Law and the Law of Pardon," in *The Metaphysical Elements of Justice* ([1798] 1965), p. 100.
5. This reasoning is picked up by Durkheim when he argues that the sacralization of the individual motivates punishment against persons who violate it but also limits such punishment owing to the humanity of the offender. Émile Durkheim, "Deux lois de l'évolution pénale" ([1899] 1969).
6. Friedrich Nietzsche, *On the Genealogy of Morals* (1887). This position is eloquently defended and extended by Didier Fassin, *Punir, une passion contemporaine* (2017), who writes: "The only satisfaction is knowing that the guilty party is suffering. There is therefore something in the act of punishment that resists rational examination . . .: a more or less repressed impulse, the effects of which society delegates to certain institutions and professions" (pp. 98–9).

Reformation is a brand of penal consequentialism.[101] It is offender-centered and oriented toward the future. It seeks to calibrate the kind and intensity of punishment to the risk of reoffending, with a view toward preventing crime while minimizing the footprint of penality. It was hegemonic in the United States from the 1920s to the 1960s and it endures as the professed philosophy of criminal justice in most advanced societies, with inflections depending on the kind of crime.[102] In the reformative view, the gravity of the act committed and strict proportionality between the crime and the sanction are residual considerations. The central concern is to tailor the penalty so as to foster the rehabilitation and reintegration of the offender and thereby diminish the likelihood of recidivism. This requires wide discretion

[101] It is not the only emanation of consequentialism: deterrence (of future criminal conduct) and incapacitation (of the offender via incarceration) are two variants of consequentialist penality. I am concerned here with characterizing the social branch of utilitarian penology.

[102] Duff and Garland (eds.), *A Reader on Punishment*, pp. 8–16. Enshrouded by strong collective and individual emotions, sexual offenses, for instance, are increasingly viewed in a retributivist light whereas drug possession is viewed through a utilitarian prism.

by prosecutors and judges to adjust criminal charges and the quantum of punishment to the specifics of the person (social profile and criminal record) and to the circumstances of the case (extenuating or aggravating). Consequentialism stands in elective affinity with the rationalist theory of punishment of the Marxist variety.

In the US penal apparatus, the consequentialist philosophy translated into a sentencing regime known as "indeterminate sentencing," whereby the court has at its disposal a range of possible sanctions, fines, probation, and prison.[103] In the case of convicts serving time, the judge sets a range (say, 5–25 years) and a parole board later decides what proportion of the sentence needs to be served depending on the prisoner's conduct behind bars, psychological progression (toward "insight" about his crime), and anticipated resources and behavior after release (for instance, the promise of a job).[104]

The Achilles' heel of consequentialist penality is that sanctions for the same crime vary across offenders depending on their personality, social and cultural capital, criminal record, and perceived progress on the path to rehabilitation. Proportionality is sacrificed to minimize sanction and maximize reintegration. But taking into account extra-judicial factors opens wide the door of discrimination based on class and ethnicity in particular (I return to this question as it plays out on the floor of the criminal court in chapter 3, pp. 329–33, 340–3). Rampant racial disparities were one of the reasons why Left advocates of just desert attacked the doctrine of rehabilitation in the wake of the Civil Rights movement. A loss of faith in the efficacy of rehabilitative programs was a compounding factor leading to the demise of reformation and the upsurge of retribution coinciding with the onset of carceral inflation after the mid-1970s.[105]

[103] The long run of changes in sentencing policy in the United States since the 1960s is retraced and explicated by Michael Tonry in *Sentencing Fragments: Penal Reform in America, 1975–2025* (2016).

[104] For a provocative ethnographic account of twenty parole hearings in California, read Victor Lund Shammas, "The Perils of Parole Hearings: California Lifers, Performative Disadvantage, and the Ideology of Insight" (2019). For a computational and interpretive study of some 10,000 transcripts of hearings, see Isaac Dalke, "I Come Before You a Changed Man: 'Insight,' Compliance, and Refurbishing Penal Practice in California" (2024). Note that indeterminate sentencing was practiced as early as the sixteenth century in the *tuchhuis* of Amsterdam, as recounted by Thorsten Sellin, *Pioneering in Penology: The Amsterdam Houses of Correction in the Sixteenth and Seventeenth Centuries* (1944).

[105] Francis A. Allen, *The Decline of the Rehabilitative Ideal: Penal Policy and Social Purpose* (1981).

Just desert is diametrically opposed to rehabilitation in that it is retrospective and offense-centered. It looks back at the crime and adjusts the penalty to the latter's severity according to strict proportionality.[106] For advocates of just desert, ascendant in the US from the mid-1970s onward, the purpose of penal sanction is not to reform the offender and alter future behavior but to inflict judicial pain commensurate with past actions. Punishment should be calibrated to the harmfulness of the offense and the degree of culpability of the offender.[107]

The discretion of judges should be reduced to its minimum to ensure consistency and strict proportionality: two people committing the same crime should suffer the same punishment, regardless of their social and judicial profile and the circumstances of their offense. When it was introduced in the US in the mid-1970s, just desert was seen as a remedy to disparity and discrimination, as when a white offender would receive a more lenient sentence than a black defendant who committed the same crime because of their different social positions and life chances, and therefore likelihood to reoffend. The Achilles' heel of just desert is the absence of clear criteria for weighing proportionality and a correlative tendency to veer into hyper-punitiveness. Retributivism stands in elective affinity with the emotionalist theory of punishment of the Durkheimian variety with its focus on the emotions of the collective whose norms of conduct have been violated.

The rich promise and paltry performance of restorative justice

Restorative justice brings into the penal equation the victim(s), individual and collective, and looks both backward and forward. Restoration combines elements of rational calibration and emotional catharsis by instituting a deliberative form of justice cracking the institutional monopoly of legal professionals over the adjudication

---

[106] An eloquent early advocate of retribution is Montesquieu in *L'Esprit des lois* (XII, 4, vol. I, p. 203): "It is the triumph of liberty when criminal laws derive each punishment from the particular nature of the crime. All arbitrariness ceases; the punishment does not come from the caprice of the legislator, but from the nature of the thing; and it is not man who does violence to man." This is also the view endorsed by Durkheim for whom punishment naturally gravitates toward proportionality (*supra*, p. 48).
[107] Andrew von Hirsch, "Penal Theories" (1999).

process. It is designed to make offender and victim work collaboratively through a face-to-face encounter aiming to foster accountability and atonement, and to repair the personal and social damage occasioned by criminal conduct. According to McCold and Wachtel's oft-cited definition, restorative justice is "a process where those primarily affected by an incident of wrongdoing come together to share their feelings, describe how they were affected and develop a plan to repair the harm done or prevent reoccurrence." It expands the individual focus of reformation to the ties frayed by the offense and, in some variants, pulls into the process the family, friends, and supporters of the offender to effect "reintegrative shaming" (1). It entails victim restitution to repair harm or compensate for loss, including the loss of dignity and self-respect; conflict resolution seeking to arrive at reconciliation; and "community rebuilding" to alleviate collective insecurity by reducing the probability of reoffending.

In the historically pristine and socially frictionless world of analytic philosophers and dispute resolution theorists, restoration has irresistible appeal as it resolves on paper multiple quandaries of state-centered justice (2). But real criminal courts do not operate in social ether. Most crime victims want nothing to do with their perpetrator; most perpetrators do not care much about the victims of their misdeeds and even less about the collateral damage they have caused. Restoration is, moreover, based on the fiction that the social and linguistic capacities needed to appropriate, and indeed dominate, the negotiation are fairly distributed – that the reconsideration of the crime is a joint narration rather than a relation of symbolic power (3). As a philosophy of punishment, restoration is weakened by the romantic notion that transforming state criminal processing can be done by salvaging and revitalizing the restorative practices that remain dormant in all societies from their multisecular past – some of its advocates even claim to trace its roots to "primate behavior that is millions of years old" (4). It is anchored by a mystical notion of "community" as a cohesive, undivided whole that makes up the natural environment of both offender and victim as well as the scene of the crime, and a populist view of the justice process that presumes moral goodwill from all parties united to birth "healing" and "reconciliation."

The foremost theoretician of restoration, the Australian criminologist John Braithwaite, counterposes the "immodest theory" and the "pessimistic theory" of this mode of justice to list its professed virtues and feared drawbacks, respectively. But his discussion studiously omits the latter altogether (5). As a result, he does not counter the common criticisms of restoration: it can apply only to a small number of cases (even if one dramatically expands judicial and para-judicial resources) and offers little or no benefit to the vast majority of victims; it assaults the self of the offender by shaming him; it turns victims into props, coerces them to forgive, and amplifies their fear of revictimization; it structurally disadvantages vulnerable categories (women, children, the poor, ethnic outsiders); and it weakens procedural safeguards. More importantly, in differentiated societies, offender and victim often do not share a social and symbolic space and thus they have little chance of "restoring harmony based on a feeling that justice has been done" (6). What if harmony was not the *status quo ante*? How can you "reintegrate" an offender who was not integrated in the first place and who is returning to an everyday position of marginality and humiliation?

Braithwaite's bold 1998 prediction that "restorative justice will come to be a profoundly influential social movement throughout the world during the next century because it appeals to universally shared values and because it responds to the defects of a centralized state criminal justice model that has been totally globalized and has utterly failed in every country where it gained ascendancy" has not come to pass (7). Restorative justice remains a marginal track in the criminal justice of advanced countries, even in those reputed for having developed a more democratic brand of penality. In Germany, *Täter-Opfer-Ausgleich* (offender-victim reconciliation) was introduced in juvenile proceedings in 1990 and in the criminal code in 1994. But, by 2020, it concerned a mere 1.5 percent of criminal cases in the state that led the country in its use (8). In France, restorative procedures have been in play since 2014 and are offered to all defendants as an optional supplement to standard judicial processing. Its advocates, such as the Institut français pour la justice restaurative (IFJR), are full of verve and hope but, despite its universal availability, it involved fewer than 1,000 cases out of a total of 544,000 criminal convictions in 2024 (9). In Norway, which is at the cutting edge of restorative justice worldwide, the police and courts have the option of calling on the local chapter of the National Mediation Service (*Konfliktrådet*), a free service staffed by volunteer mediators, either as an alternative to a trial or in lieu of a more severe sentence. In 2024, 1,265 criminal cases were resolved through mediation out of 256,000 sanctions or 57,000 sanctions excluding on-the-spot fines, for less than 2 percent of cases excluding fines and 0.5 percent of all cases. In other words, restorative justice is a decorative judicial device that is intellectually attractive as a philosophy of punishment but has little purchase on criminal processing in the real world (10).

Restorative justice is a visionary perspective without matching achievements, *a normative stance devoid of a positive outlet,* other than as a minor practical supplement to conventional justice driven by rehabilitation, deterrence, neutralization, or retribution (11). And so the theoretical and programmatic literature on the phenomenon has far outpaced its development on the ground. At this moment of justice history, the philosophy of restoration remains stuck at the margins and in the interstices of the penal state. Can it escape them and grow into a significant cog in the machinery of harm containment and resolution broadly conceived? To answer this question in the positive will require a deep rethinking of the modalities of restoration, a massive increase in material and human resources devoted to an expanded conception of criminal justice, and a clear determination of the type of offenses and offenders to be targeted.

Experiments in restoration for first-time juvenile offenders who have committed minor crimes as an alternative to a penal sanction are certainly worth conducting, but they already exist under the narrower umbrella of prosecutorial "diversion." Circles of closely monitored dialogues bringing face-to-face convicts and their victims *ex post facto* can help both reassess the import and impact of the crimes that link them. They can exercise a therapeutic effect on the latter who are yearning for the recognition of, and attention to, their suffering (12), but this pertains to reducing the mistreatment of victims by the police and the courts and not to the resolution of the crime itself. Such an enterprise in meaning-making does not in any way *breach the state monopoly over penality,* which was the initial promise of the founders of the reparative philosophy such as Howard Zehr. So much to say, then, that it is urgent to dramatically scale back expectations as to its ability to remedy the deep flaws of the current institutions of punishment.

Lately, the *avant-garde* of radical militants and theorists of penality in the US have moved from restorative justice – considered too tame and complicit with "the system" – to *transformative justice* as the true alternative to criminalization, but the notion is woefully wooly and overly capacious. Even though it has been around for more than a quarter-century, it is often mispresented as a recent innovation. It has two strands, the one derived from the international experience of "transitional justice" designed to deal with mass atrocities (as in

73

post-apartheid South Africa, Bosnia-Herzegovina after the Balkans war, and post-conflict Colombia) and the other spawned by religious visions of peace and reconciliation as an individual and collective achievement in North America (13). The fundamental idea is that justice must treat harms outside the state and at their root by confronting the "structural violence" that produces them. It aims to redistribute power by incorporating economic and social rights within the resolution of harm. It is a generous agenda but, practically, it confuses scales and means of social transformation (individual, "community," society) and involves little more than a change of language expressing a spiritual yearning for humane and peaceful relationships in a better world (14).

74

1. Paul McCold and Ted Wachtel, "Restorative Justice Theory Validation" (2002), p. 113. Another characterization is that "there are four Rs to restorative justice: repair, restore, reconcile, and reintegrate the offenders and victims to each other and to their shared community" (Carrie Menkel-Meadow, "Restorative Justice: What Is It and Does It Work?" [2007], p. 162). On the theory of "reintegrative shaming," see John Braithwaite, *Crime, Shame and Reintegration* (1989).
2. David Boonin, *The Problem of Punishment* (2008).
3. On language as a vehicle of social power, read Pierre Bourdieu, *Ce que parler veut dire. L'économie des échanges linguistiques* (1982).
4. Lawrence W. Sherman and Heather Strang, "Restorative Justice as Evidence-Based Sentencing" (2012), p. 217.
5. John Braithwaite, "Restorative Justice" (1998), pp. 324–5. For a panoramic discussion of these criticisms, read Chris Cunneen and Carolyn Hoyle, *Debating Restorative Justice* (2010).
6. Braithwaite, "Restorative Justice," p. 328.
7. Ibid., p. 336. Sherman and Strang inadvertently concede that, while there is, in their view, ample research evidence showing the efficacy of the restorative justice conference, no social movement has emerged to push for its adoption in the US, UK or Australia. "Restorative Justice as Evidence-Based Sentencing," p. 237.
8. Gerd Delattre and Christoph Willms, "After Three Decades of Restorative Justice in Germany: Thoughts on the Needs for a Strategic Re-Orientation" (2020), p. 287.
9. A three-year study found that the effect of restorative procedures on defendants was positive but thin and ephemeral. It was more lasting among correctional staff who found that these procedures gave meaning to their professional practice. Delphine Griveaud and Sandrine Lefranc, *Pratiques et effets de la justice restaurative en France* (2024). The procedure has become widely known in France thanks to the fictional movie by Jeanne Herry, *Je verrai toujours vos visages* ("All your faces" in its English-language version), which has attracted over one million viewers since 2023.
10. The gentle moralism and social irenism of restorative justice shines through:

"The underlying values of restorative justice promote a positive redemption-ist and ameliorative view of human behavior, with a positive hope that even the worst among us can be transformed to consider the common good and the best for other human beings" (Menkel-Meadow, "Restorative Justice: What Is It and Does It Work?," p. 171). The same sociological naïveté mars Danielle Sered, *Until We Reckon: Violence, Mass Incarceration, and a Road to Repair* (2019).

11. For a discussion of the thorny problem of scaling, see Menkel-Meadow, "Restorative Justice: What Is It and Does It Work?." Sherman and Strang avoid the issue altogether. They are enthused by the positive results of 12 randomized control experiments in three countries but these concern a grand total of 3,000 cases. In *Pour une autre justice. La voie restaurative* (2025), Antoine Garapon argues that restoration is best suited for incest, serial sexual assault, and mass criminality, that is, "frightful matters revealing an existential collapse of individuals and institutions." But these evidently constitute a tiny percentage of the cases routinely processed by the courts.

12. Delphine Griveaud, *Réparer la justice. Enquête sur les pratiques restauratives en France* (2025).

13. Anthony J. Nocella, "An Overview of the History and Theory of Transformative Justice" (2011), p. 8; Paul Gready and Simon Robins, "From Transitional to Transformative Justice: A New Agenda for Practice" (2014).

14. Adrienne Maree Brown, *We Will Not Cancel Us: And Other Dreams of Transformative Justice* (2020).

On paper, the opposition between reformation and retribution, rationality and emotionality, seems insurmountable but, in the every-day workings of the justice apparatus, it is overcome by applying each to a different sphere of criminality. There exists a *philosophical and practical division of the labor of punishment* inside the courthouse according to the mundane or sacred character of the offense, rein-forced by the low or high social status of the offender and victims.[108] Penal sanctions for low-level crimes, garden-variety misdemeanors such as petty theft, drug possession, driving under the influence and public-order disruption, tend toward rationality and instrumental-ity. They are emotionally "cold" and subject to a consequentialist treatment which aims at channeling mundane behavior by deterring ordinary offenses and reducing the chance of their reiteration; they partake of a *profane Benthamite penality*. By contrast, penal sanctions

---

[108] I use "sacred" in the specific Durkheimian sense of set apart from the mundane by prohibitions and elevated by shared beliefs and collective rituals. In contemporary societies, the ultimate sacred object is the individual, which is the center of a veritable cult which Émile Durkheim calls "moral individualism" (*La Science sociale et l'action* [1970]). In this sense, the person is sacred whereas material property is mundane and thus crimes against the one and against the other are treated very differently.

for grievous felonies infringing on the sanctity of the human person, such as aggravated assault, rape, and murder, are driven by "hot" emotions and partake of a *sacred Kantian penality*. The latter purports to protect sanctified values and dramatize absolute principles by casting the offender out of the human community, temporarily or permanently.[109]

Since the consequentialist and the retributivist models of punishment are both at play at the same time in the routine operation of the criminal court, instead of opposing them, we need to combine them to account for the full span of penality. Together they explain that punishment reaches an extreme when the offense is sacred, the victim of high class and status or especially vulnerable (children, women, the elderly), and the offender of low class and status; and that it sags to its lowest level when the offense is mundane, has no discernible victim and is committed by a defendant of high class and status endowed with the material and symbolic resources needed to parry penal force. Now that I have explicated the social theories and the competing philosophies of punishment as well as their homology, let me turn to theories of the state.

76

Weber, Mann, and Scott on the state: Force, penetration, legibility

I argued earlier that, with a few precious exceptions, theorists of the state have ignored penality and theorists of penality have ignored the state. Four social theorists of the state provide flexible conceptual tools for building a robust concept of the penal Leviathan: Max Weber, Michael Mann, James Scott, and Pierre Bourdieu.

1. Max Weber on "the monopoly of legitimate violence"

Weber's foundational definition of the state is expressed most clearly in the first chapter of *Wirtschaft und Gesellschaft* (1920) where we read:

---

[109] The paradigm of this excommunication is the increasingly virulent treatment of sex offenders in recent penal culture and policy, and especially paedophiles who assault the most innocent and vulnerable of victims, as shown by Roger N. Lancaster, *Sex Panic and the Punitive State* (2011), and Mark De Rond, *Dark Justice: Inside the World of Paedophile Hunters* (2025).

A compulsory political organization with continuous operations (*politischer Anstaltsbetrieb*) will be called a "state" insofar as its administrative staff successfully upholds the claim to the *monopoly* of the *legitimate* use of physical force in the enforcement of its order.[110]

Three elements attract our attention here: *force*, *staff*, and *legitimacy* (which, in turn, may be traditional, charismatic, and legal-rational). A fourth element is *territory*, which we find in Weber's correlative definition of a "compulsory political organization" as an organization whose "existence and order are continuously safeguarded within a given territorial area by the threat and application of physical force on the part of the administrative staff."[111] Weber is careful to note that violence is "not the normal or the only means of action of the state," but it is "its specific means." Other collective actors may wield acceptable violence but only insofar as the state permits it.[112]

For Weber, then, the state is characterized by its means and not its ends. This is because it can and does fulfill a multiplicity of roles. Among the "basic functions of the state," the German sociologist enumerates

> the establishment of the law (legislature); *the protection of personal safety and public order (police); the protection of vested rights (administration of justice);* the cultivation of hygienic, educational, social-welfare, and other cultural interests (the various branches of administration); and, last but not least, the organized armed protection against outside attack (military administration).[113]

Weber also notes that law differs from convention by the intercession of "the staff which could hold itself specifically ready for action meant to guarantee obedience, such as judges, prosecutors, policemen, or sheriffs."[114] But this is Weber's only passing mention of criminal jus-

77

---

[110] Max Weber, *Economy and Society: An Outline of Interpretive Sociology* ([1920] 1978), pp. 54–5, original italics. Elsewhere, Weber notes that "the relationship of the state to violence is particularly intimate" (*Le Savant et le politique* [1919] 2003, p. 118).

[111] Ibid., p. 54. See also Max Weber, *From Max Weber: Essays in Sociology* (1948), pp. 78, 82, 336. For further discussion of Weber's views of the state, see Reinhard Bendix, *Max Weber: An Intellectual Portrait* (1960), pp. 417–56; Gary L. Ulmen, "The Sociology of the State: Carl Schmitt and Max Weber" (1985); and Andreas Anter, *Max Weber's Theory of the Modern State: Origins, Structure and Significance* (2014).

[112] Max Weber, *Le Savant et le politique*, p. 118.

[113] Max Weber, *On Law in Economy and Society* (1954), p. 342, my italics.

[114] Ibid., p. 6.

tice in his treatment of the state. An extended analysis of its role in securing "personal security and public order" is nowhere to be found, despite this tantalizing remark.

This is surprising considering Weber's training as a jurist and his abiding interest in the law and its rationalization. He does treat justice in extensive empirical fashion in the sections of *Wirtschaft und Gesellschaft* devoted to the law. There, in a dazzling display of erudition, he discusses the intricacies of the Roman and Chinese systems of administration of justice, the khadi justice of Islamic law, ancient and folk forms of popular justice, the Russian and Prussian code, patriarchal and princely justice, theocratic as opposed to secular justice, the origins of natural law, and the institutionalization of formally rational justice embodied by legal professionals and the modern trial by jury, among myriad topics drawing on encyclopedic knowledge. But he also frustrates his reader by multiplying descriptive types and crisscrossing forms that are never systematized, other than through the overarching oppositions between ancient and modern, rational and irrational, formal and substantive law. Most crucially, Weber fails to integrate his considerations on the historical means and manifestations of justice in his analytic characterization of the state.[115]

Similarly, in his classic treatment of bureaucracy, Weber discusses the "concentration of the means of administration" in some detail when it comes to the "bureaucratization of organized warfare" to maintain peace or promote expansion on the foreign front. He points, *inter alia*, to the replacement of private bands of mercenaries by standing public armies, the development of military discipline and technical training, the establishment of an integrated budget, and the final monopoly of the state over military force, manifested by the generalization of the uniform.[116] There is no parallel discussion of the growing centralization, concentration, and professionalization of the means of criminal justice in the hands of the bureaucratic state to secure peace on the domestic front.

Put bluntly, Weber has no theory of the penal state specifically but we can draw on his work to begin to articulate one. I propose an amended reading which inflects the notion of force, staff, legitimacy, and territory: (i) *force* may be directed inwards as well as outwards,

---

[115] To explain this absence, it is not enough to evoke Weber's trademark analytic approach: "That Weber did not create a systematic theory of the state accords with the fact that he was no kind of systematic thinker and nowhere sought to develop large-scale theoretical constructs" (Anter, *Max Weber's Theory of the Modern State*, p. 217).
[116] Weber, *From Max Weber: Essays in Sociology*, pp. 221–4.

toward wayward members of society no less than foreign enemies, to patrol internal boundaries of difference and inequality;[117] (ii) key *staff* special to criminal justice includes the police, the prosecutor, the defense attorney, the judge, the probation officer, and the prison guard; (iii) *legitimacy* may vary such that some actors, such as law-abiding citizens and justice personnel, view punishment as justified while others, the clients of criminal court and their loved ones, experience it as arbitrary because, as Rusche noted, they do not "regard the state as their state, the law as their law";[118] (iv) the *territory* over which it rules is differentiated into regions of physical and social space, such that the deployment of force, staff, and legitimacy itself takes on a distinctive cast in what I call neighborhoods of urban relegation. Pluralizing territory pluralizes population and raises the question, where and in whose eyes is legitimacy to be assessed?

Max Weber's characterization of the modern bureaucratic state growing out of the medieval patrimonial state invites us to sketch the birth of the penal Leviathan in rough strokes. The early modern state had five main capacities: fiscal, military, diplomatic, ceremonial, and public administration requiring the early production of information about its population and territory. Since then, the prerogatives and essential roles of the Leviathan have gradually multiplied – essential in the sense that the society could not operate smoothly without their fulfillment – to coalesce and stabilize in the postwar period. They include, in rough order of appearance, minting money, ensuring police and justice, building infrastructure, deploying education, distributing social welfare, subsidizing housing, and regulating the economy. Even contemporary neoliberal states aiming to shrink public missions dispatch these functions to a minimal degree or delegate them under strict conditions. Among them, pacifying the society, enforcing public order, protecting property, and resolving conflicts by means of criminal deterrence, surveillance, and sanction are a *sine qua non* of running a large, complex, and stratified society. So much to say that the conjoining of the police, court, and prison into a coordinated penal state in the period 1750–1830 (with slightly different chronologies for different countries) marks a watershed in social and

[117] Weber notes that "the state is *valued as the agency that guarantees security*, and this is above all the case in times of external danger, when sentiments of national solidarity flare up, at least intermittently" (ibid., p. 177, my italics). I would twist this formulation to cover the internal danger posed by the criminal on the domestic front.
[118] See *supra*, p. 3.

political history. Yet it has been overlooked by influential accounts of modernity such as Michael Mann's, to which I now turn.

2. Michael Mann on "infrastructural power"

In his bold four-volume book on *The Sources of Social Power* (1986, 1988, 1993, 2013), the British sociologist Michael Mann builds a grand historical theory of the state from Neolithic to postindustrial societies shaped by the distribution of four forms of power: ideological, economic, military, and political. This theory is anchored by a fruitful distinction between "despotic power" and "infrastructural power," which I propose to apply to contemporary penality.

By *despotic power*, Mann designates "the range of actions which the elite is empowered to undertake without routine, institutionalised negotiation with civil society groups," whereas *infrastructural power* consists in "the capacity of the state to actually penetrate civil society, and to implement logistically political decisions throughout the realm."[119] He proposes that despotic power has fluctuated widely in history while infrastructural power has grown exponentially in modern societies in which the Leviathan has developed the informational, bureaucratic, and ideological capacities to monitor populations and shape individual conduct in granular fashion. "The modern state added routine, formalised, rationalised institutions of wider scope over citizens and territories. It penetrates its territories with both law and administration . . . as earlier states did not."[120]

Which were the "state infrastructures" that enabled the penetration of society and the unification of the national territory after the mid-nineteenth century? Mann gives the following enumeration:

Without many intending it, "nationally" regulated railways, roads, public utilities, public health, police forces, courts and prisons, and above all, education and discursive literacy in the dominant language of the state provided centralized-territorial infrastructures for the further flowering of the nation-states.[121]

---

[119] Michael Mann, "The Autonomous Power of the State: Its Origins, Mechanisms and Results" (1984), pp. 188, 189. See also idem, "Infrastructural Power Revisited" (2009).
[120] Michael Mann, *The Sources of Social Power*. Volume 2, *The Rise of Classes and Nation-States, 1760–1914* (1993), pp. 56–7.
[121] Ibid., p. 488.

However, criminal justice institutions are no sooner listed than they are forgotten. Mann does grant policing a major role but only in the suppression of popular unrest and not as an infrastructural capacity:

The major nineteenth-century development was the emergence of municipal, regional, and national police forces with organizational abilities paralleling armies, though without their numbers, arsenals, or potential resort to the fourth level of violence.[122]

He stays mum on the criminal court and dismisses Foucault's account of the rise of disciplinary power because "Foucault's evidence concerned *only prisons* and mental asylums, of *doubtful relevance to broader societies*."[123]

Later, in volume 4 of *The Sources of Social Power* (2013) covering the multiple "globalizations" unfolding during the period 1945–2011, Mann discusses the booming incarceration of blacks in the United States after the 1970s and flags my concept of "prisonfare," which he sees as capturing "a growth in punitive policing and incarceration."[124] But he explicitly disavows my thesis – encapsulated by that very concept – that an expanded penal apparatus partakes of the remaking of the Leviathan in the age of triumphant neoliberalism. Let me quote him for the record: "Wacquant writes convincingly about workfare and incarceration. Yet he is too functionalist when he ties the two together and claims that rising incarceration rates were caused by neoliberalism."[125] Instead, Mann views carceral expansion as a racialized moral panic specific to the US (and extending to a lesser extent to the UK)[126] and thus he overlooks the generalized burst of carceral inflation across the capitalist West in the post-Fordist era (which I discuss at length in chapter 2, *infra*, pp. 124–31). Because he adopts the narrow economistic definition of neoliberalism as entailing commodification, privatization, and financialization, he cannot

81

---

[122] Ibid., p. 404.

[123] Ibid., p. 405, my emphasis.

[124] Michael Mann, *The Sources of Social Power*. Volume 4, *Globalizations, 1945–2011* (2013), p. 151.

[125] Ibid., p. 152. The only discussion of punishment concerns the lack of criminal prosecution of the bankers responsible for the 2008 financial crisis ushering in the Great Recession (Mann, vol. 4, pp. 327, 349). I explicate the relationship between the penal state and neoliberalism in chapter 2, pp. 131–42.

[126] "The War on Drugs plus racism were less a consequence of neoliberalism than of the moral panic over drugs turned in a racist direction. This was a distinctively American rather than a neoliberal concern" (ibid., p. 152).

discern that the expansion and activation of the penal triad was a major boost to the infrastructural power of the neoliberal state after the mid-1970s, but a power selectively trained on the badlands of the polarized metropolis.

Mann makes an oblique acknowledgment that the penal triad is indeed an essential component of the Leviathan when he writes about African states that "they lack the basic health, education, communications infrastructures, and court and police institutions necessary for a modern state"; about the Soviet Union in the 1970s that "state coercion was a safety mechanism" and that "the security police were active, the courts were subordinate to the party, and prisons and labor camps remained"; and about the collapse of the police in Saddam Hussein's Iraq after the American invasion of 2002 which precipitated the military and thence political failure of occupation.[127]

Filling the gap in Mann's model, I propose that the police, court, and prison are, along with social welfare, public education, public housing, and public health, the chief means whereby the state penetrates the nether regions of social and physical space and regulates the life of the urban precariat. To put it differently, these three institutions are key vessels for the infrastructural power of the state when it comes to dispossessed populations and territories. But, remarkably, the same agencies are routinely thwarted when the authorities try to deploy them in the higher sectors of the class and urban structure. This is because the penal state is a *dual state* in the sense proposed by the legal theorist Markus Dubber: it is a *Rechtsstaat*, a state of law, for the middle and upper classes, and a *Polizeistaat*, a police state, for the working class and the subproletariat (I return to this crucial distinction in the second chapter, *infra*, pp. 183–90). If we attend to the phenomenology of penality, moreover, we also come to the realization that infrastructural power may be experienced as despotic by those at the bottom of the social order. Indeed, this is the case with young men from neighborhoods of relegation on both shores of the Atlantic who view the police as an "army of occupation."[128]

---

[127] Ibid., pp. 173, 225, 296–7.

[128] On the long history of the arbitrary and aggressive policing of the black American (hyper)ghetto, see Simon Balto, *Occupied Territory: Policing Black Chicago from Red Summer to Black Power* (2019). On the abrasive relationships between the police and young men from the French *cités* of the urban periphery, see Éric Marlière, *La France nous a lâchés! Le sentiment d'injustice chez les jeunes des cités* (2008), and Fassin, *La Force de l'ordre*.

3. James Scott on "legibility"

According to James Scott's landmark book, *Seeing like a State* (1998), modern states have designed and deployed a whole series of contraptions – maps, measures, population censuses, laws – to order nature and society, to standardize ordinary relations, and to funnel practices so as to make them "legible" and thereby regular. This argument parallels Mann's account of the rise and spread of "state infra-structures" but it diverges in that, for Scott, these contraptions are clumsy and disarticulated entities that strain to capture the complexity and messiness of the social world through administrative grids. Thus the repeated failure of what he calls "high-modernist projects" intended to revamp social institutions from the top down.

83

Among these projects, the Soviet collectivization of agriculture in the 1930s and the "villagization" program of Tanzania in the 1960s and Ethiopia in the 1980s are particularly relevant since they involved the systematic deployment of state force to displace populations and overcome local resistance. In the case of the launch of Soviet *kolk-hoz*, the resistance of the kulaks was met with fierce repression by the police and the army leading to mass deportation, mass murders, and internment in the Siberian gulags (see my discussion *infra*, p. 207). The penal triad was deployed to implement top-down institutional engineering. I draw on Scott to propose that, along with social welfare, public housing, and public health, the penal wing of the state is the "eye" that *makes legible the underbelly of the city* and provides a narrative to make its residents fit with dominant values – property, propriety, family, individual responsibility, moral respectability – as their living, walking, breathing antithesis.

> These state simplifications, the basic givens of modern statecraft, were rather like abridged maps. They did not successfully represent the actual activity of the society they depicted, nor were they intended to; they represented only that slice of it that interested the official observer. They were, moreover, not just maps. Rather, they were maps that, when allied with state power, would enable much of the reality they depicted to be remade.[129]

The vista that the police, court, and prison provide into neighbor-hoods of relegation and their inhabitants is not an accurate portrayal

[129] James C. Scott, *Seeing Like a State: How Certain Schemes to Improve the Human Condition Have Failed* (1998), p. 3.

of social conditions on the ground but a fruitful social caricature and useful moral travesty. It is fruitful in that it both facilitates and legitimates the operations of the penal state. It offers what we could call *narrative legibility*: a tale that makes sense of "the criminal element" against which society must be defended. In the United States during the final two decades of the twentieth century, the saga of the "underclass," propounded by academics, think tank experts, philanthropic foundations, and state managers, was the hegemonic discourse about the hyperghetto as a self-destructive redoubt of black danger and dereliction that propelled and justified the stupendous widening and tightening of the penal net.[130] In France over the past two decades, postcolonial immigration and Islam, and worse yet their intersection, have been at the core of the tales that make the infamous *banlieues* legible as hotbeds of "communitarianism" – thus the laws passed by parliament proclaiming to fight "separatism."[131] In Denmark, the state discourse and policy aimed at officially designated "ghettos" deployed in the past quarter-century have likewise legitimated state intrusion pegged on such indicators as the rates of immigration, female-headed household, unemployment, and recorded crime.[132] The lesson here is that the iron fist of the penal state is guided by a penal eye.

We can go one step further than James Scott by *reversing the vector of legibility* to realize that the penal triad is the primary prism through which the precariat of the city's underbelly perceives the Leviathan. Joe Soss and Vesla Weaver have shown that what they call "race-class subjugated communities" in the American metropolis are effectively governed, not by inclusive institutions of democratic consent and willful participation as mainstream political science would have it, but through exclusive institutions of "coercion, containment, repression, surveillance, regulation, predation, discipline, and violence" delivered at street level and well captured by the title of their panoramic and path-setting article: "Police Are Our Government."[133]

To varying degrees, the police, court, probation, juvenile hall, jail, prison, halfway house, parole and court-ordered supervision and "programming" are the institutions that *make the state legible* to resi-

[130] Wacquant, *The Invention of the "Underclass."*

[131] Fabien Truong, *Loyautés radicales. L'islam et les "mauvais garçons" de la nation* (2017).

[132] Anika Seemann, "The Danish 'Ghetto Initiatives' and the Changing Nature of Social Citizenship, 2004–2018" (2021).

[133] Joe Soss and Vesla Weaver, "Police Are Our Government: Politics, Political Science, and the Policing of Race–Class Subjugated Communities" (2017).

dents of neighborhoods of relegation across the capitalist West. This applies with special intensity to poor young men from denigrated ethnoracial categories while young women (their mothers, sisters, girlfriends, wives, and cousins) generally relate to the penetrative state through the mediation of immigration rules, education (when they have children), welfare, and public health.[134] The penal protrusiveness of the Leviathan fuels the collective belief, constantly reinforced by daily encounters with its crime-curating apparatus, that the state has only "one hand," the hand of castigation and discipline.[135] It nourishes sentiments of civic exclusion, cynicism toward judicial authority, and dejection toward other government institutions.

Drawing on a deep ethnography of young men residing in various declining working-class estates of the French urban periphery, the sociologist Éric Marlière insists that "the riots are only the visible part of the iceberg. The sentiment of injustice, of abandonment, of the absence of a future and the cynical perception of institutions are pervasive on an everyday basis."[136] For these men, the state is made legible and palpable by the combination of the police, the youth counselor and the employment counselor, all three of which are perceived as engaged in intrusive and humiliating surveillance that makes them feel like outsiders to the polity. The police are experienced as a repressive, violent, and racist institution. No wonder: officers routinely abuse their authority to conduct groundless "identity checks" during which they hurl ethnic and sexual slurs, provoke the youth stopped during body searches and otherwise infringe on their dignity.[137] Individual arrests often degenerate into collective mêlées that fuel a relationship of raw antagonism.

The young residents of the denigrated *banlieues* are likewise distrustful of the youth counselors tasked with crime prevention and with resolving

---

[134] On the gendered division of the labor of domination by the disciplinary state at the peak of neoliberalism, see Loïc Wacquant, "The Wedding of Workfare and Prisonfare in the 21st Century" (2012a).

[135] I discuss and diagram Pierre Bourdieu's model of the "two hands of the state," the Right hand of discipline and the Left hand of succor, later in this chapter (*infra*, pp. 99–106).

[136] Marlière, *La France nous a lâchés! Le sentiment d'injustice chez les jeunes des cités*, p. 23. On the dialectic of penalization and suspicion toward the state in the US, see Christopher Muller and Daniel Schrage, "Mass Imprisonment and Trust in the Law" (2014).

[137] Marlière, *La France nous a lâchés!*, pp. 34–44. This is not peculiar to France: similar experiences are recounted by young residents of stigmatized districts of poverty in Denmark, Sweden, and Norway, as recounted in chapter 2, see *infra*, pp. 172–6.

local conflicts and administrative problems. They are suspicious of their activities ("A cop, we know what they're for, but a counselor?"), especially when they are asked to fill forms and provide information on other youths from their estate: "They must build files on us, that's for sure ... They work for the state, they're not here for nothing."[138] So much so that they are convinced that counselors are spies, police informants, or undercover cops. Finally, jobless men develop diffident and difficult relationships with the work counselors in charge of their case at the national employment agency. They look at them as an extension of the police, entrusted with surveilling and disciplining them while artificially lowering the unemployment rate by assigning them to worthless vocational internships and enforcing arbitrary rules that make them feel like "cattle."[139]

86

Captured by the police, kept in remand detention in jail, sentenced by a judge through a fast-track procedure (whereby their case is adjudicated within 48 hours), sent away to prison: many young men from French districts of perdition are all too familiar with this punitive trajectory. But there is more: the carceral institution spills over back into the *cité*.[140] As in the American hyperghetto, going to jail or prison is a banal occurrence: nearly everyone knows someone who has been behind bars. By the time they reach their teens, most boys are already familiar with carceral culture from the tales told by their older brothers, cousins, or neighbors who have served time. The interpenetration between the neighborhood and the carceral scene is amplified by the sense of being trapped and confined in one's *cité*. Altogether, the state appears on the radar of the populations of the urban badlands through social control institutions tasked with channeling the turbid confluence between marginality, ethnicity, and territory (which is the topic of chapter 2): an omnipresent and omniscient institution whose penal arm reaches deep in the fabric of everyday life.

Now bring Michael Mann and James Scott together and you realize that there exists a *virtuous circle between infrastructural power and legibility*, whereby each amplifies and deepens the other. Infrastructural power allows state agents to insert themselves into the life of the precariat, thus fostering legibility in the form of files and records (such as the sentencing report from the probation department, which reconstructs the entire personal and family history of the defendant for purposes of sentencing). Legibility, in turn, facilitates insertion and makes it deeper and more efficient. So let us keep the idea that *the*

---

[138] Ibid., pp. 48–9.
[139] Ibid., pp. 50–60.
[140] Lise Périno, *L'Impact de la prison dans les quartiers en politique de la ville* (2013).

penal state is an infrastructural device that penetrates and makes legible the nether regions of social and physical space. Now where shall we locate the penal wing of the state? How does it fit into the architecture of the modern Leviathan? We can turn to Pierre Bourdieu to answer that question.

The three states of Pierre Bourdieu

Bourdieu wrote but a few passing lines on penality (in an influential article on the juridical field)[141] but he offers all the needed analytical tools to hone an expansive notion of criminal punishment as the public delivery of conjoint material violence (Weberian force) and symbolic violence (Goffmanian stigma). On my reading, in his lecture course at the Collège de France *Sur l'État* and related articles,[142] the French sociologist fashions not one but three models of the state, each yielding a flexible conceptual tool we can employ to forge a robust construct of the penal state.

87

1. The *genetic* model of the transition from the House of the King to the Reason of state, attendant on the rise of the bureaucratic over the dynastic mode of reproduction of rule based on the autonomization of cultural capital, yields the concept of *"bureaucratic field"* as the vehicle for the monopolization of capital over capital.
2. The *functional* model of the *"Right hand and Left hand"* of the state corresponding to the (masculine) disciplinary and (feminine) protective missions of the Leviathan, respectively, a duality that characterizes liberal democratic states across the continents.
3. The *structural* model of the state as *"central bank of symbolic capital"* which operates as the fount of efficient classification, identity, and honor, and the engine behind the invention of the "universal."

---

[141] Bourdieu, "La force du droit." A deft introduction to Bourdieu's core concept and theories for students of penality unfamiliar with his work is Victor Lund Shammas and Sveinung Sandberg, "Habitus, Capital, and Conflict: Bringing Bourdieusian Field Theory to Criminology" (2016).

[142] Pierre Bourdieu, *Sur l'État. Cours au Collège de France (1989–1992)* (2012); idem, "Esprits d'État. Genèse et structure du champ bureaucratique" (1993a); idem, "De la maison du roi à la raison d'État" (1997); idem, "On the Fundamental Ambivalence of the State" ([1993] 1998).

I draw on all three concepts to construct my model of the penal state in three steps. First, I articulate the homology between the bipolar organization of the bureaucratic field and the dual opposition between penal agents and their philosophies of punishment. Second, I locate the police, court, and prison in the Right hand of the state. Third, I focus on the double character of state classification as bestowing positive and negative credentials, aura and stigma, and thus effecting public consecration and desecration as the case may be.

1. Penality in the bureaucratic field

88

Together with the notions of political field (with which it overlaps) and of field of power (within which it is contained), the concept of bureaucratic field is a flexible and powerful tool to rethink penality and its structural dynamics.

According to Pierre Bourdieu, the state is the result of a historical process of concentration, taking place over centuries, of the various species of capital that constitute it as the holder of "capital over capital," the field that has the ability to govern other fields and their relations. These species include: (i) the capital of physical force as instruments of coercion become concentrated under the aegis of the state and differentiated into specialized agencies, the military and the police;[143] (ii) economic capital, through the creation of national markets and the establishment of fiscal capacity and policy; (iii) informational capital (of which cultural capital is a manifestation) via the deployment of the census, cartography, national accounting as well as via the codification of language and the unification of "cultural markets" leading to the creation of a national culture spread by the educational system; (iv) symbolic capital, that is, prestige, honor and legitimacy, and, more generally, "the means of imposing and inculcating durable principles of vision and division conforming to its own structures."[144] The objectified and codified form of symbolic capital is juridical capital, which is gradually monopolized by the state, effecting a transition from *de facto* legal pluralism to *de jure* legal unification under the monopoly of the Leviathan and its agencies, the police, court, and prison.

[143] "The armed forces are gradually differentiated with, on the one side, military forces destined for interstate competition, and, on the other, police forces destined to maintain internal order." Bourdieu, "Esprits d'État. Genèse et structure du champ bureaucratique," p. 52.
[144] Ibid., p. 55.

Consider now the formal properties of the bureaucratic field *qua* field. We can single out five features pertinent to our inquiry.[145]

1. *Differentiation and relative autonomy*: a field results from the gradual specialization of a space of action from the surrounding milieu. This action entails the cultivation of distinct practices and products by a body of specialists (in law, art, science, politics, etc.). Its perimeter is protected by more or less institutionalized barriers to entry. It entails the accumulation of a specific form of capital – in our case *bureaucratic capital*, the capacity to effect official acts of public authority and steer public action.

2. *Polarized space of forces*: agents who enter a field are subjected to the distinctive gravity of objective forces operating within it beyond their consciousness and will. They are located in a structure of durable and functionally interconnected positions that define the objective (im)possibilities and (im)probabilities of action.[146] Like a magnetic field, a field is organized around *two antagonistic poles*: *the locus of autonomy and the locus of heteronomy*. Agents of autonomy defend the criteria and capital specific to the field (in our case the logic of public service); agents of heteronomy seek to import external claims and values into the field (e.g., economic efficiency, political partisanship, or religious affiliation).

3. *Historical space of struggles*: a field is a battlefield born of struggles to preserve or transform the distribution of the specific capital that defines its structure. These struggles are patterned: the dominant (incumbents), who possess large volumes of this capital, are inclined to strategies of conservation while the dominated (challengers) tend to favor strategies of usurpation. All the constitutive features of a *champ*, its boundaries, barriers to entry, degree of autonomy and institutionalization, extent of internal and external differentiation, specific *doxa* (the body of notions taken for granted by its participants), and *illusio* (the point of view motivating the latter to invest their energy in its games) are at once the product, the means, and the stake of struggles.[147] These patterned battles propel the specific history of the field.

89

---

[145] This is my own synthesis of Bourdieu's theoretical clarifications as well as of his uses of the concept in empirical research, for which the best source is Pierre Bourdieu, *Microcosmes. Théorie des champs* (2022b).

[146] This is because "differentiation in relation to other fields is accompanied by a process of internal differentiation and the constitution, within each field, of positions that are differentiated but united in and by their interest and competition for the same stakes" (ibid., p. 568).

[147] Struggles take two forms: "competitive struggles which, accepting the imposed

Like all social life, the life of a field is a constant maelstrom of forces of domination and forces of resistance: "The tension resulting from the difference of potential which is constitutive of the structure of the field is a permanent principle of potential change in the structure."[148]

4. *Prismatic effects*: a field is a microcosm with the capacity to *filter and refract* external forces into internal constraints and opportunities. The more autonomous the field, the greater this prismatic capacity. A highly autonomous bureaucratic field can block or rework political demands in accordance with its own principles and values. A highly heteronomous bureaucratic field has lost this capacity, as exemplified by a hierocratic state where religious considerations rule the day.

5. *Multiscalar nesting*: a field (such as the economic field or the bureaucratic field) can contain a lower-order field (such as the financial industry or the finance ministry) organized by homologous oppositions, which harbors yet another field (a given financial firm or the tax office, captured as sites of polarized struggles between different divisions and branches) nested in each other in the manner of Russian dolls.

Figure 1 illustrates the relationship of *encompassment* or nesting between the three key concepts needed to construct the analytical notion of penal state. It shows how social space contains the field of power which in turn contains the various specialized fields corresponding to the different powers operative in a given society, including the bureaucratic field (which Bourdieu sometimes call "administrative field"), one component of which is the penal state.[149]

(i) *Social space* is the multidimensional distribution of capital in its different species, which can be collapsed into the two fundamental axes of volume of capital (vertical axis) and composition of capital (horizontal axis) running from the right-hand side, where economic capital prevails over cultural capital to the left-hand side, where cultural capital prevails over economic

categories, aim only at transforming the distribution of the stakes of competition; revolutionary struggles which, by overturning the imposed categories, aim to change the stakes, to get out of the race and propose other stakes" (ibid., p. 606).

[148] Ibid., p. 589. "The preservation and reproduction of the established order is never more than the result of an incessant struggle between the driving labor of the forces inscribed in the structure of the distribution of capital and the resistive labor that this structure itself supports and gives rise to" (ibid., p. 583).

[149] This figure is my own interpretation and combination of various diagrams sketched by Bourdieu in *La Distinction* (1979), *La Noblesse d'État* (1989b), *Les Règles de l'art* (1992) and *Raisons pratiques* (1994).

90

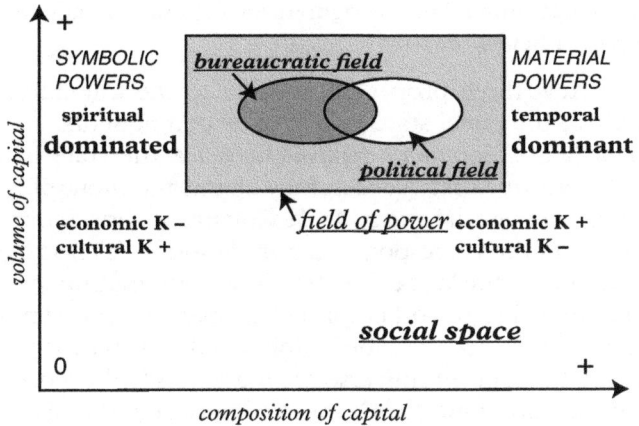

Figure 1 Social space, field of power, and bureaucratic field
in Pierre Bourdieu

capital. It is an analytic map of the geography of positions occupied by
individuals, groups, and institutions.[150]

(ii) *Field of power* is the segment of social space situated in its higher
region; it encompasses the different microcosms concentrating high volumes of the various forms of capital that compete for supremacy:[151] from
right to left, economic, political, journalistic, bureaucratic, religious,
academic, juridical, artistic, etc. (not included in the diagram so that it
remains legible). It is organized by an opposition between the dominant
pole of material (temporal) powers, on the right, and the dominated pole
of symbolic (spiritual) powers, on the left.

(iii) Among the specialized microcosms contained within the field of
power, we find the *political field and the bureaucratic field* which overlap: in
liberal democracies, politicians triumphing in their field (leading parties
and winning elections) occupy the top positions in the executive branch
of the state. The bureaucratic field stands in a barycentric position since
it mediates between the different fields and impacts their relative position.
The state is thus the locus of concentration of, and struggles over, "capital
over capital": it sets the rule of functioning of the economic, journalistic,
academic, etc., fields through administrative, fiscal, and legal regulations.

---

[150] The notion is introduced and elaborated in *La Distinction. Critique sociale du jugement* (1979), and encapsulated in Bourdieu's key article, "Social Space and Symbolic
Power" (1989a).
[151] Pierre Bourdieu, *Raisons pratiques. Sur la théorie de l'action* (1994), pp. 126–32.

The penal state is situated on the right inside the bureaucratic field as indicated in figure 4 below (p. 101).

Consider now three properties specific to the bureaucratic field, which apply to the penal state as one of its components.

1. *Monopoly over legitimate symbolic violence*: the state is, first and foremost, the agency that "successfully claims the monopoly over the legitimate use of material *and symbolic* violence in a given territory and on the totality of the corresponding population."[152] This is Bourdieu's crucial addition to the Weberian definition, one that opens up a distinctive theoretical vista and empirical agenda. *In nuce*, symbolic violence is the "soft" and "invisible" violence that is wielded whenever the dominated in a given universe are made to see the world through the eyes of the dominant. In advanced society, the school and the law are the public institutions that, respectively, inculcate and validate the categories tending to legitimize the social order by making it appear as the only possible configuration.[153] The penal triad is the agency that diffuses the negative identity of "criminal" as antonym and antagonist of the citizen (I return to this point later, *infra*, pp. 108–10).

2. *Definition and distribution of public goods*: on my reading, the bureaucratic field is the locus of the authority to specify and dispense public goods, that is, goods provided unconditionally to the entire population on a non-exclusive basis. What this entails in advanced societies depends on social struggles aimed at the state as well as bureaucratic struggles within the state which together determine the perimeter and mode of delivery of public services. Health care, for instance, is a public good in most European countries but a private good provided by market mechanisms in the United States. Likewise, access to housing can be expanded by policies such as subsidies to building or renting dwellings as a result of battles over its definition as a right or a commodity.[154]

In advanced society, punishment aimed at the production of public order, enforcement of moral propriety, staging of sovereignty and projection of legitimacy is both an *indispensable service* and a

[152] Bourdieu, "Esprits d'État. Genèse et structure du champ bureaucratique," p. 51, original italics.
[153] "If the state is able to exercise symbolic violence, it is because it is embodied both in objectivity in the form of specific structures and mechanisms, and also in 'subjectivity' or, if you like, in minds, in the form of mental structures, categories of perception and thought" (ibid., p. 51).
[154] Mary Pattillo, "Housing: Commodity versus Right" (2013); Matthew Desmond and Monica Bell, "Poverty, Housing, and the Law" (2015).

doggedly public function that every minimally functioning state must imperatively fulfill. In the terms used by Thomas Hobbes, it is part and parcel of the basic "covenant" establishing the Leviathan, a *core responsibility* of the state. No modern state can do without a penal triad, academic disquisitions on "abolition" notwithstanding. Even Scandinavian nations committed to minimalist and humane penality – they are the birthplace of modern penal abolitionism – have proved unable to do away with the police, court, and prison.

Failing states are characterized, not just by "government predation and the militarization of civil society,"[155] but by their stubborn incapacity to set up a police force, criminal courts, and carceral institutions endowed with minimal capacity, coherence, and legitimacy. When and where the penal triad does not coalesce or collapses, social relations fragment and the poor resort to "street justice" of the kind seen in South Africa and Latin America after the democratic transition in response to rampant crime, while the bourgeoisie resorts to the private provision of everyday security (gated communities, hired armed guards, neighborhood patrols, commercial surveillance, etc.).[156] This bifurcated response of street justice and private retraction, in turns, feeds violence and further delegitimizes the state.

Yet, remarkably, the leading student of failing states, Robert Bates, devotes not one line to the incapacity of African states to develop a functional penal triad. Similarly, in their synthetic study of *State Failure in the Modern World*, Zaryab Iqbal and Harvey Starr mention the police only in passing alongside the military and ignore criminal justice as a core mission of a functioning state.[157]

Thomas Hobbes and Norbert Elias were right: *only the Leviathan can durably pacify social space* through the institution and deployment of its penal wing, which is the submerged foundation for full-fledged economic development, social differentiation and psychic

93

---

[155] Robert H. Bates, "State Failure" (2008), p. 1. The disputes over the definition of "failed" or "failing" state are dissected in Zaryab Iqbal and Harvey Starr, *State Failure in the Modern World* (2015), pp. 12–27.

[156] Markus-Michael Müller, *The Punitive City: Privatized Policing and Protection in Neoliberal Mexico* (2016); Nicholas Rush Smith, *Contradictions of Democracy: Vigilantism and Rights in Post-Apartheid South Africa* (2019); Ana Villarreal, *The Two Faces of Fear: Violence and Inequality in the Mexican Metropolis* (2024). See the case studies from around the world gathered by Peter Robson and Ferdinando Spina (eds.), *Vigilante Justice in Society and Popular Culture: A Global Perspective* (2022).

[157] Robert H. Bates, *When Things Fell Apart: State Failure in Late Century Africa* (2015); Iqbal and Starr, *State Failure in the Modern World*.

individualization as demonstrated by Elias in his dissection of the "civilizing process" over eight centuries.[158]

3. The state is the *site of accumulation of "statist capital,"* that is, a "meta-capital" granting power over capital.[159] Agents of the state have garnered the capacity to act in the name of the public and to use the law and administrative regulations to influence the functioning of the various fields that compose the field of power as well as to set the "exchange rate" between the various forms of capital circulating in them: "The bureaucratic field (the state) is not a field like the others; it is the site of a power that has the means to govern the other fields."[160]

There are four takeaways from this brief presentation of the generic and specific properties of the bureaucratic field for understanding the penal state: (i) the penal triad is epicentral to the state's capacity to secure a monopoly over legitimate violence; (ii) it will be organized around a polar opposition between autonomy (the law, nothing but the law) and heteronomy (making room for social forces in the calibration and delivery of punishment); (iii) its prismatic capacity will be critical to ward off the demands of politics, the media, and interest groups to drive structure and policy; (iv) public safety and law enforcement will be the stake of patterned struggles to define the ends, means, and indicators of their provision.

Autonomy and differentiation of the penal state

A common misreading of the concept of field (*champ*) is that it necessarily implies a deeply autonomous, tightly integrated, rigidly centralized, and strongly coordinated universe, as characterizes, for instance, the academic and the bureaucratic fields studied by Pierre Bourdieu in France. Nothing could be further from the truth. In fact, the notion was elaborated by Bourdieu in part against the closed, robotic vision of the *apparatus* mechanically fulfilling a systemic function dear to the structural Marxist school, and it was first essayed to map out a weakly institutionalized case, the artistic field (1).

---

[158] Elias, *The Civilizing Process.* For an analytic complement to this historical thesis, read Ian Loader and Neil Walker, *Civilizing Security* (2007).
[159] Bourdieu, *Sur l'État*, pp. 544–5.
[160] Bourdieu, *Microcosmes*, p. 665.

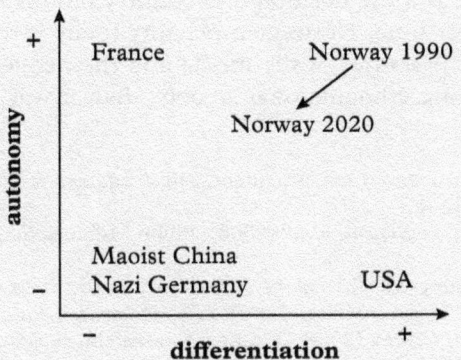

Figure 2   Autonomy and differentiation of the penal state

A field is by definition a dynamic site of patterned action and struggles that may assume a variety of configurations within structural bounds. It follows that a given penal state may be (i) strongly or weakly *autonomized*, depending on its ability to resist or rework demands emanating from rival sites of capital concentration, including the political, journalistic, juridical, and religious fields; (ii) tightly or loosely *integrated*, according to the extent of coordination and cooperation between its different constituent units; (iii) *centralized or decentralized*, depending on the degree to which a paramount authority governs the other units and imposes uniform policies and procedures from the top down across sectors and levels.

Plotting different countries along the two orthogonal *axes of autonomy and differentiation* (figure 2), we can see that France has a highly autonomous and weakly differentiated penal state: the judiciary is strongly insulated from political and popular pressure and bureaucratic units are nationally integrated and closely coordinated (2). The United States sits at the opposite end: it is weakly autonomous, since the local and national politics of crime as well as cycles of racial panic have a direct impact on penal policy; it is also highly differentiated with city, county, state, and the federal government vying for penal authority (3). Nazi Germany and Maoist China are both weakly autonomous and weakly differentiated. Penal policy in these two cases is the diligent servant of the political ruler of the day, to the point where the notion of field itself ceases to be relevant – we are back to an apparatus (4). Norway is a paradigmatic example of a penal state that traditionally sports both high autonomy and high differentiation. But the position of a country on this structural map can change over time. Norwegian penality today is much less insulated from the pressures of the media and the demands of politics, including surging ethnonational anxiety, than it was only two decades ago (5).

1. Pierre Bourdieu and Loïc Wacquant, *An Invitation to Reflexive Sociology* (1992), pp. 102–4.
2. Jean-Paul Jean, *Le Système pénal* (2008); Philip Milburn, *Sociologie de la justice pénale* (2024).
3. Stuart A. Scheingold, *The Politics of Law and Order: Street Crime and Public Policy* (1984); Lisa L. Miller, *The Perils of Federalism: Race, Poverty, and the Politics of Crime Control* (2008); Heather Schoenfeld, *Building the Prison State: Race and the Politics of Mass Incarceration* (2018).
4. Nikolaus Wachsmann, *Hitler's Prisons: Legal Terror in Nazi Germany* (2015); Frank Dikötter, *Crime, Punishment and the Prison in Modern China* (2002).
5. "Norway's penal state is growing increasingly punitive, and penal exceptionalism appears to be on the wane, evidenced by a growing incarceration rate, increasingly punitive sentiments in the population, moral panics over street crime, raised sentencing levels, the forcible detention and extradition of asylum seekers, punitive drug policies, and the creation of segregated correctional facilities for stigmatized foreign offenders." Victor Lund Shammas, "The Rise of a More Punitive State: On the Attenuation of Norwegian Penal Exceptionalism in an Era of Welfare State Transformation" (2016a), p. 57.

A critical conceptual distinction is relevant here between penal *state* and penal *field* in the Bourdieusian sense.[161] The penal field is the structured space of agents vying for the distribution of *penal capital*, that is, the set of efficient resources deployed to shape the nature, intensity, boundaries, and vehicles of public punishment. It is a broader universe of objective relations and actions which *contains* the penal state properly so-called but incorporates many more protagonists in the struggle to define and deliver official justice (see figure 3). As a first approximation, we can describe it as a *meta-field*

---

[161] In his essay on "Punishment and the Penal Field" (2013), Joshua Page draws on Bourdieu's field theory to stress the agonistic nature of correctional policies in the "penal field," but he misses the structural cast of the notion of *champ*: struggles take place in an architectured space of objective positions that transcend and, indeed, govern position-takings and social strategies. The result is an interactionist "meso-level" notion that blurs the differences between Bourdieu and advocates of strategic neo-institutionalism such as Neil Fligstein and Doug McAdam in *A Theory of Fields* (2012). Accordingly, Page presents field theory as a complement to, or extension of, other theoretical approaches rather than as an *alternative* that enables the construction of new and different objects, as cogently argued by Victor Lund Shammas in "Bourdieu's Five Lessons for Criminology" (2018).

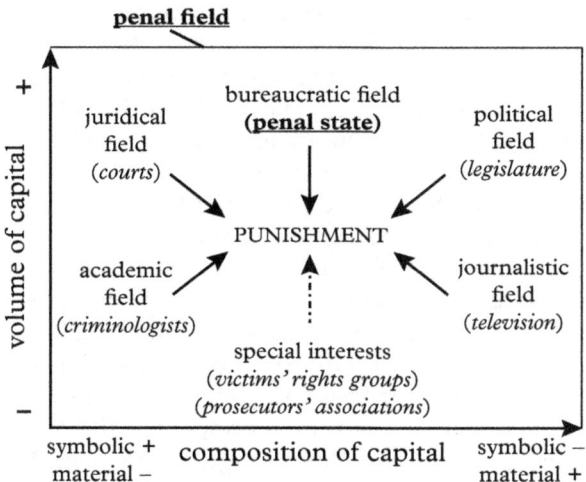

penal field

Figure 3 Penal state and penal field

or a field of fields, located on the right-hand side of the field of power, the side of temporal powers and material authority (see figure 1 *supra*, p. 91).

The penal field comprises operators embedded in the bureaucratic field (starting with the penal triad but including agencies from other ministries, such as budget, infrastructure, and health, when these intrude in the punishment chain), the juridical field (for instance, courts arbitrating the legality of penal statutes or overseeing prison conditions),[162] the political field (parties and elected officials who craft criminal legislation as well as think tanks who seek to shape it), the journalistic field (television and newspapers which mold public opinion on crime and punishment, which in turn influences the legislature, courts, and justice officials), and the academic field (policy analysts, experts, criminologists, etc.). It also includes in a subordinate position special interest groups issued from social space at large such as crime victims' outfits, prosecutors' associations, prisoners' rights groups, and human rights activists. The political and journalistic field are arrayed to the right, the side of the penal field dominated

---

[162] A textbook case is the federal court decision *Brown v. Plata* (2011), which found overcrowded conditions in California prisons in violation of the state constitution, forcing the state to speedily reduce its carceral population from 156,000 to 110,000. Jonathan Simon, *Mass Incarceration on Trial: A Remarkable Court Decision and the Future of Prisons in America* (2014).

97

by material forms of capital (indicated by "material +, symbolic –" on the horizontal axis). The juridical and academic fields are arrayed to the left, the side dominated by symbolic forms of capital ("material –, symbolic +"). Along the vertical axis charting the volume of penal capital, the juridical field has supremacy over the academic field and the political field over the journalistic field.

The test of membership in the penal field is, as with every field, whether the individual or institution considered *makes a difference* as to process and outcome. By that metric, the penal state occupies the preeminent position in the penal field; it is barycentric as it possesses by far the largest volume of penal capital in all of its forms: physical force, administrative authority, legal expertise, criminological legitimation, political connections, etc. It is, moreover, deeply institutionalized since it successfully monopolizes the organizational delivery of public punishment. But, though it may seem hegemonic, this position is but a node in a web of tension vectors and it is constantly constrained as well as disputed by the strategic action of other protagonists.

Analytically, we can distinguish between doxic (or settled) and contested (agitated) states of the penal field as well as periods during which changes come from above, say, through the dictates of politicians or officials from other state agencies, or from below, through the mobilization of "consumers" of penality and their allies, such as organizations fighting to denounce police brutality, increase resources devoted to preventing feminicide, abolish mandatory minimum sentences, or amplify punishment for sex offenders.[163] The main virtue of the concept of penal field is to give form to the material and symbolic ecology within which the penal state navigates – to situate it in an objective system of relations that determines its specific gravity. It captures both structure and strategy, viscosity and fluidity, supremacy and resistance, and it centers struggles as the principle of action and the engine of penal history, in keeping with Bourdieu's quintessentially *agonistic sociology*.

Postindustrial California offers a rich illustration of the battles producing structural change from above and from below. In *Cruel Justice: Three Strikes and the Politics of Crime in America's Golden State* (2005), Joe Domanick

---

[163] For illustrations, see, from above (by the state), Frank Dikötter, *Crime, Punishment and the Prison in Modern China* (2002), and, from below (by prisoners' rights activists), Philippe Artières et al., *Le Groupe d'information sur les prisons. Archives d'une lutte, 1970–1972* (2004).

shows how opportunistic politicians joined with sensationalistic journalists in the 1990s to seize on rare but horrific crimes (such as the home kidnapping and killing of 12-year-old Polly Klaas) to discredit experts and circumvent the authority of the courts, thereby propelling California on the road to hyperincarceration.[164] The result was a spectacular confinement boom that led the state to jump from 59,000 inmates in 1980 to 232,000 in 2000 (jail and prison together), a fourfold increase in only two decades to reach nearly five times the figure for France.

In his masterful study *The Toughest Beat: Politics, Punishment, and the Prison Officers Union in California* (2011), Joshua Page complements that story by retracing how the California prison guard union maneuvered from within to remake the imprisonment subfield in its image.[165] Surfing on carceral inflation, it morphed from fraternal club to political juggernaut. It financed and supported the electoral campaigns of tough-on-crime politicians; it blocked prison privatization to protect its members' jobs and their extravagant wages and retirement benefits; it sponsored victims rights groups pushing for punitive policies and it legitimized prison expansion through moral and emotional appeals. The union thus fundamentally altered the architecture of the Golden State's penal field.

2. The Right hand and Left hand

The second model of the state proposed by Bourdieu is the schema of the "two hands" of the state. The French sociologist broaches it in his 1991 lecture course on the topic at the Collège de France and uses it as a section title in a chapter of *La Misère du monde* (1993), but the formulation remains largely metaphorical and woefully inchoate.[166] In the lecture course, he alludes to "the permanent struggle between these two states," unfolding "in a whole series of subfields," including the bureaucratic agencies which carried out a pivotal reform of French housing policy in the 1970s favoring private over public housing.[167] Bourdieu warns that "the state of the Left hand is always threatened" and that the ongoing neoliberal revolution is seeking to

---

[164] Joe Domanick, *Cruel Justice: Three Strikes and the Politics of Crime in America's Golden State* (2005).

[165] Joshua Page, *The Toughest Beat: Politics, Punishment, and the Prison Officers Union in California* (2011).

[166] Pierre Bourdieu et al., *La Misère du monde* (1993), "La démission de l'État," pp. 221–3.

[167] Bourdieu, *Sur l'État*, pp. 581–2. Bourdieu dissects the revolution in French housing policy in *Les Structures sociales de l'économie* (2000).

Table 3
Left hand and Right hand of the state.

LEFT HAND (feminine)	RIGHT HAND (masculine)
protection	discipline
maternalist	paternalist
social rights	individual obligations
collective solutions	individual solutions
public provision	market delivery
service	commodity
solidarity	competition
(social adversity)	**(accountability)**

"demolish" the social rights built up since the eighteenth century. In a 1992 interview with *Le Monde*, Bourdieu uses the expression Left hand to refer to social workers, educators, low-level magistrates and "the ensemble of agents of the so-called spending ministries which are the trace, within the state, of the social struggles of the past." He depicts them as opposed to the Right hand incarnated by the high civil servants staffing the ministry of finance and pushing to remake the state by shrinking social support and extending the logic of the market to new domains of public provision.[168]

Let me develop this metaphorical opposition into a more articulated concept to map out the internal structure of the penal state as summed up in table 3. The functioning of the bureaucratic field is subtended by the structural opposition between the Right hand and the Left hand of the state. The Left hand is the feminine, *protective* side of Leviathan, materialized by the ministries of public education, health, housing, social welfare, and labor, that is, the ministries which offer succor to the populations shorn of economic and cultural capital. It is *maternalist* in the sense that it seeks to nurture that population and foster its collective well-being by sheltering it from the naked sanctions of the market. It embodies the social rights

---

[168] Bourdieu bemoans the fact that, pursuant to neoliberal restructuring, "the Right hand, obsessed with the question of financial balance, ignores what the Left hand does, which is confronted with the often-costly social consequences of 'budgetary cost-cutting'." Pierre Bourdieu, "La main gauche et la main droite de l'État" ([1992] 1998), pp. 13–17 and p. 13.

achieved through past historical struggles waged in social space and in the political field. It offers collective solutions and public remedies to "social problems" – for instance, build or subsidize low-income housing to tackle homelessness. It delivers public services and aims to bolster solidarity. We will see in chapter 3 that it invokes social adversity as the principle modulating remedial action when it comes to punishment.

The Right hand is the masculine, *disciplinary* side of Leviathan, entrusted with enforcing order and, in the neoliberal era, applying fiscal austerity and economic deregulation. It is *paternalist* in that it imposes authoritarian controls over individuals and prioritizes personal obligations over social rights. For Bourdieu, the Right hand is incarnated by the ministry of the budget. I fill a void in his model by inserting the military, the police, court, and prison as integral components of the Right hand of the state (figure 4). The Right hand seeks individual solutions to collective predicaments; it favors the delivery of market solutions and aims to foster competition as a principle of commodity production. On the penal front, it invokes personal accountability as the basis for punishment.

101

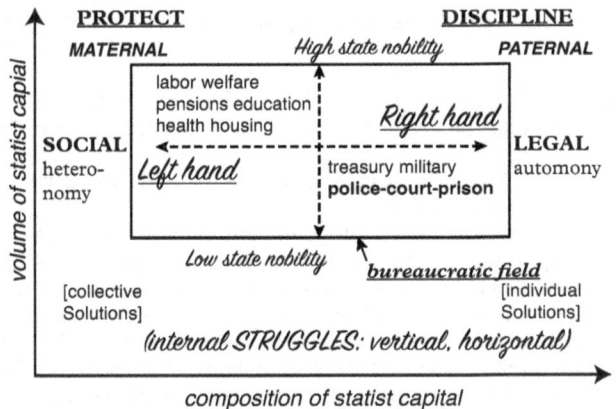

Figure 4   The location of the penal sector in the bureaucratic field

The state is traversed by two kinds of internal struggles – and this applies to the penal state specifically. The first, *horizontal struggles* pit the Left hand and the Right hand of the state, as they battle to appropriate resources (authority, budget, personnel), missions, and prerogatives. They each seek to assert their "ownership" of certain "social problems" as these emerge as priorities at the intersection of the bureaucratic, political, and journalistic fields.[169] A good example is unemployment: a Left solution is to expand jobless benefits to support the unemployed materially and occupational training to facilitate finding a new job; a Right solution is to reduce benefits and make them conditional upon filling a set of administrative requirements (such as working part-time for a nonprofit or a government agency cleaning parks and sweeping streets).[170] The former is couched in the language of social and economic rights, the latter in the idiom of the obligations of citizenship. The second, *vertical struggles* oppose what Bourdieu calls the "high state nobility" of administrative managers issued from elite schools (*haute noblesse d'État*) and the "low state nobility" of executants (*petite noblesse d'État*) who supervise street-level bureaucracies and carry out public policy in its concrete forms day-to-day.[171] In the neoliberal era, state managers have pushed to reduce public programs of support via budgetary austerity and to turn public bureaucracies handling the poor into disciplinary devices to shed recipients and effect behavioral changes.[172]

This means that we should not be naïve and equate the extension of the Left hand of the state with an unqualified expansion of rights and unconditional granting of support. Much as the two poles of

[169] On the struggles to appropriate the public treatment of social issues, see Joseph R. Gusfield, "Constructing the Ownership of Social Problems: Fun and Profit in the Welfare State" (1989).

[170] John Krinsky and Maud Simonet, *Who Cleans the Park? Public Work and Urban Governance in New York City* (2017).

[171] Bourdieu introduces the notion of "high state nobility" in *La Noblesse d'État. Grandes écoles et esprit de corps* (1989b) to designate the top tier of the bureaucratic hierarchy where elite credentials, social cooptation, and class background converge to determine positions claiming authority on merit, intelligence, and technocratic mastery. In a subsequent interview about *La Misère du monde* (1993), the French sociologist elaborates the notion of "low state nobility": "These minor functionaries of the social are the frontline antennas of a state whose Right hand does not want to know what the Left hand is doing. Worse still, the established members of the high state nobility, the *énarques* [graduates of the ENA elite school] of all political persuasions look down from on high upon this petty nobility, whom they enjoy scolding and lecturing. They ignore the fact that it plays a decisive role in maintaining a minimum of social cohesion. They should remember that the French Revolution was triggered by a revolt of the lower nobility against the upper nobility." Pierre Bourdieu, "Notre État de misère" (1993b).

[172] Delphine Serre, *Les Coulisses de l'État social. Enquête sur les signalements d'enfant en danger* (2009), and Bernardo Zacka, *When the State Meets the Street: Public Service and Moral Agency* (2017).

reformation and retribution organize the penal state, the duality of protection and discipline that cleaves the Leviathan is *replicated within the welfare arm* itself. Public aid both serves the poor and brings them under the tutelage of bureaucrats who find in their supervision an opportunity to acquire information, pass judgment, set obligations, and dictate behavior (in a logic of legibility à la James Scott and penetration à la Michael Mann). This means that the welfare wing of the state can be mobilized to pursue punitive aims. The Left hand can be colonized by the idiom, processes, and goals of the Right hand. It can be turned into an intrusive instrument of surveillance and monitoring that effectively expands discipline.[173] Indeed, this colonization was the vehicle for the meshing of workfare and prisonfare under the regime of neoliberal penality.

103

Now *zoom into the penal sector of the bureaucratic field* and you discover that the criminal justice wing of the state, minimally comprising the police, court, and prison, is itself a field stretched along the two dimensions of volume and composition of penal capital, organized by oppositions homologous to those that structure the bureaucratic field as a whole. The *Right hand of the penal state* is the masculine agent of discipline; it is anchored by the legal pole of autonomy, occupied at the criminal court level by prosecutors who prioritize juridical over social concerns. It tends to favor retribution as the philosophy of punishment. The *Left hand of the penal state* is the feminine agent of protection; it is anchored by the social pole of heteronomy, occupied by public and private defenders who battle to prioritize social over legal concerns; it tends to favor reformation as the operative philosophy of punishment (figure 5).

In the criminal court, the Left hand of the penal state strives to promote mitigation and rehabilitation. The mission of defense attorneys is to minimize punishment – that is, restrain the force of the Right hand – by weakening the legal basis of prosecution and incorporating extra-juridical factors into penal reasoning. They conceive of the defendant as a multifaceted social being, with a personal history, social ties, and a complex psychology, who cannot be reduced to the criminal act they allegedly committed (on "the worst day in their life," as public defenders like to say). They make it

---

[173] Wacquant, *Punishing the Poor*, chapter 3; Joe Soss et al., *Disciplining the Poor: Neoliberal Paternalism and the Persistent Power of Race* (2011); Leslie Paik, *Trapped in a Maze: How Social Control Institutions Drive Family Poverty and Inequality* (2021); Spencer Headworth, *Policing Welfare: Punitive Adversarialism in Public Assistance* (2021); Vincent Dubois, *Contrôler les assistés. Genèses et usages d'un mot d'ordre* (2021).

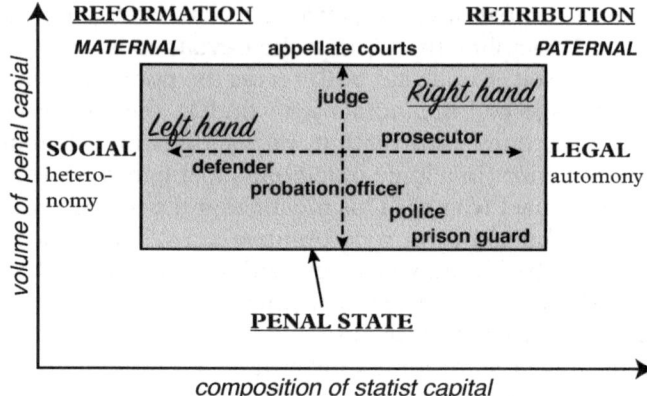

Figure 5 The structure of the penal sector in the bureaucratic field

their task to "humanize" the defendant in the eyes of the prosecutor in the hope of lessening penal sanction.

Left to its own logic, the Right wing of the penal state wants to know only the offense committed and, secondarily, the criminal background of the offender to calibrate punishment according to the philosophy of "just desert." The slant of prosecutors is to minimize the influence of extra-judicial factors ("I don't want to hear that sob story") and apply the law, nothing but the law. This polar opposition between prosecutor and defense attorney is refracted at a lower scale, for instance, *among* prosecutors inclined to litigation versus negotiation or *among* parole officers who can construe their mission either as a social worker (left pole of heteronomy turned toward social values) or as a police officer (right pole of autonomy turned toward legal values).

The fractal structure of the penal state

The opposition between the disciplinary Right hand and the protective Left hand of the state is replicated *within* the penal state itself as the opposition between the pole of retribution (Kantian penality, represented by the prosecutor) and the pole of reformation (Benthamite penality, embodied by the court-appointed defender) promoting two warring conceptions of criminal justice. I will show in chapter 3 (*infra*, pp. 252–8) that each of these poles is itself further divided into a Right and a Left hand according to a fractal logic captured by

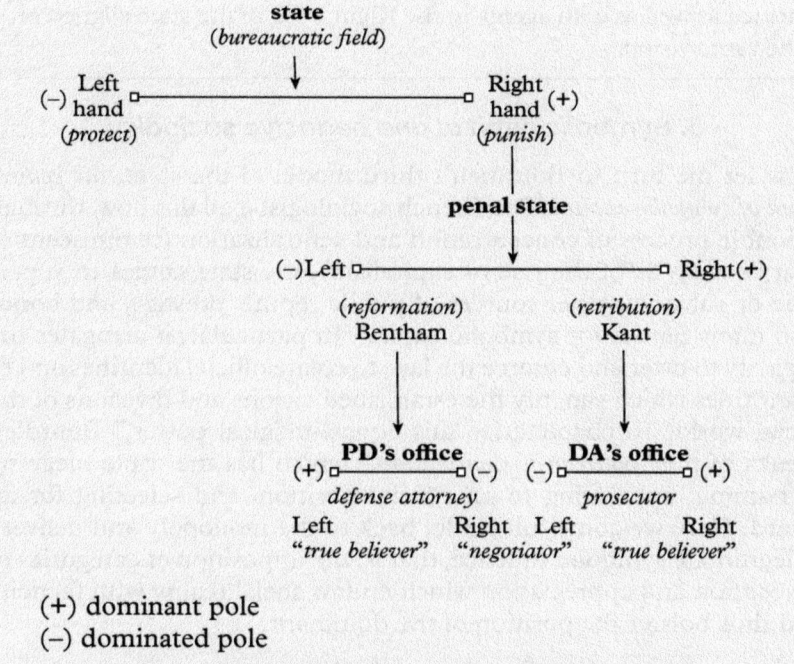

Figure 6 The fractal structure of the penal state

figure 6. Thus the office of prosecutors is organized by the opposition between "true believers" and "negotiators" (going right to left) while the office of public defenders is organized by the same opposition but inverted (going left to right).

These homological oppositions explain the *objective alliances* that exist between agents situated at the Right or Left at each of these three structural levels. Thus the "true believers" in the public defender's office occupy the "left of the left" position; they defend an "externalist," social reading of criminal cases. They are in cahoots with agents in the left wing of the penal state who push for a social vision of justice as well as with agents in the Left wing of the state such as social workers, educators, and medical specialists who provide authoritative arguments for mitigation and rehabilitation (public defenders' offices in some California counties have their own in-house social workers). The "true believers" in the District Attorney's office occupy the "right of the right" position; they defend an "internalist," strictly juridical reading of criminal cases. They are allied with agents in the right wing of the penal state who favor a strict legal conception of

> justice as well as with agents in the Right wing of the state aligned on the same vision.

3. Symbolic capital and negative sociodicy

Now let me turn to Bourdieu's third model of the state, *the central bank of symbolic capital*. The French sociologist explains how, through a double process of concentration and centralization (reminiscent of Marx's analysis of the rise of capitalism), the state comes to supersede or subsume other sources of public repute, prestige, and honor – so many names for symbolic capital. In particular, it arrogates the capacity to utter and enforce the law, to create official identities and to grant titles which sanctify the established visions and divisions of the social world. To characterize this "quasi-magical power," Bourdieu speaks of the "*pouvoir de nomination*," which has the triple meaning of naming, appointing to an official position, and selecting for an award. Here we come full circle, back to the monopoly and delivery of legitimate symbolic violence, that is, the imposition of categories of perception and appreciation which endow social reality with facticity and thus bolster the position of the dominant.

> By concentrating symbolic capital, of which the concentration of jurid-ical capital is one aspect, and which tends, for example, to replace the statutory honor of the caste of nobility with honors conferred by the central power, the state gradually establishes itself as the central bank of symbolic capital, invested with the power of *nomination* . . . The power of nomination is a power of social creation, which brings the person nominated into existence in accordance with the nomination. It is a quasi-magical power.[174]

Bourdieu focuses on the bestowal of positive symbolic capital, that is, assignment to a valorized identity elevating the person thus named or nominated in the eyes of others and attesting to their social worth and moral virtue – one of the many definitions of honor: "This process of concentration of symbolic capital operated by the state . . . culminates in the power of nomination, the power to award decorations, credentials, titles of bureaucratic nobility (such as the Legion of Honor) or academic titles."[175] But there is a dark side to the state and the power of nomination can just as well be wielded to assign a

[174] Bourdieu, *Sur l'État*, pp. 590, 432.
[175] Ibid., p. 342.

negative identity, one tarnished by official stigma and backed by the force of public bureaucracy. This is what is involved in a criminal conviction: it strips the defendant of the honor of citizenship and casts him out of the civic community, provisionally or permanently; it is an act of *negative nomination* or bureaucratic desecration. The court procedure of the entry of the guilty plea, the reading of the verdict of the jury, the sentencing of the defendant are variants of what Harold Garfinkel famously called "degradation ceremonies."[176]

It should be clear by now that punishment is not just a topic in the study of crime and deviance but a central chapter in the sociology of the state and the theory of group-making. Penal sanctions do not only inflict pain; they exact a form of *public dishonor*. This is what links them organically with ethnicity (a topic I will address in the second chapter): "race" as denegated ethnicity is also a form of public dishonor,[177] which helps explain that punishment everywhere targets populations both destitute *and stigmatized* – a dimension that materialist theories of punishment, such as neo-Marxist and neoclassical political economy, are incapable of grasping. Indeed, in the symbolic register, *penality can be understood as "negative sociodicy."*

107

The term *theodicy* was coined in 1709 by Gottfried Wilhelm Leibniz in his effort to show that the existence of evil does not contradict the goodness of God, an aporia inherited from medieval theology which vexed him throughout his life.[178] The notion was reformulated by Max Weber in his sociology of religion, which introduces a dichotomous distinction between the "theodicy of good fortune" (*Theodizee des Glückes*) and the "theodicy of suffering" or misfortune (*Theodizee des*

---

[176] This is the name given by Harold Garfinkel ("Conditions of Successful Degradation Ceremonies" [1956]: 420) to "communicative work directed to transforming an individual's total identity into an identity lower in the group's scheme of social types." A key condition of successful degradation ceremonies is that "the denouncer must make the dignity of the supra-personal values of the tribe salient and accessible to view, and his denunciation must be delivered in their name." Another is that "the denouncer must arrange to be invested with the right to speak in the name of these ultimate values." A third is that "the denounced person must be ritually separated from a place in the legitimate order, i.e., he must be defined as standing at a place opposed to it. He must be placed 'outside,' he must be made 'strange'" (ibid., p. 423).

[177] Loïc Wacquant, *Racial Domination* (2024b), pp. 86–90.

[178] Leibniz engaged with the contentious "problem of evil" in numerous texts, particularly the *Theodicy*, his only book-length writing published during his lifetime, so much so that it may be considered the core of his philosophical vision. See Paul Rateau, *La Question du mal chez Leibniz. Fondements et élaboration de la Théodicée* (2008). For a fuller genealogy of theodicy, see Bryan S. Turner, "Theodicy: The Career of a Concept" (1981).

Leidens).[179] The two theodicies serve the same function: to justify privilege at the top and deprivation at the bottom, and thereby perpetuate social hierarchy. In his work on education, Pierre Bourdieu secularizes the notion to speak of *sociodicy*: the legitimation of the existing order via the consecration of inherited cultural capital bestowed by elite schools.[180]

We can reintroduce the Weberian duality back into Bourdieu's view of the state as the fount of honor to discover that the prison operates as the fulcrum of *negative sociodicy*, the public legitimation of the dereliction of the rejects of the market, by extending to them the trope of individual (ir)responsibility and (de)merit that anchors the positive sociodicy effected by the higher education system at the other end of the class structure. The prison can thus be understood as a kind of "negative university" bestowing certificates of "discredit" justifying the truncation of the life conditions and life chances of those struck by penal law. Along with elite schools, the prison partakes of a *division of the labor of legitimation* at the two ends of the social order, in which capacity it contributes to shaping citizenship.

Elite schools provide a *positive sociodicy* of the privileges of the dominant by granting them educational credentials, honorific titles attesting to their individual merit, defined as a combination of personal talent, intelligence, hard work, and moral prowess (see table 4). They expand the life chances of their graduates and endow them with an aura that inspires collective awe on the positive side and envy on the negative side. Holders of elite diplomas are what Bourdieu calls a "state nobility," a closed and honorific group at the top of the class structure sanctified by the state and thereby separated from the common and the vulgar, that is, partaking of the sacred in the Durkheimian sense.[181]

At the other end of the social order, the prison provides a *negative sociodicy* of the social suffering and relegation of marginal populations based on the exact same criteria of merit, only in their case it allegedly sanctions their

---

[179] Weber, *From Max Weber: Essays in Sociology*, p. 271. The second variant is also characterized as a theodicy of despair, fatalism, and escape.

[180] "As the privileged instrument of bourgeois sociodicy, which confers on the privileged the supreme privilege of not appearing to themselves to be privileged, [the School] is all the more successful in convincing the underprivileged that they owe their educational and social destiny to their lack of gifts or merits as, in matters of culture, absolute dispossession excludes the awareness of dispossession." Pierre Bourdieu and Jean-Claude Passeron, *La Reproduction. Éléments pour une théorie du système d'enseignement* (1970), p. 253.

[181] Pierre Bourdieu, *La Noblesse d'État. Grandes écoles et esprit de corps* (1989b).

Table 4
Elite school and prison as complementary
institutions of legitimation.

PENALITY AS NEGATIVE SOCIODICY	
ELITE SCHOOL *positive sociodicy* *"Theodizee des Glückes"* CREDENTIAL	**PRISON** *negative sociodicy* *"Theodizee des Leidens"* CRIMINAL RECORD
privileges of dominant	deprivation of dominated
noble, at the top	ignoble, at the bottom
individual merit	individual demerit
expands life chances	shrinks life chances
honor, aura	shame, stigma
awe, envy	fear, pity
purity	pollution, danger
"state nobility"	"state pariahs"

lack of talent and intelligence, their deficient work ethic, and their moral flaws. The criminal record ("RAP sheet," *casier judiciaire, Führungszeugnis, casellario giudiziale,* etc.) justifies the dire condition and truncation of the life chances of the convict, both within and beyond carceral walls. It inflicts upon him a stigma that nourishes feelings of shame. The collective emotions evoked by the convict are fear on the negative side and pity on the positive side. Whereas elite school graduates are the embodiment of purity, prison graduates are what we could call "state pariahs." They are living bearers of pollution and incarnations of danger justifying their social ostracization and moral castigation.[182]

Just as the state vouches for the value of a university credential, it stands behind the "negative credentials" delivered by criminal justice institutions. In the United States, where an estimated one adult in three has an arrest or conviction record and one in ten a felony conviction, county, state, and federal governments make individually identified records generated by jails, courts, and prisons available on grounds of public safety, government transparency, and the

---

[182] Mary Douglas, *Purity and Danger: An Analysis of Concepts of Pollution and Taboo* (1966).

constitutional mandate of free speech.[183] Private companies mine, package, and sell justice data to employers, realtors and landlords, public bureaucracies, volunteer organizations, and the citizenry at large. Data brokers have amassed gigantic troves with files running in the billions linking judicial information with drug tests, driving records, credit profiles, as well as verification of education and employment. The criminal background check industry is worth over $5 billion, backed by the signature of the state. It impacts who gets a job, housing, welfare benefits, education and training, parental rights, the right to vote and to naturalize – confirming the inverse symbolic and organizational valence of criminality and citizenship.[184]

In England and Wales, the Disclosure and Barring Service (DBS), launched in 2012 to replace and modernize the Criminal Records Bureau, is officially tasked with conducting criminal background verification, colloquially known as "DBS checks" (similar agencies exist in Scotland and Northern Ireland). In a typical year, the DBS processes over 6 million requests, including 4 million checks mandated by law, which corresponds to 18 percent of the employed population. This represents a quadrupling in 20 years, leading criminologists to speak of a "vetting epidemic."[185] Data from the Ministry of Justice reveal that 27 percent of working-age adults have a criminal record. This is consequential: a survey commissioned by the Department for Work and Pensions in 2016 found that one-half of British businesses would decline employing someone with a criminal conviction. Discrimination based on "negative credentials" delivered by the penal apparatus is thus both enabled and validated by the state.

Three structural properties of the penal state

We now come to this definition: the penal state is the sector of the bureaucratic field that successfully *monopolizes and deploys the legit-*

---

[183] Sarah Esther Lageson, "Criminal Record Stigma and Surveillance in the Digital Age" (2022).

[184] David S. Kirk and Sara Wakefield, "Collateral Consequences of Punishment: A Critical Review and Path Forward" (2018). Criminals are the biggest losers in the great classification surge spawning what Marion Fourcade and Kieran Healy call *The Ordinal Society* (2024).

[185] Marti Rovira, "Invisible Stripes? A Field Experiment on the Disclosure of a Criminal Record in the British Labour Market and the Potential Effects of Introducing Ban-The-Box Policies" (2024), p. 829.

imate means to interpret and enforce criminal statutes, thereby curating crime in the sense that it selects, manipulates, and exhibits it for order maintenance, organizational expediency, civic instruction, and political profit. It is the *product as well as the site of patterned struggles over the meaning and means of "justice."* The enforcement of criminal statutes entails the joint delivery of concentrated material violence (Weber) and symbolic violence (Bourdieu) trained on violators, but reaching also those connected to them (social halo effect), and the spaces they inhabit (territorial effect). State force as dispensed by the penal triad penetrates (Mann) and makes legible (Scott) the underbelly of the city and its inhabitants, on whom all the urban ills and dangers of the moment are projected. Punishment draws a sharp and vivid boundary around these defamed categories and territories (Durkheim), sepa-rating them from the stable and deserving working class in the public imagination and making them available as target for public vitupera-tion and state action (Foucault), in keeping with the structural trans-formation of the economy and its destabilizing effects at the bottom of the class hierarchy (Rusche). By contraposition, the penal state traces the silhouette of the full-fledged, law-abiding citizen.

Criminal statutes are political statements about (un)acceptable conduct, conduct that tramples fundamental rights, contravenes sali-ent norms, and desecrates the moral values defining a civic commu-nity (in the sense of a collectivity of formal equals sharing core beliefs and rituals enshrined by the state). Statutes are set by the legislature, which belongs to the political and not the bureaucratic field, but they are effectively redrawn by official agents at multiple levels of the puni-tive bureaucracy (as we shall see in chapter 3). The penal state inflicts force and stigma upon the denizens of the urban badlands in order to bring them to heel and, meanwhile, projects them as a collective par-asite and menace to society, the *social refuse* of the established social and moral order. A veteran judge from San Pedrito county noted wryly about the criminal court: "We are travelling in the sewers of society on a glass-bottom boat."

Three structural properties of the penal state need highlighting here, which underlie its empirical instantiations in different coun-tries and conjunctures. First property: lodged securely in the Right hand of the state, like every field, the *penal sector is polarized* between two possible missions carried out by the pole of autonomy (pure law, tending toward retribution, incarnated by the prosecutor) and the pole of heteronomy (applied law, tending toward reformation, incar-nated by the public defender in the US and court-appointed counsel

111

in European countries). There is, at every moment, a *struggle between agents situated at these two poles* over the purpose and priority of punishment, just desert or rehabilitation, or some dynamic combination of these two philosophies.[186] This struggle plays out, not only in the field of power, between politicians, jurists, justice managers, expert scholars, and journalists vying for the authority to define "law and order," but also in the day-to-day relations between and amongst agents of justice bureaucracies at both the policy-making and policy-implementation levels. It manifests itself on the justice frontlines, for instance, in the tension that exists between prosecutors and public defenders, among judges who lean this or that way, among police who see themselves as "warriors" or as "guardians," or among prison guards and parole agents who can construe their work alternately as akin to policing or to social work.[187]

Second property: *the penal state is Janus-faced* in that it delivers two opposite services at once, the one positive and the other negative. To the citizenry at large, presumed to be law-abiding and thus deserving, it purports to provide a *public good* in the form of generalized crime prevention, the protection of property and safety, as well as firm support for individual responsibility, social propriety, and moral respectability.[188] It operates in the manner of a *shield* against disorder. To its clientele, namely, suspects, defendants, and convicts, and those close to them, who are by definition undeserving, and most of whom issue from districts of urban perdition, the penal state delivers a *private bad* in the form of targeted physical and psychic pain. It is a *sword* unsheathed to frighten would-be offenders (deterrence), neutralize scofflaws (incapacitation), retrain convicts (rehabilitation), or hurt violators (retribution). Even soft penal programs proclaiming to foster the social integration of their target population, such as

---

[186] This structural polarization underlies the historical struggles over criminal justice in America described by Philip Goodman et al. in *Breaking the Pendulum: The Long Struggle over Criminal Justice* (2017). It also animates ordinary perceptions of justice by the citizenry, as shown by Cécile Vigour et al., *La Justice en examen. Attentes et expériences citoyennes* (2022).

[187] For an illustration of this tension in the work of parole agents in California, read Robert Werth, "I Do What I'm Told, Sort Of: Reformed Subjects, Unruly Citizens, and Parole" (2012). The same alternative between repression and compassion organizes the work of probation agents in France: Yasmine Bouagga, "Le métier de conseiller d'insertion et de probation. Dans les coulisses de l'État pénal?" (2012).

[188] On the notion of "public good," that is, a good or service accessible to all once it is provided to some, regardless of one's contribution to their provision, see Mancur Olson, *The Logic of Collective Action: Public Goods and the Theory of Groups* (1965).

"therapeutic policing" in Los Angeles's Skid Row, turn out to wield panoptic forms of coercion that entrench marginality.[189] The Janus-faced nature of the penal state explains that it suffers from *structural illegitimacy*: its authority and edicts are never fully accepted by the urban precariat because, to them, it fails to deliver a positive public good (public safety) and it provides a negative private good in the form of material suasion and symbolic denigration.

This *two-sidedness is inescapable and irreducible*. It is a normal and not a pathological feature of the penal state. Thus the latter's advocates focus on the delivery of public safety, lionize the law-enforcement forces ("the thin blue line"), and push for judicial severity, while its critics decry its abuses and point to systemic injustice at every stage of the penal process. This duality maps closely onto a political opposition: right-wing analysts underestimate private pain and its asymmetric distribution while their left-wing counterparts minimize the profits of the enforcement of sociomoral order. But there is no question that, in the real world as opposed to the ether of legal theory, the poor have a vested interest in an efficacious penal state, *provided it is minimalist and unified in its actions*, such that it pursues public safety on an equitable basis and according to the same modalities across social and physical space.[190]

This is because, for readily discernible social reasons (material deprivation, family instability, emotional insecurity, and cultural conflict), the homes, streets, and neighborhoods of the poor do harbor a disproportionate share of visible crime and detectible violence. Moreover, the poor and ethnic outsiders everywhere are not just the primary perpetrators of street crime (in response to truncated or deviating opportunities); they are also its first victims. This implies that they need the state to play its role in producing the public safety they yearn for. As for the rich, if the state fails, they can always provide themselves with private security and private penality, as exemplified by gated communities and top-flight defense attorneys, and they have no need for the support of the education, welfare, and health

---

[189] Forrest Stuart, *Down, Out, and Under Arrest: Policing and Everyday Life in Skid Row* (2016). See also Forrest Stuart et al., "Legal Control of Marginal Groups" (2015).

[190] In the United States of the 2020s, it has become *de rigueur*, among left-leaning scholars, to embrace "abolition" as the new rhetoric and horizon of penal reform. I will show in the book's coda that this paper radicalism has no purchase on the actual functions and functioning of the penal state. Crucially, it ignores the urgent "security interest" of the residents of neighborhoods of relegation.

care state which are also part of the expanded apparatus of production of public safety.

Mais voilà: the penal state is emphatically not a unified institution functioning in a socially consistent manner, quite the contrary. The representations that guide it, the statutes it stipulates, and the actions it takes are systematically *differentiated by class, ethnicity and place* – and at their intersection in the neighborhoods of relegation of the postindustrial metropolis. Because this proves to be the case empirically in every society for which we have the requisite data and goes back to its budding in the late sixteenth century, it is safe to posit that the *penal state is not just polarized and two-faced but also bifurcated* – its third structural property.[191] To understand this bifurcation, it is fruitful to draw on the work of the legal scholar Markus Dubber. In his rich book *The Dual Penal State*, Dubber proposes that there are two ways of interpreting the criminal process translating into two modes of penal governance: law and police.[192] The *Rechtsstaat* is anchored in legal autonomy, equality, and interpersonal respect producing principled punishment. The *Polizeistaat* is grounded in legal heteronomy, hierarchy, and patriarchal power generating punitive discipline. These two modalities of criminal law do not exist independently of each other but through their contraposition.

However, for Dubber, this duality is juridical and not social; it is rooted in the interpretive dualism of criminal procedure. He does not realize that it expresses the dualization of penality across social and physical space. Legal governance applies to the middle and upper classes (as well as corporations), whom it treats as subjects and citizens endowed with rights guaranteed by the law (*Recht*). Police governance applies to the working class and the poor, who experience penality first and foremost as the arbitrary and capricious force of the police (*Polizei*). Those at the top are subjected to *paper penality*, for which practice closely approximates formal prerogatives; it is incarnated by the private defense attorney wending her way through court paperwork and approximates Weber's ideal type of rational law. For those at the bottom of the double hierarchy of class and status, it is an intrusive and disruptive state of constant surveillance, routine

114

---

[191] To put it differently, the *onus probandi* falls on those who treat the penal state as an integrated institution and not the other way around. This includes virtually the entire corpus of legal theory on criminal justice.

[192] Markus D. Dubber, *The Dual Penal State: The Crisis of Criminal Law in Comparative-Historical Perspective* (2018), and idem, "Criminal Process in the Dual Penal State" (2019).

brutality and personal humiliation: they are subjected to *street penality* delivered by the police.[193]

The application of street penality spawns practices and procedures that consistently deviate from, or frontally violate, official standards of justice as a matter of course (starting with fairness and individual dignity), a deviation that is normalized by bureaucratic convenience, professional omerta, and willful political ignorance or, worse, political profiteering. As I will show in the second chapter, this is especially true in the urban badlands, whose borders the penal state patrols aggressively in an effort to prevent the spillover of social and criminal disorder as well as to dramatize its commitment, if not its ability, to impose public order on the totality of its territory. Street penality is the infrastructural means whereby the Leviathan infiltrates and makes legible the nethermost regions of social and physical space, a form of Foucauldian *pouvoir-savoir* trained on the urban precariat.

My theoretical construct differs fundamentally from David Garland's elitist conception of the penal state referring only to policy-makers and decision-makers atop punishment bureaucracies, namely, "the agencies and authorities which make binding penal rules and direct their implementation," to the exclusion of the machinery and staff delivering penality in practice. Garland explicitly rules out the "apparatus of prisons, jails, correctional staff, etc.," insisting that "the 'penal state' refers instead to the penal leadership and its authority, not to the penal infrastructure that this leadership directs."[194] It thus encompasses the prison warden but not prison guards; the police commissioner but not police officers on the beat; the chief probation officer but not the probation agents; the head prosecutor but not the line attorneys who work under her authority; and consequently not the public defenders paid by the state to protect the rights of indigent defendants. Garland provides no justification, theoretical or

---

[193] For a vivid demonstration of its workings in the urban periphery of France, see Fassin, *La Force de l'ordre*, and in the American inner city, Rios, *Punished*. I elaborate the opposition between these two penalities in chapter 2, *infra*, pp. 183–90.

[194] David Garland, "Penality and the Penal State" (2013a). Garland's penal state "includes the state *legislature, executive and judiciary* acting in their penal capacity (enacting penal laws, authorizing penal budgets, or adjudicating penal issues), together with the *leadership* of penal agencies who shape penal policy and direct its day-to-day implementation (police commissioners, chief prosecutors, judicial elites, justice department chiefs, correctional commissioners, prison wardens, probation service directors, state parole board members, etc.)" (p. 496, my italics). In my conception, the legislative and executive branches of government do not belong to the penal state but to the penal field (see *supra*, figure 3, p. 97).

empirical, for this restrictive definition and he muddies the conceptual waters when he concedes in passing that police officers do belong to the penal state after all.[195]

This is a surprising top-down concept because it *leaves out the effective agents of penality* on the ground.[196] It is like saying that the welfare state does not include public aid offices and case workers; or the educational state does not encompass teachers and guidance counselors; or the public health state does not comprise clinics and nurses. But does a policeman not wield penal power when he arrests a suspect? A line prosecutor when she sets the parameters of a guilty plea offer? A prison guard when he exerts force to restrain an inmate? A parole officer sanctions a parolee for a violation sending him back being bars? Even a court clerk when she chooses to disregard a failure to pay a fine on time to give a defendant a chance to avoid further sanction? These situations do not figure among "those aspects of the state that determine penal law and direct the deployment of the power to punish,"[197] but they are clear and definite instances of penal power being activated.

This is why my concept of the penal state encompasses both the high state nobility of policy-makers and top managers, the low state nobility of local bureaucratic supervisors and the executants of penal law and policy. Michael Lipsky taught us long ago in his classic *Street-Level Bureaucracy* (1980) that the reality of a public policy resides, not in its programmatic intentions and managerial decisions, but in what ordinary civil servants do when they implement it day-to-day in direct contact with clients, when the rubber of legislative acts and executive pronouncements hits the rocky road of human reality and organizational necessity.[198]

---

[195] Garland's formal definition of the penal state excludes the police but, in a footnote, we read: "The police are state actors who, among other things, deploy penal power: they make arrests, facilitate prosecutions, issue tickets, and impose fines. In these respects, *the police form an element of the penal state*" (ibid., p. 29n30, my italics).

[196] I endeavor to show in chapter 3 that the line prosecutor working in the trenches of the criminal court is the penal state incarnate, the Leviathan turned into flesh and blood.

[197] Garland, "Penality and the Penal State," p. 495.

[198] "The decisions of street-level bureaucrats, the routines they establish, and the devices they invent to cope with uncertainties and work pressures, effectively *become* the public policies they carry out. I argue that public policy is not best understood as made in legislatures and the top-floor suites of high-ranking administrators, because in important ways it is actually made in the crowded offices and daily encounters of street-level workers" (Michael Lipsky, *Street-Level Bureaucracy: Dilemmas of the*

The structural complexity and built-in dynamism of the penal state, rooted in the contradictory pull of autonomy and heteronomy, the tension between public good and private bad, and the interplay of law and police as class-based modes of governance, explains that it can serve *multiple functions simultaneously beyond its penological mission* necessitating the coupling of consequentialist and retributivist philosophies of punishment: it curates criminality, sweeps up the urban rejects of the market (the homeless, poor addicts and the mentally ill, and irregular immigrants) and raises the cost of involvement in the street economy; brightens social boundaries and broadcasts morality; and legitimizes misfortune by the bestowal of negative credentials. Last but not least, the penal state serves to project sovereignty and shore up the deficit of legitimacy of politicians when they roll back the economic and social protections of the Leviathan established as the bedrock of citizenship during the Fordist-Keynesian era. This twin role is central to the resurgence of the prison at the forefront of the institutional horizon of advanced societies over the past half-century, a historical puzzle to which I turn in the next chapter.

117

Individual in Public Service [1980], p xii, original italics). An American illustration is the reworking of the 1996 "welfare reform" by case workers described by Celeste Watkins-Hayes, *The New Welfare Bureaucrats: Entanglements of Race, Class and Policy Reform* (2009). The same process is documented in a French welfare office by Vincent Dubois, *La Vie au guichet. Relation administrative et traitement de la misère* (1999). For a panorama of work focusing on "the people who do the work of the state, bringing identities, experiences, cognition, and cultural understandings" into focus, see Erin Metz McDonnell, "Bureaucracy in Action: The Sociology of Public Administration" (2025).

2

Marginality, Ethnicity, Territory

"The prison creates a veritable army of internal enemies."
Michel Foucault, *La Société punitive* (1974)

Throughout history, the prison has evoked dread, pain, and stigma as well as inviting voyeuristic titillation and a foreboding sense of mystery. It has stood as the materialization of the power of rulers and a vivid expression of the character of political regimes. This is illustrated by the Bastille in monarchical France, Alcatraz in prohibition-era United States, Carandiru in urban Brazil, Evin in Iran from the Shah to the ayatollahs, Saydnaya in despotic Syria, Robben Island in apartheid South Africa, Ngaragba in postcolonial Central Africa and Bastøy (the famous Prison Island) in Norway.[1] This is no different today in advanced societies. Even though only a small segment of the population of offenders is consigned behind bars at any one time, it is generally believed that incarceration is the modal state sanction. Even knowing students of penality tend to equate punishment with imprisonment, if only by granting it exclusive attention,[2] when other non-custodial

---

[1] For contrast, see Didier Bigo's portrait of "Ngaragba, 'l'impossible prison'" (1989), Drauzio Varella's chronicle of the Carandiru inmate uprising and massacre in *Estação Carandiru* (2005), and Victor Lund Shammas's peek into Norway's iconic Bastøy in "The Pains of Freedom: Assessing the Ambiguity of Scandinavian Penal Exceptionalism on Norway's Prison Island" (2014). The most infamous prison representing a failed political enterprise is without contest Abu Ghraib in Iraq under US occupation, as depicted by Philip Gourevitch and Errol Morris, *The Ballad of Abu Ghraib* (2009).

[2] Bruce Western, *Punishment and Inequality in America* (2006); Grégory Salle, *La*

forms of criminal sanction (fines, probation, court-mandating programming, public utility work, house arrest, electronic monitoring, restorative justice conferences, etc.) largely predominate. In the collective imagination, public and academic, the prison *is* the penal state.

Over the past half-century, despite its deep penological discredit, the prison has surprisingly surged to the institutional forefront of advanced societies. This is surprising because those decades were stamped by the politics and policies of state retrenchment on the social and economic fronts. Yet very few countries have escaped the carceral tropism that has fueled the runaway growth of confined populations around the globe.[3] In this chapter, I propose that carceral expansion after the mid-1970s in the capitalist West is best understood as a facet of *neoliberal state-crafting* – provided that we properly define "neoliberalism" and attend to how it actually unfolds.[4] In a nutshell, the "penal fist" of the Leviathan reinforces and complements the "invisible hand" of the market and the prison is tasked with sweeping away the human detritus generated by economic deregulation and with containing the social disorders spawned by the diffusion of social insecurity at the bottom of the hierarchy of classes, ethnicities, and places. Its aggressive deployment as part of the public policy and spectacle of "penal populism"[5] also serves to shore up the deficit of legitimacy that political elites suffer when and where they roll back the established protections of the social state.

To anchor this proposition, I turn to social history and revisit the conditions and causes of the invention of the penal prison at the close of the sixteenth century. I find that this institution of criminal confinement and moral correction arose as part and parcel of the formation of the early modern state in response to the rise and spread of marginality in the growing cities of northern Europe. The prison and

119

Part d'ombre de l'État de droit. La question carcérale en France et en République fédérale d'Allemagne depuis 1968 (2009); Thomas Ugelvik and Jane Dullum (eds.), *Penal Exceptionalism? Nordic Prison Policy and Practice* (2011); Marie Gottschalk, *Caught: The Prison State and the Lockdown of American Politics* (2016); Ignacio González Sánchez, *Neoliberalismo y castigo* (2021); Patrizia Pacini Volpe, *Il carcere, un luogo dimenticato. Una ricerca sociologia tra Italia e Francia* (2022).

[3] John Clegg et al., "Punishment in Modern Societies: The Prevalence and Causes of Incarceration around the World" (2024).

[4] Matthew Eagleton-Pierce offers a rigorous dissection of the salient facets and constructs of this regime in *Neoliberalism: The Key Concepts* (2016).

[5] Katherine Beckett, *Making Crime Pay: Law and Order in Contemporary American Politics* (1999); John Pratt, *Penal Populism* (2006); Denis Salas, *La Volonté de punir. Essai sur le populisme pénal* (2005).

urban marginality are tied at the hip since their coeval birth. To elucidate the one we must understand the other, nowadays no less than in epochs past. The penal state is a *quintessentially urban institution*, a brute fact that has been overlooked by both students of punishment and scholars of the metropolis.[6]

An excellent anthology of legal and social studies of punishment by America's most eminent scholar of the topic, Michael Tonry, asks the questions, *Why Punish? How Much?* (2010), but forgets to raise the critical query, *who to punish?*, as if the answer was self-evident or flowed logically from the motive and quantum of punishment.[7] I show that, from the late sixteenth to the early twenty-first century, the clients of the jail and prison have always been the most destitute and precarious fractions of the proletariat in the city – the urban precariat. The carceral institution captures and processes populations *doubly marginalized on grounds of class* (the poorest of the poor) and *status* (stigmatized outsiders, civic or ethnic). It is imperative, then, to hold these two dimensions together to grasp the office of penality in advanced societies. Proof is the grotesque ethnic disproportionality, ethnoracial in the United States, ethnonational in Europe, that characterizes incarceration everywhere.

What are the mechanisms that produce the carceral "overconsumption" of categories at once dispossessed and dishonored? I propose that the penal management of marginality proceeds primarily through the *targeting of territory* and that a relationship of *structural osmosis* links stigmatized districts of urban dereliction to the jails and prisons of capitalist democracies on both sides of the Atlantic. I extend this argument by developing an ideal-typical opposition between what I call "paper penality," dignified, slow-motion punishment according to the books deployed to handle bourgeois offenders, and "street penality," debasing, accelerated, and simplified punish-

---

[6] In their introduction to a special section of the *Journal of Urban History* on "Urban America and the Carceral State" (2015), Thompson and Murch note that students of the US metropolis "have not even begun to consider the ways in which our existing urban historiography might be limited by having missed such an important elephant in the room." But even they view the penal state as an external entity intruding upon the city as opposed to a building block of its institutional architecture. Heather Ann Thompson and Donna Murch, "Rethinking Urban America through the Lens of the Carceral State" (2015), p. 751.

[7] Michael Tonry, *Why Punish? How Much?* (2010). Didier Fassin tackles the "who" question head on in *Punir, une passion contemporaine* (2017). I provide an answer that is at once more granular sociologically, deeper historically, and more embedded structurally, and I uncover the key mechanisms generating the skewed profile of inmates.

ment initiated by the police which applies to the offenses of the urban precariat, an opposition which suggests that the prison is everywhere both a *class-splitting and a race-making institution.*

To further demonstrate that penality is integral to statecraft and racecraft, I turn to empire and map the distinct landscape of crime and punishment in the colonies of Western Europe from the 1830s to the 1950s. This historical excursus reveals that the police, court, and prison played a key role in enforcing the caste order, running the economy of plunder, and excluding native populations from the polity. Legal principles and provisions operative in the metropole were suspended as a matter of course to permit the routinization, intensification, and diffusion of state violence. That violence was extended by tacit or explicit delegation to a range of private agents such as planters, employers, and colonists. It had contradictory effects: it both bolstered and fragilized imperial rule by sapping its legitimacy in the eyes of the colonized. It was essential to the building of a racial state that relied heavily on the penal triad for its day-to-day functioning. I conclude by disclosing similarities – while warning against the conflation – between colonial punishment a hundred years ago and the penalization of marginality in the neighborhoods of relegation of the postindustrial city nowadays. In both cases, penality is mobilized to rule a population thrust at the margins of civic space that regards the state as illegitimate due its punitive excess and failed promise of equality.

121

The stunning return of the prison

> The days of imprisonment as a method of mass treatment of lawbreakers are largely over. What remains of it will have to employ much more scientific methods of selection and treatment in order to survive.

This pronouncement, made in 1942, did not issue from the mouth of a radical critic of incarceration. It is the prediction of Hermann Mannheim,[8] the eminent German legal scholar and pillar of mainstream penology, who after emigrating to England in 1934, taught at the London School of Economics, founded the association that later became the British Society of Criminology, and trained the leading criminologists and reformers of the British justice system after

---

[8] Hermann Mannheim, "American Criminology and Penology in War Time" (1942), p. 222.

World War II.[9] This prediction encapsulates a vision that dominated the period 1945–75, corresponding to the bloom of the Fordist-Keynesian regime, according to which the prison was on its way down and out: an institution in crisis and terminal remission, bound to recede to the organizational backstage of modern society, if not to disappear entirely.

Indeed, Mannheim's 1942 prophecy was echoed two decades later by Norval Morris, the New Zealand-born criminologist who became the most influential criminal law professor and justice advocate of his generation in the United States. In addition to writing a dozen books and heading several national commissions on justice reform, he, too, trained the major penal law scholars of the next generation, among them Franklin Zimring, Michael Tonry, Albert Alschuler, and James Jacobs. In a 1965 paper published in a "Festschrift" to Hermann Mannheim, Morris did not mince his words:

> It is confidently predicted that, before the end of this century, prison in [its current] form will become extinct, though the word may live on.[10]

A decade later, the revisionist historian of the prison David Rothman, writing against the backdrop of a slow but steady decline of the convict population and the tumultuous rise of the prisoners' rights movement in America, reasserted in *The Discovery of the Asylum* (1971) that the United States was "gradually escaping from institutional responses" to social problems, so that "one can foresee the period when incarceration will be used still more rarely than it is today." In 1972, the same Rothman published an article entitled "Of Prisons, Asylums, and Other Decaying Institutions" in the widely read quarterly *The Public Interest*, in which he announced that the combination of "basic standards of human decency and economic costs" was driving the penitentiary to its grave.[11]

[9] Two influential works by Mannheim are *Social Aspects of Crime in England between the Wars* (1940) and *Criminal Justice and Social Reconstruction* (1946). The Mannheim Center for Criminology at the London School of Economics is named after him (and not the sociologist of knowledge Karl Mannheim).

[10] Norval Morris, "Prison in Evolution" (1965), p. 268. For further reflections on the historical trajectory of incarceration at millennium's start, read Michael Tonry (ed.), *The Future of Imprisonment* (2004).

[11] David J. Rothman, *The Discovery of the Asylum: Social Order and Disorder in the New Republic* (1971), p. 295; idem, "Of Prisons, Asylums, and Other Decaying Institutions" (1972), p. 17. See also the collection of essays edited by Calvert Dodge, *A Nation Without Prisons: Alternatives to Incarceration* (1975), aimed at correctional

122

When Rothman wrote these words, the carceral population of the US had dropped to 380,000, its lowest levels in decades, following a slow but steady decline in the 1960s. Relatedly, facilities for juvenile delinquents came under the converging critiques of justice advocates, scholars, and the courts, starting with the Supreme Court decision *In Re: Gault* (1963), which condemned the arbitrary and punitive logic of youth incarceration.[12] The denunciation of the rehabilitative rhetoric as a mere façade for the castigatory nature of "juvenile halls" led to a nationwide movement of reform. The discredit falling upon the prison was further intensified by the sweeping policy of "deinstitutionalization" of psychiatric patients accelerating during the same decade following the federal Community Mental Health Act of 1963.[13] By all indications, custodial solutions to the management of problem populations were about to be replaced by "community" institutions, such as halfway houses for convicts, group homes for juvenile scofflaws, and neighborhood clinics for mental patients.

123

Then came the lightning bolt of Michel Foucault's dazzling *Surveiller et punir* (*Discipline and Punish*, 1975). Drawing the joint genealogy of the ascent of "biopower" and the "disciplinary society," Foucault found that the "penitentiary technique" was diffusing "throughout the wider social body." As surveillance, classification, examination, ordering, and coding linked the prison to the factory, the hospital, the convent, the school, and the family, they wove together a panoptic lattice that rendered the prison secondary if not expendable: "In the midst of all these apparatuses of normalization which are becoming ever tighter, the specificity of the prison and its role as hinge lose something of their raison d'être."[14]

By then, the fate of the prison seemed so gloomy that radical criminologists – such as Stanley Cohen in England, René van Swaaningen in the Netherlands, and Andrew Scull in the United States – turned to criticizing not incarceration but *decarceration*, warning of the perils of the blurring and dispersal of penal power via

professionals, which advocates radical sentencing reform prioritizing probation and halfway houses. Dodge then took his argument to the international level with a collection surveying alternatives to confinement in a half-dozen countries in *A World Without Prisons* (1979).

[12] Barry C. Feld, *Justice for Children: The Right to Counsel and the Juvenile Courts* (1993).

[13] On the intertwining of penal and mental confinement during the postwar decades, see Anne E. Parsons, *From Asylum to Prison: Deinstitutionalization and the Rise of Mass Incarceration After 1945* (2018).

[14] Michel Foucault, *Surveiller et punir. Naissance de la prison* (1975), p. 313.

"community sanctions" and stressing "the over-riding fact of proliferation, elaboration and diversification" of social control.[15] Fighting
net-strengthening, net-widening, and net-meshing beyond the penitentiary became the priority. The mushrooming of anti-prison groups
in North America and Western Europe – across Scandinavia in 1967–
8, in France and England in 1970, in the Netherlands in 1971 – and
the coalescence of abolitionism as a new paradigm in criminology
and policy advocacy,[16] the burst of activist mobilization for inmate
rights and the wave of carceral riots that struck several advanced
countries near-simultaneously in the 1970s completed this picture
of the penitentiary as a moribund institution in swift and irrevocable
decline, doomed to lose its rank as the preeminent instrument of state
punishment, if not to face extinction.[17]

124

This rosy forecast of the end of "prison as we know it" did not
come to pass. Far from "becoming extinct," the carceral institution
has made a *stunning comeback onto the institutional foreground across
the first and second worlds* over the past half-century. With precious
few exceptions (Canada, Germany, Austria, the Nordic nations, and
Japan), incarceration has steadily increased, even boomed, in all
postindustrial societies after the mid-1970s, leading to (i) the onset
of racialized hyperincarceration in the United States; (ii) robust and
continuous growth across Western Europe leading to rampant prison
overcrowding; (iii) and spectacular expansion in second-world societies such as Brazil, Mexico, Turkey, and South Africa, as well as
myriad smaller countries such as Cuba, Costa Rica, Vietnam, and
Rwanda. Worldwide, the carceral population stood at around 4 million in 1975, then jumped from just over 8 million in 1998 to exceed
11 million today (exclusive of administrative detentions in China,

---

[15] Stanley Cohen, *Visions of Social Control: Crime, Punishment and Classification*
(1985), p. 84; Andrew Scull, *Decarceration: Community Treatment and the Deviant, a
Radical View* (1977).
[16] Kevin Stenson and David Cowell (eds.), *The Politics of Crime Control* (1991),
pp. 204–7; Herman Bianchi and René van Swaaningen (eds.), *Abolitionism: Toward a
Non-Repressive Approach to Crime* (1986).
[17] Thomas Mathiesen nostalgically recalls a 1969 trip to Strasbourg where he had
gone to advocate for decarceration with the Council of Europe: "I was sitting in the
plane, looking out over the warm European landscape, rejoicing at the fact, as I saw
it then, of a Europe in my lifetime with prisons more or less as a historical relic"
("The Politics of Abolition" [1986], p. 81). Mathiesen was particularly excited at the
prospect of establishing contacts with the anti-prison outfits then mushrooming in
other countries. By the end of the 1970s, his 1974 book *The Politics of Abolition* had
appeared in three Nordic languages as well as in English, German, and French.

estimated to approach 1 million). It is safe to say that Roy Wamsley and the International Centre for Prison Studies at Birbeck College in London, who are doing a meticulous job keeping track of carceral trends around the globe, are not about to go out of business.

The tale of the stupendous prison boom in the United States has often been told and is now familiar (see the box on "Hyperincarceration in the postindustrial United States").[18] Less well known and discussed is the steady and sturdy growth of the confined population throughout Western Europe, reversing the trends of the 1960s and belying the Malthusian expectations of the analysts of the penal scene circa 1975. Two figures capture this trend well: when Michel Foucault published his canonical tome *Surveiller et punir* that year, France held 26,000 inmates; today it confines over 83,000, an all-time record, packed in a prison system with a capacity of 64,000, causing some 6,000 inmates to sleep nightly on a mattress laid on the floor.

125

Table 5 charts the rising incarceration rate (defined as the number of inmates per 100,000 residents) over the past half-century for 11 Western European nations, ranked in descending order of punitiveness for the year 2025. It shows that penal confinement grew by more than one-half in England and Wales, Scotland, and Belgium. It roughly doubled in France, Italy, and Sweden. It tripled in the Netherlands, Greece, and Ireland. It quadrupled in Portugal and grew fivefold in Spain. A second cluster of countries managed to stymie carceral inflation (table 6): Denmark, Norway, and Austria held steady while Germany sported a marginal decrease (since reunification) and Finland a spectacular drop. But, while this second cluster held the line, it failed to fulfill the universal prediction of continual carceral deflation leading to the withering away of the penitentiary formulated by the penal analysts of the postwar decades. These tendencies demonstrate that we do live in the "Third age of confinement," as feared by the abolitionist criminologist Thomas Mathiesen some 40 years ago, an age characterized by renewed prison growth, the twin failures of critique and reform, the recycling of older models of control, and the globalization of carceral inflation.[19]

---

[18] See Marc Mauer, *Race to Incarcerate* (2006), for a pedagogical primer and Loïc Wacquant, *Punishing the Poor: The Neoliberal Government of Social Insecurity* (2009b), chapters 4 and 5, for a deeper dive.

[19] Thomas Mathiesen discusses the concept of the "third age of imprisonment" in the third edition of his classic book *Prison on Trial* (2006), originally published in 1990. The First age ushered the birth and spread of the prison in the eighteenth and nineteenth centuries in keeping with Enlightenment principles. The Second age was

Table 5
Fifty years of carceral inflation in
11 Western European countries, 1975–2025.

	1975	1985	1995	2005	2015	2020	2025	increase
Scotland	95	103	110	136	143	128	150	58%
England/Wales	81	93	100	143	148	133	141	74%
France	49	78	89	91	113	119	120	145%
Spain	24	58	115	139	138	117	117 (2023)	387%
Portugal	28	82	123	123	135	111	115	310%
Belgium	67	65	74	91	100	90	106	58%
Italy	55	73	83	81	89	89	105	91%
Greece	33	35	55	85	103	102	98 (2024)	197%
Sweden	51	52	66	78	60	73	96	88%
Ireland	32	54	59	77	81	74	94	194%
Netherlands	24	34	77	124	64	60	64 (2023)	166%

Number of inmates per 100,000 residents – *Source*: World Prison Brief,
various years.

Table 6
Fifty years of carceral stability in
5 Western European countries, 1975–2025.

	1975	1985	1995	2005	2015	2020	2025	increase
Germany	★	★	77	94	76	72	68 (2023)	−12%
Norway	48	51	60	68	73	54	54	12%
Austria	100	112	84	105	99	94	102	2%
Denmark	67	65	67	71	64	70	69	3%
Finland	116	90	64	70	57	51	52 (2023)	−55%
Canada	86	118	131	107	114	103	90 (2022)	5%

Number of inmates per 100,000 residents – *Source*: World Prison Brief,
various years.

Crucially, the continuous growth of the prison population over the past 30 years diverges spectacularly from trends in criminality, especially violent criminality. In the United States, homicide, robbery, and aggravated assault increased in the 1960s, stagnated in the 1970s, rose in the 1980s, and then declined steeply and continuously from 1990 to 2005, the very period when the carceral population ballooned. Similarly, property crime dropped continuously after its peak of 1990. In the UK, carceral inflation took off after 1992, just as the incidence of crime started a three-decade-long slide. Similarly in France, violent crime has steadily decreased for 40 years even as fear of crime increased and grew into an obligatory and flammable topic in electoral politics.

Hyperincarceration in the postindustrial United States

The sudden and stupendous growth of the carceral population in the United States from 1973 to 2008, after a half-century of stability and a slow decline in the 1960s, is conventionally described as "mass incarceration." But it is better characterized as *hyperincarceration* due to its triple selectivity by class, ethnicity, and place, which makes it anything but an indiscriminate phenomenon as suggested by the notion of "mass" (1). It is a response to two epochal transformations: the collapse of the Fordist-Keynesian regime and subsequent rolling out of neoliberalism; the crumbling of the black ghetto and correlative backlash against the advances of the Civil Rights Movement. It anchors a punitive regime characterized by five structural features that makes for a one-of-a-kind penal state.

1. *Vertical expansion*: the custodial stock surged sixfold between 1973 and 2008, even as crime rates first stagnated and then declined sharply over that period (2). This propelled the country to the rank of undisputed world champion in incarceration with 2.4 million under lock at its peak in 2008 (compared to 380,000 in 1973), for a rate of 740 inmates per 100,000 residents, 5 to 14 times the rates of Western European countries.

2. *Horizontal expansion*: the number of convicts placed on probation (as an alternative to confinement) and parole (after serving

stamped by growth, bureaucratization, and professionalization in the twentieth century, closing with the critique and disillusionment about rehabilitation as a philosophy of punishment in the 1970s.

most of their prison sentence) skyrocketed from 870,000 in 1970 to 4.3 million and 866,000 respectively, for a total of 5.2 million in 2007, compared to 1.1 million and 220,000 for a total of 1.3 million in 1980. At the same time, community supervision turned from care to coercion as parole and probation agents pivoted away from supporting housing and employment to focus on surveillance (3). As a result, instead of providing alternatives to prison, probation and parole turned into pipelines to the penitentiary.

3. *Digital extension*: justice databases have undergone explosive growth, such that an estimated 78 million Americans today have a criminal record, including 19 million a felony record. Personally identifiable data are disseminated via the internet and sold by private firms for criminal "background checks" that have become generalized in the private and public sector alike, a stunning extension of penality that the sociologist and lawyer Sarah Lageson has christened "digital punishment" (4).

4. *Collateral penalties*: the swirl of digital justice data helps extend the stigma, surveillance, and sanction for crimes committed far beyond the penal state to employers, realtors, and public administrations, and even the citizenry at large. This diffusion intensifies the economic, social, and civil disabilities suffered by former convicts: their criminal record abolishes or curtails their employment and educational options, access to welfare and banking, housing and health care, parental rights and voting rights (5).

5. *Extreme selectivity by class, race and place*: incarceration strikes primarily young subproletarian black men residing in the denuded hyperghettos of the postindustrial cities, that is, the territories where the three strongest determinants of imprisonment overlap. Class first: in 2015, individuals without any college education were 27 times more likely to be admitted to prison than individuals with some college (the figure was 28 to 1 for whites and 22 to 1 for blacks) (6). Race second: the prison population circa 2008 was 38 percent black and 20 percent Latino (compared to a share of 13 percent and 16 percent in the country's population); in 2005, 5 percent of all males over 18, one black man in 9 and one young black man in 3 (18–35 years) were under correctional supervision (jail, prison, probation, or parole). Combine class and race and you discover that the lifetime probability of serving a prison sentence for African-American males without a high school diploma tripled between 1979 and 1999 to reach the astounding figure of 59% (7). Place third: the vast majority of convicts are drawn from the poorest and most segregated neigh-

borhoods of the dual city where class and race join hands to make entanglement with the penal state a banal fact of everyday life, constantly reiterated and aggravated (8).

1. Loïc Wacquant, "Class, Race and Hyperincarceration in Revanchist America" (2010a).
2. The steep and steady decrease in offending, and violent offenses in particular, starting in 1992 and continuing to this day, is known as the "Great American crime decline" (see the book by that title by Franklin Zimring, 2007). That decline is exactly contemporaneous with the most vigorous burst of carceral inflation.
3. Michelle Phelps, "Mass Probation from Micro to Macro: Tracing the Expansion and Consequences of Community Supervision" (2020); Michelle S. Phelps and Ebony L. Ruhland, "Governing Marginality: Coercion and Care in Probation" (2022); Faye Taxman, "Probation, Intermediate Sanctions, and Community-Based Corrections" (2012); Mona Lynch, "Waste Managers? The New Penology, Crime Fighting, and Parole Agent Identity" (1998).
4. Sarah Esther Lageson, *Digital Punishment: Privacy, Stigma, and the Harms of Data-Driven Criminal Justice* (2020).
5. David S. Kirk and Sara Wakefield, "Collateral Consequences of Punishment: A Critical Review and Path Forward" (2018).
6. Christopher Muller and Alexander F. Roehrkasse, "Racial and Class Inequality in US Incarceration in the Early Twenty-First Century" (2022).
7. Bruce Western, *Punishment and Inequality in America* (2006), pp. 6–27.
8. Todd R. Clear, *Imprisoning Communities: How Mass Incarceration Makes Disadvantaged Neighborhoods Worse* (2009); Robert J. Sampson and Charles Loeffler, "Punishment's Place: The Local Concentration of Mass Incarceration" (2010).

Yet the unforeseen and relentless rise of the carceral stock is only one crude, surface manifestation of the expansion and exaltation of the penal state across the Western world since the economic and political inflexion point of the mid-1970s. Six other indicators round out the picture of penalization in the age of triumphant neoliberalism.

1. The elevation of aggressive crime-fighting and judicial severity to the rank of government priority and the salience of "insecurity" (understood strictly as criminal insecurity) in the media and electoral campaigns, for which criminologists coined the term *punitive populism*, designating an abrupt turn toward "tough-on-crime" rhetoric and policies putting political profit ahead of penological efficiency and public sentiment over expert rationality.[20]

[20] The notion was forged under the label of "populist punitiveness" by the British criminologist Anthony Bottoms in "The Philosophy and Politics of Punishment and

2. Legislative hyperactivity on the criminal front: the California state assembly passed a thousand measures extending the use of the prison in the 1980s alone; New Labour instituted a stunning 3,605 new offenses in the 11 years it was in power in England in the 1990s (more than one new crime for every business day in office); France voted 24 major laws pertaining to crime and insecurity between 2002 and 2009, including a measure punishing booing during the national anthem at soccer games with a fine and a prison term.[21] A piece of crime legislation was no sooner passed than another one was proposed.

3. The virulent vituperation of criminals in public discourse accompanied by the valorization, even morbid glorification, of victims of crime and the extension of the latter's rights, resources and prerogatives in penal procedure and culture.[22]

4. The intensifying association of crime with race and with immigration, taking the form of the "blackening" of the figure of a violent "underclass" in the United States (a late avatar of the long-standing myth of the "*criminalblackman*") and the fusion of extraneity and illegality in Europe, entailing the interweaving of criminal and immigration law, for which criminologists coined the concept of *crimmigration*.[23]

5. The international diffusion of a new punitive common sense encapsulated by the catchy expression of "*zero tolerance*," incubated in the US and disseminated across the world by American think tanks and assorted experts in "law-and-order" slogans and measures ("broken windows theory," mandatory minimum sentences,

Sentencing" (1995). The diffusion of the phenomenon in the Anglophone West is documented in Julian V. Roberts et al., *Penal Populism and Public Opinion: Lessons from Five Countries* (2002). Its application to France is elaborated by Salas, *La Volonté de punir*, and to Spain by González Sánchez, *Neoliberalismo y castigo*. A cutting theoretical, empirical, and normative critique of the notion is Victor Lund Shammas, "Who's Afraid of Penal Populism? Technocracy and 'The People' in the Sociology of Punishment" (2016b).

[21] Laurent Mucchielli (ed.), *La Frénésie sécuritaire. Retour à l'ordre et nouveau contrôle social* (2008); Frank R. Baumgartner et al., "Throwing Away the Key: The Unintended Consequences of 'Tough-on-Crime' Laws" (2021).

[22] Frank Weed, *Certainty of Justice: Reform in the Crime Victim Movement* (1995); Sandrine Lefranc and Lilian Mathieu (eds.), *Mobilisations de victimes* (2015).

[23] Katheryn K. Russell, *The Color of Crime: Racial Hoaxes, White Fear, Black Protectionism, Police Harassment and Other Macroaggressions* (1998); Katja Franko Aas, *The Crimmigrant Other: Migration and Penal Power* (2019).

shock incarceration, military-style "boot camps" for juvenile delinquents, youth curfews, etc.).[24] The slow spread of negotiated justice by means of guilty pleas partakes of the growing influence of
US justice models across borders, notwithstanding its utter failure
at home.

6. The deliberate or *de facto* correctional turn away from reform and
   rehabilitation toward risk management and incapacitation applied
   to statistical categories instead of individuals – what Malcolm
   Feeley and Jonathan Simon call the "*new penology*" – due to ideological conversion or to the sheer congestion of the courts and
   overcrowding of carceral establishments, or both.[25]

Penal populism, legislative frenzy, the deserving crime victim, the
"criminalblackman" and crimmigration, zero tolerance and the
new penology: so many notions, procedures, and figures that sketch
and stretch the perimeter of the voracious and vindictive penal
state after the collapse of the Keynesian-Fordist compact in the
1970s.

Penalization as neoliberal statecraft

How to make sense of this stunning penal surge and of the sudden
ideological rehabilitation of the prison on the political scene –
encapsulated by the slogan "prison works," invoked by its advocates
in the US and the UK in the 1990s, and materialized by the drive
to build ever more carceral facilities, as with France's latest "15,000
beds plan"? Let me sketch my stance by contraposition with the main
social theories competing to explain the penal boom of the past half-
century, as summed up in table 7.[26]

In Jock Young's vision of the "exclusive society" and in David
Garland's account of the "culture of control," as well as in the Eliasian,
neo-Durkheimian, and neo-Foucauldian conceptions of penality
developed by John Pratt, Hans Bouteillier, and Pat O'Malley and

---

[24] Loïc Wacquant, *Prisons of Poverty* (2009a).
[25] Malcolm M. Feeley and Jonathan Simon, "The New Penology: Notes on the
Emerging Strategy of Corrections and its Implications" (1992).
[26] For a different contrast between four theories of the transformation of penality
in the postindustrial era, those of John Pratt, Hans Bouteillier, David Garland and
myself, read Tom Daems, *Making Sense of Penal Change* (2009).

Table 7
Competing theories of the penal surge.

"exclusive society" (Young) "culture of control" (Garland) "actuarial punishment" (Simon)	vs	neoliberal penality (proactive, politicized, pornographic)
societal stage (late modernity, postmodernity, risk society)	vs	statecraft deregulated capitalism class fragmentation
cultural formation state recedes	vs	restrictive workfare and expansive prisonfare
individualism	vs	liberal paternalism
criminal insecurity	vs	social insecurity
diffused across social space	vs	lower regions of social and urban space

Jonathan Simon, respectively,[27] the contemporary reconfiguration of punishment results from reaching a new *societal stage* – late modernity, postmodernity, the risk society. It partakes of a novel cultural constellation; it is characterized by the retraction and diminished role of the state across the board; and it seeps deep into subjectivity.[28] Penal change emerges endogenously in response to rising *criminal* insecurity and its symbolic and emotional reverberations *across social space*.

In the model that I propose, by contrast, neoliberal penality partakes of an *exercise in statecraft*. It reasserts the authority and boosts the capacity of the Leviathan to contain urban marginality and its correlates, including crime as fodder for political profiteering, and thus to deliver the material good of street security and the symbolic good of civic reassurance. It is *proactive* rather than reactive; *politicized*

---

[27] Jock Young, *The Exclusive Society: Social Exclusion, Crime and Difference in Late Modernity* (1999); idem, *The Vertigo of Late Modernity* (2007); David Garland, *The Culture of Control: Crime and Social Order in Contemporary Society* (2001); John Pratt, *Punishment and Civilization: Penal Tolerance and Intolerance in Modern Society* (2002); Hans Boutellier, *The Safety Utopia: Contemporary Discontent and Desire as to Crime and Punishment* (2004); Pat O'Malley (ed.), *Crime and the Risk Society* (1998); and Jonathan Simon, *Governing Through Crime: How the War on Crime Transformed American Democracy and Created a Culture of Fear* (2007).

[28] One of the central themes of these works is that the management of "security" has been delegated to non-state actors. We noted in chapter 1 that, for the neo-Foucauldians in particular, the penal state has been entirely supplanted by governmentality.

rather than left to the expertise of correctional professionals; and *pornographic* in the sense that it is staged, literally, as a spectacle designed to titillate the moral emotions of the viewing citizenry.[29]

In Ruschian terminology, the theater of neoliberal punishment "corresponds" to the triumph of deregulated capitalism and to the correlative fragmentation of class and dissolution of the established ethnic order (ethnoracial in the US, ethnonational in the EU). It responds to the diffusion of *social insecurity*, rather than criminal insecurity, objective among the urban proletariat and subjective in the lower-middle class, which reaches its point of maximum intensity in the badlands of the dualizing metropolis where marginality and ethnicity intersect. In Durkheimian terminology, neoliberal punishment is a "passionate reaction" to the boiling *social anxiety* that courses through the societal body as a result of the social and cultural dislocations wrought by deindustrialization and neoliberalization; it captures and channels that collective emotion onto the criminal front. The neoliberal state is, moreover, a Centaur state which obeys a bifurcated doctrine I call *liberal paternalism*: it is liberal at the top, practicing laissez-faire toward the holders of capital (both economic and cultural), and paternalistic at the bottom, toward the poor upon whom it unleashes a disciplinary combination of restrictive social policy (workfare) and expansive penal policy (prisonfare).

133

The expansion and exaltation of the police, criminal court, and prison as public services after the collapse of the Keynesian–Fordist compact are not an aberration or a temporary deviation from the coming of "small government;" on the contrary, they are an essential *block in the building of the neoliberal Leviathan*. Now, the notion of neoliberalism is a wooly and contentious one; it is often dismissed as an ideological tag or reduced to a *Kampfbegriff* suited for political critique.[30] It is also loosely identified with particular political leaders (Ronald Reagan, Margaret Thatcher, Bill Clinton, Gerhard Schröder) and their policies of deregulation, privatization, and law-and-order planks. I wish to give it a clear and concise, but expansive, analytical

---

[29] See Michelle Brown, *The Culture of Punishment: Prison, Society, and Spectacle* (2009), on the US, and Michaël Meyer (ed.), *Médiatiser la police. Policer les médias* (2012), on Western Europe.

[30] For a compact panorama of the meanings of the notion and the variants of its historical implementation, see Manfred B. Steger and Ravi K. Roy, *Neoliberalism: A Very Short Introduction* (2021), and William Davies, *The Limits of Neoliberalism: Authority, Sovereignty and the Logic of Competition* (2016). For a meticulous historical account centered on the US, read Gary Gerstle, *The Rise and Fall of the Neoliberal Order* (2023).

meaning. In particular, I propose to move beyond the thin *economistic* conception of neoliberalism as entailing the correlative retraction of the state and extension of the market to all realms of human activity and the invitation to become an entrepreneur of one's life. I elaborate a thick *sociological* construct that ties together the economic, social welfare, penal, and cultural changes materialized and fostered by the state. For, at its core, neoliberalism is a *political project* that effectively seeks to supplant politics with economics and universalize competition.[31] But, paradoxically, it cannot do so without bolstering the punitive apparatus to overcome resistance to commodification and contain the very disorders the latter generates: the "invisible hand" of the market requires the "penal fist" of the state.

134

Put crudely, the historical anthropology of neoliberalism is polarized between a hegemonic economic model anchored by variants of *market rule*, represented, in its Marxist version, by the work of the geographer David Harvey, and an insurgent approach based on derivations of the Foucauldian notion of *governmentality* as with psychologist Nikolas Rose and political theorist Wendy Brown.[32] Both conceptions obscure what is "neo" about neoliberalism: the reengineering and redeployment of the Leviathan as the core agency that sets the rules and fabricates the bureaucratic capacities, social relations, and collective representations suited to realizing markets.

I pursue a *via media* between these two approaches that draws on Bourdieu's bureaucratic field (as discussed in chapter 1, *supra*, pp. 88–99). It construes neoliberalism as an *articulation of state, market, and citizenship* that harnesses the first to impose the stamp of the second onto the third. The concept of bureaucratic field invites us to connect social and penal policies and suggests that they constitute two variants of poverty policy that must be grasped together. It reveals that neoliberalism entails not a diminution of the state, but a

---

[31] On the origins and evolving formulation of this project, see Philip Mirowski and Dieter Plehwe (eds.), *The Road from Mont Pèlerin: The Making of the Neoliberal Thought Collective* (2009); Angus Burgin, *The Great Persuasion: Reinventing Free Markets since the Depression* (2012). For a longer history that traces neoliberal thought to the collapse of the Habsburg empire, read Quinn Slobodian, *Globalists: The End of Empire and the Birth of Neoliberalism* (2020). Bernard Harcourt goes further back still and excavates the relationship between the market and punishment in eighteenth-century doctrines in *The Illusion of Free Markets: Punishment and the Myth of Natural Order* (2011).

[32] David Harvey, *A Brief History of Neoliberalism* (2007); Nikolas Rose and Peter Miller, *Governing the Present: Administering Economic, Social and Personal Life* (2008); and Wendy Brown, *Undoing the Demos. Neoliberalism's Stealth Revolution* (2015).

redrawing of its perimeter, internal architecture, and external priorities, and indeed a strengthening of its punishment apparatus.

In neo-Bourdieusian terms, the neoliberal revolution takes the form of the systematic tilting of state prerogatives from the Left hand to the Right hand, that is, *from the protective (feminine and collectivizing) pole to the disciplinary (masculine and individualizing) pole* of the bureaucratic field. This proceeds through two distinct but complementary routes: (i) the transfer of resources, programs, and populations from the social to the penal wing of the state (as when mentally ill patients get "deinstitutionalized" with the closing of hospitals and "reinstitutionalized" in jails and prisons after transitioning through homelessness); (ii) the colonization of welfare, health care, education, low-income housing, child services, etc., by the panoptic and disciplinary techniques and tropes of the Right hand (as when the unemployed are forcibly funneled into part-time jobs, public hospitals favor budgetary over medical concerns and schools put the reduction of classroom violence ahead of pedagogy and hire security guards instead of psychologists).

135

This double rightward skewing of the structure and policies of the state is emphatically *not* the product of some mysterious systemic imperative or irresistible functional necessity. Nor is it the spawn of a deliberate strategy by agents bent on effecting this grand transformation. Rather, it is the structurally conditioned but historically contingent *outcome of material and symbolic struggles,* waged inside as well from outside the bureaucratic field, over the responsibilities and modalities of operation of public authority.[33] It follows that the velocity, magnitude, and effects of this institutional torque will vary from country to country depending on its position in the international order, the makeup of its national field of power and political field, and the configuration of its social space and cultural divisions.[34]

[33] Wacquant, *Punishing the Poor,* pp. xix–xx, 67–9, 108–9, 312–13, where I supplement functional analysis with strategic explanation.

[34] For an adaptation and extension of this model of neoliberal penality as statecraft to the United Kingdom, see Peter Squires and John Lea (eds.), *Criminalisation and Advanced Marginality: Critically Exploring the Work of Loïc Wacquant* (2012); to Spain, see Ignacio González Sánchez, *Neoliberalismo y castigo* (2021); to Brazil, see Vera Malaguti Batista (ed.), *Loïc Wacquant e a questão penal no capitalismo neoliberal* (2012); and to Latin America more broadly, see Markus-Michael Müller, "The Rise of the Penal State in Latin America" (2012).

In my book *Punishing the Poor* and related papers, I forge a construct of the neoliberal state as constituted by the dynamic articulation of four policy structures and streams:[35]

1. *Imposition of market sanctions and wage precarity*: the economic plank of neoliberalism entails the "deregulation" of the economy (that is, reregulation in favor of firms), the global expansion of free trade and financialization, the shrinkage and commodification of public goods, and the spread of underpaid, insecure jobs against the backdrop of working poverty in the United States and enduring mass joblessness in the European Union.[36]

2. *Disciplinary workfare supplants protective welfare*: the social plank of neoliberalism consists in the unraveling of social protection schemes leading to the replacement of the collective right to protection from unemployment and poverty by the individual obligation to take up gainful activity ("workfare" in the US and the UK, RSA in France, the Hartz reforms in Germany, ALE jobs in Belgium, etc.) in order to impose desocialized wage labor as the normal horizon of work for the new precariat of the urban service sector.[37]

3. *Growth and glorification of the penal apparatus* recentered onto the defamed districts of the inner city and the urban periphery, which concentrate the disorders and despair spawned by the twofold movement of retrenchment of the state from the economic and social front, and where the street economy, legal and illegal, expands to fill the void left by the retraction of the wage economy. Remarkably, the hardening of penal policy aimed at street crime has been coupled with a distinct softening of punishment aimed at white-collar and corporate offenders on both sides of the Atlantic.[38]

[35] Wacquant, *Punishing the Poor*; idem, "Crafting the Neoliberal State: Workfare, Prisonfare, and Social Insecurity" (2010b); idem, "Three Steps to a Historical Anthropology of Actually Existing Neoliberalism" (2012b).

[36] Serge Paugam, *Le Salarié de la précarité. Les nouvelles formes de l'intégration professionnelle* (2007); Arne L. Kalleberg, *Good Jobs, Bad Jobs: The Rise of Polarized and Precarious Employment Systems in the United States, 1970s–2000s* (2011).

[37] A study comparing the US and eight European countries discloses that, over time, workfare programs have increased work obligations as a condition for receiving minimum income benefits, and requirements have become more individualized. Ivar Lodemel and Amilcar Moreira (eds.), *Activation or Workfare? Governance and the Neo-Liberal Convergence* (2014).

[38] John Hagan, *Who are the Criminals? The Politics of Crime Policy from the Age of*

4. *Diffusion of the trope of "individual responsibility"* as the cultural glue holding together the economic, welfare, and penal planks of the neoliberal Leviathan through the rhetoric of "merit" (for those who, endowed in economic and cultural capital, embody and enjoy social success) and "demerit" (for those who, shorn of capital, fall through the cracks of state support and into the ditches of social space).[39] Note that the very same notion of individual responsibility undergirds the penal codes of advanced societies.

Far from being antithetical to neoliberalism, then, punitive penal policy is one of its core constituents.[40] Not its *consequence*, to be clear, but one of its *building blocks*. The neoliberal revolution has brought back the prison as vacuum cleaner of the detritus of the market society; as disciplinary device to impose insecure work on the precarious fractions of the postindustrial proletariat and to deter escape into the flourishing criminal economy; and as signifying machine and moral theater to project the fortitude of the ruler and shore up the legitimacy of the politicians who organize and preach the powerlessness of the state on the economic front. A different formulation of the same thesis: rolling out a fortified penal state resolves what I christen the "problem of the two K(C)arls."

The first is the *Karl Polanyi problem*. In his landmark book *The Great Transformation: The Political and Economic Origins of Our Time* (1947), Polanyi shows that the global surge of the self-regulating market at the turn of the twentieth century, taking the form of the expanded commodification of land, labor, and money, disrupts institutions and tears at the social fabric. Economic liberalism spawns resistance which takes the form of a "protective countermovement" *from below* seeking to cushion the impact of the market and to re-embed the economy into social relations. Left-wing parties and trade unions are the chief agencies of this resistance as they push for shielding

137

Roosevelt to the Age of Reagan (2010); Pierre Lascoumes and Carla Nagels, *Sociologie des élites délinquantes. De la criminalité en col blanc à la corruption politique* (2014).

[39] Émilie Hache, "La responsabilité, une technique de gouvernementalité néolibérale?" (2007). See the discussion of the prison as a "negative university" whose "credentials" attest to individual demerit and justify social dereliction in chapter 1, *supra*, pp. 108–10.

[40] Penal bolstering is a facet of neoliberalism that the Foucauldians have entirely missed. Thus, for Brown, "neoliberal governance more generally aims to replace law, policing, punishment, and top-down directives"; "the neoliberal mobilization of law" does not aim "to repress or to punish, but to structure competition and effect 'the conduct of conduct'" (*Undoing the Demos*, pp. 141 and 148).

legislation (factory laws, retirement schemes, unemployment support, etc.) and the public provision of utilities.[41] In the late twentieth century, a new burst of economic laissez-faire again tore at the social fabric. It spawned social insecurity and despair, concentrated in the districts of dereliction of the dualizing metropolis, translating into disorders that threatened to spill over across the city. This time around, the "protective countermovement" came *from above*: it was designed and run by political elites and state managers; it flung an expanded penal dragnet to corral these urban disorders and soak up the collective anxiety coursing through the society.[42]

Next comes the *Carl Schmitt problem*. We saw in chapter 1 that, in *The Concept of the Political* ([1932] 2008), the German jurist argues that the essence of the political – as distinct from the economic, the moral, and the aesthetic – is the "antithesis of friend and enemy": the enemy is "the other, the stranger; and it is sufficient for his nature that he is, in a specially intense way, existentially something different and alien, so that in the extreme case conflicts with him are possible."[43] To stage political fortitude and project sovereignty, in an age when politicians abandon the protective mission of the state on the economic and social front established during the Fordist-Keynesian era, what better strategy than to designate as the internal enemy of the law-abiding "working family" the heinous "underclass" composed of welfare recipients, street criminals, and irregular migrants dwelling in

138

---

[41] In reaction to the self-regulating market, "a countermovement was on foot. This was more than the usual defensive behavior of a society faced with change; it was a reaction against a dislocation which attacked the fabric of society, and which would have destroyed the very organization of production that the market had called into being." Karl Polanyi, *The Great Transformation: The Political and Economic Origins of Our Time* ([1947] 2001), p. 251.

[42] There are historical precedents to the upper-class strategy which deploys punishment in response to a suffusive sense of social disquiet and urban crisis. Thus, in Victorian England, "crime was a central metaphor of disorder and loss of control in all spheres of life. Criminal and penal policy articulated the effort to counter this perception by fostering disciplined behavior and a broad ethos of respectability." Martin Joel Wiener, *Reconstructing the Criminal: Culture, Law, and Policy in England, 1830–1914* (1994), p. 11.

[43] Carl Schmitt, *The Concept of the Political* ([1932] 2008), p. 27. Note that Schmitt wishes to reserve the notion of "enemy" strictly to the political realm, but, logically, the term can be extended to the criminal inasmuch as the latter is portrayed as "existentially something different and alien" than the friend-citizen. He also labels "high points of politics" those moments in which "the enemy is, in concrete clarity, recognized as the enemy" (p. 36).

the city's underbelly?[44] This much is suggested by the spread of the militaristic trope of the "war" on crime, drugs, "antisocial behavior," and irregular migration proclaimed by the authorities in France, the US, the UK and Italy, respectively, and the use of military units to provide law enforcement in the urban badlands. This is the symbolic role of punishment: to stage the authority of the Leviathan and to draw the boundary between the honored insider and the dishonored outsider, designating the latter as the cause of the ills of the metropolis and of the fear that these ills elicit among the citizenry. Figure 7 brings these different arguments together.

Figure 7 sets out the economic, social, and penal components of neoliberal policy. It reads as follows. (i) *Economic deregulation* spawns wage-labor degradation and rampant social insecurity at the bottom of the structure of classes and places. (ii) To force people into these precarious jobs now teeming in the lower segment of the labor market, it is necessary to transition from *protective welfare to disciplinary workfare*, or else people will seek protection under the social wing of the state. This intensifies social insecurity, which fuels the street economy and spawns disorders in neighborhoods of relegation, including crime. (iii) The *penal state is then activated* to contain the disorders spurred by acute commodification (the Karl Polanyi problem) as well as to close the legitimacy gap suffered by governing elites (the Carl Schmitt problem). (iv) Social insecurity morphs into a deep current of social anxiety coursing through the society, including the fear of tomorrow among the working class and the fear of downward mobility among the middle class, which in turn deepens the deficit of legitimacy, to which state elites respond by further ramping up penalization. (v) *Social anxiety* rooted in commodification is moreover amplified by broader structural changes such as growing family instability (spawned by changing relations based on age, gender, and sexuality), intensified competition for school credentials and the ever-accelerating cycles of the news and electoral politics. (vi) *Racial division and immigration* act in the manner of a multiplier: they facilitate economic deregulation to the degree that they splinter the proletariat; they inflate class anxiety and fuel ethnic resentment among established groups (whites in the US, nationals in Western

139

---

[44] Loïc Wacquant, *The Invention of the "Underclass": A Study in the Politics of Knowledge* (2022); Christian Mouhanna and Jérôme Ferret, *Peurs sur les villes. Vers un populisme punitif à la française?* (2005). Wihtol de Wenden shows how visions of the Other in France hardened in the period 1980 to 2012 and centered on the figure of the Muslim immigrant from the Maghreb as "the internal enemy." Catherine Wihtol de Wenden, "Le contact des civilisations. Migrations et peur de l'Autre en France" (2013).

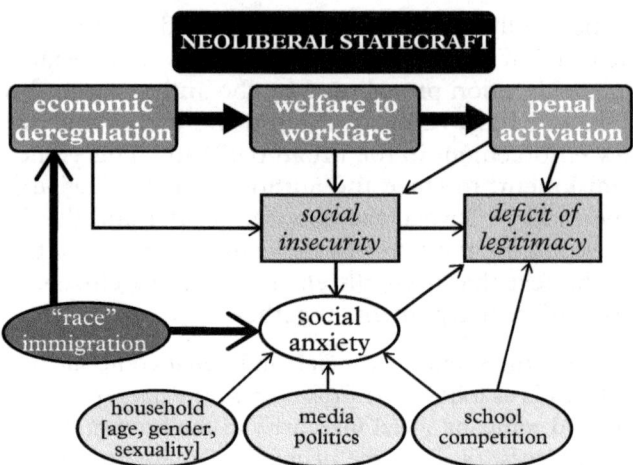

Figure 7   The economic, social, and penal planks of neoliberal statecraft

Europe) whose dominant position as protected "insiders" is threatened or collapsing.

The *geography, timing and sequencing* of policy shifts within and across nations verify the link between neoliberalism and penalization. The countries that initiated aggressive policies of economic deregulation and commodification were the first to revamp their social welfare programs in a restrictive way and they also led the international race to incarcerate. It is not by happenstance if Chile, following the economic prescriptions of the "Chicago Boys" to pursue sweeping marketization in the mid-1970s, was ahead of the pack on all three fronts, closely followed by the US, New Zealand, Australia, and the UK.[45] It is also not by happenstance if the advanced nations that have held incarceration in check are those in which economic deregulation was long restrained by deeply entrenched social welfare states and in which a corporatist political culture subtended high levels of social

---

[45] In 1974, Chile's inmate population stood at 14,500 for an incarceration rate of 142 per 100,000. A decade later, the population had jumped to 20,200 and the rate to 167 per 100,000. In 2010, the country reached its carceral peak with 53,400 and 313 per 100,000 respectively, at which time it was vying with Brazil as the leader in confinement for the continent. Chile sports the most rationalized, professionalized, and expansive punishment apparatus in Latin America. On the dynamics of the penal surge on that continent, see Paul Hathazy and Markus-Michael Müller, "The Rebirth of the Prison in Latin America: Determinants, Regimes and Social Effects" (2016).

trust in official institutions moderating the public debate on crime:[46] the Nordic nations, Germany, and Austria, countries which also managed until recently to thwart the formation of urban redoubts of ethnicized poverty. In the advanced societies of the capitalist West, *who says entrenched urban marginality says profuse penality.*[47]

It is crucial to hold together the material (economic) and symbolic (political) drivers of penal fortification. In his elaboration of the thought of Max Weber in *The Legitimation of Power*, David Beetham proposes that "those who derive their authority from the people will ignore at their peril any insistent and widespread popular current of opinion."[48] When they do so, a *legitimacy deficit* arises which undermines the authority of the rulers, eroding their ability to deploy their policies in a range of domains. I contend that such a deficit of legitimacy plagued the leaders of the states that pulled back from the mission of economic support and social protection established during the period of growth and consolidation of the Keynesian-Fordist regime, namely, the four decades from 1935 to 1975. Rolling out the penal state to deliver "security," reduced to proactive and pornographic crime-fighting, closed this legitimacy gap by demonstrating that the state was taking action to satisfy the demands of the citizenry. Anxiety about *social* insecurity was displaced and fastened onto *criminal* insecurity and the figure of the urban brigand took center stage in the public imaginary of citizenship.

My account here differs from John Pratt's in his insightful article on "Risk Control, Rights and Legitimacy in the Limited Liability State" (2016).[49] For Pratt, punitive penal policies are a response to a legitimacy deficit suffered by governing elites on the *crime* front specifically, whereas I located the origins of this deficit in the failure of the state to stem rising and diffusing *social* insecurity – a much larger and inchoate task, and for this reason one likely to generate continuing anxiety and resentment even as the crime rate slumps.

---

[46] Mick Cavadino and James Dignan, *Penal Systems: A Comparative Approach* (2005); Tapio Lappi-Seppälä, "Explaining Imprisonment in Europe" (2011).

[47] Remarkably, *The Oxford Handbook of the Social Science of Poverty* edited by David Brady and Linda Burton (2016) mentions the police, the criminal court, and the prison only in passing.

[48] David Beetham, *The Legitimation of Power* (1991), p. 36.

[49] John Pratt, "Risk Control, Rights and Legitimacy in the Limited Liability State" (2016).

Lessons from social history:
Marginality floods the city

We should not be surprised that the prison was rolled out to accompany the neoliberal restructuring of postindustrial capitalism and absorb the economic shock of labor fragmentation, the cultural tremor of ethnic dissolution, and entrenched social insecurity at the bottom of the hierarchy of classes and places in the dualizing metropolis. For curbing and containing urban marginality has been the prison's mission across the nearly 500 years of its history. To document this, it suffices to return to the invention of penal confinement in the late sixteenth century.[50]

In his masterwork, *La Potence ou la pitié. L'Europe et les pauvres du Moyen-Âge à nos jours*, the Polish historian Bronislaw Geremek reports that, "before the prison became a method of punishment and corrections of criminals on a large scale, modern Europe made it into a tool for the implementation of its social policy towards beggars" and the means for "the conspicuous affirmation of the work ethic in those countries that took the path of capitalist development."[51] The first "houses of correction" – the Bridewell of London (1555), the Tuchthuis of Amsterdam (1596), l'Hôpital général of Paris (1656) – sprang up and diffused in the period 1550–1670. They were erected as a constituent of the early modern state, not in reaction to criminality and even less serious offending, which was handled by way of corporal punishment, banishment, and death, but to the rise and

---

[50] In this section, I draw on the accounts of Georg Rusche and Otto Kirchheimer, *Punishment and Social Structure* ([1939] 2005); Thorsten Sellin, *Pioneering in Penology: The Amsterdam Houses of Correction in the Sixteenth and Seventeenth Centuries* (1944); Michel Foucault, *Folie et déraison. Histoire de la folie à l'âge classique* (1961); idem, *Surveiller et punir. Naissance de la prison* (1975); idem, *La Société punitive. Cours au Collège de France, 1972–1973* (2013); Douglas Hay et al., *Albion's Fatal Tree: Crime and Society in Eighteenth-Century England* (1975); Bronislaw Geremek, *La Potence ou la pitié. L'Europe et les pauvres du Moyen-Âge à nos jours* (1978); Catharina Lis and Hugo Soly, *Poverty and Capitalism in Pre-industrial Europe* (1979); John McMullan, *The Canting Crew: London's Criminal Underworld, 1550–1700* (1984); Jacques-Guy Petit, *Ces Peines obscures. La prison pénale en France, 1780–1875* (1990); Mary Lindemann, *Patriots and Paupers: Hamburg, 1712–1830* (1990); Pieter Spierenburg, *The Prison Experience: Disciplinary Institutions and their Inmates in Early Modern Europe* (1991); Robert Jütte, *Poverty and Deviance in Early Modern Europe* (1994); Norbert Finzsch and Robert Jütte (eds.), *Institutions of Confinement. Hospitals, Asylums, and Prisons in Western Europe and North America, 1500–1950* (1996); Paul Griffiths, *Lost Londons: Change, Crime, and Control in the Capital City, 1550–1660* (2008).

[51] Geremek, *La Potence ou la pitié*, pp. 264 and 274.

spread of urban destitution, as vagrants spawned by the collapse of the manorial economy streamed into the burgeoning cities fed by commercial capitalism. Keywords to their establishment were *idleness and immorality*. The mission of the first prisons was to clean up the streets, impose social and moral order on the disruptive poor, and discipline the nascent urban working class by setting them to labor behind bars so as to dramatize the work ethic. This historical turning point was reported in clinical terms by none other than Karl Marx in volume 1 of *Das Kapital* when he notes that displaced peasants and serfs "turned en masse into beggars, robbers, and vagabonds."[52]

"Beggars, robbers, and vagabonds"

The proletariat created by the breaking up of the bands of feudal retainers and by the forcible expropriation of the people from the soil, this "free" proletariat could not possibly be absorbed by the nascent manufactures as fast as it was thrown upon the world. On the other hand, these men, suddenly dragged from their wonted mode of life, could not as suddenly adapt themselves to the discipline of their new condition. They were turned en masse into beggars, robbers, vagabonds, partly from inclination, in most cases from stress of circumstances. Hence at the end of the fifteenth and during the whole of the sixteenth century, throughout Western Europe a bloody legislation against vagabondage. The fathers of the present working class were chastised for their enforced transformation into vagabonds and paupers. Legislation treated them as "voluntary" criminals, and assumed that it depended on their own good will to go on working under the old conditions that no longer existed.

Karl Marx, *Capital*, volume 1, p. 49, cited in David Greenberg (ed.), *Crime and Capitalism* (1980), p. 47.

England led the way with the *bridewell*.[53] In her portrait of "Prisons for the Poor: English Bridewells, 1555–1800," Joanna Innes stresses the novelty of the institution. Whereas the feudal gaols held a motley

[52] Karl Marx, "Marx and Engels on Crime and Punishment" (1991).
[53] The name bridewell comes from Bridewell Palace, a former royal palace converted into London's first house of correction in 1555. It came to designate the houses of correction that sprang up across the kingdom in the second half of the sixteenth century to form a nationwide network of urban prisons.

collection of persons detained to await criminal trial or punishment, or for failure to pay fines or debt, the bridewell was "designed for a specific clientele: for men and women drawn from the ranks of the laboring poor, guilty of no more than petty delinquencies considered to be especially characteristic of the poor: 'idle and disorderly' behaviour of various kinds, unlicensed begging, vagrancy and the like."[54]

Innes calls the bridewells "sites of punishment and reformation," "instruments of extraordinarily ambitious, even utopian, social policies," serving a *mission at once economic and moral.* They were "specifically designed to correct the faults of a servant class," especially offenses against employers such as insubordination, abandoning work while under contract, and the theft of raw materials and goods.[55] But they also served to wage a class war on the cultural front: "Fear and distaste stimulated by the pervasive presence of beggars served to spark action" and made the bridewell one element in "a more general assault on aspects of plebeian life and culture," part of a veritable "*campaign* against vice and disorder."[56] Employers and parish officers thus resorted to penal means to compel the unemployed to labor in the growing urban economy, keep the disruptive poor in public space under control and regulate behavior on the streets.[57]

But it is the *tuchthuis* or *rasphuis* of Amsterdam that served as the model for the rest of Europe.[58] Thorsten Sellin offers a painstaking account of its birth, functioning, and spread in *Pioneering in Penology* (1944). He recounts how "the house was established to deal with the young and dissolute incorrigible petty offenders, beggars, vagrants, and thieves, who might be turned into the path of civic virtue through

[54] Joanna Innes, "Prisons for the Poor: English Bridewells, 1555–1800" (1987), p. 43.
[55] Ibid., p. 47.
[56] Ibid., p. 58; for a full portrait of the clientele of the bridewell, see Griffiths, *Lost Londons*, especially the tables pp. 449–74.
[57] "How best to relieve the impotent poor, ensure that there was ample work for the able-bodied, and that there were adequate policing and disciplinary facilities to keep the 'disorderly' poor under control" were "the three questions 16th century city elites tried to resolve with the invention of the bridewell." Innes, "Prisons for the Poor," p. 50.
[58] This is duly noted by Foucault: "The oldest of these models, which is believed to have inspired all the others to a greater or lesser extent, is the Rasphuis in Amsterdam, which opened in 1596. It was originally intended for beggars or young offenders." Foucault, *Surveiller et punir*, p. 123. *Tuchthuis* means literally "house of discipline" in Dutch. The house was divided into the *rasphuis* for men (referring to the rasping of wood, the task of male inmates) and the *spinhuis* for women (referring to spinning yarn, the labor assigned to female inmates).

the treatment methods used there."[59] The earliest description of the *tuchthuis* notes that the largest contingent of inmates were professional beggars "from twenty to sixty years of age and whose crutches, bandages, straps, trusses, and wooden legs were prominently displayed on the wall of the courtyard near the whipping post as mute evidence of the curative properties of the discipline."[60] Also targeted were runaway apprentices, incorrigible children, men maltreating their wives or fallen into habitual drunkenness. The aim of incarceration was threefold: to punish, to discipline by instilling work habits, and to cleanse the city of its social refuse. In Amsterdam at the start of the seventeenth century, the street sweeping of drifters and mendicants provided "the largest clientele" of the *tuchthuis*. Sellin's description deserves quoting *in extenso*:

145

> The city ordinance of April 15, 1614, against beggars, deploring the large number of sturdy rogues in the city, both residents and transients, who because of lack of employment opportunities or because of laziness were begging, gambling, cheating at cards, drinking, or guilty of other ungodly behavior, penalized begging by six weeks in the house of correction for the first offense, and six months for the second offense, and provided penalties at the discretion of the court for those who sent children out to beg. The housing of beggars was punished by a fine which if not paid was converted to six months in the house of correction, and if anyone resisted the enforcement of the ordinance he was to be fined one hundred Charles guilders, and if unable to pay, was to be sent to the tuchthuis for three months.[61]

The most remarkable feature of the Amsterdam workhouse yet was its rapid diffusion across Europe. It mushroomed throughout the Low Countries where, according to the historian Henri Pirenne, "individuals deprived of means of subsistence could be imprisoned and compelled to work."[62] In Brussels, the city authorities built a *duchthuis* in 1623 for the incarceration, not of criminals, but of the

---

[59] Sellin, *Pioneering in Penology*, p. 41. Incarceration and forced labor were mild punishment compared to the previous registry of criminal sanctions in the Low Countries: banishment, public whipping, branding, mutilation, and death (by beheading, breaking on the wheel, hanging, and drowning), not to mention gruesome torture as a technique of investigation.

[60] Ibid., p. 42.

[61] Ibid., p. 44.

[62] Henri Pirenne, *Histoire de la Belgique*, p. 441, cited by Sellin, *Pioneering in Penology*, p. 103.

"lazy poor" loitering on city streets. The authorities of Ghent followed suit in 1627. The Amsterdam model also spread across northern Germany, in Lübeck in 1601, Bremen in 1609, Hamburg in 1618, and Danzig a decade later. It migrated to Scandinavia where the city of Stockholm ran a *tukthus* aimed at corralling beggars and drifters so as to put them to work. It was soon copied in Spain, Italy, England, and, from there, taken to the British colonies.[63] Workhouse prisons thus emerged alongside capitalism, in bustling cities in those regions of Europe that were at the forefront of the transformation of social relations of production (England, Holland, North Germany), that is, those areas where the inherited system of personal servitude was being rapidly superseded by wage labor.[64]

Geremek shows that the mounting sentiment of animosity toward mendicants that propelled the "great confinement" of disruptive poverty after the middle of the sixteenth century had its roots in the counter-reformation, for which beggarhood was a mark of impiety rather than sanctity, and in the development of the modern state, which discovered that confinement was a more efficient policy to deal with urban dereliction than expulsion.[65] This was particularly clear in Italy where, in 1566, Pope Pius V hatched a plan to remove panhandlers and vagrants from the streets and squares of Rome and to isolate them in neighborhoods reserved for the disorderly poor – extending to them the spatial solution of the ghetto applied to Jews in Venice since 1516. This hostility toward mendicants spread from the papal states throughout Catholic Europe and left a strong imprint on poverty policy that would last centuries. Thus, in France in the 1720s,

> begging was considered a criminal offence. A beggar arrested for the first time would be confined in the General Hospital for at least two months; the second time, he would be interned for at least three months and branded with the letter 'M' (for *mendiant*); for the third time, the

[63] Sellin, *Pioneering in Penology*, pp. 104–8.
[64] Muscovite Russia offers an instructive contrast here. The introduction of the prison in the seventeenth century was a major plank in state-building in that it gave the ruler a new weapon to relieve cities from the disorders of the disruptive poor. The *tiumi* (holding cell) served to confine beggars, the homeless, and the unemployed viewed as a social menace. The Russian policy diverged from the Western response to urban marginality in that it did not envisage reforming inmates, only removing troublemakers from public space. In the language of modern penology, it aimed at incapacitation without rehabilitation. Nancy Shields Kollmann, *Crime and Punishment in Early Modern Russia* (2012).
[65] Geremek, *La Potence ou la pitié*, pp. 266–70.

men risked being sent to the galleys for five years and the women being confined in the General Hospital for five years, sanctions that the court had the discretion to extend to perpetuity.[66]

In his meticulous reconstruction of *The Prison Experience* in early modern Europe, Pieter Spierenburg confirms that "prison workhouses were originally meant as solutions to problems of marginality and immorality rather than crime." Only later, during the century from 1770 to 1870, did the prison become preeminently a form of criminal punishment, as part of the general evolution of bondage and the "shift from public spectacles to privately inflicted punishment,"[67] and then its class and status recruitment hardly changed. Spierenburg stresses that the targets of houses of correction were the social derelicts and "undisciplined persons whom their families shunned," either because they were insane or immoral – the boundary between the two being fuzzy.[68] The prison had five precursors: monasteries and convents, which supplied the prototype of discipline and also employed a special cell to punish their errant members; medieval hospitals which were charitable institutions tending to the aged, the homeless, poor pilgrims, the infirm and the sick; madhouses confining persons out of their senses; jails holding debtors and convicts for later punishment; and houses for the chastisement of wayward youths.

Spierenburg also corroborates the thesis that the birth of the workhouse prison was propelled by a sea change in upper-class perception of the lower class in the sixteenth century. "Increasingly, a distinction was made between the deserving and the undeserving poor; between able-bodied and disabled beggars ... The state of poverty became a curse and the poor were considered a threat to the stability of society."[69] This new mentality fostered a secularization of the administration of charity; begging was prohibited; relief was provided only to the resident poor, compelling others to leave the city. Mendicants and vagabonds should work or scram and the authorities now had the means to compel them to labor. This is captured by an urban myth which crystallized in Amsterdam in the seventeenth century according to which the *rasphuis* contained a special cell with hermetic walls reserved for recalcitrant inmates into which water was allowed to flow and rise. This forced the

[66] Ibid., p. 288.
[67] Spierenburg, *The Prison Experience*, p. 278. On this transition, see idem, *The Spectacle of Suffering: Executions and the Evolution of Repression* (1984).
[68] Spierenburg, *The Prison Experience*, p. 19.
[69] Ibid., p. 278.

prisoner thus trapped to pump frantically on pain of drowning. The historian Simon Schama famously interpreted this myth as an expression of the Dutch ethos condemning idleness as a source of moral decay, but Spierenburg finds that the tale of the "drowning cell" actually originated in Germany where it embodied *Sozialdisciplinierung*.[70] Regardless, it stands as a vivid metaphor for the forcible regulation of the urban poor and suggests that the workhouse prison effectively *deployed space to enforce social and moral order on the streets*.[71]

In his earlier book on the transition from public to private repression, *The Spectacle of Suffering*, Spierenburg draws on Norbert Elias's theory of the "civilizing process" to spotlight three macrostructural forces driving penal innovation: state formation, the pacification of social relations leading to changing moral sensibilities among the upper class, and urbanization. Urbanization was pivotal because "cities shape the destinies of states chiefly by serving as containers and distribution points for capital. By means of capital, urban ruling classes extend their influence through the urban hinterland and across far-flung trading networks."[72] They thus accumulate the resources invested in state-building, including agencies of public force, the penal triad of police, court, and prison on the domestic front and the army on the foreign front. Cities also harbor large concentrations of the poor which make the latter more visible and more threatening as social space becomes pacified. Finally, the success of the prison was closely tied to changing attitudes toward the body, taking the form of "the gradual emergence of negative feelings vis-à-vis physical discipline and punishment" manifested in the vanishing of the theater of the scaffold, the long-term slumping of homicide rates, the privatization of the dissection of corpses and the enthusiasm for solitary confinement as a penal technique.[73]

I draw four lessons from this brief and selective account of the invention of the house of correction in the late sixteenth century for rethinking the penal state in the late twentieth century and beyond.

[70] Ibid., pp. 98–103. Simon Schama, *The Embarrassment of Riches: An Interpretation of Dutch Culture in the Golden Age* (1988). The multilayered meaning of *Sozialdisciplinierung* is laid bare by Norbert Finzsch, "Elias, Foucault, Oestreich: On a Historical Theory of Confinement" (1996).

[71] On the use of space as a means of domination comparing prison, ghetto, camp, reservation, and gated community, see Loïc Wacquant, "Designing Urban Seclusion in the Twenty-First Century: The 2009 Roth-Symonds Lecture" (2010c).

[72] Charles Tilly, "Cities and States in Europe, 1000–1800" (1989), p. 564.

[73] Pieter Spierenburg, "Four Centuries of Prison History: Punishment, Suffering, the Body and Power" (1996).

1. The birth of the correctional prison, as distinct from the gaol of detention, was *part and parcel of early modern state-building*. It was a political institution in the sense that it materialized a new mission taken up by the authorities, managing disruptive poverty in the city, which had until then been the province of the church, and asserting the expanding power of the ruler.[74] It enlarged the capacity of the state to make legible and to penetrate the city's underbelly so as to ward off the social and moral threat it presented.

2. The prison was initially *designed to manage not crime but marginality* – idleness, the problem of the "sturdy beggar," the shocking immorality of the floating proto-proletariat – during the epochal transition from feudalism to capitalism. Indeed, it defined as criminals populations cast adrift in public space. This shift was further propelled by a change in cultural orientation such that the poor were no longer perceived as idealized objects of pity and charity but seen as social parasites and vectors of political disorder.[75]

149

3. The prison started out as a *hybrid institution*, combining pity and punishment, poor relief and penal pain, assistance for the ill and the lame versus castigation for the drifter. It deployed, that is, the two faces of punishment distinguished in chapter 1, material and symbolic, economic and moral.[76] Benthamite rationality aimed at reinserting the poor into the economic circuit as capable laborers and Kantian emotionality aimed at changing character and instilling values. Then, gradually, the social question and the criminal question got separated during the long century after 1848, each giving birth to its own bureaucratic complex and claims-making track,[77] only to be fused again at the close of the millennium.

4. The prison was and is an *urban institution*, not in the superficial sense that every institution is urban because the whole society is

[74] The decades from 1530 to 1630 were "a period of extraordinarily creative and vigorous governmental activity – particularly in relation the 'the poor'." Catharina Lis and Hugo Soly, *Poverty and Capitalism in Pre-industrial Europe* (1979), pp. 82–96.

[75] Geremek, *La Potence ou la pitié*, p. 270.

[76] This is particularly clear in the case of the *hôpital général* in France, as shown by Colin Jones, *Charity and Bienfaisance: The Public and the Hospitals in Paris, 1570–1791* (1989), who stresses the moral economy of confinement and the tension between charity and control, *contra* Foucault's view of the hospital as a total institution.

[77] Marcel van der Linden, "The Social Question in Western Europe: Past and Present" (2019); Robert Castel, *Les Métamorphoses de la question sociale. Une chronique du salariat* (1995); Jacques Donzelot, *L'Invention du Social. Essai sur le déclin des passions politiques* (1984); David Garland, *Punishment and Welfare: A History of Penal Strategies* (1985); Philippe Robert, *La Question pénale* (1984).

urbanizing, but in the deep sense that (i) its very genesis was inter-twined with the consolidation of the metropolis and (ii) that it has from its origins been tasked with managing the latter's problem categories and territories. Indeed, it is during these decades that the city elites formed the vision of an "underworld" of miscreants with its own districts, culture, language, and social relations – the sixteenth-century version of today's neighborhoods of relegation.[78] Cities were nodes of penal innovation because of the large concentration of the poor they harbored, the sharper effects of cycles of boom and bust on them, and the prevalence of disease. This combined to make the poor visible and "respectable and godly citizens also reacted with distaste and alarm" to their rowdy and disorganized lives.[79]

From its origins, then, the prison has always been *deployed selectively*. To understand the transhistorical slant of criminal punishment, we can locate the Leviathan and its targets in a two-dimensional space structured by *class* (poor, rich), in the material order, and *status* or honor (insider, outsider), in the symbolic order (see figure 8).[80] As an engine of classification and stratification, the penal state is located at the point of maximum accumulation of physical and symbolic force, at the top left end of the diagram. Along the vertical axis, it strikes down at dispossessed populations, chief among them the urban precariat, because of the latter's disruptive conduct, spatial concentration, and special vulnerability to penal penetration. Along the horizontal axis, the Leviathan strikes rightward at dishonored populations, chief among them stigmatized ethnonational and ethnoracial categories, because of their outsider status: they belong to "them" and not "us" and, consequently, the state may inflict upon them kinds and volumes of punishment that it would never impose upon insider categories. Penal stigma meets and merges with ethnic stigma, each reinforcing the other. This combination spawns what I call the *vector of penalization*, which traces the direction of the delivery of state sanctions along the diagonal linking subordination by class and subordination by

---

[78] Robert Jütte, *Poverty and Deviance in Early Modern Europe* (1994); Griffiths, *Lost Londons*; Dominique Kalifa, *Les Bas-fonds. Histoire d'un imaginaire* (2013).

[79] Innes, "Prisons for the Poor," p. 52.

[80] I employ these two terms in a broad Weberian sense (see Max Weber, *Economy and Society: An Outline of Interpretive Sociology* ([1920] 1978), for which class refers to "market capacity" and status to a collectivity defined by "an effective claim to social esteem in terms of positive or negative privileges."

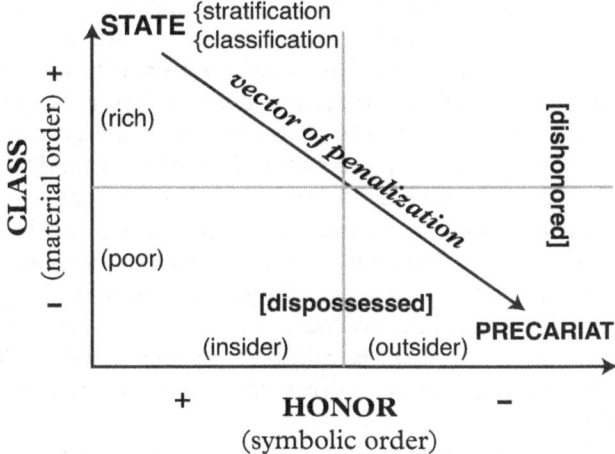

Figure 8   Class, status, and the vector of penalization

status. This diagonal captures the double selectivity of punishment in all societies organized along lines of poverty and ethnicity. The deeper these two divides, the greater the punishment.

Province of the precariat:
Class and ethnicity behind bars

All four of the propositions drawn from the social history of the genesis of the prison in early modern Europe apply today. Not only has the prison returned to the institutional forefront of advanced society as a building block of the neoliberal state. It has filled up with its most vulnerable members, the human detritus of a dualizing social order in the metropolis: the precariously employed and jobless, homeless, paperless migrants, poor drug addicts and alcoholics, the destitute mentally ill, and wards of the state, who are everywhere the "privileged clients" of custodial institutions.[81]

Change urban marginality and you change penality. The onset of the new regime of urban poverty, propelled by wage fragmentation

[81] It is revealing that the first scholarly use of the term "mass incarceration" recorded by the Institute for Scientific Information (ISI) was not to characterize the imprisonment of blacks in the US but the indiscriminate confinement of drug addicts in French jails and prisons. Jean-Paul Jean, "Mettre fin à l'incarcération de masse des toxicomanes" (1995).

and welfare retraction, and marked by ethnicization, spatial fixation, and territorial stigmatization, calls for the deployment of new penal structures and policies.[82] This functional relationship does not obtain mechanically, as a result of structural necessity as with Rusche and Kirchheimer.[83] Rather, it results from *strategic struggles* in and across the economic, bureaucratic, and political fields that tend to align the penal machinery with the need to maintain the material and symbolic order in the city's districts of dereliction to resolve the Polanyi and Schmitt problems. It establishes a correspondence not with the *mode of production* but with the *mode of stratification,* that is, the particular articulation of class and status (national or ethnic) prevailing in the metropolis. This proposition is validated by the social profile of the "penal prey" (*gibier pénal*), to borrow the apt expression of historian Michelle Perrot.[84]

As one who has written extensively on race and hyperincarceration, including a full chapter on the topic in my book *Racial Domination* (2024b), I can hardly be suspected of minimizing the role of race.[85] But the facts before us are stubborn and overwhelming: the population behind bars, *black, white, and Latino* in the United States, *national and foreign* in Europe, is composed nearly *exclusively of (sub)proletarian men* mired in deep economic precarity, early cultural exclusion, abiding social denudement, and acute mental dereliction. This is the first, *vertical dimension of penalization* along the class axis. No prison system provides a fulsome social portrait of its clients but we can patch together statistical data from the United States, the United Kingdom, and France to verify that the clients of the jail and prison are what, with Frantz Fanon, we could call the *wretched of the city.*

Consider the profile of inmates in state prisons in the United States in 2016:[86] 85 percent had only a high-school education or less, as against a mere 3 percent a college degree (compared to 38 percent nationwide). A paltry 14 percent were married compared to 50 percent for adults in the general population. One in five convicts had lived in public housing (which accounts for less than 1 percent of all

[82] For a fuller elaboration of the distinctive features of postindustrial poverty in the city, read Loïc Wacquant, *Urban Outcasts: A Comparative Sociology of Advanced Marginality* (2008), chapter 8.

[83] Georg Rusche and Otto Kirchheimer, *Punishment and Social Structure* ([1939] 2005).

[84] Michelle Perrot, *Punir et comprendre* (2023).

[85] Loïc Wacquant, *Racial Domination* (2024b), chapter 4.

[86] Lauren G. Beatty and Tracy L. Snell, *Profile of Prison Inmates, 2016* (2021)

housing) and nearly one-half reported growing up in a single-parent household (as against 23 percent for all adults). Nearly half had parents or guardians who received welfare and an astounding 17 percent had lived in a foster home, agency, or institution, eight times the national rate. To top it all, some 59 percent had family members who had been incarcerated, including 21 percent a father only and 37 percent a sibling. In short, there are no middle-class prisoners in America (as in other advanced societies): the *penitentiary is a reservation for the precariat, regardless of color.*

Now peruse the social silhouette of inmates drawn by the Prison Reform Trust for England and Wales in 2023.[87] Two-thirds of the men were without a job during the month before custody and a full 13 percent had never held a job in their lives. Growing up, one-fourth were taken into care as a child (12 times the national rate), 27 percent experienced abuse while 40 percent observed domestic violence during their childhood (four times the national rate). Fully 59 percent were regular truants from school and an astonishing 43 percent were permanently expelled from their school (compared to less than 1 percent for the country as a whole). On the mental health front, 15 percent had symptoms indicating psychosis (four times the national rate) and one in four suffered from both anxiety and depression, while two in three had used hard drugs at one time or another.

153

Finally, cross the Channel and you find a near replica in the social profile of French inmates, which confirms the economic destitution, cultural deprivation, social dispossession, and psychological distress of the confined population in advanced societies. Like their American and British counterparts, over half of them did not hold a job at the time of their arrest. Some 80 percent have less than a high school education, one-fourth have difficulty reading and writing and 10 percent qualify as fully illiterate. Some 38 percent of inmates behind bars for less than six months are addicted to narcotics and 30 percent to alcohol, and many to both at the same time. One-third suffer from generalized anxiety disorder, 40 percent from severe depression, and 21 percent from acute psychosis. All in all, only 20 percent of inmates

---

[87] Prison Reform Trust, *Bromley Briefings Prison Factfile* (2024), pp. 36 (on class), 40, 42 and 47 (on ethnicity), and pp. 56–66 (on health). An earlier study established that 83 percent of English inmates are from the working class, 43 percent left school before the age of 16 (compared to the national average of 16 percent), and over one-third were jobless while a full 13 percent were homeless at the time of their arrest. Rod Morgan, "Imprisonment: Current Concerns and a Brief History since 1945" (1997), p. 1161.

do *not* suffer from mental illness while the majority suffer from multiple afflictions simultaneously.

In short, the clients of jails and prisons at the dawn of the twenty-first century are dredged from the very bottom of the social barrel, making custodial establishments repositories for the fractions of the urban precariat living in abject poverty, destitution, and suffering. But there is more: the prison is not just a *receptacle* for the poor, but also a *crucible* of dereliction since it further impoverishes its clientele both behind and beyond bars. The cost of daily necessities bought at the prison commissary (extra food and toiletries), the rental of a television, and the payment of a fee for their uniform eat into the meager budget of inmates, who, moreover, lose their limited personal belongings when they get transferred to a different establishment.[88]

After release, a custodial sentence translates into truncated life chances as measured by higher joblessness, lower earnings, increased family dissolution, continuing addiction to drugs and alcohol, routine exposure to violence, and aggravated morbidity and mortality. Penal stigma weighs on the sense of self and warps everyday relations. Rebuilding a meaningful life in the face of moral condemnation becomes an ever-renewed obstacle course. The negative credential of the "ex-con" (*Knasti* in Germany, *ancien taulard* in France, *ex carcerato* in Italy) granted and guaranteed by the state systematically truncates life chances.[89]

The *destabilizing effects of incarceration* on the populations and places most directly put under penal tutelage include stigmatization and the sense of indignity it carries; the interruption of educational, marital, and occupational trajectories; the destabilization of families and the amputation of social networks; the deepening of social ties with protagonists of the street and criminal economy; the crystallization of a culture of resistance and even defiance of authority in the dispossessed districts where spending time behind bars is turning into a routine occurrence, even a normal stage in the life course for lower-class young men.

---

[88] The pauperizing effect of incarceration in France is painstakingly documented by Anne-Marie Marchetti, *Pauvretés en prison* (1997).

[89] Sara Wakefield and Christopher Uggen, "Incarceration and Stratification" (2010); Bruce Western, *Homeward: Life in the Year After Prison* (2018); Bernard Chaouat (ed.), *Reconstruire sa vie après la prison. Quel avenir après la sanction?* (2011); Barbara Sieferle, *Nach dem Gefängnis: Alltag und unsichtbare Bestrafungen* (2023).

The truncation of the life chances of inmates starts the minute they walk outside the gate of the penitentiary.[90] In France, 60 percent of inmates released from jail or prison are jobless, 12 percent are homeless, and over one-fourth have less than €20 in hand as they step out (the threshold below which the correctional administration acknowledges their status as "indigent" and grants them limited aid). Foreign inmates are even more destitute, with 68 percent without a job, 29 percent homeless, and 30 percent without minimal cash. Half of all released convicts never received a visit from a family member or friend during their sojourn behind bars, and nearly one-third have no one waiting for them as they reenter society. One inmate in three suffers from at least three of these handicaps, which makes "reintegration" a dubious enterprise considering the weakness of the means allocated to supporting them on the outside and the multiple obstacles faced by "ex-cons."

Let me now turn to the second, *horizontal dimension of penalization*, that of civic membership and ethnic (dis)honor. It is taken as an article of academic faith and a public fact on both sides of the Atlantic that American punishment is *uniquely racialized* in the sense of disproportionately striking at stigmatized ethnic categories, primarily African-Americans burdened by the historical stain of slavery. This is the stated rationale for the nearly exclusive focus that US scholars have accorded to racial as opposed to class inequality in incarceration – from Michael Tonry in *Malign Neglect* (1995) to Vesla Weaver in *Frontlash: Race and the Politics of Punishment* (2007) and Becky Petitt (2012) in *Invisible Men*, to Heather Schoenfeld in *Building the Prison State* (2018) and Reuben Jonathan Miller in *Halfway Home* (2021).[91]

---

[90] Maud Guilloneau et al., "Les resources des sortants de prisons" (1998). Note that the destabilizing and impoverishing effects of penal confinement do not stop at the inmate: they impact also his life partner, children and neighborhood. Incarceration also distorts civic participation and validates, even aggravates, the stratification order. Christopher Muller and Christopher Wildeman. "Punishment and Inequality" (2013).

[91] Michael Tonry, *Malign Neglect: Race, Crime, and Punishment in America* (1995); Bruce Western, *Punishment and Inequality in America* (2006); Vesla Mae Weaver, *Frontlash: Race and the Politics of Punishment* (2007); Becky Petitt, *Invisible Men: Mass Incarceration and the Myth of Black Progress* (2012); Heather Schoenfeld, *Building the Prison State: Race and the Politics of Mass Incarceration* (2018); Reuben Jonathan Miller, *Halfway Home: Race, Punishment, and the Afterlife of Mass Incarceration* (2021). See also Michael A. Hallett, *Private Prisons in America: A Critical Race Perspective* (2006); Devah Pager, *Marked: Race, Crime, and Finding Work in an Era of Mass Incarceration* (2008); Glenn C. Loury et al., *Race, Incarceration, and American Values* (2008); Naomi Murakawa, *The First Civil Right: How Liberals Built Prison America* (2014); and

Bruce Western's ground-breaking book on *Punishment and Inequality in America* (2006) is the signal exception to this stubborn bias as it consistently combines race and class in the dissection of the causes, anatomy, and consequences of incarceration. But, then again, Western is Australian and the reception of his book has focused relentlessly on the racial dimension.[92]

In his 2012 Sutherland address to the American Society for Criminology, David Garland lists among the "most distinctive characteristics" of American penality "the racial cast of America's prisons and jails." Likewise, in his Tanner Lecture, revised as *Punir, une passion contemporaine*, Didier Fassin confidently asserts that the United States is "exceptional by the exceptional severity of its penal system and the deep socioracial disparities in the distribution of punishment."[93] On the other side of the Atlantic, European criminologists have paid scant attention to the issue and generally been content to assume that their continent has escaped such severe ethnoracial bias.[94]

But a simple computation shows that, in fact, in every country of Western Europe save England, Spain, and Ireland, the ethnonational disproportionality in incarceration is *greater* than the ethnoracial disproportionality afflicting African-Americans in the United States (see table 8). In 2015, the latter comprised 36 percent of the country's carceral population as against 13 percent of the country's population, for a ratio of 2.7. If we compute the ratio of the share of foreigners behind bars divided by their share in the country's population in Europe,[95] we see that it reaches 3.4 in Germany, 3.6 in Belgium, 3.7 in Norway, 3.8 in the Netherlands and Belgium, 3.9 in Denmark, and exceeds 4 in Austria, Italy, Sweden, and Portugal. Greece leads the charge with ten times more foreigners behind bars than in its general

Sara M. Benson, *The Prison of Democracy: Race, Leavenworth, and the Culture of Law* (2019).

[92] Bruce Western, *Punishment and Inequality in America* (2006). Thus David Garland's review of the book in *Contexts* is entitled "Race and the Penal State" (2007).

[93] David Garland, "Penality and the Penal State" (2013a), p. 477; Fassin, *Punir, une passion contemporaine*, p. 114.

[94] For a thorough panorama of recent research, see Thomas Ugelvik, "The Incarceration of Foreigners in European Prisons" (2017).

[95] This simple ratio captures disproportionality without the trouble introduced by comparing ethnic categories (which vary across societies). More complex indicators, such as the modified version of the Ortona index used by Anderson to compare 18 nations, yield the same results. J.P. Anderson, "Prison Disproportion in Democracies: A Comparative Analysis" (2023).

Table 8
The overincarceration of foreigners in the prisons of Europe.

	% foreign inmates	% foreign population	ratio
Greece	59	6	9.8
Portugal	18	4	4.5
Sweden	30	7	4.3
Italy	33	8	4.1
Austria	53	13	4.1
Denmark	27	7	3.9
Netherlands	19	5	3.8
Norway	33	9	3.7
Belgium	40	11	3.6
Germany	31	9	3.4
France	19	7	2.7
United States (blacks)	**36**	**13**	**2.7**
Spain	29	11	2.6
UK	12	8	1.5
Ireland	16	12	1.3

Source: for the US: Todd D. Minton and Zhen Zeng, *Jail Inmates in 2015* (BJS, 2016); E. Ann Carson and Elizabeth Anderson, *Prisoners in 2015* (2016); for Europe, OECD, *OECD Factbook 2015–2016* (2017), Marcelo F. Aebi et al., *Key Findings of the SPACE Reports* (2022), table 3, Probation and Prisons in Europe, 2022.

population, owing to its geographical position at the border of the Balkans.

This is not a European peculiarity. In the former British settler colonies, indigenous people sport carceral disproportionality indices greater than the disproportionality suffered by African-Americans.[96] In the United States, Amerindians supply roughly 3 percent of inmates as opposed to 1 percent of the country's population for a disproportionality index exceeding 3. In Canada, native peoples constitute 4 percent of the national population but one-quarter of the prison census for an index of 6.2. In Australia, Aboriginals and Torres Strait Islanders contribute 25 percent of the population behind bars although they weigh 2 percent of the national population for an index of 12.5. In New Zealand, the Maoris supply over

[96] Christopher J. Marier and John K. Cochran, "Ethnic Diversity, Ethnic Polarization, and Incarceration Rates: A Cross-National Study" (2023), p. 481.

one-half of inmates when they represent only 12 percent of the country's population for an index of 4.2.

What is more, this measure of ethnonational disproportionality is a very crude and *conservative* figure. It vastly understates the phenomenon since it does not include the second generation of ethnic outsiders who have gained the nationality of their country of residence (generally via *jus soli*) and yet continue to be the preferential targets of the penal apparatus. Thus, for instance, the ratio of 2.7 for France excludes inmates of North and West African origins who are French citizens owing to being born in the country and to naturalization; in Germany, German inmates of Turkish and Roma parentage are not accounted for; in the Netherlands, the Moroccans and the Surinamese who have become Dutch are entirely left out; in Italy the sons and daughters of North Africans, Romanians, and Albanians; in Belgium and Portugal, inmates of North and West African origins, and so on.

This is very significant because everything indicates that, in many carceral systems, foreigners and nationals of postcolonial or foreign background together make up a majority of inmates. This is the case with La Santé at the heart of Paris, as established by Didier Fassin in his field study of France's largest jail. Fassin reports that fully three-fourths of inmates in that establishment are "visible" minorities, including one-third Arab and one-third black, 80 percent of them of French nationality.[97] Similarly, in the Netherlands, nearly two-thirds of prison inmates have at least one non-Dutch parent, compared to a ratio of one-fifth among the country's population. Inmates of mixed descent have parents who are Moroccans, Surinamese, Antilleans, and Turkish, in descending order.[98]

Another limitation of the coarse nationwide indicator reported in table 8 is that it hides spectacular variations across the country's territory and the peaks of overrepresentation reached in the major cities, congruent with my view of the penal state as manager of urban marginality. In Germany, for instance, a recent Senate study reported by *Die Welt* found that 58 percent of the inmates in the city of Hamburg are foreigners. The main nationalities are Turks, Poles, and Afghans, followed by a smattering of Algerians, Albanians, and Romanians. In Berlin, foreigners make up 56 percent of prisoners or a total of 2,110

[97] Fassin, *Punir, une passion contemporaine*, p. 117.
[98] "Most Dutch Prisoners Have a Non-Dutch Parent," *NL Times*, February 6, 2015 (https://nltimes.nl/ 2015/02/06/dutch-prisoners-non-dutch-parent).

people, led by Poles, Turks, and Eastern Europeans.[99] The far Right has been quick to weaponize these findings by decrying the putative cost of incarcerating foreigners (some €200 per day in Berlin). One group stands out for its acute disproportionate representation in nearly every European carceral system: the Romanians, most of whom are ethnic Romani, arguably the single most stigmatized and marginalized category across the continent.[100]

The association between incarceration and membership in an outsider category bearing a group stigma is a global phenomenon, detected on all five continents.[101] But we are sensitive to this form of inequality largely because it is measured or easily measurable, and because it offends our democratic sensibility – contrary to class inequality on both counts. This hides an equally prevalent pattern, the massive overrepresentation of the very poor behind bars, and the preeminence of poverty over group stigma in penal selection. How can I make this assertion? There is a simple test I call the "Skip Gates test" to determine which of the two factors, class or ethnicity, is the dominant determinant of incarceration in advanced society:[102] if a poor black (Maghrebine, immigrant, foreigner) suspect is

159

---

[99] Kaum Abschiebungen. "Mehr als die Hälfte der Hamburger Gefangenen sind Ausländer." *Die Welt*, June 17, 2024; Arbërie Shabani, "Foreigners Make Up for 58% of Prisoners in Some Germany [sic] States," *Schengen News*, June 21, 2024.

[100] Iulius Rostas and Florin Moisă, "Romani People, Policing, and Penality in Europe" (2023). One possible exception is the Travellers in Ireland, who comprise 0.6 percent of the total population but 10 percent of the carceral stock of the country (Anderson, "Prison Disproportion in Democracies: A Comparative Analysis," pp. 922–3), yielding a disproportionality score of 16.7. On the marginalization of the Roma across the continent, see Ryan Powell and John Lever, "Europe's Perennial 'Outsiders': A Processual Approach to Roma Stigmatization and Ghettoization" (2017).

[101] In "Ethnic Diversity, Ethnic Polarization, and Incarceration Rates: A Cross-National Study," Marier and Cochran report that, despite wide variation in incarceration rates, a brute fact shows "remarkable consistency around the world: the systematic lockup of racial and ethnic minorities" (p. 480).

[102] Skip Gates is a black superstar professor at Harvard University who was famously arrested in summer of 2009 while trying to break into his own house (the entrance door was jammed) by a zealous white policeman who mistook him for a burglar. The officer then found Gates to be "loud and tumultuous" as well as disrespectful (the latter would not obey his commands and insisted on calling the city's mayor instead), and so he took him in handcuffs to the police station on charges of disorderly conduct. Whereupon Gates called a top-flight lawyer (and leading black professor at the Harvard law school) and was immediately released. No charges were filed and the mayor of Cambridge issued an official apology to Gates. The incident sparked a national debate on race and policing, so much so that President Obama, a personal friend of Gates, invited both protagonists to share a beer at the White House. The

arrested, charged, and prosecuted, he can best deflect penal power and diminish criminal sanction by changing his class (money grants access to extra juridical resources such as paying bail, hiring a top-flight defense attorney, and avoiding fast-track justice) and not his race (being white/citizen and poor provides little supplemental protection). *Class shields from penal power in a way ethnicity does not.*[103]

Finally, the carceral institution has been rolled out across Europe in the form of *administrative detention centers confining irregular migrants, asylum seekers, and refugees* denied the right to stay who are awaiting deportation back to their country of origin.[104] These centers, which have mushroomed over the past 30 years to number some 130 in 2022, are plagued with squalid conditions, overcrowding, and the routine denial of rights.[105] They are effectively tasked with patrolling the external borders of the union to remedy their porosity and extirpate undesirable foreigners even as they lack the real means to do so. Their mission is supported by detention camps and temporary accommodation centers built in "gateway countries" such as Albania, Tunisia, and Libya, which are subsidized by the EU to stop and retain candidates from entering Europe. Thus, since 2016, Turkey has received some €6 billion to contain migration flows triggered by the collapse of Syria and Afghanistan as well as the stream of political refugees fleeing Iraq and Iran. The estimated 100,000 who pass through the gates of detention centers yearly, amounting to one-third of detected illegal border crossings, attest to the *de facto penalization of irregular migration* in the European Union, and thus to an extension of the penal state onto new geographical and juridical territory.[106]

According to figures compiled by Eurostat in 2022, a total of 431,000 non-EU citizens received an order to leave the EU country where they were staying, out of an estimated 1.1 million illegally pres-

---

class advantage that stopped penalization dead in its tracks went completely undiscussed.

[103] For a demonstration in the French case, read the fascinating monograph by Julien Larregue, *Au Coeur de l'Etat pénal. Les avocats de la défense sous contrainte* (2026).

[104] On the deep-seated logics of the penalization of national frontiers in the global North, see Didier Fassin, "Policing Borders, Producing Boundaries: the Governmentality of Immigration in Dark Times" (2011b).

[105] Izabella Majcher et al., *Immigration Detention in the European Union* (2020).

[106] See Nicolas Fischer, *Le Territoire de l'expulsion. La rétention administrative des étrangers et l'État de droit en France* (2017), on the mobilization, skirting, and modification of the law to run administrative retention centers in France and their reverberations in the daily life of detainees. For a superb inquiry into the past uses of centers for the confinement of foreigners, read Marc Bernardot's *Captures* (2012).

ent across the Union.[107] France led the charge with 136,000 return orders, followed by Germany (44,000), Croatia (41,000), and Greece (34,000). In France, the difficulty of enforcing OQTFs (*ordres de quitter le territoire français,* "order to leave the French territory," another state tool to deal with bodies "out of place"), due to legal, administrative, and diplomatic obstacles, has turned into an obsessive and explosive issue in the national political debate. The Right and far Right are virulently denouncing at every turn the fact that only 7% of OQTFs are executed. They claim that the "real" number pronounced exceeds 700,000 and willfully conflate the violation of immigration regulations, which are an administrative matter, with criminal offending. The image of the criminal is thus mobilized to *highlight and dramatize the boundary between the citizen and the foreigner.* In the national imagination, the latter is of darker skin and congenitally different than you and me, an incorrigible, dangerous, and treacherous other.

On both sides of the Atlantic, then, the prison in its manifold manifestations (juvenile facility, jail, penitentiary, administrative detention center) is a *race-making institution* in the sense that it validates the symbolic association between incarceration and dishonored ethnicity. The overrepresentation of persons of postcolonial origins, non-Western migrants, and asylum seekers behind bars seems to verify the collective belief in their inherent criminality and dangerosity, moral and physical, a typical feature of racialization all over the world.[108]

Managing marginality by targeting territory

Four social mechanisms can plausibly account for glaring ethnoracial and ethnonational disproportionality in incarceration on the two sides of the Atlantic, respectively, anchored by crime, class, race, and place. Let us consider the role of these four causal forces, their interrelationships and the part played by their spatial concatenation as indicated in figure 9.

---

[107] This does not mean that one-third of all irregular migrants were ordered to leave the European Union because some migrants are the target of multiple such orders. Still, it is hard to maintain that administrative detention constitutes a "last resort" as claimed by Maria Margarita Mentzelopoulou, *Detention of Migrants: A Measure of Last Resort* (2023).

[108] Wacquant, *Racial Domination,* p. 352.

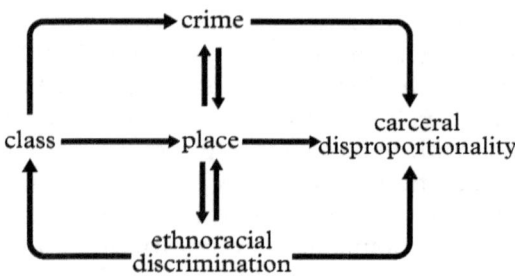

Figure 9 Crime, class, race, and place in the
production of overincarceration

1. The first cause is *differential criminality*: to the extent that African-Americans and individuals of foreign and postcolonial origins in Europe commit more crimes on average, and assuming conservatively that they are equally likely to get caught as whites and European nationals, then they will mechanically compose a higher share of inmates. There is strong evidence that much of the imprisonment disparity between blacks and whites in the United States is produced by different rates of violent offending, but the best studies leave a large "unexplained residual" of 20–39 percent for this crime category depending on the study. This residual rises to 38 percent for property crimes and 57 percent for drug offenses, suggesting that causes other than offending rates are at work behind the overincarceration of African-Americans.[109]

On the European side, there are no detailed crime data by ethnonational origins but a statistical inquiry into immigration in 17 countries found that "an increase in immigration does not affect crime victimization, but it is associated with an increase in the fear of crime, the latter being consistently and positively correlated with the natives' unfavorable attitude toward immigrants."[110] In any case, it stretches credulity to assume that foreigners in Italy, Austria, Portugal, and Sweden are over four times more likely to commit crimes than nationals (which are their overincarceration rates in these countries). An international study covering 55 countries finds no correlation between patterns of immigration and crime. Next, it reports that

[109] Cassia Spohn, "Race, Crime, and Punishment in the Twentieth and Twenty-First Centuries" (2015), p. 60.
[110] Luca Nunziata, "Immigration and Crime: Evidence from Victimization Data" (2015), p. 697.

single-country investigations turn up "no discernible causal effect of increased migration inflows" on property crimes and homicide rates. Finally, it confirms that obtaining legal status depresses the propensity of immigrants to commit offenses because it enlarges their economic opportunities in the regular labor market.[111]

Note that higher crime rates, real or perceived, contribute to territorial stigmatization to the degree that they are believed, rightly or wrongly, to afflict neighborhoods of relegation. This belief can be fed by symbolic entrepreneurs operating in the political and journalistic fields.[112] The dispossessed neighborhood, in turn, fosters criminality because of the paucity of stable jobs, the correlative dynamism of the street economy, and the weakness of proximate social controls anchored by the family. So crime impacts place which impacts justice capture. The neighborhood mediates and amplifies the relationship between offending and incarceration.[113]

2. The second cause is *differential class as well as gender and age composition*: stigmatized minorities in the European metropolis are more masculine, younger and sport a much lower class distribution than the "mainstream" population. Their abiding economic precarity explains in good measure their concentration in districts of dereliction (this is where most low-rent and public housing is located),

163

[111] Olivier Marie and Paolo Pinotti, "Immigration and Crime: An International Perspective" (2024). A panoramic review of research on the topic in the United States finds that "the immigration-crime association is negative – but very weak." Graham C. Ousey and Charis E. Kubrin, "Immigration and Crime: Assessing a Contentious Issue" (2018), p. 63.

[112] For a case study of how city newspapers "normalize and naturalize violence and crime as commonsense characteristics of everyday life" in a mixed-class black neighborhood of Chicago, see Tilman Schwarze, "Discursive Practices of Territorial Stigmatization: How Newspapers Frame Violence and Crime in a Chicago Community" (2022). A similar dynamic is documented in a declining Scottish town by Conor Wilson ("Trading Crime for Culture? Activating Territorial Stigma through Cultural Regeneration in Paisley" [2024]), and in a defamed district of a Danish city (Sune Qvotrup Jensen and Ann-Dorte Christensen, "Territorial Stigmatization and Local Belonging: A Study of the Danish Neighbourhood Aalborg East" [2012]). On the German case, see Moritz Rinn and Jan Wehrheim, "Die Produktion eines 'Problemviertels'. Mediale Diskurse, politisch-polizeiliche Interventionen und interaktive Situationsbedeutungen" (2021).

[113] This has been demonstrated time and again in the case of blacks in the American hyperghetto under the conceptual umbrella of "concentrated disadvantage." The most cogent elaborations of this thesis are William Julius Wilson, *The Truly Disadvantaged: The Underclass, the Inner City and Public Policy* ([1987] 2012), and Robert J. Sampson, *Great American City: Chicago and the Enduring Neighborhood Effect* (2012).

which makes them particularly prone to street crime and public order offenses, which in turn impacts their disproportionate incarceration. It is difficult to disentangle class and race here and perhaps we should not seek to do so through sophisticated quantitative techniques since they are deeply entwined in social reality: statistical manipulation can rely on creating fictive scenarios that just do not happen in the city (e.g., districts of immigrant high-class concentration do not exist).[114] But we do know that class is a commanding causal power from a brute fact documented in every capitalist country: there are virtually *no bourgeois inmates in jails and prisons* and the few who are behind bars are generally there for crimes of passion, which by definition are not subject to differential policing.

164

3. The third mechanism is plain old *ethnoracial discrimination*: unwarranted differential treatment by the police, prosecutors, judges, and correctional authorities ensures that, *ceteris paribus*, blacks in the United States and foreigners in Western Europe get more than their share of prison beds. There is a consensus among scholars on both shores of the Atlantic that the functioning of the penal machinery is indeed marred by ethnic bias. But there is no agreement as to how much, how consistently, and at what stage of the judicial process.[115] Moreover, studies of discrimination in the United States, which dominate research on the topic, are limited by the fact that, with precious few exceptions, they never control for class, due to the absence of readily available data on occupation, education, and housing and to the congenital blindness of American social scientists to class as a principle of social sorting.[116] So court outcomes attributed to race in

---

[114] See the subtle argument to that effect by Matthew Desmond and Bruce Western, "Poverty in America: New Directions and Debates" (2018).

[115] Fabien Jobard and René Lévy, "Police, justice et discriminations raciales en France. État des savoirs" (2011); Cassia Spohn, "Racial Disparities in Prosecution, Sentencing and Punishment" (2014); Jennifer L. Hochschild and Colin M. Brown, "Searching (with Minimal Success) for Links between Immigration and Imprisonment" (2014); Stefania Crocitti, "Immigration, Crime and Criminalization in Italy" (2014); Sveinung Sandberg, "Black Cannabis Dealers in a White Western State: Race, Politics and Street Capital in Norway" (2014); Elena Marchetti and Riley Downie, "Indigenous People and Sentencing Courts in Australia and Canada" (2014); and Julian Roberts et al., "Sentencing Members of Minority Groups: Problems and Prospects for Improvement in Four Countries" (2023), who find that sentencing causes or amplifies ethnic differentials everywhere, and that the remedies applied are weak.

[116] The rare study covering a cohort of convicts in Georgia finds that racial disparity in sentencing is virtually eliminated when one interjects class. It also shows that gradations of skin tone are a better predictor of sentence than the black/white dichotomy.

the United States may well be perfectly accountable by the built-in class bias of criminal justice. For instance, in every judicial system, defendants with a job, strong social ties, and a stable residence are routinely spared remand detention and given non-custodial sentences compared with similar defendants with precarious employment and housing, the rationale being that they are more likely to follow the orders of the court, less prone to reoffending, and the court does not want to undermine a stable social standing. European scholars suffer from the converse limitation: police, judicial, and correctional data do not record ethnicity.

Now, there is good reason to believe and some evidence to document that, while ethnic disparities in incarceration rose over the period 1970–2010, overt discrimination in policing, prosecution, and sentencing receded, even as it persisted.[117] But ethnic discrimination can work its way indirectly. Discrimination on the labor market affects class composition negatively since it increases unemployment and lowers occupational distribution. Discrimination on the housing market leads to concentration in neighborhoods of relegation with their inferior institutions, truncated life chances, and a flourishing criminal economy. So ethnoracial division can play a role in the production of carceral disproportionality even in the absence of direct discrimination by the police, prosecutors, and judges.

4. The fourth mechanism that I will argue *suffices* to account for the brunt of both class and ethnoracial/national disproportionality in incarceration and amplifies the force of the other three causal factors is *spatial targeting*.[118] Differential policing by place readily explains that

It is revealing that its author includes color but not class in the title of her article: Traci Burch, "Skin Color and the Criminal Justice System: Beyond Black-White Disparities in Sentencing" (2015). I return to this question in my discussion of class and race in prosecution in chapter 3, *infra*, pp. 331–48.

[117] Ryan D. King and Michael T. Light, "Have Racial and Ethnic Disparities in Sentencing Declined?" (2019).

[118] See Steve Herbert, "The Policing of Space: New Realities, Old Dilemmas" (2014) for a panorama of Anglophone studies and Elise C. Boddie, "Racially Territorial Policing in Black Neighborhoods" (2022), for a discussion of the legality of "racially territorial policing," whereby the police "criminalize Black spaces, ostensibly justifying them – and the people who live in or frequent them – as 'natural' targets for police activity." In Western Europe, see Marwan Mohammed and Laurent Mucchielli, "La police dans les 'quartiers sensibles'. Un profond malaise" (2007) on France; Tamara Dangelmaier and Eva Brauer, "Selektive Polizeiarbeit. Raumordnung und deren Einfluss auf das polizeiliche Handeln" (2020) on Germany; Paolo Grassi, *Barrio San Siro. Interpretare la violenza a Milano* (2022), on Italy; Otávio Raposo et al., "Negro drama. Racismo, segregação e violência policial nas periferias de Lisboa" (2019)

the clients of the prison come overwhelmingly from the dispossessed and disparaged districts of the metropolis where poor young men from stigmatized ethnic categories dominate the social scene of the street. Differential prosecution and sentencing based on place further solidify this double selectivity because defendants from poor districts are regulars of the court and typically lack the economic, social, and cultural capital that would mitigate penal sanction. Together, space-based policing and prosecution have created an *osmotic relationship between neighborhoods of relegation and the carceral apparatus* whereby these two institutions interpenetrate and feed one another. As a result, young men from these districts experience the prison as an extension of their neighborhoods and vice versa. This is demonstrated in the case of the black hyperghetto by a large body of ethnographic and statistical research.[119] I propose that a similar mechanism is at work in Western European cities, if with less intensity and depth. I return to this mechanism in the next section.

5. The last causal mechanism which makes this process self-sustaining is the *retroactive effects of overincarceration on differential policing and fast-track court processing* (figure 10). Residents of the urban badlands are more likely to be stopped and arrested when they have a criminal record (for reasons I discuss below). They are more likely to be charged with a statutory offense or with violating the conditions of a community sanction. Defendants who have already served time are more likely to be processed through fast-track dispositions and thus more likely to be sentenced to prison again and to receive longer sentences by virtue of recidivism statutes and the impatience of judges who get upset at seeing a defendant commit an offense again and again. They enter into what Western and Harding call "careers in criminalization" produced "through a mutually reinforcing process of system-induced harms and criminal justice traps that combine to prolong surveillance and penal control."[120]

Differential policing is rolled out in three spaces: neighborhoods of relegation, crossroads of public transit (such as railway stations and metro hubs), and border zones (between countries but also at the entrance and exit of public housing estates in the urban periphery

on Portugal; and the references in the box on "Policing the Precariat in the Nordic city."

[119] Wacquant, *Racial Domination*, chapter 3.

[120] Bruce Western and David J. Harding, "Careers in Criminalization: Reentry, Recidivism, and Repeated Incarceration" (2022).

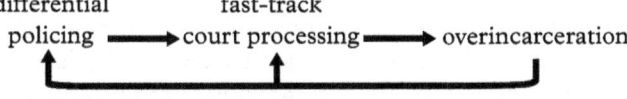

Figure 10   The causal loops between policing, court processing, and overincarceration

and along the perimeter of the black hyperghetto).[121] In these places, the police routinely conduct discriminatory stops and identity checks as well as commonly behaving in a rough and disparaging manner toward residents and passers-by, behavior that they would never engage in, and that their supervisors would never tolerate, in bourgeois districts. This is an open secret among police officers, brass, and experts that only recently has made it into public debate.[122]

Now, like it or not, it makes perfect organizational and ideological sense for the police to train their penal firepower on precincts of urban perdition, the black hyperghetto in the postindustrial United States and the districts of urban marginality in turn-of-the-century Western Europe, the *quartiers sensibles* of France, *quartieri degradati* of Italy, *Problemquartier* of Germany, *sink estates* of Great Britain, the government designated *ghettos* of Denmark, and the "vulnerable areas" (*utsatte område*) of Norway and Sweden. Several factors, cumulatively, explain the spatial selectivity that inclines the law-enforcement forces to act with special diligence, excessive force, and unbridled scorn when dealing with their residents.

1. Such areas are publicly *tarnished* by the triple stigma of place, ethnicity, and poverty. They are viewed by the broader citizenry as crucibles of social disintegration and vessels of criminality whose inhabitants are morally and socially inferior and therefore undeserving of the normal protections afforded by the law.[123] The widespread

167

---

[121] Neil and Legewie document "a higher level of police stops and lower standards of suspicion along neighborhood racial boundaries" in the implementation of the police tactic of "stop and frisk" in New York City. Roland Neil and Joscha Legewie, "Policing Neighborhood Boundaries and the Racialized Social Control of Spaces" (2024).

[122] For an account of the differential takeup of the foibles of street policing in public debate across the continent, and the political and administrative resistance to oversight, see Jacques De Maillard et al. (eds.), *The Politicization of Police Stops in Europe* (2024). For a deep case study, read Laila Abdul-Rahman et al., *Police Use of Excessive Force in Germany* (2025).

[123] Loïc Wacquant et al., "Territorial Stigmatization in Action" (2014). On differential policing in space resulting in the targeting of poor Kurds in the Turkish metropolis,

anxiety and scorn they elicit grant license to the police to act as an army of occupation rather than a force of protection.

2. Districts of perdition sport elevated levels of crime, especially public order offenses and drug possession and commerce, offenses that are out in the open and make it easy for the police to arrest people *in flagrante delicto* or claim an offense is being committed. Crime on the street is abundant and readily visible; it is low-hanging fruit compared to "crime in the suites," so it makes sense to focus on it to produce robust indicators of bureaucratic activity and success such as arrest quotas.[124]

3. The population of stigmatized zones of marginality is *judicially vulnerable*. Large numbers of young men are already entangled with the penal state. They are under correctional supervision, on probation or parole, serving community or suspended prison sentences, which can be converted into custodial sanctions with minimal bureaucratic effort. Many more have criminal records, which makes it easier for the police to arrest, book, and charge them. In the French *cités* (projects or housing estates), the police are fond of corralling "people with a *casier*" and they often know well which youths have one or not.[125] In the American hyperghetto, men on probation can be arbitrarily stopped and searched by law enforcement. They are subjected to "four-way search" clauses, which means that, *without particular motive*, the police can comb through their person, belongings, residence, and car. This makes it easy to detect marginal violations, such as possession of small amounts of narcotics or staying in an apartment harboring guns or stolen goods as well as being in the presence of another parolee (which is forbidden).

see Zeynep Gönen, *The Politics of Crime in Turkey: Neoliberalism, Police and the Urban Poor* (2016).

[124] See Peter Moskos, *Cop in the Hood: My Year Policing Baltimore's Eastern District* (2008), on the American case, and Didier Fassin, *La Force de l'ordre. Une anthropologie de la police des quartiers* (2011a), on the French case.

[125] The *casier judiciaire* is the criminal justice record attached to every individual in France: it is blank ("virgin") for those without "*antécédents judiciaires*"; it contains the list of all penal decisions for the others. It plays a key role at multiple stages in penal processing. Vanessa De Greef and Julien Pierret, *Le Casier judiciaire. Approches critiques et perspectives comparées* (2011).

"Contrôles au faciès," police profiling the French way

In France, "identity checks" (*contrôles d'identités*) are the most frequent and most discriminatory encounter between the penal state and the racialized precariat in and about the stigmatized estates of the urban periphery and at major transportation hubs. In 2021, the police conducted an estimated 47 million checks (including 15 million during a car stop). The built-in bias of these police checks, which entail stopping a person and asking them for their identification papers, and sometimes searching them (even though this is illegal according to article 78-2 of the code of penal procedure) (1), is captured by the everyday expressions *contrôle au faciès* (literally "face-based check," profiling based on phenotype) and *délit de faciès* ("face crime"). In 2007, an observational study conducted in two major Paris transport hubs (gare du Nord and the Halles) over 20 weeks and covering 525 stops showed that these checks were grossly biased by perceived origin, gender, age, dress, and the type of bag carried. A visibly black person was up to 11 times more likely to be stopped than a white person and a person perceived as Maghrebine up to 15 times more depending on the location (2). Youth dressed in typical "street" attire were 6–16 times more checked than persons in formal or casual dress. This means that black and Arab youths decked out in *banlieue* style carrying large bags were by far the preferential target of the police. The respondents who had been stopped declared being stopped "often or very often" – from 5 to 20 times in the preceding month alone.

No comparable quantitative study exists for the defamed housing projects of the urban periphery but the key variable there is the sheer *intensity and virulence* of police stops. Field reports show that the local youths are stopped and searched – a mortifying practice when it occurs in front of their friends – at astronomical rates even when police officers familiar with the neighborhood know them by sight and name. Young residents of derelict *cités* are checked so often – "every hundred meters" – that they are flooded by a sentiment of guilt: "Now, when I see the police, I feel like I have something to reproach myself for, even if I haven't done anything wrong!" Adolescents as young as 12 can be stopped and searched, asked to stand spread-eagled against a wall for frisking, and to empty their schoolbags and take off their shoes and socks to detect if they transport narcotics (3). Anthropologist Didier Fassin reveals that ID checks take on a ritualized form designed, not to achieve public safety, but to express the statutory superiority of the police, to humiliate the person checked, and thus reinforce the outside social and moral order (4). This pattern of police harassment accounts for the abrasive relationship between *banlieue* youths and the police, with boiling mutual hostility degenerating into rampant vandalism against official institutions (schools, libraries, police stations, and firefighters when they enter the estate) and street clashes exploding into periodic riots.

Long denied by state officials and politicians, the practice of discriminatory police ID-checks has been well documented and vigorously criticized over the past dozen years. Both national and European courts have condemned the French state for being biased and abusive. Legislation mandating law enforcement to produce a "stop form" (*récipissé*) recording the date, place, and motive of the check along with the ID of the police officer has been repeatedly proposed by Left parties (for instance, by François Hollande in 2012 as part of his presidential platform), but it is fiercely opposed by powerful police unions which effectively control the parameters of law enforcement at ground level. Reluctant public recognition of discriminatory police checks has thus given way to entrenched inaction (5).

1. French legislation regulating the practice is vague and multilayered, involving many procedural distinctions resulting in legal ambiguity that police officers routinely turn to their advantage. No official statistics on *contrôles d'identité* are collated and published by the authorities.
2. "The odds ratios for these minorities exceed those usually observed in comparable studies in Great Britain and the United States." René Lévy and Fabien Jobard, "Les contrôles d'identité à Paris" (2010), p. 2. The study designed by the Open Society Institute and carried out by French researchers led by Fabien Jobard and René Lévy resulted in a resounding 2009 report entitled *Police et minorités visibles. Les contrôles d'identité à Paris* (2009) that forced official acknowledgment and media endorsement of the reality of discriminatory stops.
3. On feeling guilty without reason, see Amid Khallouf and Cécile Marcel, "Vue du quartier, la prison omniprésente" (2016). On the targeting of teenagers, see Human Rights Watch, *"Ils nous parlent comme à des chiens." Contrôles de police abusifs en France* (2020).
4. Didier Fassin, *La Force de l'ordre. Une anthropologie de la police des quartiers* (2011a).
5. Magda Boutros, "Contrôles au Faciès in France: From Denial to Recognition to Inaction" (2024). For a European panorama on this question, see Jacques de Maillard et al. (eds.), *The Politicization of Police Stops in Europe* (2024).

4. A good proportion of residents are not likely to know and fully exercise their rights, such as the prerogative not to be searched without probable cause and taken to the police station without motive. Once they are brought to court, they are also inclined to accept "fast-track" justice, such as *comparution immédiate* in France and pleading guilty early in the US to get out of jail forthwith and "sleep in their own bed" or because they cannot afford the chronic disruption caused by drawn-out judicial procedures. Their precarious employment status makes it difficult to absent themselves repeatedly for court hearings; it would signal to their employers and workmates that they are embroiled with criminal justice and they could lose their jobs.[126]

171

5. In defamed districts located in the inner or outer city, the police view local teenagers and young men with open scorn and hostility. They consider them to be putative criminals if not virtual enemies. Officers assigned to these districts, most often young and inexperienced, believe that many if not most of these men are involved in street delinquency, disrespectful, hostile to them, and undeserving of standard legal protections. This is well documented across the continental countries as well as in Nordic societies (see box "Policing the precariat in the Nordic city"). As a result, police routinely engage in both physical and symbolic violence against them: they harass and bully young men, and often brutalize them; they insult them, using the informal "tu/du" term of address instead of the polite "vous/Sie" and call them racial, sexual, and social epithets (*"bougnoul"* for Arab, *"bamboula"* for black, *"pédés"* for homosexual and *"bâtard"* generically). They also provoke them to trigger misbehavior which then serves as reason for booking them at the police station under the charge of *"outrage et rébellion contre agent dépositaire de l'autorité publique."*[127] They bring them to the police station on trumped-up charges and keep them in the lockup overnight, releasing them in the morning with no charges and no record of their arrest and detention. When pursuing would-be criminals, law-enforcement personnel barge into their homes, break down doors, ransack the apartment in a search, they say, for weapons and drugs, and often rough up and disparage all residents present. In the end, "police officers consider their punitive

---

[126] Angèle Christin, *Comparutions immédiates. Enquête sur une pratique judiciaire* (2008); Issa Kohler-Hausmann, *Misdemeanorland: Criminal Courts and Social Control in an Age of Broken Windows Policing* (2018).
[127] Emmanuel Blanchard, "Contrôle au faciès. Une cérémonie de dégradation" (2014).

actions legitimate" because "they believe that justice is inefficient and judges lenient."[128]

Policing the precariat in the Nordic city

The Nordic countries are a live *experimentum crucis* on the penalization of urban marginality. They have long presented all the structural features that should mitigate if not obviate the latter: very low rates of violent crime, sharply compressed social inequalities, a strong social state, and a public culture of intolerance toward ethnic intolerance; high levels of urban civility and comparatively low levels of residential segregation; a corporatist political culture; a high degree of trust in government and law enforcement; a police that rarely use force, generally reputed for its civility and professionalism; courts following strict legal safeguards that rely broadly on noncustodial sentences; and a prison system used sparsely that offers humane conditions of reclusion and retains a real concern for rehabilitation (1). Yet, even in this region, the penal state actively targets the areas where class, ethnicity, and stigma converge to create "suitable enemies" for uses in the journalistic, political, and bureaucratic fields (2). The intensity of penalization is comparatively diminished but the processes are the same as in other advanced societies. This is particularly visible in policing as the front-stage feeder of the punishment machinery.

In Nordic societies generally, the segregated districts harboring high concentrations of non-Western immigrants and refugees and their descendants are the target of diligent and aggressive policing propelled by the public perception that young men of foreign (especially Muslim) parentage are a deviant population threatening national cohesion and in need of stern control. Youths from these districts report being stopped repeatedly by the police without plausible legal motive based on their perceived ethnicity, place of residence, manner of dress (wearing hoodies, bomber jackets, and baggy pants), or simply for hanging out in groups (e.g., in shopping malls where their phenotype and attire make them stick out) (3). It is not uncommon for them to get "logged" again and again in the police orderly book, provoking exasperation, despondency, and hostility. Repeat police contact makes these young men feel like they are criminals, even when they engage in no deviant activity, perpetually suspect in

---

[128] Fassin, *Punir, une passion contemporaine*, p. 47.

the eyes of the majority population. Being overpoliced damages their trust in law enforcement, their confidence in procedural justice, and their sense of belonging to the civic community (4).

A panoramic article reporting on "minor harassments" in Nordic nations confirms that the police and youths from the urban badlands engage in "low-level reciprocal intimidations and subtle provocations, exhibited in specific forms of body language, attitudes, and a range of expressions to convey derogatory views" of one another (5). These grating interactions partake of "a shared language of insults" that assumes a ritualized character twisting everyday relations with the police. Their periodic irruption in the media and in political debate, and their episodic explosion into full-out rioting, validates the pernicious public view that young men from these districts are miscreants involved in crime, deal drugs, and run gangs. This dynamic is rigorously identical to that observed over the past quarter-century in France's forlorn *banlieues*, except that in France urban mutinies, invariably caused by incidents between youths and the police, are more frequent and more destructive (6).

In Norway, police street stops and searches of young immigrant men living in the desolate districts of Oslo's periphery routinely result in mutual invective, resistance, and bystander involvement, leading police officers to call for reinforcement, thus escalating the conflictual situation. This pattern has now been documented for some two decades. Expressions and gestures of disrespect toward the police commonly lead to arrest – the latter call that scenario "talking your way into custody" – whereas officers feel warranted to use profanity, sexual slights, and ethnic slurs on the job (7). Targets who are "repeat customers" of law enforcement are routinely treated with more vigor and callousness than others. Ethnic profiling in the city extends to driving: a dark-skinned motorist in a luxury car is a surefire recipe for getting arrested on automatic suspicion of criminal activity, starting with vehicle theft and continuing with visions of organized crime (8). Police officers fervently insist that they are not "racist" but their work culture is replete with deprecatory ethnic stereotypes, such as the collective belief that "'Moroccans are pickpockets and never admit guilt'; 'Somalians chew khat, don't want to work and beat up their wives'; 'Kosovo Albanians are drug dealers'" (9).

In Sweden, young men from the officially designated "vulnerable areas" resent being treated differently by the police based on their place of residence. They gather from personal experience that law enforcement varies in both amenity and intensity in the different

173

parts of the city (10). First, the police are a constant presence in their neighborhoods and treat them as "suspects" regardless of their conduct. Next, when they travel in other parts of town, they are immediately spotted as men from the stigmatized redoubts of the urban periphery and thus perceived as vectors of dread and danger, to be handled accordingly. Again and again, they are treated very differently than their "blonde friend with blue eyes." Finally, they recognize that their neighborhoods are both *over*-policed, in terms of surveillance and harassment, and *under*-policed, in terms of personal safety and public tranquility. As for the police, they deflect the idea that they discriminate on grounds of race by stressing that they are policing a problematic place and not a shady people – proof positive that space serves as the crucial mediation through which the penal state enforces the social order and produces joint class and ethnic disproportionality in punishment (11).

In Denmark, young men from the government-labeled "ghettos" describe being routinely subjected by the police to the unnecessary use of force, inconsistent violence, and variegated insults (12). They complain that the actions of law enforcement are unpredictable and illegible, especially in secluded spaces such as backstreets, police cars, and the detention cells in the police station. These actions are also especially pervasive as the official designation of a neighborhood as a "ghetto" entails enhanced policing, the doubling of penal sanctions for most crimes, and increased prison sentences instead of fines (13). While they bemoan physical brutality such as body searches, it is the symbolic degradation entailed in raw law enforcement that weighs the heaviest on the targeted men. Rough policing, repeated again and again, entails an assault on their moral integrity and personal dignity. As in Norway and Sweden, the negative image of the Danish neighborhood bleeds into the devalorization of their residents which activates the excessive use of physical and symbolic force taking the form of principled suspicion, street harassment, verbal affront, and personal mortification. As for the police officers who operate in "ghetto" clusters, they insist that residents cannot be trusted and express hostility toward them despite earnest efforts to build rapport through techniques of "soft policing" (14). Insults, provocations, group fear, and emotional strain, it turns out, travel both ways.

To sum up, the manner of law enforcement in the stigmatized neighborhoods of perdition of the Nordic city demonstrates that the police apply not only special surveillance and disproportionate physical force on their residents, but also symbolic violence causing the diminution of the self and an assault on personal dignity. While mild by international standards, the *macro-aggressions* by the police are accompanied by the *micro-aggressions* of opprobrium and invalidation which, taken cumulatively over time, erode personal integrity, fray social bonds and undermine trust in the state (15). Low-level penalization effectively truncates the citizenship of its targets and contributes to creating a dual opposition between "us" and "them" pursuant to which the residents of neighborhoods of relegation are pictured in the public imagination as "the enemy within."

1. On the spirited debate about the outlier status and benignity of Nordic penality, see the elaboration of the thesis by John Pratt, "Scandinavian Exceptionalism in an Era of Penal Excess – Part I: The Nature and Roots of Scandinavian Exceptionalism" (2008a), and "Scandinavian Exceptionalism in an Era of Penal Excess – Part II: Does Scandinavian Exceptionalism Have a Future?" (2008b); Tapio Lappi-Seppälä, "Penal Policies in the Nordic Countries 1960–2010" (2012); and John Pratt and Anna Eriksson, *Contrasts in Punishment: An Explanation of Anglophone Excess and Nordic Exceptionalism* (2014). For a reassessment taking stock of adverse class, ethnic, political, and punishment trends, see Thomas Ugelvik and Jane Dullum (eds.), *Penal Exceptionalism? Nordic Prison Policy and Practice* (2011); Vanessa Barker, "Nordic Exceptionalism Revisited: Explaining the Paradox of a Janus-faced Penal Regime" (2013); Victor Lund Shammas, "The Rise of a More Punitive State: On the Attenuation of Norwegian Penal Exceptionalism in an Era of Welfare State Transformation" (2016a); John Pratt, "The Nordic Exceptionalism Thesis Revisited" (2022); and Ben Crewe et al., "Nordic Penal Exceptionalism: A Comparative Empirical Analysis" (2023).
2. I borrow the expression "suitable enemies" from Nils Christie's penetrating paper by that title (1986).
3. Randi Solhjell et al., "'We Are Seen as a Threat': Police Stops of Young Ethnic Minorities in the Nordic Countries" (2019). Strikingly, some of these youths internalize the gaze of suspecting outsiders when they concede that it is their fault that they adopt the "gangster look."
4. Elsa Saarikkomäki et al., "Dealing with Police Stops: How Young People with Ethnic Minority Backgrounds Narrate their Ways of Managing Over-Policing in the Nordic Countries" (2023).
5. Mie Birk Haller et al., "Minor Harassments: Ethnic Minority Youth in the Nordic Countries and their Perceptions of the Police" (2020a); Mie Birk Haller et al., "Experiencing Police Violence and Insults: Narratives from Ethnic Minority Men in Denmark" (2020b).
6. Carl-Ulrik Schierup et al., "Reading the Stockholm Riots – A Moment for Social Justice?" (2014); Julien Talpin, *La Colère des quartiers populaires. Enquête socio-historique à Roubaix* (2024); Fabien Truong and Gérôme Truc, *Grands ensemble. Violence, solidarité et ressentiment dans les quartiers populaires* (2025).
7. Ragnhild Sollund, "Racialisation in Police Stop and Search Practice: The Norwegian Case" (2006), p. 287.

8. In a study of the police in Gothenburg, Sweden, one of the officers explained frankly that "if you are a young immigrant man driving a dark Audi A6 and live in one of the suburbs you can expect to be stopped once a week." David Wästerfors and Veronika Burcar Alm, "'They are Harsher to Me than to my Friend who is Blonde': Police Critique among Ethnic Minority Youth in Sweden" (2020), p. 172.
9. Sollund, "Racialisation in Police Stop and Search Practice," p. 281.
10. Wästerfors and Alm, "'They are Harsher to Me than to my Friend who is Blonde'."
11. Space and race are fused in police perceptions of "problem populations," as shown by the common use of ethnic slurs, racist stereotypes, and stigmatizing shop talk among Swedish officers. Sara Uhnoo, "Within 'The Tin Bubble': The Police and Ethnic Minorities in Sweden" (2015). On the prevalence and variants of race-talk among law-enforcement officers in direct contact with stigmatized ethnic populations, read Francois Bonnet and Clotilde Caillault, "The Invader, the Enemy within and They-Who-Must-Not-Be-Named: How Police Talk about Minorities in Italy, the Netherlands and France" (2015).
12. In 2010, the Danish government published an official list of "ghettos" (*ghettoliste*), that is, clusters of more than 1,000 residents with high rates of non-Western immigrants, poverty, unemployment, social housing, educational failure, and crime, targeted by special policies aiming to prevent the formation of "parallel societies" (*parallelsamfund*). See Troels Schultz Larsen and Kristian Nagel Delica, *Fragmenting Cities: The State, Territorial Stigmatization and Urban Marginality* (2024).
13. Haller et al., "Experiencing Police Violence and Insults: Narratives from Ethnic Minority Men in Denmark" (2020b).
14. Tobias Kammersgaard et al., "Community Policing in Danish 'Ghetto' Areas: Trust and Distrust between the Police and Ethnic Minority Youth" (2023).
15. See Derald Wing Sue and Lisa Spanierman, *Microaggressions in Everyday Life* (2020), who distinguish between microassault, microinsult, and microinvalidation. Didier Fassin calls these types of assault on the self "moral violence" (*La Force de l'ordre. Une anthropologie de la police des quartiers*, 2011a).

Structural osmosis

In advanced societies, *neighborhoods of relegation and carceral institutions have become linked* by a triple relationship of structural continuity, functional equivalency, and cultural contamination through the mediation of aggressive policing, diligent prosecution, and hasty incarceration. While the *scale and intensity* of the phenomenon are vastly different on the two sides of the Atlantic, reaching a climax in the case of the black American hyperghetto,[129] the *mechanisms of*

[129] Wacquant, *Racial Domination*, chapter 4. Four factors explain this chasm: the

interpenetration and the results are the same in the United States and in Europe: the membrane between the prison, and even more so the jail, and the residential zones of racialized marginality has become porous such that young men captured by the penal state now circulate along a *carceral continuum* spanned by the two institutions.[130]

The vast majority of inmates on both shores of the Atlantic come from poor neighborhoods in large cities and, among them, a *subset* of the most derelict and defamed districts widely perceived by the broader society as crucibles of sociomoral disintegration, nests of vice and violence that call for intensive law enforcement.[131] Moreover, the higher the incarceration rate, the greater the clustering of former convicts by place. In the United States, the Million Dollar Block Project has dramatized the spatial concentration of hyper-incarceration by rendering visible its extravagant financial cost: the notion refers to a map of city blocks where the government is expending over one million dollars yearly by imprisoning an astronomical percentage of their residents.[132] These blocks are invariably located in that city's poorest and most segregated zones. A study of the geography of punishment in Chicago shows similarly that convicts are overwhelmingly recruited from the districts with the highest levels of crime, unemployment, racial isolation, high-school dropouts, female-headed households, welfare recipiency, and urban blight, and then return there upon release from the prisons located in rural areas in downstate Illinois.

177

extraordinary rates of penal confinement, the depth of poverty and segregation, the rigidity of ethnoracial division, and the strength of moralism in public life in the United States compared to Europe. The phenomenon is even more intense yet diffuse in the metropolis of the global South, where the multiplex exchanges between the prison and the neighborhood are amplified by the extreme porosity of carceral establishments (grotesquely overcrowded, underfunded, and understaffed), the prevalence of acute poverty, and the ubiquity of lumpen violence against the backdrop of informality, as shown by the Venezuelan criminologist Andrés Antillano, "In/Out: Revisiting the Relationships Between Prisons and Slums in Latin America" (2024).

[130] This thesis goes against Goffman's influential vision of the carceral world as a "total institution" closed unto itself. Erving Goffman, *Asylums: Essays on the Social Situation of Mental Patients and other Inmates* (1961). The fluidity of relations crossing prison walls is documented by Gilles Chantraine, *Par-delà les murs. Expériences et trajectoires en maison d'arrêt* (2004). A subtle study of "the activation of wide-ranging carceralized networks bringing kinship and neighborhood into the prison as well as the prison into the domestic world" in the Portuguese metropolis is Manuela Ivone Cunha, *Entre o bairro e a prisão. Tráfico e trajectos* (2002).

[131] Wacquant et al., "Territorial Stigmatization in Action."

[132] Brett Story, "The Prison in the City: Tracking the Neoliberal Life of the 'Million Dollar Block'" (2016).

Fully 54 percent of convicts going back to Chicago in 2005 settled in only seven of 77 districts, a distribution that projects almost perfectly onto the perimeter of the imploding black ghetto of the South Side and West Side.[133]

In France, a geographical study of the western periphery of Paris tracking the address of inmates aptly entitled "The prison, a '*cité*' with bars" found that areas of high incarceration were larger municipalities with a prevalence of working-class, poor, and immigrant households residing in large public housing estates (*cités*). The map of incarceration is a near-exact match with the map of "sensitive urban zones" (ZUS, the official designation for deteriorating neighborhoods targeted by the central-state policy of urban regeneration). The socio-demographic profile of their respective male populations is virtually identical. The warden of the jail serving that territory was well aware of that correspondence as he noted in his 2008 official annual report that

> the establishment is typical of the Parisian outer-city (*banlieue*), urbanized, impacted by the violence of so-called sensitive neighborhoods and by actors in the parallel economy. The problems encountered daily in the management of inmates are, moreover, directly related to the physical geography of the district, [with over half of the carceral population coming from the ZUS of the northern and southern tips of the district,] a geographical distribution that naturally fosters rivalries between bands [from these two zones] composed of young men who know each other perfectly because they grew up together and have committed crimes in highly concentrated territories based on a strong logic of identity.[134]

One of the first things that these young men do upon walking through the gates of the jail or prison is to scan the faces around them to pluck "homies" from their "stomping ground" with whom to ally, seek safety, and commiserate. They effectively reconstitute neighborhood networks of sociability, status, and protection behind bars. Stateside, Patrick Lopez-Aguado opens his ethnography of "racial

[133] Robert J. Sampson and Charles Loeffler, "Punishment's Place: The Local Concentration of Mass Incarceration" (2010); Christy Visher and Jill Farrell, *Chicago Communities and Prisoner Reentry* (2005).
[134] Annual report of the jail of Hauts-de-Seine (2008), cited by Lucie Bony, "La prison, une 'cité avec des barreaux'? Continuum socio-spatial par-delà les murs" (2015), pp. 281–2. For a fuller report, see Lise Périno, *L'Impact de la prison dans les quartiers en politique de la ville* (2013).

sorting and the spillover of carceral identity" into dispossessed districts in a poor city of California with this typical scene:

> A corrections officer finally comes for him and escorts him to a large gymnasium lined with rows of double bunks and filled with hundreds of inmates. Not sure why he's been brought here or who else is here, he sits on a bed feeling alone and unsure of what he is going to do. But hearing someone yelling behind him, Frank turns around and realizes something.
>
> He already knows a lot of the men in here. "[I hear] Hey Frank! And I look. My heart was like thank you! I was like thank you God!" So many years later Frank would laugh as he remembers how relieved he felt in that moment, and how surprised he was to see so many familiar faces in the prison with him. "[W]hen I got there, to Jamestown, I knew practically everybody in there. From all the years I was growing up, all from the Eastside. [I knew a] lotta guys there."
>
> Soon he hears more and more calls of "Frank!" "Hey man, what's going on?!" "Frank!" "What's up?!" Many remember him from high school as one of the students who always got good grades. "Man what are you doing here?" All he can think to tell them is "I got caught up." Frank finds several of the guys he grew up with in his neighborhood are already here, meaning that he won't have to face the prison alone. Their presence helps him feel much less fearful about how the next three years are going to unfold. But with the unexpected support Frank finds with this group, being associated with them also exposes him to new tensions and conflicts, and in some cases violence.[135]

Residential acquaintanceship plays a similar role in the French jail where inmates who knew each other on the outside cluster on the inside. Even when they do not have a direct personal tie, the *cité* from which they hail and its reputation ("hot" or "calm") is key to their place in the pecking order behind bars. "Where do you come from, where did you grow up?" is among the first questions that a jailee will ask a new entrant to try and locate him.[136] One of them likens affiliation with a *cité* to "forming a clan based on the neighborhood." The correctional authorities take due account of the geographical origin of inmates to distribute them in matching two-men cells and segregate them in the wings of buildings. Through informal communicative channels, the "new fish" will inform his estate buddies of his

---

[135] Patrick Lopez-Aguado, *Stick Together and Come Back Home: Racial Sorting and the Spillover of Carceral Identity* (2018), pp. 1–2.
[136] Lucie Bony, "La prison, 'une cité avec barreaux': entretien" (2016a).

arrival and then maneuver with the jail administration to be transferred to the same building, tier, or cell. So much so that the guards manipulate territorial affiliation as a means of managing bodies and securing carceral tranquility.[137]

"Prison is a 'hood' within a 'hood'"

A former inmate from the defamed periphery of eastern Paris explains: "Prison is a 'hood' within a 'hood' . . . From *cité* to *cité*, we all get to know each other over time. In fact, I found the same faces as when I was [incarcerated as] a minor. There were also people I knew from before prison. People from [the stigmatized working-class city of] Aubervilliers, but not only: I found cousins, my uncle and even my brother-in-law. Some ended up in the same cell as their father or brother!"

Observatoire International des Prisons, "João, 30 ans: 'De cité à cité, on se connaît tous avec le temps en prison'" [from estate to estate, we all get to know each other doing time in prison] (2016).

No wonder French inmates commonly analogize the prison to a "*cité*," a "big *cité*" or a "best-of the *cités*" with its exacerbated mix of sociability, rivalry, solidarity, daring, flamboyance, and hustling based on place; a milieu confined yet organically tied to the neighborhood of provenance where one will soon export the social bonds and criminal skills acquired behind walls. Residential origin is thus the basis of personal reputation, social affiliation, and cultural identification and it combines with age, carceral seniority, nationality, and the type of offense to shape the inmate hierarchy. But then, on both sides of the Atlantic, carceral experience also intensifies the distrust and disdain that the new inmates feel for the justice bureaucracy – bailiffs, attorneys, judges, and guards. They only have to look around them to see a sea of black and brown faces, with virtually no whites, to validate the sense of judicial *discrimination by race and place* they felt first-hand as they moved through the stages of penal processing. A French inmate originating from the Parisian periphery on his second stint behind bars explains: "There's a hatred of the police, of magistrates, which means that Jean-Pierre or Paul, who live downtown, got a sentence

---

[137] Bony, "La prison, une 'cité avec des barreaux'?," pp. 285–6.

three times shorter than Mamadou or Mohammed who live in a *cité*. For no apparent reason."[138]

In her fine-grained ethnography of a juvenile facility outside of Paris in the late 2000s, the anthropologist Léonore Le Caisne confirms that residence in a reputed housing estate is the primary mode of affiliation behind bars, going so far as to call the prison "an extension of the *cité*."[139] The first question the teenage inmates ask one another when they meet is, "Where you from (*T'es d'où*)?" They are stunned at first to find so many familiar faces as they come into the facility. They run into buddies, neighbors, and acquaintances from other *cités*. "At first, the reunion surprises and unsettles the boys: they are not alone in their confinement; their suffering is not unique. Then they get used to reunions, enjoy them and look forward to them feverishly. Above all, these 'acquaintances' from the outside reassure them. They are landmarks and provide some protection from the feeling of exclusion caused by incarceration. They enable them to situate themselves and others. They also open up the prison space and bring a little light into the abyss into which the boy has fallen . . . Above all, thanks to this reunion, the individual and personal experience becomes akin to a collective and social destiny for the members of an age group."[140]

To come from the same *cité* and even from the same building creates a shared history which erases the context of the prison and defeats its purpose insofar as it undermines the individual nature of punishment. A shared neighborhood origin binds the boys into a defiant collective. It creates a buffer against the correctional staff and the supervising judges and it erodes the stigma of incarceration.

Ethnicity crosscuts residential identity. Boys of North African and sub-Saharan African parentage dominate the inmate population numerically and culturally. They set themselves apart from "the Chinese" (feared and considered rich), the "Romanians" (scorned and considered poor), and the "French" (considered weak and isolated). Embedded in *cité* networks, they come to perceive their offenses, not as individual acts for which they are personally accountable, but associated with the neighborhood group and its street culture. "They persuade themselves that delinquency is common to all youths," that "everybody messes around," that passing through the prison is a normal landmark in their pathway toward adulthood and the

181

---

[138] Lucie Bony, "Sortir du continuum carcéral" (2016b), p. 104.
[139] Léonore Le Caisne, "La prison, une annexe de la cité? L'expérience collective de détenus mineurs" (2009).
[140] Ibid., p. 537.

conventional life to which they aspire once they cross the threshold of adulthood.[141]

Once they are released (from remand detention or after serving their sentence), these men typically return to the same urban badlands where rekindled social ties and renewed economic pressure combine to prod many of them to resume criminal activities that will ensnare them further in the mesh of criminal justice. They also share their prison experiences with kin, friends, and associates, serving in effect as teachers in the evolving social mores and cultural schemas of the carceral world for the next generation.[142] Even when they "go legit" ("*filer droit*" in French), they are subject again to constant and abrasive contact with the police, often triggering repeat processing by the courts, which together destabilize their life strategies and deepen their marginality as well as reviving an acute feeling of injustice. They then realize that the only way to avoid falling back into "the life" and escaping the clutches of the penal state is to leave the neighborhood for good and to relocate far beyond its reach. But, for many, the tropism of the *cité* is too strong, they miss their buddies and their family, and so they end up returning to their stomping ground, which feels like an open-air prison: "We were born here, we will die here."[143]

The black hyperghetto on the US side and the ZUS on the French side are thus deeply embroiled with the prison as shown in figure 11. They are the sites of a constant circulation of cultural constructs, social relations, and tainted bodies that cross their boundaries and make each part of the normal horizon of the other. French inmates use the metaphor of the "*engrenage*," the gearing or the cogwheel, to

182

---

[141] Ibid., p. 541.
[142] Forrest Stuart and Reuben Jonathan Miller, "The Prisonized Old Head: Intergenerational Socialization and the Fusion of Ghetto and Prison Culture" (2017). This is in contrast with young German men of Turkish parentage involved in drug dealing in one of Francfort's *Problemquartier*: they ostracize and look down upon those who have done time in jail and prison as they consider them incompetent (they got caught by the police) and untrustworthy (they may now be police snitches). Sandra Bucerius, *Unwanted: Muslim Immigrants, Dignity, and Drug Dealing* (2014), pp. 102–4.
[143] Amid Khallouf and Cécile Marcel, "Vue du quartier, la prison omniprésente" (2016). Relocation is strongly linked to the life cycle. As convicts age, they can no longer compete with "young blood" in the street economy and they get worn out by repeated prison stints. They are also more likely to find stable partners, found families, and seek to improve the everyday circumstances and educational opportunities of their children. Their aspirations typically include buying a house with a garden so their offspring will not run the streets.

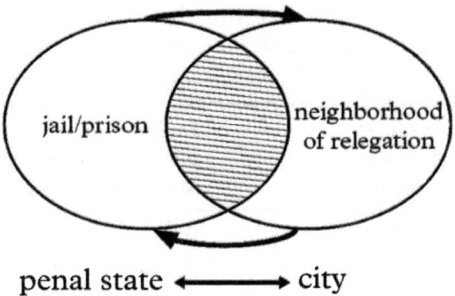

Figure 11   The interpenetration of derelict neighborhood
and voracious prison

describe their sense of being caught up in an inexorable machinery that gradually tugs them into a spiral of crime and confinement.[144] This is the existential expression of the *structural osmosis between the city's underbelly and the carceral archipelago*, resulting from the spatial bias of the penal state, which makes the jail and the prison quintessential urban institutions – something that both criminologists and sociologists of the metropolis have steadfastly ignored even as it was staring them in the face.[145]

Paper penality versus street penality

I now come to drawing out the implications of the meshing of marginality, ethnicity, and territory for the day-to-day operations of the penal state. Criminal law presents itself as a sanctified body of texts whose application is by quintessence socially invariant.[146] In the day-to-day reality of judicial work, however, it becomes split into two distinct tracks corresponding to two readings of criminal procedure, two class positions (themselves racialized) and two sets of collective expectations as to the bureaucratic handling, social relations, and

---

[144] Gilles Chantraine, "Prison, désaffiliation, stigmates. L'engrenage carcéral de l'"inutile au monde'" (2003); idem, *Par-delà les murs. Expériences et trajectoires en maison d'arrêt* (2010).
[145] Loïc Wacquant, *Bourdieu in the City: Challenging Urban Theory* (2023), pp. 137–63.
[146] The social production of neutrality as anchor for the autonomous pole of the juridical field is discussed by Pierre Bourdieu, "La force du droit. Eléments pour une sociologie du champ juridique" (1986).

Table 9

The sociolegal opposition between paper penality
and street penality.

Rechtsstaat bourgeoisie paper penality	Polizeistaat racialized precariat street penality
principled	discretionary
dignified	degrading
out of custody	in custody
private attorney	public defender
affinity, trust	distance, distrust
slow time	rushed time
open court	jail
judge	police officer
full-scale trial	fast-track processing
presumed innocent	presumed guilty

likely outcomes of cases. I call these two tracks *paper penality* and *street penality*.[147] Their ideal-typical counterposition runs as follows (see table 9).

Paper penality, or "punishment by the book," is aimed at defendants coming from the higher regions of social and physical space. Its targets belong to the *bourgeoisie* living in reputable neighborhoods so they possess the economic, cultural, and social capital needed to quickly become aware of their rights and to exercise them fully. For this, they typically appear *out of custody*, given that they can pay bail if one has been set or because they are first-time offenders. This makes a world of difference in how they are treated by the court and enables them to be patient without penalty. They hire a *private defense attorney* who has the skills, experience, and time to treat their case with due attention.

[147] As previously noted, this duality echoes Markus Dubber's distinction between *Rechtsstaat* and *Polizeistaat* as two readings of criminal procedure elaborated in his book *The Dual Penal State* (2018). But, for Dubber, this distinction is purely juridical and not social; it does not identify two socioethnic paths. The opposition between paper and street penality should not be confused with Roscoe Pound's germinal opposition between "law in books" and "law in action": both brands of punishment are law in action, only deployed differently in space, time, form and target.

They develop with this attorney a relationship based on class affinity and personal civility backed by trust in professional expertise.[148]

The defense attorney will appear on behalf of his client at pre-trial hearings, thus sparing him the loss of face, emotional stress, and practical hassle of repeated presence in court. He works all around to smooth the sharp angles of the law. Being free, bourgeois defendants can track down eventual witnesses and otherwise gather information mitigating the charges they face. They can also offer restitution to their victims or enter court-sponsored "programs" (such as an anger management class or a residential drug rehabilitation facility) on their own initiative to signal to the prosecutor and the judge that they are proactively taking steps to recognize and remedy their offense. Their attorney can "age the case," meaning push its resolution back in hopes that emotions cool down, victims and witnesses change their minds, forget key details about the crime, or otherwise move on with their lives or move out of town.[149]

The bureaucratic center of dignified paper penalty is the *open courtroom* as haven of formal neutrality and stage for the ceremonial of justice as intrinsic fairness. It enshrines the sacredness of legal texts, the imperative of procedural conformity and due process, full access by the accused to judicial resources, the autonomy of the individual, and the strict individualization of sanction. It is incarnated by the *judge*, committed to impartiality, whose behavior is impeccably professional and courteous, sometimes even apologetic and deferential – the defendant is, after all, a social equal.[150] The affinity of habituses guarantees smooth cultural agreement and behavioral concordance. The prosecutor will also be more attentive to the files of bourgeois offenders for the simple reason that they are rare and so they will pique her interest. She will wonder what led a person of such class and status to commit a crime, which she will presume was a "one-off." She will thus take due account of the "equities" of the case that may explain such unexpected deviation. Dignified paper penalty works to minimize personal hardship, bureaucratic irritation, and the collateral consequences of judicial processing. Its legal climax

185

---

[148] Matthew Clair, *Privilege and Punishment: How Race and Class Matter in Criminal Court* (2020), chapter 3.

[149] The private attorney of bourgeois defendants also has the latitude to diligently seek out prosecutors and cut "backdoor deals" before the case is even charged or reach a deferred prosecution agreement.

[150] This is one of the bases of leniency toward white-collar criminals according to Edwin H. Sutherland's classic formulation in "White Collar Criminality" (1940).

is the *trial* which maximizes the ability of the defendant to get an individualized hearing of their case and thus to obtain the most fitting outcome. The collective assumption all along is that the defendant is entitled to the presumption of innocence and will avoid prison time, especially as he is likely to have a clean prior record. Criminologists have written much about "cumulative disadvantage" in justice processing but they have not detected "cumulative *advantage*" as accrued under paper penality.[151]

Street penality is criminal law as routinely applied to defendants located at the bottom of the triple hierarchy of class, ethnicity, and place, most of whom are deemed indigent by the court and effectively presumed guilty until proven innocent. Its targets are in every country drawn from the *racialized precariat*, shorn of capital in all of its forms, chief among them the symbolic capital of self-worth, social esteem, and group prestige. These targets are first subjected to the arbitrary and discretionary application of police force translating into social degradation – whereas "paper penality" preserves the autonomy and dignity of their bourgeois counterparts. Offenders from the precariat are defended by overworked and under-resourced *court-appointed counsel* for whom one case of indigent defendant looks just like a hundred others and who, however motivated they may be, have little time to confabulate with their clients and investigate their case beyond the bare police report justifying arraignment. The relationship of the indigent defendant with his public defender is stamped by distance and distrust as well as ethnic and sexual tension, based on the assumption by the former that the latter is incompetent, uncaring, and even conspiring with the prosecutor.[152]

The bureaucratic center of degrading paper penality is the *jail* where the typical poor offender lands after arrest and will sojourn while his case slowly winds its way through the court because he cannot pay bail or otherwise proffer the "sureties" needed to be released on his own recognizance. But this brand of punishment is first delivered by the police, who routinely trample on the formal rights and social dig-

---

[151] Megan C. Kurlychek and Brian D. Johnson, "Cumulative Disadvantage in the American Criminal Justice System" (2019).

[152] Paul B. Wice, *Public Defenders and the American Justice System* (2005), pp. 134–43. Counter-intuitively, black defendants in California county court sometimes request a white male public defender because they believe that they are more competent and have more court moxie than black and female defenders. Some even request a Jewish defender based on the belief that "they are smarter." This inevitably creates durable discontent since defendants do not get to choose their court-appointed attorney.

nity of defendants caught in the urban badlands. It is amplified by the chaotic and oppressive atmosphere of the jail, where the physical integrity, self-respect, and psychological health of the defendant are under constant assault.[153] Next, it is deployed by the prosecutor who rifles through charging documents while paying more attention to the offense (to detect "proof problems") than the offender (especially if he is a "frequent flyer"); the judge who prioritizes fast processing to "clear the docket" and treats in-custody defendants with guarded impatience and subtle condescension; and the probation agent or parole officer who applies rules rigidly even when they hamper the reintegration efforts of the offender.[154] Members of the precariat have the wrong habitus to do well in open court and to navigate its extensions smoothly: they lack the cultural understanding and social skills needed to fulfill the role of the duly deferential and repentant defendant.

187

To add structural nuance, street penalty itself is further *diffracted along a class gradient internal to the urban proletariat*. The latter can be roughly divided into three fractions with labile and porous boundaries: the solid working class, the shifting precariat, and the street drifters. These fractions have different material anchorages, cultural orientations, and degrees of integration in conventional society – or distance from it – which translate into costs and benefits on the penal front because of their different ability to respond to the police on the street and to the court's class-inflected entreaties and requirements, such as having a stable job and documented residence to be released from jail pretrial, or a strong "support system" to benefit from diversion, to be put on probation, or to get a lower sentence. Their social and cultural differentiation is the foundation of the taken-for-granted class discrimination that is openly practiced by the criminal court as part of its normal functioning (a point I develop in chapter 3 in my discussion of class and race in prosecution, *infra*, pp. 318–31 and 331–49).

The most distinctive feature of street penalty is that it pushes defendants onto the fast-track adjudication of their case through streamlined procedures abridging their rights for the sake of bureaucratic efficiency: plea bargaining at the first hearing in the United States, *comparution*

---

[153] Didier Fassin, *L'Ombre du monde. Une anthropologie de la condition carcérale* (2015); Michael L. Walker, *Indefinite: Doing Time in Jail* (2022).
[154] On the drift of French probation agents from social work to correctional control, see Yasmine Bouagga, "Le métier de conseiller d'insertion et de probation. Dans les coulisses de l'État pénal?" (2012). Mona Lynch documents a similar transition among parole agents in California in "Waste Managers? The New Penology, Crime Fighting, and Parole Agent Identity" (1998).

immédiate and *plaider coupable* in France, *Verständigung* ("understanding") in Germany, *tilståelsessak* ("confession case") in Norway. Such *accelerated and simplified procedures*, evoking an assembly line even though they are in fact tailored to individual cases, mark the legal climax of street penality; they constitute a clear deviation from, if not a negation of, full-fledged justice – in the public imagination, but also in the idealized vision of court professionals, criminal justice remains epitomized by the pageantry of the trial. It also formally establishes guilt beyond doubt since the accused acknowledge their culpability.[155] For serious cases and matters involving recidivism, there was no doubt all along that the accused would serve time in jail or prison.

188

In the French fast-track procedure of *comparution immédiate*, persons accused of a flagrant low-level offense – vandalism, driving under the influence (DUI), theft, possession or distribution of narcotics, "willful violence" (against a household member or a police officer), simple burglary, insults and threats or rebellion against law enforcement, violating immigration statutes – are rushed before a court within 48 hours of their arrest (and sometimes on the same day).[156] They have a face-to-face meeting with the assistant prosecutor in their holding cell at the courthouse during which the latter notifies them of the charges filed. Next, they are subjected to a "quick social investigation" (*ESR, enquête sociale rapide*, the official name) based on an hour-long interview by a psychologist and a hasty inquiry farmed out to a third-sector agency entrusted with checking the social and family profile of the defendant.

The accused are introduced to their court-appointed defender on the spot in the morning. These attorneys are young and inexperienced because *comparution immédiate* is used as a training ground for counsel. They have neither the time nor the means to dig into the case so they look for procedural irregularities and try to glean mitigating information from their client. Defendants are then tried in the afternoon by a panel of three judges in batches of three or four in proceedings lasting 20–40 minutes for each case (for sentences of up to ten years of reclusion given recidivism laws).

[155] In the US, by pleading guilty the defendant gives up his right to an appeal. This is not so in England, Germany, and France, where the accused has ten days to file an appeal. But, in practice, poor defendants do not have the economic resources and judicial know-how to contest the outcome of their case and they typically want nothing more to do with the court.

[156] For a fuller account, read Christin, *Comparutions immédiates*, and Didier Fassin et al., *Juger, réprimer, accompagner. Essai sur la morale de l'État* (2013), chapter 1 and passim. One in five cases adjudicated by French judges in 2019 was handled through this route (Émilie Le Caignec, *L'Activité judiciaire pénale de 2012 à 2019* [2021]).

Hearings take place from 1pm to 9pm, sometimes later. "The stake of the courtroom debate in *comparution immédiate* is not so much the culpability of the defendant (the latter is considered guilty *a priori*, in the absence of proof to the contrary) as the weighing of the appropriate sanction to inflict."[157] After private deliberations, the judges renders their decision in court at the end of that same day for the dozen cases tried. They stand aloof from the whole proceedings; their main objective is to manage time and to regulate flows. Their decisions hinge crucially on their perception of the accused during the proceedings, whom they divide into two folk categories: the "dangerous perpetrator" (*prévenu dangereux*) and the "accidental offender" (*accident de parcours*).[158]

Defendants can opt out of this procedure at the outset and request a full prosecutorial inquest and trial. But the latter would take place three to six weeks down the road and so poor defendants and foreigners kept in remand detention (because they cannot provide the "sureties" indicating that they will show up at their next hearing) invariably opt for a quick resolution of their matter. As with plea bargaining in the US, pretrial detention serves as a lever to resolve cases quickly. *Comparution immédiate* is fast justice for crimes of precarity, poverty, and administrative irregularity, typically resulting in a short prison sentence, which in most cases ends up being suspended.[159] No bourgeois defendant would agree in their right mind to take this route to adjudication.

189

Paper penalty is tendentially Weberian: formal, rationalized, predictable, affectively neutral, dominated by the professional staff of the justice bureaucracy. Street penalty is recognizably Bourdieusian: patterned by social space, roiled by the clash of habituses, driven by struggles over judicial capital, a vehicle for the workings of symbolic power. Their duality partakes of the structural bifurcation of the penal state discussed in the first chapter (see *supra*, pp. 110–17). It is perceived and projected though a series of homological oppositions – sacred/profane, pure/polluted, high/low, straight/crooked, and judge's chamber/holding cell – that reinforce each other through their very contraposition. Most importantly, their *divergence is not a deviation from judicial normalcy*, as commonly conceded, but a *normal feature of criminal justice* in advanced societies. Notwithstanding the hallowed

[157] Chowra Makaremi, "Le droit de punir. L'appréciation de la peine en comparution immédiate" (2013), p. 50.
[158] Christin, *Comparutions immédiates*, p. 166.
[159] Laurent Mucchielli and Émilie Raquet, "Les comparutions immédiates au TGI de Nice, ou la prison comme unique réponse à une délinquance de misère" (2021).

self-understanding of liberal democracies, these societies lack the civic commitment to reduce urban inequality and the collective will to incorporate the precariat needed for the justice apparatus to operate in a unified manner consistent with its professed ideals.

Now, an ideal type à la Max Weber is a methodological fiction, "like a utopia which has been arrived at by the analytical accentuation of certain elements of reality . . . In its conceptual purity, this mental construct (*Gedankenbild*) cannot be found empirically anywhere in reality." Rather, its role is to "offer guidance to the construction of hypotheses" and "unambiguous means of expression for the description of reality."[160] An ideal type supplies an analytical baseline to depict and explain how and why the institutions of interest or "historical individuals" encountered in society deviate from the model. I submit that some variant of this ideal type is indispensable for understanding *social and judicial differentiation* in the actual workings of criminal courts in advanced societies in which the triad of police–court–prison anchors penality.

Theories and investigations of the penal state that do not recognize the organizational duality of "paper penality" and "street penality" do so at the cost of masking the very phenomenon that they claim to capture. This means that we must study up close the functioning of the criminal court. This is the topic of the third chapter of this book. But, before we travel to California, I propose to take a historical detour through the colonial era to scope out the distinctive features of imperial punishment for what they reveal about the deep structure and multifaceted mission of the penal state, including its handling of the dyad of ethnicity and territory in the contemporary period.

Historical excursus:
Colonial penality and the urban badlands

Colonial punishment is of special theoretical and historical interest when it comes to conceptualizing the penal state for three reasons. First, under imperial rule, *state violence is suffusive, explosive, and multifaceted,* woven into the fabric of the colonial economy, society, and polity.[161] Legal and extralegal force are closely enmeshed as are military and civilian agencies tasked with delivering them. Second, the

---

[160] Max Weber, *The Methodology of Social Sciences* (1949), p. 90.
[161] The most powerful expression of this thesis is Frantz Fanon, *Les Damnés de la terre*

colonial Leviathan is the *quintessence of the racial state*: it fashions and defends naturalized social difference and hierarchy. So its erection and operation reveal the organic connection between punishment and race as two interlocking forms of material suasion and public dishonor. Racial hierarchy finds its official expression in the juridical duality of European citizen and native subject. Third, the colonial state not only makes maximal recourse to punishment, which seeps deep into daily life, irrigates subjectivity, and stamps the institutional horizon. It also spawns an array of *crimes and criminal sanctions specific* to imperial possessions that circumvent, indeed violate, the legal provisions operative in the metropole.

My first contention in this excursus is simple and straightforward: *penality was central to colonial statecraft* and assumed distinctive forms in the European periphery – a fact not given its due by the major theorists of imperial rule and routinely ignored by its historians.[162] Thus, in her state-of-the-art review of research on African colonial states, Heather Sharkey insists on the need to cover "a wide of range of actors" involved in "the performance of colonialism" and to acknowledge the latter's violence. But she characteristically leaves out of the picture the policeman, the judge, and the prison guard, the very agents of official force.[163] To fill this gap, it is, moreover, essential to capture the labor of law enforcement carried out by the penal triad as such – police, courts, prison – as I will endeavor to do, rather than isolate one or another of its constituents.

My second claim is more controversial and delicate to formulate: the three properties set out above – suffusive official violence, racialization, and criminal specificity – infect and inflect the rolling out of the penal state in the urban badlands of advanced society, albeit in a greatly attenuated form. The intensity of criminal construction and

---

(1961), who writes: "The colonized world is a world divided in two. The dividing line, the border, is marked by barracks and police stations."

[162] See, to take three leading theorists of the colonial state, Partha Chatterjee, *The Nation and Its Fragments: Colonial and Postcolonial Histories* (1993); Crawford Young, *The African Colonial State in Comparative Perspective* (1994); Mahmood Mamdani, *Citizen and Subject: Contemporary Africa and the Legacy of Late Colonialism* (1996). An exception is Achille Mbembe's *Politique de l'inimitié* (2016, in English: *Necropolitics*, 2019), but its arguments are more allegorical than analytical.

[163] Heather J. Sharkey, "African Colonial States" (2013). The rich works of *specialist* historians of crime and punishment in the colony, on which I will rely, have not been incorporated into the conceptual canon on empire. Similarly, in his panoramic dissection of "The Sociology of Empires, Colonies, and Postcolonialism" (2014), George Steinmetz makes no mention of punishment in any of its modalities.

sanction is incomparably lower there but their operational logic is analogous so that one can *leverage the colonial experience* of a hundred years ago to better understand punishment in the underbelly of the postindustrial metropolis today even while recognizing the many historical cesuras that separate them.[164] To leverage is not to conflate: the defamed territories inhabited by the urban precariat disproportionately composed of stigmatized ethnoracial categories are emphatically *not* colonies or postcolonies. But the penal state tends to behave in them *as if they were* and it continually reactivates representations and reinvents strategies and techniques deployed erstwhile in empires because it faces the same practical quandary: *how to domesticate unruly categories that do not recognize its authority* even as they yearn for democratic acknowledgment and civic inclusion?

Sizing up the colonial state

A compact conception of the colonial Leviathan *qua* colonial can be drawn from the groundbreaking book by political scientist Crawford Young, *The African Colonial State in Comparative Perspective* (1). Young characterizes it as an artificial and coercive structure imposed by European powers in pursuit of extractive economic policies based on authoritarian governance denying political rights to indigenous populations. He further highlights three features it lacks in contrast to metropolitan states: it is a state without sovereignty, without a nation, and without recognition on the international stage.

An amplification is found in the signal works on the topic by George Steinmetz, who deploys Bourdieu's field theory in a manner germane to the model built in chapter 1 (2). Steinmetz spotlights three distinctive traits of the colonial state: it is engaged in conquest; it divides its population along ethnoracial lines as well as stipulating the congenital inferiority of the people it subjugates; it exhibits fissiparous tendencies. He then elaborates a multi-scalar account of colonial policy as the product of struggles waged in nested administrative spaces in the metropole and in the different colonies in which multiple agents vie to impose their variant of the colonial project

---

[164] For a discussion of the different mechanisms linking the colonial past to the structure and culture of contemporary societies, read Julian Go, "Reverberations of Empire: How the Colonial Past Shapes the Present" (2024a). I propose a novel one: structural homology.

based on their position in the distribution of bureaucratic and symbolic capital (3).

I propose to add to Young's and Steinmetz's roster this crucial property of the colonial state that directly impacts punishment: *juridical and thence judicial dualism* as a specification of the "legal pluralism" characteristic of empire – indeed, the latter notion was initially formulated by anthropologists to capture the two-tiered character of law in colonial societies. This means that penality is bifurcated into two tracks directed by European law and customary law, respectively. For the advocates of colonization in the nineteenth century, "the imposition of European law was a great gift, substituting law for the anarchy and fear that they believed gripped the lives of the colonized people" (4). Moreover, this "gift" does not imply a horizontal interaction between equal normative orders but the subordination of native to imperial law embedded in relations of symbolic power and bureaucratic suasion.

One last distinctive feature pertinent to penality is the interlacing of military force and civilian force as exercised by the police. In the French colonial domain, it is difficult to establish historiographically when an action is conducted by the one or by the other insofar as "terminology tends to classify military questions as mere police action and police interventions as military victories" (5). The same applies to the designation of the target of official action: is it a criminal, a rebel, a political antagonist? So, instead of seeking to disentangle them, I will stress the consistent *blurring of the line between the police and the military* as an institutional characteristic of law enforcement in the colony.

Now, we must be careful not to exaggerate the might and coherence of the colonial Leviathan. It was despotic but disarticulated, oppressive but scattered, inflexible but fumbling. Both despite and because of its extreme brutality, its control of space and people was patchy and irregular (6). The policy-making apparatus was diffuse, improvised and decentralized; it relied heavily on native intermediaries for implementation (7). Its capacity to read the colonized society à la James Scott was limited; its infrastructural power to penetrate it à la Michael Mann was weak. Indeed, the colonial state resorted to such high volumes of material violence in the mold of Weber precisely because it was unable to generate sufficient symbolic violence in the sense of Bourdieu so as to obtain the consent of the dominated with minimal expenditure of social energy. It remains the case that, however fragmented and incoherent the colonial state, the penal triad of police, courts, and prison played a pivotal role in anchoring it and consolidating its rule. For this reason, we must resist Ivarsson and Rud's call to "apply non-state-centric approaches to the analysis of the colonial state" until such time as we have a full analytical and empirical command of its apparatus of punishment (8).

1. Crawford Young, *The African Colonial State in Comparative Perspective* (1994).
2. See, in particular, George Steinmetz, "The Colonial State as a Social Field" (2008a); idem, "The Sociology of Empires, Colonies, and Postcolonialism" (2014); idem, "Social Fields, Subfields and Social Spaces at the Scale of Empires: Explaining the Colonial State and Colonial Sociology" (2016).
3. George Steinmetz, *The Devil's Handwriting: Precoloniality and the German Colonial State in Qingdao, Samoa, and Southwest Africa* (2008b).
4. Sally Engle Merry, "Legal pluralism" (1988), pp. 869–70.
5. Emmanuel Blanchard and Joël Glasman, "Le maintien de l'ordre dans l'Empire français. Une historiographie émergente" (2012), p. 12.
6. John L. Comaroff, "Reflections on the Colonial State, in South Africa and Elsewhere: Factions, Fragments, Facts and Fictions" (1998); John Parker and Richard Rathbone, *African History: A Very Short Introduction* (2007); Jane Burbank and Frederick Cooper, *Empires in World History: Power and the Politics of Difference* (2011).
7. See the scrupulous account of the administrative organization of forced labor in Senegal's hinterland in Romain Tiquet's *Travail forcé et mobilisation de la main d'oeuvre au Sénégal* (2019b).
8. Søren Ivarsson and Søren Rud, "Rethinking the Colonial State: Configurations of Power, Violence, and Agency" (2017), p. 3.

Comparative history reveals that penality resides at the very core of the colonial state. It is deployed, not just to deter, detect, and sanction crime, but also, and most crucially, to capture and pacify territory alongside military force; to organize space and limit circulation; to effect economic spoliation and labor exploitation; to extract deference, mark identity, and uphold the caste order; and to suppress native political aspirations and claims.[165] As in the metropole, it

[165] Adam Hochschild, *King Leopold's Ghost: A Story of Greed, Terror, and Heroism in Colonial Africa* (1998); Florence Bernault (ed.), *Enfermement, prison et châtiments en Afrique du 19ème siècle à nos jours* (1999); Diana Paton, *No Bond but the Law: Punishment, Race, and Gender in Jamaican State Formation, 1780–1870* (2004); Caroline Elkins, *Imperial Reckoning: The Untold Story of Britain's Gulag in Kenya* (2005); Taylor C. Sherman, *State Violence and Punishment in India* (2010); Richard Gott, *Britain's Empire: Resistance, Repression and Revolt* (2011); Daniel Neep, *Occupying Syria under the French Mandate: Insurgency, Space and State Formation* (2012); Martin Thomas, *Violence and Colonial Order: Police, Workers and Protest in the European Colonial Empires, 1918–1940* (2012); Sylvie Thénault, *Violence ordinaire dans l'Algérie coloniale. Camps, internements, assignations à résidence* (2012); Jean-Pierre Bat and Nicolas Courtin

is delivered by the official agencies of the police, courts, and prison when and where these are transplanted and adapted to deal with ordinary crimes, theft, burglary, assault, homicide, etc. But, in addition to the army, it is also meted out by variegated civil administrations and their local intermediaries entrusted specifically with the management of native populations, land, and affairs, as well as by private parties through explicit or tacit delegation. Founded on *exacerbated and special powers*, colonial penality is, moreover, in a state of *constant tension and extension* because the "colonial situation," as deftly articulated by the anthropologist Georges Balandier, is fundamentally unstable and thus inevitably threatened by the collective recalcitrance, strategies of resistance, and insurgent demands of the colonized.[166]

195

Like the study of the penal state in the metropolitan core, the study of colonial penality has been hampered by an intellectual disjuncture. On the one side, there is a rich and rapidly growing literature from imperial historians focusing on crime and punishment in colonial societies, but their work scarcely connects with the sociological and legal theories of penality (scanned in chapter 1).[167] It finds its main

(eds.), *Maintenir l'ordre colonial. Afrique et Madagascar, XIXe–XXe siècles* (2012); Peter M. Beattie, *Punishment in Paradise: Race, Slavery, Human Rights, and a Nineteenth-Century Brazilian Penal Colony* (2015); and the literature scanned by Søren Ivarsson and Søren Rud, "Rethinking the Colonial State: Configurations of Power, Violence, and Agency" (2017).

[166] The colonial situation is "a socio-historical framework that superimposes two societies, one dominant and the other dominated, in a relationship of subordination, exploitation and dependency, but also of cultural contact." This dynamic conflictuality nourishes aspirations to decolonization. Georges Balandier, "La situation coloniale. Approche théorique" (1951). For a fuller analysis stressing tension and resistance, read Georges Balandier, *Sociologie actuelle de l'Afrique noire* (1955).

[167] In addition to the studies mentioned in footnote 165, the key monographs and collections representative of this genre include David Arnold, *Police Power and Colonial Rule: Madras, 1859–1947* (1986, 2024); David M. Anderson and David Killingray (eds.), *Policing the Empire: Government, Authority and Control, 1830–1940* (1991); Thomas Holloway, *Policing Rio de Janeiro: Repression and Resistance in a Nineteenth-Century City* (1993); Gabriel Haslip-Viera, *Crime and Punishment in Late Colonial Mexico City, 1692–1810* (1999); Peter Zinoman, *The Colonial Bastille: A History of Imprisonment in Vietnam, 1862–1940* (2001); Steven Pierce and Anupama Rao (eds.), *Discipline and the Other Body: Correction, Corporeality, Colonialism* (2006); Frank Dikötter and Ian Brown (eds.), *Cultures of Confinement: A History of the Prison in Africa, Asia, and Latin America* (2007); Mark Brown, *Penal Power and Colonial Rule* (2014); Emmanuel Blanchard et al. (eds.), *Policing in Colonial Empire: Cases, Connections, Boundaries (ca. 1850–1970)* (2017); Marie Muschalek, *Violence as Usual: Policing and the Colonial State in German Southwest Africa* (2019); Radha Kumar, *Police Matters: The Everyday State and Caste Politics in South India, 1900–1975* (2021); Anastasia Dukova, *To Preserve and Protect:*

inspiration, rather, in the writings of Michel Foucault, Frantz Fanon, and Giorgio Agamben as well as in Subaltern Studies. On the other side, the colonial domain has been consistently ignored by scholars of punishment – and this criticism applies to my own work – due to the presentist cast of their investigations and the Eurocentrism of their debates. When it timidly enters their purview, it is in terms of contemporary "legacies" and "vestiges" of colonialism rather than its distinctive logics at the bloom of empire.[168] What I propose to do in this excursus is to bring the history and theory of colonial punishment together to draw lessons for the conceptualization of the penal state and for the analysis of the penal management of subordinate categories in the metropolis of the contemporary West.[169]

196

1. The penal triad in the tropics

What the historian Taylor Sherman calls "coercive networks" anchored by the state were pivotal to the establishment and running of imperial possessions: "Far from being limited to a single institution, penal practices ranged from firing on crowds and bombing from the air to dismissal from one's place of work or study, collective fines, confiscation of property, as well as imprisonment, corporal and capital punishment."[170] The colonial state was quintessentially a violent state which deployed its police, courts, and prisons alongside its military to subordinate, exploit, and exclude the populations native to the lands conquered. Its rule was extended by the leeway it granted

Policing Colonial Brisbane (2020); Samuel Kalman, *Law, Order, and Empire: Policing and Crime in Colonial Algeria, 1870–1954* (2024); Marie Houllemare, *Justices d'empire. La répression dans les colonies françaises au XVIIIe siècle* (2024); Julian Go, *Policing Empires: Militarization, Race, and the Imperial Boomerang in Britain and the US* (2024b).

[168] See, for instance, Lynsey Black et al., "Introduction: Legacies of Empire" (2021), a thematic issue of the journal *Punishment & Society* drawing on Southern and decolonial criminology. Mark Brown makes the intriguing but unnoticed argument that the penal surge of the late twentieth century in advanced society constitutes a "recursion" of punishment in past colonies: "The Politics of Penal Excess and the Echo of Colonial Penality" (2002).

[169] Needless to say, the exercise of colonial power varied greatly across empires, countries, and periods. This is why I will focus mostly on French Africa and New Caledonia (a South Pacific colony island under French rule to this day). The summary picture I draw will also necessarily exaggerate the coherence and coordination of colonial rule.

[170] Taylor C. Sherman, "Tensions of Colonial Punishment: Perspectives on Recent Developments in the Study of Coercive Networks in Asia, Africa and the Caribbean" (2009), p. 669.

local intermediaries and private parties such as settlers to use force to do likewise. No wonder the penitentiaries of the colony were prime targets of anticolonial agitation, as when Indian jails were shaken by the wave of mutinies chronicled by Clare Anderson in *The Indian Uprising of 1857–8*.[171]

The *police were an essential cog* in the machinery of imperial rule as well as a generative force in the institutional distribution and practical deployment of colonial penality, starting with material extraction. In his sweeping comparative study of the French, British, and Belgian empires during the interwar decades, Thomas Martin demonstrates that it was vital to the functioning of colonial economies: it safeguarded the flow of resources, broke strikes, and assaulted workers' movements.[172] The repression of native laborers even took priority over the suppression of nationalist aspirations. Policemen were the "violence workers" who translated the formal sovereignty of the invading power into a tangible reality at ground level through the gamut of forceful acts, from looming threats and simple arrests to savage beatings and rampant torture, designed to establish "law and order" and to impose standards of conduct imported from the metropole.[173] Torture was a choice instrument in the panoply of techniques used to instill terror and obtain obeisance from the so-called natives in the bloom of empire – and not just in its phase of open contestation and looming dislocation leading to the chaos of national independence.[174]

The law-enforcement forces were typically composed of an incoherent patchwork of personnel at odds with each other and supplemented by local operators such as guards and foremen on plantations, the private police of companies, and vigilante outfits. These operators were sometimes recruited among "minority" groups to play on ethnic divisions and often from isolated regions of the hinterland with scant

197

---

[171] Clare Anderson, *The Indian Uprising of 1857–8: Prisons, Prisoners and Rebellion* (2007). Images of the prison in the British colonies painted it as "readily recognizable space of anti-colonial struggle and trope of unfreedom." Clare Anderson and David Arnold, "Envisioning the Colonial Prison" (2007), p. 324.

[172] Thomas, *Violence and Colonial Order*.

[173] The notion of "violence worker" is elaborated by Martha Huggins and colleagues in *Violence Workers: Police Torturers and Murderers Reconstruct Brazilian Atrocities* (2002). See the creative use to which it is put by Deana Heath in *Colonial Terror: Torture and State Violence in Colonial India* (2021).

[174] Alistair Horne, *A Savage War of Peace: Algeria, 1954–1962* (1977); Georgina Sinclair, *At the End of the Line: Colonial Policing and the Imperial Endgame, 1945–80* (2006); Marnia Lazreg, *Torture and the Twilight of Empire: From Algiers to Baghdad* (2008).

opportunities to enter the capitalist sector of the colonial economy. In France's African possessions, white Frenchmen from the mainland occupied the higher ranks and oversaw African patrolmen, auxiliaries, and constables, highlighting the decisive "contribution of the natives" (*concours des indigènes*) to the ground-level enforcement of the colonial order.[175] Repeated efforts to unify and standardize procedures and practices within and across imperial possessions were largely unsuccessful and policing generally followed parochial traditions and rules. Some policemen arrived from the metropole took to learning native languages, tried their hand at ethnography, surveyed the land, and extracted data in an effort to make the social landscape legible in the interest of more efficient control.[176]

In his intriguing monograph on the genesis of the different law-enforcement occupations in Togo under German rule starting in 1884 and then French tutelage from World War I until independence in 1960, Joël Glasman confirms that the police operated as an administrative agency with a broad portfolio: to respond to crime, collect taxes, oversee native populations drawn into forced labor, and repress local revolts. For this, it unfurled military discipline and tactics that normalized violence against these populations.[177] Similarly, Marie Muschalek documents how the ordinary violence perpetrated by the *Landespolizei* was key to establishing and enforcing colonial rule in German Southwest Africa (today's Namibia) between 1907 and 1915. The banalization and bureaucratization of brutality by its uniformed force, taking the form of kicks, smacks, and beatings, with the help of shackles, whips, and guns, was integral to the construction not only of the local social order, but also of the local Leviathan itself: "Instead of being built primarily on formal, legal, and bureaucratic processes, the colonial state was produced by improvised, informal practices of violence."[178] In others words, *brutal penality drove statecraft from below*.

The colonial police typically displayed indifference and apathy when it came to crimes against indigenous individuals or groups

---

[175] Bat and Courtin (eds.), *Maintenir l'ordre colonial. Afrique et Madagascar, XIXe–XXe siècles*, p. 210. A panoramic view across empires is offered by Blanchard et al. in *Policing in Colonial Empire*.

[176] On the epistemic dimension of imperial rule, read Bernard S. Cohn, *Colonialism and its Forms of Knowledge: The British in India* (1996), and Edmund Burke, *The Ethnographic State: France and the Invention of Moroccan Islam* (2014). On making the subject population "legible," see my discussion of James Scott *supra*, pp. 83–7.

[177] Joël Glasman, *Les Corps habillés au Togo. Genèse coloniale des métiers de police* (2014).

[178] Muschalek, *Violence as Usual*, p. 26.

while displaying diligence when the victim was European. The courts acted accordingly. In the Indian subcontinent under British tutelage, white judges and white juries treated with extreme leniency the violence of unruly whites – planters, police, prison guards, soldiers, and vagrants – trained on the "natives," effectively placing the perpetrators *exlex*. The result was that arbitrary and explosive brutality was not exceptional but normal, woven into the fabric of everyday life. It upheld a shifting but omnipresent racial hierarchy that consistently placed ordinary Indians at the bottom of the scale. What is more, the vision of violence was culturally and legally bifurcated. Thus, on the plantations, "European violence was viewed as a rational and necessary mode of labor control, [while] peasant attacks were generally described as acts of insubordination, fanaticism, or insanity."[179]

Similarly, adjudication by the *courts was racially bifurcated*, with different penal codes and tribunals set up for natives and for white settlers. In the French possessions of sub-Saharan Africa, *tribunaux indigènes* run by white judges handled offenses committed among Africans and took into consideration local customs, institutionalizing "legal pluralism."[180] Matters involving Europeans were tried by a separate court applying metropolitan law only. In the former scenario, corporal punishment such as lashing, fines, short prison terms, prison labor, and death were the mainstay of criminal sentencing as sanctions stipulated by traditional African justice such as banishment, stoning, mutilation, and torture were deemed "contrary to the principles of French civilization," to cite a 1910 government decree.

199

[179] Elizabeth Kolsky, *Colonial Justice in British India: White Violence and the Rule of Law* (2010), p. 175.

[180] On this concept and its origins in the colonial domain, see Sally Engle Merry, "Legal Pluralism" (1988). There is a surprising dearth of studies of criminal courts in the colony, relative to the abundance of studies of the police and the prison. It is surprising because courts are the crucial "throughput" institution transforming police input into prison output and also because they are bureaucratic machines that produce extensive records and thus rich archives. Two exceptions are Sylvie Thénault, *Une drôle de justice. Les magistrats dans la guerre d'Algérie* (2004), but it focuses on a short period at the crumbling of empire, not its zenith; and Claude Bontems, *La Justice en Algérie, 1830–1962* (2022), which is empirically profuse (it covers civil, penal, administrative, military, and customary courts from colonial capture to national independence in the course of 600 pages) but analytically underdeveloped. Thénault notes that the sheer technical complexity of colonial law and the difficulty of access to archives in the former colonies have hampered this domain of research (personal communication with the author). I would add as a further obstacle the lack of an overarching concept of penal state tying together police, court, and prison which has trapped the historiography of tribunals into a self-contained province with a tiny readership of specialists.

This resulted in stupendous rates of incarceration for Africans, three to six times higher than in Europe. In some cities of equatorial Africa, roughly one-third of the adult male population had served days in prison in 1943.[181]

A second distinctive property of the colonial court in the French possessions of Africa was its weak institutional separation from the police and the prison and its partial short-circuiting by virtue of the native code known as *indigénat* (discussed in detail later) which made it possible to punish through an administrative route.[182] The penal triad was not clearly differentiated for the simple fact that the same person was the decision-maker for law enforcement, criminal adjudication, and incarceration, to wit, the native "chief" at the level of the village and the French civil servant responsible for overseeing a district or *cercle*. As a ground delegate of the governor trained at the École nationale de la France d'Outre-Mer and putative "expert" in indigenous mores, the *commandant de cercle* wielded a multiplex power.[183] This power was at once administrative (he supervised the native "chiefs" and translators), military (he directed the native police forces and instigated repression), judicial (he sat as judge in the native court, applied the sanctions stipulated by the native code and managed the local prison), and economic (he was entrusted with drawing the census, collecting taxes, and organizing forced labor).[184] His most crucial role when it came to the court was to implement the bifurcation of the judicial treatment of colonized (native law) and colonizer (European law).

The *colonial prison* played an integral role in establishing imperial rule, as first revealed by the historian Florence Bernault: "The prison fed the transformation of the colonized societies and consolidated the profound upheaval brought about by the conquest. A tool of disorder

[181] Florence Bernault, "The Shadow of Rule: Colonial Power and Modern Punishment in Africa" (2007), p. 62.
[182] Gregory Mann, "What was the *Indigénat*? The 'Empire of Law' in French West Africa" (2009). For a comparison with British colonies on the same continent, see Michael Crowder, *West Africa under Colonial Rule* (1968). A fine-grained study of the workings of the "native court" is Richard Roberts, *Litigants and Households: African Disputes and Colonial Courts in the French Soudan, 1895–1912* (2005).
[183] Véronique Dimier, "Le commandant de cercle: un 'expert' en administration coloniale, un 'spécialiste' de l'indigène?" (2004); Armelle Enders, "L'École nationale de la France d'Outre-Mer et la formation des administrateurs coloniaux" (1993).
[184] Jean Frimigacci, "L'État colonial français, du discours mythique aux réalités (1880–1940)" (1993), who reports that the *commandant de cercle* was viewed locally as the "king of the bush," the "true chief of empire," and an "emperor without a scepter."

rather than order, a frontier kind of carceral (in Turner's geopolitical sense), it stood as a strategic outpost, an advanced bastion of colonial supremacy."[185] In its early phase, it served to isolate and deport native political leaders until they submitted. Later, it was deployed widely to impose white domination in every realm of social life, and then to suppress indigenous rebellions and nationalist mobilization via sweeping reclusion.[186] Finally, it was enrolled in the desperate and unsuccessful effort to stem revolutionary uprisings at the crumbling of empire. In Africa, Latin America, and the South Pacific, the colonists built facilities dedicated to the internment of political dissenters, suspected insurrection leaders, and "enemy combatants." In the British dominions of Africa, the authorities used *ad hominem* ordinances to circumvent juridical rules, nullify the principle of *habeas corpus*, and permit the indefinite detention without trial of nationalist figures. The law was thus effectively turned into "lawfare," in which "law itself became the tool of conquest and oppression," rather than a protective shield against it, fuel to keep the imperial engine running.[187]

201

Colonial prisons were typically imposing, highly visible, fortress-like buildings towering over other edifices in the city, an architectural testimony to imperial might. They reinscribed racial difference and hierarchy by separating European inmates and establishing different carceral regimens for whites and "natives."[188] That these would share a cell was simply unimaginable; they even paced in separate yards. Whites enjoyed individual cells, more food, some medical care, and better clothing and sanitary facilities. They were exempt from forced labor whereas Africans were confined in collective chambers and treated as an undifferentiated human mass – it was conveniently believed that they were naturally gregarious and would not tolerate individual isolation. Native inmates were also subject to harsh corporal punishment such as flogging, which European inmates were largely

---

[185] Bernault continues: "For the conquest was not limited to the period when territories were taken possession of; it lasted well beyond that, in an ongoing effort to subjugate people and territories. The prison provided a decisive anchorage for these battles." Bernault, *Enfermement, prison et châtiments in Afrique*, pp. 39–40.

[186] The canonical book on the topic is Zinoman, *The Colonial Bastille*. An extensive bibliographic panorama is provided by Philip J. Havik et al. (eds.), *Empires and Colonial Incarceration in the Twentieth Century* (2021).

[187] Michael Lobban, *Imperial Incarceration: Detention Without Trial in the Making of British Colonial Africa* (2021), p. 15.

[188] Bernault, *Enfermement, prison et châtiments en Afrique*, pp. 42–4.

spared.[189] Indeed, the latter were often quickly repatriated in France to serve their sentence there because their continued presence among African inmates was socially incongruous and symbolically disruptive.

Penal involution in the colony: the sadistic horror of the *biribi*

The hyperbolic if paradoxical violence of the colonial state is incarnated by the sulfurous institution created to wield penal force against its own agents, the *biribi*, the mobile military prisons of the French territories of North Africa in the nineteenth century (1). These prison camps were used to punish soldiers convicted of rebellion, stubborn individuals reticent to army discipline or deemed "weak-minded," as well as former convicts, drunkards, anarchists, and homosexuals. The targeted categories, most of which came from the city's badlands and were therefore seen as threatening to "contaminate" the wholesome component of the army, were detained under horrific conditions and forced to toil until exhaustion under a blazing sun. They suffered from brutal corporal punishment, rampant malnutrition, and deficient medical care as well as constant bullying, humiliation, sadistic abuse, and even torture at the hands of non-commissioned officers. Irony of ironies and supreme humiliation, the guards who kept them in bondage were often colonial subjects.

One of the techniques of torture was the *silo*, which refers to dumping up to a dozen naked men into a deep pit for weeks. The earthen pit was so narrow that the men punished could neither sit nor lay down. It quickly turned into an infective cesspool filled with excrement and insects. Another technique was the *crapaudine*, which consisted in tying the hands and feet of the inmate behind his back, leaving him for days in an unstable crouching position reminiscent of the *crapaud* (toad). For punishment, inmates were also forced to eat their own feces, to drink soup filled up with salt and to wear leg irons that became so encrusted into their bones that the flesh had to be cut with a knife to take them off (2).

The *biribis* were part of a "punitive archipelago" that included disciplinary battalions and public-works labor camps which effectively merged military justice and criminal justice to punish delegates of

---

[189] Africans received harsher physical punishment than whites for the same offense because it was believed that they were less sensitive to physical pain and also that force was the only language they understood.

202

the state who failed in their appointed mission to wield colonial violence at ground level or who simply did not fit the social type of the colonial soldier (3). Inmates circulated from one institution to the next in a closed circuit of organized abuse and inescapable suffering. *Biribis* were geographically peripatetic and set in remote and isolated areas; the army refused inspections and oversight as well as denied journalistic reports about what its critics regularly denounced as a "state scandal." They operated largely in the shadows of the military institution and survived until the close of the Algerian war of liberation in 1962 – its last vestiges were jettisoned only in 1976. To this day, they are absent from the French collective memory of empire in spite of their visible place in popular culture into the 1920s and their central role in delivering penal punishment en masse to the "poor whites" entrusted with enforcing colonial rule (4).

The *biribi* was thus the site and means of an exacerbated penality pushed to its limit as it turned autophagous. As a vehicle for "regeneration and relegation, exclusion and redemption, rebirth and repression," it participated in the creation of the military force especially suited to the duties of conquest and empire in the French Maghreb (5).

1. Dominique Kalifa, *Biribi. Les bagnes coloniaux de l'armée française* (2009).
2. This paroxistic penality evokes the public torture lynchings of "uppity Negros" in the Deep South under Jim Crow. Loïc Wacquant, *Jim Crow. Le terrorisme de caste en Amérique* (2024a), pp. 13–19, 117–22.
3. The African battalions (*bataillons d'Afrique*) partook of the network of colonial penality. They were designed as "units of quarantine, segregation and decontamination" for removing and exiling the criminal and recidivist elements of the city's underbelly in metropolitan France. Nicola Cooper, "Biribi: Disciplining and Punishing in the French Empire" (2018), p. 323.
4. This absence is stunning in light of the impact of this institution: Kalifa estimates that nearly one million men passed through the *biribis* between 1830 and 1960. They partook of what the historian Isabelle Merle calls "the extraordinay density of penal institutions" in the colonies. Isabelle Merle, "Bagnes militaires et relégation coloniale" (2010).
5. Kalifa, *Biribi*, p. 132.

Punishment was mobilized across the colonies to *extract and discipline forced labor* in the form of mandatory work prestation and requisition (also known as *corvée*), indentured servitude and convict recruitment.[190] Forced labor in its different forms was plugged into

[190] On the varieties of forced labor and the different mechanisms of their enforcement in the French empire and beyond, see Frederick Cooper's milestone book, *Decolonization*

the local economy to remedy the endemic penury of workers caused by the formal abolition of slavery, the dispersal and low density of the population, and the latter's reticence to get drawn into the wage-labor economy. In the French empire, the *code de l'indigénat* (which I discuss in depth next) stipulated *prestation*, the obligation for indigenous males to perform a certain quantum of gratis labor (or toil for a pittance of a pay), ranging from 10 to 60 days each year – not counting "extraordinary labor requisitions."[191] The resulting workforce was dispatched to build public infrastructure such as official edifices, roads, bridges, canals, telegraph lines, and railways, as well as assigned as needed to private plantations to ensure timely harvests, to dig mines, and to unload ships and haul barges for European traders. It was organized militarily and placed under the watch of local "chiefs" and special supervisors – European and native – as well as local militias tasked with upholding the work discipline.

The police and the courts were vigilant about this obligation. To skirt the prestation was not a civil matter but an administrative matter pursuant to the code of *indigénat* which exposed one to arrest, fines, and incarceration.[192] The violator could also be beaten and flogged in informally organized public ceremonies designed to communicate to all the imperative of work and the implacability of the authorities. The latter also resorted to collective punishment, such as fining an entire "tribe" for the failure of a few men to supply their labor, seizing their crops and animals, or confiscating and destroying their property.[193] If a recalcitrant worker could not afford to pay the fine inflicted, he would be sentenced to hard labor inside the walls of the penitentiary.

With assistance from the army, the police commonly conducted raids on villages to corral the men and drag them to the worksite where they were to toil. It also arrested and sent to prison the native farmers resisting agricultural requisitions, which compelled the latter

and African Society: The Labor Question in French and British Africa (1996); Babacar Fall, *Le Travail forcé en Afrique occidentale française (1900–1946)* (1993); Romain Tiquet, *Travail forcé et mobilisation de la main d'oeuvre au Sénégal* (2019b); and Alessandro Stanziani, *Labor on the Fringes of Empire: Voice, Exit and the Law* (2018).

[191] At its origins in the seventeenth century, *corvée* was imposed both in metropolitan France and in its overseas possessions. Anne Conchon, "La corvée au XVIIIe siècle. Des formes plurielles de réquisition dans les colonies françaises" (2021).

[192] Criminal sanctions were used to enforce indentured contracts and regular employment contracts. Jean-Pierre Le Crom, "Droit du travail *vs* droit pénal. Le cas des colonies" (2020).

[193] On collective punishment, see Isabelle Merle and Adrian Muckle, *L'Indigénat. Genèses dans l'empire français, pratiques en Nouvelle-Calédonie* (2019).

to cultivate cash crops in high demand in the metropole, such as coffee, cotton, and rubber, instead of the subsistence crops they direly needed. Work conditions varied greatly but it is no exaggeration to say that they were invariably despotic and all too often catastrophic: the laying down of the Congo-Océan railway between 1921 and 1934 cost the lives of over 20,000 African workers out of 127,000, killed by exhaustion, extreme temperatures, accidents, falling rocks, mudslides, starvation, and disease, with a mortality rate peaking at 49 percent in 1926, not to mention the squalid and hazardous construction compounds and regular beatings (and murders) by supervisors. So much so that the authorities recruited an additional contingent of Chinese "coolies," reputed to be more resilient, to try and stem the human carnage.[194] African workers resisted forced labor by every means possible, including the refusal to toil, sabotage, and flight. In some large works projects, the desertion rate topped one-half of the labor force recruited – explained away by the colonialist trope of "negro laziness." As for the Kanaks of New Caledonia who, in the interwar decades, had to supply 15 days of prestation each year, they complained of being "treated like slaves."[195]

In the metropole, critics of the regime "frequently used the word 'slavery' – and images of death and dehumanization echoing those of anti-slavery propaganda – to dramatize policies that strayed beyond the bounds."[196] Forced labor scandals reverberated widely in the European press. As for its advocates, they justified the regime in its diverse forms on material and moral grounds. First, they insisted, it was required to recruit the needed workforce and ensure that the colonies would be prosperous, pay for themselves or be profitable, thus fostering the economic development of the metropole. Next, forced labor was conceived as a vehicle for "educating the native," helping him to overcome his natural lethargy and inbred "slothfulness" (*paresse*), instilling in him such personal virtues as the work ethic, a sense of discipline, and respect for authority.[197] There was a third benefit to forced labor, excavated by economic historians: it was

[194] Julia Martínez, "'Unwanted Scraps' or 'An Alert, Resolute, Resentful People'? Chinese Railroad Workers in French Congo" (2017), and James Patrick Daughton, *In the Forest of No Joy: The Congo-Océan Railroad and the Tragedy of French Colonialism* (2021).
[195] Merle and Muckle, *L'Indigénat*, pp. 340–1.
[196] Cooper, *Decolonization and African Society*, p, 27.
[197] Alice L. Conklin, *A Mission to Civilize: The Republican Idea of Empire in France and West Africa, 1895–1930* (1997).

equivalent to an "invisible tax" that build up the fiscal capacity of the early colonial state by supplying the largest share of its budget.[198] In other words, punishment subtended forced labor which built the colonial Leviathan.

Convict labor was similarly instrumental in the running of colonial economies. It served a multiplicity of purposes: first, as punishment to sustain deterrence, inflict retribution, and promote "reform"; second, to offset the cost of penal administration (especially running the carceral facilities); and third, to erect public infrastructure. Forced labor drawn from prison was also impressed into the army, farmed out to settlers, and regrouped in mobile camps, "reservoirs for frontier projects that blurred private and public need for a docile and cheap native workforce."[199]

Penal transportation and the imperial drive

Penal transportation was by itself a distinctive vehicle for colonial expansion around the world. The British, French, Dutch, Spanish, Portuguese, Danes and Swedes, Russians, Chinese, and Japanese all dispatched convicts to conquer, settle, and till new lands on four continents (1). Convicts both competed and mixed with other forced laborers such as slaves and indentured servants as well as with indigenous peoples. Their peregrinations were accompanied by flows of goods, techniques, and ideas across the oceans that tied the world together – contributing to the imperial variant of globalization.

Penal colonies were sites of intense contestation as convicts mobilized to improve their condition, which is best described as abject: brutal work regimens, vicious discipline, meager rations, and unsanitary quarters. They sometimes supported anti-colonial struggles. For the authorities also used to deport political prisoners, including Irish rebels to British rule in Botany Bay, leaders of the French Commune of 1871 to New Caledonia, anti-colonialist Indians to the Andaman islands, and Vietnamese nationalists to Côn Sơn island.

[198] Marlous Van Waijenburg, "Financing the African Colonial State: The Revenue Imperative and Forced Labor" (2018). The colonies of French Africa and Asia had to be financially self-sustaining as they received no subsidy from the metropole after 1900.
[199] Conklin, *A Mission to Civilize*, p. 69. The peregrinations of these camps rounding up convict laborers rendered the walls of the prison porous and facilitated mass escapes. Romain Tiquet, "Connecting the 'Inside' and the 'Outside' World: Convict Labour and Mobile Penal Camps in Colonial Senegal (1930s–1950s)" (2019a).

The "red virgin" of the Commune, Louise Michel, openly supported the Kanak rebellion of 1878 led by chief Ataï – she saw the Kanaks as brothers-in-arms in the fight against oppression and even wrote an ethnological monograph on Melanesian song and dance (2).

Penal transportation and confinement also played a pivotal role in the "internal colonization," economic development, and state rule of another empire: the Soviet Union under Stalin (3). The network of mobile camps and "special villages" known as the Gulag (the Russian acronym for "General Directorate of the Camps," a unit of the political police) encapsulates the arbitrariness and brutality of the regime as well as its geographical expansion. It is far and away the largest, the most systematic, and the most murderous institution of penal exile and labor ever deployed. At its peak, it confined an astonishing 3.5 percent of the country's population, for a total of 28 million inmates (known as *zek*) between 1930 and 1952. It is estimated that the normal operation of the Gulag killed 1.6 million laborers, with another million dying during transportation (4). The "special contingent," as the captive labor force put under the control of the political police was called, served a dual goal: the exploitation of the natural resources of far-away regions and the coercive industrialization of the other regions. Today, the collective memory of the Gulag in Russia and its dependencies is split, with some denouncing its horrors and others maintaining that it was necessary to modernize the country and to win the war against Nazi Germany. Regardless, empire spawned the first society of mass incarceration in history.

1. Clare Anderson (ed.), *A Global History of Convicts and Penal Colonies* (2018). An exemplary case study outside the Western ambit is Anand A. Yang, *Empire of Convicts: Indian Penal Labor in colonial Southeast Asia* (2021). For a perspective of the very *longue durée* going back to antiquity, see Christian Giuseppe De Vito and Alex Lichtenstein (eds.), *Global Convict Labour* (2015).
2. Louise Michel, *Mémoires* ([1886] 2021).
3. Juliette Cadiot and Marc Elie, *Histoire du Goulag* (2017).
4. For a rich if shocking account of the torments of life, work, and death in the camps, see Anne Applebaum, *Gulag: A History* (2003).

Race was integral to the global system of convict labor: the treatment of hands was differentiated by ethnicity, religion, and geographic provenance while racialized visions of criminality, work capacity, and moral malleability shaped European privilege.[200] White convicts were

[200] Anderson, *A Global History of Convicts and Penal Colonies*, p. x. There were exceptions, among them the French penal colonies of New Caledonia and Guyana.

viewed as reformable subjects while colored convicts – particularly enslaved populations and indigenous peoples – were cast as irredeemable or innately criminal. So much to say that the global history of punishment, race, and empire are inextricably linked. This is also a good illustration of the *multifunctionality and double-sidedness of state punishment*: at its core, it facilitates material exploitation and enforces sociosymbolic divisions.[201]

We thus come to an implacable syllogism: formal and informal punishment were vital to forced labor extraction and discipline in its many guises; forced labor was vital to the empire's self-appointed project to plunder and "uplift" the colonized; *ergo* punishment was vital to the colonial enterprise. *Without the penal force of the colonial state, however disjointed, there would have been no empire to speak of.*

2. Bringing unruly bodies to heel, or indigénat at work

One device has come to signify the ever-present menace and delivery of physical punishment and its entwinement with colonial subjugation and economic extraction in the French and Belgian possessions of black Africa: the *chicotte*, a multistranded braided whip made of raw, sun-dried animal hide used to repress crime, to discipline and drive native laborers, as well as to brutalize them when they failed to reach harvest and production quotas.[202] The device was also used liberally by colonial administrators, missionaries, and settlers to repress even minor violations of the informal racial etiquette governing the relations between colonizer and colonized and to terrorize the latter by means of public flogging ceremonies. The role of the *chicotte* was thus not just economic as commonly held: it was deemed by state officials an essential device to extract subservience to French rule and to impose cultural norms intended to "civilize the natives."

Administering the *chicotte* commonly resulted in severe injuries, massive bleeding, maiming, and even death – it was not rare for victims to receive

---

[201] This is in keeping with Georg Rusche and Otto Kirchheimer's materialist theory of punishment, *Punishment and Social Structure* ([1939] 2005), for the mobilization of labor, and Émile Durkheim's symbolic theory of penality as means of communication and community formation in *De la division du travail social* ([1893] 1990).

[202] Anne-Charlotte Martineau, "Chicotte" (2018); Jean-Pierre Le Crom and Marc Boninchi (eds.), *La Chicotte et le pécule. Les travailleurs à l'épreuve du droit colonial français (XIXe–XXe siècles)* (2021). Batons, canes, and whips were also commonly used and the authorities discussed what implement was best adapted to what category of "natives."

dozens of lashes. In *King Leopold's Ghost*, Adam Hochschild provides vivid accounts of the horrific floggings with the instrument in the Belgian Congo in the 1900s. He notes: "It took a practiced hand to administer a hundred lashes, for if they were given too quickly, the victim would die."[203] The *chicotte* was the target of an international campaign to ban it at the beginning of the twentieth century, initially centered on the Congo, launched by journalists and diplomats with the support of missionaries and former colonial officials. It was not legally banned until 1959 but its use diminished rapidly. The *chicotte* survives today in the form of the common use of flagellation by public officials as well as private citizens – fathers, husbands, teachers – in many African societies, where it is described by the verb *chicotter*.[204]

The conventional penal triad of police, court, and prison does not tell the whole story. At the heart of colonial rule sat variants of *special juridical codes and administrative authorities* regulating indigenous populations and affairs (and assimilated categories such as indentured servants), which were more or less systematized and differentially enforced by the state and its agents depending on location and period. The case of France is emblematic.[205] The set of legal rules and regulations known as *Code de l'indigénat* or *indigénat* was a distinct penal regime, running from 1881 to 1946, which was pivotal to the day-to-day enforcement of the caste order in the French empire. It was initially hatched in Algeria as a special menu of measures fit for the war of conquest for a "transitory" period of seven years deemed necessary to effect the complete "pacification" of that territory.[206] It

[203] Hochschild, *King Leopold's Ghost*, p. 120. Flogging as well as caning in the British empire are well studied. See, for instance, Stephen Peté and Annie Devenish, "Flogging, Fear and Food: Punishment and Race in Colonial Natal" (2005); David M. Anderson, "Punishment, Race and 'The Raw Native': Settler Society and Kenya's Flogging Scandals, 1895–1930" (2011); Penelope Edmonds and Hamish Maxwell-Stewart, "'The Whip Is a Very Contagious Kind of Thing': Flogging and Humanitarian Reform in Penal Australia" (2016); Steven Pierce, "The Suffering Subject: Colonial Flogging in Northern Nigeria and a Humanitarian Public, 1904–1933" (2024).

[204] On the political uses and public legitimacy of the whip in contemporary Africa, read the superb analysis of Jean-François Bayart, "Hégémonie et coercition en Afrique subsaharienne. La 'politique de la chicotte'" (2008).

[205] Mann, "What was the *Indigénat*? The 'Empire of Law' in French West Africa." For a detailed discussion of *Eingeborenenrecht* in German colonies, see Alison Redmayne and Christine Rogers, "Research on Customary Law in German East Africa" (1983).

[206] Thénault revises this account by proposing that a similar regime, more extensive and better articulated with precolonial institutions, was instituted simultaneously in Indochina as in Algeria. In both the African and the Asian case, *indigénat* was merely legalizing the existing practices of imperial authorities. Sylvie Thénault, "L'indigénat dans l'Empire français. Algérie/Cochinchine, une double matrice" (2017).

was then exported to other French colonies, as a juridical exception to metropolitan law, that is, a provisional mesh of rules, edicts, and procedures governing native populations, but it was repeatedly prorogated for seven decades.

Codifying and regularizing existing practices, *indigénat* sported three distinctive features: it stipulated specific crimes unknown in mainland France that only natives could or would commit; it dictated distinctive forms of punishment that the metropole would never impose, pursuant to special powers granted to the colonial governor; and it was enforced, not just by judicial authorities, but by colonial administrators, their underlings, and their native intermediaries, in violation of constitutional norms. Most of all, this special penality served as the institutional framework organizing the relationship between the colonizing state and the colonized population. As the historian Sylvie Thénault puts it, "these disciplinary powers were the major plank of the penal regime of *indigénat*. They were probably its most massively used component and hence they embodied colonial arbitrariness in the eyes of those who were its victims."[207]

First, *special offenses*: according to a decree of 1887 supplemented in 1892, the native crimes specific to the South Pacific colony of New Caledonia included,[208] *inter alia*, failing to obey orders proffered by administrative agents and to show proper deference to the same; skirting restrictions on travel and residence (being outside of one's assigned district without proper authorization); being in public space in the city after eight in the evening or entering a drinking establishment; violating standards of dress ("nudity" on the roads or in European settlements); practicing sorcery or accusing another *indigène* of sorcery; brush-clearing by fire and bearing native weapons in European settlements. The economic and political tenor of colonial penality was made transparent in 1915 when the code was extended to cover the refusal to provide labor prestation, to pay the head tax, to supply information requested by the authorities, and the making of "public speeches aiming to weaken the respect due to the French administration."[209] The vaguest statute concerned "causing public disorder" in European settlements, a crime that allowed the authorities to arrest and sanction any "native" virtually at will.

---

[207] Ibid., p. 23.
[208] Merle and Muckle, *L'Indigénat*.
[209] Quoted by Isabelle Merle, "De la 'légalisation' de la violence en contexte colonial. Le régime de l'indigénat en question" (2004), pp. 154–5.

Second, punishment under the native code was also exceptional in the literal sense of *evading the juridical principles and norms of the metropole*, such as the individualization of sanctions and the right of appeal. In addition to routine brutality, it included internment, which took three forms: incarceration, house arrest, and internal or external deportation; individual and collective fines; and property confiscation. Fines and days of prison were massively used to enforce labor prestation, collect the head tax, maintain spatial segregation, and curtail interethnic sociability.[210] Internment and deportation were used repeatedly to undercut rebellions and to overcome the resistance of Kanak chiefs to colonial rule – as was done in other French colonies in Africa and Asia.

Third, punishment in the colony was deployed by *specially designed agencies* beyond those of the judicial system of the metropole. In New Caledonia, the enforcement of *indigénat* was entrusted to a web of native authorities created expressly for the purpose of colonial rule, "tribes" assigned to a specific "reservation" and put under the tutelage of a "paramount chief" and a "petty chief," themselves answerable to an "inspector of native affairs."[211] After 1900, the gendarmes distributed across the island took the lead in surveilling the natives and implementing the statutes.

The forcible administration of *indigénat* was far from bureaucratic in the Weberian sense of the word. Rather, it was rife with mismanagement, maltreatment, and incompetence and it allowed wide discretion and rampant abuse by its agents, which created a climate of fear among the Kanaks. The paramount chiefs were granted the right to punish petty chiefs and the villages they oversaw. The gendarmes were entrusted with the enforcement of the law as well as the supervision of everyday interactions between European settlers and Melanesian natives to uphold racial etiquette: "A glance misinterpreted, a cap not removed, a bad-tempered gesture on the part of the *indigène* can immediately result in a penalty of up to 15 days' imprisonment and a 100-franc fine."[212] The local gendarmes could arrest whomsoever they wanted whenever they wanted on the flimsiest pretext, and inflict excessive if not extravagant sanctions by "stacking" fines and days of incarceration. Moreover, the application of the code

211

---

[210] Merle and Muckle, *L'Indigénat*, chapters 6 and 7.

[211] As in other colonies, "tribes" and "chiefs" were colonial inventions that supposedly harnessed the "customary" sociopolitical institutions of the Kanaks.

[212] Merle and Muckle, *L'Indigénat*, p. 148.

was not just capricious and arbitrary: it was without recourse. This motivated the critics of colonial law in the metropole to denounce the *indigénat* as a "juridical monstrosity."[213] Arbitrary, extreme, and plain illegal.

In some colonies, such as French Indochina, West Africa, and New Caledonia, the *indigénat* led to open conflicts between magistrates and civil administrators of native affairs. The former viewed the repressive powers wielded by the latter as "an infringement upon their prerogatives" and accused them of overextending their authority. The latter, in turn, denounced the inefficiency of judicial procedures due to the rights they granted the natives, which they deemed excessive.[214] In other colonies such as Algeria, magistrates and administrators worked hand in hand and the regime was imposed with dogged rigidity and systematic brutality.[215]

Due to its sheer harshness and capricious enforcement, *indigénat* generated collective sentiments of injustice, fear, and defiance among the Kanaks. As a result, the regime was constitutively precarious and so it had to be continually adjusted and extended. For instance, to resist the imposition of the head tax, the Kanaks not only dissimulated and manipulated their identity; they also fled and emptied their villages when the gendarmes came calling to collect it. Because it created a proclivity toward the arbitrary use of police power, *indigénat* created a tension "between the state's desire to provide itself with the means to establish and maintain domination over the colonies, and the risk of encouraging abuses of power to the point of threatening that same domination as a result of the 'exasperation of hatreds'."[216] This tension, however, did not undermine *the import of colonial penality to the fabrication of subjects in lieu of citizens.* Administrators and gendarmes wielded "a right to punish and a right to intern, arbitrary, striking here and there, and always hanging like a sword of

212

---

[213] The expression "juridical monster" was used from the beginning by metropolitan critics of the regime in the 1880s. Merle, "De la 'légalisation' de la violence en contexte colonial," p. 148. See also Olivier Le Cour Grandmaison, *De l'Indigénat, anatomie d'un "monstre juridique." Le droit colonial en Algérie et dans l'Empire français* (2015), on the debates among colonial jurists.

[214] Thénault, "L'indigénat dans l'Empire français," p. 37.

[215] Thénault, *Violence ordinaire dans l'Algérie coloniale.*

[216] Merle, "De la 'légalisation' de la violence en contexte colonial," p. 149. A similar tension characterized the deployment of punishment in India under British rule, where "violence simultaneously menaced and maintained the empire." Kolsky, *Colonial Justice in British India*, p. 146.

Damocles over the fate of the individuals potentially concerned."[217] The ever-present possibility of cruel and indiscriminate punishment diminished the material cost of ethnoracial control but it meant that colonial power could never achieve even minimal legitimacy in the eyes of its subaltern population. In the words of historian Rajit Guha, colonial penality *bought dominance but undermined hegemony*.[218]

The multifaceted deployment of the police, the ethnoracial bifurcation of the courts, the extended use of the *chicotte*, the unrestrained recourse to incarceration and special native codes disclose that colonial penality was key to the running of the imperial economy, the crystallization of the caste order of imperial possessions, and the formation of the local Leviathan. It also shaped public culture and fashioned the subjectivity of colonist and colonized alike, infusing them with precarity, anxiety, and tension.[219] *Punishment was integral to imperial rule* and its inflections help define the specificity of the colonial state.

We can synthesize the relationship between the penal state and the colonial order in diagrammatic form in figure 12. This figure applies only to the "natives" because *criminal justice is split by the juridical opposition between citizen and subject*. Indeed, punishment was, with the law, a major divider of these two categories. For the European *citizen*, endowed with full rights, the articulation of police, court, and prison is the standard linear sequence found in the metropole: police → court → prison (with feedback loops) and the penal state serves primarily to protect the social and moral order as stipulated by criminal statutes (in accordance with the model of the penal state built in chapter 1). For the "native" *subject*, the architecture of penalization is structurally different and, in addition to suppressing crime, its overt purpose is to buttress caste division and to foster economic extraction.

213

---

[217] Merle and Muckle, *L'Indigénat*, p. 219.

[218] Ranajit Guha, *Dominance without Hegemony: History and Power in Colonial India* (1997). Reflecting on the history of colonial law enforcement in imperial France, Samuel Kalman notes: "In an ironic twist, the very things that seemingly protected the imperial project – military barracks and police stations, the omnipresent *tricolore*, military parades – only heightened the desire for freedom of the colonized denizens of the empire." Samuel Kalman, "Policing the French Empire: Colonial Law Enforcement and the Search for Racial-Territorial Hegemony" (2020), p. 1.

[219] Nancy Rose Hunt, *A Nervous State: Violence, Remedies, and Rêverie in Colonial Congo* (2015). Achille Mbembe captures this abiding sense of powerlessness and ignorance of the colonial state in *Sortir de la grande nuit* (2010).

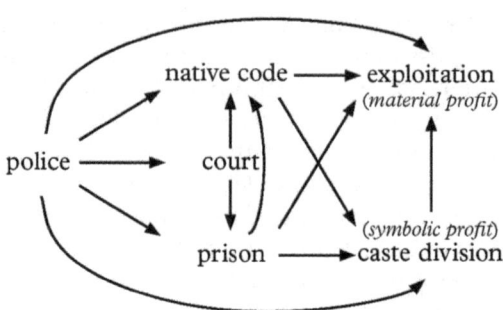

Figure 12 The architecture of colonial penality

214

The police are the most ramifying instrument in the panoply of imperial punishment. It enters into everyday life and regulates social interaction between white citizen and colored subject, bolstering the racial dualism that grants the colonizer a monopoly over ethnic honor (symbolic profit); it funnels unruly native bodies into the court and the prison; it directly subtends the native code and intrudes into the economy to facilitate exploitation (material profit). The prison also plays a multiplex role: it receives bodies from the police and the court; it supports the native code as well as ethnoracial hierarchy; it furnishes convict labor to the economy and stifles resistance from workers. As for the native code, it greases the wheels of exploitation by extracting forced labor and solidifies the caste order by stipulating racialized norms of conduct. The court plays the role of dispatcher between the police, the prison, and the native code.

Like any model, this expanded political economy of colonial punishment, taking into account both "material and ideal interests" (to speak like Max Weber), is a simplification of a dynamic complexus inflected locally by the particular configuration of agents on the ground that crucially involved native intermediaries and authorities which collaborated with imperial rule – what Mahmoud Mamdani calls "decentralized despotisms."[220] But it can serve as an analytical guide for further historical investigation and comparison between countries, epochs, and social formations, including contemporary societies. In particular, it recommends bringing together the three components of the penal triad – police, courts, and prison – along with the native code, and thus helps us to better capture the speci-

[220] Mamdani, *Citizen and Subject: Contemporary Africa and the Legacy of Late Colonialism*, p. 26.

ficity of the *colonial penal state as the very foundation and enforcement agency of the division between native and citizen.*

3. Special punishment in neighborhoods of relegation

What theoretical lesson can we draw about the penal state by scrutinizing punishment in the imperial possessions of centuries past? First, the extreme case of the colony in the gamut of social formations spotlights the *centrality of penality to state formation* and to the functioning of a society founded on a vertical dichotomy between insiders and outsiders. Punishment is rolled out by the state but, in turn, its implementation practically remakes the state from within and enlivens it as the official agency wielding material and symbolic violence. It entails the creation and deployment of specific agencies, policies, categories, and discourses that modify the structure and functioning of the bureaucratic field. There is thus a *recursive relationship* between the state and punishment which standard approaches to "law and society" and "punishment and society" miss because they cut the Leviathan out of the analytic equation.[221]

Penality is also organically connected to the structure of social and symbolic space in that the definition of crimes, the hierarchy of sanctions and their practical delivery follow, and in turn contribute to entrenching, the salient cleavages of the society – in the case at hand, the dual opposition of castes based on naturalized ethnicity buttressed by force and the law. There is thus a *correspondence between the "mode of punishment" and the "mode of stratification,"* and not the "mode of production" as Georg Rusche and Otto Kirchheimer contend in their classic tome on *Punishment and Social Structure.*[222] In particular, penality operates as an engine of racialization inasmuch that it inflicts on its targets a public stigma that marks them out as fundamentally different and vituperates them as agents of disorder, material and symbolic. It strives to contain not just dangerous classes, but also "dangerous races."[223]

215

---

[221] As noted in chapter 1, the absence of the state is characteristically conspicuous in Kitty Calavita, *Invitation to Law and Society: An Introduction to the Study of Real Law* (2016), and in Jonathan Simon and Richard Sparks (eds.), *The Sage Handbook of Punishment and Society* (2013).

[222] Georg Rusche and Otto Kirchheimer, *Punishment and Social Structure* ([1939] 2005).

[223] Loïc Wacquant, *The Invention of the "Underclass": A Study in the Politics of Knowledge* (2022), pp. 133–40.

Next, this colonial excursus confirms that penality fulfills crucial *extra-penological functions* far beyond crime control. It reveals how the penal Leviathan penetrates the lower reaches of society, makes them legible and tractable to a degree,[224] and advertises the power of the ruler to the people. Punishment sustains economic exploitation, bolsters social divisions, defends civic exclusion, and communicates normative injunctions, thus fostering the reproduction of the social and moral order at large, and not just public order and physical safety as criminologists and common sense would have it. As Émile Durkheim would predict, it tightens the social structure and *boosts solidarity*. Only this solidarity is *split*, like the colonial society itself, among the settlers as beneficiaries of judicial sanctions who form one block anchored in privilege, on the one side, and among the "natives" as their targets unified in recalcitrance and resistance, on the other.[225]

Finally, the colonial experience teaches us that the punishment apparatus is tasked, at bottom, with *capturing and corralling bodies out of place*, that is, persons and populations failing to keep their appointed position in symbolic, social, and physical space by dint of their identity, condition, or conduct.[226] Penality helps fabricate (quasi) *subjects in lieu of citizens* in that it abridges the rights and prerogatives of those it targets. This is particularly salient in the context of empire but it is just as true in advanced societies, where an arrest, criminal conviction, or incarceration translate automatically into the downgrading of one's civic status and the truncation of one's rights. By the same token, penalization generates among its target population collective emotions of dread, distrust, and defiance of authority, which paradoxically undermines the state's legitimacy and thus weakens political rule from within. This paradox expresses the structural duality of state punishment elaborated in the closing of chapter 1: it is a public good for the dominant but a private bad for the dominated.

Coming to the implications of the present analysis for the sociology of the punitive containment of urban marginality in the twenty-first century, it is imperative, *ab initio*, to resist the hasty and faulty assimilation of the zones of perdition of the postindustrial city to colonies,

---

[224] James C. Scott, *Seeing Like a State: How Certain Schemes to Improve the Human Condition Have Failed* (1998).

[225] Émile Durkheim, *De la division du travail social* ([1895] 1990).

[226] For illustrations from five colonies, see Pierce and Rao, *Discipline and the Other Body*. For a parallel with African-Americans in the postbellum South of the US, see Christopher Muller and Daniel Schrage, "The Political Economy of Incarceration in the Cotton South, 1910–1925" (2021).

archeo or neo.[227] Several properties of place and state combine to refute this equation. Four pertain to the territory policed and its population:

1. Unlike the colony, the American hyperghetto, the French *banlieues*, the British "sink estate," the German *Problemviertel*, the *utsatta områden* of Sweden, etc., do not constitute sites of economic extraction.
2. Their population is ethnically heterogeneous and class homogeneous, whereas their colonial counterpart was the obverse:[228] the different colonized ethnicities were amalgamated, in imperial eyes, into the category of the "native" and treated as such.
3. Their dwellers are formally endowed with full civil and political rights (even foreigners and refugees enjoy extended legal protections and prerogatives), which limits their possible abuse by the state.
4. The residents can and do escape the neighborhood by climbing up the class structure to lose themselves in the broader society, shedding territorial stigma and expanding their life chances, which the subaltern populations of the colony could not do.

Four key properties pertaining to the late-modern state further differentiate the predicament and treatment of the residents of neighborhoods of relegation from the subjugated populations of empire:

1. The colonial Leviathan operated largely as a "delegated state" in which non-state agents, planters, employers, militias and settlers,

217

---

[227] In France, this assimilation is defended by the Parti des indigènes de la République, for whom today's urban periphery is but an extension of the French colonies of yesteryear, as argued by Sadri Khiari, *La Contre-révolution coloniale en France. De de Gaulle à Sarkozy* (2009). In the United States, many scholars have characterized the black ghetto as a colony controlled by whites in the 1960s, starting with Kenneth Clark in *Dark Ghetto: Dilemmas of Power* (1965), Robert Blauner in "Internal Colonialism and Ghetto Revolt" (1969), and the leaders of the Black Panther Party in their political writings and memoirs: Stokely Carmichael and Charles V. Hamilton, *Black Power: The Politics of Liberation* (1967). The notion is incorporated and updated by the rhetoric of "racial capitalism," deemed operative in yesteryear's colonies as in today's metropole. It finds a hyperbolic expression in Ida Danewid, "The Fire this Time: Grenfell, Racial Capitalism and the Urbanisation of Empire" (2020).

[228] The exception here is the American hyperghetto, which is doubly segregated by race and class and therefore ethnically homogeneous, as shown in Loïc Wacquant, *The Two Faces of the Ghetto* (forthcoming), chapter 6.

wielded violence in its name, whereas the contemporary state keeps a tight hold over legitimate violence (notwithstanding exaggerated claims of devolution and privatization).

2. The late-modern state deploys not just a penal arm, but also educational, public health, housing and social welfare arms that evidently did not exist in the colony; it weaves a social and economic safety net that limits destitution and provides *de facto* entitlements; Foucauldian biopolitics supersedes necropolitics à la Mbembe.

3. The colonial state was strong in terms of "despotic power" but weak in terms of "infrastructural power;"[229] the contemporary Leviathan is the exact opposite: it can penetrate deep into the underbelly of the city through its bureaucratic tentacles but it must contend with the contrarian claims, consultation, and mobilization of civil society.

4. The contemporary Leviathan is both oppressive and protective, a source of violence and a shield against violence,[230] and state violence is correspondingly not doxic, as it was under the tropics, but *scandalous* (in the etymological sense of causing discredit and damage to reputation) whenever it demonstrably exceeds the bounds of the law.

In sum, the material foundation of relegation in today's districts of marginality is class, inflected by ethnicity and compensated by the state, whereas its basis in the past colony was race, inflected by class and sponsored by the state, and by its penal wing in particular.[231] At the same time, one cannot but be struck by the *operational parallels* between the respective justice triads of settler colony and urban badlands – with the proviso that official violence was diffuse in the former and is strictly targeted in the latter. To put it provocatively,

---

[229] This distinction is elaborated by Michael Mann in "The Autonomous Power of the State: Its Origins, Mechanisms and Results" (1984), pp. 188, 189, and discussed in chapter 1, *supra*, pp. 80–3.

[230] This is an inverted derivation from what Bourdieu calls the "fundamental ambiguity" of the state: "The State is a Janus such that one cannot enounce a positive property without simultaneously enouncing a negative property, a Hegelian property without a Marxist property, a progressive property without a regressive, oppressive property." Pierre Bourdieu, *Sur l'État. Cours au Collège de France (1989–1992)* (2012), p. 161.

[231] Here again the US hyperghetto is an exception as it follows the colonial pattern: race first, class second, and the state as aggravating institution. Wacquant, *The Two Faces of the Ghetto*, chapter 9.

in the depths of the metropolis, today's penal Leviathan *behaves like a neocolonial state without a colony,* wielding a form of authority that its targets do not recognize and delivering punishment that deviates from its own legal promulgations. Hence the constant oscillation between festering official violence fueled by routine judicial discrimination and the denunciation of official violence taking the form of seething discontent and episodic riots.[232]

Much as imperial punishment was an exception to metropolitan justice, the accelerated and simplified "street penality" abridging rights that applies to the urban precariat turns out to be a deviation from full-fledged criminal justice as experienced by bourgeois defendants – what I call "paper penality," justice administered by the books granting full substantive rights. The first procedure pertains to *Polizeistaat,* the second to *Rechtstaat.*[233] Together they constitute a *variant of "legal dualism" based on class and place* which operates as if defendants were subjected to two legalities. This dualism, observed in all advanced societies, cannot but evoke the two-tiered criminal justice based on caste characteristic of the colony with its division into European and customary law.

Special crimes, special punishment, and special administering agencies characterize colonial penality. Consider the parallels with street penality in the underbelly of the postindustrial metropolis. It comprises a *litany of special crimes* occurring out in the open such as "loitering," "causing a disturbance" (*tapage*), disorderly conduct, congregating on street corners and in the entrance hallways of buildings, acting as part of a "gang" or a "criminal association" (a vague entity in many cases), or "driving while black" (racially skewed police stops and detention pursuant to minor traffic violations) – crimes that are fictitious or nonexistent in other parts of the city.

Policing the urban badlands also involves *special punishments* such as pretextual "stop and frisk" searches followed by identity checks that are so many occasions for abusive treatment and arrests without cause and records, and body searches in public which amount

---

[232] Éric Marlière, *La France nous a lâchés! Le sentiment d'injustice chez les jeunes des cités* (2008); Julien Talpin, *La Colère des quartiers populaires. Enquête socio-historique à Roubaix* (2024). Emmanuel Blanchard notes "certain congruences" between yesterday's colony and today's urban badlands and speaks of a "family resemblance" between their respective policing methods ("The Colonial Legacy of French Policing," [2021], p. 49).

[233] Dubber, *The Dual Penal State,* with the proviso that this distinction replicates a socioethnic dualism.

to state-sponsored sexual assault.[234] Based on his ethnography of law enforcement in an impoverished *banlieue* of Paris, Didier Fassin enumerates the abrasive acts routinely suffered by its boys and men at the hands of the police: "Harassment, provocations, threats, humiliation, racist insults, unwarranted checks, unjustified searches, abusive fines, painful handcuffing, pointless arrests, arbitrary police custody, beatings that leave no trace, sometimes even the use of torture, all these documented practices being concentrated on the most vulnerable segments of the population."[235] None of these acts would be committed upon a well-to-do resident of a bourgeois neighborhood by virtue of differential policing by class and place.

220 Just as colonial penality was enforced by *dedicated agencies of the state*, policing neighborhoods of relegation relies on special units, such as the infamous BAC (Brigades Anti-Criminalité), who behave like urban cowboys in France's urban periphery, and the BRR (Brigades de Reconquête Républicaine), deployed in a selection of officially designated "Sensitive Urban Zones" targeted by national city policy,[236] the anti-crime and crime-suppression units, strategic response groups, gang units and SWAT teams (Special Weapons and Tactics), who act similarly in the United States. In both countries, there has been a surge in the militarization of policing and riot units have been dispatched for ordinary law enforcement and surveillance – mirroring the meshing of police and army in order maintenance in the colony.[237]

Everyday police abuse is in turn validated by judicial processing through accelerated tracks dedicated to low-level street crime, *com-*

---

[234] See Moskos, *Cop in the Hood*; Victor M. Rios, *Punished: Policing the Lives of Black and Latino Boys* (2011); and Forrest Stuart, *Down, Out, and Under Arrest: Policing and Everyday Life in Skid Row* (2016) on the American case. See Fassin, *La Force de l'ordre*, on the French case. Read Koshka Duff and Tom Kemp on "Strip-Searching as Abjectification: Racism and Sexual Violence in British Policing" (2025).

[235] Fassin, *Punir, une passion contemporaine*, p. 51.

[236] Created in 2018, the BRR (Brigades for Republican Reconquest) are formed by all-volunteer veteran police staff tasked with the mission to restore the authority of the state. They were assigned to some 50 QRR (Neighborhoods of Republican Reconquest), especially trained to handle tense situations of confrontation with criminals and rioters, to proactively deter crime, to fight illegal trafficking, and to back up the BAC. The designation BRR was immediately criticized for its military overtones so the Ministry of the Interior stopped using it to designate its targeted strategy of police supplementation.

[237] Fabien Jobard, "La police en banlieue après les émeutes de 2005" (2015); Trent Steidley and David M. Ramey, "Police Militarization in the United States" (2019).

parution immédiate in France and plea bargaining at the first hearing in the United States. More revealing yet, these procedures invariably convict the teenagers and men arrested for minor offenses: they are presumed guilty as charged on both sides of the Atlantic and they can rarely convince a judge that their version of the story is the truth. It is especially difficult to obtain a verdict against police abuse even when they are documented by witnesses and video recordings. Periodic police raids, called *opérations coup de poings* in France and *sweeps* in the US, wreaking social havoc and material destruction, translate into indiscriminate arrests. These are often accompanied by prearranged and sensationalistic media coverage designed to showcase the determination of the authorities to restore the law in a territory deemed beyond it. Finally, the massive show of force by law enforcement in reaction to riots roil the poor segregated districts where the police, court, and prison are the everyday visage of the state to the young jobless men who reside there. Accordingly, the first reaction of the target population of neocolonial policing is often to give up their rights and to *flee in public space to avoid contact* with law enforcement.

221

In the French urban periphery, the bitter joke is that the young boys and men run away from the police who run after them only because they run away. But the consensus among the runners is that "you should bolt before the police even when you are innocent."[238] The infraction of *refus d'ob-tempérer* (refusal to defer to a police order or refusal to come to a halt when driving, punishable by up to one year of prison, surpassing 25,000 a year) has become an obsession in the journalistic and political fields and, though this is not proffered openly, most assume that the culprits are young "Arabs and Blacks" from the stigmatized *banlieues*.[239]

Likewise, a common criminal offense in and about the poor segregated districts of Californian cities is Section 2800.2 of the California Vehicle Code, which prohibits evading the police while operating a motor vehicle and is punishable by up to four years of prison when it entails a chase demonstrating "wanton disregard for the safety of persons or property." A possible reason for refusing to heed a police order to stop is that the motorist is driving on a suspended license and thus violating his probation or parole, or the car contains drugs, weapons, or other contraband,

[238] Kamel Boukir, "Le politique au bout de la matraque. Fuir la police, obéir, résister: entre déviance et citoyenneté" (2019), p. 141.
[239] There is a strong taboo on openly mentioning the ethnicity of offenders among state officials, journalists, and the police. But the periodic link made between crime and immigration in public discourse is enough to flag it without having to verbalize it.

or parolees who are not supposed to congregate. But the refusal can just as well be motivated by the simple wish to avoid rash police intrusion and humiliation, and the fear that this routine traffic stop could escalate into lethal police violence.[240] Here again, young men in the long shadow of the penal state scamper as a matter of course when the police come onto the scene. Is this not eerily reminiscent of the Kanaks who fled their villages when the gendarmes showed up to collect the head tax?

Diligent and repeat incarceration is another modality of penalization in precincts of urban perdition that evokes the deployment of the prison in the colony in its heightened frequency if not its modality. We saw earlier that carceral facilities in advanced society are typically segregated along ethnoracial lines for purposes of order maintenance by the correctional officers and safety provision by the inmates, who regroup with co-ethnics or inmates coming from their housing estate in a bid for everyday solidarity and collective defense. As in the colonies, the belligerent penalization of poverty in the stigmatized zones of perdition of the postindustrial city *undermines the legitimacy of the state* in the eyes of their residents, especially the young jobless men who are the target of constant police harassment, insult, provocation, and degradation, as well as their family, friends, and neighbors who witness or learn of this police behavior. This fuels bitterness, resentment, and a desire for vengeance that simmers in the form of running skirmishes with law-enforcement personnel and explodes periodically into outright riots.[241]

Owing to these corrosive relations stamped by mutual scorn, these youths have come to see the police ("pigs" or "poh-poh" in the US, "*keufs*" or "*lardus*" in France) as an enemy force invading their stomping ground to impose an arbitrary rule. By routinely abridging their substantive rights as citizens or denizens, the penal Leviathan reduces them to the neocolonial status of *quasi-subjects in a republic*. This is all the more grating inasmuch as, like colonized populations before them, the residents of districts of dereliction aspire to full civic inclusion and recognition by the very authorities who ignore or mistreat them.

There is yet a final twist in the similarities between yesteryear's colony and today's urban badlands: in both problem territories, the

---

[240] Charles R. Epp et al., *Pulled Over: How Police Stops Define Race and Citizenship* (2014).
[241] Éric Marlière, "Les 'jeunes de cité' et la police. De la tension à l'émeute" (2007); Margit Mayer et al. (eds.), *Urban Uprisings: Challenging Neoliberal Urbanism in Europe* (2016); Mustafa Dikeç, *Urban Rage: The Revolt of the Excluded* (2018).

rolling out of penal policy discredits the state among its target population but, *by the same token, generates support* among the colonizer and among the broader postindustrial citizenry, respectively. For the colonizer, the delivery of wanton force and boundless brutality was rightful, reassuring, and required to effect economic spoliation, enforce caste domination, and secure political exclusion. It was demanded, approved, and amplified by the settlers. Similarly, the implementation of aggressive policing, diligent prosecution, and speedy incarceration in the defamed districts of the contemporary metropolis is requested and endorsed by broad swaths of the population (including many residents of these very districts) – a majority that is not silent but vocal in its support for "law and order" in the city's underbelly.[242] This majority views penalization as the justified means for restoring the authority of the state and for reasserting its governing mission in neighborhoods it perceives as *"zones de non-droit"* (lawless zones), fearsome redoubts of vice, violence, and civic dissension if not ethnic and religious separatism.[243]

This is illustrated by the moral panic roaring across the French political and journalistic fields in the 2020s about the alleged *"ensauvagement"* of youths and the *"décivilisation"* infecting the defamed *banlieues* against the backdrop of the constant denunciation of rampant *"islamisation."*[244] Savage, decivilized, Muslim mendacity: the language of colonial supremacy is easily reactivated in a nation that has yet to come to grips with its imperial past. The fact that the urban badlands harbor large proportions of immigrants from France's former overseas possessions gives *prima facie* validity to this alarming vision of the unruly colony coming back to exact revenge by invading the metropole – what Aimé Césaire famously called the "colonial boomerang."[245] Like punishment in the tropics a hundred years ago,

---

[242] Tracey L. Meares and Dan M. Kahan, *Urgent Times: Policing and Rights in Inner-City Communities* (1999).

[243] See, on the US case, Wacquant, *The Invention of the "Underclass,"* and, on the French case, Henri Rey, *La Peur des banlieues* (1996), and Marwan Mohammed and Julien Talpin, *Communautarisme?* (2018).

[244] Bérénice Mariau and Gaëlle Rony, "Polémique autour de l'usage de la formule ensauvagement. Tentatives de qualification d'actes de violence en France" (2024); Philippe Robert and Renée Zauberman, "Violences en France: peut-on parler de 'décivilisation'?" (2023); Abdellali Hajjat and Marwan Mohammed, *Islamophobie. Comment les élites françaises fabriquent le "problème musulman"* (2022).

[245] This vision is steeped into the "cultural repository or archive of meaning" constituted by colonialism, one of the four mechanisms whereby the imperial past shapes the present identified by Julian Go in "Reverberations of Empire" (pp. 12–13). It

the penal management of postindustrial poverty strikes ethnic outsiders and their descendants with special force and velocity by striking the neighborhoods where they tend to cluster through differential policing. *State, race, and place coalesce* to tighten the noose of urban marginality spawned by the precarization of labor and the shrinking of the social state.

Colonial penality deployed by European empires in what is now called the global South was pervasive and radiating, racialized and racializing, differentiated as well as differentiating. The same is true, with a diminished scope and at a much lower intensity, of punishment wielded by the neoliberal state to manage dispossession and dishonor in the neighborhoods of relegation of the polarized city in the contemporary global North. We must imperatively eschew the facile conflation of these two historical formations driven by the "logic of the trial," which aims to accuse and indict rather than explain and understand.[246] *Analogy is not identity, structural similarity is not genealogical necessity.* The policy of punitive containment of urban marginality in advanced society is not a "legacy," a "debris," or a "reactivation" of empire but the independent *rediscovery* of techniques of government of troubled territories that addresses the same predicament faced a century ago in the tropical possessions of Europe: how to domesticate reticent and restive categories that do not enjoy the full civic status they yearn for and which therefore regard state authority as illegitimate, bodies out of control that are projected in the public imagination as dark, deviant, and dangerous.

In the colonies, rolling out the police, court, and prison as well as special punishment regimes to subdue the indigenous population ultimately failed to secure order and consent. The same is happening today in the districts of dereliction of the postindustrial metropolis. In both cases, penality and ethnicity (caste in empire) are intricately interwoven and their nexus plays out differentially across territory.

is now intensified by the fear of the Islamist terrorist whose shadowy figure hovers over the derelict *banlieue*, as shown by Fabien Truong, *Loyautés radicales. L'islam et les "mauvais garçons" de la nation* (2017).

[246] An example of this slippage is Benjamin D. Weber, *American Purgatory: Prison Imperialism and the Rise of Mass Incarceration* (2023), which claims to establish a direct and organic connection between "empire and mass incarceration" through the "unspoken doctrine of prison imperialism." In reality, "elites around the world were generally fascinated by the penitentiary idea and eager to embrace it, rather than compelled by the dark forces of imperialism to adopt it" (Frank Dikötter and Ian Brown, *Cultures of Confinement: A History of the Prison in Africa, Asia, and Latin America* [2007], p. 3).

Beyond the analytics of penality as a vector of social classification and stratification, we ignore the slow-motion crash of the penalization of racialized poverty at our civic peril and, more urgently, at the cost of warping the lives of the urban outcasts. The core state agency driving this warping five days a week is the criminal court, the stomping ground of prosecutors, whose juridical power and professional practice are the topic of the next and final chapter.

3

Penal Power Incarnate: A Day in the Life of a Prosecutor

It is more proper that law should govern than any one of the citizens: upon the same principle, if it is advantageous to place the supreme power in some particular persons, they should be appointed to be only guardians, and the servants of the laws.

Aristotle, *Politics*, book III

Penal power is not just a theoretical abstraction necessary to think of the ways in which the state signifies its authority, regulates disruptive marginality in the city, and draws the silhouette of the citizen through the police, court, and prison.[1] It is also an everyday reality emanat-

[1] Philippe Robert, *La Question pénale* (1984); John Irwin, *The Jail: Managing the Underclass in American Society* (1985); Herbert Jacob et al., *Courts, Law, and Politics in Comparative Perspective* (1996); Salvatore Palidda, *Polizia postmoderna. Etnografia del nuovo controllo sociale* (2000); Benoit Bastard and Christian Mouhanna, *Une Justice dans l'urgence. Le traitement en temps réel des affaires pénales* (2007); Nicola Lacey, *The Prisoners' Dilemma: Political Economy and Punishment in Contemporary Democracies* (2008); Susana Durão, *Polícia e e proximidade. uma etnografia da polícia em Lisboa* (2008); Loïc Wacquant, *Punishing the Poor: The Neoliberal Government of Social Insecurity* (2009b); David Garland, *Peculiar Institution: America's Death Penalty in an Age of Abolition* (2010); Joshua Page, *The Toughest Beat: Politics, Punishment, and the Prison Officers Union in California* (2011); Didier Fassin, *La Force de l'ordre. Une anthropologie de la police des quartiers* (2011a); Amy E. Lerman and Vesla M. Weaver *Arresting Citizenship: The Democratic Consequences of American Crime Control* (2014); Yasmine Bouagga, *Humaniser la peine? Enquête en maison d'arrêt* (2015); Marie Gottschalk, *Caught: The Prison State and the Lockdown of American Politics* (2016); Forrest Stuart, *Down, Out, and Under Arrest: Policing and Everyday Life in Skid Row* (2016); Vanessa Barker, *Nordic Nationalism and Penal Order: Walling the Welfare State* (2017); Ignacio González Sánchez, *Neoliberalismo y castigo* (2021); Peter Baldwin, *Command and*

ing from the routine workings of these institutions and shaped by the mundane ways of thinking, feeling, and acting of agents of flesh and blood operating within the coils of bureaucracies of punishment. To understand the delivery of penality as legitimate material and symbolic violence trained on unruly bodies, then, it is essential to disclose and drill deep into the ordinary functioning of the criminal court as the "throughput" agency transforming the "input" of the police into the "output" of the prison and its extensions.[2]

A structural ethnography of prosecutorial practice

This chapter draws on a three-year ethnography of the day-to-day operations of two county courts in Northern California to flesh out the practical microstructure and strategic tenor of penality by following a single attorney at work negotiating guilty plea agreements. I will disclose the workings of "negotiated justice," that is, a justice system based on the extraction of guilty pleas. In a plea bargain, the prosecutor offers to lower charges and recommend a lesser sentence to the judge in exchange for an early admission of guilt by the defendant.

Persuade: Crime, Law, and the State across History (2021); Stephanie Schmidt, *Affekt und Polizei: Eine Ethnografie der Wut in der exekutiven Gewaltarbeit* (2022).
[2] Social science scholarship on punishment in the United States is overwhelmingly concentrated on policing, on the one end, and incarceration, on the other (Joe Soss and Vesla Weaver, "Police Are Our Government: Politics, Political Science, and the Policing of Race–Class Subjugated Communities" [2017]; Elizabeth Hinton and DeAnza Cook, "The Mass Criminalization of Black Americans: A Historical Overview" [2021]), leaving a gaping hole between them (Brian Forst, "Prosecution and Courts" [2017]). Rounded field studies of criminal courts are comparatively few and far between. The best ones date from some half-century ago: Arthur Rosett and Donald R. Cressey, *Justice by Consent: Plea Bargains in the American Courthouse* (1976); Milton Heumann, *Plea Bargaining: The Experiences of Prosecutors, Judges and Defense Attorneys* (1978); Malcolm M. Feeley, *The Process is the Punishment: Handling Cases in a Lower Criminal Court* (1979); Douglas W. Maynard, *Inside Plea Bargaining: The Language of Negotiation* (1982); James Eisenstein et al., *The Contours of Justice: Communities and their Courts* (1988). Three recent monographs focus exclusively on low-level offenses (Issa Kohler-Hausmann, *Misdemeanorland: Criminal Courts and Social Control in an Age of Broken Windows Policing* [2018]), view the court through the eyes of defendants (Matthew Clair, *Privilege and Punishment: How Race and Class Matter in Criminal Court* [2020]), and draw a grotesque portrait of court actors as universally racist and morally evil (Nicole Gonzalez Van Cleve, *Crook County: Racism and Injustice in America's Largest Criminal Court* [2016]). A rare effort to connect the full chain of judicial processing and its extensions is Didier Fassin et al.'s *Juger, réprimer, accompagner. Essai sur la morale de l'État* (2013).

The prosecutor gains efficiency and certainty of resolution; the defendant gets a "discount" on punishment. In the United States, 97 percent of all felony cases that resolved entailed the entry of a guilty plea. The trial by jury has been dead for nearly a century; it survives only in television series and in the movies.[3]

The present ethnography is the first to systematically triangulate the points of view of state judges, prosecutors, and defense attorneys based on a combination of biographical and observational data generated *at the point of production of punishment*.[4] It is also the first to provide a grasp of penality in the making, not from the open courtroom and public gallery, where action is largely ceremonial and bureaucratic, but from the *closed backstages* of judges' private chambers, negotiation and witness rooms, corridors and offices where the complex and contentious courtwork of criminal law-making at ground level is carried out.

By *courtwork* I mean the gamut of legal and social activities contributing to the output of the court as well as to the reproduction and transformation of its structure and functioning as an institutional microcosm. It differs from James Eisenstein and Herbert Jacob's (1977) germinal notion of "courtroom *workgroup*"[5] in that it does not limit itself to relations readily visible in "open court" but encompasses activities and sociability rooted in the wings of the courthouse and beyond: attorneys on both sides "prepping" cases in their office and negotiating deals in backrooms, judges reviewing defense motions or sentencing dossiers in the privacy of their chambers, collective practices of camaraderie among public defenders, "whiteboard sessions" of prosecutors gearing up for trial, taverns where private counsel congregate to commiserate about cases, etc. This is where the fate of criminal defendants is decided, not in the kabuki theater of the courtroom.[6]

---

[3] Mary E. Vogel, *Coercion to Compromise: Plea Bargaining, the Courts, and the Making of Political Authority* (2007); Malcolm M. Feeley and Rosann Greenspan, "The Long History of Plea Bargaining" (2024).

[4] The closest comparable study is Milton Heumann's superb monograph on *Plea Bargaining: The Experiences of Prosecutors, Judges and Defense Attorneys*. It offers a rich and subtle portrait of case disposition in six Connecticut courts that remains strikingly current and thus repays a close reading.

[5] James Eisenstein and Herbert Jacob, *Felony Justice: An Organizational Analysis of Criminal Courts* (1977), pp. 20–38.

[6] This suggests that the tradition of "courtroom ethnography" has consistently missed its object, mistaking bureaucratic ceremonial for criminal lawyering. This is glaring in the works scanned by Max Travers, "Court Ethnographies" (2021), and Sarah

More importantly, the conceptual canopy of the penal state developed in chapters 1 and 2 mandates two crucial analytical moves intended to *inject structure and history* into the analysis of occupational interactions and legal strategies in and around the courthouse.[7] The first move consists in locating prosecutors, defense attorneys and judges in the objective structure of relations of power comprising the *local judicial field* as a space of forces and a space of struggles.[8] In addition, prosecutors and public defenders must be situated in the social architecture of their respective offices, both of which are organized around a polar opposition between "true believers" and "negotiators" that mirrors the opposition between the two offices as well as the duality between the Right hand and the Left hand of the state.

229

The second analytical move consists in capturing court officers as social agents bearing and enacting an *individual and collective history*. Individual history refers to the formative influence of their originating social milieu and individual path through social space, which stamped their primary (or generic) habitus. This is captured by retracing the trajectory of attorneys from childhood to high school to law school and entry onto the court scene. Collective history refers to the professional tradition and arc of their respective offices construed as organizational entities that rework class and ethnic origins according to their own imperatives and stamp the secondary (or specific) habitus of court attorneys.[9] This allows me to avoid the twinned fallacies of

Klosterkamp and Lisa Flower, "Introduction to Courtroom Ethnography" (2023). Heumann et al. warn about the danger of "concept hagiography" and propose that the "courtroom workgroup *can* matter" for judicial outcome "but in all likelihood more on the margin." Milton Heumann et al., "Courtroom Workgroups: 'A Prosecutor, a Defense Attorney, and a Judge Walk into a Bar'" (2021), p. 286.

[7] These moves constitute a double break with the interactionist approach advocated by Jeffery T. Ulmer in his call to envisage "Criminal Courts as Inhabited Institutions: Making Sense of Difference and Similarity in Sentencing" (2019).

[8] Pierre Bourdieu, *Microcosmes. Théorie des champs* (2022b). See the discussion of the constitutive properties of a field in chapter 1, *supra*, pp. 89–90.

[9] This double historical perspective is strikingly absent from classical and contemporary field studies of the court. This reflects the strong ahistorical slant of criminological, legal, and social science studies of the law and punishment more generally. Scholars of judicial institutions who take time seriously in their theorizing are few and far between. Among them, see Douglas Hay et al. (eds.), *Albion's Fatal Tree: Crime and Society in Eighteenth-Century England* (1975); John H. Langbein, *The Origins of Adversary Criminal Trial* (2003); Lawrence Friedman, *Crime and Punishment in American History* (1994); Antoine Garapon, *Bien juger. Essai sur le rituel judiciaire* (1997); Michael Willrich, *City of Courts: Socializing Justice in Progressive Era Chicago* (2003); and James Q. Whitman, *The Origins of Reasonable Doubt: Theological Roots of*

"interactionism" and "presentism" at both the macro-level of institutions and the micro-level of face-to-face confrontations between prosecutors and defenders.[10]

The chapter runs as follows. I situate the pretrial prosecutor who negotiates plea agreements on the professional scene. I set out the methodological and empirical parameters of the study. I draw up the analytic maps of the local judicial space and of the offices of prosecutors and public defenders – the structural moment. I then take the reader through the typical day of the pretrial prosecutor and into "the trenches" of negotiated justice in an effort to give texture to his activity and capture its many stakes – the agentic moment.

230   I characterize plea bargaining as a variant of *relational contracting* in which the parties involved sustain repeated exchanges over time through minimal trust and informal norms of communication, engaging in "antagonistic cooperation" to hammer out multilayered deals resolving criminal cases. Against the conventional view of plea bargaining as an "assembly line" mechanically putting out standardized products,[11] judicial negotiation emerges as a technically *complex*, socially *embedded*, loosely *regulated*, and strikingly *collective* practice, swinging between reformation and retribution, the two poles organizing practical philosophies of punishment. It is an engine for what I call *judicial tagging*, the operation whereby bodies out of order are brought back within the control of the state.

The granular account of the judicial tagging of defendants as mechanism of penal processing both adds layers to, and challenges, conventional scholarship on criminal justice that has stressed the untrammeled if not absolute discretion prosecutors enjoy in the seemingly instrumental drive to crime control.[12] Shadowing the pretrial prosecutor in his daily activities discloses many intricacies and facets of plea bargaining that extant research ignores or underreports.[13] It

---

the *Criminal Trial* (2008). See also the thematic bibliographies in Paul Knepper and Anja Johansen (eds.), *The Oxford Handbook of the History of Crime and Criminal Justice* (2016).

[10] I discuss these fallacies in Loïc Wacquant, *The Poverty of the Ethnography of Poverty* ([2023] 2025), pp. 143–6 and 161–4.

[11] Dan Canon, *Pleading Out: How Plea Bargaining Creates a Permanent Criminal Class* (2022).

[12] Angela J. Davis, *Arbitrary Justice: The Power of the American Prosecutor* (2007); William J. Stuntz, *The Collapse of American Criminal Justice* (2011); Michael Tonry, "Prosecutors and Politics in Comparative Perspective" (2012).

[13] Brian D. Johnson et al., "Sociolegal Approaches to the Study of Guilty Pleas and Prosecution" (2016); Vanessa A. Edkins and Allison D. Redlich (eds.), *A System of*

documents the dogged search for a measure of substantive justice that attorneys on both sides of the aisle engage in despite the press of the sheer volume of cases handled. Based on these empirical findings, I propose to reorient ethnographies of the criminal court, and social studies of penality more generally, from theoretical presupposition to documented practice, output to throughput, frontstage to backstage, and from interacting agents to the dialectic of historical structures and habitus in the judicial field.

On a theoretical level, I spotlight the urgent need to take into account *class as a commanding cause* of judicial outcomes – when researchers are obnubilated by race and pliant prisoners of administrative data – as well as *class fractions* within the proletariat, because small differences in structural position translate into differences in dispositions which are in turn transmuted into differential treatment by the court.[14] I warn against confusing difference, disparity, and discrimination in prosecution, a confusion that smuggles moral judgment into the social scientific study of penality. I conclude this chapter by unpacking the thesis that the prosecutor is the human spear of the penal state, returning full circle to my opening argument on the need to wed theories of the state and theories of punishment. But, to wield its full power, the prosecutor must enroll the collusive action, not only of the defense attorney, but of the defendant himself.

231

One last prefatory note before we jump inside the office of the District Attorney (DA) of San Pedrito county in California: this chapter does not take a stance on the juridical flaws, social biases, and vexed moral valence of plea bargaining as the central engine of prosecutorial power. This omission is deliberate. The sociolegal literature is awash with principled condemnations of the practice based on how jurists and criminologists *imagine* it to work since there exists no granular first-hand account of its actual unfolding in the age of hyperincarceration.[15] Pell-mell, the procedure has been *accused* – I use the

Pleas: Social Science's Contributions to the Real Legal System (2019); Robert Schehr, *The Political Economy of Plea Bargaining* (2024).

[14] In *Privilege and Punishment*, Clair exposes "how race and class matter in criminal court" but he limits his analysis to attorney-client relations captured solely from the latter's standpoint. This phenomenology excludes from the analytic purview the ordinary actions of the key deciders, the prosecutor and the judge, and how these are shaped by their class dispositions.

[15] I call for remedying this absence in "Sealing the Fate of 'The Kid': A Field Note on the Swirl of Plea Bargaining" (2026). Mona Lynch gets us close in her reconstruction of negotiations in federal court in *Hard Bargains: The Coercive Power of Drug Laws in Federal Court* (2016).

term advisedly – of being coercive, capricious, opaque, unreviewable, and unaccountable, a violation of the fundamental rights granted by the country's sacrosanct constitution which include the right to a jury trial.[16] My position is that, before we rush to normative judgment and political conclusions about it, it is essential to capture and then unpack prosecution as the concrete deployment of penal power. That is the agenda of this chapter.

Situating the pretrial prosecutor

232

Criminal courts, which lie at the core of the penal apparatus, are organized differently in different countries, though there has been a slow drift, in recent decades, toward global alignment as manifested by the international diffusion of variants of plea bargaining and adversarial procedures borrowed from the United States.[17] In the United States, the main engine of criminal adjudication is the county or state criminal court, a local institution animated by a triad of legal professionals which processes millions of defendants each year:[18] *prosecutors*, housed by the State or District Attorney's office, who initiate action by charging cases, drive plea negotiations, and prefigure sentences;[19] *public defenders*, court-appointed lawyers generally employed by a Public Defender's office, entrusted with protecting the constitutional rights of indigent defendants accounting for some 70 percent of cases;[20] and *judges*, nominated by governors or elected to the bench by the citizenry, who arbitrate the courtroom

---

[16] An eloquent exemplar is Carissa Byrne Hessick, *Punishment Without Trial: Why Plea Bargaining is a Bad Deal* (2021), which characteristically tells "stories" castigating justice bargaining but contains not a single account of an actual plea negotiation. The flaws of plea bargaining are a central focus of the activities of the Plea Bargaining Institute founded and led by the jurist Lucian Dervan (based at Belmont University in Nashville, Tennessee).

[17] Regina Rauxloh, *Plea Bargaining in National and International Law: A Comparative Study* (2012); Erik Luna and Marianne L. Wade (eds.), *The Prosecutor in Transnational Perspective* (2012); Máximo Langer, "Plea Bargaining, Conviction Without Trial, and the Global Administratization of Criminal Convictions" (2021).

[18] Criminal courts at the county level process about 18 million cases annually whereas federal courts, which have attracted disproportionate attention from scholars of prosecution, handle barely 75,000 cases.

[19] Brian Forst, "Prosecution" (2011).

[20] Paul B. Wice, *Public Defenders and the American Justice System* (2005).

relations between prosecutors and defenders and move the bureau-cratic wheels of case adjudication.[21]

There are roughly 3,200 counties, some 2,300 prosecutors' offices and 557 public defenders' offices in the United States.[22] In large urban counties, each of these entities is in turn a complex legal and bureaucratic machinery with differentiated units and distributions of personnel, tasks, and budgets varying with county population, policy priorities, and the local profile of criminality and culture of punishment. The DA's office in the main county featured in the present article runs on a yearly budget of $90 million and employs 130 "line prosecutors" (or deputy DAs) who handle some 28,000 cases, including 7,000 felonies, in a typical year. Prosecutorial work is divided between "calendars" (the routine recording of case pro-cessing during different types of hearings) and "assignments" which include charging cases, preliminary examination, misdemeanor trial and felony trial, law and motion, as well as work on "vertical teams" handling specific offenses such as domestic violence, human traffick-ing, gang-related crimes, child sexual assault, homicide, consumer fraud, elder abuse, etc. Inspectors, victims' advocates, and technical and clerical staff support the daily work of prosecutors, for a total payroll in excess of 300.[23]

233

Gradations of criminality

Gradations of law-breaking in California entail three categories: in descending order of severity, felony, misdemeanor, and infraction. *Felonies,* which comprise serious and violent crimes such as drug traf-ficking, residential burglary, aggravated assault, robbery, kidnapping, arson, rape, and murder, are criminal offenses liable to state prison sentences of one year and more (prisoners spend an average of 2.4 years behind bars). In most cases, however, they result in probation,

[21] Cassia C. Spohn, *How Do Judges Decide: The Search for Fairness and Justice in Punishment* (2009).
[22] For a historical account of the intensely local nature and administrative insularity of these offices, see John L. Worrall, "Prosecutors in Problem-Solving Courts" (2008). For a sweeping portrait of "prosecutors in all of their contexts" in the United States, see Wright et al.'s indispensable *Oxford Handbook of Prosecutors and Prosecution* (2021).
[23] In "Prosecution in 3-D" (2012), Kay Levine and Ronald Wright make a strong case that one cannot understand prosecuting without accounting for the organization, composition, and tradition of the office in which prosecutors work.

a suspended prison sentence under supervision of a probation agent tasked with ensuring that the convict meets a series of tailored terms and conditions (regular check-ins, employment, residence, restitution, drug rehabilitation or alcohol testing, etc.) as well as "obey all laws and be of good conduct" (as in the formula read by the judge). Lasting from two to five years, probation mixes care and coercion to keep convicts on a judicial leash (1).

Misdemeanors are less serious offenses (first-time drunk driving, larceny or petty theft, drug possession, low-level domestic violence, etc.) for which the maximum punishment is a year in county jail (jail detainees spend an average of 26 days behind bars), but which typically result in fines, community service, and probation or outright dismissal because the misbehavior is inconsequential (2).

"*Wobblers*," in court lingo, are offenses (such as assault, commercial burglary, forgery, and domestic violence with injury) that may be charged either as a misdemeanor or as a felony depending on the circumstances and profile of the offender. A wobbler gives maximum latitude to the prosecutor as well as an avenue for defense attorneys to ask for a reduction in charges.

At the bottom of the scale of gravity we find *infractions* such as driving violations, parking tickets, jaywalking, littering, minor trespassing, smoking in forbidden areas, as well as violations of the gamut of municipal ordinances. They are technically not crimes and are punishable only by fines. But if they are repeated (leading, for instance, to an accumulation of traffic tickets), they can turn into misdemeanors. Offenses that can be statutorily charged either as infractions or as misdemeanors are informally called "wobblets."

1. Michelle S. Phelps and Ebony L. Ruhland, "Governing Marginality: Coercion and Care in Probation" (2022).
2. The main *de facto* sanction for most misdemeanants is the bureaucratic hassle and personal disruption of going through the court process, as shown by Malcolm Feeley in his classic study, *The Process is the Punishment: Handling Cases in a Lower Criminal Court* (1979), updated and verified by Issa Kohler-Hausmann in *Misdemeanorland: Criminal Courts and Social Control in an Age of Broken Windows Policing* (2018).

County or state prosecutors' offices vary tremendously in terms of size, resources, recruitment, demographics, legal capacities, informal culture, and courtroom tradition, not to mention the economic, ethnic, political, and criminal characteristics of the districts they cover. They are also extraordinarily insular, with very little learning and virtually no coordination across organizations. Offices in large urban counties of the type I studied are not statistically "representative" of the majority of offices which are small and medium-sized outfits dispersed across suburban and rural areas – but the "modal office" is a statistical abstraction devoid of sociological interest in any case.[24] Yet, together, they process and send to prison the majority of convicts. Small DA's offices in remote counties operating with a skeletal staff are more punitive, but the population they reel in is much smaller. Moreover, my purpose is not to make generalizable claims about prosecution nationwide but to document on-the-ground activities, probe live social relations, uncover meanings, and display some of the social and symbolic mechanisms that produce guilty pleas and articulate penal power in the flesh. In so doing, I will dispel a number of preconceptions regarding prosecutors – that they are callous cowboys thirsting for "victory" at all costs and eager to maximize punishment – and plea bargaining – that it is an "assembly line" trampling over the basic rights of defendants.

235

A central pivot in the division of judicial labor and main triage point of felony cases in the county criminal court is occupied by the *pretrial prosecutor*. Following arraignment, the initial court hearing during which the judge notifies defendants of the charges filed against them, the mission of the pretrial prosecutor is to review the cases funneled by the "charging" deputy DA (who determines the specific penal code sections violated by the accused), to make "opening offers" for a guilty plea to defendants via their defense attorney (who mediates all exchanges) and to try and close deals prior to the assignment of cases to trial (thus the adjective "pretrial"). It also entails coordinating with, and checking on, the work of the team of younger prosecutors tasked with preparing "preliminary examinations" for these same cases in the event that plea negotiations prove fruitless.[25] The

[24] For a statistical portrait of state prosecutors' offices (exclusive of attorneys in municipal and city courts handling only misdemeanors and infractions), see Steven W. Perry and Duren Banks, *Prosecutors in State Courts, 2007. Statistical Tables* (2011). A few highlights: offices served districts with populations ranging from 500 to 10 million; 15 percent were part-time offices; yearly operating budgets ranged from $536,000 to $49 million; the largest offices (Los Angeles and Chicago) employed more than 600 prosecutors while the smallest ones had only a single prosecutor. See Ronald Wright and Kay Levine's extended argument that "Place Matters in Prosecution Research" (2016).

[25] In California criminal procedure, a preliminary examination hearing (known as "prelim" or "PX") is a sort of abbreviated mini trial (lasting a couple of hours to a day) during which the prosecutor must show enough incriminating evidence to convince a judge that the defendant should be "held to answer" and that the case should be "bound over" to the next stage. The next stage is assignment to the felony

pretrial prosecutor is at the center of a neuralgic nexus where penality is concretized, materialized in time, space, discourse, and decision (to inflict stigma, probation, or prison), and so its study offers what Robert Merton calls "strategic research materials" for capturing the penal state in action.[26]

In San Pedrito county, all pretrial felony pleas are *centralized in the hands of only two deputy DAs*, one each for the western and eastern parts of the county. This guarantees a measure of consistency across cases in each region, but it comes with notable differences across individuals and across regions. Prosecutors differ widely in how they assess cases and use their discretion.[27] Some are particularly intolerant of certain offenses (e.g., the sale of narcotics or mass identity theft) and thus make comparatively "high" offers on them; some refuse to make offers on certain cases (brutal homicides or child sexual assaults); some bend over backward to offer felony probation to meritorious defendants. The fate of the accused at any given time thus depends in part on the professional and moral inclinations of the pretrial DA on duty at that moment.[28] But, getting into the guts of negotiated justice, we are going to discern how these individual variations are shaped and channeled by nested social structures, symbolic frames, and interactional loops.

As for geography, the western region of the county contains Alphaville, a large multiethnic city home to a black hyperghetto plagued by rampant drug dealing, routine gang activity, and high rates of violent crime, including street robbery, sexual assault, and homicide. Correspondingly, the pretrial DA there navigates a torrent of serious offenses, even as most cases are "garden-variety felonies" involving little or no violence. To resolve these cases speedily, he habitually makes comparatively "low offers," meaning offers more favorable to the defendant so that scarce resources in personnel, time, and

---

trial calendar in preparation for a possible trial – but, in fact, most of these cases will still be resolved by further plea negotiations. For an explication of the full chain of criminal adjudication, see *infra*, pp. 238–41.

[26] Robert K. Merton, "Three Fragments from a Sociologist's Notebooks: Establishing the Phenomenon, Specified Ignorance, and Strategic Research Materials" (1987).

[27] Megan S. Wright et al., "Inside the Black Box of Prosecutor Discretion" (2022).

[28] This variability is confirmed by Wright et al.'s (ibid.) survey of 500 prosecutors recruited nationwide which documents the seemingly capricious nature of prosecutorial judgment. But the study does not relate judgments to variations in social background, professional experience, office culture, and jurisdiction, and so it is not possible to dismiss the notion that these variations are actually patterned rather than random.

courtroom may be directed at the more grievous and complex cases. The eastern region is more mixed ecologically and dispersed in settlement with many suburban developments and semi-rural towns; crime there is less prevalent and thus collective intolerance for offending is greater and judges are more severe. The pretrial DA is expected and in a position to make higher offers, meaning that the standard punishment or "going rate" – a key folk concept – for committing a given offense is greater than in the western region. Attorneys in the eastern district sometimes joke that many crimes they prosecute as felonies would be "Alphaville misdemeanors." The assignment of pretrial DA changed four times while I was in the field, creating as many natural experiments on "resetting the price of crime" in the county and its effects on plea negotiations, relations with defense attorneys, and ultimately on defendants as well as on office and courthouse reputation.

The pretrial DA must be a *seasoned* attorney with extensive and recent trial experience.[29] He must know what quantum of punishment judges will consistently impose after conviction for the different categories of crimes so he can evaluate the "worth of a case" from the endpoint of the prosecution chain. The *worth of a case is a central folk category* of judicial work in the criminal court.[30] It is constantly invoked and haggled over by prosecutors and defense attorneys. It is an evolving estimate of the fitting quantum of punishment that anchors negotiations, based on offense, offender's age and record, circumstances and impact, provability and the current "going rate," set against the operational resources of the court. It is the central stake of negotiations. Typically, the prosecutor sees that value as higher than the defender, but not always, and the purpose of negotiation is to come to a shared valuation.[31]

It is an *honor* for a prosecutor to be assigned to the position of pretrial negotiator, a mark of professional expertise and a vote of personal confidence from "the elected" (the chief DA) which generally

237

[29] I use the masculine because five of the six pretrial and head trial DAs active in San Pedrito during my three years in the field were men. Three of them were mid-career attorneys (with a dozen years of experience) and two were veterans (with some 30 years in the office).

[30] Rosett and Cressey, *Justice by Consent*; Milton Heumann, *Plea Bargaining*; Feeley, *The Process is the Punishment*; Debra S. Emmelman, *Justice for the Poor: A Study of Criminal Defence Work* (2003); Peter F. Nardulli et al., *The Tenor of Justice: Criminal Courts and the Guilty Plea Process* (1988).

[31] The "going rate" is the generic value of a crime type or category on the punishment scale. The "worth of a case" is an application of this value to the specifics of that case. I return to these notions later, *infra*, pp. 291–2, 294–5.

signals a climb up the occupational hierarchy. For younger prosecutors, it marks them out as a "rising star in the office" who may one day become part of "management." It comes with a small increase in salary and a great increase in prestige. But it is also a *burden*: the volume of activities is crushing, the pace of labor torrid, and the complexity of the work daunting. The pretrial DA must be prepared to put in long days of work (a good ten hours) and come into the office all day on Saturday or Sunday to pore over paper files, listen to audio recordings, and view video evidence of criminal activity to hone his offers. He must deal face-to-face with a constant stream of defense attorneys, public and private, who can be difficult to get along with, as well as follow the trajectory of the cases he "deals" as they go through preliminary examination ("PX") on their way to resolution or trial. Some seasoned prosecutors would rather be spared the honor, especially the "trial dogs," DAs who relish taking serious cases to trial, including homicide, child sexual assaults (the most delicate and taxing matters), and rape – the dictum at the main courthouse of San Pedrito county is that trials are reserved for "sex and death." Finally, the prosecutor "dealing" cases is tangibly wielding penal power; in serious matters, he can alter the life of the defendant in dramatic and irreversible fashion. Contrary to the public and academic stereotype, not every deputy DA is comfortable with shouldering that responsibility. Discretion confers power but it also imposes a burden at once professional, moral, and emotional.

238

From arrest to prosecution to punishment, the California way

The criminal processing of cases in California county court unfolds in a multiplicity of tracks with manifold exits and graduated forms of punishment. It may be simplified into eight stages.

1. The police *arrest* a suspect either during the commission of a crime, as a result of an investigation, or on a court warrant. The suspect is *booked* in jail and kept behind bars or released to appear in court within 48 hours.
2. The police report (which includes a narrative of the event, statements by suspects and witnesses, material evidence, observations by the officer, and recommended charges) is submitted to the District Attorney's office where a charging deputy *files* the case or

declines to file due to insufficient evidence or because the misconduct is minor or difficult to characterize as criminal. The standard
for charging is that the prosecutor should be able to prove the case
"beyond a reasonable doubt" to a jury of 12 people.

3. The suspect goes through *arraignment*, a court hearing during
which the judge notifies him of the charges filed against him, sets
bail, and refers the defendant to the Public Defender's office (the
vast majority of defendants do not have the means to hire a private
attorney). In nine cases out of ten, the defendant enters a plea of
not guilty.

4. The case goes through a succession of *pretrial hearings* (PTH)
during which the defendant's attorney and the line prosecutor
assigned to the case meet to share evidence about the case ("discovery"), litigate motions if any, and negotiate a plea agreement.
The number of hearings is set by local tradition and by the judge
running the master felony calendar and it varies from one to four
or five scheduled about three weeks apart each.

5. If the DA and defendant cannot agree, the case is sent to *preliminary examination* (called PX in court lingo) (1), a contested hearing resembling a mini-trial (lasting an hour to a day, typically a
couple of hours) during which the prosecutor must show sufficient
evidence ("probable cause") for the judge to decide that the case
should go forward to trial. The PX judge may validate, reduce, or
dismiss the charges.

6. If the defendant is "bound over," the case is sent to *felony trial
negotiation*. These hearings, one to four of them, are the last opportunity to "resolve" the case by a plea agreement.

7. If it does not resolve, the case is assigned to a *trial judge* and the
two parties prepare for trial. The trial follows a set formula: preliminary motions (to dismiss the case, suppress evidence, etc.), opening statements by the two parties, evidence, closing statements,
jury deliberation. But plea deals can still be struck before and even
during the trial itself, so long as the jury has not concluded its
deliberations.

8. The *sentence*, which is prefigured in the plea agreement, is decided
later by a different judge and served in the form of probation, jail
time, or prison time accompanied by a litany of fines and fees and
assorted administrative obligations.

The vast majority of matters find a negotiated resolution at the
pretrial stage (2). As a rule, the plea offer gets less and less favorable

as the case climbs from one judicial step to the next, to give the defendant an *incentive to settle early*. Then the latter benefits from a punishment "discount" and early release while the court benefits from securing a conviction, "clearing the docket," and economizing limited collective resources (in personnel, time, and courtroom space). A crucial early bifurcation separates defendants *"in custody"* (in remand detention in the local jail) during the proceedings and defendants *released* on bail or on their "own recognizance" ("OR'ed," meaning on the promise to appear in court at the next hearing). Aside from the seriousness of the offense, the factors deciding custody status are *all class-related*: whether the defendant has a job, a stable financial situation and regular residence, a supporting family and social ties to the community such as membership in a church (3). These factors are viewed by the arraignment judge as presumptive indicators that the defendant will not endanger the citizenry and will dutifully appear in court at his subsequent hearings. It is part and parcel of the judicial doxa, a notion taken for granted by all court actors that inscribes class discrimination at the heart of the punishment apparatus as I will show later (*infra*, pp. 320–4, 329–31).

Ceteris paribus, a defendant in custody is far more likely to quickly accept a plea deal in order to be released from jail than a defendant who appears "out of custody" and to receive a less favorable sentence (4). Another crucial decision is whether or not the defendant "waives time," that is, forgoes his right to a preliminary hearing within ten court days of his initial arraignment and the right to a jury trial within 60 calendar days of his arraignment after preliminary examination. Most defendants "waive 10 and 60" because they need time to gather and process evidence for their defense or wish to negotiate a plea agreement which will take a few weeks to hammer out. Many are simply "aging the case" in hopes that the passage of time will weaken the evidence against them and yield a better offer from the DA.

1. Preliminary hearings are held only for felonies. On paper, misdemeanor cases go directly from pretrial to trial. But, in reality, misdemeanors rarely reach the trial stage as they are resolved by a plea, diversion, or dismissal. The standard of evidence for the defendant to be "held to answer" at PX is "probable cause" and not "beyond a reasonable doubt" as for jury trials. For a dissection of the treatment of misdemeanors and infractions, see Issa Kohler-Hausmann, "Don't Call It a Comeback: The Criminological and Sociological Study of Subfelonies" (2022).

2. The resolution rate varies by county in and out of California, but it exceeds

90 percent nearly everywhere. In major cities around the country, 94 percent of felony convictions result from a plea agreement. Brian A. Reaves, *Felony Defendants in Large Urban Counties, 2009* (2013).

3. Joshua Page and Christine S. Scott-Hayward, "Bail and Pretrial Justice in the United States: A Field of Possibility" (2022).

4. Stacie St. Louis, "The Pretrial Detention Penalty: A Systematic Review and Meta-Analysis of Pretrial Detention and Case Outcomes" (2024). A study of pretrial detention in misdemeanor cases in Houston, Texas, found that defendants in custody were 25 percent more likely to plead guilty than similarly situated defendants out of custody and 43 percent more likely to be sentenced to jail time for average sentences that were twice as long. Paul Heaton et al., "The Downstream Consequences of Misdemeanor Pretrial Detention" (2017).

"The Professor" comes to court

This chapter is based on an ethnographic study of 30 months stretched over a three-year period during which I embedded myself in two county criminal courts of Northern California I call San Pedrito county and Carnival county. I gained entry into the field by volunteering as an intern for pretrial services (whose mission is to facilitate the release of defendants "on their own recognizance" or low money bail so that they do not remain in jail while waiting for their case to be adjudicated) and by studying up close a "problem-solving court" aimed at clearing the matters of homeless persons embroiled with the law due to minor cases.[32] After eight months of slow and cautious diplomacy, I obtained permission from the chief District Attorney of San Pedrito county to interview and shadow line prosecutors (known colloquially as "DAs") in their ordinary round. I obtained a similar permission from the chief Public Defender of the county in three months using the same tactic of indirect approach.[33]

[32] See John L. Worrall, "Prosecutors in Problem-Solving Courts" (2008) on the bureaucratic rationale and role of the prosecutor in such courts.

[33] I produced an extensive dossier on the head DA and head PD, their background, policies, and social and political views. I identified, obtained information from, and garnered the support of people who knew them professionally or personally, and could influence their judgment. I prepared a short presentation of my project highlighting its scholarly, civic, and policy potential and defended it during a lengthy interview. I never hid from prosecutors the fact that I had written a book entitled *Punishing the Poor* (2009b), but I also did not foreground it. I put forth as model for my future monograph on the court my ethnography of prizefighting. I personally offered a copy of my book *Body and Soul: Notebooks of an Apprentice Boxer* ([2004] 2022) to the office leaders and to the attorneys I interviewed on both sides of the aisle. Only one prosecutor out of one hundred mentioned googling me and finding "compromising"

I developed trusting ties with two important judges assigned to pivotal calendars (arraignment in one courthouse and the master felony calendar in another) who acted as my "ambassadors" to the bench and to attorneys on both sides of the aisle. This allowed me to interview, observe, and consort with a dozen judges in their courtrooms and private chambers before, during, and after hearings, so they could tutor me on the fine points of "judgecraft" and on the functioning of the court more generally.[34] I observed up close the gamut of hearings from both front- and backstages. Finally, I conducted formal, sit-down, semi-structured interviews with 100 prosecutors and 100 public defenders in the two counties as well as with 20 private defense attorneys active in the San Pedrito court, not counting repeated interviews with a veteran "star" attorney and a younger attorney new to the county. I also interviewed a dozen judges and shadowed a couple of them in and out of the courtroom. To all, I presented my study as aiming to do for the court what I had done for the boxing gym a decade earlier in my book: to depict the mundane workings of the institution, to document its mores, and to uncover what makes agents on the scene tick.[35]

In this chapter, I focus on plea bargaining as the pivot of judicial treatment and outcome: in California, only 2 percent of felony cases are resolved by jury trial; the rest result in a plea of guilty (or *nolo contendere*) or are otherwise dismissed at some point in the judicial process. I conducted live observation of 17 pretrial negotiation sessions before PX (each lasting two or three hours) in three different courthouses with four different prosecutors whom I knew well since I had previously interviewed them at length about their social trajectories, occupational activities, and professional values, as well as followed them in court and in their offices. These semi-structured interviews were part of the batch of 100 in-office interviews with prosecutors that each lasted an average of 2.5 hours generating about 4,000 printed pages of transcripts in total. I also observed 20 negotiation sessions conducted by two veteran prosecutors after PX at the felony trial stage, the last judicial step before cases are "set" for presentation to a jury.

During these sessions, I was given access to the negotiation chamber, a nondescript windowless room inside the DA's office. I was

evidence on my personal web page. We discussed the themes and intent of my prior work on punishment and how the study of the court would not just amplify, but also challenge that work, and the interview proceeded smoothly.

[34] Richard Moorhead and Dave Cowan, "Judgecraft: An Introduction" (2007).

[35] Wacquant, *Body and Soul* ([2004] 2022).

Photo 1 The tools of the Professor

allowed to sit at or near the edge of the negotiating table to scruti-
nize the interactions between attorneys, take handwritten notes in a
pocket notebook sitting on one thigh along with my pocket watch,
and record conversations with a small digital voice recorder (Olympus
VN5200PC) sitting on my other thigh. Altogether, I recorded over
80 hours of plea negotiations. The digital tapes were first "scripted,"
meaning that a rundown of interlocutors, cases, conversational turns,
prosodic and embodied behavior as well as the comings and goings
of attorneys in the room was established based on the notes and diagrams couched in my field notebook. Scripts run 8–18 pages single-
spaced. The script was then used to transcribe the verbal exchanges
in full, taking note of tone, manner, and emotion, at which time the
names of attorneys, defendants, and other identifying information
were changed or stripped (in accordance with the requirements of

my university's Institutional Review Board).[36] The full transcript of pretrial negotiation sessions typically runs to about 50–70 pages, for a total in excess of 2,000 pages of printed text. For three of the five attorneys I observed at work, the negotiation sessions were preceded by in-office discussion of that morning's cases and followed by an afternoon debrief during which I was able to ask for clarifications and follow up on issues of tactics and strategy as well as on questions of character and policy.

I use the ten plea bargaining sessions I attended with the same pretrial attorney who had recently been assigned to the post, a conjuncture which offered a unique opportunity to reveal the "rules of the game" as they came to be contested and reset. These sessions of ten felony plea negotiations covering some 300 cases yielded a total of 22 hours of recordings and nearly 500 pages of transcripts. To the best of my knowledge, this is the second time a social scientist has been able to both observe and tape plea bargaining in an American criminal court *in vivo*. The first time was the ethnomethodological and conversation-analytic study by Douglas Maynard (1984), *Inside Plea Bargaining: The Language of Negotiation*.[37] Taping was indispensable to make sense of the technical and social aspects of fast-flowing conversations mentioning at machine-gun speed penal code sections, previous court cases, names of attorneys, places, and courthouse stories and rumors involving prosecutors, judges, public defenders, and private defense attorneys. It was also indispensable for the investigator to *know the people behind the names*, otherwise the meaning of these stories would remain opaque at best. It was similarly essential to know something of the social personality and professional style

---

[36] The transcription of interviews and digital fieldnotes was performed by my research assistant David Showalter, an astute sociologist with a musician's ear, who produced documents incomparable for their precision and richness, capturing the subtle social dynamics of conversation as well as contributing provocative reactions and queries about the materials transcribed.

[37] Maynard dissects ten hours of recorded plea negotiations on 52 cases taking place in 1978 in three misdemeanor courts in a city on the outskirts of Los Angeles, backed up by three months of ethnographic observation. The only other study of live plea bargaining I was able to track down in the limited empirical literature on negotiated justice is Deirdre Bowen's 2009 article "Calling your Bluff: How Prosecutors and Defense Attorneys Adapt Plea Bargaining Strategies to Increased Formalization," based on the observation of the plea negotiations for 42 cases in Seattle, Washington. But it contains no description of the setting and participants and it quotes all of 41 lines of bargaining, suggesting that the negotiations were not taped or written up systematically.

of the different court attorneys involved to interpret their demeanor and deeds in the closed space of the negotiation room. Finally, as I will show later, it was crucial to be able to situate the prosecutors and public defenders observed on the map of objective positions they occupied in their respective office in terms of trajectory, expertise, reputation, and seniority.

When I was granted permission to observe plea negotiations, I had been conducting fieldwork in three of the five courthouses of San Pedrito county for over a year and I was about to embark on comparative fieldwork in Carnival county. I had thus become fully acquainted with the local scene; made myself known and accepted among attorneys, judges, clerks, court reporters, and bailiffs as "The Professor" doing a field study of "The social life of the county criminal court" (a capsule both accurate and suitably vague); and established personal relations with a plurality of the protagonists I followed on both sides of the aisle. This deep embeddedness allowed me to observe with minimal interference with the phenomenon.

245

Court attorneys are intensely focused on their work, always pressed for time, and used to dealing swiftly with disruptions of all sorts. Having a sociologist around was surprising at first but irrelevant to their purpose and inconsequential for their activity once they were given appropriate guarantees of confidentiality and anonymity. Any concerns they might have had were allayed by the fact that I was "warranted" by veteran judges and attorneys on both sides, in addition to having secured official permission from the head of their office and the presiding judge of the court. Prosecutors and defense lawyers took their cues from the pretrial DA running the negotiation session and soon treated me as a normal fixture of the scene.[38] Public defenders who appeared regularly during these sessions were initially reticent, a reflection of the paranoid collective mentality of the office. But, as soon as they knew of my identity and purpose, they welcomed my presence because they believed that a sociologist was a "natural ally" – although I was diligent in conveying to them as to prosecutors that it was imperative that my work not "take sides."[39] When a private

[38] To a young female PD who was asking who I was, a supervising DA responded: "Oh, Loïc is just joining us, he's shadowing everybody here today," to which she retorted flatly, "Okay, okay."

[39] During their negotiation with the head of the felony trial team, some PDs would jokingly turn to me and ask if I could intercede to get them a better deal. In our formal interviews, one of them voiced the unfounded belief that she was getting lower offers when I was in the room because the DA did not want to appear as a callous "cowboy"

attorney I did not know entered the room, I would whisper to them aside that I was a "Berkeley professor of sociology doing a study of the court" and I asked them to participate by agreeing to a later interview (which they nearly always did by giving me their business card as they found the invitation flattering).[40]

A few times in the negotiation room, I was mistaken for a defense attorney from out of town, and a PD or private counsel whose turn it was to step up to the pretrial desk would point at me and demur, muttering "That's his turn," to which the pretrial DA Julius would retort matter-of-factly, "He's not an attorney, he's a sociologist," to the quiet amusement and nodding of those in the know. I was understandably misidentified as a prosecutor when I sat at their desk in open court. I was also confused for an attorney by defendants many times in the elevators because I wore a suit and looked serious, and because I am white whereas virtually all defendants were people of color. But an experienced prosecutor once told me that he knew right away when he saw me in the courtroom that I was not an attorney because I was smiling and so he also gave me advice on straightening my tie.

After about a year in the field, I had become a regular on the work scene in three courthouses. So much so that Julius once remarked that "you're running everywhere. They'll have to give you an office." Attorneys on both sides often remarked approvingly of my growing court knowledge and technical prowess. A rookie PD assigned to the misdemeanor trial team in Alphaville quipped with commendation, "You're gonna have to give some trainings to the new recruits!" A veteran DA running the preliminary trial team likewise noted with glee: "If you lose your job at UC, we can hire you!" Another prosecutor echoed, "You've gotta give up your research, we need you to deal these cases." When I ran into my second year of fieldwork,

---

in the eyes of a renowned Berkeley professor. Lynn Mather reports a similar dilemma in her ethnography of the Los Angeles court: she made "a conscious effort to spend equal time with attorneys on both sides" to signal that she was not aligned with either. Lynn M. Mather, *Plea Bargaining or Trial?* (1979), pp. 7–8.

[40] My presence in the plea negotiation room created a breach of normalcy only twice. In the first episode, a female private attorney first asked what my digital recorder was doing on the prosecutor's desk, which gave me an opening to introduce myself. She was pleased by my response but then she abruptly changed her mind and asked that I not tape her discussion. In the second episode, a young female public defender whom I had not yet interviewed started her exchange with the pretrial prosecutor by stating that she was not comfortable with being taped and asked that I leave the room, which I did. The incident was quickly resolved with the head PD later that week. My permission to attend and record plea negotiation sessions was confirmed.

attorneys asked me impatiently when I would be done and produce the promised monograph. They were dumbfounded and impressed at the same time that I would burrow so deep into my field site. One of them groused with a wide grin, "When will you write your book, I'll die before it's published?" My response was, "Would you rather I spend three months and do a hatchet job?" or I joked, "I'm aging the case" (a vernacular expression referring to a defense tactic of deferring resolution). Attorneys and judges were also impressed by my assiduity and dedication to getting as close as possible to the action. To which I would note with a chuckle: "I'm the hardest working attorney in the county and I'm not even an attorney."

In this chapter, I limit myself to only one of the three pretrial prosecutors whom I observed at work. I joined Julius during a total of nine plea negotiation sessions carried out in the same courthouse.[41] These sessions cover 22 hours of observation, 300-odd cases, involving some 68 different attorneys, 18 of them public defenders and 53 private attorneys. In addition to field notes, recordings, photos, and documents produced during these sessions, I had conducted five two-hour-long interviews with Julius beforehand. Lastly, I shadowed him on his assignment from morning to evening for a full week by rotating days over a five-week period. It would have been too exhausting to cover him on consecutive days: when my day in court with him was over, I was completely spent and my left hand was nearly paralyzed from furiously writing in my notebook. I needed to recover, debrief, and develop my field jottings into field notes. I also jumped on the fly at opportunities for interviews with DAs, PDs, and private attorneys met during these sessions.

After he was "rotated" back to his favorite assignment, the felony trial team to tackle homicides, I consorted and consulted extensively with Julius on all matters prosecutorial whenever I visited the office to shadow another "trial dog," who was his closest colleague and best friend in the office assigned to consecutive murder cases. This allowed me to make numerous short interviews and record myriad office conversations on the fly that provide the naturalistic backdrop to my reading of the negotiation sessions.

Years after our time together in the courthouse, Julius and I met at my place and I shared with him a draft of the present chapter.

---

[41] For the fourth of the ten sessions, Julius was attending the sentencing hearing for a double murder he had tried in another courthouse and he was subbed by a veteran prosecutor supervising the PX team, which offered a stimulative contrast in substance and style.

I obtained his permission to feature him as its central character and to include a sketch of his social biography. I was anxious about his reaction: Julius is a very private person and so he could have been uncomfortable about it all and I would have to rewrite parts of the chapter and possibly reorganize it. I was relieved when, after a pause, he said that I did not need to disguise him further. Instead of being reticent, he verbalized that he felt "honored to be in the book." In addition to gaining Julius's consent, I was able to verify critical information and to garner additional data extending key episodes recounted in these pages. Remarkably, Julius spontaneously evoked twists and turns in prosecutorial work as well as shared experiences we had in the plea negotiation room that were already in the chapter, which I took as validating my choice to focus on them.

248

The epistemological approach that guided my fieldwork and informs my interpretation of the data it generated is what, in neo-Bourdieusian language, I call *thick construction*.[42] Asserting the primacy of reason over sensation in knowledge production, this approach mandates a flexible and dynamic relation between theory and observation, concept and percept, aimed at putting the social phenomenon considered into a new light. Against both Geertzian "thick description" and the "grounded theory" of symbolic interactionists,[43] thick construction asserts that all ethnographic work, no matter how descriptive and narrative it may appear *prima facie*, is anchored by theoretical commitments and propelled by a simplified model, explicit or implicit, of the slice of reality it carves out and reworks. Against the "extended case method" codified by Michael Burawoy,[44] it deploys theory for the purpose of producing *novel empirical objects*, not returning to that theory in an effort to verify or falsify it. In contrast with "abductive theorizing" as expounded by

---

[42] Wacquant, *The Poverty of the Ethnography of Poverty*, pp. 155–7. "Thick construction" is an extension to ethnography of Pierre Bourdieu's sociological epistemology – anchored by the famous formula: "The social fact is conquered, constructed, constated" (Pierre Bourdieu et al., *Le Métier de sociologue. Préalables épistémologiques* [1968, 1973, 2021]) – which is itself an extension to the social sciences of Gaston Bachelard's *rationalisme appliqué* elaborated for physics and chemistry. For a compact discussion of Bachelard in the stream of twentieth-century epistemology, see Hans-Jörg Rheinberger's *On Historizing Epistemology* (2010).

[43] Clifford Geertz, "Thick Description: Toward an Interpretive Theory of Culture" (1973); Barney G. Glaser and Anselm L. Strauss, *The Discovery of Grounded Theory: Strategies for Qualitative Research* (1967).

[44] Michael Burawoy, "The Extended Case Method" (1998).

Iddo Tavory and Stefan Timmermans,[45] it stresses that the task of the ethnographer is to carry out a *construction squared*: an analytic construction of the ordinary construction of the agents observed on the ground. This means that the answer to the reader's objection that my account of prosecuting is selective and partial is to plead guilty on all counts: social science is the art of fruitful simplification for purposes of description, explanation, and interpretation.[46]

Anatomy of the local judicial field

To understand the professional conduct of court attorneys and their strategic interactions with one another as with judges, it is essential to first locate them on a map charting their location and possible peregrinations. Deploying the topological mode of reasoning, one can construct the *local judicial field* defined as the structure of objective positions occupied by the court protagonists in their everyday struggle to impose their definition of justice and thus shape process and output in the courthouse accordingly.[47] This *invisible structure* is based on the distribution of judicial capital or resources efficient in the universe considered (positional authority, technical expertise, professional reputation) and on the embedding of the court into the local bureaucratic field of the county. It underlies a set of homological oppositions, material and symbolic, and determines the strategies and styles of lawyering on the ground.

249

The diagrams that follow picture a purified judicial world reduced to these fundamental divisions and deliberately stripped of its organizational complexity and interactional dynamism – a visual "ideal type," in Max Weber's sense of the term, that provides a benchmark with which to orient inquiry and measure reality.[48] We shall see later how and why these oppositions are rolled out, inflected, and

[45] Iddo Tavory and Stefan Timmermans, *Abductive Analysis: Theorizing Qualitative Research* (2014).
[46] Loïc Wacquant, "In Praise of 'Thick Construction'" (2025).
[47] On the construction of social space as an *analytic prerequisite* to the study of social practices and strategies, see Pierre Bourdieu, *Sociologie générale*, volume 2 (2016), especially pp. 1127–8 and 1177–8.
[48] On the methodology and epistemic virtues of the Weberian ideal type, read Richard Swedberg, "How to Use Max Weber's Ideal Type in Sociological Analysis" (2018). On the use of diagrams as a tool for theorizing, read Daniel Silver, "Figure It Out!" (2020).

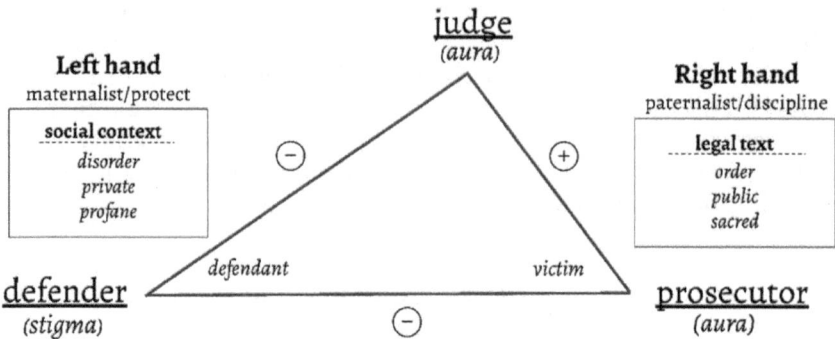

Figure 13   The judicial triangle

sometimes breached in practice, and how collusion and cooperation set in between positional antagonists. The point here is that *structure governs interaction* – a theoretical position that goes against the grain of the long tradition of court ethnographies that focus narrowly on face-to-face encounters within the courtroom, thereby committing the *fallacy of interactionism*.[49]

As a first approximation, we may represent the *judicial triad* formed by the prosecutor, the defender (public or private) and the judge as a triangle with the opposition between DA and PD (or court-appointed counsel) forming the base and the judge situated at the summit (figure 13). This triangle is *scalene* because the distance between judge and DA is shorter than the distance between judge and PD for reasons that will quickly become clear.[50] The prosecutor occupies the *domi-*

[49] For an extended discussion of this fallacy, precipitated by "ethnographism," the tendency to describe, interpret and explain a phenomenon based solely on the data gathered in the field site, see Wacquant, *The Poverty of the Ethnography of Poverty*, pp. 143–5. This is where neo-Bourdieusian ethnography both resembles and parts with "relational ethnography," which focuses on "concrete transactions" among "multiple actors and agencies who are engaged with one another." Agents in a *champ* as an invisible structure need not be engaging with one another to be located and produce effects in it. The Bourdieusian concept is *topological*: it mandates constructing the multiscalar space of positions to which agents bring dispositions. The Desmondian take is *transactional*: capture the visible exchanges between tangible agents from the two ends of the relation. Matthew Desmond, "Relational Ethnography" (2014), especially pp. 563–4.

[50] It is only after drawing an equilateral triangle to figure the judge–prosecutor–defender triad that I realized that the distance between them is not equal. The empirical shape of the triangle at a given moment is affected by the local political climate. In counties and periods where the ethos of "law and order" prevails prevail, the position of the judge slides further to the right, giving added authority to the prosecu-

nant pole of the local judicial field because he initiates action, drives proceedings, and enjoys considerable discretion and leverage in the use of state authority. He is located on the Right, politically, semantically, and metaphorically, on the public side of the law, which he is entrusted with enforcing. He incarnates the Right hand of the state, the *masculine or paternal hand* of discipline and castigation, delivered in the name of deserving citizens, incarnated by the victim, and of the public good.[51] He is the guarantor of social and moral order.

The defender occupies the *dominated pole* of the local judicial field. She stands on the Left, politically, semantically, and metaphorically, on the private side of the putative violator of the law, whom she shields from the wrath of the Leviathan. She incarnates the Left hand of the state, the *feminine or maternal hand* that protects and nurtures categories shorn of capital and suspected of being undeserving by dint of their conduct.[52] The public as well as private defender react to the initiatives of the prosecutor and the pronouncements of the judge; she suffers from her absence of independent authority – a word derived from the Latin *auctor*, meaning master, leader, author.

The judge occupies a seemingly neutral and overhanging position, but he is clearly leaning toward the right, the side of social and public order. This is because he is entrusted with seeing that this very order is properly restored – insofar as it has been breached by the defendant. He shares many *positional properties* with the prosecutor: both are public agents who act in the name and for the benefit of the citizenry at large.[53] Both are endowed with *aura* insofar as they are delegated by the state to act in its name. They stand on the side of the sacred

251

tor. In counties and periods where progressive penality prevails in public debate, the judge inches toward the center, nay the left, giving more weight to public and private defenders. But, even in progressive phases, he remains the guarantor of order and therefore a creature of the Right.

[51] Even "victimless crimes" such as drug consumption, public drunkenness, and vagrancy can be shown to have victims, if only moral ones, in that they create trouble in public space and violate societal norms, thus infringing on what Durkheim would call "strong and definite states of the collective conscience." A stimulative analysis of this category offense is Edwin M. Schur, *Crimes Without Victims: Deviant Behavior and Public Policy – Abortion, Homosexuality, Drug Addiction* (1965).

[52] On the emplacement of the penal institution in the Right hand of the penal state, see Loïc Wacquant, *Punishing the Poor: The Neoliberal Government of Social Insecurity* (2009b), pp. 289–91, and chapter 1 *supra*, pp. 101–2.

[53] In the US, judges and the head DA are both elected and serve at the will of "the people," whereas the chief public defender is typically appointed by county supervisors and subject to their political whims.

embodied by the law – more precisely, by the penal code treated as scripture.[54] This is the basis for their *structural collusion* (marked by the + sign), which accounts for the ordinary perception of their complicity among court agents and defendants and does not depend on the personalities of individual judges.

The defenders, public and private, stand on the side of the profane: their mission is to thwart the actions of the DA who represents "the people";[55] they act, not in the name of a sanctified collective but a singular individual who has allegedly desecrated that whole by their conduct. The very expression "client" suggests a venal and private relationship. Defenders protect agents of disorder and are, for this reason, themselves suspected of fomenting disorder. They stand in a relation of *submissive diffidence* with the judge, whom they approach as supplicants, and *collusive antagonism* with the DA. Antagonism because, in an adversarial system, their task is to derail the strategies and blunt the authority of the prosecutor. Collusive because, for reasons of volume and process, they must collaborate with the latter to resolve cases in the best interest of their client. The mission of the public defender is enshrouded in *stigma* due to the lowly character and errant behavior of the population she serves; her profession is disgraced even in the eyes of the offender she serves.[56] In the professional imaginary, the qualities that DAs and PDs collectively valorize are inverted: the former are "tough" toward the criminal and "caring" toward the crime victim; the latter "tough" toward the state and "caring" toward the offender.

The structural opposition between the disciplinary Right hand and the protective Left hand of the state that I elaborated in chapter 1 is thus replicated within the local judicial field by the opposition *between*

[54] I follow here the structuralist definition of the sacred by Émile Durkheim as that which is separate from the mundane, distinct in time, place, and ceremonial. Émile Durkheim, *Les Formes élémentaires de la vie religieuse* ([1912] 1982). This is signified by the black robe that judges wear, which separates them from other court agents, their central position under the American flag draped on the wall behind him, and the physical elevation of the bench, which allows them to speak *down* to the attorneys and the defendant.

[55] A normative critique of the appropriation of "the people" by the prosecutor is Jocelyn Simonson, "The Place of 'The People' in Criminal Procedure" (2019).

[56] Indigent defendants commonly disparage their public defenders. They refer to them as "public dumpsters" and "public pretenders." They believe that court-appointed counsel are subpar lawyers – or else they would be prosecutors or private attorneys. In their eyes, the fact that their legal service is provided free of charge is proof positive that it is worthless.

the prosecutor and the public defender, as well as *within* the spaces of prosecutors and public defenders by the opposition between the left wing and the right wing of each office. Consider the first antinomy. The prosecutor affirms the priority of the law and is inclined to give primacy to the *text over social context*. He is the agent of autonomy; he wields the power of the state in the name of the people – thus, when the DA goes "on the record" at the beginning of every hearing, prompted by the judge, he utters the mandatory formula, "For the people, your honor," before elocuting his name. He serves the public good. Pushed to its extreme, his purview is closed and narrowly focused on the offense and the relevant legal statutes: "Apply the law to the facts" is the phrase learned in law school by court attorneys and repeated with relish. His penal philosophy centers on the offense and tends structurally toward just desert or retribution, the retrospective delivery of punishment fitting the crime, regardless of the profile of the offender. In his pure form, he is the progenitor of Kantian penality.[57]

253

The public defender is in every way diametrically opposed: she wishes to broaden the purview, project her client as a full social being, and prioritizes *social context over legal text*. She is the agent of heteronomy in that she brings extra-judicial considerations (of work, family, and community) into the judicial field and acts on behalf of a private individual and not for the benefit of a collective asking to be made whole. This is most visible when the defender is a private defense attorney, since the latter's motivation is pecuniary, but it remains true with the public defender who is a paradoxical being since she is *paid by the state to battle against the state*. She is a public creature turned back against the public.[58] Her penal philosophy centers on the offender and is animated by a prospective commitment to rehabilitation. She is the progenitor of Benthamite penality. Thus, when they look at the defendant, the prosecutor and the public defender see a very different silhouette: the former a judicial profile (the criminal justice background materialized by the RAP sheet and associated court records of prior convictions); the latter a human profile and a social background (a being with myriad social ties as student, son,

---

[57] On the opposition between prospective and retrospective philosophies of punishment, see the luminous discussion of Andrew von Hirsch, "Penal Theories" (1999), and chapter 1, *supra*, pp. 64–6.

[58] Thus the predicament of the "cocktail question": at parties, people will often ask a public defender, upon learning their occupation, "How can you defend these people?" Lisa J. McIntyre, *The Public Defender: The Practice of Law in the Shadows of Repute* (1987).

brother, worker, neighbor, etc., who cannot be reduced to "the worst thing he ever did on the worst day of his life").[59]

As noted earlier, the opposition between DA and PD in the local judicial field is deeply gendered.[60] Together, the attorneys on the two sides of the aisle are positioned like the *two parents in a patriarchal family* facing the task of handling their unruly children – defendants are consistently infantilized by criminal procedure, even as they are held to be fully accountable for their actions.[61] In terms of cultural coding, the DA is the stern father who chastises and disciplines; he wields the sword of the state; he is a disembodied agent following his head, guided by cold reason in pursuit of the public good (public safety, group morality, individual accountability). Even when he shows mercy, it is as an expression of his fatherly authority tinged with benevolence. The PD is the loving mother who cares for the defendant as a wayward child; she holds the shield also of the state, which makes her a paradoxical legal agent; she is an embodied creature guided by her heart; she is driven by hot passion in defense of a private interest. Thus it is not uncommon for female public defenders to come out of court crying upon losing a trial in which a client risks a long prison sentence, or to hurry back to their office with a stoic face only to burst in tears in the arms of their colleagues.[62] Prosecutors have no inclination and no reason to cry. Whether delivered by a male or female prosecutor and judge, *punishment is symbolically encrypted as masculine*. It is striking that the women who reach the status of "trial dogs" in the DA's office are endowed with a masculine habitus.

---

[59] The latter perspective is brought to its institutional conclusion by those public defenders' offices which adopt "holistic defense" as their operational philosophy, under which an interdisciplinary team of specialists (including social workers, specialist lawyers, and advocates) respond to their clients' underlying needs (housing, employment, drug treatment, mental health care, etc.). See James M. Anderson et al., "The Effects of Holistic Defense on Criminal Justice Outcomes" (2019), and Ronald Wright and Jenny Roberts, "Expanded Criminal Defense Lawyering" (2023), for a description and evaluation of holistic defense.

[60] An early feminist critique of law as a gendered discursive system instituting masculine norms and values is Carol Smart, *Feminism and the Power of Law* (1989).

[61] This is not specific to the criminal court. Infantilization applies to other precarious populations supervised by the state, such as the clients of welfare agencies, who must demonstrate obedience and subservience in their relation to street-level bureaucrats, as shown by Vincent Dubois, *La Vie au guichet. Relation administrative et traitement de la misère* (1999).

[62] The opposition is actually more complex: the PD also bears masculine qualities by virtue of being a creature of the Leviathan who wields the law against the law, but this is not the place to address this symbolic layering.

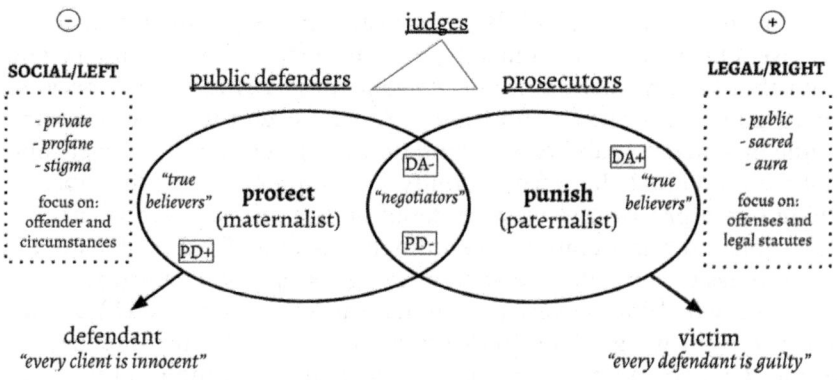

Figure 14 The structure of the local judicial field

Now consider the *internal anatomy* of each of the two offices set out in figure 14. They can both be represented by an oblong organized around two opposed poles aligned with the antinomy organizing the two poles of the local judicial field: the right of the DA's office (right-right) and the left of the PD's office (left-left) are the poles of autonomy in their respective spaces (represented by the plus sign); the left of the DA's office (left-right) and the right of the PD's office (right-left) are the poles of heteronomy in their respective spaces (represented by the minus sign). The two oblongs overlap to form a Venn diagram. Remarkably, the lawyers occupying the autonomous pole in the two offices are both called "true believers" in court lingo, an exonym that speaks volume about their passion and inflexibility. A seasoned true believer in the DA's office assures me that he would "rather be a dog catcher" than a defense attorney, public or private. A veteran true believer in the PD's office exclaims that she would "rather drink poison" than turn into a DA. The DA true believer trains his affection on the victim; the PD true believer loves each and every one of her clients.

On the far right-hand side, the hardened prosecutors believe that "every defendant is guilty" (of some crime, if not exactly the one they are accused of) and should pay the price on grounds of *individual responsibility*. Their priority is "winning," which means securing a conviction (and not racking up years of prison, as commonly believed, since even serious offenders are rarely incarcerated).[63] At their purest,

---

[63] In California, only 10 percent of all felony arrests lead to a prison sentence. Only one in five convicted felons serves time in a state penitentiary.

they are advocates for retribution: punishment commensurate with the offense. On the far left-hand side, the hardened public defenders who hold that "every client is innocent" and deserves to "walk" because social conditions and circumstances explain even the most gruesome crime in which culpability is beyond doubt.[64] For them, it is society and not the individual client who is guilty. Punishment should therefore be guided by a prospective view centered on the offender to foster rehabilitation and reintegration. Accordingly, the aim of public defender is to suppress or mitigate punishment by invoking *social adversity*.

These two oblongs overlap such that the left wing of the DA's office and the right wing of the PD's office intersect.[65] At this intersection reside what we may call *hybrid attorneys* (my terminology) who are two-sided: prosecutors who are sensitive to the stance of the defense and could even have become public defenders themselves, and public defenders who acknowledge the righteous mission of the prosecutor and could have become one themselves, but for the accidents of personal, academic, and professional life.[66] Some hybrid DAs even apprenticed in a PD's office as a summer law clerk before getting their bar card; some PDs worked for a DA's office in another county earlier in their legal career. But both keep that information strictly confidential because it would undermine their professional credibility and dent their status in their office, and so they swore me to absolute secrecy.[67] These two-sided attorneys are the "negotiators" who help resolve cases smoothly because they are disposed to dialogue and endowed with empathy for the opposing party. This is also the structural location occupied by prosecutors and public defenders who view being a court attorney as a stepping stone in their career plan to become a judge.

256

[64] This is not true of the private attorneys, who have a jaundiced view of their clients in sharp contrast with the exalted view of the public defenders.

[65] The two poles of "true believers" and "negotiators" are of equal size in the figure for purposes of analytical and visual clarity. In actuality, the population of true believers is generally much smaller than the population of negotiators.

[66] For reasons to be discussed later, there is an asymmetry here: it is easier for prosecutors to see the world through the eyes of defenders than the opposite. Indeed, it is not uncommon for experienced prosecutors to leave the DA's office to "hang their shingle" and become private defense attorneys, solo or in small firms.

[67] Thus the predicament of those prosecutors and public defenders married with a court attorney from "the other side." In their study of nine DA's offices in the Southeast, Wright et al. found many prosecutors who had a background in defense work and who openly envisaged doing that work again. Ronald F. Wright et al., "The Many Faces of Prosecution" (2014), p. 44.

The space of prosecutors is traversed by a tension between the attorneys who prioritize the *penal* or reactive mission of the office (the right of the Right) and those who see value in its *social* or proactive purpose (the left of the Right). The former relish the assignments that put them in a position to fight serious crime: they are part of the "gang unit," volunteer for the "sexual assault team," and are prepared to "rack twelve" to take to trial the toughest rape and murder cases. The latter set store by programs of diversion, crime prevention, and public education; they favor negotiation over litigation and have little taste for the highwire of trial.[68] The "trial dogs" are dismissive of them when they insist that "prosecutors are not social workers." They hold the upper hand in terms of prestige even in an office leaning on negotiation, in part because the social imaginary of criminal justice remains grounded in the pageantry of the jury trial.[69] They view their colleagues who "hide" on calendar assignments as "yellow prosecutors" (a term so deprecating that some veteran prosecutors claimed that they had never heard it).

The space of public defenders is traversed by a tension between what I call the "populists" (located on the left of the Left, the side of PD autonomy, society, context) and the "constitutionalists" (located on the right of the Left, the side of PD heteronomy, the law, text). The *populists*, as their name indicates, see themselves as defending "the people" against the encroachment of the state. They are the "extreme left," champions of the underdogs, fierce critics of society and of the built-in biases of the justice machinery, which they see as irretrievably "broken." They are prepared to use all the tools at their disposal, and even to skirt the bounds of the law, to protect and support their clients. They have close, motherly, affective relationships with the latter. "I love my clients" is a professional as much as an existential leitmotiv. The *constitutionalists* are located on the far right of the office, in the zone of overlap with the space of prosecutors. They see themselves as upholding the constitutional rights of their clients – one PD points

257

[68] Contrary to a commonly held view, many if not most prosecutors in a mid-sized office are not eager to take cases to trial. A trial is an intense, risky, and exacting stretch that demands full devotion and is physically, psychologically, emotionally, and socially costly. A seasoned supervisor of the felony trial team quipped mockingly, "That should be the title of your book: I don't want to go to trial." Not everyone is born a "trial dog" (or "trial horse").

[69] This is true even though the trial has been supplanted by negotiated justice for nearly a century, as shown by George Fisher, *Plea Bargaining's Triumph: A History of Plea Bargaining in America* (2003), and Vogel, *Coercion to Compromise*.

to a huge poster of the US Constitution on his office wall when I ask him what motivates him to come to work every morning. They are the skilled negotiators of the office by taste and necessity.

The Venn diagram reminds us that *"justice" is not an absolute but the historical product of patterned struggles*, raging both *between as well as within the two offices*, over the overarching philosophy as well as the day-to-day priorities of the prosecutor and the public defender. It suggests that attorneys similarly positioned in their respective organization will have structural affinities affecting their strategies: "negotiators" can recognize one another and act accordingly; DAs on the far right can intuitively grasp the unyielding passion of PDs on the far left and vice versa, even as they clash fiercely, as both fend off the forces of heteronomy within their organizational space (the intrusion of "society" for the DAs, the hegemony of "law" for the PD).[70]

The diagram also tells us also that the pretrial prosecutor cannot be a "true believer" or the machinery of plea bargaining will come to a screeching halt. If the DA's office is committed to a culture of negotiation, as opposed to a culture of litigation that would quickly clog up the court,[71] it will nominate a centrist or center-left prosecutor with a track record of respectful yet firm relationship with the opposing office and a court reputation as a "straight shooter" – the expression is used on both sides to characterize an attorney who is forthcoming, measured, and trustworthy. But, if that prosecutor leans too far toward the defender's side, it will antagonize the veteran DAs positioned to his right, especially the mid-career "trial dogs" who sit atop the symbolic hierarchy of the office. Ideally, the pretrial DA must be able to hear the arguments, comprehend the reasoning, and accommodate the concerns of defense attorneys while staying resolutely committed to his mission: to enforce the "price of crime," exact a measure of pain, and "keep the public safe." Another imperative about this nomination is to not fray the relationship of precedence between the generations of attorneys in the office. *Seniority is a par-*

---

[70] "Two agents who interact are two positions that interact, or, better, it is the objective relation between their two positions that commands their interaction; but they are also two agents who manage this relation by investing the two positions with feelings, desires, and, more precisely, by giving each other a representation of their position, hence of the relation, determined by the representation they have of their respective positions." Bourdieu, *Microcosmes*, p. 564.

[71] Plea resolution itself also runs the spectrum from "adversary bargaining" to "collaborative negotiation" as incarnated by two coastal counties studied in the 1970s by Pamela J. Utz, *Settling the Facts: Discretion and Negotiation in Criminal Court* (1978).

amount principle of stratification within offices of court lawyers. This became apparent when the chief DA of San Pedrito county replaced Albert (who had succeeded Julius) with a younger gung-ho prosecutor known for his abrasive personality and short fuse, to the disbelief of attorneys on both sides of the aisle.

The pretrial morning has ended and the witness room which serves as negotiation chamber has emptied. It's just me and Albert, the pretrial prosecutor who is leaving the office next month to open his own shop as a private defense attorney. For the past three weeks, the courthouse has been abuzz with fervid rumors about who will be his successor. Ben, trial dog supreme, comes in, takes a seat and bends forward in confidence. I gear up to leave the two of them.

Ben: [to LW] You can sit down.
Albert: [nodding] Yeah, you can sit.
Ben: Yeah, you can sit. The reason why, to me it's an interesting dynamic that he can appreciate, and the Professor keeps it [a secret].
Albert: [thumping on the desk in frustration] *What the fuck, man!*
Ben: So, we know who's taking this spot, Mason Lundberg, from Metro City. (LW in disbelief: Whaaat!?) And he's very high-stress, high-energy, very closed-minded as far as what he thinks should happen with cases. He has a split personality, because on the other hand, he wants everybody to love him and he wants people to think that he's somebody – so that's why *we* know he's taking the place . . .
Albert: [his voice rising] Ben, *it's gonna be fucking fire* coming out of this room, like – okay, fucking Rachel Sandhorn, [inaudible name], Geraldo, Fanny Gastard [three true believers in the PD's office], *they're gonna be at each other's fucking throats every day!*
Ben: But see, what's gonna temper it is the fact that he wants everybody to like him. He has this *overriding desire* to have people like him, so that's why it's gonna be alright.
Albert: [exploding] *Oh, what the fuck!* Why, why would he [the chief DA], oh, here's the list of everyone who works in our office, who would be a really good fit, who's well-tempered, well-liked, who really gets along with people well – oh, [sarcastic] *Mason Lundberg*, that sounds good, well he's free – oh, no, he's in a fucking trial right now in Metro City! . . . Which is *fucked* . . . It's gonna be like, it's gonna be a *feeding frenzy* before Lundberg comes in. I feel like most defense attorneys can't stand to work with him, because he's the way he is in trial, you know what I mean?

. . .

LW: So it's a surprising assignment?

Ben: To everybody who's heard it, except –
Albert: That's an understatement!
Ben: – *except for the corner office.*
(Field notebook, 12 December 2016)

Years later, Julius remembers that episode well because it stunned everyone in the office for another reason: despite the initial announcement, Mason Lundberg ended up *not* taking up the position of pretrial prosecutor after pushback from within the office as well as from the public defender's office. The head PD probably got the head DA on the phone and pressure from all sides nixed the move. Julius roars with delight as he elaborates: "The other side's got to trust you, they gotta respect you, they gotta really be able to feel like they can talk to you and you will listen. He was a *terrible choice* [laughter]. He never got that job. One-hundred percent he *never ever* did pretrial. He's so like *tightly wound*, he would yell at people – I could not see him in that role."

Julius recalls that, when he finished his stint as the felony pretrial prosecutor to rotate back to the trial team, an experienced public defender came to thank him and, much to his surprise, told him, [in a little voice] "I'm going to really miss you." He asked her why and she said, "It's not that I loved your offers, it's because you were always *fair* and you were *predictable*, and you would always *listen*." Julius replied to her, "'Cos I'm not always right and I'm trying to do the best I can do." He continues: "Now Lundberg is the *opposite of that*: he's always right, and he would never listen, and he would talk *at* people, not *to* them. Because sometimes – you were in that room – when we weren't negotiating we would laugh, we'd be talking, making jokes: it's gotta be that way."
(Field notebook, 24 August 2025)

A day in the life

Tracking Julius during a routine day at the office gives us a prism through which to refract and capture the nature of his activity, its technical and social organization, and the practical dilemmas and professional challenges it presents day-to-day. It provides insight into the microsociology of punishment as *meaningful collective action by agents of the penal state* and into the *organized malleability of criminal law*, that is, the patterned variations in the interpretation and application of legal statutes rooted in the inherent social complexity of justice lawyering as a form of *people-processing and people-tagging* resulting in

260

the calibrated application of material and symbolic force.[72] It also discloses the multiple signposts and filters that angle, channel, and limit the discretion of the prosecutor. Far from being absolute, as commonly alleged in the prevalent legal literature on plea negotiation, the prosecutor exercises *bounded discretion*, embedded as he is in a web of nested social spaces and symbolic structures that encase his professional authority.

There is an efflorescent branch of legal research on criminal justice grounded in the *a priori* notion that prosecutors are nefarious agents that must be castigated and reined in, if not stopped altogether. This moralizing approach, based largely on theoretical models, legal texts, and newspaper anecdotes, is an obstacle to grasping prosecution as it actually works.

In this literature, the power of the DA is self-evidently portrayed as "unilateral," "arbitrary," "unbridled," "tyrannical," "vindictive," as well as "unethical and unconstitutional."[73] The defense attorneys and judges are portrayed as utterly powerless or absent from the scene altogether. The prosecutor is depicted as a solo actor maximizing punishment instead of an embedded agent pursuing a satisficing goal – conviction, first and foremost – and ready to lower his target if the case requires it (for instance, if "proof problems" emerge in the course of negotiation). Empirical ignorance creates a void filled with moral vituperation and normative considerations that scarcely connect with the multilayered and dynamic reality of negotiated justice at ground level.

Julius's dispositions as a prosecutor, his propensity to think, feel, and act in a patterned and predictable manner as a court attorney are grafted onto his *primary habitus* acquired in early childhood and adolescence as a result of the class and ethnic forces he was exposed

---

[72] Yeheskel Hasenfeld, "People Processing Organizations: An Exchange Approach" (1972). I develop the notion of "people-tagging" later in this chapter, *infra*, pp. 352–4.
[73] For a sample of this scholarship, see Davis, *Arbitrary Justice* (2007); Paul Craig Roberts and Lawrence M. Stratton, *The Tyranny of Good Intentions: How Prosecutors and Law Enforcement are Trampling the Constitution in the Name of Justice* (2008); Leigh Goodmark, "The Impact of Prosecutorial Misconduct, Overreach, and Misuse of Discretion on Gender Violence Victims" (2018); Monroe H. Freedman, "The Use of Unethical and Unconstitutional Practices and Policies by Prosecutors' Offices" (2012); Doug Lieb, "Vindicating Vindictiveness: Prosecutorial Discretion and Plea Bargaining, Past and Future" (2013); and the literature surveyed by David Sklansky in the appositely titled article, "The Problems with Prosecutors" (2018). For comparison with a justice system that does grant near-absolute power to the prosecutor, see David Johnson's meticulous dissection of *The Japanese Way of Justice: Prosecuting Crime in Japan* (2002).

to in the family, the school, the neighborhood, and the peer group.[74] His early biography perfectly captures the mix of ingredients that produce *prosecutors driven by passion*, enchanted by and engrossed in their mission as servants of the law and protectors of the citizenry, the attorneys who "wear the white hat" in the theater of the courtroom: a lower-middle-class upbringing stressing hard work and individual merit; living a rule-bound existence shaped by disciplinarian parents and the protracted practice of competitive sport; fervent religion and an unquestioning respect for authority and the police; all of which feeds into a clear and rigid morality painting the world in black and white, with little grey to go, tempered by a sense of compassion for those who bend under the weight of social adversity. This translates into a polarized vision of offenders, with "bad dudes" deserving of severe punishment, at one end, and "kids who made a mistake" and call for clemency, on the other. The prosecutors for whom the job is a *vocation rather than an occupation*, even when they discover it late and by circuitous routes, typically endorse the criminal justice system and reject the criticism that portrays it as bloated, virulent, and biased.

262

"Find me a better justice system than the one we have"

Find me a better justice system than the one we have. I was a legal studies major [in college]. *Find me a better one! Show me another one* that's better, where citizens are involved, and the process is one where a prosecutor has the burden of proving you guilty. Whereas there are systems in this world where you have to prove your innocence. I don't know of a better system. *I embrace our system and I come from the inner city.* Nothing is gonna be one hundred percent foolproof . . .

One of the biggest problems with this system is that we get people on the *back end*. Meaning, we get people *after* they've committed crimes. And we don't address what is the source of the crime, where does it come from. Most of our offenders, they're under the influence of alcohol or drugs – *that's* a problem. Our inner-city schools – *that's* a problem. If you go to North Alphaville, one of the reasons why

---

[74] On the concept of habitus as the system of acquired, durable, and transposable categories of perception, appreciation, and action characterizing an agent or a class of agents, see Pierre Bourdieu, *Esquisse d'une théorie de la pratique, précédé de trois études d'ethnologie kabyle* (1972), and Loïc Wacquant, "Habitus as Topic and Tool: Reflections on Becoming a Prizefighter" (2011), and idem, "A Concise Genealogy and Anatomy of Habitus" (2016).

those kids commit so much crime at a young age is they don't see *hope*. There's *despair*. I mean, that's where *I came from*, an area where there was despair. When you're in school, there's no books, and the school is ratty, and the teachers don't care, and the students don't care – it just *festers*.

[When President Obama expresses concern about long prison sentences for nonviolent drug offenses] *he is right*. But this is what I would tell him: most of our violent crimes are connected with drugs, you know, turf wars. You can't blame the *end of the road* for what's happening at the *beginning of the road* . . . He's missing *everything* – it's not about the criminal justice system being broken, it's about *society itself* having all these *cracks*.

Because of racial segregation, Julius grew up at the heart of a poor, crime-infested black district of Uberville known as Bird Hill, and many of his childhood buddies fell into delinquency and drift – some are now dead, others are on drugs, and yet others served time in prison: "That was the norm, that was my world." His parents, dad an insurance adjuster and mom a clerk who studied later in life to become a teacher, both of them first-generation high-school graduates, were "strict when it came to education." They did not allow him to run the streets and insisted that he pick his friends with caution. In every activity, he had to prioritize personal *accountability* – a key category in the moral vocabulary of prosecutors. Julius "didn't become a statistic in the neighborhood," he insists, because he "tried to make the right choices." He admired his parents deeply, especially his father who was "really big and intimidating" (he had served in the military and fought as an amateur boxer in the heavyweight division), and Julius would do everything to not let them down.

Julius's family relied on faith to steer its ship in the right direction: "Religion was our life. It's kind of the foundation of who I am. It's one of the reasons why, *I believe*, I didn't get into trouble." His moral compass was shaped, not just by his parents, but also by his grandparents: when Julius and his three siblings vacationed with them in Houston, Texas, his grandfather, a deacon, and his grandmother, a treasurer for the congregation, took them to church three times a week. Religion shapes his professional practice today: "It's part of your *soul*. I mean, part of being a prosecutor is not just trying cases, but it's also *having compassion for people*, and being able to use your discretion." Deference for authority was a given in the family: "My parents, they *respected the law* and they expected us to respect it. They respected other people and they expected us to do it." As a result, he followed academic rules to a tee and he was always a good student. A socially constituted taste for order, a trained reverence for authority, and punctilious morality learned from multiple sources: the three core constituent ingredients of the prosecutorial habitus were laid down early in Julius's life.

Another source of individual and collective discipline was high-school and college football, at which Julius excelled. On the gridiron he learned grit, fairness, and the love of winning. He makes a spontaneous parallel between prosecution and athletic competition under the aegis of the category of sportsmanship: "*That's* the way I see the courtroom: I see it more as *an arena, a competition*, and it's never personal. I never see the defense attorney as *my enemy*. I see us as having opposing *points of view*. I see us as *advocating* for one side or the other. Being a good sport, to me, is the most important part of it." He recognizes that "defense attorneys are necessary for the system to work." He respects their mission, which is essential to the smooth negotiation of criminal cases.

Julius attended a local college on an academic scholarship majoring in legal studies out of a love of history, which got him thinking about the law. After graduation, however, he "moved right back in my neighborhood because that's all I knew." His homecoming was spoiled by the death of his best friend who was murdered on the street that year. Julius soon settled into a life of work and family; he got married and fathered three children. He earned a good living first as truck driver for a neighborhood company that ran an outreach program for inner-city youth; then he was promoted to office clerk in the purchasing department before the company trained him to be a plumber, a skilled job in high demand and with a solid pay. His next career move was becoming a housing inspector for a nearby city, a job he held for four years.

Intrigued by his experience of jury service and aiming to get his license as a contractor, while working by day, Julius took night classes at a local community college and grew "really jazzed up for the law." Being rather reserved, he also signed up for a class in public speaking, something he had never done and "it really felt good." This took him to law school at a large public university in the city – he wanted to stay close to his family – where he threw himself into learning every possible kind of law, thinking he would go into housing litigation. But a school internship at the San Pedrito county District Attorney's office would decide otherwise. When he hit the courtroom that summer as a law clerk, he had an epiphany:[75] "I just *knew* that was what I was made for. This is where I wanted to be. It's weird how life works." His one trial capping the internship was a difficult drunken-driving case. All at once, he found himself moving "on autopilot" and going "back to my roots, using my common sense. Stuff is comin' out of my mouth, you know? [joyously] I have been told that *I sound like a preacher*. And I felt *so good* afterwards. I *knew* it was what I should be doing. I *knew* I was gonna get a job offer."

Could he have become a public defender if he had interned on that side of the aisle? Julius takes a moment to ponder the question. Perhaps at the time because he was genuinely naive about criminal law but no longer, realizing the impact of crime on victims: "Now my *moral compass has been shaped a certain way* that it would almost be impossible." He could not find it in himself to defend a murderer, a rapist, or a child molester knowing the suffering they inflict, he muses, and a defendant needs the fulsome commitment of his attorney. It is clear, in any case, that the social and moral forces that converged to shape his primary habitus predestined him to join the prosecutors, righteous knights of order, and not the rebels in the courthouse known as public defenders.

Julius's parents are immensely proud of him, as of the academic and professional success of his two brothers (one is a real estate businessman, the other a military officer) and one sister (who teaches in a community college): "They wanted us to be productive citizens, they wanted us to good people." But his childhood neighborhood friends are distant and "don't know how to relate" to him because he now stands on the "other side" of the law: he is "The Man."[76] So they gingerly step around the topic and never mention his job: "I've never told *any of my friends* what I do. They *know* what I do, but no one really talks to me about it. They know that I'm a professional, they know that I'm a lawyer, but they don't talk about the fact that I'm a

265

[75] A summer law clerk is a law school student who has completed one or two year of studies and works over the summertime break providing administrative support, preparing cases, and observing hearings in court. The capstone of their training stint in some counties is to try a misdemeanor case before a real jury under the supervision of a veteran prosecutor. The position serves as a pipeline for recruitment. Some DA's offices hire all of their attorneys through this route because it guarantees that they will immediately fit into the culture of the office.

[76] This expression from the black street vernacular designates the police or the authorities of the dominant white society in general. It evokes racial oppression and implacable injustice. Its classic explication is in *Soul on Ice* (1968), the memoir by Eldridge Cleaver, co-founder of the Black Panther Party.

prosecutor. It's a kind of a pact." This silence pains him but neither side will break it.

It took Julius sustained emotional work of his own to bring himself to admit that, yes, his job makes him part of the law-enforcement apparatus. Being a black prosecutor is to stand at the turbulent point of confluence of multiple cultural contradictions, legal paradoxes, and competing political demands for justice. The long history of penal oppression of African-Americans and, as a result, their deep distrust of, and disdain toward, the police, the court, and the prison creates a cultural stigma and triggers a wide reaction of social rejection of the occupations associated with state authority among the black population.[77] This is a major obstacle to recruiting, training, and retaining African-American prosecutors. But does having more of them result in more impartial outcomes and more acceptance of verdicts, as Julius thinks, or does it simply camouflage the systemic biases of the justice machinery under a thin coat of "diversity"?

"When you see a black prosecutor"

I tried a triple homicide, I want to say it was like over a year ago. And all three defendants were African-American *young men*. And, of course, the families are all black, of both the victims and the defendants. Even the defendants' side, to see a prosecutor who's African-American brings some *legitimacy to the process itself*. It's like, they sometimes think it's *The Man, The System, against them*. And when you see a black prosecutor – and when I'm in court, I feel like I sound like *me*, just the way I'm talking to you right now is the way I talk to juries. And there is something about that that makes, *I believe*, some families believe that they're getting a fair shake. Which, I think, for most people of color, it's *really important*.

---

[77] This cynical mistrust, rooted in a long history of rampant government abuse, applies to the gamut of state agencies such as child services, housing, welfare, and health care. For instance, three-quarters of black Americans hold that the police deliberately let guns flood their neighborhoods. A full 55 percent believe that medical researchers carry out experiments on black people without their knowledge or consent. The same percentage agree with the notion that "the government encourages single motherhood among Black women to eliminate the need for Black men." Half believe that "the government promotes birth control and abortion to keep the Black population small." Kiana Cox, *Most Black Americans Believe U.S. Institutions Were Designed to Hold Black People Back* (2024).

In the office, Julius threw himself into work with abandon – "If you come from the streets, if you come from where I came from, to make it in this world you've got to outwork the other person." He soon became a master of the preliminary examination; shone on the felony trial team; and honed his negotiation and courtroom skills on the vertical team handling child sexual assault, an assignment that he credits with making him an all-around better lawyer in spite of the emotional toll it inflicts upon prosecutors. This capped the sequence of life experiences and professional missions that have made him a "victim-centered" prosecutor whose core mission is to serve the community by ensuring public safety and holding defendants accountable for the harm they cause – a mix of Benthamite incapacitation and Kantian retribution.[78] Now a mid-career DA with a dozen years of experience and 45 trials under his belt (including 18 homicides), Julius belongs to the small minority of attorneys known in the office as "trial dogs" – self-evaluated at under 15 per cent – who relish taking hard cases to a jury. Whether he is weighing the "value" of cases for purposes of bargaining, advising the "baby DAs" on their assignment, or crusading in front of a jury, Julius is a happy man: "I love my job, I love what I do."

So when "the elected" called him into his office to announce to him in person that he was "promoting" him to pretrial attorney, Julius was of two minds. On the one hand, he loved his current assignment on the felony trial team in the courthouse of Metro City where he had just wrapped up a horrific double murder case leading to two "LWOP" convictions.[79] On the other hand, he could see how the elected wanted to have "a black man from Alphaville handling crime in Alphaville." The head DA did not give him specific instructions

267

---

[78] In their rich interview study of 267 prosecutors in nine offices in the Southeast US, Wright and Levine disclose four main professional motivations: bolstering an absolutist identity anchored by a righteous commitment to order, accountability, and morality; delivering a valuable public service; gaining courtroom skills and trial experience; and seeking professional stability and camaraderie as well as maintaining a work-life balance. Julius fits in the first and second categories. Ronald F. Wright and Kay L. Levine, "Career Motivations of State Prosecutors" (2018).

[79] LWOP is the abbreviation for Life Without the Possibility of Parole. It is a sentence usually meted out only for extreme sex crimes and the gravest cases of first-degree murder ("with special circumstances" such as lying in wait, multiple victims or involving torture, multiple murders, or murder of a law-enforcement agent, judge, or juror). A more common sentence for the latter is 25 or 50 years to life (when involving a gun), which is tantamount to the same in actuality, but it does not carry the symbolic weight of LWOP since the latter forecloses any future avenue for exit from prison.

as to how to do his job, but it was tacitly understood that he would uphold the standards and abide by the culture of the office, which stresses negotiation for all but the most serious offenses which need airing in open court. This is the first restraint on prosecutorial discretion: the *expectations of, and policies set by, the chief District Attorney* who can appoint, "rotate," and dismiss deputy DAs at will if they do not perform as expected.

"The victim was wronged!"

I had a public defender say to me, like their whole mantra now is that they want everybody to get treatment. Every case I get, "Oh, he robbed somebody, but he's got a drug problem, so he needs treatment," and I'm like, maybe he does! But I'm trying to *hold him accountable* for what he *did.* That may be his motivation behind doing it, but what about the victim? I mean, so we're supposed to ignore the victim because your guy has a drug problem? No! That's not how this system works, that's not how we dispense justice, we don't ignore the victim, *the victim has rights!* The victim was *wronged!*

I had a public defender tell me that this crime should be a misdemeanor because the car that was stolen was a Honda Civic and it was a piece of crap, and I told her, "That piece of crap is worth more to that person than my car is worth to me," because guess what? I can afford for your guy to steal my car because I have insurance, and my insurance gives me a rental. Probably that person only had liability insurance, when you take away their car, how do they get their kid to school, or to a doctor's appointment? How will they get to work? It's like, you're missing the point: it's not the value of the car, *it's the crime the person committed!* That's ultimately what the criminal justice system should be looking at, everyone should be treated the same: a rich defendant should be treated like a poor defendant, a rich victim treated like a poor victim, it doesn't – station and race and all the other stuff just doesn't matter.

Even though this assignment would not be his personal choice, Julius presents all the individual properties required of a good pretrial prosecutor:[80] he is calm, knowledgeable, and level-headed – in short,

---

[80] A fellow pretrial prosecutor in another courthouse is not sure Julius fits the bill: "He essentially *does not like the process* of bargaining, haggling . . . Julius is, I think,

"reasonable," a term attorneys on both sides of the aisle use sparingly and approvingly. He has the gift of the gab but he is restrained in his expression. He is not argumentative but he can entertain an argument and is prepared to change his mind when presented with valid reasons and contrary evidence. This is in sharp contrast with one of his predecessors (another "trial dog" miffed at being rotated to this assignment) who, instead of engaging defenders in discussion, shocked one and all by pinning yellow stickies on the bare wall of the negotiation room with the name of the defendant and the script corresponding to the offer scribbled on it. After a couple of months of constant recrimination and rising discontent from defense attorneys and judges, he was rotated again to a different assignment. This is a second constraint on the discretion of the pretrial DA: *collective pushback from the defense bar and the bench.*

Julius is a centrist (leaning to the Right) in terms of his location in the social space of the office. This puts him in a position to tangle productively with defense attorneys for whom he has respect – except for those whose representation of their cases cannot be trusted. He is equally respected by them as an attorney and esteemed as a person. After about a year occupying this position, Julius knows what he likes most about it: exchanging daily with the young deputies of the PX team (who "prep" the cases he negotiates in the event that no plea deal is reached on them), teaching them the fine points of preliminary examination, and boosting their professional ego. "Part of this process is learning from *what is a weak case and what is a strong case.* Some of the time it's testing yourself, and pushing yourself, and going out on really hard cases." He is especially excited at detecting potential "trial dogs" and taking them under his wing. Julius also knows what he dislikes: being immobile, sitting all day in the same places; missing lunch with colleagues to read cases during the mid-day break; the fact that "these cases don't *belong to me.* So I can't really *work 'em up* the way that I would"; and the difficult personalities of some defense attorneys he has to tangle with.

The pace of work "can become *overwhelming,* especially if you do this job the way that I do it," turning over every piece of evidence to weigh the "worth of the case." This is so he "can have an *intelligent* conversation, and an *informed* conversation" with defense attorneys and "the *competitor* in me doesn't want them to have the upper hand."

more temperamentally suited to doing *trials.* I don't think he likes the *give-and-take.* I think Julius would *rather* be in court crusading, trying a case."

Another downer is the misrepresentation and deceitfulness of the other party: "People aren't honest with you. They try to get one over on you. And I know they're advocates for their clients [but] *I don't like the dishonesty side of it.* So it's not that I dislike the individual, I just don't like *tactics.*" He does his best to not get irritated by fishy stories spun by defense attorneys and sometimes he uses humor to signal that he is not being fooled: "I know all the bull, and I'm not fallin' for it."

Otherwise, Julius has principled respect for the defense bar and periodically reminds himself as well as his interlocutors that "it's not personal." Plea bargaining works best when the prosecutors "are not trying to be *punitive,* not trying to be *emotional,* but everyone in the room is trying to evaluate a case." Julius was irritated when public defenders started showing up wearing "Black Lives Matter" t-shirts – a conspicuous violation of the code of formal dress in the courtroom: "Coming from where I come from, Black Lives Matter aren't just the defendants, it's the victims, and I've never heard them talk about the victims of crime."[81]

The daily round of the pretrial DA

8:00–9am: Driving to the office near the downtown courthouse, catching up office phone messages, chatting with colleagues, checking with the "baby DAs" on the PX team, verifying with the clerk that his cart of cases is ready.

9–11am: Plea bargaining session with anywhere from 10 to 20 defense attorneys, public and private, covering about 30–50 cases, leading to a handful of agreements on the spot. PDs and private attorneys come and go to talk to their clients in custody in the secure booths at the back of the courthouse and return with decisions to resolve or "continue" the case, or "set it" for PX.

---

[81] Katheryn Russell discusses the various tropes circulating around blacks as victims and perpetrators of intra-racial crime in *The Color of Crime: Racial Hoaxes, White Fear, Black Protectionism, Police Harassment and Other Macroaggressions* (1998). Michelle Phelps documents how many black community organizations have fought interpersonal violence for decades prior to the emergence of BLM in *The Minneapolis Reckoning: Race, Violence, and the Politics of Policing in America* (2024), chapter 6.

270

11am–12pm: Open court in Department 315 where judge Judy Meredith handles the law-and-motion calendar as well as the felony plea calendar. Brief whispered conversations by the side of his desk with private and public defenders who want to move their cases forward or resolve them.

12–12:30pm: Staying at the DA's desk in the empty courtroom to fill out the paperwork for the cases resolved that morning.

12:30–2pm: Returning to the office, picking a new batch of felony cases in the mail sorter, eating some fruit at his desk (no time for lunch) while checking his email, reading more files, screening the cases that will require much time reviewing evidence (which he will do on his week-end day at the office), chasing the specifics of penal code sections, talking to the "baby DAs" about their cases and hearings of the morning, coaching others on the phone about their ongoing trials.

2–4:30pm: Open court again in Department 315 to finish the calendar for the day. PDs and private lawyers keep coming to him for whispered conversations; reading tomorrow's case files during lulls in court action; entry of the pleas agreed upon during the day by the judge: "It's a wrap."

4:30–5:00pm: Back to the office, conferring with the PX team supervisor about the run of the day, about salient or complex cases, and discussing the outcome of their PX with the "baby DAs" and other cases with veteran attorneys doing complex "prelims."

5:00–7:00: Reading a batch of new files for his negotiations for the next morning, taking notes, working out the opening offers, more conversation with "baby DAs" on the cases they "prep"; closing shop for the day. Time to go home, mentally and physically drained, often with a headache, which he hates because he has no energy left to play with his young son ("I can't explain it, it's like talking to people all day just, always being *on*, I think that's what it is").

Monday is a comparatively slow day (the charging deputies are catching up with arrests and bookings made over the weekend), Tuesday and Wednesday are intense and Thursday is the peak. On Fridays, the court is "dark" (meaning that the courtrooms are closed and no hearings are scheduled) to allow attorneys, judges, clerks, and court reporters to catch up with late work and to prepare for the week ahead. This allows Julius to read a big batch of cases for the following week.

271

Every day, Julius drives from home in his brand new silver Mercedes, a half-hour away, into the public parking garage next to the courthouse and comes into the office through a secure stairwell and back door connected to the garage at about 8:45am.[82] He walks into the drab corridor lined with small rectangular offices on both sides where the PX team of eight attorneys is holed up. Time permitting, he quickly checks office phone messages, banters with colleagues gearing up for the day's work, and chats with "baby DAs" he has taken under his wing. They are nervous and rushed: they will be holding "prelims" that morning for defendants who have so far refused to "take a deal." So they keep Julius in the loop as to the "strength of the case," possible "proof problems," and the evolving position of the defense. This will help Julius recalibrate his offers as needed.

At 9am sharp, he rolls in through the back door of the 10-by-4 meter windowless room that serves as pretrial negotiation chamber pushing a metal cart packed with 40–50 blue folders containing the cases to be discussed that morning.[83] He sits on a padded swivel chair behind a wooden L-shaped desk, clear except for a white digital clock and two copies of the thick blue California Penal Code for the parties to consult if needed. On the bare white walls, taped cutouts from the local newspaper show a series of annual maps of homicides in Alphaville and an article on a rash of burglaries in the county. Julius's predecessor in the negotiation room liked to point to them in jest to remind the defense attorneys of the trouble they deal with. As a veteran colleague who "deals" serious cases put it, "We're in the badness business."

Defense attorneys are already there anxiously waiting for him, a mix of hurried private attorneys handling a single case or two – for them time is money, they need to run out to travel and appear in another courthouse soon – and stolid public defenders who each handle anywhere from three to ten cases filed in this courthouse. Ages

---

[82] Prosecutors never come into the courthouse through the front entrance because they could run into defense attorneys as well as defendants and their families. In another courthouse, they also exit through a side door closed to the public. This contributes to their sense of collective aloofness and elevation.

[83] This room sits near the secure front entrance to the DA's office (controlled by two amiable secretaries in a glass booth), opposite three small cube-like rooms used for interviewing witnesses and adjacent to a waiting room for witnesses summoned for the "prelims" of the day. Police officers called to appear at hearings have their own separate waiting room located deeper inside the office, materializing the trust and bond they enjoy with the DA's office.

Photo 2   The pretrial negotiation room as seen from the attorneys'
entrance

range from the early thirties to the late sixties. Most are white but
public defenders include many attorneys of color spanning the ethnic
gamut. The men are dressed in dark tailored suits, mono-colored
shirts and matching ties (sea blue is a favorite hue); the women are
elegantly attired, in mute-colored dresses or pantsuits, with scarves
and discreet jewelry. The men wear stock leather shoes, the women
are often in high heels (the novice attorneys are warned early against
showing "toe cleavage"). They lug a special rolling suitcase with a
lock or carry a leather satchel bursting with the folders of their clients
for that day.

Defense attorneys chit-chat amicably among themselves; two are
sitting on the chairs facing the prosecutor's desk, two more on chairs
nearer to the front wall (the sociologist sits on the last chair in the
corner), while another couple of attorneys stand in the frame of the
main door, conversing in a low voice. The topics run from court cases
and politics, vacationing in Italy to basketball and family news – some
attorneys have been friends for decades. Negotiations and decisions
concerning crimes that break the norm are a favorite. The courthouse
is a beehive of tall tales and fast rumors. The public defenders are
a tight fraternity, the private defense attorneys a loose one; there is

Photo 3 The blue folders of cases set for plea bargaining that morning

mutual respect among them, although the latter have been known to dump difficult cases onto the former in mid-stream, once they have drained all the money they can out of their private clients. The atmosphere is formal but relaxed; it will get tense at times when attorneys discuss their cases and they are surprised or despondent at the "deal" offered by Julius, or when the matter discussed is a very "heavy" one. They will feign a little indignation, but not too much. The tone remains professional if not cordial: there is nothing to gain in aggravating the pretrial DA. Even attorneys otherwise known for their aggressive "take-no-prisoner" style have to modulate their behavior accordingly.[84]

The door at the back is open at all times on a corridor leading to the main room of the office occupied by clerks in their cubicles. This allows the female staff to come in and hand over documents while negotiations are going on. The young DAs who are doing preliminary

[84] Professional cordiality in the negotiation chamber does not extend to closeness outside the courthouse: prosecutors and defense attorneys do not go to lunch together, share drinks, or otherwise consort in public places as a matter of culture and practicality. Public defenders, in particular, worry about the impression this would create among defendants who *already* believe that they are "in bed with the prosecutor."

hearings three floors up in the same building that morning can pop in to inform Julius of any development that bears on the bargaining of the case they handle. If the PX does not go the prosecutor's way, disclosing unforeseen "proof problems," or if the judge unexpectedly reduces the charges, Julius will lower the offer in cases where he believes that some kind of criminal conviction is still warranted. If the preliminary examination is favorable to the DA, the defendant will often take the offer in a hurry or even a higher offer if the conduct documented turned out to be worse than the charges.[85] But that offer must be accepted on the spot as it is "open" only that day by 4pm.

Plea bargaining setups vary widely across locations within and across counties. In Metro City, negotiations take place individually with attorneys sitting across a small desk set at the back of the courtroom handling the misdemeanor calendar while the court is in session, creating a noisy environment in which it is hard to hear clearly the back and forth of the negotiation. In the modern courthouse of Nicetown, the pretrial prosecutor meets with defenders sitting in clusters of three or four in a small windowless witness room by the entrance of a courtroom, again creating aural confusion (periodically, a clerk from that courtroom comes out to ask that we lower the volume). In Carnival county, the opening felony offer is made and briefly discussed by email and then face-to-face bargaining takes place one pair of attorneys at a time in the private chambers of the judge in the latter's presence.

One can find more variants traveling around the country.[86] In an Arizona county, weekly group sessions, informally called "sharkfests," involved multiple pairs of prosecutors and defense attorneys negotiating with each other in a large room, within earshot of one another, sometimes in the presence of a judge who intervened by opining on the viability of evidence and the fairness of the deal proposed. In a Georgia county, multiple defense attorneys sat around an oval table and took turns presenting their case to a junior prosecutor who had little authority to depart from formulaic

---

[85] In many cases of violence against persons, the defendant hopes that the victim or witness will not show up at the PX and thus that the case will be weakened and reevaluated downward or even dropped with all charges dismissed. When that expectation is not realized, the computation of risk and punishment changes radically and might lead a defendant to hurry to take a deal. Occasionally, a frantic defense attorney barges into the negotiation chamber, apologizes to all for interrupting the proceedings, and beseeches Julius to accept a guilty plea based on the offer made prior to setting the unfavorable PX.

[86] Kay L. Levine et al., "Sharkfests and Databases: Crowdsourcing Plea Bargains" (2018), pp. 657–8.

deals under the watch of a supervisor who did not know the cases. In a Texas county, the judge took the initiative to proactively shape deals so as to move the caseload and reduce jail overcrowding.[87] So far as to say that the physical and social setup of plea bargaining is flexible and diverse with different degrees of involvement by the judge as mediator or active protagonist intent on forcing deals.

"Down in the trenches"

A plea bargaining session with Julius is a fast-flowing two-hour mix of technical talk, legal argumentation, social conversation, court news, professional rumor, and light banter. It mingles the routine and the shocking, the banal and the stunning, the hilarious and the tragic, the droning and the jaw-dropping, and everything in between. Mostly, it is consistently unpredictable and frequently florid. A veteran private attorney from a far-away suburban town puts it this way: "All I do is criminal defense, I've done it for 22 years, every day is something new, *every day is like, 'Oh my Lord!'*"[88] To which a female colleague from Alphaville chimed in, "We couldn't make it up."

Of course, the tenor and tone of negotiation depend largely on the individual personality and occupational persona of the pretrial prosecutor, who sets the parameters of the ongoing barter. But haggling is a two-way street: the latter must also get to know and accommodate the skills, style and temperament of the public defenders and private defense attorneys who fill the room and take turns on the chair facing his desk. Moreover, the idioculture of the county criminal court favors negotiation over litigation. As a result, plea bargaining is stamped with professional cordiality, which helps keep strong disagreements in check and defuse episodic tension. The exchanges are

---

[87] Nancy J. King and Ronald F. Wright, "Managerial Judging and Judicial Plea Negotiations" (2017).

[88] This is a view voiced in stock expressions, the most common of which is, "You couldn't invent this stuff!" Another is, "You could make a movie out of this stuff." Indeed, a public defender in Carnival county kept a notebook of scribbled summaries of her cases in hopes of turning them into a scenario for a television series. Court attorneys often mention that this is a major attraction of their job, one that keeps them coming back energized day after day, which they compare favorably with the boring, slow, and repetitive work of corporate lawyers who spend their work time buried under mounds of paper in their offices and never appear in court.

swift, making references to multiple strands of conversation couched in legalese, to past exchanges about the current or earlier cases and to future possibilities should the case not resolve on this day ("put it over" for another pretrial hearing or "set it" for PX in two to three weeks thence).

"I love being in that room"

I love being in that room, there's always something going on, you jump from the mundane to the dramatic and from the silly to the ordinary to the unbelievable, the mix and match of personalities and styles and cases is constantly changing. It is really nonstop entertainment. It's better than reality TV. I can see how somebody would want to make a show out of that!
  (Field notebook, 21 December 2015)

277

There is no particular order in which cases are discussed; the rule is first-come, first-serve, and attorneys are careful to stay in line. There is also no set duration for discussing a case; some take a couple of minutes, or less when an agreement is validated or a confirmation is given that the case will go to preliminary examination, or the corresponding file is missing (which happens once or twice every morning). Others take five minutes, up to ten more rarely – which is a long stretch to contrast competing evaluations of a file that boils down to charges, circumstances, and offender profile and that a prosecutor on the PX team is actively working on. Public defenders who generally have a satchel full of cases will ask private attorneys how many they have and sometimes let them cut the line so that they can get on with their next hearing in another courthouse. When they have haggled over their offer, defense attorneys leave to go into the secure part of the courthouse to discuss the offer with their clients in a holding cell. There is thus a constant Brownian movement of bodies in and out of the room and multiple conversations going on at the same time. For instance, my eighth bargaining session involved 22 people (not counting the sociologist), among them six prosecutors, one staff person, two receptionists, six public defenders and six private defense attorneys (including two from out of county).

The prosecutors who successively handle the case write down their notes in the "activity" column on the inside of the file folder. The form records the name of the defendant, docket number, name of the private attorney or public defender, and the actions taken by the DA at each step. Julius scribbles his offers in office lingo. In matters that involve co-defendants, the business cards of the private attorneys hired are stapled at the bottom of the folder. The contents of the folder is considered "work product," that is, information proprietary to the office that is not part of "discovery," materials that the prosecutor is legally obligated to share with defense counsel.

The offers are made verbally; no written documents are exchanged. Surprisingly, this rarely leads to miscommunication. This is because attorneys are vigilant and incited to be honest by the tight social and symbolic mesh of the court: their professional reputation depends on it and reputation is their most precious asset. They are constantly under the gaze of colleagues and antagonists. A lapse would undermine their credibility, that is, the collective belief in their honesty and competence – credibility comes from *credere*, to believe.[89] Julius keeps track of the negotiations by handwriting notes on the inside flap cover of the case folder. His *modus operandi* is to ask defense counsel what resolution they propose to the case, to voice where he stands (based on memory or by quickly checking the folder flap), and then the two dig into the specifics of their disagreement. Among his stock phrases: "Tell me what you want"; "Tell me what you're thinking of"; "Lemme think about it." Julius tersely explains his reasoning on the case while defense attorneys cycle through a litany of reasons why he should lower his offer, as one after another gets pushed aside. An effective defense attorney is one who properly weighs the "value" of the case and has a resolution in mind, even better, a resolution that she has already cleared with her client. Malcolm Feeley rightly characterizes the attitude of the prosecutor as one of "dynamic passivity": he "knows where he wants to go and it is up to others to convince him to depart from it."[90]

278

---

[89] When a defense attorney behaves in an errant way that suggests dishonesty, news of her conduct and character quickly spreads through the District Attorney's office and all prosecutors adjust their conduct accordingly. Wariness becomes an obstacle to smooth and efficient professional relations in all manner of hearings. A veteran pretrial DA once pulled aside a novice PD who was flirting with the bounds of fraudulence and warned him of the irreversible consequences of continued misbehavior of the sort: "I told him he's got to decide what kind of attorney he wants to be."

[90] Feeley, *The Process is the Punishment*, p. 178.

> ### "I'm always willing to do something different"
>
> If you want me to do something, you gotta *tell me something about your client*. Like the young defendant that I told you about, I told him to pull up his pants in the courtroom: I told the attorney, "Well, tell me what is he doing: Is he in school? Does he have a job? What's his support group?" I'm like, "If you want me to do something out of the ordinary, I'm not gonna do it because you tell me to do it. I'll do it because you're telling me that he has a support system, or *you have a plan* on how to make sure this guy doesn't come back here." I'm always willing to do something *different*, but in order to do something different, *they* have to do the legwork. I want you to *give me information!* I can't tell you how to do your job. Just do your job!

Attorneys on both sides are on the *honor system* for everything that they represent to their antagonist and to the bench. For instance, if defense counsel tells Julius that they talked to judge Santucci (who handles felony sentencing) and that the latter is agreeable to a certain resolution of the case being haggled over, then Julius will go by their word. Defense attorneys, for their part, take great care to differentiate what they personally know to be documented fact and what their clients claim. For instance, they will tell Julius, "my client tells me that he has a job at a Target warehouse," rather than "my client has a job," if they were not able to personally verify it by reaching the putative employer on the phone. But the temptation to fudge facts is irresistible and an *artful defense attorney will make the line fuzzy and then toe it.* The less skilled lawyers will cross it, inadvertently or deliberately, and eventually incur the corresponding loss in symbolic capital which greatly hampers their ability to get favorable deals going forward.

Legal scholarship on criminal lawyering is replete with articles questioning the ethical conduct and standards of prosecutors under the heading of "prosecutorial misconduct."[91] There is no corresponding body of research impugning the professional morals of defense counsel even though the controls over their conduct are lax at best. The closest counterpart would be "ineffective assistance of counsel," which points to incompetence rather

---

[91] A classic statement is Angela J. Davis, "The American Prosecutor – Power, Discretion, and Misconduct" (2008). A valiant but flawed attempt at documenting and measuring the phenomenon based on appellate court rulings, court decisions, and media accounts is Kathleen M. Ridolfi and Maurice Possley, *Preventable Error: A Report on Prosecutorial Misconduct in California 1997–2009* (2010).

than immorality and the deliberate violation of professional ethics in search of "winning" at all costs. Yet one of the flaws of plea bargaining which its critics overlook resides in the possible professional ineptitude of the defense attorney who does not know how to properly strategize on behalf of his client. This is not uncommon in smaller jurisdictions in rural areas without a public defender's office which rely on substandard private attorneys under county contract.

Julius will agree to set a new pretrial hearing so long as he feels that progress is being made on the matter and that the attorney is not just "aging the case" – a common delaying tactic aimed at eroding the charges as time goes by. A new hearing may be set because the defense attorney is trying hard but cannot get his client to take what is deemed a favorable offer. Private counsel may also ask for yet another pretrial because they cannot get their client to pay up the money they are owed. If no movement toward resolution is made after four pretrials, Julius will push for "setting" the case for preliminary examination: time for the DAs on the PX team to take over and then send the case sailing toward trial with confirmed or revised charges.[92] "Heavy cases" always take longer because the stakes are much higher and human lives are literally at stake. A premeditated murder will commonly take two years to go to trial as the investigation unfolds and the attorneys tangle to find common ground.

The span of gravity of the cases negotiated is vertiginous: some matters are trifling, as banal as selling marijuana or stealing a car, and will routinely be "busted down" to misdemeanors with or without time behind bars; others are life-overturning for the defendant (as for the victim), such as carjacking, child sexual assault, rape, or homicide, for which punishment is measured in dozens of years and more. When the latter are discussed, the banter stops, the room becomes quiet, the mood turns somber and Julius reclaims the helm of negotiation. In very serious and violent cases exposing the defendant to "big numbers," he will wait for defense counsel to notify him whether the latter wants to bargain or not: "If you tell me you want one, I'll make an offer, I'll figure it out, but you usually have to come to me because *they* know their clients, 'I've been talking to this guy about pleading, so can you give me an offer, something that he can, that somehow, *he can have a life*,' and I say, sure! But if they don't come to me, it's not

---

[92] The easier cases are generally handled by the novice DAs (who are assigned to this team three to five years into the job) and the more complex ones by veterans coming on the team for the second or third time.

worth my while even writing anything down." The case will be sent to preliminary examination on its way to trial – those are among the rare cases that will see a jury.

The pretrial DA has considerable latitude to craft his offers, playing with the charges, recommended sentences, and facts pled to. He can revise his offer up or down depending upon new information and evidence dug up by the DA from the PX team to whom the case was assigned as the matter slowly winds its way from one hearing to the next. A typical instance is this: in the course of bargaining, Julius found out that the victim of an assault with a deadly weapon (known at "ADW," Penal Code section 245, a "wobbler" punishable by up to 4 years of prison if charged as a felony) was still in hospital a full month after the crime. This led him to "amend the complaint" by including the enhancement of "GBI" (Penal Code section 12022.7), a clause of "great bodily injury" adding a consecutive term of 3, 4, or 5 years of prison to the defendant's exposure (of 4, 8, or 12 years). In another case, Julius had made a low offer with no prison time to a first-time burglar. But, a few weeks later, he was notified by the office that the defendant had allegedly committed a second burglary, so he combined the two burglaries and revised his offer to two years of state prison. A third example is the case of a premeditated attempted murder (Penal Code section 664/187, punishable by life in prison) on which Julius's predecessor on the job had made an offer of 26 years. Upon reexamination, Julius found out that the victims of this street gun down had stopped working with the office in view of a possible trial and so he made an offer of 19 years "open" only until the next pretrial. Notwithstanding the frantic efforts of his counsel, the defendant did not take the offer and would live to regret it: the victims changed their mind and decided to cooperate again and so the offer was "pulled" and scaled back up to the original 26 years – a costly tactical mistake.[93]

Offers can also be revalued down when "proof problems" materialize, the conduct turns out to be less serious than originally charged, or new facts emerge that color the criminal and social profile of the defendant to his benefit. Julius can use his broad discretion to the benefit of the defendant, something he does often in cases involving young offenders with no criminal record – *age is the single most impactful variable* at this stage of adjudication. This was consistent

[93] A pretrial prosecutor will always honor the offer on a case made by his predecessor on the job, absent new elements necessitating a recalibration of the proposed plea.

across pretrial prosecutors and counties. Everywhere 21 years was considered the cutoff point after which a defendant is "old" and no longer deserving of advantageous treatment because beyond salvage. Defense attorneys hope to play on this variable when they keep calling their client "the kid" or "my kid" (even when the latter is well into his twenties).[94]

In addition to adjusting charges, Julius has a whole menu of items to check on or off, including "enhancements" and "strikes," that allow him to vary punishment from minimal (misdemeanor probation with no custody time) to extreme (life without the possibility of parole), depending on the specifics of the case.[95] I discuss the eight parameters of plea negotiation later, but just to give a typical example: on an armed robbery committed by a recidivist, Julius can make an offer discounting the fact that the defendant used a gun, which would automatically trigger an enhancement adding 10 years of prison (for handling a gun), 20 years (for firing the gun, known as "big use") and 25 years to life (for causing injury or death with the gun); he can disregard the fact that the action was part of gang activity; he can erase "enhancements" in the criminal record of the defendant (known as "strikes" or "prison priors") for purposes of computing the suggested sentence as an incentive for the defendant to settle, or "in furtherance of justice" if the case calls for veering off the standard course. This latitude gives him considerable leverage in negotiations, but this leverage is nonetheless circumscribed.

To say that the pretrial prosecutor has discretion does not mean that he can invoke these elements at will and on a whim.[96] For he is *embedded in a series of nested webs of social ties and symbolic frames* that extend well beyond the courtroom workgroup and transmute absolute discretion into what, following Herbert Simon's (1957) famous critique of the neoclassical conception of the rational actor, one may

[94] Loïc Wacquant, "Sealing the Fate of 'The Kid': A Field Note on the Swirl of Plea Bargaining" (2026).
[95] California has the death penalty on the books but it does not apply it. In addition, it is exceedingly rare for the District Attorneys of San Pedrito county and Carnival county to recommend it at trial. Such cases are subjected to painstaking review by a special committee composed of the seniormost prosecutors in the office.
[96] See Forst, "Prosecution," for a selection of, and guide to, research on prosecutorial discretion. The conventional complaint is that the prosecutor has way too much discretion and exercises it whimsically in ways that perpetuate the usual biases of criminal justice, chief among them racial. This complaint is typically made mechanically without any supporting evidence. But see the counterargument of Jeffrey Bellin, "The Power of Prosecutors" (2019).

call *bounded discretion* (after Simon's "bounded rationality").[97] The constraining factors that shape the prosecutor's evaluation of any given case take the form of a series of concentric circles of magnetic force. They include his habitus (especially his visceral moral values), which leads him to perceive and evaluate facts in a certain light; the penal algorithm he uses to compute exposure; the "going rate" for similar cases and the "price of crime" in the region of his county; pushback from the defense bar, especially public defenders who act collectively via their office; membership in a team and his supervisor, who double-checks salient matters and with whom he is in constant communication; office culture and policy; the sentencing judge who has to validate the plea agreement; courthouse tradition and county criminal politics; and finally legal statutes.

The bargaining strategies of the prosecutor and defender are, not surprisingly, diametrically opposed. The former seeks to *narrow* the perimeter of negotiation to focus on the offense, its circumstances and its impacts, and the defendant's criminal past if he has one. The latter strives to *expand* the scope of the confabulation to center on the offender, his social biography, and his current circumstances.[98] The prosecutor tends to be *charge-oriented* in keeping with a Kantian, just-desert philosophy of punishment seeking retribution (or neutralization motivated by the seriousness of the crime alleged) while the defender tends to be *character-oriented* according to a Benthamite, consequentialist philosophy whose goal is reformation. But these are mere tendencies and, in practice, Julius will readily acknowledge and reckon with the social profile and predicament of the defendant. Defense attorneys, on the other hand, never veer away from stressing social context over legal text. Their focus on minimizing and excusing the alleged criminal conduct is relentless. This effectively recognizes the guilt of their client, which the negotiators take as a tacit

[97] In *Models of Man* (1957), Herbert A. Simon develops the concept of "bounded rationality" – the cornerstone of behavioral economics – in response to two restraints on individual rationality. The first is cognitive: the limitations of the human brain make it impossible to acquire and process all the information needed to behave in the manner of a perfect utility maximizer. The second is social: the human agent is not a solitary being acting as a monad but a social creature situated in "an environment of choice" replete with institutional pressures.

[98] "While the prosecutor develops a rough notion of a 'normal crime', the defense attorney must break down this stereotype and individualize the charge and the defendant. In essence, he does this by providing reasons why the case should not be treated 'normally'" (Feeley, *The Process is the Punishment*, p. 179).

presumption of their confrontation. (I return to this point in the conclusion to this chapter, *infra*, pp. 363–4.)

In some cases, plea bargaining effectively entails not one but two negotiations: the one between the prosecutor and the defense attorney to craft an offer, the other between the defense attorney and the defendant to validate it. In serious matters where the parties are discussing "big numbers," it is not uncommon for counsel to have difficulty getting their client to realize that the deal on the table is the best they will get – sometimes it is a sweetheart deal – and that they should not risk going to trial based on the facts of the case and the abundance of proof as to their guilt. But some defendants are scared, hard-headed, misadvised (by cell mates and "jailhouse lawyers"), overconfident, in denial, or downright delusional and they cannot rationally weigh their options.[99]

284

Julius recalls the case of a 19-year-old defendant with a long prior record charged with 43 counts of armed robbery who was facing life behind bars. He was offered a plea deal of 19 years of prison, of which he would likely end up serving 16 ("He was getting the same amount of time as he had been on the face of this earth"). He passed up on the offer and kept insisting instead that he should be offered probation and a "program" of diversion (which he had gotten earlier on a previous case). He went to trial against the better judgment of his attorney. He was found guilty on all counts by the jury and the judge sentenced him to 130 years of prison.

"I gave him a three-year offer, he's doing 30 to life"

"It happens *all the time* [that defense attorneys cannot convince their client to take a deal they should jump on]. I'm on the sexual assault team, so I'm talking to this attorney. It's a vertical assignment, so I negotiate my own cases. And I make this defendant a three-year offer on a sexual assault case against his daughter, *that he confessed to*. And I did it because the mom asked me to, and because I didn't want the little girl to testify (1).

---

[99] The material conditions of social stress, emotional pressure, and cognitive distortion under which defendants decide to accept or decline a plea offer in serious cases suffice to invalidate the reigning theoretical model developed by criminologists according to which bargaining is a rational evaluation by both parties proceeding "in the shadow of the trial." Shawn D. Bushway, "Defendant Decision-Making in Plea Bargains" (2019).

We're pretrying this case for like, we come back week after week. And finally I said, "I can't justify coming back here, talking about something, when this isn't moving." This guy says, "I want to talk to my mom, and then I'll come back and I'll give you my decision." [annoyed] Forty-something year old man going to talk to his mom! Well, he comes back and he says, "No" (2). And I look at the attorney, and he looks at me. And he says, [defeated] "Julius, I don't know what else to do." Anyway, he ended up firing his attorney, *hiring* an attorney that would do what he wanted, *what he wanted her to do*. She and I went to trial. I gave him a three-year offer, he's doing 30 to life. [thud, pause] And that's because sometimes, no matter what you do as a defense attorney, you can't make this guy take this time. He has to decide he wants to do it himself."

285

"Oh, I'll never forget that case." A decade later, Julius remembers it vividly and for a reason: the convict father applied for an early parole release on medical grounds after serving 12 years of his sentence (3). That means that he would appear before a parole board where the victim and the prosecutor are called to present their response to the request (4). Julius contacted the daughter, now a grown woman in her mid-twenties, but the matter was still too painful for her to attend the hearing. She did not want to see her father and she fiercely opposed his release and so she asked Julius to appear on her behalf, which he did. When the convict father came into the room and saw Julius there, he immediately exited and withdrew his petition: "I was about to hammer him."

Julius also recalls the trial well because the accused father was appearing "out of custody," which is rare in such cases: his mother had paid bail in the amount of $400,000. "He confessed, it was a *slam dunk case*. But it wasn't about me. If I had just wanted to put notches on my belt, I would have just went out" straight to trial. Instead Julius made a plea offer because the daughter did not want to testify but "the father made her do it" by insisting on taking the matter to a jury.

At the trial, the father called a false-confession expert, in vain. "I think he was selfish, think about the mentality of a father who would do that to his own daughter. He thought he would get away with it. He wasn't man enough to take responsibility." The defendant's mother sat immobile in the courtroom gallery as she watched the video of her son's confession to the police playing on a giant flat screen. "It's one of those cases where it's hard to understand why do people do the things they do. People will admit a murder before they admit sexual assault," which runs the gamut of class and ethnicity, rich, poor, black, white, latino: "People who hurt kids, they come from every walk of life."

1. Child sexual assault cases are the single most difficult cases to negotiate and litigate because they generally entail relying on the testimony of a traumatized child who would be retraumatized should the matter go to preliminary examination and to trial, at which the defense attorney skewers them to produce inconsistent statements and instill doubt about culpability. When the victim will not put up with this emotional ordeal, the prosecutor has to "deal" the case. For the same reason, most allegations of sexual assaults against children never make it past the investigation stage.
2. Child sexual abusers often cannot bring themselves to plead guilty in the face of overwhelming evidence of culpability (including their own confession and material proofs), not just because these offenses involve "big numbers" (prison sentences measured in decades), but because this would amount to a symbolic suicide in the eyes of their loved ones, especially when the assault targeted a member of the family.
3. In California, "medical parole" can be granted to prisoners who are permanently incapacitated and thus presumably do not pose a threat to public safety, pursuant to Penal Code section 3550. "Compassionate release" can be granted to inmates who are terminally ill with less than six months to live pursuant to Penal Code section 1170(e).
4. For a pointillist account of the social and juridical dynamics of these hearings, read Victor Lund Shammas, "The Perils of Parole Hearings: California Lifers, Performative Disadvantage, and the Ideology of Insight" (2019).
5. In California, the jury must be unanimous (12 to 0) to convict the defendant and the DA's office gets "two bites at the apple," meaning it can take the case to trial again after a mistrial due to a "hung jury." The prosecutor can simultaneously negotiate a new plea offer while the second trial is set and ongoing. For a meticulous account from the inside of a trial and jury deliberation, read D. Graham Burnett, *A Trial by Jury* (2022).

The possible outcomes of a pretrial hearing for any given defense attorney are varied and typically set off a chain of future bargaining exchanges. They include receiving an initial offer; discussing a possible plea and "putting the case over"; agreeing to an offer and getting set to enter the plea in open court later that afternoon; modifying an offer (facts, charge, sentence, enhancements, restitution, probation conditions, etc.); being referred to diversion or to a problem-solving court (drug, behavioral health); setting the case for PX (preliminary examination); "kicking" the case because the file is missing; and, in rare instances, dismissing the case outright.

Capturing the conduct, reasoning, and emotions of the pretrial prosecutor at ground level based on close-up observation of routine activities in his ordinary setting instantly *deconstructs monolithic portraits of the penal state* – including my own in this very book. It invites us to enrich and reformulate the major questions tackled by extant research on plea bargaining, including the press of caseloads, the collective nature and temporal texture of bargaining, the calibration of offers, the weight of the criminal record, the role of the sentencing judge, and the very purpose of punishment. Standard accounts of guilty pleas center on two core elements: charges and sentence.[100] Let me set them into a broader spectrum of twelve steps and stakes of a plea negotiation.

Theorizing from afar and from above is wont to produce overly coherent, cohesive, and streamlined visions of reality. A great virtue of ethnography is that it forces the investigator to face the raw phenomenon at ground level in all of its complexity and fluidity, and thus to reconsider how his analytic constructs fare in the heat of historical practice. Another is to put the sociologist in direct personal contact with the agents of flesh and blood who "act out" the institution and thus enable her to capture both its structural necessity and its practical contingency in the very movement of their articulation. It also reveals the sensual and moral tenor of conduct in the universe under examination – a dimension sorely lacking in standardized social science accounts.

Fieldwork can thus serve as an instrument of double rupture with both folk and scholarly common sense, inspiring nuance and inviting new conceptualization and observation in a spiraling movement of epistemic ascent.[101] Spending three years in the county criminal court definitely convinced me that most of the scholarship on prosecutors deals with an *imaginary character* (in the triple sense of fictional person in a play, moral disposition, and reputation), idealized or (more often) demonized, because of its shocking lack of observational grounding. This scholarly fiction is echoed by the caricatural vision guiding the mobilization of justice militants for whom prosecutors are mindless and callous automatons in the penal machinery – "blue-eyed devils," as a veteran prosecutor puts it. Academic and activist caricatures support one another but jointly obscure the occupational and moral intricacy of justice in action.

---

[100] Kay L. Levine, "Prosecutorial discretion" (2014).
[101] On this point, see Loïc Wacquant, *The Poverty of the Ethnography of Poverty* ([2023] 2025), chapter 3, especially pp. 154–8.

1. Quantity, quality, and information asymmetry

The first dilemma that Julius must resolve is the sheer volume of files he has to process and the knowledge asymmetry he must contend with. On any one morning, the attorneys he faces negotiate a single case each (for most private defense attorneys) or a handful of cases (typically four to seven for public defenders) which they have had the time to "prep" in some depth on the preceding days or earlier that morning. By contrast, Julius must devote most of his time to reading new files and keep at his command the facts concerning three to five dozen cases that morning, old and new, and not just in broad outline because the devil is in the details. What attorneys call the "equities of the case" – the extra-legal particulars of the offender and crime calling for mitigation or aggravation – inflect the offers he makes and the negotiation stance he takes.

If he is unprepared, Julius will get "rolled" by defense attorneys who will rule the roost.[102] This is why "it's always been my practice that I want to know *more* than they know." Alas, this is mission impossible: Julius grouses that defense attorneys "are talking to me about this *singular case*, and I handle like, *hundreds of cases a week.*" Moreover, defense attorneys generally have more and better information about the matter at hand because they have talked to their client and witnesses while the DA must rely largely on the bare police report augmented by whatever information the PX prosecutor assigned to the case has been able to garner in haste, if any.[103] As a result, it is public and private counsel who paint the picture of the case that morning and drive the direction of the negotiation. This is why Julius must strike a balance between quality (digging into a particular case) and quantity (not getting submerged by the endless flow of cases). A long-standing critique of the bloated criminal justice apparatus is that public defenders have too many cases and too little time to devote to each defendant, amounting to *de facto* "ineffective assistance of

---

[102] This was the case in another courthouse where the pretrial DA was notoriously unprepared and defense attorneys had the upper hand in negotiations. Public defenders relished discussing cases with him. When rumor about this imbalance reached the office head, that DA was rotated to a different assignment.

[103] In very "heavy" cases such as murder, the prosecutor is supported by an inspector (also called an investigator) who goes out to the field, gathers additional evidence, serves subpoenas for records, verifies information, tracks down and reinterviews witnesses, and otherwise helps prepare the case for trial. But this support is not available for "garden-variety felonies."

counsel."[104] But the same is true, and to a greater extent, of prose-cutors.[105] Another critique is that prosecutors drive bargaining: the opposite can be true when the defense counsel has a richer picture of the case.

2. Judicial pedagogy

All the attorneys present in the room and standing in the entrance corridor, typically numbering from three to seven, can hear the details of the cases that are verbalized as well as follow the run of bar-gaining between Julius and the defender facing him at the desk. This infringement on confidentiality might seem surprising but it serves an important *pedagogical function*: it educates the lawyers on the legal standards, mode of thinking, and negotiating style of Julius.[106] They can sample his demeanor; they hear him chortle at the offenses that are his pet-peeves; they find out that he has little patience for the usual "sob stories" concocted by defense attorneys. More crucially, they learn what he expects them to do to agree to lower an offer: pre-pare a "mitigation package" providing evidence that the defendant has a job, goes to school, is checked into a "program" related to his offense (such as a residential facility for alcohol or drug treatment), or is otherwise meritorious. In short, by observing other negotiations as they unfold, defense attorneys learn salient facets of Julius's *prose-cutorial habitus*, forged day-to-day within the office, the categories of legal perception and moral evaluation that guide his work, and they can thus anticipate how best to engage him.

289

Julius's judicial taste includes these five tenets: (i) when the defendant has "graduated" to prison time on a felony conviction, there is "no going

---

[104] Laurence A. Benner, "The Presumption of Guilt: Systemic Factors that Contribute to Ineffective Assistance of Counsel in California" (2008).

[105] In total, prosecutors handle more cases than public defenders because some defendants (circa 20 percent) hire private attorneys and because, in matters involving multiple co-defendants ("codees"), the Public Defender's office handles the case of the "Defendant A" while the other defendants (B, C, etc.) are handled by private attorneys contracted by the county to avoid creating a conflict of interest for the office.

[106] This is confirmed by a veteran DA in charge of plea bargaining after preliminary examination who opines: "I don't like all this stuff being done in private. I think this should be done publicly. *There should be no secrets, no agendas,* I want every defense attorney to see how I act with everybody else. I'm not biased to my friends or biased to a good-looking girl or whoever. It's a healthier environment when everybody is around there. And then they also start to see my likes, my dislikes."

back to misdemeanorland;" (ii) drug dealing offenses are serious crimes because they create collateral danger and victims: they will not be dealt "cheap;" (iii) he does not offer DEOJ (deferred entry of judgment) and does not give infractions ("I don't even know this word"), meaning that he will never reduce a felony to the offense category below misdemeanor: he would rather dismiss it; (iv) he will not make offers on cases in which a victim was seriously harmed until the PX team prosecutor has conferred with the latter; (v) he is especially repulsed by defense attorneys who minimize the gravity of child sexual assault (the "dirty grandpa" trope) because he was a member of the vertical team that handles these cases for three years and it transformed him as a lawyer and a father. Defense attorneys, public and private, had better know these principles and act accordingly or else their negotiation with Julius will drag on or derail.

The semi-public setup of judicial bargaining also exerts a *framing effect* by narrowing the range of offers. It elevates the lower bound and lowers the upper bound of plea deals. If Julius started making overly favorable offers on some category of crimes or to a particular attorney, this would be duly noted by all those present in the room and quickly enter into the communication channels of the court.[107] The communal nature of the bargaining scene creates a bargaining floor. It also gives the witnessing attorneys an opportunity to intervene in the discussion, as when a public defender interjects an argument in favor of one of his colleagues who faces Julius at the negotiating desk. At times, the whole audience seems to converge to press Julius on a deal, as if its member were waging a coordinated campaign of attrition on him. So much to say that plea bargaining is not carried out on an island by an isolated and punctual pair of attorneys but by a fluid couple surrounded by an audience which monitors and influences the process.

[VN520764] *PD Garzon is negotiating the case of a defendant who embezzled $7,248 from an acquaintance (Penal code section 487, a "wobbler" punishable by 16 months, 2 or 3 years of prison). A bench warrant was issued to arrest him after he failed to show up in court for his hearing. The offer on the table is a felony but, if the defendant reimburses the full sum, the conviction will be retroactively reduced to a misdemeanor. Garzon insists that his client is doing all he can to pay up but he's got living expenses to cover; that he's half-way there (it's not true,*

290

---

[107] Levine et al. detect a similar "audience effect" in their study of "group negotiation sessions" ("Sharkfests and Databases").

he's only reimbursed $700); and that "he's crushin' it." Julius does not fall for the claim and takes the room as witness of the fairness of his offer, inviting other attorneys to chime in and thus restrain Garzon. They demur because they don't want to undermine a colleague.

DA Julius: Dude, this is what I'm saying: he's making a great effort to do it, **the case is getting *old***, why don't we just plead him to the felony, and he's gonna have to wait the three years, once he pays it off, he comes in and shows proof that he's paid it off, and it's reduced to a misdemeanor.

PD Garzon: I think **he's gonna *lose his job* if he pleads to the felony**.

DA Julius: **I'm just asking the room, is that a fair offer?**

Private attorney Bastillo: Aw shit, [inaudible, maybe says "I wasn't listening"]

PD Garzon: Yeah, he's not gonna say anything, he knows better!

[DA Julius crows loudly, almost shouting in delight]

Private attorney Bastillo: I've been trained well!

DA Julius: I mean, that's all I can do, other than that, dude, **we gotta set it** [for PX]. [pretrial supervisor] **Mike wrote "set it" in the file, so I have to set it.**

PD Garzon: [stunned] You want to set a PX?

DA Julius: [adamant] Yep.

Long silence.

3. *"Setting the price of crime"*

With his plea offers, the pretrial DA effectively "sets the price of crime" for the territory under his authority – to use the court vernacular. This price, also known as "the going rate," is the customary quantum of punishment attached to each offense category for a generic offender absent case specifics – for example, 180 days of jail for being illegally in possession of a firearm, three years of state prison for a second robbery, or five-year felony probation for a first residential burglary. It is a *local value* which varies with geography: courthouses in different cities in the same county will price a given offense category differently; the variation across counties is even more pronounced. For instance, the punishment for a first-time DUI (driving under the influence) in the eastern region of San Pedrito county is "standard one plus ten," meaning ten mandatory days in jail in addition to "standard one," the baseline set by Alphaville in the western region of the county. The greatest unwarranted disparity in criminal adjudication is not race – which has obsessed scholars of punishment – but place.[108] The same felonies that routinely receive probation in large urban coastal counties are just as routinely sanctioned by long prison terms in small rural counties of California inland due to differences in the sheer volume of cases, the overall gravity of the crime profile, and the punitiveness of the local population.[109]

The "price of crime" is not the spawn of a whimsical wish or personal taste. It is the dynamic product of court precedent, office policy, the volume of cases, the balance of power between the offices of the DA and the PD, and the sentencing scale of the judges. The individual pretrial DA can inflect it, but not change it drastically by going against the *weight of collective expectations* as defined, not just in the county, but in each individual courthouse in different localities.[110] Proof: on his very first morning on the job, a half-dozen defense attorneys, public and private, conspired to try and vehemently convince Julius that the price of crime for drug offenses was lower than what he personally envisioned.[111] He detected their tactics ("I felt like they came in with an agenda, because it's my first day here") and he drew a line in the sand, revealing why he would prove inflexible on narcotics offenses by calling on his biography.

> "My *first day here*, I'm giving offers and *they were trying to punk me*! And they were like, 'No one cares about drugs, so your offers on drug cases should be lower.' And I told them, [unflinching] 'You are talking to the wrong dude about that.' And I gave them a *lecture* – it was like a room full of private and public defenders. Uh-uh, *first day*! I was sitting around, first day! (LW: How many attorneys did you have?) It had to be, like, five or six of them, and some standing up. And I was like, [piqued] 'Hey! *Lemme*

---

[108] In the comprehensive collective volume edited by Edkins and Redlich on *A System of Pleas: Social Sciences Contributions to the Real Legal System* (2019), one finds the obligatory chapter on race but no discussion of inequality by place. The same goes for the thick *Research Handbook on Plea Bargaining and Criminal Justice* edited by Máximo Langer et al. (2024) and Wright et al.'s *The Oxford Handbook of Prosecutors and Prosecution* (2021).

[109] For instance, prosecutors in inland counties of the central valley or the mountainous inland will seek the death penalty for a single murder, whereas prosecutors in the urban coastal counties will not do so even in the case of multiple murders.

[110] On the role of "collective expectations" in setting the paths for social action, see the classic essays in social psychology by Marcel Mauss, *Sociologie, psychologie, physiologie* (2021).

[111] This was amplified by the fact that Julius had been stationed for several years in the eastern part of the country, where the punishment scale is higher, and was now operating in the western side, where "garden-variety" felonies received milder punishment due to the sheer volume of violent crime.

tell you about drugs. *Lemme tell you* about the impact of drugs. *I lived that!*' I have *friends* who are addicted to drugs. I grew up in a neighborhood [crabby] where you couldn't even *walk to the corner store* because of drug dealers, you know? Don't tell me about that! Don't try to *preach* what *society* thinks about drugs ... But don't tell me it doesn't *matter*, because it matters to people who I know. It matters to me, and it *certainly matters to this community*, because as we know, Alphaville is an *extremely violent city* ...

I mean, [pugnacious] *I'm from the streets!* I can see when I'm *bein' played!* I'm like, you picked the *wrong guy!* There's a reason why [head DA] Nick put me here. And I told Nick, I said, 'You know, they may not like me. Because I come with a different experience, my foundation is different.' It's totally different from [my predecessor on the job] Rob's. Rob had been in this office for almost thirty years! I'm comin' in here, this stuff is *fresh* to me, because *I lived it!*."

A decade later, Julius roars with laughter as we recount this episode, which he remembers vividly: "The fix was in, I remember that [laughter] – the fix was in, *they were all out to get me*. Because it was a rite of passage. And then they knew, [despondent] "Oh-oh, it's not gonna work." Then I think I threw [the fearsome district of] Bird Hill at them, where I grew up. I started talking to them about drugs in my neighborhood and what comes from it. And like, most of them didn't grow up where I grew up, so how do they counteract that, how do they debate that?"

For a couple of months, relations in the negotiating room were tense and deals on narcotics cases hard to hammer out. Yet, for all his indignation at the attempt to "roll him," Julius did yield and lower his offers some when the defense attorneys came up and thus deals were struck again. There is pressure on both sides: the prosecutor cannot let cases accumulate and clog up the pipeline to the next stage of adjudication; the defenders cannot let their client stew behind bars with no resolution in sight. Julius put the resistance of defense attorneys in perspective: "You're *penalizing your clients*, because this system *doesn't work* unless there's plea bargaining, unless you talk and try to lessen the exposure for your client. And it's not *a game*. It's someone's *life* that you're dealing with." So both parties have to soften their stance and realign their action to come to what Erving Goffman calls a "working consensus."[112] The price of crime in Alphaville had

---

[112] In everyday interaction, "there is often a kind of division of definitional labor. Each participant contributes to a single overall definition of the situation which involves not so much a real agreement as a working consensus." Erving Goffman, *The Presentation of Self in Everyday Life* (1959), p. 10.

effectively been reset but this was a *collective achievement and not an individual action.*

4. Calibrating offers, the not-so-secret sauce

There is one more source of consistency and predictability which reduces discretion. Pretrial prosecutors commonly use an *informal penal algorithm* to peg their initial plea offers. A common formula is to decide whether the case is a "probation case" or a "prison case" and, if the latter, compute "total exposure" – the sum of the maximum number of years of prison incurred if the defendant was found guilty on all counts – and to divide that number by three (or by two in the case of violent offenses). The offer can then be adjusted by adding or subtracting a year or two of prison depending on the age and record of the defendant (21 is considered old), the circumstances of the crime, the attitude of the victim, and "proof problems." This algorithm is tantamount to a *self-imposed limit on latitude.* Defense attorneys know it is in play and invoke it in their bargaining argumentation, calling out the prosecutor when she hands out offers that are out of line with its calculation.[113]

Next, and crucially, the decisions of the pretrial DA who makes opening plea offers and his subsequent moves are anchored by the *"going rate"* for each category of crime, that is, the customary punishment meted out for the type of offense at hand in a given county and even city within a county, given notable geographic variations in case resolution.[114] If she deviates notably from that value, the prosecutor will be subjected to reactions and pressures from a variety of court actors, starting with defense attorneys, public and private. Prosecutorial discretion is thus limited by insertion in a web of transactional relations unfolding over time with members of the "courtroom workgroup" which turn plea bargaining from a one-sided spot

[113] A veteran prosecutor notes that "if the offer is more than half the exposure, it's not really an offer," meaning that it communicates a refusal to negotiate by the pretrial DA: take it or go to PX.

[114] Feeley, *The Process is the Punishment;* Eisenstein et al., *The Contours of Justice;* Denise Leifker and Lisa L. Sample, "Do Judges Follow Sentencing Recommendations, or Do Recommendations Simply Reflect what Judges Want to Hear? An Examination of One State Court" (2010); Christi Metcalfe, "The Role of Courtroom Workgroups in Felony Case Dispositions: An Analysis of Workgroup Familiarity and Similarity" (2016); Don Stemen and Gipsy Escobar, "Whither the Prosecutor? Prosecutor and County Effects on Guilty Plea Outcomes in Wisconsin" (2018).

Photo 4   Reading cases and crafting offers during the lunch break

decision-making into a form of "relational contracting" involving repeated exchanges over time by the same pair aimed at problem-solving that build some measure of trust and cooperation between the DA and most defense attorneys, even the more combative ones.[115]

The "going rate" and relational contracting create *structural hysteresis*: current cases are evaluated in the shadow of prior cases woven into the fabric of past and ongoing relationships. This invalidates the idea that plea bargaining is an instantaneous process taking into account only the specifics of the case at hand, as assumed in many quantitative studies of plea bargaining that fail to capture the cross-case temporal flow and the moving sociocognitive ecology of judicial negotiation. Every case is unique, but every case is also an instance of a type that was previously dealt with, a variant of a configuration already sanctioned as well as an anticipation of future similar cases.

Most felonies processed by Julius in the negotiation chamber are "busted down" to misdemeanors and then sentenced leniently. Dealing the felony will also commonly come with dropping the

---

[115] Ian R. Macneil, "Contracts: Adjustment of Long-Term Economic Relations under Classical, Neoclassical, and Relational Contract Law" (1977).

"trailing misdemeanors" the defendant may have been charged with. The most common sentence agreed upon is "CTS @ S," meaning credit for time served at sentencing, followed by a term of probation. So the study of *prison sentences*, their length and determinants, which dominates both juridical and statistical research on plea bargaining, works on a small and skewed subset of all felony cases. This is congruent with statewide statistical data showing that, in 2011, 78 percent of felony arrests in California led to filing a complaint, 52 percent led to a conviction and only 10 percent led to a prison sentence, the other 40 percent resulting in probation or county jail, which indicates that many were resolved as misdemeanors.[116] Moreover, a significant portion of felony offenses are *not* funneled into felony prosecution but handled via probation violation, which is quicker and more economical (I return to this point below).

An ordinary morning in the plea negotiation chamber

The third session of plea negotiation I observed involved, aside from Julius and myself, four line prosecutors coming in and out of the room, four public defenders, 11 private attorneys (including three from out of county), one private investigator and one staff person. During this light morning, the 31 cases discussed ran as follows, based on the "top count" or principal charge:

- One case by white out-of-county private attorney Burawoy: welfare fraud, case sent to the vertical fraud prosecution team.
- Two cases by white veteran PD Lockard: three-striker bringing a gun to court; multiple counts of burglary.
- Seven cases by Latino PD Rodriguez: possession of multiple guns and drugs in the course of gang activity; running a "chop shop" (dismantling stolen cars); missing file; selling marijuana; selling marijuana; fourth DUI (driving under the influence); felon in possession of a firearm.
- One case by white private attorney Shammas: grand theft.
- One case by white out-of-county private attorney Tugal (accompanied by a private detective): armed robbery at an ATM.
- One case by white private attorney Fourcade: child sexual assault, no plea offer, case assigned to the specialized vertical unit.

---

[116] Mac Taylor, *California's Criminal Justice: A Primer* (2013), p. 34.

- One case by Latino private attorney Sanchez: illegal possession of a gun.
- One case by white out-of-county private attorney Muller: rap artist arrested in his limousine with very large quantities of marijuana and $3,200 in crisp twenties.
- One case by Asian private attorney Long: revisiting a plea deal rejected by the sentencing judge because it did not include state prison time.
- One case by white private attorney Loveman: second-degree robbery.
- Four cases by Latina PD Canizales: two counts of robbery; failure to register as sex offender; missing discovery, put over to next month; shipping marijuana via airline.
- Eight cases by black PD Dumonnier: car crash caused by DUI; missing file; driving without a license (case with immigration consequences); codefendant on an armed robbery; defendant threatened his brother with a knife, accusing him of cashing his disability check, mental health issues; codefendant on a case of felon in possession of a gun; missing discovery, date of PX confirmed; gun possession; codee on unidentified charge.
- Two cases broached by black private attorney Byers as we take the elevator and walk down the hallway to the courtroom, with Julius pushing his cart whose wheels are gently squeaking (conversation interrupted to be resumed at the DA's desk).

5. Span and stakes of negotiation

The legal and social science literature on plea bargaining generally limits its purview to two outcomes: charge and sentence, with the latter measured in years of prison.[117] This draws a woefully incomplete picture of the span, stakes, and paths of negotiation and it *misses*

---

[117] "Pervasive measurement issues continue to plague plea bargaining research. For example, most studies are limited to binary measures that capture only whether or not a guilty plea or charge reduction occurs. Few studies carefully investigate the processes that generate guilty pleas or their impact on downstream punishment outcomes. Prosecutors design plea offers from an extensive array of charging and punishment options available within the 'depth and distance' of the criminal code. Narrowly focusing on single charging outcomes misses the nuance of charging concessions, sentencing enhancements, and the complexity of plea bargaining. It also risks faulty conclusions regarding fairness and equality" (Brian D. Johnson and Raquel Hernandez, "Prosecutors and Plea Bargaining" [2021], p. 86).

the majority of felony cases processed by the criminal court (since only one in ten felony arrests result in a prison sentence). In San Pedrito county, the prosecutor and the defense attorney routinely haggle over eight elements:

(i) *Charges*: the DA can drop or add charges, lower counts, or lower charges by replacing them by one or another "lesser included offense." This requires, first, crafting a shared characterization of the incriminated conduct, that is, negotiating facts (as when the prosecutor agrees to "overlook" the fact that a robbery was committed with a firearm). In some serious cases, if the haggling yields an agreement on the length of the prison sentence, the negotiating DA may "reverse-engineer" a corresponding set of charges, some of which can be unrelated to the actual behavior initially incriminated. As new information becomes available at the pretrial stage, the prosecutor may "amend" the charges. One implication of the practice of "busting down" cases is that the criminal profile of the prison population is a juridical artifact that misrepresents the actual criminal behavior of convicts. It systematically underestimates the seriousness of the offenses they were charged with or committed.[118]

(ii) *Sentence*: the prosecutor can agree to recommend a sentence by choosing the "low term" of the sentencing triad (in California, every felony on the books is punishable by a middle term, a low term or a high term depending on mitigating or aggravating factors, for instance 2/3/5 years for robbery). In most cases, if it falls within her acceptable range given the conduct and the defendant's background, the sentencing judge will rubber stamp this recommendation on the presumption that the two negotiating attorneys know the case better than she does. But, as we shall see later, the judge can also reject certain types of deals and send the case back to the pretrial prosecutor.

(iii) *Facts*: as indicated above, the prosecutor and the defendant agree to stipulate certain facts and to erase others from the record. They forge a sanitized and stylized narrative of "what happened" for juridical purposes, different from what actually happened: a legal fiction built through mutual interest. For instance, the parties can agree to omit the use of a gun and to exclude the elements of "force and fear" in a robbery to lower the charge from armed robbery (PC

[118] For instance, many and perhaps most prison convicts incarcerated on paper for possession of drugs were in fact charged, and in most cases factually guilty, of possession with intent to distribute or other equally serious charges that were "busted down." This distorting effect makes the justice system appear systematically more severe than it actually is.

298

section 211, a "strike" with an exposure of 12–15 years of prison with the gun enhancement) to grand theft (PC section 487 a "nonstrike" with an exposure of 3 years).[119] Counties vary on this front: in San Pedrito County, fact bargaining is routine; in Carnival County, it is rare as the DA insists on keeping the "factual basis" of the plea close to the police report.

(iv) *Sentence enhancements*: the law stipulates a number of factors that automatically increase the punishment by adding years to the base sentence. The California penal code specifies no fewer than 118 enhancements (compared to six in 1977). In 2023, over two-thirds of California prisoners had at least one enhancement applied to their sentence. Four accounted for over 80 percent of all felony enhancements: three strikes (43%), use of a firearm (22%), prior one- and five-year prison terms (15%), and commission of a crime in the course of gang activity (6%).[120]

The prosecutor can "allege" the enhancements (that is, include them in the sentence computation) or exclude them from the charges. They are typically two-step supplements: they increase exposure and thus sanction for the case being discussed but for future criminal cases as well. Because of their delayed action, enhancements are the single most consequential component in offenses leading to prison terms and they are intensely fought over during plea bargaining. Quantitative studies of sentencing output measure the impact of enhancements when they are attached to the charges, but they omit those enhancements that were struck from the charges, so they both overestimate the severity of punishment and miss out on a key stake of bargaining.

[119] On the legal mechanics, strategic benefits, and moral quandaries of fact bargaining pushed to its extreme, see Thea Johnson, "Fictional Pleas" (2019). Defendants charged with sex crimes are particular keen to "fact bargain" to erase the nature of their crime from the record so as to dodge collateral consequences (such as lifetime registration and yearly reporting to the police) and avoid the shame of a sexual conviction.
[120] For a statistical and regional breakdown of felony enhancements, see Mia Bird et al., *Sentence Enhancement in California* (2023). Enhancements are applied very unevenly across California counties, with the lowest application rates in urban coastal counties in the Bay Area and Southern California, and the highest rates among far Northern rural counties and in the Central Valley and Inland Empire regions. See Julian V. Roberts and Richard S. Frase, *Paying for the Past: The Case Against Prior Record Sentence Enhancements* (2019), for a thorough examination of the nature, application, and consequences of enhancements based on prior record.

(v) *Site of execution of a custodial sentence*: the convict may be allowed to serve his time "in the box" (county jail) as opposed to far away in state prison. This alternative matters, not just for its social impact (staying close to home makes it easier to maintain family and romantic ties),[121] but also because jail inmates can earn 50 percent off their sentence for good behavior whereas state convicts must serve 66 percent of their sentence for "serious felonies" and 85 percent of their sentence for "violent felonies."[122] In addition, serving locally makes it possible to get a "split sentence" combining a county jail term and a term of probation.

(vi) *Probation terms*: the most common sentence for run-of-the-mill felonies is probation, not prison time, so that the parameters of probation supervision loom large in negotiations.[123] These include whether probation is formal or summary (supervised by a probation agent or merely via court reporting), the duration of supervision (from one to five years), search and seizure clauses (up to four-way: the right to search person, belongings, vehicle, and residence), and myriad stipulations such as drug and alcohol testing, curfew and stay-away orders, as well as the obligation to follow court-mandated programs and obligations (classes in anger management, parenting or theft awareness; community service, obtaining the GED (General Educational Development test), drug counseling, etc.). Defense counsel will make every effort to get a deal short of probation because they know full well that most of their clients will not successfully complete it. They will also go to battle to limit the search clause, making it "three-way" by arguing that the vehicle or domicile should be excluded because it does not have the requisite "nexus to the crime."[124]

---

[121] Megan Comfort, *Doing Time Together: Love and Family in the Shadow of the Prison* (2007).

[122] Nonetheless, surprisingly, many convicts are eager to "get to state" because they find the prison regimen more predictable and less stringent than conditions at the county jail where the inmates are more unruly, food is awful, and "privileges" are few and far between.

[123] In 2014, the total probation population of California (297,000) was more than twice the prison population (123,000), nearly four times the jail population (81,000) and six times the parole population of 50,000. Ryken Grattet and Brandon Martin, *Probation in California* (2015).

[124] The defense will often be successful in cases that do not involve weapons or drugs. Defendants who have a strong employment record and a stable residence are more likely to avoid a search clause (another facet of overt class discrimination in the courthouse, as analyzed *infra*, pp. 320–4). Probation deals reached after preliminary examination will nearly always include a search clause. Local practice varies both across and within counties.

(vii) *Time of release*: the defendant may be allowed to walk out of jail immediately upon the entry of plea (on what is called a "Cruz waiver") or have to wait in custody until the sentencing hearing one to two months down the road. The Cruz waiver stipulates that the terms of the plea may be withdrawn and more severe punishment imposed if the defendant fails to abide by the law or to show up at his sentencing hearing.

(viii) *Restitution, fines and fees*: some of the fines are statutory, others are discretionary. The prosecutor cannot negotiate or waive restitution to the victim and to the state restitution fund (ranging from $200 to $10,000) or court operations fees and conviction assessment. But he can sweeten the plea agreement by foregoing the "base fines" attached to specific offenses (e.g., first-degree robbery is punishable by prison, a fine of up to $10,000, or both).[125] He can also impose the forfeiture of contraband, money, weapons, and the personal phone of the defendant seized at the time of arrest.

6. The probation and parole violation route

In addition to *plea packages* combining these eight different ingredients in different doses, a great many felony cases do not make it into the pretrial funnel: they are processed *via the detour through probation and parole violation*. It is estimated that one in five adult criminal arrests in California involve suspects on probation or parole. It is quite often simpler and more economical for the prosecution as well as the bench to deal with recidivism that way. By committing a new crime, the defendant has by definition violated the terms of his probation or parole.[126] The DA may decide to pursue sanctions through a probation revocation hearing rather than by filing new charges; or he may combine a probation violation with the new case. The same applies to parolees who have violated their terms and conditions, but their numbers are much smaller.

---

[125] In San Pedrito County, judges never impose discretionary fines except in white-collar crimes. But in Carnival County, prosecutors frequently attach such fines to probation deals and judges will impose them routinely in cases of theft (especially repeat retail theft and burglary theft), drug possession for sale, and property crimes motivated by profit, the rationale being that fines are part of accountability.

[126] In California, fully 47 percent of defendants put under probation supervision were booked in county jail within a year, leading to an automatic probation revocation. Viet Nguyen, Ryken Grattet, and Mia Bird, *California Probation in the Era of Reform* (2017).

The advantages of the probation revocation route for the prosecutor are fourfold: the defendant is automatically kept in custody, which pressures him to plead early; the burden of proof is "preponderance of the evidence" and not "beyond a reasonable doubt" as for a new felony charge; the matter is decided by a judge and not a jury; there is no statutory deadline for holding the revocation hearing so that defendants typically "admit" their violation as part of the plea deal. As a result, the case resolves faster through that path.[127] The court can then impose on the defendant the original sentence whose execution had been suspended by activating the "years hanging over his head," extend probation, terminate and reinstate probation under new terms, or impose new sanctions. Knowing the *probation status and specifics of a defendant is key.* The pretrial DA working in Metro City gleefully voiced the office fantasy of "putting half of the population of the county on probation."

7. The vertical prosecution grinder

One last branching point impacts process and outcome which is not taken into account by extant research on plea bargaining: whether the case is handled by a team dedicated to pursuing that particular offense type (domestic violence, elder abuse, environmental crime, gang crime, etc.) through what is known as *vertical prosecution,* whereby the same DA handles the case from start to finish, as opposed to the case moving from one DA to the next along the prosecutorial chain (charging, arraignment, pretrial, PX, trial, sentencing) in "horizontal" fashion.[128]

A case routed to the vertical team is *a priori* considered to be more serious (even if it is not); it will receive more focused attention, absorb more attorney time and lead to more involved negotiations based on a broader evidentiary basis, all of which is typically to the

---

[127] In serious cases, the DA will do both: initiate a probation violation proceeding and file new felony charges. In this scenario, the pretrial prosecutor will seek to resolve both in the same deal. Some offenders are under multiple terms of probation at the same time, which can be consolidated and terminated and/or reinstated. This is an unexplored complexity of plea bargaining and sentencing that concerns a large proportion of offenders, perhaps as many as one-half of repeat offenders.

[128] On the design and deployment of specialized tracks and units, see Cassia Spohn, "Specialized Units and Vertical Prosecution Approaches" (2021). Research on their impact is very limited and focuses on charging, not bargaining. There are no robust empirical studies comparing vertical and horizontal prosecution.

defendant's disadvantage if he is guilty as it is likely to produce a higher plea offer than would have resulted from being submerged in the broader stream of horizontal prosecution. Yet assignment to vertical prosecution results in part from the (bad) luck of the draw: when the specialized team has filled its docket, cases that qualify for take-up on factual grounds stay in the horizontal prosecution pipeline. Defense attorneys dread learning that their client's fate is in the hands of a DA on the vertical team who will "cast more serious eyes" on their case, have more time to drill deep into it, and is more likely to go to trial in case negotiations stall, and so they breathe a sigh of relief when they find out it is not. Contrary to conventional wisdom and scholarly expectations, many if not most defendants would rather their case receive cursory instead of focused attention: granularity generally works to their legal detriment.

303

The vast majority of felonies, then, are *"busted down" to misdemeanors, resolved with probation or handled via the probation violation route* with no new charges as a matter of administrative economy. They do not lead to a prison sentence, let alone a long prison sentence for which the number of years takes on significance. This implies that quantitative studies that probe court felony output working "backward" from the features of the carceral population to their social and legal determinants are capturing a small and truncated subset of cases and are therefore missing most of the action of prosecutors. It also means that statistical studies that work "forward" by following cases from arraignment to adjudication to sentencing but do not include whether the resulting sentence is a misdemeanor or a felony obscure the bright boundary between these two outcomes which defense attorneys work feverishly not to cross.[129] Finally, it suggest that principled critiques about the rigidity, severity, and arbitrary character of sentencing in the United States overstate their case.[130] They also miss their mark to the degree that they focus on the carceral tip of the penal iceberg and overlook the submerged body of non-custodial sanctions imposed on defendants found guilty of a felony, not to mention a misdemeanor.[131]

---

[129] Thus the exemplary study by John Sutton on "Structural Bias in the Sentencing of Felony Defendants" (2013) uses as a scale for the severity of punishment the trichotomy noncustodial sentence (probation or fine), jail, or prison. But it omits the most crucial variable for the future: whether the conviction is for a felony or a misdemeanor.
[130] Michael Tonry, "Sentencing in America, 1975–2025" (2013).
[131] Michelle Phelps draws a comprehensive map of the landscape of probation, its causes, composition, and consequences, but she overlooks the central role of probation

8. Playing with time

When defendants are arraigned, they typically "waive time," meaning that they suspend their right to a preliminary examination within ten court days and to a trial within 60 calendar days of the entry of plea. The judge will commonly allow for up to four pretrial hearings spaced about three to four weeks apart to give time to the two parties to "prep" and haggle over the matter. The prosecutor has a vested interest in settling a case as rapidly as possible. If he is in custody, as is the case with most indigent defendants, the accused has an urgent desire to get out of jail. But it may not be to his interest to do so.

Much is made by critics of the criminal court about the pressure to plead put on defendants by keeping them in jail while their case is processed. But many felony defendants are rightly advised by their attorney to "sit" behind bars in hopes of obtaining the rebate generated by a good plea offer, because doing some pretrial detention will mollify the prosecutor and the judge (they will then receive "credit for time served" known as CTS).[132] In very "heavy" matters, moreover, their interest is to "age the case," as court lingo has it, to let the dust settle and allow emotions to cool off, in the hopes that evidence gets misplaced, witnesses forget or move to a different city, and victims think twice about testifying at PX or trial. Contrary to common perception, the more serious the case, the less the defendant has an interest in a speedy resolution (unless he is evidently innocent). As a veteran private attorney who tries only first-degree murders put it with a chuckle, "Speed kills." Time is manipulated by both parties. The defendant can threaten to "pull time" and ask for his PX or speedy trial right at a moment's notice if he senses that the prosecutor would not be ready to go before a jury. As for the pretrial DA, he can make bargain offers "open only today," meaning that they have to be accepted by the defendant before the late afternoon, after which the next offer, if any, will be higher.[133] This creates a sense

violation in the extraction of guilty pleas. Michelle S. Phelps, "Mass Probation from Micro to Macro: Tracing the Expansion and Consequences of Community Supervision" (2020).

[132] In low-level cases, delay is "often a highly effective strategy" whereby defense counsel seeks to "wear down" the prosecutor and obtain a cheap resolution, as shown by Feeley, *The Process is the Punishment*, p. 223.

[133] In other counties, a plea offer with an expiration date is sometimes called an "exploding offer" or a "vanishing offer." In some jurisdictions, it is used systematically by the prosecutor as leverage to force an early resolution.

of urgency and pressures the defendant into taking the deal on the table.

There is one unexpected twist in the manipulation of time: some pleas *punish, not the current crime, but future probable crimes*. The pretrial prosecutor will sometimes put on the table this kind of dilemmatic offer: a misdemeanor conviction with 90 days in jail *or* a felony conviction with probation for five years (akin to a suspended prison sentence that will be activated in case of violation, known as "years hanging over your head") plus credit for time served (CTS) leading to an immediate release. This creates a painful quandary for the defense attorney. One public defender huffs, "How do you talk somebody *not* to get out as soon as possible, it's like the *hardest conversation* to have! I died a little bit about that, that tore me up a little bit" to have to present that offer to her client and argue that they should choose the first option, stay behind bars and serve the 60 days. Why? The defendant, understandably, wants to "sleep in his own bed" *subito* and will plead to five years of felony probation in a snap to get out. But, by doing so, he nearly guarantees that he will serve the "years hanging over his head" in prison soon enough because, coming from the urban precariat residing in neighborhoods of relegation, his chance of getting through probation without a violation is very low.[134] In effect, he trades the assurance of "no jail now" for the near certainty of "prison later."

In addition, the defendant will have a felony conviction on their record, which will mechanically increase plea offers on future cases – there will be no going back to "misdemeanorland" – as well as carrying a host of economic penalties, social restrictions, and civic disabilities.[135] The public defender knows too well that their clients are released today only to be recaptured tomorrow because of technical violations of probation or ongoing criminal activity due to relentless life pressures and, for some, the sensual and moral allure of criminal

[134] There is no recent statistical data on this point, but a study covering the period 1986 to 1989 found that 43 percent of felony probationers were rearrested for a new offense within three years (Patrick A. Langan and Mark A. Cunniff, *Recidivism of Felons on Probation, 1986–89* [1992]), to which one must add the probationers sent behind bars because they technically violated one or another condition of their release (to pass a drug test, comply with a treatment program, keep a job, report on time to their probation officer, not travel outside of their county of assignation, not associate with another felon, duly register as a sex offender, pay restitution and fees imposed by the court, etc.).

[135] David S. Kirk and Sara Wakefield, "Collateral Consequences of Punishment: A Critical Review and Path Forward" (2018).

305

life. Likewise, as part of a deal, the pretrial prosecutor will sometimes ask a recidivist defendant to "eat a strike," that is, insist on a felony plea that includes the first admission of a violent or serious offense that automatically *escalates not current sanction but future punishment.*[136]

9. The soft side of the criminal record

Statistical research on plea bargaining and sentencing treats the criminal record of the defendants as a hard variable supposed to uniformly and automatically influence outcomes.[137] In sit-down interviews, pretrial prosecutors unanimously insist that they take the criminal profile of the defendant into due consideration from the get-go. But live observation reveals that, in the give-and-take of haggling in the pretrial room, that same record is routinely inflected, backgrounded, and sometimes marginally pertinent or even dismissed as irrelevant. The run of prior offenses proves to be a *soft, multidimensional variable* that may or may not impact bargaining. What matters most is whether the defendant has a criminal background *or not*; then, for the vast majority who do, the matter can turn out surprisingly flexible.

Defense attorneys are quick to say about their client, "She doesn't have a record," meaning a felony record; to stress that "her record is super old" (by which is meant over a decade; in addition, certain felony convictions technically "wash out" in ten years and are thus automatically discounted); or to emphasize that there is no escalation in the seriousness of the offenses even as they are repeated. The impact of the past record of the defendant can also be manipulated because the prosecutor has the latitude to "allege" or not a number of enhancements linked specifically to recidivism. For instance, a defendant who has already served time in prison is liable to an extra year of incarceration tacked onto his sentence (colloquially known as a "bullet"). The DA can agree to not allege the "prison prior" and to lower the suggested sentence accordingly. He can propose to discount a strike, that is, disregard the fact that the defendant already has a conviction for a serious or violent crime that would double his

[136] Under the California penal code, a second "strike" will double the next prison term and a third "strike" for a serious or violent crime will trigger an automatic prison sentence of 25 years to life. See Franklin E. Zimring et al., *Punishment and Democracy: Three Strikes and You're Out in California* (2001), on the penological (il)logics of California's exceptionally punitive variant of "Three Strikes."

[137] Shawn D. Bushway et al., "An Explicit Test of Plea Bargaining in the Shadow of the Trial" (2014).

prison exposure.[138] The pretrial DA may also offer a favorable sentence now in exchange for the defendant "eating a strike," that is, pleading to a serious or violent felony that will determine aggravated punishment later.

As for prior convictions in "juvie" (juvenile court), they are off limits unless they include serious and violent offenses, in particular if they involved weapons and gang activity. Prior convictions become salient, however, when they are recent and repetitive. It is the *timing, sequencing and reiteration of specific past offenses* that make them matter. Prosecutors and judges are particularly irritated, for instance, by a repeat convict for automobile theft (PC 487(d)) who is caught again and again stealing cars (more so than if the latest offense was commercial burglary for a change, for instance). For these cases, Judge Santucci will routinely reject deals made by Julius that only result in felony probation with a short stint in the local jail: he will ask for prison time. So much to say that the criminal record is a soft, fungible, and disputed property entering in the plea bargaining equation.

10. In the shadow of the PX

Every once in a while comes a case that is not just complex and contentious but, more simply, *befuddling*: the police report and additional information gathered by the DA assigned to the case make it difficult to characterize the conduct, to weigh the circumstances and the robustness of the evidence, and to capture the intent of the defendant. Julius will acknowledge such cases and confess to the defense attorney: "I'll be honest with you, *I don't know how to read this case.* I made a two-year offer, but I don't know what this case is really about." To resolve this ambiguity, "it's probably a case you have to put on" for PX because "I don't even feel comfortable making this offer." Indeed, preliminary examination is a judicial device to resolve questions of identity ("whoisit"), clear up ambiguity ("whatisit"), assess the evidence, test victim and witnesses, detect "proof" problems, and channel contestation (persistent disagreement) about cases.

Yet all parties typically would rather avoid "putting on the PX": the DA's office and the PD's office because they are costly in time and

---

[138] The judge can do the same by electing to "Romero a strike," a colloquial expression referring to the California Supreme court decision *People v. Superior Court (Romero)* (1996) giving judges the discretion to disregard a prior serious or violent felony conviction on the record "in furtherance of justice" (Penal Code section 1385).

personnel; private attorneys because they lose money when they are tied up in court for hours on end on a single case; and the defendant because the trial-like hearing will generally validate the charges he faces and his attorney advises that the plea offer subsequently will be raised. Those defendants who wish to go to PX typically face serious charges with high offers, wish to test the evidence and perhaps "knock off" some charges, or hope that the victims and the witnesses will not show up or withstand the pressure of courtroom interrogation, so that the charges will be downgraded if not dismissed outright. This happens frequently in matters of domestic violence in which the woman who initially pressed charges against her intimate partner now refuses to testify or otherwise cooperate with the DA's office; when she fails to appear at the PX, the prosecutor has no option but to dismiss the case (unless there is strong independent evidence such as 911 calls, medical records or video footage). This is why, when the time limit gets nearer, the negotiation often assumes the form of a *game of chicken* in which each party dares the other to go to PX by holding out on an offer when neither of them really wishes to do so.[139]

Students of judicial negotiation who rely on theoretical models of formal rationality inspired by economics have proposed that plea bargaining occurs "in the shadow of the trial."[140] By this, they mean that the accused seek to maximize their utility by anticipating the likely outcome of a trial and comparing this outcome with the plea offer on the table.[141] The reasoning postulated is the following: "A defendant

---

[139] That game of chicken will be played again when the case is set for trial: in many instances, both parties are hoping that the other will flinch on the eve of calling a jury, which neither really wants to happen.

[140] Johnson et al., "Sociolegal Approaches to the Study of Guilty Pleas and Prosecution," pp. 484–6.

[141] This approach is commonly traced back to the influential paper by William M. Landes, "An Economic Analysis of the Court" (1971). Its most surreal postulate is that *both defendant and prosecutor* are rational actors maximizing their utility, measured, for the latter, by the aggregate number of years of prison she generates: "Let the prosecutor's decision rule be to maximize the expected number of convictions weighted by their respective sentences – he prefers longer to shorter sentences – subject to a constraint on the resources or budget available to his office. This decision rule coincides with the social optimum in the following sense. If expected sentences are regarded as prices the community charges for various offenses, then the prosecutor's behavior is equivalent to maximizing the community's welfare for a given resource level." Indeed, the court itself is assumed to be a rational organization optimizing the use of its resources and the benefits it produces for the citizenry. As often with economic models based on utility theory, reality is sacrificed on the altar of formal elegance, analytical transparency, and predictability. The fact that the model neither describes process nor predicts outcomes is conveniently overlooked.

pleads guilty if the offered sentence is less than or equal to his or her expected value of the trial. For example, if the expected sentence for a conviction at trial is 20 years and the defendant believes his or her probability of conviction at trial is 0.8, then a plea to a sentence of no more than 16 years (80 percent of 20) represents a rational choice for a risk-neutral defendant."[142] This model is alluring owing to its parsimony, logical clarity, and practical utility for mathematical modeling and statistical sorting, but it does not connect with the crude and messy world of bargaining as it actually happens.

First, even if it did, the "shadow-of-the-trial" model would apply only for prison cases whereas the vast majority of felony plea offers yield non-custodial sentences and plea negotiations involve a multiplicity of variables, not just the proposed sentence, as shown earlier, with particular impact granted to conditions of probation. Second, the decisions of the pretrial prosecutor are shaped by myriad social and organizational factors that belie the notion of rational choice. Where he exerts discretion, he is animated, not by the abstract goal of maximizing punishment, but by a combination of organizational routine, "going rates," evolving caseload, local convention, and personal feelings about what substantive justice entails in the particular case at hand. Third, a defendant placed in the psychological and emotional pressure-cooker of custody is anything but a rational decision-maker. His desire to get out of jail at once will lead him to greatly and gravely discount future punishment. Fourth, defendants are not "risk neutral" and generally hold wildly unrealistic views of how a trial proceeds (due to the influence of television series such as *Law and Order* and *CSI*). They have no reliable indicator of the probable sentence should they be found guilty, other than the informed supputations of their defense attorney made murky by court rumors and jailhouse lawyering. Fifth and relatedly, defense counsel plays a decisive role in framing the offer and steering their client toward a choice, which is also influenced by the exhortations of family, friends, and loved ones such that the decision is made by a moving collective of interlinked agents and not a monadic individual engaging in a two-variable computation.[143]

309

[142] Bushway et al., "An Explicit Test of Plea Bargaining in the Shadow of the Trial," p. 724.

[143] How much and how to influence the plea decisions of the defendant is a crucial professional dilemma for defense attorneys, particularly public defenders who get emotionally attached to their clients. They are forever worried that they are trespassing on the latter's agency. More experienced PDs sometimes openly assume

But there is more: the decisive crossroad on the judicial horizon in striking plea deals for felonies is *not the trial but the preliminary examination.* This is the looming test that needs to be passed. It will determine what charges "stick" and set the stage for the possibility of a trial as well as define its parameters. At the pretrial stage, the trial is a far-off eventuality that does not enter into the equation because everyone knows well, defendant included, that very few cases get to be litigated before a jury. There is no doubt a *social rationale* to plea bargaining, then, but the latter is not *rational* in the economist's narrow sense of the term.[144] Its logic can be unpacked by paying due attention to the *social and cognitive embeddedness* of the prosecutor, defense attorney, judge, and defendant in real time and space – and not by postulating some abstract rationality whose conditions of possibility are excluded by the situation of constant urgency, the setup of the criminal court, and the social properties of the people it processes.

11. Playing cat and mouse with the sentencing judge

A key filter extraneous to the negotiating pair is manned by the *sentencing judge who must review and approve* all plea agreements and is wont to cast out deals falling outside of the norm of the court and even of the particular courthouse where he officiates.[145] The judge has the latitude to reject plea agreements because the charges are not right or the proposed sentence is too low, thus sending the case back to the pretrial prosecutor, for whom this rejection is a black mark. He can also decide not to follow the sentencing recommendation of the DA, although he will do so in the vast majority of cases: there is a pragmatic presumption that the prosecutor and defense attorney know the case best and thus found the most sensible resolution. In addition, the pretrial attorney has deliberately calibrated his offer after the judge's standards as he perceives them. The judge can also override the deal and offer the defendant the option to "plead to the sheet," meaning to plead guilty to all the charges for a reduced sentence, thus cutting the prosecutor out of the equation.

a stance of "benevolent paternalism" in steering their clients out of their judicial predicament.

[144] For a thoroughgoing critique of rational choice models in economics and the social sciences more generally, read Pierre Bourdieu, *Anthropologie économique* (2017).

[145] In both San Pedrito and Carnival, felony sentencing is centralized in the hands of only two judges, to achieve consistency. In San Pedrito county, each judge pronounces about 12–15 sentences per court day.

Finally, the judge has pet peeves of her own, certain crimes that she regards as more serious than the court generally allows and for which she will exact higher punishment than was negotiated. Or he is particularly irritated by reiterating recidivists, that is, defendants who commit the same crime as before – for instance, offenders who keep stealing cars again and again, disregarding the repeated sanctions and warnings of the court. The pretrial DA must *anticipate the expectations of the sentencing judge* and factor them into his offers, which reduces his own latitude and channels his thinking and negotiation. Indeed, he will tell public defenders that the reason why he cannot give one such lenient deal is that he knows that the sentencing judge would throw it back in his face.[146] Occasionally, Julius will conspire with a veteran defense attorney he holds in high regard in crafting an offer that both of them hope will sail past the judge unnoticed.

311

This demonstrates that the prosecutor negotiating pleas is not a *solo decider* based on personal taste and fancy but, rather, a networked agent making fluid choices in a dynamic sociocognitive space of relations that both constrain and enable definite lines of action.[147] The unilateral individualism postulated as a matter of course – and caricature – by conventional legal scholarship on prosecution collapses under ethnographic scrutiny to reveal *multilateral relationalism*. What is more, any present scene locked in the here-and-now is, notwithstanding appearances to the contrary, *triply historical*: it is driven by the personal and professional biographies of the negotiating attorneys which shape their moral compass and legal expertise; it is embedded in a sequence of past and future negotiations (a point I develop later in my elaboration of "relational contracting," *infra*, p. 355); and it is

---

[146] Another proof that the criminal court is not the rational organization postulated by economists: Julius has never had a personal meeting or any direct communication with judge Santucci to clarify the latter's judicial standards and sentencing norms (even though he officiates in a courthouse only a couple of miles away). So he is left with guessing what they are through trial and error and by consulting with other prosecutors who know the judge well (in particular the deputy DA who sits on the master felony calendar and observes judge Santucci in action daily).

[147] Jeffery Ulmer rightfully criticizes studies that seek "to isolate the discretion of this or that courtroom actor or sponsoring organization, because almost every case decision-making stage is interactive in some sense" ("Criminal Courts as Inhabited Institutions: Making Sense of Difference and Similarity in Sentencing" [2019], p. 510). Where I part with Ulmer is that this *distribution of discretion* is not an emergent "interactional" effect in the mold of Anselm Strauss or Bruno Latour. The interaction itself is the historical precipitate of a meeting of objective positions in intersecting social spaces à la Bourdieu.

framed by the broader history of the objective relations between the office of prosecutors, the defense bar and the bench, relations which are themselves influenced by the bureaucratic and political history of the county. Structure and history together assign its place to agency.

Public defender Boyish moves up to the desk, puts her file on top of LW's recorder (!), and calls the case of Jameson, a client accused of stealing cars, a "wobbler." Julius is deeply annoyed that this is the third time in a year that he sees this defendant, whom he had previously pled to misdemeanors and who, moreover, was on probation on another case. Now Jameson has to take a felony, plus serve time behind bars. Julius regrets his earlier leniency: "He should've got his felony the last time, and someone made a pitch, I caved." He agrees to reduce the sentence from 180 to 120 days but stays firm on the principle of a jail component because, he contends, judge Santucci will want a felony conviction plus time.

Here we discern how decisions made over time get interwoven and how the current offer is inflected by past offers and the overall criminal trajectory of the defendant. We see how both attorneys make moral appeals to justify their position. This excerpt also captures a decisive fork in judicial careers: the moment a defendant tumbles from "misdemeanorland" into "felonyland," with dire consequences both in and out of the court. Once that border is crossed, there is no going back.

PD Boyish: So yeah, I just feel like **if he's gonna have to take his first felony ever**, and then you're gonna have him on **felony probation**, that he shouldn't have to take the time, *or* he should take 180 [days of jail] on a misdemeanor. But doing this time *plus* the felony –

DA Julius: *Lemme stop you.* (PD Boyish: Okay) So he had . . . a prior 10851 [ten-eight-fifty-one, car theft] prior to the one he's on probation for, right? (PD Boyish: Yeah) In 2015. *Then* someone in your office made the pitch that you're making right now, so I *gave him* (PD Boyish: The misdo) a misdemeanor 10851. (PD Boyish: Right) So I haven't been here a year, and this is the third 10851 in less than a year.

PD Boyish: And I *hear that*, but this would still be his *first felony conviction*.

DA Julius: *Yeah*, **he should've got his felony the last time, and *someone made a pitch*, I caved**, I put time on the PV [parole violation], and I said, "If I see him again . . ."

PD Boyish: [finishing his sentence] He's gonna have a *felony*, which is why I'm not arguing with you about the felony! [chuckles]

DA Julius: – And he's getting time [behind bars], he's getting time, that's how this works. I've only been here – I haven't been here 11 months yet, and I've seen him three times [inaudible].

PD Boyish: Which is why I'm not pitching for a misdemeanor, and I think he probably *does* have to take his first felony conviction, but if he *takes that* –

DA Julius: [sternly] He, *he's taking time, too* – I mean, I don't know how else to put it. When I see my name on a dispo sheet . . . and then I talk to [DA] Sam about this too, 'cause she did the one in Metro City, and **we pled him like, back-to-back**, and I said, "Are you giving him time?" And she said, "No," and I said, "Okay, I'm gonna give him a little time on his PV [parole violation], but if I see him again, it's not good," and I saw him again.

PD Boyish: Which is why – I understand why, if he's gonna deal, he's gonna have to deal to **a felony, but I think 180 [days] is a lot of time** to get him **if he's *also* changing his life, becoming a felon**, you're gonna have him on felony probation, you're gonna wanna violate that if he messes up again. I mean, he's gonna **go from a 25-year-old with a misdemeanor record to a 25-year-old felon and be on 5-year felony probation** –

DA Julius: [raising his voice] It's his fault! **I gave him a break, *it's his fault*.** *I gave him a break.* [pause] It's his fault.

PD Boyish: [seven-second pause] [measured] Yeah, he did drive the car, um –

DA Julius [insistent]: He did *steal the car*. (PD Boyish: Well, I don't think there's any evidence of that) And he stole – **that's *three cars* in less than a year**.

PD Boyish: I don't think there's any evidence of that in this case [i.e., stealing as opposed to driving a stolen car].

DA Julius: [dismissively] Okay, I mean, I don't know what to say, I mean –

PD Boyish: **Will you come down on the time?** That's a lot of time.

DA Julius: I'll do **120 [days], nothing less** than that. I mean, this guy has three cars in less than a year, three convictions, possibly, in less than a year. He's gotta do some time – **I have to send this up to Santucci showing that he *is* getting some time**, and that's kinda just the way it is.

PD Zara (sitting at the back, interjects in a sing-song voice): **You know *Santucci loves you, man*, he doesn't turn down any of your deals** –

DA Julius: *Shiiit!* [all laugh] I should link you to my emails when he says, "*Deal rejected*," I want you to see, **I'm gonna forward all my "Deal rejected" to you** –

PD Zara (amused): You send 'em [inaudible], I'll work it out, I'll talk to Santucci for you, don't worry!

DA Julius: He's just, that guy, I mean, I gave him a chance.

PD Boyish (conceding): Alright.

(Field notebook, 8 February 2016)

In another case of repeat car theft, Julius consorts with PD Jankowski, a veteran of the office known for his legal savvy and extensive trial experience, which means he ranks very high in Julius's esteem. The case is set to go to PX the next day, so this is the last chance to strike a deal. Julius agrees to craft a guilty deal without jail time (what he had denied PD Boyish) and to let Jankowski see if it will fly under judge Santucci's radar. Experience, expertise, and status pay off dividends at the negotiation table.

PD Jankowski: Uh, well, you offered him 16 [months], he'll take a bullet [one year behind bars], I talked to him yesterday.

DA Julius: [skeptical] Mmm . . . [5 seconds] Probation, probation, uh . . . [5 seconds] (PD Jankowski: You know, it's basically) I can't, he's got *two* 10851s [car thefts].

PD Jankowski: But it's an old – I mean, this is an *old Honda*, it's *parked*.

DA Julius: [dismissive] Yeah, that doesn't matter.

PD Jankowski: Yeah, it does, (DA Julius: No, it doesn't) 'cause **a 1996 Honda, a five-year-old could steal it.** With a screwdriver.

DA Julius: Yeah, but it doesn't matter – [talking over the laughter] Especially when you've stolen two cars prior to that!

PD Jankowski: I'm not nominating him for probationer of the year, but if your offer is 16 [months] and you're not ready –

DA Julius: I just did 16 because **I've had 'em rejected with priors from Santucci** –

PD Jankowski: But not on a 10th-day PX, 'cause I [inaudible] Santucci that, you know, this was the 10th day, they weren't ready, it was gonna go over . . . I think the guy gets more screwed – to tell you the truth, I advised him not to take it, because he's gonna be on *felony probation* for five years.

DA Julius: But he's on, [chuckling] he's on felony probation already, right?

PD Jankowski: [casually] Yeah. [pause] Again, I'm not nominating him for probationer of the year, that's almost everything –

DA Julius: If you follow it, **I'm fine if you get it through,** but I'm telling you –

PD Jankowski: Yeah, I'll follow it, and I'll get it through, (DA Julius: Alright) believe me, **I'll get it through.**

(Field notebook, 21 January 2018)

12. Building reputation and maintaining face

Like actors on a stage, court attorneys are constantly under the gaze of their antagonists, colleagues, and other courthouse personnel. They are keen to maintain face and protect their courthouse persona and office reputation – as a veteran DA puts it, "Credibility is everything. If you lose your credibility in this line of work, *you are finished.*"[148] In the pretrial negotiation room, this means being on guard and defending one's image in the face of potentially offensive moves. It also means that the actions of others are weighed in turn by their status, determined by legal prowess, occupational experience, and court standing.

Two episodes illustrate the premium put on professional standing in negotiation. The first one involves a private attorney from out of the county, which means that he was unfamiliar with the labile social hierarchies, bureaucratic rules, and punishment scale specific to the Alphaville courthouse. He is frustrated that Julius cannot accelerate the resolution of his case and he inquires about contacting Julius's supervisor, only to be firmly rebuffed. If Julius was seen yielding to this request, other defense attorneys would soon attempt to take the same route, Julius's authority would be undermined and his reputation diminished. In addition, this is a sensitive case involving mental illness and death threats which could turn sour and so Julius is extra cautious.

315

Private defense attorney Phil Hammer is a newcomer. He has traveled all the way from Groundsville in an adjacent county and this is his first venture in this courthouse. So he proceeds cautiously. His client is deeply psychotic and in custody after being arrested for repeatedly threatening to behead a long-time friend by way of postal mail. (In California, making death threats as defined by Penal Code section 422 is a "wobbler" punishable by up to 4 years in prison if charged as a felony). The defendant's arraignment was delayed again and again until he was stabilized with the appropriate medications, and so he has already spent 79 days in jail. Hammer managed to convince the family to not *bail him out so he could try and get a better pretrial deal, perhaps a misdemeanor, in light of him being in custody.*

Attorney Hammer: So what *we're* looking to do, quite frankly, and what I would *like* to accomplish maybe even *before* we resolve it, is **get him OR'ed [released] to a residential, locked, treatment facility** ... [His family] is working really hard to try to find the appropriate facility. What I was *hoping, maybe,* 'cause it might expedite things, is **we get him**

---

[148] On the dynamics of "face" and "face work" in interpersonal encounters, see Erving Goffman, *Interaction Ritual: Essays on Face-to-Face Behavior* (1967), chapter 1. Goffman is insightful on the subtleties of interaction but he is blind to the structural determinants of interactional strategies.

into the *behavioral health court*, 'cause they can help *coordinate and transfer* him to a locked facility, and I know that the county's got contracts with at least two facilities: one that has a bed available *now*, and one we're not sure of. (DA Julius: Right) So I know the charges are not *normally what we would see* in behavioral health court (DA Julius: Right), and I've never done it in your county, but I know that it's a good program, and I know that that will help us do what we want to do, which is **get him into a facility**.

DA Julius: I can tell you, I'm **not prepared to do anything on it** *today*, (attorney Hammer, his voice dropping: Okay) I want Rosetta [the PX team DA assigned to the case] **to contact the victim**, (attorney Hammer: Sure) and I want to get as much information as I can, so then we can decide, **after input from the victim, how to proceed**.

Hammer keeps pressing: he has a diagnosis and medical documentation from a Doggy University psychiatrist who also made recommendations. The defendant is "a very bright man" able to support himself, except that "when he's not on his meds, he's way over the top," but he has never been dangerous before. Julius cautiously retreats behind the victim, arguing that he cannot move on the case until she has been consulted.[149]

Attorney Hammer: Yeah, oh yeah, I mean, **if I had got those letters, I'd be scared shitless**.

DA Julius: I know, **talking about cutting off somebody's head**, and stuff like that –

Attorney Hammer: Yeah, yeah, no, I mean, what was interesting about 'em is they were, if you've read 'em, they're in *rhyme*, they're lyrical –

DA Julius: [chuckling] Yeah, I saw that one!

Attorney Hammer: . . . Again, what I'm *really* wanting to try to do now is get him *into* a – **rather than just warehousing him in the jail**, I mean, he's *okay*, and he's taking his meds – is **get into an actual** *treatment facility*.

DA Julius: Well, I'm **not prepared to do that yet**, uh, (attorney Hammer: Okay) I don't want to do anything that will . . . (attorney Hammer: Even if it's locked?) go against the wishes of this victim at this point – (attorney Hammer: Sure) I need to, **I need to have some input, 'cause this could blow up in** *my* **face** (attorney Hammer: No, I understand), and

---

[149] A 2008 amendment to the California Constitution (the California Victims' Bill of Rights Act, known as "Marsy's Law") approved by a popular vote institutes the right for victims to be informed and consulted about a plea offer made to the offender before it is finalized. The right does not include vetoing or otherwise blocking the deal.

that's my major concern. I'm not saying – I don't disagree with anything that you've said –

Attorney Hammer: No, I got you (DA Julius: Yeah), is **there anybody – all due respect – in the chain of command** upwards that you'd – I mean, I know [chief prosecutor] Nick –

DA Julius (forcefully): *No, it starts with me* (attorney Hammer: Okay) **this is *my job*, this is what *I do*.**

(Field notebook, 21 January 2016)

The second episode involves an attorney dissatisfied with Julius's offers who went around his back all the way up the chain of command to the "elected." This furtive move potentially threatened Julius's standing with the office brass. But the latter's assessment validated Julius's prosecutorial judgment and he further reassured himself by noting that the attorney in question was not a *bona fide* "trial attorney" – meaning, an attorney who has the will and skills to take cases to a jury as opposed to negotiating pleas. This episode also illustrates how information travels across informal channels to get vetted by multiple members of the office.

Yesterday Julius learned from a work mate who had information from another office colleague that "a defense attorney went to [chief prosecutor] Nick to complain about one of my offers, saying my offers were too *high*." Nick talked to Donald, the office's most experienced DA handling plea negotiation at the felony trial stage, who reassured him that "'Julius's offers aren't high at all, he's in the norm.' And [upset, slowing down] it kinda *bothered me* that this attorney made it his mission to go up, to complain about it" rather than bring up the matter with him: "I'm from a place where you go *man-to-man*, and you talk to someone and you tell 'em, 'Okay, I'm dissatisfied, I think your offers are too high'. . .

But then I had to put it in perspective, think about the attorney and think, '*Is he a trial attorney?*' No, I realized, [snickers] I can't remember the last time he *ever went to trial*, which makes me think that his *complaint* was that I wasn't seeing things *his way*. Where I'm from, *men* don't do that, they just don't, everything is, 'I'm in your face, I'm talking to you.' [LW note: it was all indirect, information travels fast. I bet it is Kevin who talked to Donald who talked to Nick who talked back to Kevin who eventually talked to Julius.] So I talked to other DAs who had my position, and I'm like, 'Does this ever happen?' He's like, 'Yeah, it happens all the time,' and I'm like, okay, then I'm not even gonna worry about it, it's like, it's the norm: if you're doing your job *the right way*, this *should happen*. And I said, 'Okay, then I feel good about it.'"

All in all, then, Julius does not stand alone and act on his own. He is a "team member" and not an "independent contractor" as portrayed in the prevalent literature on prosecution.[150] He sits at the epicenter of a web of interactional chains linking him to defense attorneys (public and private, who are themselves intricately tied to one another); other prosecutors up and down the judicial line and office hierarchy (the charging DA, the "baby DAs" on the PX team and their supervisor, the head of the felony trial team who handles the next stage of negotiations), all the way to "management" (the head DA and his assistants), not to mention other veteran attorneys who entered the office in the same cohort as he did;[151] and, finally, the judges who enter pleas and weigh sentences. These visible interactions are encased in the invisible structure of objective relations organizing the social space of the DA's office, the PD's office, and the bench, as well as shaped by the evolving balance of power between them. Time is another force that molds and channels the discretion of the pretrial DA: the lattice of relations within which he is enmeshed is rooted in past exchanges, constrains current dealings, and anticipates future transactions.

The splintering of punishment across class fractions

Ethnographic observation thus reveals or confirms that the following variables are pivotal to plea bargaining as a fluid yet patterned system of collective action and have yet to be detected or properly reckoned with by quantitative studies of negotiated justice: the age of the defendant defined as over or under 21 years (and not treated as a continuous variable); his probation status and the number of "years hanging over his head"; class, which, *ceteris paribus*, determines whether the defendant appears in or out of custody, hires a private attorney, proffers assurances as to future conduct, and possesses the time and resources to gather remedial information and to put together a credible "mitigation package";[152] whether the case is adju-

---

[150] This duality is linked to office size, architecture, and recruitment strategy, according to Wright et al., "The Many Faces of Prosecution" (2014), p. 41.

[151] Professional friendships are especially strong among attorneys who entered the office at the same time as young graduates fresh out of law school and who went through the rigors of early rotations together.

[152] Hiring private counsel is not always an advantage for poor defendants. A solo practitioner cannot draw on the collective store of knowledge and court connections

dicated through the probation violation route (or via both a probation violation and charging a new case); whether the case is prosecuted vertically or horizontally; whether the case is "busted down" to misdemeanor; the present and future impact of specific enhancements; where a custodial sentence will be served (county jail or state prison); the use of probation as penal mesh flung out to detect and sanction future criminal conduct; the terms of probation; the timing of release from custody; whether the offense negotiated is a repeat of immediately prior offenses; the geographical location of the courthouse in relation to its social (urban) and political (electoral) environment; the experience, seniority, and position of the pretrial prosecutor in the social space of the DA's office; and whether the latter centralizes plea bargaining in the hands of a few veteran prosecutors or delegates the task to a broader cadre of deputies who have the latitude to deal their own cases.

Conspicuously absent from the ethnographic foreground is race – central to mainstream studies of inequality in negotiated justice, to the point of obsession, even when the empirical studies that explicitly focus on it are rare, flawed, and inconsistent.[153] This is what one would expect: overt mention would be culturally shocking, a glaring violation of the professional ethos of impartiality, not to mention anti-discrimination statutes. But this remains in sharp contrast with class, which is frequently and openly invoked, as when a judge justifies treating a defendant out of custody with clemency by exclaiming in open court that "his job is his saving grace" or when the pretrial DA considers a "mitigation package" composed of class resources assembled by his defense attorney. No one in that courtroom thinks that there is anything odd, objectionable, or scandalous about that justification. Imagine the moral outrage, the professional commotion, and the legal sanctions triggered if the same judge said of a white defendant, "his race is his saving grace."

---

available to public defenders via their office. Private attorneys are also a highly heterogeneous population and there is no reliable external indicator of professional proficiency. Prosecutors in San Pedrito county were unanimous in praising the skills of public defenders and uniformly ranked them above their private counterparts.

[153] Contrary to the conventional view found in the sociolegal literature on negotiated justice and in public discussion, the scant statistical evidence of racial disparities in plea bargaining is mixed, with some studies finding that African-American defendants receive more favorable outcomes than whites. Brian D. Johnson and Rebecca Richardson, "Race and Plea Bargaining" (2019), pp. 91–2; Brian D. Johnson and Raquel Hernandez, "Prosecutors and Plea Bargaining" (2021), p. 82.

All court actors adhere to the doxic tenet that offenders who have a job, a stable residence, pursue an education, and support a family are more pliant and responsive, and therefore deserve a measure of leniency – without hard evidence thereof *in the particular case at hand.* They effectively practice "statistical discrimination" in the rigorous sense of the term, using social status as a proxy for future (un)lawful conduct.[154] But not only: the possession of minimal economic, cultural, and social capital translates into the automatic presumption of moral character, since social standing in America is construed as the result of one's individual exertion and personal virtues, which in turn translates into diminished punishment. This translation is rarely examined, let alone challenged, by legal professionals, jurists, and social scientists.

320

Why class discrimination is invisible

Why have the social sciences failed to develop a robust concept of class discrimination – defined as differential treatment and unwarranted disparate impact based on class origins or membership – on an equal analytical footing with racial discrimination and gender discrimination?

The first reason resides in the inherent differences between these constructs as "social principles of vision and division" (to use Bourdieu's language) (1). By and large, race and gender are readily *visible, clearly bounded,* and their boundaries largely agreed upon (2). By contrast, class refers to largely invisible categories – external symbols of class position are easily manipulable – whose foundations and demarcations are fuzzy and disputed, in academia no less than in private life and public culture. Classes are, moreover, doxically construed as gradational entities with continuous features whereas race and gender designate discrete categories (3).

Second, social sex and naturalized ethnicity are both believed to be *inherited, embodied, and fixed for life* whereas class is inherited, but position can be lost or gained based on variations in the volume of economic, cultural, social, and symbolic capital garnered within and

[154] The founding article of Edmund S. Phelps, "The Statistical Theory of Racism and Sexism" (1972) repays a close reading. Note that it does not include class but two categorical identities officially recognized by the state and protected by legal statutes included in fresh legislation (title IV of the Civil Rights Act of 1964).

across generations. Granted, there is a class habitus but it is malleable to a degree: think of a provincial – say, a person born and raised in the South both in the US and in France – who successfully works to lose their twangy accent. The belief in meritocracy, which many scholars embrace as they feel that their own biography exemplifies it, reinforces the collective view that class is achieved and therefore fair, whereas race and gender are ascribed and therefore should not be detrimental to their members in keeping with the liberal values of equality and liberty. The bestowal of academic credentials, largely based on cultural capital accrued in the family, sanctifies class inequality. No formal institution similarly legitimates ethnoracial and gender inequality any longer.

321

Third, in the US, race and gender, while fluid to a degree, have both been *officialized and frozen by the state* (in European societies, ethnicity enjoys varying degrees of official recognition). They serve as the unquestioned basis for the production of individual identity and oceans of administrative data so that there is a built-in incentive for persons and researchers to use and to think in terms of these rigid bureaucratic categories. Not so for class, which does not have an official existence, although organizations and mobilizations often rely on it, if quietly. Thought experiment: imagine how different academic and public debate would be if government agencies routinely produced administrative data coded by class (using some combination of education, occupation, income, assets, and housing status) alongside ethnicity on both sides of the Atlantic.

Fourth, in capitalist societies, class discrimination is normalized by tacit or explicit *appeal to the market* as a fair distributor of material and symbolic rewards. The thorough and agile review of social science research on discrimination by Issa Kohler-Haussman published in "Oxford Bibliographies online" (4) notes the difficulty of defining the phenomenon and addresses "discrimination against specific socially salient groups defined on the basis of race, sex, sexual orientation, ethnicity and national origin, religion, age, and disability." Conspicuously missing is class, which appears edgewise to be implicitly dismissed when she writes: "Discrimination is typically considered something antithetical to norms of fair and equal treatment in a democratic market society." This suggests that market outcomes are "fair and equal," the main ideological pillar legitimating class discrimination.

A fifth, related, reason for the absence of class in debates on discrimination pertains to the possibility, probability, and *politics of categorical mobility*: members of aggrieved ethnic and sexual categories are inclined to "voice" their collective discontent because they are trapped, as it were, inside their classificatory box, whereas members of the lower class are able and inclined to "exit" individually to rise into the middle class (5). State canonization and collective mobilization stand in a mutually reinforcing relationship. Indeed, the reason why race and gender discrimination are so firmly established in social science is that they have been made salient and actionable as juridical categories by the insurgent movements of African-American and women rising up against subaltern relegation and unfair treatment. No similar mass movement against bourgeois rule has emerged and endured in advanced societies since the mid-twentieth century. Indeed, we live in an era in which class mobilization and politics have been eroded, to be replaced, in a growing number of advanced countries, by some variant of autocratic ethno-populism (6), and this in the face of an unprecedented polarization of the class structure.

The invisibility of class discrimination in social science is also rooted in the peculiarities of American society as the global center of sociological production. It is a society descended from an agrarian settler colony bordered by slavery, on one side, and a moving frontier based on genocide, on the other. As a result, racialized ethnicity has been inscribed as a fundamental cleavage of social space and public culture (7). Class divisions, though deep and brutal, have been further muted by the collective belief in "American exceptionalism" anchored by the notion of social openness and fluidity constructed against the image of old Europe as closed, rigid, and class-ridden, a belief that has deeply shaped US social sciences from their origins (8). Thus there is a long and distinguished lineage of research documenting and explaining why American workers have failed to develop a strong class consciousness, identifying instead as "middle class" and aspiring to move up the existing status ladder instead of mobilizing collectively for social transformation (9).

Finally, perhaps controversially, I submit that there is a deeper problem: the social sciences have quite simply failed to develop a *properly analytic concept of discrimination*, of whatever kind, relying instead on a mix of legal and commonsensical notions surreptitiously insinuating moral values into social scientific reasoning such that detrimental discrimination is equated with discrimination *tout court* (which can in fact be positive or negative) and is routinely confused with other elementary forms of racial domination, to wit, categorization (including prejudice, bias, and stigma), segregation, ghettoization, and violence (10).

It goes without saying – but it is better said to avoid confusion – that to attend to *class* discrimination neither negates nor neglects ethnoracial discrimination or its gender cousin (indeed, discrimination based on any principle of social vision and division, visible or invisible, informal or recognized by the state). On the contrary: the point is to elaborate the former precisely to conjugate it with the latter to get the fullest possible picture of differential treatment, positive or negative, warranted and unwarranted, in the court of law and beyond.

1. For a theoretical elaboration of the question of classification in society and history, that is, the classification of social creatures who are themselves "classified and classifying," and the "classification struggles" that ensue, see Pierre Bourdieu, *Sociologie générale*, volume 1, *Cours au Collège de France 1981–1983* (2015), pp. 18–29, 52–3, 67–75, 84–7, 93–6 and 126–39.
2. On the comparative malleability and porosity of racial and sexual boundaries and their recent contestation, read Rogers Brubaker, *Trans: Gender and Race in an Age of Unsettled Identities* (2016).
3. These are modal tendencies. Ethnoracial classification can assume a gradational form, as with the color continuum in Brazil and the Caribbean. Class theory is split between gradational conceptions (say, the six strata of Lloyd Warner and Wisconsin-style status attainment research) and relational conceptions (Marxist constructs such as Erik Olin Wright's discrete categories mixing exploitation and authority).
4. Issa Kohler-Haussmann, "Discrimination" (Oxford Bibliographies online, 2019).
5. This is an application of the classic schema elaborated by Albert O. Hirschman in *Exit, Voice, Loyalty: Responses to Decline in Firms, Organizations, and States* (1972).
6. Cihan Tuğal, "Populism Studies: The Case for Theoretical and Comparative Reconstruction" (2021).
7. David R. Roediger, *How Race Survived U.S. History* (2019).
8. Dorothy Ross, *The Origins of American Social Science* (1991).
9. Werner Sombart, *Warum gibt es in den Vereinigten Staaten keinen Sozialismus?* (1906); Richard Centers, *The Psychology of Social Classes* (1949); Mary R. Jackman and Robert W. Jackman, *Class Awareness in the United States* (1983); Erik Olin Wright, *Class Counts: Comparative Studies in Class Analysis* (1997).
10. On the five elementary forms of ethnoracial domination and their combinations, see Loïc Wacquant, *Racial Domination* (2024b), pp. 113–60.

Put brutally, the working principle seems to be that if you have a conventional life, the penal institution should bend over backward to allow you to preserve it, whereas if you live a wretched existence, you can absorb the full force of state sanction because there is nothing much to damage there. This is the foundation of the bifurcation of criminal processing into dignified "paper penalty" and degrading "street penalty." Bourgeois standing deserves protection; proletarian status gets no reprieve. *Class discrimination runs rampant* in criminal court and is hiding in plain sight. This opposition is, moreover, replicated *within* the proletariat itself. Punishment is differentially distributed and accentuated, not just at the "macro" level of large socioeconomic gaps between bourgeoisie and proletariat, but also, and most commonly given the social composition of the penal clientele, at the "micro" level of small gradations between the *three class fractions composing the proletariat* in the postindustrial city. I call them the solid working class, the shifting precariat, and the street drifters occupying the "zone of integration," the "zone of vulnerability," and the "zone of disaffiliation," respectively.[155] These are not rigidly separated and neatly separable populations, but we can differentiate their structural position and cultural inclinations as follows.

The *solid working class* is, so to speak, the "bourgeoisie" within the proletariat. It sports reliable markers of social integration: steady employment, regular income, secure housing along with a stable nuclear family, valuable social ties (membership in a church, a union, a neighborhood group, a sports club) and an embrace of order and conventional morality.[156] These markers are appreciated by the prosecutor and the judge and thus earn punishment discounts as a matter of course in the give-and-take of adjudication. Much like the middle class, members of this class fraction and their offspring are worthy candidates for release from remand detention, for sentencing to probation, and for assignment to assorted "court programming" insofar as they broadcast clear signals that they are inclined to "obey all laws and be of good conduct" (in the formulaic words of the judge at arraignment) while their case winds its way through the court maze.[157]

[155] On these three zones and their distinctive properties, see Robert Castel, *Les Métamorphoses de la question sociale. Une chronique du salariat* (1995), pp. 15–16. For a kaleidoscopic portrait of the three fractions, sample the pertinent chapters in Pierre Bourdieu et al., *La Misère du monde* (1993).

[156] Its anchors and culture are probed on the two sides of the Atlantic by Olivier Schwartz, *Le Monde privé des ouvriers. Hommes et femmes du Nord* (1990), and Elijah Anderson, *Code of the Street: Decency, Violence, and the Moral Life of the Inner City* (2000).

[157] This is manifested most clearly and early in the decision to release (or not) the defendant "on their own recognizance." In serious cases, release is mechanically denied to those devoid of minimal work, housing, and social ties because this lack is read as a precursor sign that the defendant will not show up at his next hearing. This

As its name indicates, the *shifting precariat* is composed of members of the proletariat living in material precarity due to being trapped in insecure, low-pay, part-time, and short-term wage labor or being sporadically unemployed.[158] It suffers from economic insecurity, housing instability, and family fragility despite solidarity, which means that it lacks the capitals (economic, cultural, social, and especially moral) that punishment professionals value and reward as predictive of law-abiding behavior. Its members engage in episodic or sustained crime as a matter of material necessity, cultural immersion, and social persistence. As a result, they become regular clients of the penal state and accrue extensive records.[159] The court and the jail are a normal fixture of their life horizon and major determinants of their personal trajectories until they age out of crime. Given this profile, their defense attorneys are hard pressed to put together the "mitigation package" or the makeshift "CV" that yield better offers in plea negotiations.

325

The *street drifters* accumulate and circulate in the nethermost regions of social and physical space in the metropolis. They include all manner of human derelicts: the hard-core jobless and chronic homeless, former convicts and wards of the state, the poor addicted and mentally ill, the crippled and the variously unemployables who fall through the cracks of the social and medical safety net and whose extended family cannot or will not save from their wretched fate – in short, the social refuse of the market society.[160] The category also

becomes self-perpetuating as defendants with multiple FTAs ("failure to appear") from previous cases are routinely detained pretrial.

[158] For a conceptual elaboration, see Loïc Wacquant, *The Invention of the "Underclass": A Study in the Politics of Knowledge* (2022), pp. 162–8. A vivid account of Harlem's precariat is Katherine S. Newman, *No Shame in my Game: The Working Poor in the Inner City* (2001). For a picture of everyday life and social strategies across generations, see Jean-François Laé and Numa Murard, *Deux Générations dans la débine. Enquête dans la pauvreté ouvrière* (2012), and Collectif Rosa Bonheur, *La Ville vue d'en bas. Travail et production de l'espace populaire* (2020). A surprising collection of experiential narratives by prison writers is Zeke Caligiuri (ed.), *American Precariat: Parables of Exclusion* (2023).

[159] John Irwin, *The Jail: Managing the Underclass in American Society* (1985).

[160] Patrick Bruneteaux, *L'Arrière-cour de la mondialisation. Ethnographie des paupérisés* (2010); Teresa Gowan, *Hobos, Hustlers, and Backsliders: Homeless in San Francisco* (2010); Matthew Desmond, *Evicted: Poverty and Profit in the American City* (2017). This means that the volume, composition, and persistence of this population, and by implication its penal involvement, are a direct function of the type and extension of the social state. No wonder it is largest, growing, and nearly intractable in the US metropolis, the country where deep poverty is institutionalized by the toxic confluence of market rule and state abandonment.

encompasses the petty entrepreneurs of the street economy: hustlers, sex workers, panhandlers, trash recyclers, professional robbers and burglars, gang members and the foot soldiers of criminal business such as the rank-and-file of the drug trade.[161]

As we saw in chapter 2 (*supra*, pp. 151–61), along the precariat from which they issue, the street outcasts and operators are massively overrepresented behind bars. The reason is that their very dereliction turns them into an annoyance or a threat in public space; their festering criminal activity is readily visible, which makes them the privileged prey of the police.[162] They have nothing to offer and redeem at the prosecutorial counter. Along with the precariat, they are the "frequent flyers" who clog the justice system as they cycle in and out of the criminal court, jail, prison, city shelter, and county hospital. In these two lowermost class fractions, incarceration runs in the family: fathers, sons, and cousins churn before the same judge who gets to know them by name, inquires about their kin and realizes well, when he sentences them, that they will very soon be back.[163] They get the worst judicial deals because of their long criminal records and, due to their cultural disrepute and lack of social attachments, they can proffer no positive assurances as to future behavior. Indeed, the default assumption is that they will reoffend as soon as the opportunity arises. They are viewed as walking, talking, breathing criminality waiting to happen.

Race and immigrant status are a crucial secondary variable that crosscuts class fraction, with the proportion of stigmatized ethnic categories, national and foreign, peaking among the precariat locked in degraded and informal employment where they toil without social protection or legal recognition. Ethnic labor market segmentation increases downward economic pressure on blacks and Latinos in the US and on postcolonial migrants in Western Europe, increasing the likelihood of criminal involvement. Immigrants often escape the street thanks to stronger networks of family and group solidarity than the native precariat, but they face the *double contingency* of

---

[161] For a rich analysis of the immersion of "stick-up artists" in street life and culture, read Richard T. Wright and Scott H. Decker, *Armed Robbers in Action: Stick-ups and Street Culture* (1997).

[162] Philippe Bourgois and Jeff Schonberg, *Righteous Dopefiend* (2009); Peter Moskos, *Cop in the Hood: My Year Policing Baltimore's Eastern District* (2008); Forrest Stuart, *Down, Out, and Under Arrest: Policing and Everyday Life in Skid Row* (2016).

[163] An eloquent call to think of criminal desistance as well as escalation in terms of both individuals and generations is Christopher Wildeman and Robert J. Sampson, "Desistance as an Intergenerational Process" (2024).

labor market and nationality. They must worry about the joint enforcement of criminal law and immigration law whose violation can lead them to be arrested, detained, and deported at any moment.[164]

A third relevant variable is gender: women are, again, vastly overrepresented among the precariat and bear the double burden of degraded labor inside and outside the household as well as care work within the family under conditions of acute precarity.[165] But they benefit from court leniency across the board as a matter of course. Next comes age: roughly put, the steady working class is older, the precariat younger, and the street population a mix of young and old. Some members of each class fraction will find a path of upward intra-class mobility as they transition from youth to adulthood; others will take a structural fall as they approach senior status. The gang members, robbers, and hustlers age out quickly: criminal enterprise on the streets is a young man's game.[166] The hard-core homeless do not get old: the street kills them before they do.

Finally, the three fractions of the urban proletariat are not sharply differentiated by neighborhood, although the solid working class often own their homes and seek to create spatial distance from the precariat and the street population. In the case of African-Americans, due to inflexible racial segregation, all three categories tend to reside interspersed among each other in the hyperghetto and its vicinity; the major dividing line is between the proletariat as a whole, on the one hand, and the middle class which has typically moved away, on the other. When the black middle class invades poor segregated districts via gentrification, the result is acute cultural dis-

327

---

[164] Salvatore Palidda, *Devianza e vittimizzazione tra i migranti* (2001); Cecilia Menjívar and Daniel Kanstroom (eds.), *Constructing Immigrant "Illegality": Critiques, Experiences, and Responses* (2013); Ruth Milkman, *Immigrant Labor and the New Precariat* (2020). In *Unwanted*, Sandra Bucerius shows that young Turkish, Moroccan and Kosovar-Albanian men involved in the street economy of Frankfurt were further marginalized by their lack of citizenship such that their penal exposure was compounded by the constant threat of deportation.

[165] Christelle Avril, *Les Aides à domicile. Un autre monde populaire* (2014); Arne Kalleberg, *Precarious Lives: Job Insecurity and Well-Being in Rich Democracies* (2018).

[166] One of the main changes in gang culture and economy in the US metropolis over the past quarter-century is that its members do not "age out" of the gang as they used to, due to the lack of economic alternatives and robust social ties linked to the degradation of the employment market (affecting jobs) and the shrinking of the social safety net (affecting family formation). See Martin Sánchez-Jankowski, *Cracks in the Pavement: Social Change and Resilience in Poor Neighborhoods* (2008), and Randol Contreras, *The Marvelous Ones: Drugs, Gang Violence, and Resistance in East Los Angeles* (2024). Meanwhile, participation in the illegal street economy in Western Europe has gone in the opposite direction, with participants getting younger over time, as shown in the case of France by Nasser Tafferant, *Le Bizness. Une économie souterraine* (2007).

sension and brewing conflict over the uses of public space.[167] In Western Europe, social classes and ethnic categories are not as sharply segregated residentially as in the US, except for the established bourgeoisie at the top. In France, the main spatial opposition of relevance to penality and class formation at the bottom is between large public housing estates, which concentrate street crime and vulnerable families, and single-family homes in the nearby housing tracts of the urban periphery.[168]

In the neoliberal era, however, with working-class decomposition in full swing, what animates all three class fractions is the *fear of downward mobility*. The solid working class anguishes about sinking into precarity as its work conditions deteriorate, its employment security wanes, and part-time employment spreads. The precariat dreads losing its shaky hold on meager work, welfare, and family, and then falling into the street. Even the homeless, who seem radically denuded, have something to lose, their scanty belongings and personal papers, the brittle social ties that keep them afloat day-to-day, the safe spot where they sleep, and their fast-eroding bodily capital.[169] As the expression from the black hyperghetto goes, "there is always somebody doing worser than you." Criminal money-making is sought as a social parachute at every level before it becomes an episodic activity or an economic mainstay. Embroilment with the punishment apparatus is a consequence that, in turn, becomes one more cause of enduring marginality.

To repeat, the boundaries between these three proletarian class fractions are not hard and fast but labile and permeable – though the line between the sturdy working class and the other two categories is more firmly drawn. There is a continuous flow of bodies, relationships, objects, and signs back and forth between them. The same family or household will often harbor members of the three fractions. Each has its own material and symbolic center of gravity, but the solid working class sets the material and symbolic standards to which the other two fractions aspire. Crucially, its cultural contours stand

---

[167] Mary Pattillo, *Black on the Block: The Politics of Race and Class in the City* (2010).

[168] Marie-Hélène Bacqué et al., "Des territoires entre ascension et déclin. Trajectoires sociales dans la mosaïque périurbaine" (2016).

[169] Matthew Desmond, "Disposable Ties and the Urban Poor" (2012); Giuseppe Scandurra, *Tutti a casa. Il Carracci: etnografia dei senza fissa dimora a Bologna* (2005); Gisèle Dambuyant-Wargny, *Quand on n'a plus que son corps. Soin et non-soin de soi en situation de précarité* (2006); Nora Sellner, *Alltägliche Bewältigungspraxen obdachloser Menschen* (2021).

in a relation of elective affinity with the moral code of the court such that they benefit from relative magnanimity.

This triad is key to understanding the work of *sociosymbolic sorting* that punishment professionals effect in their daily work and the differential responsiveness of prosecutors and judges to the *slightly* different profiles presented by defendants. The habitus of the prosecutor and judge, anchored by a taste for order, a reverence for authority, and a yearning for morality, lead them to *dramatize these small differences* to deliver disparate treatment to the three class fractions, which get further amplified through the logic of cumulative disadvantage along the penal chain. This is the mechanism through which the criminal triage effected by the court reproduces and even accentuates social stratification.[170]

329

Class advantage is not limited to objective *position* defined by the volume and composition of capital (economic with a job, cultural with education, social with family attachments, and symbolic with categorical prestige). It extends to subjective *disposition*, according to a logic of conditioning and embodiment described by Pierre Bourdieu in his classic book *La Distinction*.[171] Small markers of class (fraction) displayed in the courtroom, such as dress (for defendants appearing out of custody), bodily posture and facial expression, learned (or not) in the family and cultivated (or reproved) by the peer group, are read by penal professionals as outward signs of (dis)respect for conventional authority.[172]

They buy the defendant minimal compassion and a small discount on punishment because they signal a modicum of social reverence and moral pliancy to the prosecutor. Through their accoutrement and conduct ("the blazer and the tie"), the defendants effectively *recognize* judicial power as such and they submit, as expected by the Leviathan. As with all symbolic powers, recognition begets a measure of magnanimity. By contrast, no special consideration is forthcoming for those defendants who cannot tame their street habitus in the courtroom.

---

[170] This validates my contention that punishment "corresponds," not to the mode of *production*, as claimed by Georg Rusche and Otto Kirchheimer, but to the mode of *stratification* (see *supra*, p. 152).

[171] Pierre Bourdieu, *La Distinction. Critique sociale du jugement* (1979).

[172] In his painstaking study of the policing of LA's Skid Row, Forrest Stuart shows that the homeless deploy the same public performances of social docility and moral propriety on the street, as manifested by dress, demeanor, body care, and body language, "in hopes of escaping officers' default assumptions of criminality." Stuart, *Down, Out, and Under Arrest*, p. 127.

"That's what the guy in the blazer tells me"

DA Julius: I do have a level of respect for a defendant when he comes into court, if he has a tie on, [chuckles] or you know, a blazer. It doesn't even have to *fit him*, you know? The fact is that what they're saying is, "I respect this room, I respect this process, and I want you to know I *understand* what I did was wrong." *Without saying it, they show it.* And I mean, when I *see someone* like that, I *do* have like, a little bit of compassion for that person, 'cause I'm thinking, "Well, at least this person is taking this process seriously."

The Professor: Whereas if they walk in with their shoes unlaced . . .

DA Julius: And their pants down and their pants all the way down –

The Professor: Sometimes I've even seen young guys in the hallway who wear t-shirts (DA Julius: Exactly) that read, not "Fuck the Police," but pretty much! (1)

DA Julius: They're kind of *expressing that*. And you're saying, "What am I seeing? Someone who I'm gonna see again." And to me, these young people – 'cause most of 'em are young – eventually are *gonna get it*. Or they're gonna be *old-time felons*, with *no life*, and with *no future* . . . And like, at some point you say, "Well, I'm never gonna do this again, I'm *never* gonna be back here again. *I don't like it here*," you know? That's what the guy in the blazer and the tie tells me.

1. I once caught sight in the courtroom gallery of a young black couple wearing matching red outfits with oversize grey sweaters with large block letters blaring "NO RULES, NO MASTER" on the front and "MEN OF MAYHEM" on the sleeves. My fieldnotes from that day read: "This is beyond absurd: this is the outfit that you wear to court to face a judge who has the power to send you to the slammer? I presume they realize the disrespect this entails! (Later I'll learn via the web that this is the outfit of characters in a TV series about an outlaw motorcycle gang in Central California, 'Sons of Anarchy')."

Instead of the Freudian "narcissism of small differences" cultivated by the poor themselves, then, we get a Bourdieusian "amplification of small differences" cultivated by the institution, whereby punishment professionals seize on minor distinctions between defendants to make them juridically consequential and thus to separate what they take to be the social wheat from the chaff of society – people who have committed a crime but "get up in the morning to go to work" and can be reintegrated into the law-abiding citizenry with moderate punishment versus the human parasites who "lead a feral existence" and therefore deserve neither compassion nor mercy.

To sum up, close-up observation of plea bargaining and in-depth interviews of prosecutors in action reveal the two mechanisms of production of doxic class discrimination in the courthouse. The first mechanism producing the class diffraction of punishment is *objective*; *it is rooted in capital*: the prosecutor reads the portfolio of resources of the defendant as indicative of future law-breaking or law-abiding conduct. Does he possess the economic capital of a job, the cultural capital of schooling, the social capital of family or marriage, the symbolic capital of morality as attested by a letter from a teacher or pastor? If he does, he is entitled to a punishment discount. This is what I call the "mitigation-package" or the "CV" formula.

331

The second mechanism explaining penal differentiation across class and class fractions is *subjective*; *it is rooted in habitus* (as capital embodied): by his dress, deportment, demeanor, and elocution, the defendant earns a downward deviation of sanction by expressing or faking humility, contrition, and deference to the punishment professionals in the courtroom. This is what I call the "blazer-and-tie" formula. The two mechanisms reinforce each other: defendants who possess some quantum of capital are also more likely to have the inner inclination and outward capacity to bow before penal power. Conversely, their counterparts who have no capital are also more likely to lack the disposition to submit to the latter. The CV and the blazer work together, to the detriment of those who lack both.

A cautionary note on race and prosecution

The fact that, unlike class and age, race is absent from the phenomenological forefront of the *process* of criminal prosecution does not mean that it does not enter in indirect and subtle ways into the causal determination of plea *outcomes*. The possible causal routes include biased cognition by court protagonists (prosecutor, defense counsel, and judge), name and place association (the location of law-breaking crops up in haggling), crime association (certain offenses, say, carjacking or the manufacture of methamphetamine, are presumed to be "typical" of certain ethnic categories), seemingly neutral organizational routines with ethnoracially disparate impact (such as setting bail), and the spillover of "cumulative disadvantage" from earlier stages of penal processing and earlier life experiences going back decades.[173] It does mean that the kind of crude, glaring and suffusive discrimination in *process*, readily perceptible on the judicial stage, denounced by scholars fixated on race, may well be the result of selective (in)attention and affective projection.

Racial fixation in Chicago's penal colony and the Nebraska test

In Nicole Gonzalez Van Cleve's *Crook County: Racism and Injustice in America's Largest Criminal Court* (2016), a deep insider account of everyday work in Chicago's criminal courthouse, "a space that has the look and feel of the Jim Crow era," race is *on the surface* (1). It saturates every scene; it infiltrates every nook and cranny of the institution; it is *hypervisible* – Van Cleve claims to "see it" time and time again. Racism refers, pell-mell and without clarity, to biased cognition, emotion, disposition, interaction, segregation and discrimination, materiality and ideology, architecture and culture, code and system, process and outcome, cause and consequence. It propels practices that are not just unfair, unethical, and illegal but downright cruel and even sadistic, *unfolding in plain sight*.

There is no outside to this nightmarish regime of "state-sanctioned racial violence" in the courtroom and no one but Gonzalez Van Cleve dares to "shatter the code of silence" and denounce it (pp. 146, 148–9, 183, 185, 189–90). The justice professionals in leadership positions, including the presiding judge, chief prosecutor, and chief public defender, are all people of color; the courthouse is the workplace of hundreds of black and Latino attorneys. All are said to keep mum and to play along as actively or passively complicit actors in this racial theater of the absurd (p. 57) (2).

The notions that "the courtroom is completely racially biased" and that the "power lines were racially divided" are first formulated by an impressionable 19-year-old undergraduate doing a class project (p. 27). They become the *thesis* to be hammered at every turn and not the *hypothesis* to be tested – a textbook logical fallacy of "begging the question." All the rich and rare data patiently gathered

---

[173] Besiki Luka Kutateladze et al., "Cumulative Disadvantage: Examining Racial and Ethnic Disparity in Prosecution and Sentencing" (2014); Robert J. Sampson and Roland Neil, "The Social Foundations of Racial Inequalities in Arrest over the Life Course and in Changing Times" (2024).

years later for a doctoral dissertation are read through, and forcibly fitted, into a dichotomous racial lens: black defendants are systematically portrayed as *black first* and defendants second (if at all); white court professionals are depicted as *white first* and court professionals second (if at all). The result is that every material condition, practical disposition, bureaucratic action, and judicial decision made by the court is automatically attributed to racial animus, humiliation, and oppression – down to the dilapidated corridors, sticky floors, and missing toilet paper in the building's public bathrooms (p. 27). "Us versus them" refers not to justice professionals versus criminal suspects, *as it does in every courthouse in every advanced society*, but to white versus people of color (pp. 22–8). For instance, the silencing and disciplining of people sitting in the gallery is not a matter of courtroom decorum enforced to uphold the authority of the judge and to signify the grandeur of the law but a remanence of the Jim Crow era (p. 40). The sentencing hearing is not a ritual that debases the defendant as a criminal but a "racial degradation ceremony" (as if white defendants were not similarly degraded, pp. 52–3) (3).

Strikingly, Gonzalez Van Cleve provides ample evidence of class bias in court proceedings but she consistently misinterprets her own data to reassert again and again the sinister primacy of race – made more plausible by generously sprinkling her text with the words "racial," "racialized," and "of color" (4). When class is overtly staged and signaled, she insists, it is to signify the insidious office of race: "Whiteness had to be performed convincingly by exhibiting middle-class capital, dialects, degrees, or other signifiers that could verify class membership" (p. 67). Could it be that middle-class capital was exhibited *for itself* because it counters the presumption of immorality and criminal propensity so that it earns a punishment "discount"? Even "poor ethnic whites" are "racialized and punished for racial difference" and not because they are poor (p. 89). The transparently class and moral folk category of "mope" (designating the disorganized and underserving poor wallowing in crime, black, white, and Latino) (5) is racialized not by the actors on the scene but by Gonzalez Van Cleve. In her view – blinded by racial obsession – every status or condition, from class and poverty to education, morality, and criminality, becomes an automatic *proxy for race*.

Gonzalez Van Cleve's fixation on race is such that she cannot see this fundamental contradiction in her account of its workings: racial oppression is both gross and subtle, at once blatant and discreet,

333

by turns evident and hidden, simultaneously visible and invisible. Thus, on the one hand, "racism has staying power; it merges with life so as to be nearly invisible to those embedded in it . . . *Real life*, in the Cook County Courts, is *real racism*" (p. 134, original italics). But, on the other, to "rectify the type of racial violence inflicted by the courts," "the answer is simple: *go*. Go to the courts. Bear witness to what attorneys and judges are doing and bear witness en masse" (p. 189) because racial domination is there for anyone to see with the naked eye.

The question arises, then, as to why *Crook County* was met with an enthusiastic reception, in the academy as well as in the general media, and won multiple book awards. Aside from public ignorance about the topic and misunderstanding about the method, the answer is straightforward. Gonzalez Van Cleve tells her readers the ghoulish story they wish to hear with the run-up of the Black Lives Matter movement because it validates their worst inner fears: that criminal justice in America is a racial grinding machine worthy of Franz Kafka's harrow in *The Penal Colony*. This is a classic case of what the logicians call the "bandwagon fallacy."

There is an object lesson to be drawn here that motivates the present dissection: failing to *separate the analytics from the politics of race* leads to grievous scientific errors and paves the way for political confusion and policy misdirection (6). It is essential to document and explain racial domination, to use clear theoretical language, to decompose the phenomenon, to ferret out mechanisms, and to consider counterfactuals (7). To do the latter, we can apply what I call the *Nebraska test* (after the Great Plains state whose population was until recently nearly exclusively white): are the practices observed in Chicago also observed in Lincoln? Is courtroom decorum not imposed on the sitting public there? Are defendants not degraded by the judges? Do bailiffs and attorneys not disparage the accused in the backstage of the courthouse? If the answer is positive, then chances are the practices observed are not racial in character and one needs to go back to the drawing board to disclose the social principles of vision and division that drive them.

1. Nicole Gonzalez Van Cleve's *Crook County: Racism and Injustice in America's Largest Criminal Court* (2016).
2. Gonzalez Van Cleve castigates defense attorneys *ad unum omnes* as "ambassadors of racialized justice" (p. 162). One wonders why no local journalist has written an exposé on this spectacular racial scandal, since it is out in the open, and why the *Chicago Tribune* did not detect it in its award-winning report on

"Stalled Justice" (2023) focusing on the logjams and delays plaguing Cook County court.

3. "Race is everywhere but nowhere, in the structural arrangements, in the policing of boundaries, in the recoding of rhetoric, and in the delineation of defendants as 'deserving' or 'undeserving'. By wielding morality as a currency, professionals create 'sincere fictions' that rationalize the 'doing of justice' and the 'doing of racism'" (pp. 53–4).

4. Gonzalez Van Cleve is not one to shy away from inflammatory rhetoric. Thus, for defense counsel, "the moral pricing of the defendant requires seeing your clients through the racialized lenses of the Cook County Courts, much like placing a price on slaves and gauging their worth" (p. 161). In her concluding chapter, she likens the legal practices in Chicago's courts to public torture lynching under Jim Crow and insists on the "symbolic continuity between popular justice of the past and racialized justice of the present" (pp. 187–8).

5. "Work ethic, competency, and motivation are central elements of court culture ... 'Mope' is shorthand for a person who violates these values" (p. 58). The term is used to categorize defendants but can also be employed to designate judges and attorneys who are not competent and hard-working. What is racial about it? Yet Gonzalez Van Cleve overinterprets it as racially coded, as if whites were to a man diligent and capable workers.

6. For instance, to go sit in the gallery of the courtroom to "bear witness" serves no purpose other than warming the heart of justice activists keen on making themselves useful. The real courtwork is carried out in the wings of the courthouse and in particular in the private chambers of the judge. Groups that engage in "court-watching" are essentially burning militant energy for naught.

7. For a historical illustration of these principles put to work, see Loïc Wacquant, *Racial Domination* (2024b), chapter 3, "Jim Crow as Caste Terrorism."

More broadly, to propose that race and criminal justice are "mutually constitutive" – the latest avatar of what Andreas Wimmer aptly calls "race-centrism"[174] – is an *analytical cop-out*: it presupposes resolved the very conundrum in need of clear conceptual articulation and tailored empirical inquiry. It stops inquiry right where it should get started; it skews it when it should remain on a straightforward track leading to all possible bifurcations.[175] It also ignores the fact

[174] Andreas Wimmer, "Race-Centrism: A Critique and a Research Agenda" (2015).
[175] This conceptual legerdemain is in evidence in Laura E. Gómez, "Understanding Law and Race as Mutually Constitutive: An Invitation to Explore an Emerging Field" (2010); Naomi Murakawa and Katherine Beckett, "The Penology of Racial Innocence: The Erasure of Racism in the Study and Practice of Punishment" (2010); Nicole Gonzalez Van Cleve and Lauren Mayes, "Criminal Justice through 'Colorblind' Lenses: A Call to Examine the Mutual Constitution of Race and Criminal Justice" (2015); Hedwig Lee, "How does Structural Racism Operate (in) the Contemporary US Criminal Justice System?" (2024); and Lily Hu and Issa Kohler-Hausmann, "What is Perceived when Race is Perceived and Why it Matters for Causal Inference and Discrimination Studies" (2025).

that race is never alone in shaping law and law in shaping race, and that their articulation is *historical and not ontological.* Fueled by political passion and moral indignation, the principled affirmation of the omnipresence and omnipotence of race by Critical Race Theory and its derivatives – sometimes expressed by the magical formula "race is baked in" – gets in the way of identifying the stages, modalities, and devices that interject and ingrain ethnoracial division into criminal justice structure and process, *or not.*[176]

In this quest, the notion of systemic or "structural racism" is part of the problem and not the solution.[177] The racialization of law and the juridification of race are two distinct if intertwined processes that are perfectly open to historical recapitulation and methodical investigation, but rash sloganeering passed off as enlightened theory gets in the way. Their study must assiduously eschew the twin traps of *presentism* and *groupism,* which takes for granted the existence, the boundaries, and the basis of classification of particular collectives in a given society at the present time.[178] Here the principles of historicist-analytical sociology must be duly recalled and implemented: define your concepts clearly and use theoretical terminology cautiously, disaggregate instead of lumping phenomena and their constituents, identify mechanisms – themselves racial and nonracial – and think historically and counterfactually.

An exemplary case of the fallacy of *petitio principii* is the resounding article by Heather Schoenfeld at al. on "Criminal Justice as Racialized Organizations" (2025) published in the flagship journal *Criminology.* The authors write: "To move beyond research on racial disparities, define racism structurally rather than individually, and elaborate mechanisms, criminologists need new frameworks and theories that can unpack the *unyielding and undeniable link* between race/racism and the criminal justice system" (p. 5, my italics). If the link is undeniable, why waste energy inquiring into it? They continue: "The

---

[176] The latest avatar of this theological way of thinking which *posits* the dogma that race (in its commonsensical American variant) invades and invests every nook and cranny of the punishment apparatus is the mystified and mystifying notion of "racialized organization" developed by Victor Ray and applied by Heather Schoenfeld et al., "Criminal Justice as Racialized Organizations: Evidence from Ethnographies of Police, Courts, and Jails" (2025).

[177] See Wacquant, *Racial Domination,* pp. 174–88 (for a generic dissection) and pp. 188–97 (for a specific application to race and punishment).

[178] On groupism, read the indispensable critique of Rogers Brubaker in *Ethnicity Without Groups* (2004).

theory of racialized organizations posits that organizational power and resources 'encode racial processes' through their everyday functioning, *and it is these interactions, practices, and policies* that constitute race" (p. 6, original italics). In sum, the theory *posits* the phenomenon and proposes that racialized institutions encode and constitute race: is that not a definitional tautology?

As for evidence, Schoenfeld et al. selected seven ethnographies of the police, the court, and jails, and "coded the books for ethnographic vignettes that fit components of the theory" (p. 10) while conveniently disregarding those that did not fit. Is that not the elementary methodological mistake of selecting on the dependent variable? Worse, Schoenfeld et al. *project* into these ethnographies arguments and findings about race that are simply not there. This is particularly glaring in the case of Issa Kohler-Hausmann's *Misdemeanorland*, a masterful study of case processing in New York City's lower criminal courts that does not address the topic, even in passing.[179] A close reading reveals that there is not a shred of data in *Misdemeanorland* that validates the notion that the court is a "racialized institution" in Victor Ray's doctrinal sense of the term, whereas there is plenty of evidence of the role of class from arrest to conviction. Kohler-Hausmann quotes a veteran supervisor in the DA's office who openly justifies class discrimination: "*A huge factor that we always take into consideration is whether or not the person is employed.* We don't want to see people losing their jobs, especially not in today's economy. We do not penalize someone for not having a job, but it certainly is a plus, and we always take it into consideration in forming dispositions."[180]

Schoenfeld et al. effectively propose to move from the *sociology to the theology of race* in criminal justice.[181] Empirical research is superfluous

---

[179] Issa Kohler-Hausmann, *Misdemeanorland: Criminal Courts and Social Control in an Age of Broken Windows Policing* (2018). The only place where Kohler-Hausmann discusses race pertains to the question of the spatial targeting of the police (not the court), where she is careful to tie together race and class: "Quality-of-life policing is intensely focused in black and Hispanic spaces . . . [M]isdemeanor arrests have been overwhelmingly concentrated in precincts that have 60 percent or more black or Hispanic population. Arrests from these spaces have a social meaning, one that translates into a presumption of need for social control over the people who are brought from them to misdemeanorland. Precincts with high concentrations of minority residents tend also to be low-income spaces marked by other forms of social disadvantage. Therefore, misdemeanor arrests are not only concentrated by gender, race, and ethnicity but also by socioeconomic class" (p. 53).

[180] Ibid., pp. 151–2, my italics.

[181] Schoenfeld et al., "Criminal Justice as Racialized Organizations" (2025), pp. 21–2.

if we simply postulate the phenomenon from the outset: "The theory of racialized organizations moves scholars beyond the preoccupation with demonstrating and accounting for racially disparate outcomes. By *positing* the expectation of racial disparities across Criminal Legal Organizations and related organizations, it makes racism (rather than no racism) the null hypothesis."[182] *Abracadabra*: the burden of proof is disappeared in a methodological sleight of hand. Schoenfeld et al. go one step further, proposing to build on research when it demonstrates ethnoracial impact (under the coded concept of "slow violence") but to disregard it when it explains racial differences in judicial output by nonracial factors:

338

> As an alternative to studying racial disparities, researchers can direct their attention to uncovering the daily organizational mechanisms of the criminal legal system that create racial harm. This focus would problematize the negative consequences of criminal legal system involvement *regardless of whether research can account for racial disparities with "warranted" factors*. It would also take seriously the "slow violence" of the criminal legal system on Race-Class-Subjugated individuals and communities.[183]

This is a clear violation of the principle of epistemological symmetry according to which you must accept the findings of social inquiry when they disprove as well as prove your thesis.

There is no question that the penal state inflicts grievous harms, reduces, nay annihilates, the agency of its client population and powerfully legitimizes inequality, but it does this *regardless of the ethnicity of suspects, defendants, and convicts*. All three of these processes apply to white populations in multiethnic cities as well as to the all-white populations of the rural regions of the American heartland. The proposition that the justice apparatus is inherently "racialized" simply does not pass the "Nebraska test" (as defined above, see *supra*, p. 334). Now, as we saw in chapter 2, penalization does have an *elective affinity* with racialization in the Weberian sense of *Wahlverwandtschaft*: both are state-enforced variants of public dishonor or, to borrow the language of Pierre Bourdieu, negative symbolic capital, so they tend to attract one another and interweave when they are both present. But affinity is not identity; articulation is not amalgamation; reciprocal reinforcement is not teleological imbroglio.

[182] Ibid., pp. 21–2, my italics.
[183] Ibid., p. 22, my italics.

Lastly, there is the triple empirical puzzle, set up by the landmark article by Chris Muller and Alex Roehrkasse, that the theory of "racialized Criminal Legal Institution" is hard pressed to resolve.[184] First, the carceral population of the US has declined steeply from its peak of 2.32 million in 2008 to reach 1.84 million in 2024, with the black inmate population falling faster than the white in both absolute and relative numbers; next, the white–black racial disparity in prison admissions has *collapsed* from 1 to 9 in 1993 to settle at 1 to 2.7 in 2015; meanwhile, class disparity as measured by the crude educational divide "some college" versus "no college" has *ballooned*, jumping from 1 to 6 to surpass 1 to 25. Does this abrupt triple turn not suggest that the link between race and punishment is deep yet historically contingent – as a theory of racial domination sensitive to the temporal dynamics of classification and stratification as the two dialectical dimensions of group-making would suggest?[185]

I submit that, instead of postulating a "null hypothesis" that aggravates them, students of prosecution must remain alert to the possibility that plea bargaining simply *passes on* ethnoracial differentials it inherits – from differential offending and policing or from the earlier prosecutorial steps of "screening" police reports and "charging" (or "filing") cases – without *adding* to them, or even *reduces* differentials when negotiating prosecutors are animated by a sense of substantive justice, as many are.[186] In a shrewdly designed statistical study of 203 deputy DAs in North Carolina linking individual surveys to the outcome of their cases, Hannah Shaffer finds that "prosecutors who attribute disparities to racial bias in the system have lower prison rates for Black defendants with criminal records than facially similar white defendants, thereby offsetting past disparities."[187] Blanket *a priori* statements about plea bargaining and ethnoracial gaps conveniently overlook the ideological and professional heterogeneity of the population of prosecutors as well as offices. This intra- and inter-office

339

[184] Christopher Muller and Alexander F. Roehrkasse, "Racial and Class Inequality in US Incarceration in the Early Twenty-First Century" (2022).
[185] Wacquant, *Racial Domination*.
[186] We also cannot *presume* systematic bias at earlier stages in the prosecutorial process. Research on racial bias in charging is mixed, turning up small and inconsistent gaps; studies of class bias are few and inconclusive. The most systematic study is a randomized controlled experiment using vignettes with 467 line DAs nationwide which found no detectable prejudicial effect of the race or class of the defendant on charging decisions. Christopher Robertson et al., "Race and Class: A Randomized Experiment with Prosecutors" (2019).
[187] Hannah Shaffer, "Prosecutors, Race, and the Criminal Pipeline" (2023), p. 1889.

heterogeneity undermines the popular claim that "race neutrality" necessarily contributes to the aggravation of racial disparity in the absence of probative evidence to this effect.[188]

A thorough review of the small, uneven, and dispersed body of research that touches on ethnoracial discrepancies in plea bargaining published in the authoritative volume *A System of Pleas: Social Science's Contributions to the Real Legal System* edited by the psychologist Vanessa Edkins and the criminologist Allison Redlich (2019) reveals, first, that the phenomenon has yet to be solidly established and, second, that its potential causal springs, assuming it is established, are plural and remain to be identified. The mishmash of studies gathered across time periods and locations, covering federal and state justice and lumping together felonies and misdemeanors, reveals "scarce," "mixed," and "inconsistent" results whose interpretation rests on multiple conditionals.[189] Observable gaps between blacks and Latinos, on the one side, and whites, on the other, are small when they show up at all, and they sometimes favor blacks. It is not demonstrated that they are generated in plea negotiation as opposed to being the downstream effects of "cumulative disadvantage" at earlier stages of case processing.[190]

As for theoretical predictions, they are equally dispersed and weak. "Critical race" perspectives issued out of legal scholarship have not yielded testable hypotheses, only rhetorical flourishes. "Focal concern" theory inspired by criminology has not been properly operationalized. "Implicit bias" as developed by psychology has yet to

340

[188] This claim is made without a shred of evidence by R. R. Dunlea, "'No Idea Whether He's Black, White, or Purple': Colorblindness and Cultural Scripting in Prosecution" (2022). It will no doubt be repeated because it conforms to a prevalent preconception shared by court scholars.

[189] Brian D. Johnson and Rebecca Richardson, "Race and Plea Bargaining" (2019). An earlier meta-analysis commissioned by the Vera Institute covering 34 studies examining six discretion points in prosecution (charging, pretrial release or bail procedure, dismissal, charge reduction, guilty plea, and sentencing) similarly reports that "the findings are complex and somewhat difficult to interpret. Overall, research finds that the effect of race and ethnicity on prosecutorial decision-making is *inconsistent*, and it *not always blacks or Latinos who are treated more punitively*" (Kutateladze et al., *Do Race and Ethnicity Matter in Prosecution?* [2012], p. 7, my italics). In the section on guilty plea, the authors point to only one study documenting that black defendants are less likely to plead guilty than their white counterparts (p. 14). They also warn that "it is possible that studies finding differences by race and ethnicity were more likely to be published and thus are overrepresented in this review (p. 17).

[190] Megan C. Kurlychek and Brian D. Johnson, "Cumulative Disadvantage in the American Criminal Justice System" (2019).

be empirically linked to plea outcomes. The "shadow-of-the-trial" model driven by economics flatly ignores race. Altogether, there is "little evidence of widespread and overt discrimination in guilty plea processes"; "evidence of racial disparity in negotiated pleas remains decidedly mixed"; "few studies explain the underlying reasons for racial differences in pleading guilty, or their potential to contribute to systemic disparity in punishment."[191]

In total, Johnson and Richardson are forced to concede that extant scholarship works with a grossly simplified version of plea bargaining (there is not even an agreement across authors as to what constitutes it); that bargaining "may be a fertile ground for implicit bias" but there is no evidence thereof; that racial differentials in negotiating power in the broader society "may extend" to plea negotiation but there are no data to this effect; and that racial differences in plea discounts "may contribute to patterns of racial inequality" but we just do not know. So should the burden of proof not fall on those who *assume* that plea bargaining is consistently skewed by race? Meanwhile, critics of negotiated justice as coercive and secretive should take heart from one consistent finding: African-American and Latino defendants are less likely than their white counterparts to plead guilty and thus more likely to go to trial, which these same critics assume embodies "true justice."[192] But no one knows why for sure and with what results.

341

There are several plausible mechanisms for why African-American defendants decline to plead at a higher rate than whites: the plea offer they received from the pretrial prosecutor is higher than the offer tendered to facially similar whites; they distrust the process of negotiation more; and they are more likely to make the wrong bet on expected punishment at trial. In turn, the reason why they receive less favorable offers from the DA might be that their attorney is less zealous in their defense and prone to recommend taking higher offers. Indeed, an experimental study using vignettes found that "practicing defense attorneys displayed a tendency

---

[191] Johnson and Richardson, "Race and Plea Bargaining" (2019), pp. 88–9, 92, and 93.

[192] It is taken as an article of blind faith by legal scholars critical of plea bargaining that the constitutional right to a jury trial is the true incarnation of justice (see, for instance, Carissa Byrne Hessick's *Punishment Without Trial: Why Plea Bargaining is a Bad Deal* [2021]). But why should one trust the judgment of 12 random strangers culled from the voting rolls more than the expert deliberation of seasoned court professionals to determine guilt and set the quantum of punishment?

to recommend plea bargains for African-Americans that were longer than those that they would recommend for Caucasian clients."[193]

It could also be that counsel is zealous but anticipates a higher probability of a guilty verdict at trial due to the perceived racial bias of jurors or other factors that would increase this risk (for example, defending a client who does not "present" well visually, e.g., one who wears visible tattoos on his hands, neck, or face commonly associated with gangs), in which case they would recommend taking a higher offer which, perversely, might lead their client to go to trial, the very outcome they worked to prevent. One final mechanism: black defendants may be less likely to follow advice from counsel to take the offer on the table – the proverbial "client control" problem – because of a generalized distrust of attorneys, and of public defenders specifically, especially if that attorney is white.[194]

Clearly, multiple causal processes can impact a plea outcome to the detriment of black defendants outside of differential treatment by the prosecutor based on ethnic markers. The agent responsible for the added disparity – if there is one – may be the DA, defense counsel, the judge (who validates and otherwise shapes the plea), or the defendant himself, or some dynamic combination of this interacting quartet, not to forget the victim (who wields some influence on the trajectory of cases by pressing the prosecutor to pursue them and by resisting a given resolution). All of this suggest, at minimum, that the reflex accusation of the DA – I use the term "accusation" advisedly[195] – may be methodologically hasty and factually wrong multiple times over.

Note that, in San Pedrito county, the pretrial attorney crafts his opening offers with knowledge of the defendant's ethnic identity. The complaint he reviews contains a rubric with a small color picture taken at booking in the jail as well as a racial code (B for black, H for Hispanic, W for white, AP for Asian and Pacific Islanders, O for other).[196] When she sits in open court during the pretrial hearings, the prosecutor sees dozens of defendants for just a few short min-

---

[193] Vanessa A. Edkins, "Defense Attorney Plea Recommendations and Client Race: Does Zealous Representation Apply Equally to All?" (2011), p. 422.

[194] Matthew Clair explores the attorney-client dynamic in *Privilege and Punishment: How Race and Class Matter in Criminal Court* (2020), but his research design does not allow him to isolate the distinct impact of the race of defense counsel.

[195] A paradigmatic illustration is Angela J. Davis, "In Search of Racial Justice: The Role of the Prosecutor" (2013).

[196] That rubric lists height, weight, hair color, eye color, race, sex, build, baldness, and "complexion." The information is taken from the CRIMS database (Criminal Records Information Management System) managed by the state.

utes each over the course of the week and, by then, the offer on their case has already solidified. In the courtroom, crucially, the defendants who stick out visually are the rare whites. So students of plea bargaining – and criminal justice more generally – should look for *mechanisms that advantage whites* rather than mechanisms that disadvantage blacks. *White leniency and not black severity* is the puzzle that needs resolving. Note, moreover, that, in continuing negotiations after preliminary examination and before trial is set, the "prepped" file does not contain any racial identifier so the head of the trial team is crafting his last-ditch offers from behind a veil of ethnic ignorance.

It should further be stressed that the American criminology of court outcomes almost *never considers nor controls for class* as a matter of course, with the excuse that official data do not record class or its empirical indicators (occupation, education, employment, material assets, and housing status), let alone class fraction (which we saw creates critical differentiations). But it does not stop to reflect seriously on this fundamental design flaw which invalidates the vast majority of statistical studies of racial disparity in punishment using the method of residuals.[197] Indeed, it may well turn out that race in plea bargaining is in many cases a *proxy for class* – rather than the other way around – since color is closely associated with subproletarian status, which is itself commonly perceived as resulting from social profligacy and moral inferiority as springs for a disorganized life conducive to crime. Nothing sinks a defendant deeper than the intimation of a flawed moral character.

In the single most ambitious and rigorous statistical study on the topic, Besiki Kutateladze and colleagues make a valiant but ultimately feeble attempt at capturing "socioeconomic status" in their study of ethnoracial "cumulative disadvantage" in prosecution and sentencing in New York county by using as proxies the type of defense attorney (public or private) and the characteristics of the neighborhood of arrest.[198] They find that both factors significantly reduce racial disparities but do not eliminate them. But these proxies are poor and patently unreliable (to be sure, Kutateladze

343

[197] For a ruthless critique of the studied ignorance of class in conventional studies of crime, read John Hagan's 1991 presidential address to the American Society of Criminology, which could as well be delivered today: "The Poverty of a Classless Criminology" (1992). This critique is even more apposite for punishment.

[198] Kutateladze et al., "Cumulative Disadvantage: Examining Racial and Ethnic Disparity in Prosecution and Sentencing." No other study covering prosecutorial process and outcomes controls for class, according to the leading student of the topic (personal communication with Besiki Kutateladze).

et al. call them "rough" and ritually concede the need for "improved measurements").

The vast majority of defendants are poor and rely on public defenders so this is hardly a differentiating indicator sorting class and class fraction. Blacks are more likely to be arrested for minor offenses for which it would make little sense to hire private counsel even if they could. Along with class position, a crucial variable is whether the defendant was employed or not at the time of arrest, which is not available. The neighborhood of arrest is not always the neighborhood of residence (that information was not used because it was missing for half of the cases, suggesting a significant population of homeless defendants); poor segregated districts are also subject to more intense policing, which confounds the effects of place and differential law enforcement. Moreover, the study divides all of Manhattan, which hosts a population surpassing 600,000, into only four "neighborhoods," which indicates that the geographical units used drown the ability of residence to stand for class.

Finally, it is crucial to use *finely stratified indicators of class to capture gradations within the proletariat,* including differences between the stable working class, the precariat properly so-called, and the floating population of the street. We know from entire libraries of statistics on the labor and housing markets that blacks and whites are not similarly distributed across these three class fractions. This is the distribution that matters most if we are to reconstruct the mesh of extra-legal variables that commingle to shape prosecutorial outcomes. To achieve this distribution, we would need data on four variables: employment (yes/no), occupation (coded in three modalities), education (highest level), and housing status (owns, rents, homeless). If correctional administrations cannot produce them, a focused survey of the population in a given jail or prison could.

Kutateladze et al. conclude their study by very cautiously reporting "some tentative support for the expectation that racial differences in case processing might be partially tied to socioeconomic differences."[199] "Some," "tentative," "might," "partially": the importance of class is not

---

[199] Ibid., p. 540. Kutateladze and his colleagues overlook the landmark book by Bruce Western, *Punishment and Inequality in America* (2006), which demonstrates the steep and systematic impact of class on punishment (using education as a proxy for class and imprisonment as the main judicial outcome), from its incidence to its concentration to its consequences. This impact has been further substantiated since by Muller and Roehrkasse in "Racial and Class Inequality in US Incarceration in the Early Twenty-First Century" (2022), who show that class produces a much steeper gradient of inequality in punishment than race does. How could class so powerfully shape judicial outcomes without shaping prosecution?

established by pointing to the *social mechanisms* that determine its impact on punishment (starting with deciding whether the defendant is in or out of custody during pretrial proceedings, which powerfully influences plea and sentence downstream), but by the small magnitude of its statistical effect in the quantitative weighing of predictive variables. As for race, the use of the quartet white, black, Hispanic, and Asian confounds the effect of *skin tone* as applied to blacks and whites, which has consistently been shown to be a better predictor of criminal justice outcomes than the black/white dichotomy, with light-skinned African-Americans receiving about the same amount of punishment as whites.[200] Finally, while the statistical impact of race is significant, its substantive impact is very minimal: the distribution of whites and blacks across combinations of punitive outcomes at the end of the judicial course is virtually identical except for the most punitive combination (defendants who were both detained pretrial and sentenced to incarceration), for which the white–black disparity is a meager 1 to 1.18, not far from parity.[201]

345

One last note of warning about quantitative studies of race and prosecution based on administrative data. These data are riddled with inconsistencies and missing information, with racial identification varying across justice agencies and across the stages of penal processing. It is not uncommon for the same individual to be classified differently by the police (an etic *categorization* by the arresting officer based on visual cues), the jail (where "booking" involves asking the detainee for his emic *identification*), the court's case tracking system (in California, CINI, Criminal Information Index, recently replaced by CRIMS, Criminal Records Information Management System and Odyssey, the internal portal that borrows its race data from the jail), the prosecutor's filing database (which takes race from the police but includes prior criminal cases and therefore prior classifications that may differ), and the probation intake form (based on a face-to-face interview during which race may be determined by either the officer or the convict depending on the parties), not to mention the prison data management system (ARMS, Automated Reentry Management

---

[200] Traci Burch, "Skin Color and the Criminal Justice System: Beyond Black-White Disparities in Sentencing" (2015); Ryan D. King and Brian D. Johnson, "A Punishing Look: Skin Tone and Afrocentric Features in the Halls of Justice" (2016); Ellis P. Monk, Jr., "The Color of Punishment: African Americans, Skin Tone, and the Criminal Justice System" (2019); Kenneth Barideaux Jr et al., "Colorism and Criminality: The Effects of Skin Tone and Crime Type on Judgements of Guilt" (2021).
[201] Kutateladze et al., "Cumulative Disadvantage: Examining Racial and Ethnic Disparity in Prosecution and Sentencing," table 4, last panel on the right, p. 536.

System) which uses its own ethnic palette and features a mix of identification and categorization, or recategorization if the correctional case record staff person deems it necessary at "reception" (for instance, if the latest jail booking classification does not match prior prison classification).[202]

The result is proliferating ethnic misalignment, particularly pronounced for light-skinned African-Americans, Latinos, Middle Easterners, and persons of ambiguous phenotype or who have been in justice databases for decades (across which administrative classifications have changed). The result is that the prosecutor, the defense attorney, and the judge may have different racial readings of a given defendant. The latter's ethnoracial label may also change from penal input to output: an Afro-Latino arrested as "black" by the police may be sentenced as "Latino"; a defendant may be prosecuted as "white" only to be placed on probation as "Middle-Easterner"; a Cape Verdean mischaracterized as Latino by the police may serve time as black according to prison data.[203] Even if these inconsistencies in racial classification concern a small proportion of defendants or convicts, racial disparities are also small, so nothing indicates that they are not affected by these inconsistencies. In his fine-grained qualitative study of defendant–attorney relations in the Boston courts, Matthew Clair dug deep into administrative data for one courthouse and found them so "incomplete and imprecise" that he decided not to use them for ethnic distribution and to estimate how "race" impacted legal outcomes.[204] A methodological alarm needs to be sounded.

---

[202] In the general US population, Saperstein and Penner document racial mobility in classification over time whereby successful or high-status individuals are redefined as white (or not black) and unsuccessful or low-status individuals as black (or not white) (Aliya Saperstein and Andrew M. Penner, "Racial Fluidity and Inequality in the United States" [2012]). More crucially, they also demonstrate that contact with the punishment apparatus (police arrest, criminal conviction, or incarceration) increases the probability that a person is categorized as black (Aliya Saperstein et al., "The Criminal Justice System and the Racialization of Perceptions" [2014]). If penalization results in "blackening" on the outside, there is reason to believe that it has the same effect inside and along the stages of criminal processing.

[203] On the ground-level tussles over racial categorization inside California jails and prisons, institutional and micro-interactional, see Philip Goodman's stunning article, "'It's just Black, White, or Hispanic': An Observational Study of Racializing Moves in California's Segregated Prison Reception Centers" (2008), and the equally provocative piece by Michael L. Walker, "Race Making in a Penal Institution" (2016).

[204] Clair, *Privilege and Punishment*, p. 204.

To recapitulate: *race hides skin tone and class is missing* (and, with it, class fraction). Yet the cottage industry of research on "racial disparities" in punishment using the former and ignoring the latter continues to flourish as if nothing were the matter.[205] My point here is not to defend one thesis or another and especially not the idea of some kind of ontological priority of race or class as principle of social vision and division – that is decided by historical struggles waged in social space, the bureaucratic field, and the field of power.[206] It is to suggest that the study of class, race, and penal processing and sanction is in dire *need of epistemological reflection, conceptual clarification and methodological reformulation,* starting with the very terms commonly (mis)used to examine bias in the operation of criminal justice.

347

Three seemingly self-evident terms are at play here: the "three Ds" of difference, disparity, and discrimination; but their meaning is imprecise and their interrelations complex and often confused in extant research. In addition, all three are connected in non-obvious ways to the category of inequality standing at the epicenter of the social sciences, but which itself is also far from obvious, as demonstrated in Amartya Sen's lucid *Inequality Reexamined.*[207] A brief analytical excursus is in order here for the sake of clarity.

When does a *difference,* defined as a measurable gap in outcome between categories, turn into a *disparity:* when it defies our collective expectations, when it offends our moral sensibility, when it violates legal statutes, or when it cannot be satisfactorily explained by background factors and institutional processes? But if the latter do not infringe on morality or legality, why do we not continue to talk of difference or switch to the neutral language of inequality? If a disparity is an *unfair difference,* which is generally implied, whose standard of fairness is at play and measured by what scale? For instance, as commonly defined, the "disparity" in imprisonment between whites and blacks in the US in the 1990s was 1 to 7, but 80 percent of it was fully accounted for by differences in rates of violent offending:[208] so

[205] Shawn Bushway et al., "Understanding Race Disparities in Criminal Court Outcomes" (2025).

[206] Wacquant, *Racial Domination,* pp. 197–205.

[207] Amartya Sen, *Inequality Reexamined* (1992). For a cogent demonstration of the centrality and multidimensionality of inequality in human societies defined, not just as distributed resources but as an affront to human dignity, read Göran Therborn's bold tome on *The Killing Fields of Inequality* (2013).

[208] Michael Tonry, *Malign Neglect: Race, Crime, and Punishment in America* (1995). To add complexity, this differential propensity to violent crime is itself accountable in terms of class, race, space, and state.

should disparity not be the 20 percent residual of 1 to 1.4 and should we then consider it large or small? Certainly it is much closer to parity than the disparities between Euro-Americans and African-Americans of 1 to 2.2 for their unemployment rates and 1 to 9 for their economic assets.

Another complication: should we use as our measuring stick of inequality in punishment *relative* disparity (a ratio of measures) or *absolute* disparity (the gap between them)? Imagine that a black defendant is offered a guilty plea deal for 30 years of prison on a carjacking case while a facially similar white defendant is offered a 10-year deal: the relative disparity is 1 to 3 and the absolute disparity is 20 years – and, in this hypothetical, a product of prosecutorial discrimination. Now consider a second scenario where the African-American defendant is tendered a 9-year deal and his Euro-American counterpart 3 years. The relative disparity is still 1 to 3 but the absolute disparity falls down to 6 years. Clearly, these two disparity scenarios are not equivalent from a sociological, moral, and policy standpoint. The lower the penalties, the less impactful discrimination. Does relative disparity matter as much when absolute disparity is limited or diminishing?

Is the opposite of disparity equality or is it equity, which would imply a difference of treatment needed to achieve a fair outcome? But then we are back to square one with difference, except that it is now burdened with moral judgment.[209] But it is a mistake to equate difference with inequality. In his perspicacious critique and provocative revision of Charles Tilly's influential tome on *Durable Inequality*, Rogers Brubaker argues conclusively that "ascribed categorical differences are not *intrinsically* linked to inequality; *different* does not necessarily imply *unequal*. The relation between difference and inequality is contingent, not necessary; it is empirical, not conceptual."[210]

Next, what is the relationship between disparity and discrimination? This is where the confusion peaks. Many analysts assume that every difference is a disparity and that every disparity (especially when dealing with race in the punishment apparatus) is proof positive of discrimination. This overlooks the demonstrable fact that unequal outcomes can be produced by a multiplicity of mechanisms, many of

---

[209] Over the past dozen years in the US, the fashionable term promoted by philanthrocapitalist foundations and unthinkingly borrowed by many scholars is the moral category of "inequity" – so much more innocuous than good old inequality and better suited to signaling virtue in the current racial climate.

[210] Rogers Brubaker, *Grounds for Difference* (2015), p. 11, original italics; Charles Tilly, *Durable Inequality* (1998).

which do not entail differential treatment based on real or putative categorical membership (as when ethnic income differences rooted in the labor market translate into residential segregation).[211] Finally, does disparity that is fully explained by non-discriminatory factors cease to be one and therefore revert to the status of "mere" difference? Is there such a thing as a warranted disparity or is it a *contradictio in adjecto*?

All of this is to say that students of race, class, and prosecution, or punishment more generally, need to engage in a collective work of clarification without which they will continue to conflate difference, inequality, disparity, discrimination, and "inequity" in accordance with the fluctuating parameters of scholarly common sense and public debate. They will continue, that is, to confuse analytical, empirical, ethical, and political argumentation violating a fundamental tenet of social science: that it eschew moralism.

349

Judicial tagging and relational contracting

By taking the reader to the point of production of punishment, I have documented in granular detail the technical intricacy, social configuration, and symbolic frames that both channel and sustain negotiated justice as an ongoing collective achievement. Plea bargaining stands at *the epicenter of courtwork*, that is, the social and legal labor collectively expended to transform judicial input into output – a body out of place into a body tagged and disciplined. In the case at hand, it differs from the activities of the "courtroom workgroup" canonized by the court community perspective rooted in the path-setting work of James Eisenstein and Herbert Jacob.[212]

---

[211] For a conceptual précis on discrimination and a discussion of non-ethnic mechanisms that produce ethnic "disparities," see Wacquant, *Racial Domination*, pp. 123–30, and Andreas Wimmer, *Ethnic Boundary Making: Institutions, Power, Networks* (2013).

[212] The trio of James Eisenstein, Roy Flemming and Peter Nardulli are the authors of a trilogy, formed by *The Contours of Justice* (1988), *The Tenor of Justice* (1988) and *The Craft of Justice: Politics and Work in Criminal Court Communities* (1992), which builds on Eisenstein and Jacob's *Felony Justice* (1977). This trilogy stands as the touchstone for social studies of the county criminal court one half-century later, along with Malcolm Feeley's *The Process is the Punishment* (1979), which complements the "community" perspective with an "open systems" approach. See also the monograph by Jeffery T. Ulmer, *Social Worlds of Sentencing: Court Communities Under Sentencing Guidelines* (1997), for an extension of the "courtroom workgroup" approach drawing on symbolic interactionism.

For the authors of *Felony Justice*, taking an organizational perspective, the "courtroom workgroup" is the stable set of actors who *visibly* come in *direct interaction* in *open court* to process cases; it includes "prosecutors, defense counsel, clerks, bailiffs, and to a limited extent defendants." It is based on consensual norms and values – enshrined by the warm and fuzzy notion of "community" – that make it possible to achieve four goals: dispose of the caseload, reduce uncertainty, maintain group cohesion, and do justice.[213] By contrast, I propose that courtwork is organized by the *invisible structure* of the local judicial field, anchored in the *semi-private wings* of the court, extended to the offices of the District Attorney, Public Defender, and private counsel, and centered on the *trio* of prosecutor, defense attorney, and judge. Crucially, courtwork is the result, stake, and instrument of *ongoing struggles over the ends and means of justice*, a relation of material and symbolic power between the members of the trio and their respective sponsoring institutions that cannot be reduced to observable face-to-face encounters.[214] Beneath the veneer of consensus lurks conflict over the primary mission of the court: restore victims and rehabilitate offenders (Left hand of the penal state) or neutralize and sanction miscreants (Right hand of the penal state); reformation or retribution; Benthamite rationality or Kantian deontology. Those two competing readings of criminal law are always in the cards, even when retributive prosecutors and punitive judges rule the roost, as each can be activated by the right alignment of actors.[215]

---

[213] Eisenstein and Jacob, *Felony Justice*, pp. 24–8.

[214] Here we must beware of the danger of "concept hagiography": "Courtroom workgroup *can* matter" for judicial outcomes "but in all likelihood more on the margin." Milton Heumann et al., "Courtroom Workgroups: 'A Prosecutor, a Defense Attorney, and a Judge Walk into a Bar'" (2021), p. 286.

[215] This is demonstrated by the rise of "reform prosecutors" in a number of left-leaning cities across the United States after the mid-2010s, as recounted by Emily Bazelon, *Charged: The New Movement to Transform American Prosecution and End Mass Incarceration* (2020). This sprouting has created a lot of excitement among opponents of "mass incarceration" and skepticism among abolitionists, but it remains to be seen whether it will endure, spread, and fulfill its promise. The jurisdictions concerned so far are a miniscule percentage of all counties even if they include large cities. Reform prosecutors have faced intense internal resistance and external pushback from governors, legislatures, and rich donors. A number of them in California (including Los Angeles, San Francisco, and Alameda county) have been recalled during their term or lost subsequent elections. Benjamin Levin, "Imagining the Progressive Prosecutor" (2020), and Ojmarrh Mitchell and Nick Petersen, "The Rise of Progressive Prosecutors in the United States: Politics, Prospects, and Perils" (2025).

It seems generous, perhaps even democratic, to include the ancillary support staff of the courthouse in the courtroom workgroup, as Eisenstein and Jacobs do, but then where do we stop? Why not include the court reporter, the bail bondsman, the probation officer sitting at the attorneys' desk, the social worker dispatched by the Public Defender's office, the behavioral health specialist advocating for diversion, the summer law clerk, the representative of pretrial services, the intake technician from the court-assigned residential treatment program who shows up to pick up defendants upon their conditional release, the arresting police officer who testifies against a motion to dismiss, the witness taking the stand, and the victim or victim's kin who come to elocute an impact statement at sentencing?[216] The deciding factor here has to be, not do they make an *appearance* in the courtroom, but do they make a *difference* in judicial output? In the two California counties I studied, when these characters show up on the scene, the plea bargaining decision has been sealed. What happens in the courtroom is a matter of bureaucratic packaging and ceremonial delivery.

351

In San Pedrito county, courtwork takes place, not in open court,[217] but in the wings of the courthouse, in a closed perimeter controlled by the DA's office – away from the gaze of the courtroom observer that anchors and thus hampers the conventional ethnography of the judicial institution, which rests on a continuous conflation of court, courthouse, and courtroom.[218] It also involves the judge as a prospective regulator and final arbiter, whose decisions are anticipated by the negotiators against the backdrop of past exchanges – which means that he does not have to act to influence outcomes. As for the defendant, whom Eisenstein and Jacob include in the courtroom workgroup, she is the *object rather than the subject of judicial tagging and penal processing*. Courtwork also serves not just to adjudicate cases, but also to reaffirm and reproduce the structural relationship of power between

---

[216] A strong case can certainly be made for the bail bondsman, as argued by Joshua Page and Christine S. Scott-Hayward, "Bail and Pretrial Justice in the United States: A Field of Possibility" (2022).

[217] This is the case in Carnival county as well as in the many counties depicted by Levine et al., "Sharkfests and Databases." It is safe to say that, as a rule, plea bargaining in large urban jurisdictions happens *in camera* and not in public, which implies that most cases pled overall are not resolved within eyesight of an external observer, undercutting the claims of the conventional ethnography of the courtroom (Lisa Flower and Sarah Klosterkamp, eds., *Courtroom Ethnography: Exploring Contemporary Approaches, Fieldwork and Challenges* [2023]).

[218] Leslie Paik and Alexes Harris, "Court Ethnographies" (2015); Carla J. Barrett, "Doing Court Ethnography: How I Learned to Study the Law in Action" (2018); Travers, "Court Ethnographies."

the DA's office, the PD's office and the bench that anchors the train of face-to-face interactions between attorneys.

In the courthouse, the crucial operation for the disposal of unruly bodies is *judicial tagging*. Tagging is a graduated process and a collective activity carried out by way of plea negotiation. It consists in the disputed assignation of the defendant to a penal category (comprising the crime acknowledged and the attendant punishment) recognized by the court and its agents: the transmutation of a human being in all of her biographical idiosyncrasy and behavioral complexity into a simplified legal designation recorded by the prosecutorial script of the plea, such as "11351 / 5FP / CTS / 4X / 296 /11590 / RFF." As we have seen, the terms of this script and their combination are a matter of contention stretched over time and shaped by the positional properties of the attorneys involved. Plea bargaining consists in people-tagging designed to facilitate people-processing by the penal machinery and thus bring disobedient bodies to heel.[219] It brings together the symbolic and material powers of the penal state as classification and stratification machine.

352

O → 11351 / 5FP / CTS / 4X / 296 / 11590 / RFF
Forfeit cash & contraband

Offer is to plead guilty to violation of Health and Safety Code section 11351 ("eleven-three-fifty-one"): possession of narcotics with intent to distribute; 5 years felony probation (and no prison time); credit for time served (in jail while awaiting resolution); four-way search (the police officer or probation agent has the right to search without warrant or motive the body, belongings, vehicle, and residence of the defendant); provide DNA sample for the California Department of Justice databank (two specimens of blood, a saliva sample, right thumbprints and full palm print impression of each hand); register under section 11590 as a "drug user" (for at least 5 years); pay restitution fund fines (a financial penalty ranging from $300 to $10,000); forfeit currency and drugs seized during the arrest.

---

[219] This validates Foucault's insight into penal sanction as a political economy of organisms reticent to social norms and economic dictates: "The systems of punishment are to be situated in a certain 'political economy' of the body: even when they do not make use of violent or bloody punishment, even if they use 'lenient' methods involving confinement or correction, it is always the body that is indeed at issue – the body and its forces, their utility and their docility, their distribution and their submission." Michel Foucault, *Surveiller et punir. Naissance de la prison* (1975), p. 30.

O → 496 / 2Y SP / 296 / Rest / RFF

Offer is to plead guilty to a violation of Penal Code section 496 ("four-ninety-six"): knowingly receiving, concealing, or selling stolen property (colloquially known as "fencing"), a "wobbler" here charged as a felony (due to the defendant already having an earlier misdemeanor conviction for the same offense); two years of state prison; provide DNA sample to the California Department of Justice databank; payment of direct restitution to the victim for the material losses caused by the crime plus state restitution fund fines.

O → 2800.2 (a) / 5FP / NSP / 4X / 296 / REST RFF

Offer is to plead guilty to a violation of Vehicle Code section 2880.2 (a): reckless evading of a police officer while driving (with a willful or wanton disregard for the safety of people or property); 5 years of felony probation; no physical state prison; four-way search; provide DNA sample to the California Department of Justice databank; pay state restitution fees.

Tagging results from the professional tug of war between the pretrial prosecutor and the defense attorney, with the judge playing the role of the referee or tipping the scales of punishment, thereby altering the tag (for instance, substituting 2YSP = two years of state prison for NPSP = no physical state prison). The mission of the defense attorney in plea bargaining is to fight tagging by minimizing the conduct and reminding the prosecutor that, behind the tag, there is a person with a history whose many facets are obscured by the script and by chipping away at its looser elements. The tag is a *judicial fiction* in the etymological sense of "fabrication" (from the Latin *fingere*, to knead and form out of clay) and in the bureaucratic sense that it always misrepresents the nature and severity of the conduct (as when three counts of robbery are pled down as one count, or when the crime of burglary is pled down to the lesser-included offense of trespassing, or when the use of a gun is effaced from the plea), but a fiction with consequences since it determines the further peregrinations of the defendant turned convict through the maze of the penal apparatus.[220]

---

[220] Bourdieu captures this effect of legal condensation thus: "Juridical fiction reduces the biological individual to the juridical personality it constitutes, abstracting all individual particularities, such as a constant relationship to property, a relationship that

Once a defendant is tagged in the give-and-take of plea negotiations, she literally disappears behind her tag. The tag *simplifies and signifies reality* by translating verdicts about conduct and person into legal and bureaucratic constructs for the sake of court processing. It is fashioned for *internal consumption* and follows the defendant for the rest of his court life since it can be retrieved later if the defendant reenters the penal funnel. It is different from the "RAP sheet" (Record of Arrest and Prosecution) and summary judgment which are accessible by outside actors, such as employers, realtors, financial institutions, or, for some categories of offenders, the broad citizenry.[221] Tagging is a form of *consequential categorization* that ultimately rests on the successful claim of court attorneys to the legitimate use of state power to apply force and stigma to the defendant morphing into convict. People-tagging is a *graduated, contested, and ongoing activity*. In the manner of a graffito, the tag is scrawled, partly effaced and possibly rewritten from hearing to hearing at the pretrial stage until the plea offer is accepted and duly entered into the record.

In terms of the theories of state power articulated in chapter 1, judicial tagging is an exercise in *symbolic violence* (Pierre Bourdieu) by a delegate of the Leviathan that leads to the delivery of legitimate *physical violence* (Max Weber). It is a technique for making criminal conduct *legible* and thus organizationally actionable for the state (James Scott). It sits at the core of the *infrastructural chain* flung by the penal Leviathan that reaches deep into the lives of the urban precariat (Michael Mann), its target of choice.

Judicial negotiation is best understood, then, not through the metaphor of the *market*, where supply meets demand punctually,[222] but

defines the owner, the donee, the usufructuary or the heir, but also the high-school graduate, the university graduate or the *agrégé*, or even the duke and the viscount, thus eternalized in a kind of timeless and transpersonal essence: the subject of law is nothing more than *a title* which, being a product of social magic, founded on social belief, transcends the individuals who bear it, simultaneously or successively." Pierre Bourdieu, *Microcosmes*, p. 612.

[221] Sarah Esther Lageson, "Criminal Record Stigma and Surveillance in the Digital Age" (2022).

[222] Use of the "marketplace" analogy is common in legal scholarship, especially by critics of negotiated justice: Feeley, *The Process is the Punishment*; Darryl K. Brown, *Free Market Criminal Justice: How Democracy and Laissez Faire Undermine the Rule of Law* [2016]; Thomas J. Miceli, *The Paradox of Punishment: Reflections on the Economics of Criminal Justice* [2019]). Its most ardent exponent is Stephanos Bibas (*The Machinery of Criminal Justice* [2012]), who argues that plea bargaining operates in the manner of an imbalanced and distorted market. For a broader discussion of the ins and outs of

with the concept of *relational contracting* coined a half-century ago by the legal scholar Ian Macneil. Macneil built on the classic article by Stewart Macaulay on routine transactions among industrial firms supplying goods and services to one another and the notion was further elaborated by the "transaction cost economics" of Oliver Williamson.[223] Surprisingly, it has never been deployed to analyze plea bargaining despite its obvious fit both theoretical and empirical.

Relational contracting characterizes a sequence of exchanges sustained by an ongoing social relationship premised on mutual trust and tacit norms that compensate for the lack of a formal contract. The present transaction is crucially informed by the trace of past exchanges and by the expectation of future exchanges between the same parties. This describes well the social organization and temporal tenor of the interactions between attorneys in Alphaville's pretrial room. Consider that the same public defender comes every week on the same day to negotiate her batch of cases. This means that, over a year's time, Julius and that attorney will have faced each other some 50 times and negotiated in the order of 250 cases. Moreover, they will have done so in an enclosed physical space with its own idioculture where other repeat actors will have witnessed their exchanges, and sometimes intervened in them.

355

No wonder prosecutors and defense counsel evolve minimal reliance and collaborative relations based on informal norms to keep the wheels of bargaining going, *non obstante* the adversarial framework within which they formally operate. In these repeated exchanges, the two attorneys gain a sense of each other's judicial personality, personal temperament, and moral proclivities. They gain the capacity to anticipate and smoothly adjust to the peculiarities of the other's rhetorical tactics and negotiation strategies. They can, in short, engage in *antagonistic cooperation* and reap its dual benefits – the definitive resolution and practical disposal of cases for the prosecutor, a discount on current punishment and its future consequences for the defense attorney – and extend their relationship into the future.[224]

---

plea bargaining as contract, which, remarkably, does *not* include relational contracting, see Robert E. Scott and William J. Stuntz, "Plea Bargaining as Contract" (1992).
[223] Macneil, "Contracts: Adjustment of Long-Term Economic Relations under Classical, Neoclassical, and Relational Contract Law"; Stewart Macaulay, "Non-Contractual Relations in Business: A Preliminary Study" (1963); Oliver Williamson, *Markets and Hierarchies: Analysis and Antitrust Implications* (1975).
[224] The notion of "antagonistic cooperation" was developed by a now-forgotten early American sociologist, William Graham Sumner (1840–1910), a passionate advocate

The prosecutor and public defender thus act as two agents of the state, the one to deliver punishment and the other to restrain it, whose *structural complicity*, inscribed in the positions they occupy in the local judicial field, makes it possible for the state to regain dispatching control over bodies out of place.

Structural position matters: the relations between the prosecutor and the public defenders take on a different tone and tenor depending on their location in the social architecture of the office. The exchanges between "negotiators," who occupy the left wing of the space of DAs, with "negotiators," who occupy the right wing of the space of PDs, are smooth and fruitful, while transactions involving "true believers" on either side tend to be fractious and even acrimonious – when they do not break down entirely. In one instance, Julius clashed openly with Roy, a veteran public defender known for his blunt manner and aggressive negotiation style, who, following the confrontation previously narrated (see *supra*, pp. 292–3), had stopped seeking offers for his clients to mark his discontent. Julius invited him into the negotiating room for a one-on-one face-off to clear the air: "He huffed and puffed and walked away, and it's like, *we're adults*, come on, this isn't *personal to me*, it's like, hey, I have a *job to do*." It took another couple of weeks for Roy to come around and reengage productively with Julius. This happened only after the two attorneys had an opportunity, on a slow morning, for an extended one-on-one social chat (in the presence of the sociologist), during which they hit on a shared interest in home improvement projects to do the "repair work" needed to restart their professional relationship.[225]

The first, *horizontal*, coordinate of position in the social space of the office is location on the axis running from "true believers" on the right to "negotiators" on the left. The second, *vertical*, coordinate is *seniority*: as they gain experience, with the exception of the principled "true believers" whose *certitudo sui* leads them to endure as such, attorneys on both sides of the aisle tend to tack to the middle.[226] They grow less anxious to demonstrate with fracas their ironclad commit-

of social Darwinism who also coined the concepts of folkways, mores, in-group and out-group, and ethnocentrism.

[225] For Goffman (*Interaction Ritual*, p. 112), "face-work" is a collaborative effort designed to restore the standing of persons involved in face-to-face encounters, giving social structure its "elasticity."

[226] For most prosecutors, being a true believer is an early *stage* in their professional trajectory which they outgrow as they gain experience and complete their training rotation across assignments. For a sizeable minority, it is a permanent *identity* with deep roots in their primary habitus that they will not relinquish.

ment to their professional mission, as they were in their younger days. Through the years, they gain experience and confidence in their technical abilities and social skills in court. They let go of the exaggerated adversarial posture they adopted as a novice and acquire a reputation as a "reasonable" player in the game. They realize that the run-of-the-mill matters they deal with are not "the crime of the century." They learn to pick their fights and so they are more likely to engage the other side productively. The gradual *positional convergence* that prosecutors and public defenders make as they gain seniority facilitates negotiated justice. Thus, in the give-and-take of the bargaining room, Julius notes that, while the "more seasoned" attorneys can get "a little overbearing," they are easier to get to an agreement with. The younger guns, "there's a lot of me saying, 'No, no, no' to them."

357

The "young prosecutor's syndrome" detected by Ronald Wright and Kay Levine is actually a *young court attorney's syndrome*: it applies to inexperienced defense attorneys, public and private.[227] Public defenders in particular have to let go of the romance of the trial and abandon their illusions about the innocence of their clients. They compensate by being aggressive and inflexible in negotiations: they file motions, they insist on holding more pretrial hearings when no agreement is made, and they hold on to an unrealistic evaluation of the "worth of the case."

There is also a "young judge's syndrome," not in terms of biological age but in terms of seniority in that job. Newly appointed judges are often nervous and insecure on the bench. They feel isolated (they no longer belong to an office) and vulnerable (everyone's behavior toward them has changed overnight due to their new role). They are wont to sweat a lot, speak too loudly and second-guess themselves (some will interrupt a hearing to dash to their chambers and discreetly check a legal technicality on their computer). They want to err on the side of caution and end up overshooting, as when judges who are former public defenders unwittingly take harsh decisions favoring the prosecution just to prove that they are not beholden to their long-time office.

Social affinity between the pretrial prosecutor and defense counsel based on class, ethnicity, and gender further facilitates negotiation as it provides shared categories of perception and communication

---

[227] Ronald F. Wright and Kay L. Levine, "The Cure for Young Prosecutors' Syndrome" (2014). Heumann reports similar observations in his 1978 book on *Plea Bargaining* (pp. 96–7): the new prosecutor adopts a rigid negotiation stance; he is cautious and afraid to make mistakes; he is wary of defense attorneys, about whom he has not build a baseline of information and a modicum of functional trust; and he is anxious about being fooled.

rooted in the primary habitus of attorneys. Julius will be more patient and "take more flak" as well as laugh more easily with black and Latino defense attorneys – some of whom he addresses as "bro" or "buddy," a term they reciprocate. There is also a level of social comfort and cultural confidence with defense attorneys who grew up in or near poor segregated neighborhoods and therefore have first-hand knowledge of the street culture in which most defendants are steeped.[228] Communication is more technical and subtly more formal with "white knights from the suburbs," that is, defense attorneys with a privileged social background who went straight "from their mama's house to college and law school and have never lived a real life." Prosecutors with a working-class background resent the fact that public defenders who were born "with a silver spoon in their mouth" take the side of the proverbial underdog.

The mainstream literature on prosecution focuses on the positional properties of the defendant to try to detect bias and discrimination. It overlooks the role played by the social trajectory and position of the negotiating attorneys in shaping judicial process and product. That literature focuses nearly exclusively on the impact of the defendant's race (anchored by the black/white dichotomy, thus disregarding color gradations that have been shown to be a better predictor of punishment) because race is a national obsession mirrored in scholarship and because all bureaucratic data are precoded by race.[229] If a class variable was made available (via occupation, education, and housing status at the time of arrest), this entire domain of inquiry would be revolutionized.

The human spear of the state

The prosecutor who runs plea bargaining is the human spear of the state. He is the penal state incarnate. He is the judicial Leviathan in action. (Remember the two-sided argument of the first chapter that penality is a core state capacity and that the state is the exclusive agency tasked with delivering legal punishment.) Out of the daily tussle with the bar and bench, he effectively rewrites criminal law at ground level and

[228] This is a major asset for attorneys on both sides. Those who have primary familiarity with the rules of street culture have a different depth and range of relations with defendants and victims who may respect them for that.

[229] See Jawjeong Wu, "Racial/Ethnic Discrimination and Prosecution: A Meta-Analysis" (2016), for a conventional panorama.

pinpoints the delivery of properly authorized material and symbolic violence. Pay attention to the terms of this carefully worded proposition. My argument here is emphatically *not* that the power of the prosecutor is "unlimited," "excessive," or "arbitrary," as commonly argued by legal analysts and social critics of the American justice apparatus, nor that the guilty plea is an adulteration of judicial equity.[230] On the contrary, the close-up analysis of plea negotiation sessions as they unfold at ground level demonstrates that the power of the prosecutor is finely calibrated, socially bounded, and impeccably legitimate.

Calibrated: "A court is not an assembly line and court officials are not automatons mindlessly stamping out endless copies of the same product."[231] Punishment is painstakingly adjusted to the specifics of cases, tailored to the facts at hand, angled by policy directives, and inflected by the tenor of the extended mesh of social exchanges between the pretrial prosecutor and the defense bar and bench. "Excessive" presumes some "normal" quantum of power, but set by what or whom? The cases that are resolved through negotiation never match the maximum or even the medium stipulated by criminal statutes – even when the defendant "pleads to the sheet" (that is, admits to all charges) in hopes that the judge will offer him a better deal than the pretrial prosecutor does. If there is excess, then, it is promulgated by legislators, not spawned by prosecutors, and the problem is distinctively political, not judicial.[232] If punitiveness rules (but, then again, using whose scale?), it is validated by the social demand of the citizenry in the jurisdiction in question,[233] and so the problem now resides in the extreme fragmentation and hyperlocalism of the bureaucratic field.

Bounded: The prosecutor is deeply embedded in a series of nested social spaces that shape her cognition, inform her emotions, and circumvent her conduct, starting with her team, supervisor, and work mates, continuing with defense attorneys and judges, and closing with courthouse tradition and the politics of crime in the county. Her

359

---

[230] A paradigmatic expression of this position is Davis, *Arbitrary Justice*, a book written by a former public defender. A popular account is Amy Bach, *Ordinary Injustice: How America Holds Court* (2009). Carissa Hessick argues that plea bargaining is "a bad deal" that has "undermined justice at every turn" by setting it against an idealized conception of the trial as the materialization of equity and fairness that is totally fictitious (*Punishment Without Trial: Why Plea Bargaining is a Bad Deal* [2021]).

[231] Feeley, *The Process is the Punishment*, p. 12.

[232] Even in DA's offices that refuse to bargain on charges as a matter of policy, as in Carnival county, haggling over sentences still results in significant discounts on the legally prescribed punishment.

[233] Máximo Langer and David Alan Sklansky (eds.), *Prosecutors and Democracy: A Cross-National Study* (2017).

discretion is real, but circumscribed; her power is considerable, but nonetheless constrained; her substantive sense of justice is pertinent, but shared and checked. For the line DA is not a "lonesome cowboy" riding the horse of his individual taste and impulses but an intensely social animal actualizing the possibilities of a structural position in a professional and judicial space that both contains and explains her strategic action.[234] She has a courthouse and office reputation which took her years to build and which can be lost in a day if she misuses her judicial power.

Legitimate: The prosecutor is dressed in the garb of the state and, so long as he follows his oath and grants the defendant minimal "due process," his actions are unimpeachable.[235] Formal rationality in the Weberian sense is his impersonal justification. Here the defense attorney plays a key role in *partnering* with him to roll out the ceremonial of equity. The public defender is especially pivotal, for she is employed, paid, and tasked by the state to limit the wrath of the same toward indigent citizens, wayward creatures of the dreaded underbelly of the city: she is the *state turning against the state* – the state, again, in action.[236]

The legitimacy of prosecutorial power is reinforced and validated by the judicial deportment and deeds of the defendant in court. The latter is, first, *rendered mute*: pursuant to the rules of criminal procedure in an adversarial system, he is spoken by his attorney.[237] According to plan, he never has any verbal exchange with the prosecutor and only

360

[234] The horror stories of gross penal abuse, blatant judicial excess, and outright illegality that fascinate, even hypnotize, scholars of the court (their articles teem with such anecdotes, generally culled from newspaper articles) and scandalize the general public are bound to happen in a disarticulated quasi-bureaucratic machinery processing some 17 million cases each year, and moreover a clientele receiving a service it did not ask for. The same horror stories could be told about mistreatment in schools, hospitals, or child protection agencies. The task of the sociology of prosecution as a people-tagging institution is to focus on the unremarkable normal case, not the outrageous anomaly.

[235] "The lowliest judge – or, to trace the relation to its final links, the police officer or the prison guard – is tied to the theorist of pure law and to the specialist in constitutional law by a *chain of legitimacy* that removes his acts from the state of arbitrary violence" (Bourdieu, "La force du droit," as reprinted in *Microcosmes*, p. 332).

[236] The long history of legal, professional, and social struggles that resulted in the state taking over indigent defense in the United States is chronicled by Sara Mayeux, *Free Justice: A History of the Public Defender in Twentieth-Century America* (2020).

[237] Contrast with the French criminal trial, whose overriding purpose is to press the defendant to speak, and to speak volumes, as shown by Christiane Besnier, *La Vérité côté cour. Une ethnologue aux assises* (2017), and Philip Milburn, *Sociologie de la justice pénale* (2024).

faint communication with the judge – he utters "yes" or "no," or, better, "yes your honor," when asked about the different stipulations of the guilty plea, thereby acknowledging that the judge is deputized by the state as "fount of honor."[238] In the daily work of the court, the defendant is virtually unseen and unheard from; he is held away in jail or kept in holding pens in the secure area of the courthouse, only to make a brief and formalistic appearance in the courtroom, dressed in a jail uniform that erases his individuality. His fate is decided in confabulations happening in the corridors, witness rooms, and judge's chambers, not in the bureaucratic ceremonial of open court; he fades into the background of judicial action. Indeed, there are few things that irritate the bench and bar more than a defendant who chooses to go *pro se*, that is, waives their right to legal representation to fend for themselves in court and recover their voice, however faint.

361

While he ultimately decides to accept or reject a plea deal, the defendant does not set its terms and his choice is strictly circumscribed by "circumstances not of his own choosing" (to invoke Marx's celebrated formula capturing the structural determinants of history). His decision is, moreover, largely prefigured by the casting that his counsel gives to the plea offer on the table. Like it or not, the defendant is simply not a player but a prop in the legal dance, contrary to populist accounts who wish to generously endow him with "agency" in the courthouse.[239] He is just a body out of place, whose most salient and consequential properties are age and class, not race.

Except, and this is my second point, that the defendant is *made into the agent of his own condemnation*: by agreeing, albeit under duress, to plead guilty or no contest, regardless of whether he is factually guilty or not, he becomes a *de facto delegate of the state*. He is made to literally impose upon himself a criminal sanction – and to lock it in, since, in most jurisdictions, by entering a guilty plea he gives up his right to an appeal.[240] This allows the penal apparatus to proclaim, with good

---

[238] "It is the state which, acting in the manner of a central bank of symbolic capital, guarantees all acts of authority." Pierre Bourdieu, "Esprits d'État. Genèse et structure du champ bureaucratique" (1993a), p. 122.

[239] It is not happenstance if Matthew Clair's book, *Privilege and Punishment: How Race and Class Matter in Criminal Court* (2020), centers on conduct unfolding mostly outside the courthouse. Clair wishes to recover and foreground the agency of defendants (p. 12) but a close reading reveals a tale of *agency denied*. This is striking because the matters he discusses are all low-level misdemeanors with minor stakes, for which his informants appear out of custody, which should have given them great latitude.

[240] See Alexandra W. Reimelt, "An Unjust Bargain: Plea Bargains and Waiver of the Right to Appeal" (2010), for a typical denunciation of this "unjust bargain" because it "violates due process and contract law principles." This denunciation overlooks

reason, that rights are respected, proper procedure is followed, due process is implemented, and the wheels of justice appropriately spun, regardless of the substantive outcome. Did the accused not wield the sword of "justice" himself?

Students of negotiated justice, most of whom have never observed a prosecutor in action, have been transfixed by *two scholastic dualities: the trial versus plea bargain trade-off and the guilty versus innocent dilemma.* The trouble is that neither of these alternatives is pertinent to the day-to-day work of the criminal court. The first dualism is moot and has been for a long time:[241] everyone in the courthouse, whatever their role and defendant included, knows full well that the overwhelming majority of cases will be "dealt"; that only especially grievous crimes or spectacular crimes that have made media headlines will be decided by a jury; or matters in which particularly "hard-headed" defendants cannot be convinced to take the plea deal on the table, however favorable, and insist on going to trial against the better judgment of the court actors involved. In any case, most defendants who are in custody are not prepared to wait for their matter to come to trial – ten court days after initial arraignment (on complaint) plus 60 calendar days after PX (called arraignment on information) translate into a minimum of 74 days behind bars, which is an eternity, especially for members of the precariat whose life is disorganized and insecure and whose temporal horizon scarcely extends beyond a few weeks thence. Getting out of jail quickly is, moreover, essential to not losing your unstable job if you have one, your car left parked where you were initially arrested, and your housing for failure to pay rent on time.

The notion that bargaining is taking place "in the shadow of the trial" is a paper fiction concocted by legal scholars who are "too comfortable in their ivory tower," in the words of a veteran prosecutor in San Pedrito county.[242] If there is a "shadow" in which the plea is nego-

362

---

the power of juridical language: in the ceremonial of the entry of plea, the defendant affirms that he is pleading guilty "knowingly, intelligently, and voluntarily" (according to the script read by the judge), as well as attesting to the veracity of the factual specifics of his guilt. So, in terms of legal formalism, his culpability is placed beyond dispute.

[241] For a demonstration, see Feeley and Greenspan, "The Long History of Plea Bargaining."

[242] For a discussion of this theory, see Johnson et al., "Sociolegal Approaches to the Study of Guilty Pleas and Prosecution," pp. 484–6. A rare empirical critique is Shawn D. Bushway and Allison D. Redlich, "Is Plea Bargaining in the 'Shadow of the Trial' a Mirage?" (2012).

tiated, it is the shadow of the preliminary examination, the abbreviated preview of the trial during which the prosecutor must present sufficient evidence to the judge for the defendant to be "bound over" onto the path to felony trial. But, again, while the alleged offender has a right to a PX within ten court days, he almost never exercises it because he needs time to review "discovery" (the evidence bearing on the case), assemble the elements of a defense but, mostly, because "going to PX" will likely solidify or aggravate the charges he faces, which will result in the plea offer being raised. Most defendants want nothing to do with a trial given the strength of the evidence against them and, in serious matters, their attorney does their best to "age the case" in hopes that a better offer is forthcoming.

The second dualism is similarly irrelevant: everyone in the courthouse fully understands that the bulk of cases are handled and resolved on the *tacit presumption of guilt* – even as defendants insist ritually on their innocence to protect their dignity and save their self-image. Honest defense attorneys will readily concede that most of their clients are guilty in any event and they could not care less. Public defenders, in particular, make it a point of professional pride to provide "zealous representation" on behalf of their clients regardless of the specifics of the matter that landed them in court. Guilt does not matter one way or another, except in the cases in which the defendant is the wrong person and then, suddenly, the stakes of the game change, but these are few and far between. This is why, as a professional rule, the proficient defense attorney never asks her client whether he is guilty of the offenses with which he is charged. In any case, honest veteran public defenders and private counsel agree that the proportion of innocent defendants does not reach 5 percent.

For the compromise reached by the pretrial prosecutor and the defender typically centers on "whatisit" and not "whodunit." Haggling turns on the characterization of the alleged criminal conduct and the judicial profile of the suspect: is it a possession of narcotics for sale or simple possession, a robbery or theft, a burglary or trespassing, a homicide or manslaughter? Does the defendant have a record, "prison priors," or "strikes" that will automatically increase his sentence, and will the prosecutor formally allege them or not? If the prosecutor deems that his evidentiary basis is weak, if the case is a "garden-variety" felony or has been "knocking around" for a while, he will "deal it cheap" or sometimes dismiss it outright. Even a "slam dunk" may routinely be dealt "cheap" to make sure that matters are being "moved" efficiently. The criminal court is in the business of

363

churning out cases and turning up "proof" (or its silhouette), not "truth." The prolific cottage industry of research on the conviction of innocents is generous in spirit, but it is pursuing a beautified image of the court, a platonic ideal of justice that has little connection with the ordinary realities of criminal processing – in the United States or anywhere else.

By tracking the daily activities of the DA "dealing cases," the core of the judicial reactor in county criminal court, we discover how the penal state operates at ground level and we breathe life into the theoretical abstractions necessary to sketch its social architecture. We rearticulate structure and agent, position and interaction, the invisible and the visible, the concept and the percept. We capture the technical complexity and legal flexibility of prosecutorial work and peel away the layers of material and symbolic filters that circumscribe and channel discretion. We discover, finally, that the public defender and the defendant himself, who steadfastly oppose the prosecutor, also act as *de facto* delegates of criminal authority. Everywhere we turn, we discover situated, knowing, and skilled agents pursuing their professional mission and their personal aims who are nonetheless creatures of the penal state.

Coda

The Parable of Marx's Hangman and the Aporias of Abolitionism

"We are entitled to a portion of utopia within the limits of the possible."
— Pierre Bourdieu, *Le Sociologue et l'historien*, 1988

Time to wrap up my efforts to rethink the meshing of the state and punishment in the metropolis by joining the analytical and the empirical, the abstract and the concrete, the historical and the ethnographic. The penal Leviathan is central to the construction of the social order in modern societies: it institutes, dramatizes, and patrols the division between citizen and criminal. The citizen is a full-fledged member of the civic community; she stands on a *horizontal* plane of equality with others in that community; she enjoys the rights granted and the protections guaranteed by the state, starting with the provision of physical security and the defense of private property fostering peace in public space and safety in the home.[1] The convicted criminal is a truncated social being who stands in a *vertical* relationship of

---

[1] "Citizenship is a status bestowed on those who are full members of a community. All who possess the status are equal with respect to the rights and duties with which the status is endowed. There is no universal principle that determines what those rights and duties shall be, but societies in which citizenship is a developing institution create an image of an ideal citizenship against which achievement can be measured and towards which aspiration can be directed." This conflicts with social class which undergirds a system of inequality. T.H. Marshall, *Citizenship and Social Class* (1949), p. 18.

inequality to the citizen. He is submitted to the wrath of that same state; he is stained and struck by the calibrated force of its penal arm which effectively curtails his rights and prerogatives. He is the bearer of a temporary or permanent "discrediting differentness," to recall Erving Goffman's definition of stigma.[2] The convict is akin to an internal deportee in the domestic province of the state.

But the penal Leviathan remains a figurative entity until we pay attention to the skilled agents of flesh and blood who actualize its manifold powers day-to-day, as with the intelligent social and juridical machinery that is the criminal court: the power to penetrate the nether regions of the city's social and physical space, to render legible and hence manageable their populations, and to deploy legitimate physical and psychic violence to corral, tag, and dispatch unruly bodies. Yet, in advanced societies that sacralize the individual, the penal state holds within itself, as dormant potential or actual programs of public action, the two opposite philosophies of punishment descended from the Enlightenment: rational reformation premised on utility (Bentham) and emotive retribution derived from morality (Kant).[3]

Which of these two philosophies comes to drive the macro-level formulation and the micro-level implementation of criminal law and policy depends on *multiscalar struggles*, waged in social space, in the political and bureaucratic fields and, most importantly, within the penal state itself, by the gamut of agents engaged in a chain of interlinked confrontations over the meanings and means of "justice."[4] Police officers, prosecutors, victims' advocates, defense attorneys, judges, probation agents, and prison guards as well as immigration officials high and low are the organizational creatures who set in motion, dose, and steer penal power, effectively rewriting criminal law from the ground up. Yet their latitude is structurally circumscribed by the objective positions they occupy in the local judicial

---

[2] Erving Goffman, *Stigma: Notes on the Management of Spoiled Identity* (1963). Goffman also talks of "shameful," "stigmatic," "undesired," and "exotic" differentness.

[3] Remarkably, Montesquieu combined utilitarian and retributivist arguments in *L'Esprit des lois* (1748), as shown by David Carrithers, "Montesquieu's Philosophy of Punishment" (1998).

[4] Three illustrations of these internecine struggles are Didier Fassin et al., *Juger, réprimer, accompagner. Essai sur la morale de l'État* (2013); Emily Bazelon, *Charged: The New Movement to Transform American Prosecution and End Mass Incarceration* (2020); and Ezequiel Kostenwein (ed.), *Mundos judiciales y dinámicas sociales. Aproximaciones al funcionamiento de la justicia penal* (2023).

field and by the personal and professional trajectories that shaped their dispositions to tap this or that potentiality deposited in the punishment apparatus by past historical battles. This implies that the historicization of penal institutions must imperatively be supplemented by the historicization of the agents who populate them.[5]

The historical detour through empire disclosed that Sally Engle Merry's notion of "legal pluralism," forged to capture the hybrid character of the law in the colonies,[6] can be fruitfully adapted to grasp the deployment of penality in advanced society. The notion suggests that, whereas the law asserts itself as a unified body of neutral rules and formal processes, it is substantively differentiated along gradients of class and status (honor, civic membership, racial rank, or caste). Everywhere, albeit with varying intensities depending on country and epoch, there exist tendentially two regimes of punishment cohabiting under the same state canopy, one for the bourgeoisie and another for the precariat, especially when the latter is ethnically stigmatized and splintered: in ideal-typical terms, decorous justice *by the book* for the former and debasing justice *by the hook* for the latter.

Nicolas Herpin is the first sociologist to provide a multi-method account of the production of the social dualism of penality in advanced society belying the constitutional promise of isonomy. In *L'Application de la loi. Deux poids, deux mesures*, published way back in 1977 when the social studies of punishment had yet to emerge as a distinct domain of research, the French sociologist weds the ethnomethodological observation of 400 trials in open court with a full-bore quantitative analysis of the social determinants of criminal sanctions revealing the systematic and converging impacts of class, occupation, age, sex, and extraneity.[7] A decade later, the results of his inquiry were confirmed

367

---

[5] On the former, see Markus D. Dubber and Lindsay Farmer (eds.), *Modern Histories of Crime and Punishment* (2007). The latter task remains to be tackled through systematic social biographies of the protagonists of criminal law, but see the data in Paul B. Wice, *Criminal Lawyers: An Endangered Species* (1978); idem, *Public Defenders and the American Justice System* (2005), chapter 4; and Tore Bjørgo and Marie-Louise Damen (eds.), *The Making of a Police Officer: Comparative Perspectives on Police Education and Recruitment* (2023).

[6] Sally Engle Merry, "Legal Pluralism" (1988).

[7] Nicolas Herpin, *L'Application de la loi. Deux poids, deux mesures* (1977, roughly translating as *Enforcing the Law: Double Standards*). Herpin's originality is threefold: he mates direct observation and statistics; he encompasses the social properties of magistrates in his model; and he includes multiple measurements of class and its influence on multiple sentencing outcomes. By contrast, American scholars, such as Alfred Blumstein writing at about the same time, ignored class for both practical reasons

and deepened by the criminologist Bruno Aubusson de Cavarlay who proposed, in a striking formulation, that "the fine is bourgeois, suspended prison sentence proletarian, and firm prison sentence subproletarian."[8] My claim about the built-in dualism of penality goes three steps further than Herpin and his recent successors who have probed the statistical relationship between punishment and inequality. I contend that the organizational bifurcation of criminal sanction is anchored by routine statistical discrimination based on class; that it is essential to the political management of urban marginality and arises from the spatial targeting of the city's underbelly; and that it sanctifies the very inequalities it has a mission to protect and project. Penality, marginality, sociodicy: the analytical circle is complete.

Urban marginality, penal policy, and social rights

Now, I must disappoint the reader who is expecting me to close with extended normative meditations or smart critical reflections. My aim in this book has been not philosophical or practical but: (i) *theoretical* – to elaborate a sturdy concept of the penal state so as to put punishment on the map of students of the state and the state in the sights of scholars of punishment; (ii) *historical* – to dig out the roots of the prison in the sixteenth century to capture its original and perennial role as regulator of urban marginality as well as indispensable vehicle for the colonial project, an outlier case which throws light on the logic of penalization today; and (iii) *ethnographic* – to document in fine grain how punishment is assembled and deployed in the innards of the criminal court as the key throughput apparatus of criminal sanction.

There are dozens of recent articles and books making clever and pointed proposals to reform criminal justice on both sides of

(the variable is absent from administrative data) and ideological motives (US scholars tend to be class-blind and obnubilated by race), and they focused on incarceration severity as the main outcome, omitting non-custodial sentences even though these are by far prevalent. Hagan's 1974 comprehensive review of research on the impact of the social properties of offenders on criminal sanctions confirms this diagnosis: his discussion of studies using race as their independent variable runs over 12 pages as against two pages for studies considering socioeconomic status (using only occupation as variable). John Hagan, "Extra-Legal Attributes and Criminal Sentencing: An Assessment of a Sociological Viewpoint" (1974).

[8] Bruno Aubusson de Cavarlay, "Hommes, peines et infractions. La légalité de l'inégalité" (1985), p. 277.

the Atlantic, and little need to add more.[9] But let me nonetheless put some suggestions on the table based on tracking the penal state historically, comparatively, and ethnographically. In my view, the obvious candidates are to shrink the spectrum of conducts and situations defined as crimes; to redefine the mission of the police putting peace-keeping on a par with crime-fighting; to curtail differential policing by place (as the chief vehicle for class and ethnic disparities); to eliminate bail and otherwise reduce remand detention; to invest massively in the educational and social treatment of juvenile delinquency; to divert systematically defendants suffering from psychiatric disorders and alcohol and drug dependency or living on the streets; to boost funding for court-appointed attorneys defending indigent offenders; to maximize alternatives to incarceration such as community service, day fines, and restitution;[10] to deploy day prison and home custody while being mindful of "net widening"; to generalize deferred prosecution agreements and probationary judgments; to create a dedicated track for the processing of domestic violence in conjunction with women's rights protection, family counseling, and parenting classes; to banish mandatory minimums and limit the use of sentencing enhancements; to reduce prison terms across the board; to put a cap on the confined population and call a moratorium on the building of new carceral facilities (except for replacing slumlike establishments); to make those facilities less decrepit, chaotic, and hostile; to banish disciplinary wards and "supermax" facilities; to ramp up suicide prevention behind bars; to introduce or generalize

369

[9] The foibles of deliberate judicial change and its counterintuitive effects are anatomized in Malcolm M. Feeley's *Court Reform on Trial: Why Simple Solutions Fail* (1983), written over 40 years ago but more current than ever. An imaginative catalog of measures adapted to the US context is drawn up by Premal Dharia et al. (eds.), *Dismantling Mass Incarceration: A Handbook for Change* (2024). A more conventional multi-prong approach is advocated by Katherine Beckett, *Ending Mass Incarceration: Why It Persists and How to Achieve Meaningful Reform* (2022), and Franklin E. Zimring, *The Insidious Momentum of American Mass Incarceration* (2023). The possible futures of sentencing are mapped out by Michael Tonry, *Sentencing Fragments: Penal Reform in America, 1975–2025* (2016), chapter 6. On the French case, read Jean Bérard and Jean-Marie Delarue, *Prisons, quel avenir?* (2016); on the Italian case Luigi Manconi and Giovanni Torrente, *La pena e i diritti. Il carcere nella crisi italiana* (2015); on the Portuguese case, António João Latas (ed.), *Mudar a justiça penal. Linhas de reforma do processo penal português* (2012).

[10] Variants of "community service" exist in most advanced countries, *travail d'intérêt général* in France, *Gemeinnützige Arbeit* in Germany, *lavoro di pubblica utilità* in Italy, *samfunnsstraff* in Norway, etc., but it is everywhere vastly underutilized. It should be systematized for first-time offenders.

schooling for prisoners to stamp out illiteracy and change everyday life inside the walls; to radically improve medical services and mental health care (including for tackling depression *caused* by incarceration); to provide real resources for inmate amelioration and reentry instead of merely paying lip service to rehabilitation; and to roll back the collateral penalties attached to a criminal record and expunge the latter by statute after a set maximum of years.

Even implementing a small subset of these measures would result in a sea change in penal input, throughput, and output. The problem with justice reform, however, has never been the lack of practical solutions but the lack of political will to implement them. If I was minister of justice, my three most urgent measures would be to ramp up community service, day prison in lieu of jailing, and schooling behind bars.

Add to this the requirement of *democratic transparency and accountability* at key stages of the penal process. Every year, the police, court, and jail/prison should be required to publish data on key indicators of activity (input, throughput, output, budget allotment, staff allocation, spatial distribution, etc.), including the class, ethnic, and geographic profile of their clientele and their differential treatment at the successive stages of the penal process. This yearly publication would be subjected to biannual scientific evaluation and public debate. Policies and priorities would be clarified and elected officials would then be required to provide an assessment and present a plan to remedy glaring problems such as the incidence of police brutality, insufficient numbers of trial judges, ineffective assistance of counsel, sordid conditions of detention, unwarranted disparities, etc. Transparency is no silver bullet but opacity is definitely a hindrance to the civic oversight of the penal state.

Making the penal state transparent

A number of US states have attached a "racial impact statement" to criminal legislation mandating consideration of the possible disparities caused by the proposed laws – but, remarkably, no "social class impact statement" has been envisaged (1). "Progressive prosecutors" also in the US have made data availability one of their priorities, which is not without dangers and difficulties because these data are tricky and difficult to interpret, but it is a step in the right direction (2). A third-party monitor could be tasked with evaluating and reporting on the functioning of the police and the court.

France has an independent office for the "oversight of places of confinement" (*contrôleur général des lieux de privation de liberté*) which publishes an annual report submitted to the presidency and to parliament. Its prerogatives could be expanded and parliament required to debate the report and act on its recommendations or justify inaction. It could be granted a sanctioning power, rather than a mere reporting role (3). Italy has a similar agency, the *garante nazionale dei diritti delle persone private della libertà personale*, endowed with the authority to visit and oversee all institutions of detention and which formulates critiques and recommendations to the relevant agencies. Its work is complemented by Antigone, an association mandated by the Italian Ministry of Justice to visit prisons which produces a compendium of its observations annually.

In Norway, the national correctional services, court administration, and police are required to publish yearly reports with indicators of bureaucratic performance. But the population data focus on nationality, region, age, and gender and do not include the crucial variables of class and ethnicity. The Parliamentary Ombudsman for Scrutiny of the Public Administration (*Sivilombuds-mannen*) regularly inspects the country's prisons on multi-day visits yielding compact factual and often critical reports scrutinizing the everyday procedures and institutional facts of carceral life. But these reports are rarely included in the academic and public debates on criminal justice, showing that the availability of data is not by itself sufficient to create policy clarity.

1. Nicole D. Porter, *Racial Impact Statements* (2021).
2. Caitlin Glass et al., "Prosecutorial Data Transparency and Data Justice" (2024). The Prosecutor Performance Indicators (PPI) program run by Besiki Luka Kutateladze at Florida International University has elaborated metrics by which to assess the output of DA's offices. A warning: it is easy to get mesmerized by percentages and graphics, but they falsely isolate the actions of prosecutors when output results from a mix of factors, most of which are beyond the control of the DA, such as the quality of the police complaints, trends in crime, a penury of clerks or judges, budget allowances, etc.
3. Nicolas Fischer, "Entre droit et savoirs professionnels. L'action des membres du contrôleur général des lieux de privation de liberté français" (2016).

All these measures fall into the material register and they are immediately actionable to produce effects in the short term. Some of them require political decisions or legislative action; others can be taken through simple bureaucratic fiat. Symbolic changes are also needed to thwart penalization as marginality management, such as reducing the stigma of judicial conviction, loosening the discursive entwining of ethnicity and criminality, or changing representations of poor segregated neighborhoods as cauldrons of moral perdition bubbling with depravity and brutality. But these mental changes are typically slower and more difficult to accomplish as they involve altering collective categories of perception and appreciation, political work that can take up to a generation as it is hindered by the hysteresis of symbolic structures rooted in historical encounters going back decades.[11] At the same time, material turns can foster symbolic transformations, which means that there is a Gramscian battle to be waged on the cultural front over the sulfurous association of class, ethnicity, dangerosity, and penality in the city.

Yet the social theory, history, and ethnography of the penal state converge to teach us that many of these reforms will have minimal or temporary effects when it comes to the hard core of penal outcasts. They will fail to resorb it so long as marginality continues to fester and to intersect with denigrated ethnicity in the defamed districts of dispossession of the metropolis: the American hyperghetto, the French *banlieue*, the British "sink estate," the "*utsatta områden*" of Sweden, etc., which are the primary purveyors of "penal prey." One last diagram helps us visualize this claim by charting the *vicious cycle of unruly marginalization and reactive penalization* (figure 15). When the state lets social precarity diffuse and urban dereliction brew, it feeds social, moral, and symbolic disorder as well as the collective imaginary of fear and loathing associated with the city's badlands,[12] to which it then responds by rolling out its penal apparatus to contain local trouble and assuage public concern. But the penalization of disruptive poverty only aggravates urban destitution, disorder, and dread, thus further entrenching marginality, which festers again, and the causal carousel keeps on turning.

---

[11] This is demonstrated by Khalil Gibran Muhammad, *The Condemnation of Blackness: Race, Crime, and the Making of Modern Urban America* (2011), in the case of African-Americans coming into northern cities at the start of the twentieth century, and Emmanuel Blanchard, *La Police parisienne et les Algériens (1944–1962)* (2011), in the case of the Algerians residing in metropolitan France at the dusk of colonial rule.
[12] Loïc Wacquant, *The Invention of the "Underclass": A Study in the Politics of Knowledge* (2022); Henri Rey, *La Peur des banlieues* (1996); Miguel Chaves, *Casal Ventoso: Da gandaia ao narcotráfico. Marginalidade económica e dominação simbólica em Lisboa* (1999); Paolo Grassi, *Barrio San Siro. Interpretare la violenza a Milano* (2022); Bernd Belina, *Gefährliche Abstraktionen: Regieren mittels Kriminalisierung und Raum* (2023).

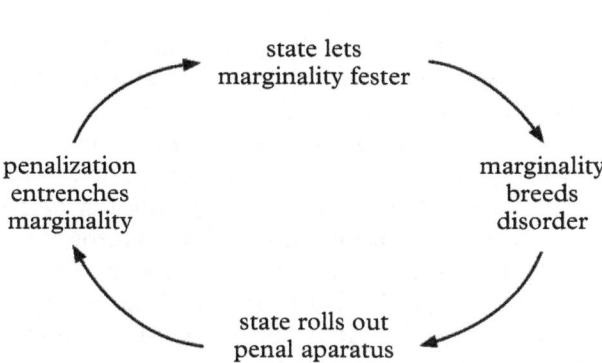

Figure 15 The vicious cycle of urban marginalization and penalization

373

So I will escape with a theoretical pirouette by invoking what we could call the parable of Marx's hangman. In an article on the death penalty published in the *New York Daily Tribune* in 1853, Karl Marx writes: "Is there not a necessity for deeply reflecting upon an alteration of the system that breeds these crimes, instead of glorifying the hangman who executes a lot of criminals to make room only for the supply of new ones?"[13] Marx's formulation suggests that the best criminal justice reform is to act upstream and *stanch the flow of offenders entering the penal funnel*. It recommends "switching hands," so to speak, and strengthening the Left hand of the state by building its organizational and ideological capacity to reduce social inequality, curb dispossession, and attenuate ethnic division in the polarized metropolis.

Thus the most efficient measures to shrink the societal footprint and minimize the repercussive effects of state punishment do not concern the penal apparatus itself.[14] They include providing free daycare and universal preschool; eliminating childhood exposure to environmental hazards (air and water pollution, lead, noise) that gravely impair human development; reducing academic truancy and boosting high-school completion rates; offering summertime jobs for teenagers; enhancing employment among young men sidelined by their lack of skills, hiring discrimination, and the structural degradation of the low-wage labor market (all of which makes the street economy

[13] Karl Marx, "Marx and Engels on Crime and Punishment" (1991), p. 55.
[14] A powerful argument for the economic, social, and medical treatment of criminality based on clear causal reasoning and evidence is Randi Hjalmarsson, *Social Policies as Crime Control* (2022).

irresistibly attractive); providing drug and alcohol rehabilitation on demand; and offering mental health care and universal family counseling to reduce domestic violence, the most insidious source of criminality within and across generations, direct and indirect.

These measures, which amount to expanding and *institutionalizing social rights*, can be bundled together and pointed at neighborhoods of relegation to ensure maximum impact. If the vector of penalization is spatially targeted, so must the measures designed to derail it. In the metropolis of the capitalist West, *engrained marginality walks hand in hand with prolific penality.*[15] It is not happenstance if the countries that have best curbed carceral inflation are those that have managed to prevent the formation of isolated, leprous and hypersegregated redoubts of ethnicized poverty in their cities in which an intricate street economy flourishes: Germany, Austria, Finland, and Canada.

The historical and comparative sociology of punishment reveals that *penality is foundational to the state* and that *the modern bureaucratic state remains the paramount fount of criminal deterrence, surveillance, and sanction*, notwithstanding attempts at, and claims of, devolution, privatization, and "governmentalization."[16] In particular, the liberal

[15] Remarkably, to take panoramic articles each reviewing a broad spectrum of research, the prevalence, persistence, and depth of (racialized) urban marginality do not figure among the core causes of penal policy put forth by Nicola Lacey et al., "Understanding the Determinants of Penal Policy: Crime, Culture, and Comparative Political Economy" (2018), and by Michael Tonry, "Punishments, Politics, and Prisons in Western countries" (2022). They are also absent from Sara Wakefield and Christopher Uggen's discussion of "Incarceration and Stratification" (2010), Michael Campbell and Heather Schoenfeld's model of "The Transformation of America's Penal Order: A Historicized Political Sociology of Punishment" (2013), and Katherine Beckett's reconsideration of "The Politics, Promise, and Peril of Criminal Justice Reform in the Context of Mass Incarceration" (2018). Even Jessica Simes et al.'s call to study "Policing, Punishment, and Place: Spatial-Contextual Analyses of the Criminal Legal System" (2023) decenters the metropolis and its badlands in favor of a catholic geographical approach. The rare scholar who insists on the role of neighborhoods of urban relegation and their distinctive social ecology is Robert Sampson, as in "Criminal Justice Processing and the Social Matrix of Adversity" (2014) and a stream of related publications on doubly segregated redoubts of "concentrated disadvantage" and "correlated adversities." This line of work is also mined by Sampson's erstwhile student Patrick Sharkey in *Uneasy Peace: The Great Crime Decline, the Renewal of City Life, and the Next War on Violence* (2018).

[16] To extend and adapt these two propositions beyond the United States and Western Europe, read Frank Dikötter, *Crime, Punishment and the Prison in Modern China* (2002); Daniel V. Botsman, *Punishment and Power in the Making of Modern Japan* (2013); David T. Johnson, *The Japanese Way of Justice: Prosecuting Crime in Japan* (2002); Sinclair Dinnen, *Law and Order in a Weak State: Crime and Politics in Papua*

democratic Leviathan cannot secure its rule in the absence of a properly functioning and minimally legitimate triad of police, court, and prison. This is demonstrated *a contrario* by the runaway violence, suffusive legal cynicism, and criminal justice dysfunction in the black American hyperghetto, where death, drugs, and brutality, starting with police brutality, rule the streets, making the racialized core of the US metropolis akin to the high-mortality shantytowns of the mega-cities of the global South where failing official justice feeds proliferating vigilante justice and the runaway growth of the private security industry.[17]

The state must imperatively gain and maintain its monopoly over judicial force and stigma because penality is the chief practical and discursive means for tracing the bright border separating the law-abiding and therefore deserving, worthy, and moral citizen from the undeserving, unworthy, and immoral lawbreaker – the "enemy of society." In *Der Begriff des Politischen*, Carl Schmitt proposes that the core of the political as a distinct domain of social existence resides

375

New Guinea (2000); David H. Bayley, *Police and Political Development in India* ([1969] 2015); Beatrice Jauregui, *Provisional Authority: Police, Order, and Security in India* (2019); Takashi Shiraishi, *The Phantom World of Digul: Policing as Politics in Colonial Indonesia, 1926–1941* (2021); Fariba Zarinebaf, *Crime and Punishment in Istanbul, 1700–1800* (2010); Zeynep Gönen, *The Politics of Crime in Turkey: Neoliberalism, Police and the Urban Poor* (2016); Nancy Shields Kollmann, *Crime and Punishment in Early Modern Russia* (2012); Florence Bernault (ed.), *Enfermement, prison et châtiments en Afrique du 19e siècle à nos jours* (1999); Samuel Kalman, *Law, Order, and Empire: Policing and Crime in Colonial Algeria, 1870–1954* (2024); Jean Comaroff and John L. Comaroff (eds.), *Law and Disorder in the Postcolony* (2007); Gail Super, *Governing through Crime in South Africa: The Politics of Race and Class in Neoliberalizing Regimes* (2016); Marcelo Bergman and Gustavo Fondevila, *Prisons and Crime in Latin America* (2021); Luiz Dal Santo and Máximo Sozzo (eds.), *Punishment in Latin America: Explorations from the Margins* (2024); Daniel M. Goldstein, *Outlawed: Between Security and Rights in a Bolivian City* (2012); Esteban Rodriguez Alzueta and Fabián Viegas (eds.), *Circuitos carcelarios. Estudios sobre la cárcel argentina* (2015); Graham Denyer Willis, *The Killing Consensus: Police, Organized Crime, and the Regulation of Life and Death in Urban Brazil* (2015); Michel Misse, *Malandros, marginais e vagabundos. A acumulação social da violência no Rio de Janeiro* (2023).

[17] George Karandinos et al., "The Moral Economy of Violence in the US Inner City" (2014); Jill Leovy, *Ghettoside: A True Story of Murder in America* (2015); and Randol Contreras, *The Marvelous Ones: Drugs, Gang Violence, and Resistance in East Los Angeles* (2024). For an exemplary study of the ramifying consequences of the state's failure to monopolize and deliver criminal punishment, read Laurent Fourchard, *Trier, exclure et policer. Vies urbaines en Afrique du Sud et au Nigeria* (2018), and, for comparison, Javier Auyero and María Fernanda Berti, *In Harm's Way: The Dynamics of Urban Violence* (2015) in the margins of the Argentinian metropolis, and Markus-Michael Müller, *The Punitive City: Privatized Policing and Protection in Neoliberal Mexico* (2016).

precisely in the distinction between "friend" and "enemy," a dichotomy he sees as central to the formation and defense of collective identity.[18] In this perspective, the criminal is, along with the pauper and the foreigner, the *Feind* who defines and sanctifies via contraposition the full-fledged member of the civic community by concentrating and embodying pollution, danger, and dereliction.[19] He is the living, breathing *anti-citizen* lurking in the shadowy depths of the city's underbelly, all the more feared when he wears a dark skin, speaks a foreign language, and practices an alien religion. The daily delivery of punishment in its manifold forms, starting with street policing, is also the chief means whereby state officials, bureaucratic and political, manufacture minimal legitimacy among the citizenry by turning safety and security into a service and a spectacle. Penality is the perfect vehicle for staging the fortitude of the Leviathan – or the shared illusion of fortitude. Meshing law and order, at bottom, is at once practical endeavor and civic theater.

Abolitionism as penal millenarism

It is perplexing, in this regard, that the country which has developed the most bloated and most severe penal apparatus of the capitalist West has also spawned the most vibrant, small but vocal, web of activists and intellectuals advocating for its outright eradication, rather than piecemeal amelioration or partial take-down.[20] Perhaps the very enormity of the former and its imperviousness to piecemeal alteration has pressed the latter to philosophical extremity. Keeanga-Yamahtta Taylor suggests as much when she recounts "the sanguinary and absurd cycle of racist police violence" that no reform seems able to stop.[21] Regardless, abolition is "good to think with" and fruitful as a suite of *Gedankenexperimente* in the manner of Max Weber designed

---

[18] Carl Schmitt, *The Concept of the Political* ([1932] 2008). For a critique of the ambiguities and aporias of his conception of the "enemy," see Benjamin Arditi, "On the Political: Schmitt contra Schmitt" (2008).

[19] "The criminal harms society above all else; by breaking the social contract, he establishes himself as an enemy within." Michel Foucault, *La Société punitive. Cours au Collège de France, 1972–1973*, p. 260.

[20] For a wide survey and documentation of the issue, see Michael J. Coyle and David Scott (eds.), *The Routledge International Handbook of Penal Abolition* (2021).

[21] Keeanga-Yamahtta Taylor, "The Emerging Movement for Police and Prison Abolition" (2021).

to stretch the mind and envisage novel configurations and institutions of punishment, as well as alternatives to the same.[22] It also eloquently reminds us of the variety and scale of the social harms caused by the penal state. But mind games played in a universe of abstractions must not be mistaken for plausible historical options.

This is not to gainsay the political engagement and everyday work of abolitionist activists on the ground in the US, many of them people of color (especially women) who have suffered at the hands of the penal state and who have founded, lead, or otherwise participate in myriad organizations such as Critical Resistance, INCITE! (women of color survivors of violence), Survived and Punished (formerly incarcerated individuals), She Safe We Safe (militants adopting a black queer feminist perspective) and Project NIA (incarcerated youth of color).[23] These organizations engage in varied forms of local mobilization; design and run diverse interventions that tug at the penal state; provide a safe space for debate and much needed services for people embroiled in the justice apparatus and their loved ones; and produce field reports and educational toolkits. They give a bullhorn to subaltern voices silenced by the conventional parameters of public discussion about punishment and bestow value upon the knowledge of penalized people.[24] The point of my critique is not to disaffirm this work but to push its intellectuals, organic and academic, to better articulate the abolitionist position, which I find philosophically alluring but logically inconsistent, sociologically untenable, and politically counterproductive.[25]

377

Responding to the urgency of the political moment and untethered from reality owing to their willful and watertight isolation from policy and

[22] In *The Idea of Prison Abolition* (2022), philosopher Tommie Shelby finds value in the project of ending incarceration, which he ultimately deems utopian, as a "framework for ethical reflection" (p. 190).
[23] See Angela Y. Davis et al., *Abolition. Feminism. Now* (2022), for a roster and collective genealogy. The work of justice abolitionists partakes of a long tradition of African-American thought and activism as retraced by Robin D. G. Kelley in *Freedom Dreams: The Black Radical Imagination* ([2002] 2022).
[24] Mariame Kaba, *We Do This 'Til We Free Us: Abolitionist Organizing and Transforming Justice* (2021). For a sanguine appraisal of such knowledge and discussion of "community-derived, bottom up" safety strategies, see David J. Knight and Vesla M. Weaver, "Black Political Mobilization and the US Carceral State: How Tracing Community Struggles for Safety Changes the Policing Narrative" (2025).
[25] A cogent discussion of the steep strategic downside of abolitionist advocacy is Rachel E. Barkow, "Promise or Peril? The Political Path of Prison Abolition in America" (2023).

administrative circles, American advocates of penal abolition argue in bliss-
ful ignorance of the first wave of modern prison abolitionism which arose
in the tow of Nils Christie and Thomas Mathiesen in Scandinavia and
Louk Hulsman in the Netherlands in the 1960s and 1970s, as well as the
kindred works of Ruth Rittenhouse Morris in Canada and Eugenio Rául
Zaffaroni in Argentina.[26] The canonical text here is Thomas Mathiesen,
The Politics of Abolition ([1971] 1974), which was translated into multiple
languages in Europe shortly after its publication in English in 1974.[27] It is
rarely cited and never seriously discussed by American abolitionists, who
trace their thought back to Angela Y. Davis's *Are Prisons Obsolete?* (2003),
and from Davis back to the W.E.B. Du Bois of *Black Reconstruction* (1935)
and to the slavery abolitionists of the ante-bellum United States.[28]

378

 This ignorance deprives them of the lessons of past experiments and
causes them to repeat the strategic mistakes of the earlier generation
of abolitionists, such as not supporting incremental steps or rolling out
the untenable distinction between "positive" and "negative" reforms,
reworked as the duality of "reformist reform" and "non-reformist reform"
(itself borrowed from the French ecologist philosopher André Gorz). It
reinforces the tunnel vision rooted in the principled prioritizing of race
as a vector of penality – for instance, by postulating that the link between
slavery and prison, as well as their abolition, is organic when it is historically contingent, neither necessary nor sufficient to motivate the radical
critique of the penal state (I return to this neuralgic question later, *infra*,
pp. 387–9). If American abolitionists engaged the Scandinavian tradition
of prison abolition, they might ask why the criminologist Nils Christie, one
of the founding figures and leading lights of this intellectual and political
strand, moved to advocating penal minimalism in a country where the total
carceral population has never reached 4,000 inmates – the size of a single
California prison.[29]

---

[26] Máximo Langer, "Penal Abolitionism and Criminal Law Minimalism: Here and
There, Now and Then" (2020); Gwenola Ricordeau, *Crimes et peines. Penser l'abolitionnisme pénal avec Nils Christie, Louk Hulsman et Ruth Morris* (2021). A comprehensive account of the origins and evolution of penal abolitionism across borders
is Joël Charbit et al., *Brique par brique, mur par mur. Une histoire de l'abolitionnisme
pénal* (2024). See also Vincenzo Ruggiero, *Penal Abolitionism* (2010), on the northern
European strand and Herman Bianchi and René van Swaaningen (eds.), *Abolitionism:
Toward a Non-Repressive Approach to Crime* (1986), for key texts that remain current.
[27] Thomas Mathiesen, *The Politics of Abolition* ([1971] 1974).
[28] Davis et al., *Abolition. Feminism. Now*, pp. 54–8; Angela Y. Davis, *Are Prisons
Obsolete?* (2003); W.E.B. Du Bois, *Black Reconstruction* (1935).
[29] Nils Christie, *A Suitable Amount of Crime* (2004), pp. 213–14.

Coda

Abolition aiming to eliminate the penal state *in toto* is particularly attractive to scholars – and especially graduate students and professors eager to curry favor with them – who walk the safe and cushy corridors of academia and benefit from the genteel police patrolling of their campus and middle-class home neighborhoods allowing for normalized public peace and normative civility. Stateside, in the wake of the Black Live Matters mobilization and the public torture killing of George Floyd, abolition has become a new rhetorical badge of civic courage and political progressivism among scholars and activists of law, race, and inequality.[30] The word has turned into a shibboleth and spawned multiple derivations beyond penality: school abolition, social work abolition, debt abolition, poverty abolition, border abolition, abolition geography, abolition democracy, etc. But pluralizing the word does not bolster its analytics nor clarify its politics. Consider six troublesome features of penal abolitionism as propounded by American intellectuals and militants, whose friendly but unsparing critique can serve to highlight perennial issues and possible paths in the (re)organization of penality.[31]

1. Hyper- and hypo-penalization

Police, court, and prison abolitionists conveniently background or flatly ignore the hard fact that crime is more prevalent, more penetrating, and more corrosive of the social fabric in stigmatized neighborhoods of relegation doubly segregated by race and class – some

---

[30] From the flood of recent US books on criminal justice, see Lydia Pelot-Hobbs, *Prison Capital: Mass Incarceration and Struggles for Abolition Democracy in Louisiana* (2023), for a historical case study; Tommie Shelby, *The Idea of Prison Abolition* (2022), for an examination through the lens of analytic philosophy; Rachel Herzing and Justin Piché, *How to Abolish Prisons: Lessons from the Movement Against Imprisonment* (2024), for the view of activist organizers; and Derecka Purnell, *Becoming Abolitionists: Police, Protests, and the Pursuit of Freedom* (2022), for a memoir. Elite universities were prompt to jump on the bandwagon and to fund conferences, workshops, and events on the topic, such as the "Abolitionist Politics, Practices, and Horizons Speaker Series" at Harvard University in the Fall of 2023.

[31] Abolitionists present themselves as "a movement" – "a growing and internationalist abolition feminist ecosystem," in the words of Angela Y. Davis et al. in *Abolition. Feminism. Now* (2022, p. 6) – but they are more like a rhizomatic constellation of activists and intellectuals, lay and professional, who do not always agree on goals and means. I direct my criticism at advocates of *penal* abolition who argue for the *elimination* of all three constituents of the penal triad, and not their mere shrinkage, which, *horresco referens*, would make them penal minimalists.

even deny the seriousness of crime there.[32] Their residents suffer from conjoint *over*-policing (as surveillance and force) and *under*-policing (as prevention and protection), not to mention mishandling by underfunded and understaffed courts. Indeed the category that suffers the most from both in the American hyperghetto is poor black women.[33] In Minneapolis, epicenter of the collective protest against brutal and discriminatory law enforcement in the American metropolis circa 2020, the established leaders of the black population and many residents of the city's African-American district mobilized *against* "defund the police," much to the dismay of activists from out of town.[34]

A long line of black civil rights leaders have fought hard for over a century to gain equal protection under penal authority, including an end to police indifference to crime in African-American settlements and the protection of the courts from the racial violence of whites. One of the pillars of the regime of caste terrorism known as Jim Crow in the American South was the exclusion of African-Americans from judicial institutions, which made it impossible for them to resort to the court to safeguard minimal physical integrity and public safety.[35] At the same time, many black rebellions such as the ghetto uprisings of the 1960s were triggered by police surveillance and violence. The two seemingly contradictory demands cohabit over time, across space and within the same population, attesting to a long-standing pattern of joint over-penalization and under-penalization. The black jurist Trevor Gardner demonstrates that abolitionism disregards the "security interest" of the citizenry and in particular "the primary interest of African-Americans in penal administration." This interest is twofold: "A security interest (in relation to private violence) and a democratic interest (in regard to the group's influence over penal institutions)."[36]

[32] "The fear for our public safety is based less on real harm than on hype that blows the threat of harm out of proportion." Critical Resistance, "Abolition Organizing Toolkit (Selections)" (2021), p. 448.

[33] Lisa Avalos, "The Under-Policing of Crimes Against Black Women" (2022). For a broader consideration, see Aaron Chalfin and Justin McCrary, "Are US Cities Underpoliced? Theory and Evidence" (2018); Hunter M. Boehme et al., "Citizens' Perceptions of Over- and Under-Policing: A Look at Race, Ethnicity, and Community Characteristics" (2022).

[34] Michelle Phelps, *The Minneapolis Reckoning: Race, Violence, and the Politics of Policing in America* (2024).

[35] Loïc Wacquant, *Jim Crow. Le terrorisme de caste en Amérique* (2024a), pp. 97–105.

[36] Trevor George Gardner, "The Conflict Among African American Penal Interests: Rethinking Racial Equity in Criminal Procedure" (2022), p. 1700.

2. *"Community" fetishism*

Advocates of abolition rely on the populist invocation of an *idealized "community"* (and its rhetorical cousin, the romanticized "grassroots") that would be the natural repository of judicial wisdom and a unified force for organized resistance against the penal state, provided people are properly educated by enlightened militants through patient "base-building," "mutual aid," and "narrative shifting."[37] They magically presume that this "community" is cohesive rather than fractured and stratified, organically disposed to direct democracy rather than autocracy, constitutively inclined to judicial temperance rather than severity, and moved by principled solidarity with offenders because of the adverse social circumstances the latter have suffered – a staple of abolitionist discussions is that the offender/victim binary is arbitrary.[38]

381

The "community" is not just idealized but downright idolized by some abolitionists, as when the jurist and former public defender Cynthia Godsoe proposes to "shift power from professionals to communities" and to "center community expertise" by listening to "the voices of the community."[39] But concretely who gets to speak: the business owner or the store thief, the landlord or the homeless person, the mother of three children or the streetcorner drug dealer who terrorizes them, the teacher or the truant youth, the police officer who lives in the neighborhood or the gang member who controls its streets? What if the celebrated voices are a cacophony of discordant diagnoses and contradictory demands? What if the loudest ones ask for retribution? This adoration for the community as benevolent cocoon and progressive body overlooks the fact that it has all too often been the boiling crucible of racial separation, class selectivity, and cultural tyranny as well as a hardened bunker for conservatism and regressive resistance to urban change. The feminist political theorist Iris Marion

---

[37] The word "community" appears no fewer than 96 times in the 41-page article by Rachel Foran et al., "Abolitionist Principles for Prosecutor Organizing: Origins and Next Steps" (2021), and 97 times in the 47-page article by Matthew Clair and Amanda Woog, "Courts and the Abolition Movement" (2022). Abolition itself is bafflingly defined by Foran et al. as "a process of re-imagining communities" (p. 535).

[38] We will see later that, by contrast, "minimalism does not idealize all social and non-criminal responses to crime since they can be harsher or more burdensome on freedom than criminal law." Máximo Langer, "What Is Penal Minimalism?" (2024), p. 2052.

[39] Cynthia Godsoe, "The Place of the Prosecutor in Abolitionist Praxis" (2022), pp. 214–22.

Young reminds us in *Justice and the Politics of Difference* that "the myth of community operates strongly to produce defensive exclusionary behavior" that reproduces structures of domination in the city.[40] As to "marginalized communities," many of their residents aspire to leave them behind and they often do so when they garner the resources to migrate to a better neighborhood, first of all to escape crime. Exit and not voice is their preferred political option.

This irenic vision of *Gemeinschaft* leading to the placid prevention and peaceful resolution of criminality based on intra-racial comity and class maternalism does not withstand historical scrutiny. The racial politics of punishment in the American metropolis during the era of carceral hyperinflation suffices to demonstrate it. The black jurist and former public defender James Forman shows in his landmark book *Locking Up Our Own* that, for two decades after the ebbing of the Civil Rights Movement, the black working and middle classes strongly supported "tough-on-crime" policies, including intensified policing and brutal prison sentences for the black drug dealers and assorted street criminals sowing disorder in and about their segregated neighborhoods. They saw these outlaws not as victims of oppression and race brothers but as "black-faced traitors" and the "enemy within."[41] They viewed the need to protect themselves from crimes committed by the black precariat as a new civil rights frontier – the expression "black-on-black crime" was not the spawn of white racists but of the black magazine *Ebony* which featured it on its August 1979 cover. The African-American leaders and middle class were incensed by what they deemed to be lax policing and lenient courts; they denounced drug dealers as "the scourge of the earth" who "deserved to roast and to fry" and even compared them to the Ku Klux Klan.[42] Crucially, black officials at the city level carefully maneuvered to point penal force toward the hyperghetto, sparing their own neighborhoods from increased punishment.[43]

---

[40] Iris Marion Young, *Justice and the Politics of Difference* (1990), p. 235.

[41] James Forman, *Locking Up Our Own: Crime and Punishment in Black America* (2017), pp. 29 and 32. One crucial addendum: established black citizens and organizations simultaneously supported economic, social, and educational investment in their neighborhoods. In response, the state delivered punitive penal policies without the "Marshall Plan for Urban America" demanded by African-American leaders.

[42] Ibid., pp. 131 and 158.

[43] This confirms my thesis that differential policing and punishment by place is crucial to the rolling out of the penal state in the metropolis and to its class-race selectivity. Spatial targeting aimed at the hyperghetto and sparing black middle-class districts explains why the lifetime probability of serving a prison sentence went down for

This argument is amplified by Michael Javen Fortner's meticulous history of the incubation and implementation of New York's stringent "Rockefeller Drug Laws" in the 1970s in *Black Silent Majority*.[44] It reveals the deep class schisms within and across African-American neighborhoods that led most blacks to support super-punitive policies fueling hyperincarceration – for instance, 75 percent of black and Puerto Rican residents of New York City favored prison for life for narcotics dealers. Just because a population is the priority target of penalization does not mean that it will rise in unison against the state. The fact that people in districts of dereliction *distrust* the police owing to the latter's brutal, hostile, and discriminatory conduct does not imply that they want to *eliminate* it. Indeed, 56 percent of residents of "fragile communities" and 59 percent of black respondents to a 2019 Gallup poll on *The State of Opportunity in America* wanted *more* police presence in their neighborhood, not less. In addition, fully 56 percent of members of "fragile communities" also reported that most people in their area viewed the police positively or very positively.[45]

Relatedly, sociologist and legal scholar Monica Bell takes a step toward the deconstruction of the falsely unitary notion of "community" when she shows that responses to criminal legal institutions among residents of segregated neighborhoods of relegation vary systematically along the two cross-cutting gradients of agency and stigma, yielding four stances she labels subordination, consumption, resistance, and transformation (individual and collective), only the last of which fits the scenario of abolitionists.[46] Bell also reminds us of a well-established fact: African-Americans, women, and residents of districts of dereliction are more likely to call the police than other demographics *after controlling for crime rates*. Black women,

---

blacks with some college education to reach 5 percent during the closing two decades of the century, while it tripled to reach 59 percent for blacks who did not finish high school. Bruce Western, *Punishment and Inequality in America* (2006), p. 27.

[44] Michael Javen Fortner, *Black Silent Majority: The Rockefeller Drug Laws and the Politics of Punishment* (2015). These laws mandated prison terms of 15 years to life for simple possession of two ounces or more of heroin or cocaine, equal to the penalty for second-degree murder.

[45] Gallup with the Thurgood Marshall College Fund, *The State of Opportunity in America: Understanding Barriers and Identifying Solutions* (2019), pp. 20 and 23. This compares with 50 percent for whites and 59 percent for Hispanics.

[46] Monica C. Bell, "The Community in Criminal Justice: Subordination, Consumption, Resistance, and Transformation" (2019). Bell is politically cautious and ends up clinging to the notion of "community" even after her own analysis has undermined it.

in particular, are wont to trigger police intervention as a means of regaining control over their intimate partners and children despite their disdain and distrust for the justice apparatus. They rework legal cynicism into "situational trust," an unexpected twist that underlines the layered complexity of the relationship of the urban precariat to the penal state.[47]

One last problem with *community fetishism*: abolitionists propose "shifting authority away from government representatives" to "place power in the hands of local communities."[48] But would this shift not apply then to wealthy white "communities" as well as suburban and rural "communities"? In a democratic polity, it is hard to see why the latter would not be entitled to shaping the penal state in accordance with their own needs and preferences, thereby bringing the abolitionist project to a screeching halt even if it did take hold in "marginalized communities" since bourgeois whites generally dominate county and state politics. Considering the fragmentation of the bureaucratic field in the US, the populist tenet of the local control of punishment is no guaranteed path to penal deflation. Indeed, it is one of the key mechanisms that drove sweeping policing, aggressive prosecution, and runaway incarceration for 40 years and a surefire recipe for the continued sidelining of the concerns of poor black residents of the metropolis.[49]

3. The demonic myth of the PIC

Advocates of police and prison abolition buy into the *Left demonology of the "Prison Industrial Complex"* lock, stock, and barrel, perpetuating a fiendish myth based on a flawed parallelism and imaginary symbiosis with the "Military Industrial Complex" that obscures the structure and functioning of the penal Leviathan as a distinctly political organization of public force.[50]

[47] Monica C. Bell, "Situational Trust: How Disadvantaged Mothers Reconceive Legal Cynicism" (2016).

[48] Clair and Woog, "Courts and the Abolition Movement," p. 30.

[49] David Garland, *Law and Order Leviathan: America's Extraordinary Regime of Policing and Punishment* (2025).

[50] The militant myth is articulated in its full glory in Angela Y. Davis, *Are Prisons Obsolete?* (2003), chapter 3, and distilled in James Braxton Peterson, *Prison Industrial Complex for Beginners* (2016). The latest recasting of this dark legend, pushed to the point of absurdity by the pseudo-concepts of "institutional cross-pollination" and "mimetic connections," is Jacob Swanson and Mary Fainsod Katzenstein, "From the Battlefield to Behind Bars: Rethinking the Relationship between the Military-

Coda

The tale of the PIC, assuming verisimilitude from being incessantly told and retold among militants and scholars alike, misses the fact that the carceral boom in post-Civil Rights America results not from profit-seeking but from state-crafting; that the "prison industry" is not an industry, and still less a global industry, while corrections as a whole are a miniscule and marginal sector of the economy (under 0.5 percent of the United States GDP and undetectable on a world scale) driven by bureaucratic regulations and not market mechanisms; that hyperincarceration is economically irrational and not a vehicle for the capitalist exploitation of penal labor (fewer than 5,000 inmates out of 2.3 million were working for private firms behind bars at peak use circa 2005);[51] that firms providing food services, medical care, security, and communications make money as a consequence, and not a cause, of prison expansion; that, of all government functions and services, punishment remains doggedly public, unlike education, welfare, and health, which have all been partially captured by private operators (for-profit prisons account for a paltry 8 percent of available beds); and that penal institutions in the US are so dispersed and disarticulated that they do not compose a "system" with a single lever of control as does the military.[52] Abolitionists consistently conflate punishment, prison, the state, capitalism, militarism, colonialism, and racial domination – even "cis-hetero-patriarchy," transphobia, and ableism are brought into the picture for no perceptible reason other than to be politically catholic.[53]

and Prison-Industrial Complexes" (2025). Incredibly, this article was published in *Daedalus*, the journal of the venerable American Academy of Arts and Sciences, catapulting the PIC from the lunatic fringe to the respectable center.

[51] Thanks to activist crusades preaching the catechism of the Prison Industrial Complex, the delusional notion that the boom in penal confinement is driven by the profit motive is broadly diffused among the African-American population as a mainstay of racial conspiracies: fully 74 percent of African-Americans believe that blacks are more likely than whites to be incarcerated because prisons are run to make money on the backs of black people. Kiana Cox, *Most Black Americans Believe U.S. Institutions Were Designed to Hold Black People Back* (2024), p. 7.

[52] A fuller, step-by-step dismantling of the diabolical legend of the PIC is Loïc Wacquant, "Prisoner Reentry as Myth and Ceremony" (2010d).

[53] Calvin John Smiley, *Defund: Conversations toward Abolition* (2023). "These systems of punishment rely on, reinforce, and perpetuate structures of oppression: white supremacy, patriarchy, capitalism, settler colonialism, xenophobia, ableism, transphobia, and heterosexism. We aim to abolish these systems, not reform them" (Foran et al., "Abolitionist Principles for Prosecutor Organizing," pp. 517–18). But what about ageism, looksism, sizeism and speciesism? And the list goes on.

This fiery rhetoric riding on leftist pieties about power structures cannot hide the lack of understanding of the inner workings of the machinery of punishment. Thus the guide proposed by the "Digital Resource Hub" of Beyond Criminal Courts (an activist project led by Critical Resistance) available at https://beyondcourts.org/en/court_101 is chock-full of inaccuracies, overgeneralizations, and flat-out errors about the way the criminal court functions.

One example: "No matter how 'progressive,' at its core, the job [of prosecutors] is to put people in cages" and "that is why prosecution can never be progressive." In reality, the vast majority of defendants resolve their case through dismissal, diversion, or plea offers that entail no incarceration; remember that, in California, only 10 percent of felony arrests and only 20 percent of felony convictions result in a prison sentence. Abolitionists buy into the public caricature of prosecutors as righteous cowboys and blind zealots of law and order. But a comprehensive study of the motivations of 260 line DAs in nine offices found that, in addition to enforcing criminal statutes, most are driven to "serve their community"; invest professional "pride in being the person who dispenses mercy instead of punishment"; "recognize defendants as *members* of the community, and not just as *threats* to the community"; and put fairness and "doing justice" over "winning."[54]

Another example: in a guilty plea, "the accused is giving up their right to trial, without even getting the benefit of a reduced sentence." In fact, guilty pleas typically result from bargaining, which entails a substantial "discount" on punishment for the defendant – pegged at one-half to two-thirds of their exposure in San Pedrito county. Yet another: when they charge cases, prosecutors "are motivated to rack up convictions to advance their careers." But a charging deputy must make sure that the elements of the crime are present and provable or the case will flounder, which means that she should *not* include "any and all crimes that could conceivably be charged based on what a cop or witnesses describe."[55] In mid-sized to large offices, the deputy who charges cases does not negotiate them and thus she cannot "rack up convictions" of her own. Finally, in these offices promotion is based on experience and seniority so there is no advancement to be had by being especially punitive.

---

[54] Ronald F. Wright and Kay L. Levine, "Career Motivations of State Prosecutors" (2018), pp. 1689–93.

[55] There is great heterogeneity and dispersion in practices and policies of charging across the land. Many offices have policies against "stacking"; others commonly charge felonies as misdemeanors (especially for first-time offenders); yet others decline to prosecute large numbers of cases to entice the police to improve their investigations. Megan S. Wright et al., "Inside the Black Box of Prosecutor Discretion" (2022).

Another error: funding for the prosecutor's office does not depend on the rate of conviction (a meaningless statistic since it is easily manipulated), but on the evolving volume of cases, staffing needs, the profile and media coverage of crime in the county, grants from the state, and new criminal laws to enforce. Lastly, the portrait of plea bargaining painted by the same guide is a grotesque caricature presenting as standard operating procedure the worst-case scenarios at every step in the process (with the prosecutor threatening the death penalty on a whim!) and flatly ignores the legal, bureaucratic, and social checks circumscribing the power of the prosecutor documented in chapter 3 as well as other research.[56]

4. Contingent versus necessary institutions and the fictitious link to slavery

American abolitionists who want to get rid, not just of the prison, but of the police and the court as well, frequently make an analogy between slavery and the penal state to argue that, just as the overturning of the former was once unthinkable but eventually happened, the elimination of the latter is currently inconceivable but could nonetheless be achieved. This is a false analogy that disregards the crucial distinction between *historically contingent* institutions and *structurally necessary* institutions.[57] Another way to put it: there have always existed societies without slavery or where human bondage was a marginal institution, but no societies without punishment, which takes us to the alternative between private and public punishment, that is, in the case of advanced countries, to the penal state. Moreover, in the specific case of the US, making the prison the spawn of slavery and a building block of "racial capitalism," as the abolitionists do with aplomb, is historical nonsense. But this mythical genealogy is widely believed in through sheer force of repetition and because of its congruence with their race-centric faith.

---

[56] Jeffrey Bellin, "The Power of Prosecutors" (2019).

[57] The historical contingency of slavery in spite of its global diffusion across the millennia is established by Orlando Patterson, *Enslavement, Past and Present* (2025). An account of the rocky expansion and retraction of slavery in the Americas belying its historical necessity is Seymour Drescher, *Abolition: A History of Slavery and Antislavery* (2009).

The myth of the genealogical link between slavery and the prison

In *Abolition. Feminism. Now*, Angela Y. Davis et al. claim that there is a *genealogical relationship*, and not just an analogy, between the prison and racial slavery – a mantra of abolitionist scholars and militants. This proposition is reaffirmed as matter of course in a lead article published in the *Harvard Law Review* by the preeminent jurist of race and punishment Dorothy Roberts, "Abolition Constitutionalism": "Today's carceral punishment system can be traced back to slavery and the racial capitalist system it relied on and sustained" (1). But, to make this claim, Davis and Roberts have to twist historical facts three times.

First, the prison was *not* rolled out as a functional substitute for human bondage either before or after abolition in the South. In fact, rates of black incarceration after the Civil War were lowest in the cotton-growing counties where human bondage once predominated. For a simple reason conclusively demonstrated by the sociologist Chris Muller: driven by economic interest, planters strove to keep their slaves out of penal custody and they did the same when the latter turned into formally free agricultural laborers (2).

Second, the development of penitentiaries in the United States sprouted in the North of the country during the Jacksonian era, that is, in the decades after 1820 when the authorities deployed closed institutions to manage the gamut of problem populations spawned by accelerating social changes, among them brewing urbanization and its correlates, slum housing, moral dissipation, street crime, ethnic dissension, and overt class conflict. As in Europe a century earlier, the prison was (re)invented and mobilized to absorb social troubles in the city, which political and intellectual elites viewed as threatening the very existence of the young republic (3). Jacksonian innovation involved the concurrent creation and diffusion of "penitentiaries for the criminal, asylums for the insane, almshouses for the poor, orphan asylums for homeless children, and reformatories for delinquents" (4). No link with slavery, apparent or subterranean, figures among the precursors of the American prison.

Third, even contractual penal servitude, which, on first blush, evokes slaves toiling on a plantation and the infamous "convict lease system" that succeeded human bondage in the South, as described by W.E.B. Du Bois in *Black Reconstruction* (1935), was first deployed in the Northern states after the 1820s, long before abolition. Class and labor exploitation were epicentral to the formation of the American penal state, not race (5). It is true that there is a distinctly Southern carceral paradigm shaped by the ramifying remanence of slavery and its successor regime of Jim Crow terrorism. Past slavery helps explain both the virulence of ethnoracial division, the depth of racialized poverty, the atrophy of the social state, and the corresponding hypertrophy of the penal state as manifested by extreme levels of incarceration and brutal conditions of confinement across that region. But the South is neither at the origin, nor the pattern followed by, the country as asserted by Robert Perkinson in *Texas Tough: The Rise of America's Prison Empire*, and Angela Y. Davis et al. after him (6). The South is like a country of its own when it comes to crime and punishment, one that other regions and nations are hard pressed to imitate.

389

1. Davis et al., *Abolition. Feminism. Now*, p. 60; Dorothy E. Roberts, "Abolition Constitutionalism" (2019) p. 7.
2. Christopher Muller, "Exclusion and Exploitation: The Incarceration of Black Americans from Slavery to the Present" (2021).
3. Paul Boyer, *Urban Masses and Moral Order in America, 1820–1920* (1978).
4. David J. Rothman, *The Discovery of the Asylum: Social Order and Disorder in the New Republic* (1971), p. xiii.
5. Rebecca McLennan, *The Crisis of Imprisonment. Protest, Politics and the Making of the American Penal State (1776–1941)* (2009), chapter 2.
6. Robert Perkinson, *Texas Tough: The Rise of America's Prison Empire* (2010).

5. A political cul de sac

For abolition to be more than a gratuitous intellectual exercise geared toward providing moral self-gratification, it has to find a *plausible political path*. Where is that path at a moment when punitive populism as both political strategy and collective sentiment is deeply entrenched or making a comeback across advanced societies?[58] Even in some hypothetical long run – one is reminded of John Maynard Keynes's

[58] Vincent Sizaire, *Sortir de l'imposture sécuritaire* (2016); Kirstin Drenkhahn et al., "Zum Stand der Punitivitätsforschung in Deutschland und darüber hinaus" (2020); Susanne Karstedt and Rebecca Endtricht, "Crime and Punishment: Public Opinion and Political Law-And-Order Rhetoric in Europe 1996–2019" (2022); Amanda Hernández, "'Tough-On-Crime' Policies are Back in Some Places that had Reimagined Criminal Justice" (2024). For a fruitful elaboration of the notion of "punitive moment" as extended temporal frame and political-policy momentum, see Didier Fassin, *Punir, une passion contemporaine* (2017), pp. 11–15.

quip that "in the long run we are all dead" – how realistic is it to expect to disappear the penal state in its entirety when small-scale reforms to parts of the justice apparatus prove so difficult to achieve and engrave?

In the case of the United States, which owns the world's most bloated punishment apparatus, how could it possibly accomplish transformations of a kind and on a scale that the most progressive countries endowed with formidable social states and very low rates of violent crime – such as the Netherlands in the 1980s, Denmark in the 1990s, and Finland in the 2000s – were unable to accomplish?[59] Consider the prison alone. It is one thing for Thomas Mathiesen to push for "negative reforms" designed to undermine the legitimacy of penal institutions in 1971 when Norway, an ethnically homogeneous country of 4 million with a majority then living in rural areas and small towns, sported an incarceration rate of 44 inmates per 100,000 residents for all of 1,700 prisoners (this is not a typo).[60] It is another to make that same move in 2025 in the United States, with a population of 347 million with 80 percent living in cities deeply divided along ethnoracial lines, which confines 580 convicts per 100,000 residents for a staggering total approaching two million. The raw difference in scale is exactly 1 to 1,063.

6. Waiting for Godot and the elusive substitute

Do abolitionists not abandon or hurt the very constituency they claim to defend and serve? Victims of police violence, prosecutorial severity, and harsh confinement cannot wait until "the system" is defeated and dismantled in some grand uchronic overhaul.[61] They need practical recourse and concrete remedies *now*, suited to alleviating their imme-

---

[59] Illusion turns into delusion when such minor individual interventions as "paying bail for a stranger, using social media to let the public know what everyday courtroom proceedings are like, making a video about someone's life for a criminal court judge, [and] presenting a budget proposal to the city council" are portrayed as undermining the penal Leviathan, as in Jocelyn Simonson, *Radical Acts of Justice: How Ordinary People are Dismantling Mass Incarceration* (2023).

[60] Thomas Mathiesen, *The Politics of Abolition* ([1971] 1974).

[61] "As abolitionists, we are working towards a future where people are no longer prosecuted and therefore where prosecutors do not exist. *That future is a long way off.* To get there, our movements need to build significant power through a variety of organizing interventions while remaining pointedly focused on shrinking the power, size, and scope of the prosecuting office." Foran et al., "Abolitionist Principles for Prosecutor Organizing: Origins and Next Steps," p. 535, my italics.

diate predicament, and not mind games tailored for the byzantine eristic of the law-school seminar or suited to militant grand-standing at "grassroots" meetings.

Abolitionists oppose many immediate steps that would benefit offenders and victims alike on grounds that they reinforce "the system." For instance, "prosecuting offices should not receive more resources to provide social services or survivor/victim support," nor divert offenders to problem-solving courts such as drug courts on grounds that "giving more resources to death-making institutions is not abolitionist. It only cements and increases power and also cloaks the system in legitimacy."[62] Waiting for the advent of a brave new society in which social harm will have vanished and punishment been rendered superfluous is waiting for Godot. Moreover, as legal scholar Máximo Langer has argued, a society without state punishment "can itself be unfair, discriminatory, and inhumane; deprive the weak of protection against the powerful; harm the communities and individuals affected by these situations; and enable more of these harmful situations in the future."[63]

One of the favorite verbs of abolitionists is "re-imagine,"[64] but at some point imagination must connect with historical reality lest it fuel a flight into the ether of social oneirism. This is their greatest failure yet: after decades of incubation, it is still unclear what abolitionists would replace the penal state with – other than an assortment of homilies to "community" and paeans to "life-affirming institutions."[65] Foran et al. advocate eliminating the prosecutorial function altogether without so much as adumbrating what they would put in

391

---

[62] Ibid., p. 519.

[63] Langer, "Penal Abolitionism and Criminal Law Minimalism: Here and There, Now and Then," p. 40.

[64] "Let's begin our abolitionist journey not with the question 'What do we have now, and how can we make it better?' Instead, let's ask 'What can we imagine for ourselves and the world?'." Mariame Kaba, *We Do This 'Til We Free Us*, p. 5. Imagining is a survival strategy for militants fighting a losing battle in the crevices of the penal state. As an enthusiastic reviewer of Kaba's book puts it, "removing the imagination from the work we do can lead us to severe levels of burnout, anguish, and ultimately feeling hopeless about whether or not we can reach that liberated world." Alycia Kamil, "Community Review of Mariame Kaba's We Do This 'Til We Free Us'" (2023).

[65] Davis et al., *Abolition. Feminism. Now*, p. 58. The expression is that of Ruth Wilson Gilmore, the prophet of "abolition geography." The authors of the same book endorse the catch-all and positively tinged notion of "voluntary, accessible, community run services and infrastructures" (p. 195).

its place. Instead, they invoke the nebulous notion of "community-driven methods of justice" without further elaboration.[66]

Sociologist Matthew Clair and attorney-scholar Amanda Woog propose "abolishing criminal courts as sites of coercion, violence, and exploitation and replacing them with other social institutions, such as community-based restorative justice and peacemaking programs, while investing in the robust provision of social, political, and economic resources in marginalized communities." They extol "Indigenous methods that have been used for centuries to make communities whole" but they fail to dispel the mystery surrounding them. They therefore also fail to consider their inapplicability to large societies characterized by what Durkheim calls "organic solidarity" featuring high social density, a complex division of labor, deep individualism, and moral diversity.[67] Sentimentalizing First Nations, Critical Resistance likewise makes a vague and passing gesture toward the harm-resolution "circles" of the Amerindians of the Yukon and the Qjibway tribe of Hollow Water in Canada presented as "humane forms of accountability." But the same First Nations are ravaged by crime and incarceration in every British former settler colony, proof that their hallowed harm-resolution methods are hardly a workable response to offending.[68]

Sociological realism versus Rousseauist idealism

The doggedly sociological realism guiding my friendly critique of abolitionism diverges fundamentally from reasoning based on the postulation of a perfect world that effaces history, removes all organizational constraints, and eliminates domination as a prevalent if not constitutive feature of human society by a stroke of the pen to give free rein to the moral imagination. This is the mode of

---

[66] Foran et al., "Abolitionist Principles for Prosecutor Organizing," p. 505. They also mention "building life-affirming institutions and support systems so people have what they need to thrive and feel safe" (p. 521), and "funding community-led endeavors for wellness, safety and healing" (p. 532), notions that are just as vague.

[67] Émile Durkheim, *De la division du travail social* ([1893] 1990). Clair and Woog, "Courts and the Abolition Movement," pp. 7 and 38. A similar argument is made by Cynthia Godsoe, "The Place of the Prosecutor in Abolitionist Praxis," for whom abolishing the prosecutor amounts to "ceding power to communities." She sternly opposes "'reformist reform' which risks reentrenching and relegitimating the criminal system under a new cover" (p. 165).

[68] Critical Resistance, "Abolition Organizing Toolkit (Selections)," p. 447.

reasoning deployed by Bernard Harcourt in his bold but bemusing book *Cooperation: A Political, Economic, and Social Theory* (2023). It is a provocative and revealing work in that it skillfully theorizes the social vision tacitly underlying abolitionist thinking – which Harcourt lionizes – and thus exposes the latter's sheer implausibility.

Harcourt proposes to "transcend the punishment paradigm of the punitive society" by "achieving a new society based on cooperation." He fantasizes about "an entirely different world, one in which everyone treats all others with equal dignity, true respect, and humanity, where everyone regards others as truly equals, as their own, as people to care about . . . a world where people cooperate in all dimensions of consumption, work, housing, aid, and support, regardless of race or ethnicity as well as gender, sexuality, poverty, or class" (1). On principle, who could possibly object to such an irenic vision of society, reminiscent of Charles Fourier's *phalanstère* and Robert Owen's communal village? But then what is the theoretical or practical use of such unimpeachable ruminations and how relevant are they for large, complex, and vertical societies? And did Marx and Engels not rip to pieces this naïve, ahistorical, and moralizing vision – "fantastic pictures of future society" – in *The Communist Manifesto* under the heading of "utopian socialism"? (2). Do we really need a Little Icaria for the twenty-first century?

Harcourt continues in this Rousseauist vein: "An ethic of care and cooperation would displace the punitive paradigm. It would render obsolete the notion of enforcing the criminal law. Instead of punishment, there would be a panoply of measures of care, well-being, education, and support to help individuals work through problems. These measures would take us beyond punishment practices" (3). But what if acquisitive, domineering, immoral, or otherwise riotous individuals refuse these measures? What if victims of crime insist on retribution, do they undergo "reeducation" into the right ideological frame? What about those who consistently violate the principle of cooperation to take advantage of others? Harcourt again: "In a society based on coöperism, when someone deviates from the norm, others would likely interpret that as a call for care and assistance" (4). But what if this interpretation is plain wrong? How do we ensure that care is not coercion by another name, assistance discipline by another name, harm crime by another name? This is pie in the penal sky which evokes the eschatological vision of Saint Augustine's *City of God* (*De Civitate Dei*, 426 AD), in which people live in harmony according to Christian principles more than Foucault's conception

393

of society as a tension-riven system of power-knowledge traversing the social and individual body – which Harcourt takes as his starting inspiration. At least, St. Augustine was consistent in that the City of God could be achieved only in the heavens and not by transforming the earthly city based on selfishness and vanity.

1. Bernard Harcourt, *Cooperation: A Political, Economic, and Social Theory* (2023), p. 155.
2. Karl Marx and Friedrich Engels, *The Manifesto of the Communist Party* ([1848] 1998), pp. 47–50. "Ultimately, when stubborn historical facts had dispersed all intoxicating effects of self-deception, this form of Socialism ended in a miserable hangover" (p. 41).
3. Harcourt, *Cooperation*, p. 161.
4. Ibid., p. 161.

Aside from the sociological vacuity of such an angelic vision of "community," I highlighted in chapter 1 the deep flaws and high improbability of scaling up miniscule programs of restorative justice that concern under 2 percent of the justice caseloads in the countries that use them the most – unless one massively expanded the resources of criminal justice broadly conceived, which abolitionists oppose. Restorative justice is at best a *minor supplement* to, and certainly not a wholesale *replacement* for, the penal state. And what, concretely, are "peacemaking programs" and what use are they when you have to *respond, in the moment,* to organized larceny, repeat DUI, mass identity theft, ongoing domestic violence, a street robbery, a home-invasion burglary in progress, suspected child sexual abuse, or a cold-blooded murder?

The leading abolitionist organization Critical Resistance concedes that "so far, abolitionists have not created practical ways of providing the alternative to the police," but it nonetheless advises against calling them because they are "a catchall solution for what are normally specific problems." They recommend instead "calling someone else – a neighbor, a family member, or friend," a practical and legal absurdity in the face of an imminent criminal threat.[69] In his rigorous elaboration of what he calls "real utopias," the late sociologist Erik Olin Wright stresses that an "emancipatory social science" must develop "an account of viable alternatives in response to the critique" of existing institutions, emphasis on *viable*.[70] That account is conspicuously missing from the *argumentarium* of abolitionists.

[69] Ibid., pp. 448, 449.
[70] Erik Olin Wright, "Transforming Capitalism through Real Utopias" (2013), p. 1.

Abolitionists expend much of their energy striving to differentiate themselves from "reformists" so as to maintain their moral
purity, judicial righteousness, mutual commitment, and oppositional
culture – so many properties that characterize a sect according to
Max Weber.[71] But when they are pressed for "actionable strategies"
fostering abolition, they mention "richer investments in social services that can prevent conditions that enable crime in the first place,"
"boosting resources for community," and "invest in people and communities,"[72] in other words, the standard fare of reformists focused
on reinforcing the social state. To call court watching, participatory
defense hubs, and community bail funds "partial abolitions" and
measures that "shift power" from the state to the "community" is to
wildly exaggerate the impact of these local interventions and to play
on words.[73] The rhetoric is abolitionist, the practice minimalist.

395

The ten tenets of radical penal minimalism

So what is the alternative to abolitionism that progressives should
embrace? Over a century ago, the founder of modern sociology Émile
Durkheim showed that crime, construed as an "infringement on clear
and definite states of the collective conscience," is a normal and necessary fact of social life: even in the simplest social formations, the
assertion of a collective norm mechanically produces deviance – there
are always individuals who ignore, skirt, or violate the rule, if under
the sway of passion.[74] Crime reminds the collectivity of that shared

---

[71] Max Weber, *The Sociology of Religion* ([1920] 1993). This sense of purity and exclu-
sivity is expressed by McDowell and Fernandez when they insist that "the contemporary abolitionist movement contains the potential to radically transform society"
and that it is aimed at "dismantling the racial-capitalist order [while] *adopting uncom-
promising positions* that resist liberal attempts at co-optation, incorporation, and/or
reconciliation" so as "to create *alternative democratic spaces* that directly challenge the
legitimacy of the police." Meghan G. McDowell and Luis A. Fernandez, "'Disband,
Disempower, and Disarm': Amplifying the Theory and Practice of Police Abolition"
(2018), p. 373, my italics.
[72] Foran et al., "Abolitionist Principles for Prosecutor Organizing," pp. 521 and 529.
[73] Clair and Moog, "Courts and the Abolition Movement," pp. 34–6.
[74] "Crime is necessary; it is linked to the fundamental conditions of all social life and,
by that very fact, it is useful, because these conditions, of which it is the consequence,
are themselves indispensable to the normal evolution of morality and law" (Émile
Durkheim, *Les Règles de la méthode sociologique* ([1895] 2001, p. 70). Durkheim again:
"By the very fact that a certain amount of activity deriving from the passions is always

standard of conduct, which produces the social reaction to deviance that we call punishment, which in turn rekindles social solidarity. In Durkheimian language, then, *punishment is normal and necessary*, and not pathological as some Left critics hastily assert when they confound scholarly conjecture with sociohistorical reality. It follows that to seek to eliminate penality is as naïve as it is futile – a sociological impossibility.

Now, there are three possible options for delivering criminal sanctions: *private* vendetta and *community* vigilantism and reprisal, on the one hand, and *public* authority, with the possibility of legal safeguards and democratic accountability, on the other. The flaws, horrors, and self-sustaining dynamics of the private and communal delivery of punishment are well documented in countries where the state has failed to set up a minimally functional and legitimate penal apparatus. To consider murder, think of "honor killings" in Pakistan, "necklacing" in the townships of South Africa, the "*linchamientos*" of rural bandits in the backcountry of Guatemala and, closer to home, the lethal cycles of attacks and retaliation among street gangs in the US metropolis.[75] Where it prevails, communal justice proves retributive, harsh, and arbitrary as well as bereft of juridical guardrails and democratic accountability. So the domain of potential transformative action centers, first, on the perimeter of criminality and, second, on the nature and modalities of the public delivery of criminal sanction, not on its necessity. This is the bifurcation point between minimalism and abolitionism: the former is anchored in comparative history; the second is what Durkheim would call a "sociological heresy."

A grounded sociology of the penal state recommends, not abolitionism, which is socially implausible and whose first losers would be the residents of districts of urban perdition, but *radical penal minimalism* applied uniformly across social and physical space while taking into account both individual responsibility and social adversity at every stage in the designation and processing of offenders.[76] This approach

---

inevitable, crimes are always occurring" (*Leçons de sociologie. Physique des mœurs et du droit* [1950], p. 97).

[75] Nafisa Shah, *Honour and Violence: Gender, Power and Law in Southern Pakistan* (2016); Nicholas Rush Smith, *Contradictions of Democracy: Vigilantism and Rights in Post-Apartheid South Africa* (2015); Angelina Snodgrass Godoy, *Popular Injustice: Violence, Community, and Law in Latin America* (2006); Martín Sánchez-Jankowski, *Islands in the Street: Gangs and American Urban Society* (1991), and Laurence Ralph, *Renegade Dreams: Living Through Injury in Gangland Chicago* (2014).

[76] For a deft doctrinal account and appraisal of the three variants of minimalism, read

to the political organization of criminal sanction rests on ten tenets. The first five lay the foundation for the minimalist Leviathan on the punishment front:

1. The necessity of the penal state is affirmed. In large, dense, and differentiated societies characterized by what Durkheim calls "organic solidarity" rooted in an extensive division of labor, *there is no pathway around or step beyond the penal state* as the agency officially entrusted with deploying legitimate force to implement criminal statutes.[77]

2. The province of criminal conduct is sharply shrunk to avoid "overcriminalization" as defined by the analytical philosopher Douglas Husak.[78] One of its juridical translations is the principle legal theorists call *de minimis*: that the court should disregard conduct that is technically wrongful but minor and socially harmless.

3. The unleashing of punishment is only ever a last resort, taken after every other modality of preventative and remedial action (social, economic, educational, family, housing, medical, etc.) has been exhausted. As clarified by the jurist Máximo Langer, this is the principle legal theorists call *ultima ratio*.[79]

4. Incarceration is drastically reduced to its bare minimum. It is

Máximo Langer, "What Is Penal Minimalism?" (2024). Langer builds on the work of the Italian jurist Luigio Ferrajoli and the American philosopher Douglas Husak to develop his own approach, on which I draw in turn to develop mine with the help of Durkheim's foundational sociology of crime and punishment. Early elements of minimalism as applied to sentencing – but not statecraft itself – were proposed under the label of "parsimony" by H.L.A. Hart, Norval Morris, Andrew von Hirsch, and Michael Tonry, *inter alia*. But the unsung precursor of minimalism is the Norwegian criminologist Nils Christie who spotlights the social cost of "pain delivery" by the state and advocates for its scarcity in *Limits to Pain: The Role of Punishment in Penal Policy* ([1961] 1981, pp. 94, 95): "The amount of pain inflicted in the name of punishment should always be kept as low as possible . . . Prison should be reserved for the few, for those very few situations where no other sanction will serve."

[77] Durkheim, *De la division du travail social*. Put simply, state punishment is a structural-functional requirement of differentiated social formations. A subtle reading of Durkheim on this point is David Garland, "Punishment and Social Solidarity" (2013b).

[78] The notion is far from self-evident and raises thorny questions of penal philosophy and policy, as discussed by Douglas Husak, "Six Questions About Overcriminalization" (2023). See also the elaboration of doctrinal versus enforcement minimalism in W. Robert Thomas, "Does the State Have an Obligation Not to Enforce the Law?" (2023).

[79] Langer, "What Is Penal Minimalism?." This principle also applies to the definition of the perimeter of criminality (point 2 above).

reserved for the *incapacitation* of the most dangerous criminals liable to cause violent wrongful harms.[80] Imagine a carceral population of, say, 180,000 in the US, one-tenth of the current figure.[81] In any case, the penal state is emphatically not reducible to the "carceral state": even in today's US with its gargantuan custodial archipelago, confinement concerns only a small minority of offenders (even serious offenders).

5. The conventional opposition between state sanction and its proposed alternatives is revoked in principle and in practice whenever they can be combined.

398

Radical penal minimalism, as I construe it, deploys the full palette of measures suited to *resolving a criminal act before, during, and after its commission*: multi-sited prevention, targeted mentorship, conflict mediation, violence interruption, restitution, *and* criminal sanction, itself spanning the gamut from fines and community service to restoration and reparation, probation and incarceration – and, again, incarceration only as a frugal final recourse for a small subpopulation of offenders.

As the jurist Benjamin Levin shows, there are no *a priori* criteria for defining the proper scope (targets) and scale (intensity) of minimization.[82] These will necessarily be fought over inside and outside of the penal state by the range of agents vying to calibrate and direct judicial force. Minimalism can serve as a framework for

[80] Christopher Slobogin makes that argument on the pragmatic basis of "risk management" in "The Minimalist Alternative to Abolitionism: Focusing on the Non-Dangerous Many" (2024). But risk management itself is deeply problematic, as shown by Bernard Harcourt, *Against Prediction: Profiling, Policing, and Punishing in an Actuarial Age* (2007).

[81] To get a sense of scale, there are roughly 23,000 homicides, 31,000 carjackings, and 140,000 reported rapes in the US during a typical year. Only a fraction of these crimes leads to an arrest (roughly one-half for homicides, one-fourth for carjacking and under 5 percent for reported rapes), and an even smaller proportion still to a conviction. So every year under 15,000 convicts for these three serious and violent offenses would walk in through prison gates. The same carceral computation yields a prison population of 8,500 in France and in England and Wales, 6,300 in Italy, and 5,700 in Spain.

[82] Levin lists seven graduated targets of minimization: the number of substantive criminal laws, their scope, incarceration (covering its frequency and conditions of confinement), policing, social control, structural inequality, and the cultural vilification of criminals. Benjamin Levin, "Criminal Law Minimalisms" (2024), pp. 1777–92. He omits the key variable to minimize, regardless of the other targets: the number of individuals entering the penal funnel.

these debates informed by the collective realization that state punishment is a form of material and symbolic violence, albeit legitimate: it infringes upon the dignity, integrity, and membership of the suspect-turned-defendant-turned-convict, which is a private *and* public bad regardless of the act he has committed since it frays the social bond.[83] Therefore it is a *reluctant penal philosophy* which actively strives to question itself and to shrink the perimeter of its intervention, first and foremost by reducing the size of its clientele.

Realizing that no complex and deeply stratified social formation can do without a penal state, radical penal minimalism draws the lessons from the theoretical, historical, and ethnographic study of punishment developed in the present book. What makes it *radical* is its sociological effort to articulate punishment and social structure as spelled out by these five additional criteria:

399

6. Radical penal minimalism is keenly aware that penality is targeted at *urban marginality* and so it works to blunt the effects of this built-in selectivity by ensuring that the legal and geographical perimeter of criminalization is as narrow as possible and focused strictly on conduct and not on place and circumstances.

7. It acknowledges the ideological and institutional *bifurcation* of punishment into principled "paper penality" (for the bourgeoisie) versus arbitrary "street penality" (for the racialized precariat) and works methodically to narrow that gap: as regards policing, the cardinal rule is that officers should behave toward the most marginal members of the society as they would toward its most privileged; as regards judicial processing, recourse to fast-track procedures should be curtailed; as regards probation, support should be maximized and coercion minimized; as regards incarceration, non-custodial alternatives should be the default option for all but the most serious violent offenses.

8. It recognizes that *class and ethnicity* are key drivers of penal sanction and so it builds protocols at every stage in the legal process to disclose and diminish this double bias (especially class discrimination, which has largely escaped scholarly and public scrutiny even though it is hyper visible and decisive in the courthouse).

[83] Contrary to a common belief, prosecutors in San Pedrito county who successfully try a murder case to a guilty verdict – the peak of professional achievement – do not feel that they have scored "a victory." They feel *relief* for the family of the deceased and from the hard emotional, intellectual, and physical labor they invested in the case. They readily confess that "there are no winners" in these cases.

9. It appreciates that penalization, socialization, and medicalization are three competing strategies for the regulation of the precariat in the metropolis but, while ceding priority on principle to the latter two alternatives, it is mindful of the potentially *perverse effects of their interweaving* (as when the psychiatric treatment of homeless persons, for instance, serves as a vehicle for surveillance and sanction or further entrenches their penal entanglement).[84]

10. It actively worries that punishment is a means of signaling state sovereignty on the domestic front and a vehicle for public officials to generate everyday legitimacy among the citizenry. So it strives to preserve the autonomy of justice officials by shielding them from political and journalistic influences. Indeed, the diligent *defense of the autonomy of the judicial subfield* within the bureaucratic field and within the broader field of power is the precondition for pursuing the four aforementioned goals.[85]

Most importantly, radical penal minimalism is not a static state but a dynamic process, not so much a paper doctrine as a regulative ideal to guide the ordinary functioning of the penal state at ground level. It immediately translates into judicial checkpoints and administrative measures,[86] such as the curtailing of remand detention and the expanded use of public utility work as baseline sanction for low-level offenses. While the legislature can act to shrink the perimeter of criminal acts and abridge sanctions across the board, the primary engine of penal minimalism is the court because it is the critical decision point in the penal chain. It is relatively insulated from direct popular pressure – even in the US, where the elections of judges and prosecutors are typically pro forma affairs in which the incumbent runs unopposed or

[84] Philippe Bourgois and Jeff Schonberg, *Righteous Dopefiend* (2009); Mary Ellen Stitt, *Trial by Treatment: Punishing Illness in an Age of Criminal Legal Reform* (2025).

[85] I diverge on this point with the leading authority on prosecution in the US, Ronald Wright, who argues in "Reinventing American Prosecution Systems" (2017) that, in that country, autonomy from local society and politics is neither feasible nor desirable. The eminent William J. Stuntz famously lionizes local control in *The Collapse of American Criminal Justice* (2011). The same argument was made a half-century ago by James Eisenstein et al. (*The Contours of Justice: Communities and their Courts* [1988], p. 295): "A centralized and uniform criminal justice system strikes Americans as an unthinkable vision, almost un-American" and definitely "unrealistic." In my view, localism is a multiplier of both punitiveness and disparity that needs to be mitigated to the greatest degree possible, as it is in many European countries by the architecture of judicial institutions.

[86] Trevor George Gardner, "Auditing Criminal Justice Minimalism" (2025).

400

opposed by weak candidates. The judge makes a determination case by case and thus can dismiss charges when they target minor criminal conduct (the *de minimis* principle); divert cases when non-penal treatment is recommended and available (the *ultima ratio* principle); and show parsimony in sentencing (the penal restraint principle).[87]

Penal transformation and the "ethic of responsibility"

What are the social and political conditions of possibility of radical penal minimalism once its principles have been formulated on paper? Abolitionism is an *eschatology*: a form of penal millenarism unspooling in the frictionless world of moral wish and political longing for a perfect society to come in which punishment will have vanished out of thin air.[88] It deliberately pushes aside as "reformist" and thus pointless the question of concrete means and "objective possibility" in the Weberian sense. By contrast, radical penal minimalism draws prosaically on *sociology* to find real institutional anchors and to trace plausible pathways within the imperfect society that history has bequeathed us.

I proposed in chapter 1 that, to understand penality, we need to grasp the structural bifurcation and functional rivalry between the Leviathan's paternalist "Right hand" of discipline and its maternalist "Left hand" of succor. I further argued in chapter 2 that penal policy is best conceptualized as one plank in the dual design of poverty policy in the city alongside the second plank of social policy. Putting these two propositions together points to an inverse relationship between the punitive and the supportive treatment of urban marginality – between punishment and welfare, castigation and protection, penal severity and social generosity – both within and across advanced countries. This means that every measure that bolsters the social state is a measure that curtails the penal state. *Radical penal minimalism is premised upon and permitted by radical social maximalism.* To achieve the one we must fight to institute the other, in steps both big and small. This returns us to the agenda which prioritizes tackling urban marginality via the expansion and institutionalization of social and economic rights.

[87] For a clear formulation and convincing discussion of these three principles, see Yoav Sapir and Guy Rubinstein, "Minimalist Criminal Courts" (2023).
[88] The theoretical version of that argument in conceptual language is Bernard Harcourt, *Cooperation: A Political, Economic, and Social Theory* (2023). The practical version in everyday language is Mariame Kaba, *We Do This 'Til We Free Us: Abolitionist Organizing and Transforming Justice* (2021).

401

Conversely, *social minimalism is a built-in obstacle to penal minimalism.* The brute material conditions of the urban precariat are set by the welfare state and they, in turn, shape the range of punishment options available to the criminal court. In the US, many measures designed to contain crime while diminishing the penal load commonly used in European countries, such as "day fines" (pegged on the income of the convict),[89] are not workable because *the American poor are simply too poor* to make non-custodial responses viable. County judges cannot routinely resort to fines in lieu of short jail stays because the income of defendants is too meager for them to pay such fines. He cannot use home detention because their housing situation is too precarious or they cannot afford the cost of electronic home detention (an administrative enrollment fee of $150 and a monthly charge of $865 in Carnival county, which effectively reserves that option for the solid working class and middle class). He cannot successfully divert offenders to drug or alcohol treatment programs because many of them lack the life stability and meager monies needed to cover the bus fare to go to the clinic, not to mention the cost of the weekly drug test.[90]

Yet, perversely, the county court automatically hits convicts with a litany of administrative fees, surcharges, and payments to the state restitution fund as a *supplement* to jail and prison sentences, such that extra "financial legal obligations" further impoverish the poorest defendants and extend their punishment in the form of legal debt for years after they have served their sentence.[91] So much to confirm that the miserly social state and the gargantuan penal state are the two sides of the frowning visage of the American Leviathan.

[89] Elena Kantorowicz-Reznichenko and Michael Faure (eds.), *Day Fines in Europe: Assessing Income-Based Sanctions in Criminal Justice Systems* (2021). Half of the countries in the European Union employ day fines as an alternative to short custodial sentences because they are more effective, less costly, more transparent, and fairer. Yet even on that continent that option is under-utilized. In Germany, which leads the charge on that front, the *Tagessatz* was introduced in 1975 as an alternative to prison sentences of less than 6 months. It is determined through a point system pegged on the severity of the offense and the offender's income. It allows the vast majority of low-level offenders to avoid incarceration and helps explain the low and stable prison rate of the country. As for fine defaulters, they are given the option of paying their due in community service or doing time behind bars. Hans-Joerg Albrecht, "Day Fines in Germany" (2021).
[90] Mary Ellen Stitt, *Trial by Treatment: Punishing Illness in an Age of Criminal Legal Reform* (2025), pp. 1–2. On the social and political determinants of the wretched state of the American precariat and its offshoot, a homeless population officially estimated at 770,000, read Matthew Desmond, *Poverty, by America* (2023), especially pp. 13–23.
[91] Alexes Harris, *A Pound of Flesh: Monetary Sanctions as Punishment for the Poor* (2016); Joshua Page and Joe Soss, *Legal Plunder: The Predatory Dimensions of Criminal Justice* (2025).

Coda

Abolitionists ride on a false alternative between law and order fueling hyperincarceration, on the one hand, and the elimination of justice institutions, on the other, as if no practically viable, morally desirable, and socially progressive option existed between these two extremes. But, logically, *every abolitionist should be a penal minimalist* since shrinking the penal state is a stage on the road toward its eventual elimination – a necessary stage, to boot, unless one holds on to a fantastic "big-bang theory" of judicial change by which the penal Leviathan vanishes overnight. Yet some abolitionists insist on opposing measures that would result in the progressive modulation of penal power in favor of "non-reformist reforms" designed to undermine the reproduction and legitimacy of "the system." In so doing they lock themselves into a practical endorsement of the status quo. Pierre Bourdieu's warning is apposite here: "*Messianic hope is one of the great obstacles to transformation.* To this messianic illusion, we must substitute entirely moderate rational hopes, which were often discredited as reformist, as compromises, etc., even though there exist forms of them that are very, very radical."[92]

Here is a judicial reform that would most benefit the regular clientele of the penal apparatus and the residents of the city's underbelly from which they issue, which abolitionists would fiercely oppose on principle: dramatically increase the budget for local courts, say, by a factor of three, to give them the resources needed to process cases according to their professed principles of dignity, impartiality, and constitutionality – while also establishing conflict resolution boards to handle minor disputes, enlarging prosecutorial diversion, and supporting "expanded criminal defense."[93] Allocations of court funds and personnel are in nearly every country woefully insufficient. In large urban counties in the US, even serious criminal cases *have* to resolve through plea bargaining for the simple reason that there just are not enough courtrooms, not enough judges to sit a jury, not enough attorneys on both sides of the aisle to go to trial, and not enough clerks and court reporters to support their work. In some counties, defendants are forced to languish in jail for weeks because of a dearth of court-appointed attorneys to take up their case. Abolitionist activists wish to "starve the beast," not realizing that the court is already famished for finance and staff to the point where it undermines its constitutional mandate.[94]

---

[92] Pierre Bourdieu (with Roger Chartier), *Le Sociologue et l'historien*, p. 54, my italics.
[93] Ronald Wright and Jenny Roberts, "Expanded Criminal Defense Lawyering" (2023).
[94] Michael J. Graetz, "Trusting the Courts: Redressing the State Court Funding

A related measure would be to triple the number of public defenders or court-appointed counsel assigned to indigent defendants to reduce their caseload and to boost their pay and make the job more attractive to well-trained lawyers. Expanded funding would make it possible to include in their offices immigration specialists, social workers, mental health professionals, housing navigators, and family counselors as well as to build a bridge to non-judicial programs to treat alcohol and drug addiction (which are entailed in a majority of crimes).[95]

In New York City, as in a dozen major cities around the country, legal aid providers and justice-focused non-profit associations such as the Osborne Association employ "mitigation specialists," skilled assistants trained in social work, forensics, and the law tasked with preparing meticulous reports (typically running to a dozen pages) on the childhood, family, school, work, and health profile of defendants as well as their plans to firm up their social integration. These reports are submitted to the prosecutor pre-plea and to the judge pre-sentencing to incline them to moderate punishment. Such specialists are commonly used in death penalty cases pursuant to the guidelines of the American Bar Association. Their numbers could be greatly expanded and their use generalized to cover all defendants accused of felonies pre-plea and to advocate for the early jail release of persons accused of misdemeanors. This is another reason to massively augment funding for the courts: expand the size of the penal state to the immediate benefit of defendants and correlatively shrink the population placed under its tutelage.

But abolitionists are strident about the need to "defund" or "deresource" criminal justice institutions and consistently push for shrinking their budgets with dire potential consequences for the penalized population. Some flatly oppose publicly funded defense attorneys on grounds that "it invests the criminal justice system with a veneer of impartiality and

Crisis" (2014). At the end of the year in Carnival county, the court puts its entire staff on furlough and closes the courthouse for a week because its budget has run out. Hearings are rescheduled to the new year and cases are delayed accordingly to the detriment of defendants first and foremost.

[95] The varied and generally sorry state of California's system of public defense is mapped out by Laurence A. Benner, "The Presumption of Guilt: Systemic Factors that Contribute to Ineffective Assistance of Counsel in California" (2008). Note that, in coastal urban counties, public defenders are well paid and work in diversified offices with a strong *esprit de corps*, which allows these offices to recruit, train, and retain skilled and motivated lawyers. According to prosecutors in San Pedrito county, public defenders are superior court attorneys to private counsel. But their ranks are still not sufficient to absorb the high volume of cases that characterize urban jurisdictions.

respectability it does not deserve."[96] So should we leave defendants to fend for themselves without counsel just to make an ideological point?

Here is an everyday dilemma in the mission of court-appointed defenders: by protecting the judicial interests of individual defendants at the micro-level, they prop up the judicial institution at the meso-level. This dilemma is not unique to public defenders; it is built into all the occupations housed by the Left hand of the state (social workers, teachers, housing advocates, health providers, labor inspectors, etc.) who reproduce through their daily activities a "system" they rightfully find deeply deficient, nay intolerably flawed. It is insuperable and so public defenders must learn to live with it while engaging in collective forms of activism aimed at changing the institution from within.

405

Radical penal minimalism is paradoxical, then, in that, at least for an extended phase of transition, it requires that we simultaneously *increase* the budgets and personnel allocated to the court, jail, prison, and their administrative extensions, which are woefully insufficient relative to the volume of judicial labor on both sides of the Atlantic (save for Scandinavian countries, Germany, Austria, and Canada), and *decrease* the population processed by the penal chain. The most redundant observation running through reports on judicial institutions in most advanced countries is that they are submerged by the human tide they face, their staff crushed by the workload they carry, their services buried by enormous backlogs. They operate in a constant state of organizational emergency due to the grotesque dearth of human and material resources on a daily basis.[97]

---

[96] Paul D. Butler, "Poor People Lose: *Gideon* and the Critique of Rights" (2012), pp. 2178–9. One wonders if Butler, an eminent law professor, former prosecutor, and renowned television guest commentator, would let his brother, son, or nephew face a felony charge on his own.

[97] Read the shocking account of police detectives working on 20 homicides at a time in the black hyperghetto of Los Angeles in Jill Leovy's *Ghettoside*: they lack desks, working phones, and functioning printers in their decrepit offices, gas to travel to their crime sites and recorders to tape witnesses. Unlike in TV series, they have to make do without forensic support, DNA testing, and timely surveillance video footage. This gross penury of means attests to the institutional abandonment of poor black crime victims. See also the description of *comparution immédiate* (fast-track judicial processing) by Chowra Makaremi, "Le droit de punir. L'appréciation de la peine en comparution immédiate" (2013), which discloses a similar deficit of material and human resources in French criminal courts.

Build prisons, close prisons, and diminish the influx of inmates

The two most urgent issues faced by the French carceral system are shocking overcrowding and the utterly dilapidated and even dangerous state of much of its physical plant. The national occupancy rate of custodial facilities is 135 percent but it exceeds 150 percent in 97 of 188 prisons and even 200 percent in 29 establishments. Every night, 6,000 of the country's 85,000 inmates sleep on a thin portable mattress laid on the floor of cells designed for two but confining three or even four inmates (1). Correctional staff unions have alerted the authorities again and again about the impossibility of providing basic safety and security, let alone support "reinsertion," under such conditions: in some penitentiaries, the number of inmates per guard has doubled in a decade. Overpopulation mechanically deteriorates access to all the amenities and activities behind bars, food, yard time, medical and psychiatric care, schooling, religious services, etc., and translates into rising tension and endemic violence.

The country was twice condemned by the European Court of Human Rights in 2020 and 2022 for the "degrading and inhumane conditions" of detention caused by the dilapidation of its custodial facilities (2). Nearly half of French prisons were built before 1940 and establishments erected in the nineteenth century are still in operation. Many are so decrepit that parts of them are closed down because they are unsafe or unfit for human habitation. Rodents, bed bugs, saltpetre, lead shards, asbestos paint, mold, deficient ventilation, dysfunctional sanitary systems, defective electrical wiring and plumbing, and water leaks are the daily fare of thousands of inmates. In many prisons, cells are frigid in the winter, sweltering in the summer, and toxic and suffocating year around.

"Defunding" the national correctional system under this scenario would be downright calamitous for the inmate population. Paradox of paradox, then, France *urgently needs to build new prisons* – to provide more beds, safe buildings, and salubrious cells that are the baseline minimum for human dignity (3), *close and decommission older prisons* while *convicting fewer felons on shorter sentences*, and expanding the use of pretrial release and alternative sentences such as community work, home detention, and electronic monitoring. To do that, it needs to massively increase its criminal justice budget, not decrease it, and set a goal of shuttering first two and then three

406

old prisons for every new one it opens. The government should also forego economies of scale and build smaller prisons as these are less impersonal, less bureaucratic, less anomic, and less violent than large establishments. Human-scale institutions cushion to a degree the psycho-socio-biological shock of incarceration and limit the crush of "prisonization." Finally, increasing justice finance would bankroll expanding the ranks of the *agents d'insertion et de probation* who handle the supervision of noncustodial sentences and support the reentry of convicts after they have served their sentence. The winning formula boils down to a bigger budget for fewer prisons and more correctional personnel for fewer inmates.

1. These conditions are further deteriorated in the French overseas dominions issued from colonization, where incarceration rates are double and triple the national average and custodial facilities are even worse. In 2022, in the jail of Saint-Denis on the Réunion island, some inmates had nothing to sleep on but the bare floor – not even a mattress.
2. Observatoire international des prisons, *Dignité en prison* (2022).
3. Ian Loader makes dignity a yardstick of "penal moderation," alongside parsimony and restraint, in "For Penal Moderation: Notes Towards a Public Philosophy of Punishment" (2010).

As for the police, a country-by-country or city-by-city audit is necessary to determine whether more officers are needed per unit of crime alongside drastic qualitative changes to shift from crime-fighting to peace-keeping, warrior to protector.[98] Redeploying the force should be sufficient in many cases since police spend much of their schedule doing administrative chores and, when called out on the street, they devote most of their dispatch time to handling noise complaints, traffic infractions, wellness checks, and mental health crises – tasks that could be better handled by mobile social service and medical brigades. In any case, law enforcement should at all time prioritize personal dignity, procedural fairness, and de-escalation for better prevention and reduced brutality.

The rationale for this scissor-like movement – increase organizational means, decrease the human flow into the penal funnel – is to boost the number of prosecutors, public defenders, and judges per

[98] In the outlier case of the US, given the routinization of extreme violence, rampant militarization, and bureaucratic fragmentation of law enforcement agencies, legal, procedural, and cultural changes need to be implemented *prior* to any eventual increase in personnel. Meanwhile, the latter can be redeployed to focus on preventative policing and detective work focused on serious criminal cases.

defendant for better adjudication respecting fundamental rights; the personnel handling probation and assorted alternatives to incarceration to deliver support over surveillance; and the number of prison guards per inmate to increase safety and dignity for both behind bars. Abolitionists cannot grasp this paradox because they misconstrue the absolute size of the penal state (measured by its budget and staffing) as the root cause of penal excess when the way to curb the latter is to *augment size while diminishing scope*. To effect this double move requires a campaign to come to the collective realization that *criminal adjudication is a core public service* and, as such, requires a collective investment on a par with the essential mission it purports to accomplish.

408

Consider the differential human means devoted to criminal justice across borders: the US has ten state and county prosecutors for every 100,000 residents, while France (which sits at the low end of European countries on this count) has three, Germany has six and Norway 18, even though these four countries have comparable levels of crime save for violent offences.[99] The differences per homicide are shockingly larger and attest to the outlier status of the US on the international scene when it comes to handling the more serious offenses: the US sports 0.6 state prosecutors per murder, as against 2.3 for France, 7.3 for Germany and an astounding 30 for Norway.

The US does not need to abolish prosecutors: it needs to hire them by the bushel, alongside battalions of police detectives, if homicide cases are to be resolved. They need to be assigned pronto to cities with large poor black and Hispanic populations where the clearance rate for homicides is abysmally low in neighborhoods of relegation.[100] On the South

---

[99] The US estimate is based on 35,000 full-time state and county prosecutors. It does not include 6,000 federal prosecutors because they do not handle run-of-the-mill offenses, concentrating instead on a tiny number of complex crimes falling in their restricted jurisdiction (amounting to less than one-third of 1 percent of the total number of criminal cases in the country). It also omits municipal prosecutors, whose exact numbers are unknown (estimates range from 5,000 to 10,000) because they typically handle mostly infractions and city-ordinances violations.

[100] Richard Stansfield and Karen F. Parker, "A Neighborhood Analysis of US Homicide Clearances in 50 Cities: Examining Race and Disadvantage across Neighborhood Types" (2025). "Clearance" does not mean that the murderer was convicted, only that someone was arrested and charged in the case. To be sure, the shockingly low murder resolution rate in the hyperghetto is affected, not just by the insufficient number of prosecutors and police detectives but, critically, by the deep distrust and disdain of the local population for the justice apparatus as well as by the collective fear of street retaliation against those who would participate in investigations and prosecution: no one wants to "wear a snitch jacket." This disdain is itself

Side of Chicago, in Brooklyn's Brownsville, in West Baltimore, in North Philadelphia, and in South Central LA, the majority of murderers walk unscathed. In 2011, the homicide clearance rate for Oakland, home of the Bay Area largest black hyperghetto, was a shocking 29 percent compared to a California average of 64 percent. In East and West Oakland, the two poor black districts of the city which concentrate two homicides in three, it was probably half that, even though most killers are well identified in the neighborhood.

All in all, the ideal of abolitionists is philosophically attractive and morally unimpeachable. It is hands down the best penal policy for some small-scale, socially and culturally homogeneous, imaginary society from which harm would have magically disappeared or could be resolved by amicable means – a society run by Jean-Jacques Rousseau instead of Thomas Hobbes. But, placed in the American context, and even in the most progressive European societies, it is practically self-defeating and turns into a sectarian practice promoting *penal stasis*: it ensures the perpetuation of the status quo by rejecting small steps toward real changes – what Didier Fassin calls "little utopias" by contrast to "grand utopias"[101] – in favor of the sociologically absurd and thus politically illusory goal of the wholesale dismantlement of the penal Leviathan devoid of viable replacement.

There is, admittedly, a *tension* between the theses propounded in the first two chapters of this book, according to which the penal state is structurally bifurcated by class and ethnicity, targets populations by place, and spawns in every advanced society a dual set of punishment regimes, one for the bourgeoisie and another for the racialized precariat, and what will seem to some readers a relative reserve on the proposed path to penal change – *radical reform* rather than fictive revolution, to put it in simple political terms, that is, multiprong reform aimed at "softening" the penal state to make it smaller in scope, reflexive, and reticent. This tension is resolved by the unavoidable

---

fed by the rampant indifference of the authorities to black suffering generated by crime.

[101] Didier Fassin, "La faculté de punir," 9th lecture at the Collège de France, Paris, May 2024. Fassin gives as an example of a little utopia allowing inmates to have cell phones and regulating their use, instead of prohibiting them while knowing full well that they circulate en masse behind bars. This might seem trivial but having a personal phone would allow the prisoner to maintain contact with his loved ones and his attorney, break monotony and isolation, improve his mental health, economize on communication costs, and avoid violence linked to the illegal economy of phones, which are the most sought-after piece of contraband in custodial facilities.

compromise that every analyst and activist of criminal justice must strike between what Max Weber calls the "ethic of conviction" (*Gesinnungsethik*), which commands fierce obedience to ideal absolutes, and the "ethic of responsibility" (*Verantwortungsethik*), which takes into pragmatic account possible paths and likely outcomes.[102] In matters involving human suffering, when it comes to action, I incline toward the latter.

Radical penal minimalism is a political and moral imperative for a simple reason: the penal state is not just a "people-processing" institution, as elaborated in the classic article by Yeheskel Hasenfeld,[103] but also a *people-damaging institution* – and, left to its own compulsion, it damages populations that are already the most precarious and vulnerable categories in the city. Decades of research have amply documented the acute psychological and social injuries of incarceration, from emotional deadening and hypervigilance to interpersonal distrust and generalized anxiety to the gamut of post-traumatic stress disorders that make it exceedingly difficult to function as a human being during and after confinement.[104]

Punishment need not be severe to inflict harm, as with the machine in Franz Kafka's *Penal Colony*. The gentlest carceral regimens, such as that implemented by the famed "prison island" of Bastøy in Norway, rasp the character and twist the social relations of their inmates. The residents of this Norwegian penal facility without walls who live in self-organized cottages and enjoy nearly unfettered movement find that "freedom" under correctional supervision feels "ambiguous, bittersweet or tainted."[105] But there is more: even when the police arrest proves in error, the overnight stay in jail ends, the criminal case is dismissed by the prosecutor, or the sentence by the judge turns out to be lenient, punishment wounds the self and rends the human fabric.

---

[102] Max Weber, *Le Savant et le politique* ([1917, 1919] 2003), p. 192. "The believer in an ethic of conviction feels 'responsible' only for seeing to it that the flame of pure intentions is not quelched: for example, the flame of protest against the injustice of the social order. To rekindle the flame ever anew is the purpose of his actions, thoroughly irrational if we judge them from the standpoint of their possible results" (p. 193).

[103] Yeheskel Hasenfeld, "People Processing Organizations: An Exchange Approach" (1972).

[104] Craig Haney, "The Psychological Impact of Incarceration: Implications for Post-Prison Adjustment" (2003). In its most extreme forms in the US, long-term solitary confinement, it amounts to torture as documented by Atul Gawande, "Hellhole" (2009).

[105] Victor Lund Shammas, "The Pains of Freedom: Assessing the Ambiguity of Scandinavian Penal Exceptionalism on Norway's Prison Island" (2014), p. 104.

Once it is set in motion, penalization leaves its poisonous stain, indelible. It follows that any measure that curtails the reach and reduces the scope of the penal state is a measure of public salubrity and civic urgency. This urgency is the reason why the intellectual and militant Left should forsake the righteous chimera of penal abolitionism and embrace radical penal minimalism.

Return to urban marginality: progressive scholars are typically unwilling to acknowledge the brute fact of suffusive danger and brewing insecurity in racialized districts of dereliction in the metropolis because it would seem to incriminate the black and immigrant poor and thus to lend support to conservative or reactionary interpretations of criminality and penality. It is easier to swim with the political tide sweeping academia and to embrace the rhetoric of abolition as the latest language game signaling moral virtue. But it is essential to eschew the logic of the trial which impels one to indict institutions – in this case, the penal triad – instead of striving to understand them, "their force of resistance and their infinite variability" (to quote Durkheim again), and to face historical reality in all of its vexing complexities.

Let me close on a provocation: when it comes to crime and punishment, the intellectual Left should go further and reclaim the sulfurous dyad of "law and order" – fight fire with fire. It should unpack its coupling and to give it a fully sociological reckoning, tightly tying criminal and social insecurity, instead of abandoning it as the rhetorical ploy and tactical province of the Right, neoconservative, neoliberal, or neonativist.[106] It should then attach the provision of safety and security to an expansive notion of justice centered on the concrete realization of human capabilities and the real-life removal of unjust states of affairs, as construed by Amartya Sen, and on the bestowal and protection of dignity, as proposed by Martha Nussbaum.[107] It should hold criminal justice to the standards of social justice. *Law, order, and justice*: that triad has a dissonant ring and I realize full well that many readers will find it jarring beyond salvage – even political

---

[106] A fruitful theoretical elaboration of the notion, defined minimally as "a negative form of peace secured through some combination of police and policy," is Nick Cheesman, "Law and Order" (2022), p. 275. Its recent crystallization as political slogan is recapitulated by Michael W. Flamm, *Law and Order: Street Crime, Civil Unrest, and the Crisis of Liberalism in the 1960s* (2005), for the US, and Laurent Bonelli, *La France a peur. Une histoire sociale de "l'insécurité."* (2010), for France.

[107] Amartya Sen, *The Idea of Justice* (2009); Martha C. Nussbaum, *Creating Capabilities: The Human Development Approach* (2011).

anathema. But it can be made to work in a progressive key and applied to penality by providing this guidance for its deployment: pacify social relations by pacific means, minimize unjust states, and diminish infringements on dignity.

This entails amplifying and seizing on the progressive side of the law as shield against danger and oppression, including oppression by penal institutions, for, like the state itself, the law is a Janus-faced institution than can both coerce and protect, exclude and include, disable and enable, subjugate and liberate.[108] It means recognizing the requirement of order as a social good, especially in districts of urban perdition where everyday life is warped by criminal turmoil (fed by the invasive economy of street drugs), the crucial question being whose order and enforced by what means. There can be such a thing as a just order defined as the democratic provision of safety and security, rather than its despotic distortion and imposition, or worse its absence due to the failings of the state. Living under the rule of law in an inclusive sense should not be a class privilege of the bourgeoisie in its secluded districts and of flaneurs in pacified downtowns revamped for the pleasures of commercial consumption. Neighborhoods of relegation should not be relegated to lawless zones, real or imagined.

In their masterful book *Civilizing Security*, Ian Loader and Neil Walker demonstrate, first, that security is "a constitutive social good" that underpins the "social" and the "public" as well as the "we-feeling" of a human collectivity; and second, that "the democratic state has a necessary and virtuous role to play in the production of this good."[109] To change the valence and deploy the triad of law, order, and justice, then, progressive thinkers and activists must start by acknowledging the indispensable *need for the penal state*, albeit one *drastically downsized and profoundly transformed* by organizational restraint, procedural accountability, and democratic legitimacy.[110]

---

[108] The double-sidedness of the law as instrument of oppression and social conservation, on the one side, and lever for institutional redesign and liberatory agency, on the other, is captured by Unger's distinction between a "structure-preserving structure" and a "structure-denying structure," that is, an open-ended institution that promotes its own critique and revision, thus supporting democratic experimentation. Roberto Mangabeira Unger, *False Necessity: Anti-Necessitarian Social Theory in the Service of Radical Democracy* (1987).

[109] Ian Loader and Neil Walker, *Civilizing Security* (2007), pp. 161–6 and p. 6.

[110] On the promise and pitfalls of procedural justice as the foundation of democratic penality, see Tom R. Tyler, "Whither Legitimacy? Legal Authority in the Twenty-First Century" (2023).

Coda

There is an urgent battle to be waged for gradual but real gains on all three fronts – law, security, justice. For, contrary to the image it strives to project and that militant scholars too hastily adopt,[111] the Leviathan is not a monolith mechanically geared toward fulfilling a single invariant function of tyranny but a multidimensional space of patterned struggles that can secure and expand life chances under its canopy. We can mobilize one sector of the bureaucratic field against another, enroll the law to fight the law, activate the Left hand to tame the Right hand at multiple scales, in the quest to make the state own up to its promise and to take steps, however small and halting, toward realizing its professed ideals, starting with the ideal of justice as essential civic value and fragile historical achievement.[112]

---

[111] For a one-dimensional account of penal law as exclusively, fiercely, and increasingly oppressive, see Vanessa Codaccioni, *Comment les États répriment. Une courte histoire du pouvoir de punir* (2025). This vision reduces the bureaucratic field to an apparatus by effacing the struggles that spawn its dynamics.

[112] The distinctive role of jurists in these battles is excavated by Pierre Bourdieu, *L'Intérêt au désintéressement. Cours au Collège de France (1987–1989)* (2022a). The constitutive fragility and ambiguity of justice are explored by Hannah Arendt, *Eichmann in Jerusalem: A Report on the Banality of Evil* (1963).

Acknowledgments

This book was written as the "long version" of the three lectures presented as the Adorno-Vorlesungen at Goethe-Universität in Frankfurt in November of 2024. I would like to thank the Institüt für Sozialforschung (especially Stefan Lessenich and Almut Poppinga) for this honorific and intimidating invitation to contribute to the continuing vibrancy of critical theory in its most varied forms. When I was an undergraduate student at the University of Paris in the 1980s, I had an abiding fascination for the Frankfurt School. I would never have dreamt then that one day I would be asked to speak in the haunts of Theodor Adorno, Max Horkheimer, Erich Fromm, and Jürgen Habermas. I am especially appreciative of the warm welcome I received from the scholars, students, and other interested listeners during and after the three lectures. I hope that the unusual combination of social theory, history, and ethnography I devised to respond to the challenge of the moment invites the specialists of each of these domains to sample and better appreciate the others and spawns imitators.

I would like to express my gratitude to the colleagues and intellectual fellow travelers who took the time to read and react to earlier chunks and versions of the chapters of this book, among them (with apologies for those I am inadvertently forgetting) Javier Auyero, Vanessa Barker, François Bonnet, Jérôme Bourdieu, Rogers Brubaker, Sandra Bucerius, Jenae Carpenter, Manuela Cunha, Julian Go, Ignacio González Sánchez, Ricarda Hammer, Christian Sandberg Hansen, Bernard Harcourt, Laurie Kain Hart, Paul Hathazy, Milton Heumann, Cathy Hu, Troels Schultz Larsen, Kay Levine, Ian Loader, Douglas Maynard, Ellis Monk Jr., Nazli Ökten, Sonia Paone, Virgílio Borges Pereira, Jill Pöggel, Annick Prieur, Dylan Riley, Daniel

Acknowledgments

Sabbagh, Grégory Salle, Rob Sampson, Martín Sánchez-Jankowski, Fatinha Santos, Heather Schoenfeld, Dahlia Showalter, Jonathan Simon, George Steinmetz, Michael Tonry, Bruce Western, Andreas Wimmer, and Michael Zanger-Tishler. David Garland and Máximo Langer deserve special thanks for commenting fruitfully on the entire manuscript and Malcolm Feeley for his constant intellectual backing and smart suggestions to various iterations of chapter 3.

For the "excursus" on colonial penality, I benefited greatly from the magnanimous encouragement and pointed suggestions of colleague historians, among them Florence Bernault, Emmanuel Blanchard, Joël Glasman, Jean-Pierre Le Crom, Isabelle Merle, Sylvie Thénault, and Romain Tiquet.

For the ethnographic chapter on penal power in the courthouse, I am deeply indebted to the prosecutors, public defenders and private counsel, judges and ancillary court staff who graciously took me under their wings and patiently taught me the ropes of criminal justice as a collective happening. I regret that I cannot thank them by name to maintain my promise of confidentiality but they know who they are and they know how much I value their many-sided contributions to this research enterprise. My gratitude goes to Julius Atkins (a pseudonym) for welcoming me in the pretrial negotiation chamber in Alphaville and making me feel at home among hurried and harried criminal lawyers. Max Silver (a pseudonym) merits special commendation, not only for tutoring me in the fine arts of plea bargaining in Metro City, but also for patiently combing his way through chapter 3 to save me from errant claims on the technical front. Any remaining mistakes and misinterpretations are mine alone.

Once again, Chris Muller and Victor Lund Shammas went far beyond the call of duty, reading and reacting in real time to multiple drafts of every section of the book as I was writing them. I am most appreciative of their sharp minds, stimulating support, and intellectual generosity. To say that they handled the endless avalanche of queries, sorties, and worries filling their mailboxes in Cambridge and Oslo with poise, patience, and precision does not begin to capture the luscious cast of our feverish exchanges across the continents. Last but not least, I thank Tamar Young for superior office support; Harry Jude for drafting many versions of the figures until we got them right; and the Berkeley undergraduate students who took the inaugural version of SOC 149 – The Penal State in the spring of 2024, willing guinea pigs who kept me focused and honest. As ever, Sophie's presence was steadfast and essential.

References

Abdul-Rahman, Laila, Hannah Espín Grau, Luise Klaus, and Tobias Singelnstein. 2025. *Police Use of Excessive Force in Germany*. Berlin: Campus Verlag.

Aebi, Marcelo F., Edoardo Cocco, and Yuji Z. Hashimoto. 2022. *Key Findings of the SPACE Reports*. Brussels: Council of Europe.

Albrecht, Hans-Joerg. 2021. "Day Fines in Germany." Pp. 85–121 in *Day Fines in Europe: Assessing Income-Based Sanctions in Criminal Justice Systems*. Edited by Elena Kantorowicz-Reznichenko and Michael Faure. Cambridge: Cambridge University Press.

Alford, C. Fred. 2000. "What Would It Matter if Everything Foucault Said About Prison Were Wrong? *Discipline and Punish* After 20 Years." *Theory & Society* 29 (1): 125–46.

Allen, Francis A. 1981. *The Decline of the Rehabilitative Ideal: Penal Policy and Social Purpose*. New Haven, CT: Yale University Press.

Althusser, Louis. 1971. *Pour Marx*. Paris: Maspéro.

Anderson, Clare. 2007. *The Indian Uprising of 1857–8: Prisons, Prisoners and Rebellion*. London: Anthem.

Anderson, Clare (ed.). 2018. *A Global History of Convicts and Penal Colonies*. London: Bloomsbury Academic.

Anderson, Clare and David Arnold. 2007. "Envisioning the Colonial Prison." Pp. 304–31 in *Cultures of Confinement: A History of the Prison in Africa, Asia, and Latin America*. Edited by Frank Dikötter and Ian Brown. Ithaca, NY: Cornell University Press.

Anderson, David M. 2011. "Punishment, Race and 'The Raw Native': Settler Society and Kenya's Flogging Scandals, 1895–1930." *Journal of Southern African Studies* 37 (3): 479–97.

Anderson, David M. and David Killingray (eds.). 1991. *Policing the Empire: Government, Authority and Control, 1830–1940*. Manchester: Manchester University Press.

References

Anderson, Elijah. 2000. *Code of the Street: Decency, Violence, and the Moral Life of the Inner City*. New York: Norton.

Anderson, J.P. 2023. "Prison Disproportion in Democracies: A Comparative Analysis." *Law & Social Inquiry* 48 (3): 906–36.

Anderson, James M., Maya Buenaventura, and Paul Heaton. 2019. "The Effects of Holistic Defense on Criminal Justice Outcomes." *Harvard Law Review* 132 (3): 819–93.

Anter, Andreas. 2014. *Max Weber's Theory of the Modern State: Origins, Structure and Significance*. London: Palgrave Macmillan.

Antillano, Andrés. 2024. "In/Out: Revisiting the Relationships Between Prisons and Slums in Latin America." Pp. 109–29 in *Punishment in Latin America: Explorations from the Margins*. Edited by Luiz Dal Santo and Máximo Sozzo. Leeds: Emerald Publishing.

Applebaum, Anne. 2003. *Gulag: A History*. New York: Doubleday.

Arditi, Benjamin. 2008. "On the Political: Schmitt contra Schmitt." *Telos* 142: 7–28.

Arendt, Hannah. 1963. *Eichmann in Jerusalem: A Report on the Banality of Evil*. New York: Penguin.

Arnold, David. 1986. *Police Power and Colonial Rule: Madras, 1859–1947*. London: Primus, expanded edition, 2024.

Artières, Philippe, Laurent Quéro, and Michelle Zancarin (eds.). 2004. *Le Groupe d'information sur les prisons. Archives d'une lutte, 1970–1972*. Paris: Decitre.

Aubusson de Cavarlay, Bruno. 1985. "Hommes, peines et infractions. La légalité de l'inégalité." *L'Année sociologique* 35: 275–309.

Auyero, Javier and María Fernanda Berti. 2015. *In Harm's Way: The Dynamics of Urban Violence*. Princeton, NJ: Princeton University Press.

Avalos, Lisa. 2022. "The Under-Policing of Crimes Against Black Women." *Case Western Reserve Law Review* 73: 795–842.

Avril, Christelle. 2014. *Les Aides à domicile. Un autre monde populaire*. Paris: La Dispute.

Bach, Amy. 2009. *Ordinary Injustice: How America Holds Court*. New York: Holt.

Bacqué, Marie-Hélène, Éric Charmes, and Lydie Fol. 2016. "Des territoires entre ascension et déclin. Trajectoires sociales dans la mosaïque périurbaine." *Revue française de sociologie* 57 (4): 681–715.

Balandier, Georges. 1951. "La situation coloniale. Approche théorique." *Cahiers internationaux de sociologie* 11 (1): 44–79.

Balandier, Georges. 1955. *Sociologie actuelle de l'Afrique noire*. Paris: PUF.

Baldwin, Peter. 2021. *Command and Persuade: Crime, Law, and the State across History*. Cambridge, MA: MIT Press.

Balto, Simon. 2019. *Occupied Territory: Policing Black Chicago from Red Summer to Black Power*. Chapel Hill, NC: UNC Press.

Barideaux Jr, Kenneth, Alexandra Crossby, and Dondre Crosby. 2021.

"Colorism and Criminality: The Effects of Skin Tone and Crime Type on Judgements of Guilt." *Applied Psychology in Criminal Justice* 16 (2): 181–99.

Barker, Vanessa. 2009. *The Politics of Imprisonment: How the Democratic Process Shapes the Way America Punishes Offenders*. New York: Oxford University Press.

Barker, Vanessa. 2013. "Nordic Exceptionalism Revisited: Explaining the Paradox of a Janus-faced Penal Regime." *Theoretical Criminology* 17 (1): 5–25.

Barker, Vanessa. 2017. *Nordic Nationalism and Penal Order: Walling the Welfare State*. London: Routledge.

Barker, Vanessa and Lisa L. Miller. 2017. "Introduction to the Special Issue on the State of the State." *Theoretical Criminology* 21 (4): 417–21.

Barkow, Rachel E. 2023. "Promise or Peril? The Political Path of Prison Abolition in America." *Wake Forest Law Review* 58 (1): 245–320.

Barrett, Carla J. 2018. "Doing Court Ethnography: How I Learned to Study the Law in Action." Pp. 21–8 in *Doing Ethnography in Criminology: Discovery through Fieldwork*. Edited by Stephen K. Rice and Michael D. Maltz. Berlin: Springer.

Bastard, Benoit and Christian Mouhanna. 2007. *Une Justice dans l'urgence. Le traitement en temps réel des affaires pénales*. Paris: PUF.

Bat, Jean-Pierre and Nicolas Courtin (eds.). 2012. *Maintenir l'ordre colonial. Afrique et Madagascar, XIXe–XXe siècles*. Rennes: Presses Universitaires de Rennes.

Bates, Robert H. 2008. "State Failure." *Annual Review of Political Science* 11: 1–12.

Bates, Robert H. 2015. *When Things Fell Apart: State Failure in Late Century Africa*. Cambridge: Cambridge University Press.

Baumgartner, Frank R., Tamira Daniely, Kalley Huang, et al. 2021. "Throwing Away the Key: The Unintended Consequences of 'Tough-on-Crime' Laws." *Perspectives on Politics* 19 (4) (Special Issue: "Race and Politics in America"): 1233–46.

Bayart, Jean-François. 2008. "Hégémonie et coercition en Afrique subsaharienne. La 'politique de la chicotte'." *Politique africaine* 110 (2): 123–52.

Bayley, David H. [1969] 2015. *Police and Political Development in India*. Princeton, NJ: Princeton University Press.

Bazelon, Emily. 2020. *Charged: The New Movement to Transform American Prosecution and End Mass Incarceration*. New York: Random House.

Beattie, Peter M. 2015. *Punishment in Paradise: Race, Slavery, Human Rights, and a Nineteenth-Century Brazilian Penal Colony*. Durham, NC: Duke University Press

Beatty, Lauren G. and Tracy L. Snell. 2021. *Profile of Prison Inmates, 2016*. Washington, DC: Bureau of Justice Statistics.

Beckett, Katherine. 1999. *Making Crime Pay: Law and Order in Contemporary American Politics*. New York: Oxford University Press.

References

Beckett, Katherine. 2018. "The Politics, Promise, and Peril of Criminal Justice Reform in the Context of Mass Incarceration." *Annual Review of Criminology* 1: 235–59.

Beckett, Katherine. 2022. *Ending Mass Incarceration: Why It Persists and How to Achieve Meaningful Reform*. New York: Oxford University Press.

Beetham, David. 1991. *The Legitimation of Power*. London: Palgrave Macmillan.

Belina, Bernd. 2023. *Gefährliche Abstraktionen: Regieren mittels Kriminalisierung und Raum; Beiträge 2005–2023*. Münster: Verlag Westfälisches Dampfboot.

Bell, Monica C. 2016. "Situational Trust: How Disadvantaged Mothers Reconceive Legal Cynicism." *Law & Society Review* 50 (2): 314–47.

Bell, Monica C. 2019. "The Community in Criminal Justice: Subordination, Consumption, Resistance, and Transformation." *Du Bois Review: Social Science Research on Race* 16 (1): 197–220.

Bellin, Jeffrey. 2019. "The Power of Prosecutors." *New York University Law Review* 94 (2): 171–212.

Bendix, Reinhard. 1960. *Max Weber: An Intellectual Portrait*. Berkeley: University of California Press.

Benner, Laurence A. 2008. "The Presumption of Guilt: Systemic Factors that Contribute to Ineffective Assistance of Counsel in California." *California Western Law Review* 45 (2): 263–362.

Bensaïd, Daniel. 2007. *Les Dépossédés. Karl Marx, les voleurs de bois et le droit des pauvres*. Paris: La Fabrique.

Benson, Sara M. 2019. *The Prison of Democracy: Race, Leavenworth, and the Culture of Law*. Berkeley: University of California Press.

Bérard, Jean and Jean-Marie Delarue. 2016. *Prisons, quel avenir?* Paris: PUF.

Bergman, Marcelo and Gustavo Fondevila. 2021. *Prisons and Crime in Latin America*. Cambridge: Cambridge University Press.

Bernardot, Marc. 2012. *Captures*. Bellecombe-en-Bauges: Éditions du Croquant.

Bernault, Florence (ed.). 1999. *Enfermement, prison et châtiments en Afrique du 19ème siècle à nos jours*. Paris: Karthala.

Bernault, Florence. 2007. "The Shadow of Rule: Colonial Power and Modern Punishment in Africa." Pp. 55–94 in *Cultures of Confinement: A History of the Prison in Africa, Asia, and Latin America*. Edited by Frank Dikötter and Ian Brown. Ithaca, NY: Cornell University Press.

Besnier, Christiane. 2017. *La Vérité côté cour. Une ethnologue aux assises*. Paris: La Découverte.

Bessone, Magali (ed.). 2000. *La Justice*. Paris: Flammarion.

Bianchi, Herman and René van Swaaningen (eds.). 1986. *Abolitionism: Toward a Non-Repressive Approach to Crime*. Amsterdam: Free University Press.

Bibas, Stephanos. 2012. *The Machinery of Criminal Justice*. New York: Oxford University Press.

References

Bigo, Didier. 1989. "Ngaragba, l'impossible prison'." *Revue française de science politique* 39 (6): 867–86.

Bird, Mia, Omair Gill, Johanna Lacoe, Molly Pickard, Steven Raphael, and Alissa Skog 2023. *Sentence Enhancements in California*. Berkeley: California Policy Lab.

Bjørgo, Tore and Marie-Louise Damen (eds.). 2023. *The Making of a Police Officer: Comparative Perspectives on Police Education and Recruitment*. London: Routledge.

Black, Lynsey, Lizzie Seal, Florence Seemungal, Bharat Malkani, and Roger Ball. 2021. "Introduction: Legacies of Empire." *Punishment & Society* 23 (5): 609–12.

Blanchard, Emmanuel. 2011. *La Police parisienne et les Algériens (1944–1962)*. Paris: Nouveau Monde Éditions.

Blanchard, Emmanuel. 2014. "Contrôle au faciès. Une cérémonie de dégradation." *Plein droit* 4: 11–15.

Blanchard, Emmanuel. 2021. "The Colonial Legacy of French Policing." Pp. 39–53 in *Policing in France*. Edited by Jacques de Maillard and Wesley Skogan. London: Routledge.

Blanchard, Emmanuel and Joël Glasman. 2012. "Le maintien de l'ordre dans l'Empire français: une historiographie émergente." Pp. 11–41 in *Maintenir l'ordre colonial. Afrique, Madagascar, XIXᵉ–XXᵉ siècles*. Edited by Jean-Pierre Bat and Nicolas Courtin. Rennes: Presses Universitaires de Rennes.

Blanchard, Emmanuel, Marieke Bloembergen, and Amandine Lauro (eds.). 2017. *Policing in Colonial Empire: Cases, Connections, Boundaries (ca. 1850–1970)*. Berlin: Peter Lang.

Blauner, Robert. 1969. "Internal Colonialism and Ghetto Revolt." *Social Problems* 16 (4): 393–408.

Boddie, Elise C. 2022. "Racially Territorial Policing in Black Neighborhoods." *University of Chicago Law Review* 89: 477–98.

Boehme, Hunter M., Deanna Cann, and Deena A. Isom. 2022. "Citizens' Perceptions of Over- and Under-Policing: A Look at Race, Ethnicity, and Community Characteristics." *Crime & Delinquency* 68 (1): 123–54.

Bond, Sarah. 2014. "Altering Infamy: Status, Violence, and Civic Exclusion in Late Antiquity." *Classical Antiquity* 33 (1): 1–30.

Bonelli, Laurent. 2010. *La France a peur. Une histoire sociale de "l'insécurité."* Paris: La Découverte.

Bonnet, François. 2019. *The Upper Limit: How Low-Wage Work Defines Punishment and Welfare*. Berkeley: University of California Press.

Bonnet, Francois and Clotilde Caillault. 2015. "The Invader, the Enemy within and They-Who-Must-Not-Be-Named: How Police Talk about Minorities in Italy, the Netherlands and France." *Ethnic & Racial Studies* 38 (7): 1185–201.

Bontems, Claude. 2022. *La Justice en Algérie, 1830–1962*. Geneva: Slatkine Érudition.

References

Bony, Lucie. 2015. "La prison, une 'cité avec des barreaux'? Continuum socio-spatial par-delà les murs." *Annales de géographie* 702: 275–99.

Bony, Lucie. 2016a. "La prison, 'une cité avec des barreaux': entretien." *Dedans Dehors* 92.

Bony, Lucie. 2016b. "Sortir du continuum carcéral." *Mouvements* 88 (4): 101–8.

Boonin, David. 2008. *The Problem of Punishment.* Cambridge: Cambridge University Press.

Botsman, Daniel V. 2013. *Punishment and Power in the Making of Modern Japan.* Princeton, NJ: Princeton University Press.

Bottoms, Anthony. 1995. "The Philosophy and Politics of Punishment and Sentencing." Pp. 17–50 in *The Politics of Sentencing Reform.* Edited by Chris Clarkson and Rod Morgan. Oxford: Clarendon Press.

Bouagga, Yasmine. 2012. "Le métier de conseiller d'insertion et de probation. Dans les coulisses de l'État pénal?." *Sociologie du travail* 54 (3): 317–37.

Bouagga, Yasmine. 2015. *Humaniser la peine? Enquête en maison d'arrêt.* Rennes: Presses Universitaires de Rennes.

Boukir, Kamel. 2019. "Le politique au bout de la matraque. Fuir la police, obéir, résister: entre déviance et citoyenneté." *Politix* 125: 135–59.

Boukli, Avi and Justin Kotzé (eds.). 2018. *Zemiology: Reconnecting Crime and Social Harm.* London: Palgrave Macmillan.

Bourdieu, Pierre. 1972. *Esquisse d'une théorie de la pratique, précédé de trois études d'ethnologie kabyle.* Geneva: Droz.

Bourdieu, Pierre. 1979. *La Distinction. Critique sociale du jugement.* Paris: Minuit.

Bourdieu, Pierre. 1982. *Ce que parler veut dire. L'économie des échanges linguistiques.* Paris: Fayard.

Bourdieu, Pierre. 1986. "La force du droit. Éléments pour une sociologie du champ juridique." *Actes de la recherche en sciences sociales* 64: 3–19.

Bourdieu, Pierre. 1989a. "Social Space and Symbolic Power." *Sociological Theory* 7 (1): 14–25.

Bourdieu, Pierre. 1989b. *La Noblesse d'État. Grandes écoles et esprit de corps.* Paris: Minuit.

Bourdieu, Pierre. 1992. *Les Règles de l'art. Genèse et structure du champ littéraire.* Paris: Seuil.

Bourdieu, Pierre. 1993a. "Esprits d'État. Genèse et structure du champ bureaucratique." *Actes de la recherche en sciences sociales* 96: 49–62.

Bourdieu, Pierre. 1993b. "Notre État de misère" (interview with Sylvian Pasquier). *L'Express,* March 18.

Bourdieu, Pierre. 1994. *Raisons pratiques. Sur la théorie de l'action.* Paris: Seuil.

Bourdieu, Pierre. 1997. "De la maison du roi à la raison d'État." *Actes de la recherche en sciences sociales* 118: 55–68.

Bourdieu, Pierre. 1998. *Méditations pascaliennes.* Paris: Seuil.

References

Bourdieu, Pierre. [1992] 1998. "La main gauche et la main droite de l'État." Pp. 9–17 in *Contre-feux*. Paris: Raisons d'agir Éditions.

Bourdieu, Pierre. [1993] 1998. "On the Fundamental Ambivalence of the State." *Polygraph: An International Journal of Culture and Politics* 10 (1): 21–32

Bourdieu, Pierre. 2000. *Les Structures sociales de l'économie*. Paris: Seuil.

Bourdieu, Pierre. 2001. *Langage et pouvoir symbolique*. Paris: Seuil.

Bourdieu, Pierre. 2011. "Champ du pouvoir et division du travail de domination." *Actes de la recherche en sciences sociales* 190: 126–39.

Bourdieu, Pierre. 2012. *Sur l'État. Cours au Collège de France (1989–1992)*. Paris: Seuil and Raisons d'agir Éditions.

Bourdieu, Pierre. 2015. *Sociologie générale,* Volume 1: *Cours au Collège de France 1981–1983*. Paris: Seuil and Raisons d'agir Éditions.

Bourdieu, Pierre. 2016. *Sociologie générale,* Volume 2: *Cours au Collège de France 1983–1986*. Paris: Seuil and Raisons d'agir Éditions.

Bourdieu, Pierre. 2017. *Anthropologie économique. Cours au Collège de France 1992–1993*. Paris: Seuil and Raisons d'agir Éditions.

Bourdieu, Pierre. 2022a. *L'Intérêt au désintéressement. Cours au Collège de France (1987–1989)*. Paris: Seuil and Raisons d'agir Éditions.

Bourdieu, Pierre. 2022b. *Microcosmes. Théorie des champs*. Paris: Raisons d'agir Éditions.

Bourdieu, Pierre and Roger Chartier. [1988] 2011. *Le Sociologue et l'historien*. Marseilles: Agone.

Bourdieu, Pierre and Jean-Claude Passeron. 1970. *La Reproduction. Éléments pour une théorie du système d'enseignement*. Paris: Minuit.

Bourdieu, Pierre and Loïc Wacquant. 1992. *An Invitation to Reflexive Sociology*. Chicago: University of Chicago Press.

Bourdieu, Pierre, Jean-Claude Chamboredon, and Jean-Claude Passeron. 1968, 1973, 2021. *Le Métier de sociologue. Préalables épistémologiques*. Paris: Éditions de l'EHESS.

Bourdieu, Pierre et al. 1993. *La Misère du monde*. Paris: Seuil.

Bourgois, Philippe and Jeff Schonberg. 2009. *Righteous Dopefiend*. Berkeley: University of California Press.

Boutellier, Hans. 2000. *Crime and Morality: The Significance of Criminal Justice in Post-Modern Culture*. Dordrecht: Kluwer.

Boutellier, Hans. 2004. *The Safety Utopia: Contemporary Discontent and Desire as to Crime and Punishment*. Dordrecht: Kluwer.

Boutros, Magda. 2024. "Contrôles au Faciès in France: From Denial to Recognition to Inaction." Pp. 123–46 in *The Politicization of Police Stops in Europe: Public Issues and Police Reform*. Edited by Jacques De Maillard, Kristof Verfaillie, and Mike Rowe. London: Palgrave Macmillan.

Bowen, Deirdre. 2009. "Calling your Bluff: How Prosecutors and Defense Attorneys Adapt Plea Bargaining Strategies to Increased Formalization." *Justice Quarterly* 26 (1): 2–29.

422

References

Boyer, Paul. 1978. *Urban Masses and Moral Order in America, 1820–1920*. Cambridge, MA: Harvard University Press.

Brady, David and Linda M. Burton (eds.). 2016. *The Oxford Handbook of the Social Science of Poverty*. New York: Oxford University Press.

Braithwaite, John. 1989. *Crime, Shame and Reintegration*. Cambridge: Cambridge University Press.

Braithwaite, John. 1998. "Restorative Justice." Pp. 323–44 in *The Handbook of Crime and Punishment*. Edited by Michael Tonry. New York: Oxford University Press.

Braxton Peterson, James. 2016. *Prison Industrial Complex for Beginners*. Danbury, CT: For Beginners.

Brenner, Neil. 1994. "Foucault's New Functionalism." *Theory & Society* 23 (5): 679–709.

Brown, Adrienne Maree. 2020. *We Will Not Cancel Us: And Other Dreams of Transformative Justice*. Chico, CA: AK Press.

Brown, Darryl K. 2016. *Free Market Criminal Justice: How Democracy and Laissez Faire Undermine the Rule of Law*. New York: Oxford University Press.

Brown, Mark. 2002. "The Politics of Penal Excess and the Echo of Colonial Penality." *Punishment & Society* 4 (4): 403–23.

Brown, Mark. 2014. *Penal Power and Colonial Rule*. New York: Routledge.

Brown, Michelle. 2009. *The Culture of Punishment: Prison, Society, and Spectacle*. New York: NYU Press.

Brown, Wendy. 2015. *Undoing the Demos. Neoliberalism's Stealth Revolution*. Cambridge, MA: MIT Press.

Brubaker, Rogers. 1992. *Citizenship and Nationhood in France and Germany*. Cambridge, MA: Harvard University Press.

Brubaker, Rogers. 2004. *Ethnicity Without Groups*. Cambridge, MA: Harvard University Press.

Brubaker, Rogers. 2015. *Grounds for Difference*. Cambridge, MA: Harvard University Press.

Brubaker, Rogers. 2016. *Trans: Gender and Race in an Age of Unsettled Identities*. Princeton, NJ: Princeton University Press.

Bruneteaux, Patrick. 2010. *L'Arrière-cour de la mondialisation. Ethnographie des paupérisés*. Paris: Éditions du Croquant.

Bucerius, Sandra M. 2014. *Unwanted: Muslim Immigrants, Dignity, and Drug Dealing*. New York: Oxford University Press.

Buffington, Robert M. 2000. *Criminal and Citizen in Modern Mexico*. Lincoln, NE: University of Nebraska Press.

Burawoy, Michael. 1998. "The Extended Case Method." *American Sociological Review* 16 (1): 4–33.

Burbank, Jane and Frederick Cooper. 2011. *Empires in World History: Power and the Politics of Difference*. Princeton, NJ: Princeton University Press.

Burch, Traci. 2015. "Skin Color and the Criminal Justice System: Beyond

References

Black-White Disparities in Sentencing." *Journal of Empirical Legal Studies* 12 (3): 395–420.

Burgin, Angus. 2012. *The Great Persuasion: Reinventing Free Markets since the Depression.* Cambridge, MA: Harvard University Press.

Burke, Edmund. 2014. *The Ethnographic State: France and the Invention of Moroccan Islam.* Berkeley: University of California Press.

Burnett, D. Graham. 2022. *A Trial by Jury.* New York: Vintage.

Bushway, Shawn D. 2019. "Defendant Decision-Making in Plea Bargains." Pp. 24–36 in *A System of Pleas: Social Science's Contributions to the Real Legal System.* Edited by Vanessa A. Edkins and Allison D. Redlich. New York: Oxford University Press.

Bushway, Shawn D. and Allison D. Redlich. 2012. "Is Plea Bargaining in the 'Shadow of the Trial' a Mirage?" *Journal of Quantitative Criminology* 28: 437–54.

Bushway, Shawn D., Allison D. Redlich, and Robert J. Norris. 2014. "An Explicit Test of Plea Bargaining in the Shadow of the Trial." *Criminology* 52 (4): 723–54.

Bushway, Shawn, Andrew Jordan, Derek Neal, and Steven Raphael. 2025. "Understanding Race Disparities in Criminal Court Outcomes." *RSF: The Russell Sage Foundation Journal of the Social Sciences* 11 (3): 86–135.

Butler, Paul D. 2012. "Poor People Lose: *Gideon* and the Critique of Rights." *Yale Law Journal* 122 (8): 2176–204.

Cadiot, Juliette and Marc Elie. 2017. *Histoire du Goulag.* Paris: La Découverte.

Calavita, Kitty. 2016. *Invitation to Law and Society: An Introduction to the Study of Real Law.* Chicago: University of Chicago Press.

Caligiuri, Zeke (ed.). 2023. *American Precariat: Parables of Exclusion.* Minneapolis, MN: Coffee House Press.

Caloz-Tschopp, Marie-Claire. 2004. *Les Étrangers aux frontières de l'Europe et le spectre des camps.* Paris: La Dispute.

Campbell, Michael C. 2018. "Varieties of Mass Incarceration: What We Learn from State Histories." *Annual Review of Criminology* 1: 219–34.

Campbell, Michael C. and Heather Schoenfeld. 2013. "The Transformation of America's Penal Order: A Historicized Political Sociology of Punishment." *American Journal of Sociology* 118 (5): 1375–423.

Canon, Dan. 2022. *Pleading Out: How Plea Bargaining Creates a Permanent Criminal Class.* New York: Basic Books.

Carmichael, Stokely and Charles V. Hamilton. 1967. *Black Power: The Politics of Liberation.* New York: Vintage.

Carrithers, David. 1998. "Montesquieu's Philosophy of Punishment." *History of Political Thought* 19 (2): 213–40.

Carson, E. Ann and Elizabeth Anderson. 2016. *Prisoners in 2015.* Washington, DC: Bureau of Justice Statistics.

Castel, Robert. 1995. *Les Métamorphoses de la question sociale. Une chronique du salariat.* Paris: Fayard.

References

Cavadino, Michael. 2010. "Penology." Pp. 447–63 in *The Sage Handbook of Criminological Theory*. Edited by Eugene McLaughlin and Tim Newburn. London: Sage.

Cavadino, Michael and James Dignan. 2005. *Penal Systems: A Comparative Approach*. London: Sage.

Cefaï, Daniel and Édouard Gardella. 2011. *L'Urgence sociale en action. Ethnographie du Samu social de Paris*. Paris: La Découverte.

Centers, Richard. 1949. *The Psychology of Social Classes*. Princeton, NJ: Princeton University Press.

Chalfin, Aaron and Justin McCrary. 2018. "Are US Cities Underpoliced? Theory and Evidence." *Review of Economics and Statistics* 100 (1): 167–86.

Chantraine, Gilles. 2003. "Prison, désaffiliation, stigmates. L'engrenage carcéral de l'"inutile au monde'." *Déviance et société* 27 (4): 363–87.

Chantraine, Gilles. 2004. *Par-delà les murs. Expériences et trajectoires en maison d'arrêt*. Paris: PUF.

Chaouat, Bernard (ed.). 2011. *Reconstruire sa vie après la prison. Quel avenir après la sanction?* Paris: Éditions de l'Atelier.

Charbit, Joël, Shaïn Morisse, and Gwenola Ricordeau. 2024. *Brique par brique, mur par mur. Une histoire de l'abolitionnisme pénal*. Montréal: Lux Éditeur.

Chatterjee, Partha. 1993. *The Nation and Its Fragments: Colonial and Postcolonial Histories*. Princeton, NJ: Princeton University Press.

Chaves, Miguel. 1999. *Casal Ventoso: Da gandaia ao narcotráfico. Marginalidade económica e dominação simbólica em Lisboa*. Lisbon: Imprensa de Ciências Sociais.

Cheesman, Nick. 2022. "Law and Order." *Annual Review of Law and Social Science* 18: 263–81.

Chevalier, Louis. 1958. *Classes laborieuses et classes dangereuses à Paris pendant la première moitié du XIXᵉ siècle*. Paris: Plon.

Christie, Nils. [1961] 1981. *Limits to Pain: The Role of Punishment in Penal Policy*. Oxford: Martin Robertson.

Christie, Nils. 1986. "Suitable Enemies." Pp. 42–54 in *Abolitionism: Towards a Non-Repressive Approach to Crime*. Edited by Herman Bianchi and René van Swaaningen. Amsterdam: Free University Press.

Christie, Nils. 2004. *A Suitable Amount of Crime*. London: Routledge.

Christin, Angèle. 2008. *Comparutions immédiates. Enquête sur une pratique judiciaire*. Paris: La Découverte.

Clair, Matthew. 2020. *Privilege and Punishment: How Race and Class Matter in Criminal Court*. Princeton, NJ: Princeton University Press.

Clair, Matthew and Amanda Woog. 2022. "Courts and the Abolition Movement." *California Law Review* 110: 1–45.

Clark, Kenneth. 1965. *Dark Ghetto: Dilemmas of Power*. New York: Harper & Row.

Clear, Todd R. 2009. *Imprisoning Communities: How Mass Incarceration Makes Disadvantaged Neighborhoods Worse.* New York: Oxford University Press.

Cleaver, Eldridge. 1968. *Soul on Ice.* New York: Delta.

Clegg, John, Sebastian Spitz, Adaner Usmani, and Annalena Wolcke. 2024. "Punishment in Modern Societies: The Prevalence and Causes of Incarceration Around the World." *Annual Review of Criminology* 7: 211–31.

Codaccioni, Vanessa. 2025. *Comment les États répriment. Une courte histoire du pouvoir de punir.* Paris: Éditions Divergence.

Cohen, Elizabeth F. 2009. *Semi-Citizenship in Democratic Politics.* Cambridge: Cambridge University Press.

Cohen, Stanley. 1985. *Visions of Social Control: Crime, Punishment and Classification.* Cambridge: Polity Press.

Cohen, Stanley. 1996. "Crime and Politics: Spot the Difference." *The British Journal of Sociology* 47 (1): 1–21.

Cohn, Bernard. 1996. *Colonialism and its Forms of Knowledge: The British in India.* Princeton, NJ: Princeton University Press.

Collectif Rosa Bonheur. 2020. *La Ville vue d'en bas. Travail et production de l'espace populaire.* Paris: Editions Amsterdam.

Comaroff, John L. 1998. "Reflections on the Colonial State, in South Africa and Elsewhere: Factions, Fragments, Facts and Fictions." *Social Identities* 4 (3): 321–61.

Comaroff, Jean and John L. Comaroff (eds.). 2007. *Law and Disorder in the Postcolony.* Chicago: University of Chicago Press.

Comfort, Megan. 2007. *Doing Time Together: Love and Family in the Shadow of the Prison.* Chicago: University of Chicago Press.

Conchon, Anne. 2021. "La corvée au XVIIIe siècle. Des formes plurielles de réquisition dans les colonies françaises." Pp. 77–94 in *Travail servile et dynamiques économiques XVIᵉ–XXᵉ siècle.* Edited by Anne Conchon, Myriam Cottias, and Alessandro Stanziani. Paris: IDPDE.

Conklin, Alice L. 1997. *A Mission to Civilize: The Republican Idea of Empire in France and West Africa, 1895–1930.* Stanford, CA: Stanford University Press.

Contreras, Randol. 2024. *The Marvelous Ones: Drugs, Gang Violence, and Resistance in East Los Angeles.* Berkeley: University of California Press.

Cooper, Frederick. 1996. *Decolonization and African Society: The Labor Question in French and British Africa.* Cambridge: Cambridge University Press.

Cooper, Nicola. 2018. "Biribi: Disciplining and Punishing in the French Empire." *French Cultural Studies* 29 (4): 321–9.

Cox, Kiana. 2024. *Most Black Americans Believe U.S. Institutions Were Designed to Hold Black People Back.* Washington, DC: Pew Research Center.

Coyle, Michael J. and David Scott (eds.). 2021. *The Routledge International Handbook of Penal Abolition.* London: Routledge.

References

Crewe, Ben, Alice Ievins, Simon Larmour, Julie Laursen, Kristian Mjåland, and Anna Schliehe. 2023. "Nordic Penal Exceptionalism: A Comparative, Empirical Analysis." *The British Journal of Criminology* 63 (2): 424–43.

Critical Resistance. 2021. "Abolition Organizing Toolkit (Selections)." Pp. 438–50 in *The Routledge International Handbook of Penal Abolition*. Edited by Michael J. Coyle and David Scott. London: Routledge.

Crocitti, Stefania. 2014. "Immigration, Crime and Criminalization in Italy." Pp. 791–833 in *The Oxford Handbook of Ethnicity, Crime, and Immigration*. Edited by Sandra M. Bucerius and Michael H. Tonry. Oxford: Oxford University Press.

Crowder, Michael. 1968. *West Africa under Colonial Rule*. Evanston, IL: Northwestern University Press.

Cunha, Manuela Ivone. 2002. *Entre o bairro e a prisão. Tráfico e trajectos.* Lisbon: Fim de Século.

Cunneen, Chris and Carolyn Hoyle. 2010. *Debating Restorative Justice*. London: Bloomsbury Academic.

Daems, Tom. 2009. *Making Sense of Penal Change*. Oxford: Clarendon Press.

Dal Santo, Luiz and Máximo Sozzo (eds.). 2024. *Punishment in Latin America: Explorations from the Margins*. Leeds: Emerald Publishing.

Dalke, Isaac. 2024. "I Come Before You a Changed Man: 'Insight,' Compliance, and Refurbishing Penal Practice in California." *Law & Social Inquiry* 49 (2): 1138–68.

Dambuyant-Wargny, Gisèle. 2006. *Quand on n'a plus que son corps. Soin et non-soin de soi en situation de précarité*. Paris: Armand Colin.

Danewid, Ida. 2020. "The Fire this Time: Grenfell, Racial Capitalism and the Urbanisation of Empire." *European Journal of International Relations* 26 (1): 289–313.

Dangelmaier, Tamara and Eva Brauer. 2020. "Selektive Polizeiarbeit. Raumordnung und deren Einfluss auf das polizeiliche Handeln." Pp. 213–33 in *Polizeiarbeit zwischen Praxishandeln und Rechtsordnung*. Edited by Daniela Hunod and Andreas Ruch. Wiesbaden: Springer.

Daughton, James Patrick. 2021. *In the Forest of No Joy: The Congo-Océan Railroad and the Tragedy of French Colonialism*. New York: Norton.

Davenport, Christian. 2017. "Performing Order: An Examination of the Seemingly Impossible Task of Subjugating Large Numbers of People, Everywhere, All the Time." Pp. 258–83 in *The Many Hands of the State: Theorizing Political Authority and Social Control*. Edited by Kimberly J. Morgan and Ann Shola Orloff. Cambridge: Cambridge University Press.

Davies, William. 2016. *The Limits of Neoliberalism: Authority, Sovereignty and the Logic of Competition*. London: Sage.

Davis, Angela J. 2007. *Arbitrary Justice: The Power of the American Prosecutor*. New York: Oxford University Press.

Davis, Angela J. 2008. "The American Prosecutor – Power, Discretion, and Misconduct." *Criminal Justice* 23 (1): 25–37.

References

Davis, Angela J. 2013. "In Search of Racial Justice: The Role of the Prosecutor." *New York University Journal of Legislation & Public Policy* 16: 821–51.

Davis, Angela Y. 2003. *Are Prisons Obsolete?* New York: Seven Stories Press.

Davis, Angela Y., Gina Dent, Erika R. Meiners, and Beth Richie. 2022. *Abolition. Feminism. Now.* Chicago: Haymarket Books.

De Giorgi, Alessandro. 2006. *Re-thinking the Political Economy of Punishment: Perspectives on Post-Fordism and Penal Politics.* London: Ashgate.

De Greef, Vanessa and Julien Pierret. 2011. *Le Casier judiciaire. Approches critiques et perspectives comparées.* Brussels: Larcier.

De Maillard, Jacques, Kristof Verfaillie, and Mike Rowe (eds.). 2024. *The Politicization of Police Stops in Europe.* London: Palgrave Macmillan.

De Rond, Mark. 2025. *Dark Justice: Inside the World of Paedophile Hunters.* Cambridge: Cambridge University Press.

De Vito, Christian Giuseppe and Alex Lichtenstein (eds.). 2015. *Global Convict Labour.* Leiden: Brill.

Delattre, Gerd and Christoph Willms. 2020. "After Three Decades of Restorative Justice in Germany: Thoughts on the Needs for a Strategic Re-Orientation." *International Journal of Restorative Justice* 3 (2): 282–94.

Desmond, Matthew. 2012. "Disposable Ties and the Urban Poor." *American Journal of Sociology* 117 (5): 1295–335.

Desmond, Matthew. 2014. "Relational Ethnography." *Theory & Society* 43 (5): 547–79.

Desmond, Matthew. 2017. *Evicted: Poverty and Profit in the American City.* New York: Crown.

Desmond, Matthew. 2023. *Poverty, by America.* New York: Crown Books.

Desmond, Matthew and Monica Bell. 2015. "Poverty, Housing, and the Law." *Annual Review of Law and Social Science* 11: 15–35.

Desmond, Matthew and Bruce Western. 2018. "Poverty in America: New Directions and Debates." *Annual Review of Sociology* 44: 305–18.

Dharia, Premal, James Forman Jr., and Maria Hawilo (eds.). 2024. *Dismantling Mass Incarceration: A Handbook for Change.* New York: Farrar, Straus and Giroux.

Dikeç, Mustafa. 2018. *Urban Rage: The Revolt of the Excluded.* New Haven, CT: Yale University Press.

Dikötter, Frank. 2002. *Crime, Punishment and the Prison in Modern China.* New York: Columbia University Press.

Dikötter, Frank and Ian Brown (eds.). 2007. *Cultures of Confinement: A History of the Prison in Africa, Asia, and Latin America.* Ithaca, NY: Cornell University Press.

DiMaggio, Paul J. and Walter W. Powell. 1983. "The Iron Cage Revisited: Institutional Isomorphism and Collective Rationality in Organizational Fields." *American Sociological Review* 48 (2): 147–60.

References

Dimier, Véronique. 2004. "Le commandant de cercle: un 'expert' en administration coloniale, un 'spécialiste' de l'indigène?." *Revue d'histoire des sciences humaines* 10 (1): 39–57.

Dinnen, Sinclair. 2000. *Law and Order in a Weak State: Crime and Politics in Papua New Guinea.* Honolulu, HI: University of Hawaii Press.

Dodge, Calvert R. (ed.). 1975. *A Nation Without Prisons: Alternatives to Incarceration.* Lexington, MA: Lexington Books.

Dodge, Calvert R. (ed.). 1979. *A World Without Prisons: Alternatives to Incarceration Throughout the World.* Lexington, MA: Lexington Books.

Domanick, Joe. 2005. *Cruel Justice: Three Strikes and the Politics of Crime in America's Golden State.* Berkeley: University of California Press.

Donzelot, Jacques. 1984. *L'Invention du Social. Essai sur le déclin des passions politiques.* Paris: Fayard.

Douglas, Mary. 1966. *Purity and Danger: An Analysis of Concepts of Pollution and Taboo.* London: Routledge, reprint 2003.

Draper, Tony. 2002. "An Introduction to Jeremy Bentham's Theory of Punishment." *Journal of Bentham Studies* 5: 1–17.

Drenkhahn, Kirstin, Julia Habermann, Lukas Huthmann, et al. 2020. "Zum Stand der Punitivitätsforschung in Deutschland und darüber hinaus." *Kriminalpolitische Zeitschrift* 5 (2): 104–7.

Drescher, Seymour. 2009. *Abolition: A History of Slavery and Antislavery.* Cambridge: Cambridge University Press.

Du Bois, W.E.B. 1935. *Black Reconstruction.* New York: Harcourt, Brace and Co.

Dubber, Markus D. 2010. "Citizenship and Penal Law." *New Criminal Law Review: An International and Interdisciplinary Journal* 13 (2): 190–215.

Dubber, Markus D. 2018. *The Dual Penal State: The Crisis of Criminal Law in Comparative-Historical Perspective.* New York: Oxford University Press.

Dubber, Markus D. 2019. "Criminal Process in the Dual Penal State." Pp. 3–24 in *The Oxford Handbook of Criminal Process.* Edited by Darryl K. Brown, Jenia Iontcheva Turner, and Bettina Weisser. Oxford: Oxford University Press.

Dubber, Markus D. and Lindsay Farmer (eds.). 2007. *Modern Histories of Crime and Punishment.* Stanford, CA: Stanford University Press.

Dubois, Vincent. 1999. *La Vie au guichet. Relation administrative et traitement de la misère.* Paris: Économica.

Dubois, Vincent. 2021. *Contrôler les assistés. Genèses et usages d'un mot d'ordre.* Paris: Raisons d'agir Éditions.

Duff, Antony and David Garland (eds.). 1994. *A Reader on Punishment.* Oxford: Oxford University Press.

Duff, Koshka and Tom Kemp. 2025. "Strip-Searching as Abjectification: Racism and Sexual Violence in British Policing." *Theoretical Criminology* 29 (1): 65–90.

References

Dukova, Anastasia. 2020. *To Preserve and Protect: Policing Colonial Brisbane.* Brisbane: University of Queensland Press.

Dunlea, R. R. 2022. "'No Idea Whether He's Black, White, or Purple': Colorblindness and Cultural Scripting in Prosecution." *Criminology* 60 (2): 237–62.

Durão, Susana. 2008. *Polícia e proximidade: uma etnografia da polícia em Lisboa.* Coimbra: Almedina.

Durkheim, Émile. [1893] 1990. *De la division du travail social.* Paris: PUF.

Durkheim, Émile. 1895. "Crime et santé mentale." Pp. 175–80 in *Textes.* Volume 2: *Religion, morale, anomie.* Paris: Minuit.

Durkheim, Émile, [1895] 2001. *Les Règles de la méthode sociologique.* Paris: PUF.

Durkheim, Émile. [1897] 1990. *Le Suicide. Étude sociologique.* Paris: PUF.

Durkheim, Émile. [1899] 1969. "Deux lois de l'évolution pénale." *Journal sociologique* 4: 245–73.

Durkheim, Émile. [1900] 1975. "L'État." Pp. 172–8 in *Textes.* Volume 3: *Fonctions sociales et institutions.* Paris: Minuit.

Durkheim, Émile. [1912] 1982. *Les Formes élémentaires de la vie religieuse.* Paris: PUF.

Durkheim, Émile. 1925. *L'Éducation morale.* Paris: PUF.

Durkheim, Émile. 1950. *Leçons de sociologie. Physique des mœurs et du droit.* Paris: PUF.

Durkheim, Émile. 1970. *La Science sociale et l'action.* Paris: PUF.

Eagleton-Pierce, Matthew. 2016. *Neoliberalism: The Key Concepts.* London: Routledge.

Edkins, Vanessa A. 2011. "Defense Attorney Plea Recommendations and Client Race: Does Zealous Representation Apply Equally to All?" *Law and Human Behavior* 35 (5): 413–25.

Edkins, Vanessa A. and Allison D. Redlich (eds.). 2019. *A System of Pleas: Social Science's Contributions to the Real Legal System.* New York: Oxford University Press.

Edmonds, Penelope and Hamish Maxwell-Stewart. 2016. "'The Whip Is a Very Contagious Kind of Thing': Flogging and Humanitarian Reform in Penal Australia." *Journal of Colonialism and Colonial History* 17 (1): 1–16.

Eisenstein, James and Herbert Jacob. 1977. *Felony Justice: An Organizational Analysis of Criminal Courts.* Boston: Little, Brown.

Eisenstein, James, Roy B. Flemming, and Peter F. Nardulli. 1988. *The Contours of Justice: Communities and their Courts.* Boston, MA: Little, Brown.

Elias, Norbert. [1939] 2000. *The Civilizing Process: Sociogenetic and Psychogenetic Investigations.* Cambridge, MA: Blackwell.

Elkins, Caroline. 2005. *Imperial Reckoning: The Untold Story of Britain's Gulag in Kenya.* London: Macmillan.

Emmelman, Debra S. 2003. *Justice for the Poor: A Study of Criminal Defence Work*. New York: Routledge.

Enders, Armelle. 1993. "L'École nationale de la France d'Outre-Mer et la formation des administrateurs coloniaux." *Revue d'histoire moderne et contemporaine* 40 (2): 272–88.

Engels, Friedrich. [1845] 1987. *The Condition of the Working Class in England*. London: Penguin Classics.

Epp, Charles R., Steven Maynard-Moody, and Donald Haider-Markel. 2014. *Pulled Over: How Police Stops Define Race and Citizenship*. Chicago: University of Chicago Press.

Erikson, Kai. 1966. *Wayward Puritans: A Study in the Sociology of Deviance*. New York: Wiley.

Evans, Richard J. 1998. *Tales from the German Underworld: Crime and Punishment in the Nineteenth Century*. New Haven, CT: Yale University Press.

Fall, Babacar. 1993. *Le Travail forcé en Afrique occidentale française (1900–1946)*. Paris: Karthala.

Fanon, Frantz. 1961. *Les Damnés de la terre*. Paris: La Découverte.

Fassin, Didier. 2011a. *La Force de l'ordre. Une anthropologie de la police des quartiers*. Paris: Seuil.

Fassin, Didier. 2011b. "Policing Borders, Producing Boundaries: The Governmentality of Immigration in Dark Times." *Annual Review of Anthropology* 40: 213–26.

Fassin, Didier. 2015. *L'Ombre du monde. Une anthropologie de la condition carcérale*. Paris: Seuil.

Fassin, Didier. 2017. *Punir, une passion contemporaine*. Paris: Seuil.

Fassin, Didier. 2018. "Punishment." Pp. 26–33 in *Political Concepts: A Critical Lexicon*. Edited by J.M. Bernstein, Adi M. Ophir, and Ann Laura Stoler. New York: Fordham University Press.

Fassin, Didier. 2024. "La faculté de punir." 9th lecture at the Collège de France, Paris, May 21, available at: https://www.youtube.com/watch?v=pU4H-BJyIHU.

Fassin, Didier, Yasmine Bouagga, Isabelle Coutant, et al. 2013. *Juger, réprimer, accompagner. Essai sur la morale de l'État*. Paris: Seuil.

Feeley, Malcolm M. 1979. *The Process is the Punishment: Handling Cases in a Lower Criminal Court*. New York: Russell Sage Foundation.

Feeley, Malcolm M. 1983. *Court Reform on Trial: Why Simple Solutions Fail*. New York: Basic Books.

Feeley, Malcolm M. and Rosann Greenspan. 2024. "The Long History of Plea Bargaining." Pp. 441–72 in *Research Handbook on Plea Bargaining and Criminal Justice*. Edited by Máximo Langer, Mike McConville, and Luke Marsh. Cheltenham: Edward Elgar Publishing.

Feeley, Malcolm M. and Jonathan Simon. 1992. "The New Penology: Notes on the Emerging Strategy of Corrections and its Implications." *Criminology* 30 (4): 449–74.

431

References

Feld, Barry C. 1993. *Justice for Children: The Right to Counsel and the Juvenile Courts*. Chicago: University of Chicago Press.

Finzsch, Norbert. 1996. "Elias, Foucault, Oestreich: On a Historical Theory of Confinement." Pp. 3–16 in *Institutions of Confinement. Hospitals, Asylums, and Prisons in Western Europe and North America, 1500–1950*. Edited by Norbert Finzsch and Robert Jütte. Cambridge: Cambridge University Press.

Finzsch, Norbert and Robert Jütte (eds.). 1996. *Institutions of Confinement. Hospitals, Asylums, and Prisons in Western Europe and North America, 1500–1950*. Cambridge: Cambridge University Press.

Fischer, Nicolas. 2016. "Entre droit et savoirs professionnels. L'action des membres du contrôleur général des lieux de privation de liberté française." *Déviance et Société* 40 (4): 411–32.

Fischer, Nicolas. 2017. *Le Territoire de l'expulsion. La rétention administrative des étrangers et l'État de droit en France*. Paris: ENS Éditions.

Fisher, George. 2003. *Plea Bargaining's Triumph: A History of Plea Bargaining in America*. Palo Alto, CA: Stanford University Press.

Flamm, Michael W. 2005. *Law and Order: Street Crime, Civil Unrest, and the Crisis of Liberalism in the 1960s*. New York: Columbia University Press.

Flemming, Roy B., Peter F. Nardulli, and James Eisenstein. 1992. *The Craft of Justice: Politics and Work in Criminal Court Communities*. Philadelphia, PA: University of Pennsylvania Press.

Fligstein, Neil and Doug McAdam. 2012. *A Theory of Fields*. New York: Oxford University Press.

Flower, Lisa and Sarah Klosterkamp (eds.). 2023. *Courtroom Ethnography: Exploring Contemporary Approaches, Fieldwork and Challenges*. Cham, Switzerland: Palgrave Macmillan.

Foran, Rachel, Mariame Kaba, and Katy Naples-Mitchell. 2021. "Abolitionist Principles for Prosecutor Organizing: Origins and Next Steps." *Stanford Journal of Civil Rights & Civil Liberties* 16 (3): 496–536.

Forman, James. 2017. *Locking Up Our Own: Crime and Punishment in Black America*. New York: Farrar, Straus & Giroux.

Forst, Brian. 2011. "Prosecution." Pp. 437–66 in *Crime and Public Policy*. Edited by James Q. Wilson and Joan Petersilia. New York: Oxford University Press.

Forst, Brian. 2017. "Prosecution and Courts." *Oxford Bibliographies online*.

Fortner, Michael Javen. 2015. *Black Silent Majority: The Rockefeller Drug Laws and the Politics of Punishment*. Cambridge, MA: Harvard University Press.

Foucault, Michel. 1961. *Folie et déraison. Histoire de la folie à l'âge classique*. Paris: Gallimard.

Foucault, Michel. 1969. *L'Archéologie du savoir*. Paris: Gallimard.

Foucault, Michel. 1975. *Surveiller et punir. Naissance de la prison*. Paris: Gallimard.

References

Foucault, Michel. 1976. *La Volonté de savoir. Histoire de la sexualité, I.* Paris: Gallimard.

Foucault, Michel. 1980. *Power/Knowledge: Selected Interviews and Other Writings, 1972–1977.* New York: Pantheon.

Foucault, Michel. 2004. *Sécurité, territoire, population. Cours au Collège de France, 1977–1978.* Paris: Gallimard, Seuil.

Foucault, Michel. 2013. *La Société punitive. Cours au Collège de France, 1972–1973.* Paris: EHESS, Gallimard.

Foucault, Michel. 2021. *Théories et institutions pénales. Cours au Collège de France 1971–1972.* Paris: Seuil.

Fourcade, Marion and Kieran Healy. 2024. *The Ordinal Society.* Cambridge, MA: Harvard University Press.

Fourchard, Laurent. 2018. *Trier, exclure et policer. Vies urbaines en Afrique du Sud et au Nigeria.* Paris: Presses de Sciences Po.

Franko Aas, Katja. 2010. "Global Criminology." Pp. 427–46 in *The Sage Handbook of Criminological Theory.* Edited by Eugene McLaughlin and Tim Newburn. London: Sage.

Franko Aas, Katja. 2019. *The Crimmigrant Other: Migration and Penal Power.* London: Routledge.

Franko Aas, Katja and Mary Bosworth (eds.). 2013. *The Borders of Punishment: Migration, Citizenship, and Social Exclusion.* Oxford: Oxford University Press.

Freedman, Monroe H. 2012. "The Use of Unethical and Unconstitutional Practices and Policies by Prosecutors' Offices." *Washburn Law Journal* 52: 1–21.

Friedman, Lawrence. 1994. *Crime and Punishment in American History.* New York: Perseus.

Frimigacci, Jean. 1993. "L'État colonial français, du discours mythique aux réalités (1880–1940)." *Matériaux pour l'histoire de notre temps* 32 (1): 27–35.

Gallup with the Thurgood Marshall College Fund. 2019. *The State of Opportunity in America: Understanding Barriers and Identifying Solutions.* Washington, DC: Gallup.

Garapon, Antoine. 1997. *Bien juger. Essai sur le rituel judiciaire.* Paris: Odile Jacob.

Garapon, Antoine. 2025. *Pour une autre justice. La voie restaurative.* Paris: PUF.

Gardner, Trevor George. 2022. "The Conflict Among African American Penal Interests: Rethinking Racial Equity in Criminal Procedure." *University of Pennsylvania Law Review* 171: 1699–770.

Gardner, Trevor George. 2025. "Auditing Criminal Justice Minimalism." *Washington University Journal of Law and Policy* 78 (1): 147–57.

Garfinkel, Harold. 1956. "Conditions of Successful Degradation Ceremonies." *American Journal of Sociology* 61 (5): 420–4.

References

Garland, David. 1985. *Punishment and Welfare: A History of Penal Strategies.* Aldershot, UK: Gower.

Garland, David. 1990. *Punishment and Modern Society: A Study in Social Theory.* Chicago: University of Chicago Press.

Garland, David. 2001. *The Culture of Control: Crime and Social Order in Contemporary Society.* Chicago: University of Chicago Press.

Garland, David. 2007. "Race and the Penal State." *Contexts* 6 (1): 62–4.

Garland, David. 2010. *Peculiar Institution: America's Death Penalty in an Age of Abolition.* Cambridge, MA: Harvard University Press.

Garland, David. 2013a. "Penality and the Penal State." *Criminology* 51 (3): 475–517.

Garland, David. 2013b. "Punishment and Social Solidarity." Pp. 23–39 in *The Sage Handbook of Punishment and Society.* Edited by Jonathan Simon and Richard Sparks. London: Sage.

Garland, David. 2014a. *The Welfare State: A Very Short Introduction.* Oxford: Oxford University Press.

Garland, David. 2014b. "What is a 'History of the Present'? On Foucault's Genealogies and their Critical Preconditions." *Punishment & Society* 16 (4): 365–84.

Garland, David. 2018. "Theoretical Advances and Problems in the Sociology of Punishment." *Punishment & Society* 20 (1): 8–33.

Garland, David. 2025. *Law and Order Leviathan: America's Extraordinary Regime of Policing and Punishment.* Princeton, NJ: Princeton University Press.

Gawande, Atul. 2009. "Hellhole." *The New Yorker,* March 30: 36–45.

Geertz, Clifford. 1973. "Thick Description: Toward an Interpretive Theory of Culture." Pp. 3–30 in *The Interpretation of Cultures.* New York: Basic Books.

Georgi, Fabian. 2025. *Grenzen und Bewegungsfreiheit: Eine kritische Einführung.* Berlin: Bertz & Fischer.

Geremek, Bronislaw. [1978] 1987. *La Potence ou la pitié. L'Europe et les pauvres du Moyen-Âge à nos jours.* Paris: Gallimard.

Gerstle, Gary. 2023. *The Rise and Fall of the Neoliberal Order.* Oxford: Oxford University Press.

Glaser, Barney G. and Anselm L. Strauss. 1967. *The Discovery of Grounded Theory: Strategies for Qualitative Research.* Chicago: Aldine.

Glasman, Joël. 2014. *Les Corps habillés au Togo. Genèse coloniale des métiers de police.* Paris: Karthala.

Glass, Caitlin, Kat M. Albrecht, and Perry Moriearty. 2024. "Prosecutorial Data Transparency and Data Justice." *Northwestern University Law Review* 119 (1): 193–220.

Go, Julian. 2024a. "Reverberations of Empire: How the Colonial Past Shapes the Present." *Social Science History* 48 (1): 1–18.

Go, Julian. 2024b. *Policing Empires: Militarization, Race, and the Imperial*

Boomerang in Britain and the US. New York: Oxford University Press.

Godoy, Angelina Snodgrass. 2006. *Popular Injustice: Violence, Community, and Law in Latin America*. Stanford, CA: Stanford University Press.

Godsoe, Cynthia. 2022. "The Place of the Prosecutor in Abolitionist Praxis." *UCLA Law Review* 69: 164–239.

Goffman, Erving. 1959. *The Presentation of Self in Everyday Life*. New York: Doubleday.

Goffman, Erving. 1961. *Asylums: Essays on the Social Situation of Mental Patients and other Inmates*. New York: Anchor Books.

Goffman, Erving. 1963. *Stigma: Notes on the Management of Spoiled Identity*. New York: Prentice-Hall.

Goffman, Erving. 1967. *Interaction Ritual: Essays on Face-to-Face Behavior*. New York: Pantheon.

Goldstein, Daniel M. 2012. *Outlawed: Between Security and Rights in a Bolivian City*. Durham, NC: Duke University Press.

Goldstein, Jan Ellen (ed.). 1994. *Foucault and the Writing of History*. Chicago: University of Chicago Press.

Gómez, Laura E. 2010. "Understanding Law and Race as Mutually Constitutive: An Invitation to Explore an Emerging Field." *Annual Review of Law and Social Science* 6: 487–505.

Gönen, Zeynep. 2016. *The Politics of Crime in Turkey: Neoliberalism, Police and the Urban Poor*. London: I.B. Tauris.

González Sánchez, Ignacio. 2021. *Neoliberalismo y castigo*. Barcelona: Bellaterra Edicions.

Goodman, Philip. 2008. "'It's just Black, White, or Hispanic': An Observational Study of Racializing Moves in California's Segregated Prison Reception Centers." *Law & Society Review* 42 (4): 735–70.

Goodman Philip, Joshua Page, and Michelle Phelps. 2017. *Breaking the Pendulum: The Long Struggle over Criminal Justice*. New York: Oxford University Press.

Goodman, Sara Wallace. 2023. "Citizenship Studies: Policy Causes and Consequences." *Annual Review of Political Science* 26: 135–52.

Goodmark, Leigh. 2018. "The Impact of Prosecutorial Misconduct, Overreach, and Misuse of Discretion on Gender Violence Victims." *Dickinson Law Review* 123: 627–59.

Gott, Richard. 2011. *Britain's Empire: Resistance, Repression and Revolt*. London: Verso.

Gottschalk, Marie. 2008. "Hiding in Plain Sight: American Politics and the Carceral State." *Annual Review of Political Science* 11: 235–60.

Gottschalk, Marie. 2016. *Caught: The Prison State and the Lockdown of American Politics*. Princeton, NJ: Princeton University Press.

Gourevitch, Philip and Errol Morris. 2009. *The Ballad of Abu Ghraib*. New York: Penguin.

Gowan, Teresa. 2010. *Hobos, Hustlers, and Backsliders: Homeless in San Francisco.* Minneapolis, MN: University of Minnesota Press.

Graetz, Michael J. 2014. "Trusting the Courts: Redressing the State Court Funding Crisis." *Daedalus* 143 (3): 96–104.

Gramsci, Antonio. 1992–2007. *Prison Notebooks.* Edited and translated by Joseph A. Buttigieg. New York: Columbia University Press.

Grassi, Paolo. 2022. *Barrio San Siro. Interpretare la violenza a Milano.* Milano: FrancoAngeli.

Grattet, Ryken and Brandon Martin. 2015. *Probation in California.* Berkeley: Public Policy Institute of California.

Gready, Paul and Simon Robins. 2014. "From Transitional to Transformative Justice: A New Agenda for Practice." *International Journal of Transitional Justice* 8 (3): 339–61.

Greenberg, David (ed.). *Crime and Capitalism: Readings in Marxist Criminology.* Philadelphia, PA: Temple University Press.

Griffiths, Paul. 2008. *Lost Londons: Change, Crime, and Control in the Capital City, 1550–1660.* Cambridge: Cambridge University Press.

Griveaud, Delphine. 2025. *Réparer la justice. Enquête sur les pratiques restauratives en France.* Paris: La Découverte.

Griveaud, Delphine and Sandrine Lefranc. 2024. *Pratiques et effets de la justice restaurative en France.* Paris: Institut des études et de la recherche sur le droit et la justice.

Guha, Ranajit. 1997. *Dominance without Hegemony: History and Power in Colonial India.* Cambridge, MA: Harvard University Press.

Guilloneau, Maud, Annie Kensey, and Philippe Mazuet. 1998. "Les resources des sortants de prisons." *Cahiers de démographie pénitentiaire* 5, February.

Gusfield, Joseph R. 1981. *The Culture of Public Problems: Drinking-Driving and the Symbolic Order.* Chicago: University of Chicago Press.

Gusfield, Joseph R. 1989. "Constructing the Ownership of Social Problems: Fun and Profit in the Welfare State." *Social Problems* 36 (5): 431–41.

Gustafson, Kaaryn S. 2011. *Cheating Welfare: Public Assistance and the Criminalization of Poverty.* New York: NYU Press.

Hache, Émilie. 2007. "La responsabilité, une technique de gouvernementalité néolibérale?." *Raisons politiques* 28 (4): 49–65.

Hagan, John. 1974. "Extra-Legal Attributes and Criminal Sentencing: An Assessment of a Sociological Viewpoint." *Law & Society Review* 8 (3): 357–84.

Hagan, John. 1992. "The Poverty of a Classless of Criminology: The American Society of Criminology 1991 Presidential Address." *Criminology* 30 (1): 1–20.

Hagan, John. 2010. *Who Are the Criminals? The Politics of Crime Policy from the Age of Roosevelt to the Age of Reagan.* Princeton, NJ: Princeton University Press.

References

Hajjat, Abdellali and Marwan Mohammed. 2022. *Islamophobie. Comment les élites françaises fabriquent le "problème musulman."* Paris: La Découverte.

Haller, Mie Birk, Randi Solhjell, Elsa Saarikkomäki, Torsten Kolind, Geoffrey Hunt, and David Wästerfors. 2020a. "Minor Harassments: Ethnic Minority Youth in the Nordic Countries and their Perceptions of the Police." *Criminology & Criminal Justice* 20 (1): 3–20.

Haller, Mie Birk, Torsten Kolind, Geoffrey Hunt, and Thomas Friis Søgaard. 2020b. "Experiencing Police Violence and Insults: Narratives from Ethnic Minority Men in Denmark." *Nordic Journal of Criminology* 21 (2): 170–85.

Hallett, Michael A. 2006. *Private Prisons in America: A Critical Race Perspective.* Urbana, IL: University of Illinois Press.

Haney, Craig. 2003. "The Psychological Impact of Incarceration: Implications for Post-Prison Adjustment." Pp. 33–66 in *Prisoners Once Removed: The Impact of Incarceration and Reentry on Children, Families, and Communities.* Edited by Jeremy Travis and Michelle Waul. Washington, DC: The Urban Institute.

Harcourt, Bernard. 2007. *Against Prediction: Profiling, Policing, and Punishing in an Actuarial Age.* Chicago: University of Chicago Press.

Harcourt, Bernard E. 2011. *The Illusion of Free Markets: Punishment and the Myth of Natural Order.* Cambridge, MA: Harvard University Press.

Harcourt, Bernard E. 2023. *Cooperation: A Political, Economic, and Social Theory.* New York: Columbia University Press.

Harris, Alexes. 2016. *A Pound of Flesh: Monetary Sanctions as Punishment for the Poor.* New York: Russell Sage Foundation.

Harvey, David. 2007. *A Brief History of Neoliberalism.* New York: Oxford University Press.

Hasenfeld, Yeheskel. 1972. "People Processing Organizations: An Exchange Approach." *American Sociological Review* 37 (3): 256–63.

Haslip-Viera, Gabriel. 1999. *Crime and Punishment in Late Colonial Mexico City, 1692–1810.* Albuquerque, NM: University of New Mexico Press.

Hathazy, Paul and Markus-Michael Müller. 2016. "The Rebirth of the Prison in Latin America: Determinants, Regimes and Social Effects." *Crime, Law and Social Change* 65: 113–35.

Havik, Philip J., Helena Pinto Janeiro, Pedro Aires Oliveira, and Irene Pimentel (eds.). 2021. *Empires and Colonial Incarceration in the Twentieth Century.* London: Routledge.

Hawthorn, Geoffrey. 1993. *Plausible Worlds: Possibility and Understanding in History and the Social Sciences.* Cambridge: Cambridge University Press.

Hay, Colin, Michael Lister, and David Marsh (eds.). 2022. *The State: Theories and Issues.* Basingstoke: Palgrave Macmillan.

Hay, Douglas, Peter Linebaugh, John G. Rule, E.P. Thompson, and Cal Winslow (eds.). 1975. *Albion's Fatal Tree: Crime and Society in Eighteenth-Century England.* London: Allen Lane.

Headworth, Spencer. 2021. *Policing Welfare: Punitive Adversarialism in Public Assistance*. Chicago: University of Chicago Press.

Heath, Deana. 2021. *Colonial Terror: Torture and State Violence in Colonial India*. Oxford: Oxford University Press.

Heaton, Paul, Sandra Mayson, and Megan Stevenson. 2017. "The Downstream Consequences of Misdemeanor Pretrial Detention." *Stanford Law Review* 69 (3): 711–94.

Hedström, Peter and Peter Bearman (eds.). 2009. *The Oxford Handbook of Analytical Sociology*. New York: Oxford University Press.

Herbert, Steve. 2014. "The Policing of Space: New Realities, Old Dilemmas." Pp. 589–605 in *The Oxford Handbook of Police and Policing*. Edited by Michael D. Reisig and Robert J. Kane. New York: Oxford University Press.

Hernández, Amanda. 2024. "'Tough-On-Crime' Policies are Back in Some Places that had Reimagined Criminal Justice." *Stateline*, March 18 (accessible at stateline.org).

Hernández, Kelly Lytle, Heather Ann Thompson, and Khalil Gibran Muhammad (eds.). 2015. Special issue on "Historians and the Carceral State." *Journal of American History* 102 (1).

Herpin, Nicolas. 1977. *L'Application de la loi. Deux poids, deux mesures*. Paris: Seuil.

Herzing, Rachel and Justin Piché. 2024. *How to Abolish Prisons: Lessons from the Movement Against Imprisonment*. Chicago: Haymarket Books.

Hessick, Carissa Byrne. 2021. *Punishment Without Trial: Why Plea Bargaining is a Bad Deal*. New York: Abrams.

Heumann, Milton. 1978. *Plea Bargaining: The Experiences of Prosecutors, Judges and Defense Attorneys*. Chicago: University of Chicago Press.

Heumann, Milton, Rick Cavin, and Anu Chug. 2021. "Courtroom Workgroups: 'A Prosecutor, a Defense Attorney, and a Judge Walk into a Bar'." Pp. 273–89 in *The Oxford Handbook of Prosecutors and Prosecution*. Edited by Ronald F. Wright, Kay L. Levine, and Russell M. Gold. New York: Oxford University Press.

Hinton, Elizabeth and DeAnza Cook. 2021. "The Mass Criminalization of Black Americans: A Historical Overview." *Annual Review of Criminology* 4: 261–86.

Hirschman, Albert O. 1972. *Exit, Voice, and Loyalty: Responses to Decline in Firms, Organizations, and States*. Cambridge, MA: Harvard University Press.

Hjalmarsson, Randi. 2022. *Social Policies as Crime Control*. Stockholm: SNS.

Hochschild, Adam. 1998. *King Leopold's Ghost: A Story of Greed, Terror, and Heroism in Colonial Africa*. New York: Mariner Books.

Hochschild, Jennifer L. and Colin Brown. 2014. "Searching (With Minimal Success) for Links Between Immigration and Imprisonment." Pp. 663–707 in *The Oxford Handbook of Ethnicity, Crime, and Immigration*. Edited by Sandra M. Bucerius and Michael Tonry. Oxford: Oxford University Press.

References

Holloway, Thomas. 1993. *Policing Rio de Janeiro: Repression and Resistance in a Nineteenth-Century City*. Stanford, CA: Stanford University Press.

Hopkins, Zachary and Antony Duff. 2021. "Legal Punishment." *Stanford Encyclopedia of Philosophy*, https://plato.stanford.edu/entries/legal-punishment/.

Horne, Alistair. 1977. *A Savage War of Peace: Algeria, 1954–1962*. New York: NYRB Classics.

Houllemare, Marie. 2024. *Justices d'empire. La répression dans les colonies françaises au XVIIIe siècle*. Paris: PUF.

Hu, Lily and Issa Kohler-Hausmann. 2025. "What is Perceived when Race is Perceived and Why it Matters for Causal Inference and Discrimination Studies." *Law & Society Review* 59 (2): 239–64.

Huggins, Martha, Philip Zimbardo, and Mika Haritos-Fatouros. 2002. *Violence Workers: Police Torturers and Murderers Reconstruct Brazilian Atrocities*. Berkeley: University of California Press.

Human Rights Watch. 2020. *"Ils nous parlent comme à des chiens." Contrôles de police abusifs en France*. Paris: Human Rights Watch.

Hunt, Nancy Rose. 2015. *A Nervous State: Violence, Remedies, and Rêverie in Colonial Congo*. Durham, NC: Duke University Press.

Husak, Douglas. 2023. "Six Questions About Overcriminalization." *Annual Review of Criminology* 6: 265–84.

Innes, Joanna. 1987. "Prisons for the Poor: English Bridewells, 1555–1800." Pp. 42–122 in *Labour, Law, and Crime: An Historical Perspective*. Edited by Francis Snyder and Douglas Hay. London: Tavistock.

Iqbal, Zaryab and Harvey Starr. 2015. *State Failure in the Modern World*. Stanford, CA: Stanford University Press.

Irwin, John. 1985. *The Jail: Managing the Underclass in American Society*. Berkeley: University of California Press.

Isin, Engin F. 2009. "Citizenship in Flux: The Figure of the Activist Citizen." *Subjectivity* 29 (1): 367–88.

Ivarsson, Søren and Søren Rud. 2017. "Rethinking the Colonial State: Configurations of Power, Violence, and Agency." *Political Power & Social Theory* 33: 1–19.

Jackman, Mary R. and Robert W. Jackman. 1983. *Class Awareness in the United States*. Berkeley: University of California Press.

Jacob, Herbert, Erhard Blankenburg, Herbert M. Kritzer, Doris Marie Provine, and Joseph Sanders. 1996. *Courts, Law, and Politics in Comparative Perspective*. New Haven, CT: Yale University Press.

Jauregui, Beatrice. 2019. *Provisional Authority: Police, Order, and Security in India*. Chicago: University of Chicago Press.

Jean, Jean-Paul. 1995. "Mettre fin à l'incarcération de masse des toxicomanes." *Esprit* 10 (3): 130–1.

Jean, Jean-Paul. 2008. *Le Système pénal*. Paris: La Découverte.

Jensen, Sune Qvotrup and Ann-Dorte Christensen. 2012. "Territorial

439

Stigmatization and Local Belonging: A Study of the Danish Neighbourhood Aalborg East." *City* 16 (1–2): 74–92.

Jessop, Bob. 2015. *The State: Past, Present, Future.* Cambridge: Polity Press.

Jobard, Fabien. 2015. "La police en banlieue après les émeutes de 2005." *Mouvements* 83 (3): 75–86.

Jobard, Fabien and René Lévy. 2009. *Police et minorités visibles. Les contrôles d'identité à Paris.* New York: Open Society Institute.

Jobard, Fabien and René Lévy. 2011. "Police, justice et discriminations raciales en France. État des savoirs." Pp. 167–98 in *La Lutte contre le racisme, l'antisémitisme et la xénophobie, année 2010.* Paris: La Documentation française.

Johnson, Brian D. and Raquel Hernandez. 2021. "Prosecutors and Plea Bargaining." Pp. 75–100 in *The Oxford Handbook of Prosecutors and Prosecution.* Edited by Ronald F. Wright, Kay L. Levine, and Russell M. Gold. New York: Oxford University Press.

Johnson, Brian D. and Rebecca Richardson. 2019. "Race and Plea Bargaining." Pp. 83–106 in *A System of Pleas: Social Science's Contributions to the Real Legal System.* Edited by Vanessa A. Edkins and Allison D. Redlich. New York: Oxford University Press.

Johnson, Brian D., Ryan D. King, and Cassia Spohn. 2016. "Sociolegal Approaches to the Study of Guilty Pleas and Prosecution." *Annual Review of Law and Social Science* 12: 479–95.

Johnson, David T. 2002. *The Japanese Way of Justice: Prosecuting Crime in Japan.* New York: Oxford University Press.

Johnson, Thea. 2019. "Fictional Pleas." *Indiana Law Journal* 94 (3): 855–900.

Jones, Colin. 1989. *The Charitable Imperative: Hospitals and Nursing in Ancien Régime and Revolutionary France.* London: Routledge.

Jütte, Robert. 1994. *Poverty and Deviance in Early Modern Europe.* Cambridge: Cambridge University Press.

Kaba, Mariame. 2021. *We Do This 'Til We Free Us: Abolitionist Organizing and Transforming Justice.* Chicago: Haymarket Books.

Kalifa, Dominique. 2009. *Biribi. Les bagnes coloniaux de l'armée française.* Paris: Perrin.

Kalifa, Dominique. 2013. *Les Bas-fonds. Histoire d'un imaginaire.* Paris: Seuil.

Kalleberg, Arne L. 2011. *Good Jobs, Bad Jobs: The Rise of Polarized and Precarious Employment Systems in the United States, 1970s–2000s.* New York: Russell Sage Foundation.

Kalleberg, Arne. 2018. *Precarious Lives: Job Insecurity and Well-Being in Rich Democracies.* Cambridge: Polity.

Kalman, Samuel. 2020. "Policing the French Empire: Colonial Law Enforcement and the Search for Racial-Territorial Hegemony." *Historical Reflections/Réflexions Historiques* 46 (2): 1–8.

Kalman, Samuel. 2024. *Law, Order, and Empire: Policing and Crime in Colonial Algeria, 1870–1954.* Ithaca, NY: Cornell University Press.

Kamil, Alycia. 2023. "Community Review of Mariame Kaba's 'We Do This 'Til We Free Us'." *South Side Weekly*, July 27.

Kammersgaard, Tobias, Thomas Friis Søgaard, Mie Birk Haller, Torsten Kolind, and Geoffrey Hunt. 2023. "Community Policing in Danish 'Ghetto' Areas: Trust and Distrust between the Police and Ethnic Minority Youth." *Criminology & Criminal Justice* 23 (1): 98–116.

Kant, Immanuel. [1798] 1965. "The Penal Law and the Law of Pardon." Pp. 137–44 in *The Metaphysical Elements of Justice*. Indianapolis, IN: Bobbs-Merrill.

Kantorowicz-Reznichenko, Elena and Michael Faure (eds.). 2021. *Day Fines in Europe: Assessing Income-Based Sanctions in Criminal Justice Systems*. Cambridge: Cambridge University Press.

Karandinos, George, Laurie Kain Hart, Fernando Montero Castrillo, and Philippe Bourgois. 2014. "The Moral Economy of Violence in the US Inner City." *Current Anthropology* 55 (1): 1–22.

Karstedt, Susanne and Rebecca Endtricht. 2022. "Crime and Punishment: Public Opinion and Political Law-And-Order Rhetoric in Europe 1996–2019." *The British Journal of Criminology* 62 (5): 1116–35.

Kelley, Robin D. G. [2002] 2022. *Freedom Dreams: The Black Radical Imagination*. Boston, MA: Beacon Press.

Khallouf, Amid and Cécile Marcel. 2016. "Vue du quartier, la prison omni-présente." *Dedans Dehors* 92.

Khiari, Sadri. 2009. *La Contre-révolution coloniale en France. De de Gaulle à Sarkozy*. Paris: La Fabrique.

King, Desmond and Robert C. Lieberman. 2017. "The Civil Rights State: How the American State Develops Itself." Pp. 178–202 in *The Many Hands of the State: Theorizing Political Authority and Social Control*. Edited by Kimberly J. Morgan and Ann Shola Orloff. Cambridge: Cambridge University Press.

King, Nancy J. and Ronald F. Wright. 2017. "Managerial Judging and Judicial Plea Negotiations: Further Evidence." Available at SSRN: http://dx.doi.org/10.2139/ssrn.2972294.

King, Ryan D. and Brian D. Johnson. 2016. "A Punishing Look: Skin Tone and Afrocentric Features in the Halls of Justice." *American Journal of Sociology* 122 (1): 90–124.

King, Ryan D. and Michael T. Light. 2019. "Have Racial and Ethnic Disparities in Sentencing Declined?" *Crime & Justice* 48: 365–437.

Kirk, David S. and Sara Wakefield. 2018. "Collateral Consequences of Punishment: A Critical Review and Path Forward." *Annual Review of Criminology* 1: 171–94.

Klosterkamp, Sarah and Lisa Flower. 2023. "Introduction to Courtroom Ethnography." Pp. 1–13 in *Courtroom Ethnography: Exploring Contemporary Approaches, Fieldwork and Challenges*. Edited by Lisa Flower and Sarah Klosterkamp. Berlin: Springer.

Knepper, Paul and Anja Johansen (eds.). 2016. *The Oxford Handbook of the History of Crime and Criminal Justice*. Oxford: Oxford University Press.

Knight, David J. and Vesla M. Weaver. 2025. "Black Political Mobilization and the US Carceral State: How Tracing Community Struggles for Safety Changes the Policing Narrative." *Annual Review of Criminology* 8: 25–52.

Kohler-Hausmann, Issa. 2018. *Misdemeanorland: Criminal Courts and Social Control in an Age of Broken Windows Policing*. Princeton, NJ: Princeton University Press.

Kohler-Hausmann, Issa. 2022. "Don't Call It a Comeback: The Criminological and Sociological Study of Subfelonies." *Annual Review of Criminology* 5: 229–53.

Kollmann, Nancy Shields. 2012. *Crime and Punishment in Early Modern Russia*. Cambridge: Cambridge University Press.

Kolsky, Elizabeth. 2010. *Colonial Justice in British India: White Violence and the Rule of Law*. Cambridge: Cambridge University Press.

Koselleck, Reinhart. [1979] 2004. *Futures Past: On the Semantics of Historical Time*. New York: Columbia University Press.

Kostenwein, Ezequiel (ed.). 2023. *Mundos judiciales y dinámicas sociales. Aproximaciones al funcionamiento de la justicia penal*. Buenos Aires: Fabián Di Plácido Editor.

Krinsky, John and Maud Simonet. 2017. *Who Cleans the Park? Public Work and Urban Governance in New York City*. Chicago: University of Chicago Press.

Kumar, Radha. 2021. *Police Matters: The Everyday State and Caste Politics in South India, 1900–1975*. Ithaca, NY: Cornell University Press.

Kurlychek, Megan C. and Brian D. Johnson. 2019. "Cumulative Disadvantage in the American Criminal Justice System." *Annual Review of Criminology* 2: 291–319.

Kutateladze, Besiki, Whitney Tymas, and Mary Crowley. 2012. *Do Race and Ethnicity Matter in Prosecution?* New York: Vera Institute of Justice.

Kutateladze, Besiki Luka, Nancy R. Andiloro, Brian D. Johnson, and Cassia C. Spohn. 2014. "Cumulative Disadvantage: Examining Racial and Ethnic Disparity in Prosecution and Sentencing." *Criminology* 52 (3): 514–51.

Lacey, Nicola. 1988. *State Punishment: Political Principles and Community Values*. London: Routledge.

Lacey, Nicola. 2008. *The Prisoners' Dilemma: Political Economy and Punishment in Contemporary Democracies*. Cambridge: Cambridge University Press.

Lacey, Nicola, David Soskice, and David Hope. 2018. "Understanding the Determinants of Penal Policy: Crime, Culture, and Comparative Political Economy." *Annual Review of Criminology* 1: 195–217.

Laë, Jean-François and Numa Murard. 2012. *Deux Générations dans la débine. Enquête dans la pauvreté ouvrière*. Paris: Bayard.

Lageson, Sarah Esther. 2020. *Digital Punishment: Privacy, Stigma, and the*

442

Harms of Data-Driven Criminal Justice. New York: Oxford University Press.

Lageson, Sarah Esther. 2022. "Criminal Record Stigma and Surveillance in the Digital Age." *Annual Review of Criminology* 5: 67–90.

Lancaster, Roger N. 2011. *Sex Panic and the Punitive State.* Berkeley: University of California Press.

Landes, William M. 1971. "An Economic Analysis of the Courts." *The Journal of Law and Economics* 14 (1): 61–107.

Langan, Patrick A. and Mark A. Cunniff. 1992. *Recidivism of Felons on Probation, 1986–89.* Washington, DC: Bureau of Justice Statistics.

Langbein, John H. 2003. *The Origins of Adversary Criminal Trial.* New York: Oxford University Press.

Langer, Máximo. 2020. "Penal Abolitionism and Criminal Law Minimalism: Here and There, Now and Then." *Harvard Law Review* 134: 42–77.

Langer, Máximo. 2021. "Plea Bargaining, Conviction Without Trial, and the Global Administratization of Criminal Convictions." *Annual Review of Criminology* 4: 377–411.

Langer, Máximo. 2024. "What Is Penal Minimalism?" *Washington University Law Review* 101: 2031–77.

Langer, Máximo and David Alan Sklansky (eds.). 2017. *Prosecutors and Democracy: A Cross-National Study.* New York: Cambridge University Press.

Langer, Máximo, Mike McConville, and Luke Marsh (eds.). 2024. *Research Handbook on Plea Bargaining and Criminal Justice.* Cheltenham: Edward Elgar Publishing.

Lappi-Seppälä, Tapio. 2011. "Explaining Imprisonment in Europe." *European Journal of Criminology* 8 (4): 303–28.

Lappi-Seppälä, Tapio. 2012. "Penal Policies in the Nordic Countries 1960–2010." *Journal of Scandinavian Studies in Criminology and Crime Prevention* 13 (1): 85–111.

Larregue, Julien. 2026. *Au Coeur de l'Etat pénal. Les avocats de la défense sous contrainte.* Paris: Raisons d'Agir Éditions.

Larsen, Troels Schultz and Kristian Nagel Delica. 2024. *Fragmenting Cities: The State, Territorial Stigmatization and Urban Marginality.* Cheltenham: Edward Elgar Publishing.

Lascoumes, Pierre and Carla Nagels. 2014. *Sociologie des élites délinquantes. De la criminalité en col blanc à la corruption politique.* Paris: Armand Colin.

Latas, António João (ed.). 2012. *Mudar a justiça penal. Linhas de reforma do processo penal português.* Coimbra: Almedina.

Lazar, Sian (ed.). 2013. *The Anthropology of Citizenship: A Reader.* Chichester: John Wiley & Sons.

Lazreg, Marnia. 2008. *Torture and the Twilight of Empire: From Algiers to Baghdad.* Princeton, NJ: Princeton University Press.

Le Caignec, Émilie. 2021. *L'Activité judiciaire pénale de 2012 à 2019: une baisse des délais de traitement induite par la progression des procédures simplifies.* Paris: Ministère de la Justice, SDSE.

Le Caisne, Léonore. 2009. "La prison, une annexe de la cité? L'expérience collective de détenus mineurs." *Ethnologie française* 39 (3): 535–46.

Le Caisne, Léonore. 2014. *Un Inceste ordinaire. Et pourtant tout le monde savait.* Paris: Belin.

Le Cour Grandmaison, Olivier. 2015. *De l'Indigénat, anatomie d'un "monstre juridique." Le droit colonial en Algérie et dans l'Empire français.* Paris: Zones.

Le Crom, Jean-Pierre. 2020. "Droit du travail *vs* droit pénal: le cas des colonies." Pp. 457–69 in *Les Mots du droit, les choses de justice. Dire le droit, écrire la justice, défendre les hommes.* Paris: Dalloz.

Le Crom, Jean-Pierre and Marc Boninchi (eds.). 2021. *La Chicotte et le pécule. Les travailleurs à l'épreuve du droit colonial français (XIX*ᵉ*–XX*ᵉ *siècles).* Rennes: Presses Universitaires de Rennes.

Lee, Hedwig. 2024. "How does Structural Racism Operate (in) the Contemporary US Criminal Justice System?" *Annual Review of Criminology* 7: 233–55.

Lefranc, Sandrine and Lilian Mathieu (eds.). 2015. *Mobilisations de victimes.* Rennes: Presses Universitaires de Rennes.

Leibfried, Stephan, Evelyne Huber, Matthew Lange, Jonah D. Levy, Frank Nullmeier, and John D. Stephens (eds.). 2015. *The Oxford Handbook of Transformations of the State.* Oxford: Oxford University Press.

Leifker, Denise and Lisa L. Sample. 2010. "Do Judges Follow Sentencing Recommendations, or Do Recommendations Simply Reflect what Judges Want to Hear? An Examination of One State Court." *Journal of Crime and Justice* 33 (2): 127–51.

Lenin, V.I. [1917] 2024. *The State and Revolution.* Introduction by Antonio Negri. London: Verso.

Leovy, Jill. 2015. *Ghettoside: A True Story of Murder in America.* New York: Spiegel and Grau.

Lerman, Amy E. and Vesla M. Weaver. 2014. *Arresting Citizenship: The Democratic Consequences of American Crime Control.* Chicago: University of Chicago Press.

Levin, Benjamin. 2020. "Imagining the Progressive Prosecutor." *Minnesota Law Review* 105 (3): 1415–51.

Levin, Benjamin. 2024. "Criminal Law Minimalisms." *Washington University Law Review* 101 (6): 1771–803.

Levine, Kay L. 2014. "Prosecutorial Discretion." Pp. 4081–9 in *Encyclopedia of Criminology and Criminal Justice.* Edited by Gerben Bruinsma and David Weisburd. New York: Springer.

Levine, Kay L. and Ronald F. Wright. 2012. "Prosecution in 3-D." *Journal of Criminal Law & Criminology* 102 (1): 1233–75.

Levine, Kay L., Ronald F. Wright, Nancy J. King, and Marc L. Miller. 2018.

References

"Sharkfests and Databases: Crowdsourcing Plea Bargains." *Texas A&M Law Review* 6: 653–70.

Lévy, René and Fabien Jobard. 2010. "Les contrôles d'identité à Paris." *Questions pénales, CESDIP* 23 (1): 1–4.

Lieb, Doug. 2013. "Vindicating Vindictiveness: Prosecutorial Discretion and Plea Bargaining, Past and Future." *Yale Law Journal* 123: 1014–69.

Lindemann, Mary. 1990. *Patriots and Paupers: Hamburg, 1712–1830.* New York: Oxford University Press.

Linebaugh, Peter. 1976. "Karl Marx, the Theft of Wood, and Working Class Composition: A Contribution to the Current Debate." *Crime & Social Justice* 6: 5–16.

Linebaugh, Peter. 2001. *The London Hanged: Crime and Civil Society in the Eighteenth Century.* London: Verso.

Lipsky, Michael. 1980. *Street-level Bureaucracy: Dilemmas of the Individual in Public Service.* New York: Russell Sage Foundation.

Lis, Catharina and Hugo Soly 1979. *Poverty and Capitalism in Pre-industrial Europe.* Atlantic Heights, NJ: Humanities Press.

Loader, Ian. 2010. "For Penal Moderation: Notes Towards a Public Philosophy of Punishment." *Theoretical Criminology* 14 (3): 349–67.

Loader, Ian and Neil Walker. 2007. *Civilizing Security.* Cambridge: Cambridge University Press.

Lobban, Michael. 2021. *Imperial Incarceration: Detention Without Trial in the Making of British Colonial Africa.* Cambridge: Cambridge University Press.

Lodemel, Ivar and Amilcar Moreira (eds.). 2014. *Activation or Workfare? Governance and the Neo-Liberal Convergence.* Oxford: Oxford University Press.

Lombardini, John. 2013. "Isonomia and the Public Sphere in Democratic Athens." *History of Political Thought* 34 (3): 393–420.

Lopez-Aguado, Patrick. 2018. *Stick Together and Come Back Home: Racial Sorting and the Spillover of Carceral Identity.* Berkeley: University of California Press.

Loury, Glenn C. et al. 2008. *Race, Incarceration, and American Values.* Cambridge, MA: MIT Press.

Luna, Erik and Marianne L. Wade (eds.). 2012. *The Prosecutor in Transnational Perspective.* Oxford: Oxford University Press.

Lynch, Mona. 1998. "Waste Managers? The New Penology, Crime Fighting, and Parole Agent Identity." *Law & Society Review* 32 (4): 839–70.

Lynch, Mona. 2016. *Hard Bargains: The Coercive Power of Drug Laws in Federal Court.* New York: Russell Sage Foundation.

Macaulay, Stewart. 1963. "Non-Contractual Relations in Business: A Preliminary Study." *American Sociological Review* 28 (1): 55–67.

Macneil, Ian R. 1977. "Contracts: Adjustment of Long-Term Economic Relations under Classical, Neoclassical, and Relational Contract Law." *Northwestern University Law Review* 72 (5): 854–905.

Maelicke, Bernd and Stefan Suhling (eds.). 2017. *Das Gefängnis auf dem Prüfstand: Zustand und Zukunft des Strafvollzugs*. Berlin: Springer.

Majcher, Izabella, Michael Flynn, and Mariette Grange. 2020. *Immigration Detention in the European Union*. Berlin: Springer.

Makaremi, Chowra. 2013. "Le droit de punir. L'appréciation de la peine en comparution immédiate." Pp. 29–62 in Didier Fassin et al., *Juger, réprimer, accompagner. Essai sur la morale de l'État*. Paris: Seuil.

Malaguti Batista, Vera (ed.). 2012. *Loïc Wacquant e a questão penal no capitalismo neoliberal*. Rio de Janeiro: Editora Revan.

Mamdani, Mahmood. 1996. *Citizen and Subject: Contemporary Africa and the Legacy of Late Colonialism*. Princeton, NJ: Princeton University Press.

Manconi, Luigi and Giovanni Torrente. 2015. *La pena e i diritti. Il carcere nella crisi italiana*. Roma: Carocci.

Mangabeira Unger, Roberto. 1987. *False Necessity: Anti-Necessitarian Social Theory in the Service of Radical Democracy*. Cambridge: Cambridge University Press.

Mann, Gregory. 2009. "What was the *Indigénat*? The 'Empire of Law' in French West Africa." *The Journal of African History* 50 (3): 331–53.

Mann, Michael. 1984. "The Autonomous Power of the State: Its Origins, Mechanisms and Results." *European Journal of Sociology/Archives européennes de sociologie* 25 (2): 185–213.

Mann, Michael. 1993. *The Sources of Social Power*. Volume 2, *The Rise of Classes and Nation-States, 1760–1914*. Cambridge: Cambridge University Press.

Mann, Michael. 2009. "Infrastructural Power Revisited." *Studies in Comparative International Development* 43 (3): 355–65.

Mann, Michael. 2013. *The Sources of Social Power*. Volume 4, *Globalizations, 1945–2011*. Cambridge: Cambridge University Press.

Mannheim, Hermann. 1940. *Social Aspects of Crime in England between the Wars*. London: Routledge.

Mannheim, Hermann. 1942. "American Criminology and Penology in War Time." *The Sociological Review* 34 (3–4): 222–34.

Mannheim, Hermann. 1946. *Criminal Justice and Social Reconstruction*. London: Routledge.

Marchetti, Anne-Marie. 1997. *Pauvretés en prison*. Toulouse: Érès.

Marchetti, Elena and Riley Downie. 2014. "Indigenous People and Sentencing Courts in Australia and Canada." Pp. 360–85 in *The Oxford Handbook of Ethnicity, Crime, and Immigration*. Edited by Sandra M. Bucerius and Michael H. Tonry. Oxford: Oxford University Press.

Mariau, Bérénice and Gaëlle Rony. 2024. "Polémique autour de l'usage de la formule ensauvagement. Tentatives de qualification d'actes de violence en France." *Mots. Les langages du politique* 136 (3): 63–78.

Marie, Olivier and Paolo Pinotti. 2024. "Immigration and Crime: An

International Perspective." *Journal of Economic Perspectives* 38 (1): 181–200.

Marier, Christopher J. and John K. Cochran. 2023. "Ethnic Diversity, Ethnic Polarization, and Incarceration Rates: A Cross-National Study." *Justice Quarterly* 40 (4): 478–505.

Marlière, Éric. 2007. "Les 'jeunes de cité' et la police. De la tension à l'émeute." *Empan* 67 (3): 26–9.

Marlière, Éric. 2008. *La France nous a lâchés! Le sentiment d'injustice chez les jeunes des cités*. Paris: Fayard.

Marshall, T.H. 1940. "Review of Rusche and Kirchheimer, *Punishment and Social Structure*." *The Economic Journal* 50: 126–7.

Marshall, T.H. 1949. *Citizenship and Social Class*. Cambridge: Cambridge University Press. Republished in 1992 by Pluto Press.

Martineau, Anne-Charlotte. 2018. "Chicotte." Pp. 182–190 in *International Law's Objects*. Edited by Jessie Hohmann and Daniel Joyce. Oxford: Oxford University Press.

Martínez, Julia. 2017. "'Unwanted Scraps' or 'An Alert, Resolute, Resentful People'? Chinese Railroad Workers in French Congo." *International Labor and Working-Class History* 91: 79–98.

Marx, Karl. [1842] 2017. "Debates on the Law on Thefts of Wood." Pp. 128–39 in *The Sociology of Law*. Edited by A. Javier Trevino. London: Routledge.

Marx, Karl. 1991. "Marx and Engels on Crime and Punishment." Pp. 45–56 in *Crime and Capitalism: Readings in Marxist Criminology*. Edited by David Greenberg. Palo Alto, CA: Mayfield.

Marx, Karl and Friedrich Engels. [1848] 1998. *The Manifesto of the Communist Party*. London: Signet Classic.

Mather, Lynn M. 1979. *Plea Bargaining or Trial?* Lanham, MD: Lexington Books.

Mathiesen, Thomas. [1971] 1974. *The Politics of Abolition*. London: Martin Robertson.

Mathiesen, Thomas. 1986. "The Politics of Abolition." *Contemporary Crises* 10: 81–94.

Mathiesen, Thomas. [1990] 2006. *Prison on Trial: A Critical Assessment*. London: Waterside Press.

Matza, David. 1961. "Poverty and Disrepute." Pp. 619–69 in *Contemporary Social Problems*. Edited by Robert K. Merton and Robert A. Nisbet. New York: Harcourt Brace Jovanovich.

Matza, David. 1969. *Becoming Deviant*. Englewood Cliffs, NJ: Prentice-Hall.

Mauer, Marc. 2006. *Race to Incarcerate*. New York: New Press.

Mauss, Marcel. 2021. *Sociologie, psychologie, physiologie*. Paris: PUF.

Mayer, Margit, Catharina Thörn, and Håkan Thörn (eds.). 2016. *Urban Uprisings: Challenging Neoliberal Urbanism in Europe*. London: Palgrave Macmillan.

447

References

Mayeux, Sara. 2020. *Free Justice: A History of the Public Defender in Twentieth-Century America*. Chapel Hill, NC: UNC Press.

Maynard, Douglas W. 1982. *Inside Plea Bargaining: The Language of Negotiation*. New York: Plenum.

Mbembe, Achille. 2010. *Sortir de la grande nuit. Essais sur l'Afrique décolonisée*. Paris: La Découverte.

Mbembe, Achille. 2016. *Politique de l'inimitié*. Paris: La Découverte. (English, *Necropolitics*, Durham, NC: Duke University Press, 2019).

McBride, Keally. 2007. *Punishment and Political Order*. Ann Arbor, MI: University of Michigan Press.

McCold, Paul and Ted Wachtel. 2002. "Restorative Justice Theory Validation." Pp. 110–42 in *Restorative Justice: Theoretical Foundations*. Edited by Elmar Weitekamp and Hans-Jürgen Kerner. London: Routledge.

McDonnell, Erin Metz. 2025. "Bureaucracy in Action: The Sociology of Public Administration." *Annual Review of Sociology* 51: 191–211.

McDowell, Meghan G. and Luis A. Fernandez. 2018. "'Disband, Disempower, and Disarm': Amplifying the Theory and Practice of Police Abolition." *Critical Criminology* 26: 373–91.

McIntyre, Lisa J. 1987. *The Public Defender: The Practice of Law in the Shadows of Repute*. Chicago: University of Chicago Press.

McLennan, Rebecca. 2009. *The Crisis of Imprisonment. Protest, Politics and the Making of the American Penal State (1776–1941)*. Cambridge: Cambridge University Press.

McLaughlin, Eugene and Tim Newburn (eds.). 2010. *The Sage Handbook of Criminological Theory*. London: Sage.

McMullan, John. 1984. *The Canting Crew: London's Criminal Underworld, 1550–1700*. New Brunswick, NJ: Rutgers University Press.

Meares, Tracey L. and Dan M. Kahan. 1999. *Urgent Times: Policing and Rights in Inner-City Communities*. Boston, MA: Beacon Press.

Melossi, Dario. 1980. "Georg Rusche: A Biographical Essay." *Crime & Social Justice* 14: 51–63.

Melossi, Dario and Massimo Pavarini. 1981. *The Prison and the Factory: Origins of the Penitentiary System*. Totowa, NJ: Barnes & Noble.

Melossi, Dario, Máximo Sozzo, and José Brandariz García (eds.). 2017. *The Political Economy of Punishment Today: Visions, Debates and Challenges*. London: Routledge.

Menjívar, Cecilia and Daniel Kanstroom (eds.). 2013. *Constructing Immigrant "Illegality": Critiques, Experiences, and Responses*. Cambridge: Cambridge University Press.

Menkel-Meadow, Carrie. 2007. "Restorative Justice: What Is It and Does It Work?" *Annual Review of Law and Social Science* 3: 161–87.

Mentzelopoulou, Maria Margarita. 2023. *Detention of Migrants: A Measure of Last Resort*. Brussels: European Parliamentary Research Service.

Merle, Isabelle. 2004. "De la 'légalisation' de la violence en contexte colonial.

Le régime de l'indigénat en question." *Politix. Revue des sciences sociales du politique* 17 (66): 137–62.

Merle, Isabelle. 2010. "Bagnes militaires et relégation coloniale." *La Vie des idées*, March 29.

Merle, Isabelle and Adrian Muckle. 2019. *L'Indigénat. Genèses dans l'empire français, pratiques en Nouvelle-Calédonie.* Paris: CNRS Éditions.

Merry, Sally Engle. 1988. "Legal Pluralism." *Law & Society Review* 22 (5): 869–96.

Merton, Robert K. 1987. "Three Fragments from a Sociologist's Notebooks: Establishing the Phenomenon, Specified Ignorance, and Strategic Research Materials." *Annual Review of Sociology* 13: 1–29.

Metcalfe, Christi. 2016. "The Role of Courtroom Workgroups in Felony Case Dispositions: An Analysis of Workgroup Familiarity and Similarity." *Law & Society Review* 50 (3): 637–73.

Meyer, Michaël (ed.). 2012. *Médiatiser la police. Policer les médias.* Lausanne: Antipodes.

Miceli, Thomas J. 2019. *The Paradox of Punishment: Reflections on the Economics of Criminal Justice.* London: Palgrave Macmillan.

Michel, Louise. [1886] 2021. *Mémoires.* Paris: Folio.

Milburn, Philip. 2024. *Sociologie de la justice pénale.* Paris: Armand Colin.

Miliband, Ralph. 1969. *The State in Capitalist Society.* London: Merlin.

Milkman, Ruth. 2020. *Immigrant Labor and the New Precariat.* Cambridge: Polity Press.

Miller, Lisa L. 2008. *The Perils of Federalism: Race, Poverty, and the Politics of Crime Control.* Oxford: Oxford University Press.

Miller, Reuben Jonathan. 2021. *Halfway Home: Race, Punishment, and the Afterlife of Mass Incarceration.* Boston, MA: Little, Brown.

Miller, Reuben Jonathan and Forrest Stuart. 2017. "Carceral Citizenship: Race, Rights and Responsibility in the Age of Mass Supervision." *Theoretical Criminology* 21 (4): 532–48.

Mirowski, Philip and Dieter Plehwe (eds.). 2009. *The Road from Mont Pèlerin: The Making of the Neoliberal Thought Collective.* Cambridge, MA: Harvard University Press.

Misse, Michel. 2023. *Malandros, marginais e vagabundos. A acumulação social da violência no Rio de Janeiro.* Rio de Janeiro: Editora Lamparina.

Mitchell, Ojmarrh and Nick Petersen. 2025. "The Rise of Progressive Prosecutors in the United States: Politics, Prospects, and Perils." *Annual Review of Criminology* 8: 459–84.

Mohammed, Marwan and Laurent Mucchielli. 2007. "La police dans les 'quartiers sensibles'. Un profond malaise." Pp. 104–25 in *Quand les banlieues brûlent. Retour sur les émeutes de novembre 2005.* Edited by Laurent Mucchielli and Véronique Le Goaziou. Paris: La Découverte.

Mohammed, Marwan and Julien Talpin. 2018. *Communautarisme?* Paris: PUF.

449

Monk, Ellis P. Jr. 2019. "The Color of Punishment: African Americans, Skin Tone, and the Criminal Justice System." *Ethnic & Racial Studies* 42 (10): 1593–612.

Monkkonen, Eric H. 1975. *The Dangerous Class: Crime and Poverty in Columbus, Ohio, 1860–1885.* Cambridge, MA: Harvard University Press.

Monkkonen, Eric H. 1992. "History of Urban Police." *Crime & Justice* 15: 547–80.

Moorhead, Richard and Dave Cowan. 2007. "Judgecraft: An Introduction." *Social & Legal Studies* 16 (3): 315–20.

Morgan, Kimberly J. and Ann Shola Orloff (eds.). 2017. *The Many Hands of the State: Theorizing Political Authority and Social Control.* Cambridge: Cambridge University Press.

Morgan, Rod. 1997. "Imprisonment: Current Concerns and a Brief History since 1945." Pp. 1137–95 in *The Oxford Handbook of Criminology.* Edited by Mike Maguire, Rod Morgan, and Robert Reiner. Oxford: Oxford University Press.

Morris, Christopher W. 1998. *An Essay on the Modern State.* Cambridge: Cambridge University Press.

Morris, Christopher W. 2004. "The Modern State." Pp. 195–209 in *Handbook of Political Theory.* Edited by Gerald F. Gaus and Chandran Kukathas. London: Sage.

Morris, Norval. 1965. "Prison in Evolution." Pp. 26–46 in *Criminology in Transition: Essays in Honor of Herman Mannheim.* Edited by Tadeusz Grygier, Howard Jones, and John C. Spencer. London: Tavistock.

Moskos, Peter. 2008. *Cop in the Hood: My Year Policing Baltimore's Eastern District.* Princeton, NJ: Princeton University Press.

Mossberger, Karen, Susan E. Clarke, and Peter John (eds.). 2015. *The Oxford Handbook of Urban Politics.* New York: Oxford University Press.

Mouhanna, Christian and Jérôme Ferret. 2005. *Peurs sur les villes. Vers un populisme punitif à la française?* Paris: PUF.

Mucchielli, Laurent (ed.). 2008. *La Frénésie sécuritaire. Retour à l'ordre et nouveau contrôle social.* Paris: La Découverte.

Mucchielli, Laurent and Émilie Raquet. 2021. "Les comparutions immédiates au TGI de Nice, ou la prison comme unique réponse à une délinquance de misère." Pp. 201–20 in *Délinquances, police, justice. Enquêtes à Marseille et en région PACA.* Edited by Laurent Mucchiel and Émilie Raquet. Aix-en-Provence: Presses Universitaires de Provence.

Muhammad, Khalil Gibran. 2011. *The Condemnation of Blackness: Race, Crime, and the Making of Modern Urban America.* Cambridge, MA: Harvard University Press.

Muller, Christopher. 2021. "Exclusion and Exploitation: The Incarceration of Black Americans from Slavery to the Present." *Science* 374 (6565): 282–6.

Muller, Christopher and Alexander F. Roehrkasse. 2022. "Racial and Class

References

Inequality in US Incarceration in the Early Twenty-First Century." *Social Forces* 101 (2): 803–28.

Muller, Christopher and Daniel Schrage. 2014. "Mass Imprisonment and Trust in the Law." *The Annals of the American Academy of Political and Social Science* 651 (1): 139–58.

Muller, Christopher, and Daniel Schrage. 2021. "The Political Economy of Incarceration in the Cotton South, 1910–1925." *American Journal of Sociology* 127 (3): 828–66.

Muller, Christopher and Christopher Wildeman. 2013. "Punishment and Inequality." Pp. 170–85 in *The Sage Handbook of Punishment and Society*. Edited by Jonathan Simon and Richard Sparks. London: Sage.

Müller, Markus-Michael. 2012. "The Rise of the Penal State in Latin America." *Contemporary Justice Review* 15 (1): 57–76.

Müller, Markus-Michael. 2016. *The Punitive City: Privatized Policing and Protection in Neoliberal Mexico*. London: Bloomsbury.

Murakawa, Naomi. 2014. *The First Civil Right: How Liberals Built Prison America*. New York: Oxford University Press.

Murakawa, Naomi and Katherine Beckett. 2010. "The Penology of Racial Innocence: The Erasure of Racism in the Study and Practice of Punishment." *Law & Society Review* 44 (3–4): 695–730.

Muschalek, Marie. 2019. *Violence as Usual: Policing and the Colonial State in German Southwest Africa*. Ithaca, NY: Cornell University Press.

Mygdal, Joel S. and Klaus Schlichte. 2016. "Rethinking the State." Pp. 1–40 in *The Dynamics of States: The Formation and Crises of State Domination*. Edited by Klaus Schlichte. London: Routledge.

Nardulli, Peter F., James Eisenstein, and Roy B. Flemming. 1988. *The Tenor of Justice: Criminal Courts and the Guilty Plea Process*. Urbana, IL: University of Illinois Press.

Neep, Daniel. 2012. *Occupying Syria under the French Mandate. Insurgency, Space and State Formation*. Cambridge: Cambridge University Press.

Neil, Roland and Joscha Legewie. 2024. "Policing Neighborhood Boundaries and the Racialized Social Control of Spaces." *Law & Society Review* 58 (2): 192–215.

Nelken, David. 2010. "Denouncing the Penal State." *Criminology & Criminal Justice* 10 (4): 331–40.

Newman, Katherine S. 2001. *No Shame in my Game: The Working Poor in the Inner City*. New York: Vintage.

Nguyen, Viet, Ryken Grattet, and Mia Bird. 2017. *California Probation in the Era of Reform*. Berkeley: Public Policy Institute of California.

Nocella, Anthony J. 2011. "An Overview of the History and Theory of Transformative Justice." *Peace & Conflict Review* 6 (1): 1–10.

Noiriel, Gérard. 1996. *Sur la "crise" de l'histoire*. Paris: Belin.

Norrie, Alan 1984. "Thomas Hobbes and the Philosophy of Punishment." *Law and Philosophy* 3: 299–320.

Novak, William J. 2008. "The Myth of the 'Weak' American State." *American Historical Review* 113 (3): 752–72.

Nunziata, Luca. 2015. "Immigration and Crime: Evidence from Victimization Data." *Journal of Population Economics* 28: 697–736.

Nussbaum, Martha C. 2011. *Creating Capabilities: The Human Development Approach*. Cambridge, MA: Harvard University Press.

O'Malley, Pat (ed.). 1998. *Crime and the Risk Society*. Aldershot: Ashgate.

O'Malley, Pat. 2010. "Governmental Criminology." Pp. 319–36 in *The Sage Handbook of Criminological Theory*. Edited by Eugene McLaughlin and Tim Newburn. London: Sage.

Observatoire International des Prisons. 2016. "João, 30 ans: 'De cité à cité, on se connaît tous avec le temps en prison'." *Dedans Dehors* 26.

OECD. 2017. *OECD Factbook 2015–2016*. Paris: OECD.

Olson, Mancur. 1965. *The Logic of Collective Action: Public Goods and the Theory of Groups*. Cambridge, MA: Harvard University Press.

Ousey, Graham C. and Charis E. Kubrin. 2018. "Immigration and Crime: Assessing a Contentious Issue." *Annual Review of Criminology* 1: 63–84.

Page, Joshua. 2011. *The Toughest Beat: Politics, Punishment, and the Prison Officers Union in California*. New York: Oxford University Press

Page, Joshua. 2013. "Punishment and the Penal Field." Pp. 152–66 in *The Sage Handbook of Punishment and Society*. Edited by Jonathan Simon and Richard Sparks. London: Sage.

Page, Joshua and Christine S. Scott-Hayward. 2022. "Bail and Pretrial Justice in the United States: A Field of Possibility." *Annual Review of Criminology* 5: 91–113.

Page, Joshua and Joe Soss. 2025. *Legal Plunder: The Predatory Dimensions of Criminal Justice*. Chicago: University of Chicago Press.

Pager, Devah. 2008. *Marked: Race, Crime, and Finding Work in an Era of Mass Incarceration*. Chicago: University of Chicago Press.

Paik, Leslie. 2021. *Trapped in a Maze: How Social Control Institutions Drive Family Poverty and Inequality*. Berkeley: University of California Press.

Paik, Leslie and Alexes Harris. 2015. "Court Ethnographies." Pp. 283–95 in *The Routledge Handbook of Qualitative Criminology*. Edited by Heith Copes and J. Mitchell Miller. London: Routledge.

Palidda, Salvatore. 2000. *Polizia postmoderna. Etnografia del nuovo controllo sociale*. Rome: Feltrinelli.

Palidda, Salvatore. 2001. *Devianza e vittimizzazione tra i migranti*. Rome: FrancoAngeli.

Paone, Sonia. 2008. *Città in frantumi. Sicurezza, emergenza e produzione dello spazio*. Milan: FrancoAngeli.

Parisot, James. 2025. "Marx and Engels on Prisons and Capitalism." *Journal of Classical Sociology*, https://doi.org/10.1177/1468795X241308818.

Parker, John and Richard Rathbone. 2007. *African History: A Very Short Introduction*. Oxford: Oxford University Press.

References

Parsons, Anne E. 2018. *From Asylum to Prison: Deinstitutionalization and the Rise of Mass Incarceration After 1945*. Chapel Hill, NC: UNC Press.

Paton, Diana. 2004. *No Bond but the Law: Punishment, Race, and Gender in Jamaican State Formation, 1780–1870*. Durham, NC: Duke University Press.

Patterson, Orlando. 2025. *Enslavement, Past and Present*. Cambridge: Polity Press.

Pattillo, Mary. 2010. *Black on the Block: The Politics of Race and Class in the City*. Chicago: University of Chicago Press.

Pattillo, Mary. 2013. "Housing: Commodity versus Right." *Annual Review of Sociology* 39: 509–31.

Paugam, Serge. 2007. *Le Salarié de la précarité. Les nouvelles formes de l'intégration professionnelle*. Paris: PUF.

Pelot-Hobbs, Lydia. 2023. *Prison Capital: Mass Incarceration and Struggles for Abolition Democracy in Louisiana*. Chapel Hill, NC: UNC Press.

Périno, Lise. 2013. *L'Impact de la prison dans les quartiers en politique de la ville*. Paris: Observatoire International des Prisons.

Perkinson, Robert. 2010. *Texas Tough: The Rise of America's Prison Empire*. New York: Metropolitan Books.

Perrot, Michelle (ed.). 1980. *L'Impossible prison. Recherches sur le système pénitentiaire au XIXe siècle*. Paris: Seuil.

Perrot, Michelle. 2023. *Punir et comprendre*. Rennes: Presses Universitaires de Rennes.

Perry, Steven W. and Duren Banks. 2011. *Prosecutors in State Courts, 2007. Statistical Tables*. Washington, DC: Bureau of Justice Statistics.

Peté, Stephen and Annie Devenish. 2005. "Flogging, Fear and Food: Punishment and Race in Colonial Natal." *Journal of Southern African Studies* 31 (1): 3–21.

Petit, Jacques-Guy. 1990. *Ces Peines obscures. La prison pénale en France (1780–1875)*. Paris: Fayard.

Petitt, Becky. 2012. *Invisible Men: Mass Incarceration and the Myth of Black Progress*. New York: Russell Sage Foundation.

Phelps, Edmund S. 1972. "The Statistical Theory of Racism and Sexism." *The American Economic Review* 62 (4): 659–61.

Phelps, Michelle S. 2020. "Mass Probation from Micro to Macro: Tracing the Expansion and Consequences of Community Supervision." *Annual Review of Criminology* 3: 261–79.

Phelps, Michelle. 2024. *The Minneapolis Reckoning: Race, Violence, and the Politics of Policing in America*. Princeton, NJ: Princeton University Press.

Phelps, Michelle S. and Ebony L. Ruhland. 2022. "Governing Marginality: Coercion and Care in Probation." *Social Problems* 69 (3): 799–816.

Picatto, Pablo. 2001. *City of Suspects: Crime in Mexico City, 1900–1931*. Durham, NC: Duke University Press.

453

References

Pierce, Steven. 2024. "The Suffering Subject: Colonial Flogging in Northern Nigeria and a Humanitarian Public, 1904–1933." *Comparative Studies in Society & History* 66 (2): 319–41.

Pierce, Steven and Anupama Rao (eds.). 2006. *Discipline and the Other Body: Correction, Corporeality, Colonialism*. Durham, NC: Duke University Press.

Pitt-Rivers, Julian. 2011. "The Place of Grace in Anthropology." *HAU: Journal of Ethnographic Theory* 1 (1): 423–50.

Polanyi, Karl. [1947] 2001. *The Great Transformation: The Political and Economic Origins of Our Time*. Boston, MA: Beacon Press.

Porter, Nicole D. 2021. *Racial Impact Statements*. Washington, DC: The Sentencing Project.

Potter, Nelson. 2009. "Kant on Punishment." Pp. 179–95 in *The Blackwell Guide to Kant's Ethics*. Edited by Thomas E. Hill. Cambridge: Blackwell.

Powell, Ryan and John Lever. 2017. "Europe's Perennial 'Outsiders': A Processual Approach to Roma Stigmatization and Ghettoization." *Current Sociology* 65 (5): 680–99.

Pratt, John. 1993. "'This is Not a Prison': Foucault, the Panopticon and Pentonville." *Social & Legal Studies* 2 (4): 373–95.

Pratt, John. 2002. *Punishment and Civilization: Penal Tolerance and Intolerance in Modern Society*. London: Sage.

Pratt, John. 2006. *Penal Populism*. London: Routledge.

Pratt, John 2008a. "Scandinavian Exceptionalism in an Era of Penal Excess – Part I: The Nature and Roots of Scandinavian Exceptionalism." *The British Journal of Criminology* 48 (2): 119–37.

Pratt, John 2008b. "Scandinavian Exceptionalism in an Era of Penal Excess – Part II: Does Scandinavian Exceptionalism Have a Future?" *The British Journal of Criminology* 48 (3): 275–92.

Pratt, John. 2013. "Punishment and the Civilizing Process." Pp. 90–113 in *The Sage Handbook of Punishment and Society*. Edited by Jonathan Simon and Richard Sparks. London: Sage.

Pratt, John. 2016. "Risk Control, Rights and Legitimacy in the Limited Liability State." *British Journal of Criminology* 57 (6): 1322–39.

Pratt, John. 2022. "The Nordic Exceptionalism Thesis Revisited." Pp. 109–25 in *Research Handbook of Comparative Criminal Justice*. Edited by David Nelken and Claire Hamilton. Cheltenham: Edward Elgar Publishing.

Pratt, John and Anna Eriksson. 2014. *Contrasts in Punishment: An Explanation of Anglophone Excess and Nordic Exceptionalism*. London: Routledge.

Presser, Lois and Sweinung Sandberg (eds.). 2015. *Narrative Criminology: Understanding Stories of Crime*. New York: NYU Press.

Prison Reform Trust. 2024. *Bromley Briefings Prison Factfile*. London: Prison Reform Trust.

Purnell, Derecka. 2022. *Becoming Abolitionists: Police, Protests, and the Pursuit of Freedom*. New York: Penguin Random House.

Quinney, Richard. 1974. *Critique of the Legal Order: Crime Control in Capitalist Society*. London: Routledge.

References

Ralph, Laurence. 2014. *Renegade Dreams: Living Through Injury in Gangland Chicago.* Chicago: University of Chicago Press.

Raposo, Otávio, Ana Rita Alves, Pedro Varela, and Cristina Roldão. 2019. "Negro drama. Racismo, segregação e violência policial nas periferias de Lisboa." *Revista Crítica de Ciências Sociais* 119: 5–28.

Rateau, Paul. 2008. *La Question du mal chez Leibniz. Fondements et élaboration de la Théodicée.* Paris: Editions Honoré Champion.

Rauxloh, Regina. 2012. *Plea Bargaining in National and International Law: A Comparative Study.* London: Routledge.

Reaves, Brian A. 2013. *Felony Defendants in Large Urban Counties, 2009.* Washington, DC: Bureau of Justice Statistics.

Redmayne, Alison and Christine Rogers. 1983. "Research on Customary Law in German East Africa." *Journal of African Law* 27 (1): 22–41.

Reimelt, Alexandra W. 2010. "An Unjust Bargain: Plea Bargains and Waiver of the Right to Appeal." *Boston College Law Review* 51: 871–904.

Reitz, Kevin R. (ed.). 2017. *American Exceptionalism in Crime and Punishment.* New York: Oxford University Press.

Rey, Henri. 1996. *La Peur des banlieues.* Paris: Presses de Science-Po.

Rheinberger, Hans-Jörg. 2010. *On Historicizing Epistemology: An Essay.* Stanford, CA: Stanford University Press.

Ricordeau, Gwenola. 2021. *Crimes et peines. Penser l'abolitionnisme pénal avec Nils Christie, Louk Hulsman et Ruth Morris.* Paris: Grevis.

Ridolfi, Kathleen M. and Maurice Possley. 2010. *Preventable Error: A Report on Prosecutorial Misconduct in California 1997–2009.* Santa Clara, CA: Veritas.

Rinn, Moritz and Jan Wehrheim. 2021. "Die Produktion eines 'Problemviertels'. Mediale Diskurse, politisch-polizeiliche Interventionen und interaktive Situationsbedeutungen." *Berliner Journal für Soziologie* 31 (2): 249–78.

Rios, Victor M. 2011. *Punished: Policing the Lives of Black and Latino Boys.* New York: NYU Press.

Robert, Philippe. 1984. *La Question pénale.* Geneva: Librairie Droz.

Robert, Philippe and Renée Zauberman. 2023. "Violences en France. Peut-on parler de 'décivilisation'?" *Sciences Humaines* 362 (9): 25–31.

Roberts, Dorothy E. 2019. "Abolition Constitutionalism." *Harvard Law Review* 133 (1): 1–122.

Roberts, Julian V. and Richard S. Frase. 2019. *Paying for the Past: The Case Against Prior Record Sentence Enhancements.* Oxford: Oxford University Press.

Roberts, Julian V., Loretta J. Stalans, David Indermaur, and Mike Hough. 2002. *Penal Populism and Public Opinion: Lessons from Five Countries.* Oxford: Oxford University Press.

Roberts, Julian V., Gabrielle Watson, and Rhys Hester. 2023. "Sentencing Members of Minority Groups: Problems and Prospects for Improvement in Four Countries." *Crime & Justice* 52: 343–93.

455

References

Roberts, Paul Craig and Lawrence M. Stratton. 2008. *The Tyranny of Good Intentions: How Prosecutors and Law Enforcement are Trampling the Constitution in the Name of Justice.* New York: Crown.

Roberts, Richard. 2005. *Litigants and Households: African Disputes and Colonial Courts in the French Soudan, 1895–1912.* Portsmouth, NH: Heinemann.

Robertson, Christopher, Shima Baradaran Baughman, and Megan S. Wright. 2019. "Race and Class: A Randomized Experiment with Prosecutors." *Journal of Empirical Legal Studies* 16 (4): 807–47.

Robson, Peter and Ferdinando Spina (eds.). 2022. *Vigilante Justice in Society and Popular Culture: A Global Perspective.* Vancouver: Fairleigh Dickinson University Press.

Rodriguez Alzueta, Esteban and Fabián Viegas (eds.). 2015. *Circuitos carcelarios. Estudios sobre la cárcel argentina.* La Plata: UNLP.

Roediger, David R. 2019. *How Race Survived U.S. History: From Settlement and Slavery to the Twenty-First Century.* New York: Verso.

Rose, Nikolas and Peter Miller. 2008. *Governing the Present: Administering Economic, Social and Personal Life.* Cambridge: Polity Press.

Rosenberg, Clifford D. 2006. *Policing Paris: The Origins of Modern Immigration Control between the Wars.* Ithaca, NY: Cornell University Press.

Rosett, Arthur and Donald R. Cressey. 1976. *Justice by Consent: Plea Bargains in the American Courthouse.* Philadelphia: J.B. Lippincott.

Ross, Dorothy. 1991. *The Origins of American Social Science.* Chicago: University of Chicago Press.

Rostas, Iulius and Florin Moisă. 2023. "Romani People, Policing, and Penality in Europe." Pp. 113–23 in *The Routledge International Handbook on Decolonizing Justice.* Edited by Chris Cunneen, Antje Deckert, Amanda Porter, Juan Tauri, and Robert Webb. London: Routledge.

Rothman, David J. 1971. *The Discovery of the Asylum: Social Order and Disorder in the New Republic.* London: Routledge.

Rothman, David J. 1972. "Of Prisons, Asylums, and other Decaying Institutions." *The Public Interest* 26: 3–17.

Rovira, Marti. 2024. "Invisible Stripes? A Field Experiment on the Disclosure of a Criminal Record in the British Labour Market and the Potential Effects of Introducing Ban-The-Box Policies." *The British Journal of Criminology* 64 (4): 827–45.

Rubin, Ashley and Michelle S. Phelps. 2017. "Fracturing the Penal State: State Actors and the Role of Conflict in Penal Change." *Theoretical Criminology* 21 (4): 422–40.

Rueschemeyer, Dietrich, Theda Skocpol, and Peter B. Evans (eds.). 1985. *Bringing the State Back In.* New York: Cambridge University Press.

Ruggiero, Vincenzo. 2010. *Penal Abolitionism.* Oxford: Oxford University Press.

Rusche, Georg. [1933] 1978. "Labor Market and Penal Sanction: Thoughts on the Sociology of Criminal Justice." *Crime & Social Justice* 10: 2–8.

References

Rusche Georg and Otto Kirchheimer. [1939] 2005. *Punishment and Social Structure*. New Brunswick, NJ: Transaction.

Russell, Katheryn K. 1998. *The Color of Crime: Racial Hoaxes, White Fear, Black Protectionism, Police Harassment and Other Macroaggressions*. New York: NYU Press.

Ryberg, Jesper (ed.). 2024. *The Oxford Handbook of the Philosophy of Punishment*. Oxford: Oxford University Press.

Saarikkomäki, Elsa, Randi Solhjell, and David Wästerfors. 2023. "Dealing with Police Stops: How Young People with Ethnic Minority Backgrounds Narrate their Ways of Managing Over-Policing in the Nordic Countries." *Policing & Society* 33 (8): 937–52.

Salas, Denis. 2005. *La Volonté de punir. Essai sur le populisme pénal*. Paris: Pluriel.

Salle, Grégory. 2009. *La Part d'ombre de l'État de droit. La question carcérale en France et en République fédérale d'Allemagne depuis 1968*. Paris: Éditions de l'EHESS.

Salvatore, Ricardo D., Carlos Aguirre, and Gilbert M. Joseph (eds.). 2001. *Crime and Punishment in Latin America: Law and Society since Late Colonial Times*. Durham, NC: Duke University Press.

Sampson, Robert J. 2012. *Great American City: Chicago and the Enduring Neighborhood Effect*. Chicago: University of Chicago Press.

Sampson, Robert J. 2014. "Criminal Justice Processing and the Social Matrix of Adversity." *The Annals of the American Academy of Political and Social Science* 651 (1): 296–301.

Sampson, Robert J. and Charles Loeffler. 2010. "Punishment's Place: The Local Concentration of Mass Incarceration." *Daedalus* 139 (3): 20–31.

Sampson, Robert J. and Roland Neil. 2024. "The Social Foundations of Racial Inequalities in Arrest over the Life Course and in Changing Times." *Criminology* 62 (2): 177–204.

Sánchez-Jankowski, Martín. 1991. *Islands in the Street: Gangs and American Urban Society*. Berkeley: University of California Press.

Sánchez-Jankowski, Martin. 2008. *Cracks in the Pavement: Social Change and Resilience in Poor Neighborhoods*. Berkeley: University of California Press.

Sandberg, Sveinung. 2014. "Black Cannabis Dealers in a White Western State: Race, Politics and Street Capital in Norway." *The British Journal of Criminology* 48 (5): 604–19.

Saperstein, Aliya and Andrew M. Penner. 2012. "Racial Fluidity and Inequality in the United States." *American Journal of Sociology* 118 (3): 676–727.

Saperstein, Aliya, Andrew M. Penner, and Jessica M. Kizer. 2014. "The Criminal Justice System and the Racialization of Perceptions." *The Annals of the American Academy of Political and Social Science* 651 (1): 104–21.

Sapir, Yoav and Guy Rubinstein. 2023. "Minimalist Criminal Courts." *Washington University Law Review* 101: 1955–84.

References

Scandurra, Giuseppe. 2005. *Tutti a casa. Il Carracci: etnografia dei senza fissa dimora a Bologna*. Roma: Garaldi.

Schama, Simon. 1988. *The Embarrassment of Riches: An Interpretation of Dutch Culture in the Golden Age*. Berkeley: University of California Press.

Schehr, Robert. 2024. *The Political Economy of Plea Bargaining*. New York: Routledge.

Scheingold, Stuart A. 1984. *The Politics of Law and Order: Street Crime and Public Policy*. New York: Longman.

Schierup, Carl-Ulrik, Aleksandra Ålund, and Lisa Kings. 2014. "Reading the Stockholm Riots – A Moment for Social Justice?" *Race & Class* 55 (3): 1–21.

Schmidt, Stephanie. 2022. *Affekt und Polizei: Eine Ethnografie der Wut in der exekutiven Gewaltarbeit*. Berlin: Transcript Verlag.

Schmitt, Carl. [1932] 2008. *The Concept of the Political*. Chicago: University of Chicago Press.

Schoenfeld, Heather. 2018. *Building the Prison State: Race and the Politics of Mass Incarceration*. Chicago: University of Chicago Press.

Schoenfeld, Heather, Chas Walker, and Marielis Rosa. 2025. "Criminal Justice as Racialized Organizations: Evidence from Ethnographies of Police, Courts, and Jails." *Criminology* 63 (1): 122–54.

Schur, Edwin M. 1965. *Crimes Without Victims: Deviant Behavior and Public Policy – Abortion, Homosexuality, Drug Addiction*. Englewood Cliffs, NJ: Prentice-Hall.

Schwartz, Olivier. 1990. *Le Monde privé des ouvriers. Hommes et femmes du Nord*. Paris: PUF.

Schwarze, Tilman. 2022. "Discursive Practices of Territorial Stigmatization: How Newspapers Frame Violence and Crime in a Chicago Community." *Urban Geography* 43 (9): 1415–36.

Scott, James C. 1998. *Seeing Like a State: How Certain Schemes to Improve the Human Condition Have Failed*. New Haven, CT: Yale University Press.

Scott, Robert E. and William J. Stuntz. 1992. "Plea Bargaining as Contract." *Yale Law Journal* 101: 1909–68.

Scull, Andrew. 1977. *Decarceration: Community Treatment and the Deviant, a Radical View*. Englewood Cliffs, NJ: Prentice-Hall.

Seemann, Anika. 2021. "The Danish 'Ghetto Initiatives' and the Changing Nature of Social Citizenship, 2004–2018." *Critical Social Policy* 41 (4): 586–605.

Sellin, Thorsten. 1944. *Pioneering in Penology: The Amsterdam Houses of Correction in the Sixteenth and Seventeenth Centuries*. Philadelphia, PA: University of Pennsylvania Press.

Sellin, Thorsten. 1976. *Slavery and the Penal System*. New York: Elsevier.

Sellner, Nora. 2021. *Alltägliche Bewältigungspraxen obdachloser Menschen*. Berlin: Verlag Barbara Budrich.

Sen, Amartya. 1992. *Inequality Reexamined*. Oxford: Oxford University Press.

References

Sen, Amartya. 2009. *The Idea of Justice*. Cambridge, MA: Harvard University Press.

Sered, Danielle. 2019. *Until We Reckon: Violence, Mass Incarceration, and a Road to Repair*. New York: New Press.

Serre, Delphine. 2009. *Les Coulisses de l'État social. Enquête sur les signalements d'enfant en danger*. Paris: Raisons d'agir Éditions.

Shachar, Ayelet, Rainer Bauböck, Irene Bloemraad, and Maarten Vink (eds.). 2017. *The Oxford Handbook of Citizenship*. Oxford: Oxford University Press.

Shaffer, Hannah. 2023. "Prosecutors, Race, and the Criminal Pipeline." *University of Chicago Law Review* 90: 1889–965.

Shah, Nafisa. 2016. *Honour and Violence: Gender, Power and Law in Southern Pakistan*. New York: Berghahn.

Shammas, Victor Lund. 2014. "The Pains of Freedom: Assessing the Ambiguity of Scandinavian Penal Exceptionalism on Norway's Prison Island." *Punishment & Society* 16 (1): 104–23.

Shammas, Victor Lund. 2016a. "The Rise of a More Punitive State: On the Attenuation of Norwegian Penal Exceptionalism in an Era of Welfare State Transformation." *Critical Criminology* 24 (1): 57–74.

Shammas, Victor Lund. 2016b. "Who's Afraid of Penal Populism? Technocracy and 'the People' in the Sociology of Punishment." *Contemporary Justice Review* 19 (3): 325–46.

Shammas, Victor Lund. 2018. "Bourdieu's Five Lessons for Criminology." *Law & Critique* 29 (2): 201–19.

Shammas, Victor Lund. 2019. "The Perils of Parole Hearings: California Lifers, Performative Disadvantage, and the Ideology of Insight." *PoLAR: Political and Legal Anthropology Review* 42 (1): 142–60.

Shammas, Victor Lund and Sveinung Sandberg. 2016. "Habitus, Capital, and Conflict: Bringing Bourdieusian Field Theory to Criminology." *Criminology & Criminal Justice* 16 (2): 195–213.

Sharkey, Heather J. 2013. "African Colonial States." Pp. 151–70 in *The Oxford Handbook of Modern African History*. Edited by John Parker and Richard Reid. New York: Oxford University Press.

Sharkey, Patrick. 2018. *Uneasy Peace: The Great Crime Decline, the Renewal of City Life, and the Next War on Violence*. New York: Norton.

Shelby, Tommie. 2022. *The Idea of Prison Abolition*. Princeton, NJ: Princeton University Press.

Sherman, Lawrence W. and Heather Strang. 2012. "Restorative Justice as Evidence-Based Sentencing." Pp. 215–43 in *The Oxford Handbook of Sentencing and Corrections*. Edited by Joan Petersilia and Kevin R. Reitz. New York: Oxford University Press.

Sherman, Taylor C. 2009. "Tensions of Colonial Punishment: Perspectives on Recent Developments in the Study of Coercive Networks in Asia, Africa and the Caribbean." *History Compass* 7 (3): 659–77.

Sherman, Taylor C. 2010. *State Violence and Punishment in India*. London: Routledge.

Shiraishi, Takashi. 2021. *The Phantom World of Digul: Policing as Politics in Colonial Indonesia, 1926–1941*. Singapore: National University of Singapore Press.

Sieferle, Barbara. 2023. *Nach dem Gefängnis: Alltag und unsichtbare Bestrafungen*. Berlin: Transcript Verlag.

Sierra-Arévalo, Michael. 2024. *The Danger Imperative: Violence, Death, and the Soul of Policing*. New York: Columbia University Press.

Silver, Daniel. 2020. "Figure It Out!" *Sociological Methods & Research* 49 (4): 868–905.

Simes, Jessica T., Brenden Beck and John M. Eason. 2023. "Policing, Punishment, and Place: Spatial-Contextual Analyses of the Criminal Legal System." *Annual Review of Sociology* 49: 221–40.

Simon, Herbert A. 1957. *Models of Man*. New York: John Wiley.

Simon, Jonathan. 2007. *Governing Through Crime: How the War on Crime Transformed American Democracy and Created a Culture of Fear*. New York: Oxford University Press.

Simon, Jonathan. 2013. "Punishment and the Political Technologies of the Body." Pp. 60–89 in *The Sage Handbook of Punishment and Society*. Edited by Jonathan Simon and Richard Sparks. London: Sage.

Simon, Jonathan. 2014. *Mass Incarceration on Trial: A Remarkable Court Decision and the Future of Prisons in America*. New York: Free Press.

Simon, Jonathan. 2019. "For a Human Rights Approach to Reforming the American Penal State." *Journal of Human Rights Practice* 11 (2): 346–56.

Simon, Jonathan and Richard Sparks (eds.). 2013. *The Sage Handbook of Punishment and Society*. London: Sage.

Simonson, Jocelyn. 2019. "The Place of 'the People' in Criminal Procedure." *Columbia Law Review* 119 (1): 249–308.

Simonson, Jocelyn. 2023. *Radical Acts of Justice: How Ordinary People Are Dismantling Mass Incarceration*. New York: New Press.

Sinclair, Georgina. 2006. *At the End of the Line: Colonial Policing and the Imperial Endgame, 1945–80*. Manchester: Manchester University Press.

Sizaire, Vincent. 2016. *Sortir de l'imposture sécuritaire*. Paris: La Dispute.

Sklansky, David Alan. 2018. "The Problems with Prosecutors." *Annual Review of Criminology* 1: 451–69.

Slobodian, Quinn. 2020. *Globalists: The End of Empire and the Birth of Neoliberalism*. Cambridge, MA: Harvard University Press.

Slobogin, Christopher. 2024. "The Minimalist Alternative to Abolitionism: Focusing on the Non-Dangerous Many." *Vanderbilt Law Review* 77: 531–60.

Smart, Carol. 1989. *Feminism and the Power of Law*. London: Routledge.

Smiley, Calvin John. 2023. *Defund: Conversations toward Abolition*. Chicago: Haymarket Books.

460

References

Smith, Nicholas Rush. 2019. *Contradictions of Democracy: Vigilantism and Rights in Post-Apartheid South Africa*. New York: Oxford University Press.

Smith, Philip. 2008. *Punishment and Culture*. Chicago: University of Chicago Press.

Snacken, Sonja. 2021. "Human Dignity and Prisoners' Rights in Europe." *Crime & Justice* 50: 301–51.

Solhjell, Randi, Elsa Saarikkomäki, Mie Birk Haller, David Wästerfors, and Torsten Kolind. 2019. "'We Are Seen as a Threat': Police Stops of Young Ethnic Minorities in the Nordic Countries." *Critical Criminology* 27 (3): 347–61.

Sollund, Ragnhild. 2006. "Racialisation in Police Stop and Search Practice: The Norwegian Case." *Critical Criminology* 14 (3): 265–92.

Sombart, Werner. 1906. *Warum gibt es in den Vereinigten Staaten keinen Sozialismus?* Tubingen: J.C.B. Mohr.

Soss, Joe and Vesla Weaver. 2017. "Police Are Our Government: Politics, Political Science, and the Policing of Race–Class Subjugated Communities." *Annual Review of Political Science* 20: 565–91.

Soss, Joe, Richard C. Fording, and Sanford Schram. 2011. *Disciplining the Poor: Neoliberal Paternalism and the Persistent Power of Race*. Chicago: University of Chicago Press.

Spierenburg, Pieter. 1984. *The Spectacle of Suffering: Executions and the Evolution of Repression – From a Preindustrial Metropolis to the European Experience*. Cambridge: Cambridge University Press.

Spierenburg, Pieter. 1991. *The Prison Experience: Disciplinary Institutions and their Inmates in Early Modern Europe*. New Brunswick, NJ: Rutgers University Press.

Spierenburg, Pieter. 1996. "Four Centuries of Prison History: Punishment, Suffering, the Body, and Power." Pp. 17–35 in *Institutions of Confinement: Hospitals, Asylums, and Prisons in Western Europe and North America, 1500–1950*. Edited by Norbert Finzsch and Robert Jütte. Cambridge: Cambridge University Press.

Spierenburg, Pieter. 2004. "Punishment, Power, and History: Foucault and Elias." *Social Science History* 28 (4): 607–36.

Spitzer, Steven. 1975. "Toward a Marxian Theory of Deviance." *Social Problems* 22 (5): 638–51.

Spohn, Cassia. 2009. *How Do Judges Decide: The Search for Fairness and Justice in Punishment*. Newbury Park, CA: Sage.

Spohn, Cassia. 2014. "Racial Disparities in Prosecution, Sentencing and Punishment." Pp. 166–93 in *The Oxford Handbook of Ethnicity, Crime, and Immigration*. Edited by Sandra M. Bucerius and Michael H. Tonry. Oxford: Oxford University Press.

Spohn, Cassia. 2015. "Race, Crime, and Punishment in the Twentieth and Twenty-First Centuries." *Crime & Justice* 44: 49–97.

Spohn, Cassia. 2021. "Specialized Units and Vertical Prosecution

Approaches." Pp. 259–71 in *The Oxford Handbook of Prosecutors and Prosecution*. Edited by Ronald F. Wright, Kay L. Levine, and Russell M. Gold. New York: Oxford University Press.

Squires, Peter and John Lea (eds.). 2012. *Criminalisation and Advanced Marginality: Critically Exploring the Work of Loïc Wacquant*. Bristol: Policy Press.

St. Louis, Stacie. 2024. "The Pretrial Detention Penalty: A Systematic Review and Meta-Analysis of Pretrial Detention and Case Outcomes." *Justice Quarterly* 41 (3): 347–70.

Stansfield, Richard and Karen F. Parker. 2025. "A Neighborhood Analysis of US Homicide Clearances in 50 Cities: Examining Race and Disadvantage across Neighborhood Types." *Journal of Criminal Justice* 98: online first.

Stanziani, Alessandro. 2018. *Labor on the Fringes of Empire: Voice, Exit and the Law*. London: Palgrave Macmillan.

Stedman Jones, Gareth. 1971. *Outcast London: A Study in the Relationship Between Classes in Victorian Society*. Oxford: Clarendon Press.

Steger, Manfred B. and Ravi K. Roy. 2021. *Neoliberalism: A Very Short Introduction*. Oxford: Oxford University Press.

Steidley, Trent and David M. Ramey. 2019. "Police Militarization in the United States." *Sociology Compass* 13 (4): e12674.

Steinmetz George. 2008a. "The Colonial State as a Social Field." *American Sociological Review* 73 (3): 589–61.

Steinmetz, George. 2008b. *The Devil's Handwriting: Precoloniality and the German Colonial State in Qingdao, Samoa, and Southwest Africa*. Chicago: University of Chicago Press.

Steinmetz, George. 2014. "The Sociology of Empires, Colonies, and Postcolonialism." *Annual Review of Sociology* 40: 77–103.

Steinmetz, George. 2016. "Social Fields, Subfields and Social Spaces at the Scale of Empires: Explaining the Colonial State and Colonial Sociology." *The Sociological Review* 64 (2): 98–123.

Stemen, Don and Gipsy Escobar. 2018. "Whither the Prosecutor? Prosecutor and County Effects on Guilty Plea Outcomes in Wisconsin." *Justice Quarterly* 35 (7): 1166–94.

Stenson, Kevin and David Cowell (eds.). 1991. *The Politics of Crime Control*. London: Sage.

Stitt, Mary Ellen. 2025. *Trial by Treatment: Punishing Illness in an Age of Criminal Legal Reform*. Chicago: University of Chicago Press.

Story, Brett. 2016. "The Prison in the City: Tracking the Neoliberal Life of the 'Million Dollar Block'." *Theoretical Criminology* 20 (3): 257–76.

Stuart, Forrest. 2016. *Down, Out, and Under Arrest: Policing and Everyday Life in Skid Row*. Chicago: University of Chicago Press.

Stuart, Forrest and Reuben Jonathan Miller. 2017. "The Prisonized Old Head: Intergenerational Socialization and the Fusion of Ghetto and Prison Culture." *Journal of Contemporary Ethnography* 46 (6): 673–98.

References

Stuart, Forrest, Amada Armenta, and Melissa Osborne. 2015. "Legal Control of Marginal Groups." *Annual Review of Law and Social Science* 11 (1): 235–54.

Stuntz, William J. 2011. *The Collapse of American Criminal Justice*. Cambridge, MA: Belknap Press.

Sue, Derald Wing and Lisa Spanierman. 2020. *Microaggressions in Everyday Life*. New York: Wiley.

Super, Gail. 2016. *Governing through Crime in South Africa: The Politics of Race and Class in Neoliberalizing Regimes*. London: Routledge.

Sutherland, Edwin H. 1940. "White Collar Criminality." *American Sociological Review* 5 (1): 1–12.

Sutton, John R. 2013. "Structural Bias in the Sentencing of Felony Defendants." *Social Science Research* 42 (5): 1207–21.

Swanson, Jacob, and Mary Fainsod Katzenstein. 2025. "From the Battlefield to Behind Bars: Rethinking the Relationship between the Military- and Prison-Industrial Complexes." *Daedalus* 154 (4): 295–311.

Swedberg, Richard. 2018. "How to Use Max Weber's Ideal Type in Sociological Analysis." *Journal of Classical Sociology* 18 (3): 181–96.

Tafferant, Nasser. 2007. *Le Bizness. Une économie souterraine*. Paris: PUF.

Talpin, Julien. 2024. *La Colère des quartiers populaires. Enquête socio-historique à Roubaix*. Paris: PUF.

Tannenbaum, Frank. 1938. *Crime and the Community*. New York: Columbia University Press.

Tavory, Iddo and Stefan Timmermans. 2014. *Abductive Analysis: Theorizing Qualitative Research*. Chicago: University of Chicago Press.

Taxman, Faye. 2012. "Probation, Intermediate Sanctions, and Community-Based Corrections." Pp. 363–86 in *The Oxford Handbook of Sentencing and Corrections*. Edited by Joan Petersilia and Kevin R. Reitz. New York: Oxford University Press.

Taylor, Keeanga-Yamahtta. 2021. "The Emerging Movement for Police and Prison Abolition." *The New Yorker*, May 7.

Taylor, Mac. 2013. *California's Criminal Justice: A Primer*. Sacramento, CA: Legislative Analyst's Office.

Thénault, Sylvie. 2004. *Une drôle de justice. Les magistrats dans la guerre d'Algérie*. Paris: La Découverte.

Thénault, Sylvie. 2012. *Violence ordinaire dans l'Algérie coloniale. Camps, internements, assignations à résidence*. Paris: Odile Jacob.

Thénault, Sylvie. 2017. "L'indigénat dans l'Empire français. Algérie/Cochinchine, une double matrice." *Monde(s)* 12 (2): 21–40.

Therborn, Göran. 2013. *The Killing Fields of Inequality*. Cambridge: Polity.

Thomas, Martin. 2012. *Violence and Colonial Order: Police, Workers and Protest in the European Colonial Empires, 1918–1940*. New York: Cambridge University Press.

References

Thomas, W. Robert. 2023. "Does the State Have an Obligation Not to Enforce the Law?" *Washington University Law Review* 101: 1883–913.

Thompson, E.P. 1975. *Whigs and Hunters: The Origin of the Black Act.* London: Allen Lane.

Thompson, Heather Ann and Donna Murch. 2015. "Rethinking Urban America through the Lens of the Carceral State." *Journal of Urban History* 41 (5): 751–5.

Tilly, Charles. 1989. "Cities and States in Europe, 1000–1800." *Theory & Society* 18 (5): 563–84.

Tilly, Charles. 1993. *Coercion, Capital, and European States, AD 990–1990.* Cambridge, MA: Blackwell.

Tilly, Charles. 1998. *Durable Inequality.* Berkeley: University of California Press.

Tiquet, Romain. 2019a. "Connecting the 'Inside' and the 'Outside' World: Convict Labour and Mobile Penal Camps in Colonial Senegal (1930s–1950s)." *International Review of Social History* 64 (3): 473–91.

Tiquet, Romain. 2019b. *Travail forcé et mobilisation de la main d'oeuvre au Sénégal.* Rennes: Presses Universitaires de Rennes.

Tonry, Michael. 1995. *Malign Neglect: Race, Crime, and Punishment in America.* New York: Oxford University Press.

Tonry, Michael (ed.). 2004. *The Future of Imprisonment.* New York: Oxford University Press.

Tonry, Michael (ed.). 2010. *Why Punish? How Much? A Reader on Punishment.* Oxford: Oxford University Press.

Tonry, Michael. 2012. "Prosecutors and Politics in Comparative Perspective." *Crime and Justice* 41: 1–33.

Tonry, Michael. 2013. "Sentencing in America, 1975–2025." *Crime & Justice* 42: 141–98.

Tonry, Michael. 2016. *Sentencing Fragments: Penal Reform in America, 1975–2025.* New York: Oxford University Press.

Tonry, Michael. 2022. "Punishments, Politics, and Prisons in Western Countries." *Crime & Justice* 51: 7–57.

Travers, Max. 2021. "Court Ethnographies." Pp. 512–29 in *The Oxford Handbook of Ethnographies of Crime and Criminal Justice.* Edited by Sandra M. Bucerius, Kevin D. Haggerty, and Luca Berardi. New York: Oxford University Press.

Tripkovic, Milena. 2019. *Punishment and Citizenship: A Theory of Criminal Disenfranchisement.* New York: Oxford University Press.

Truong, Fabien. 2017. *Loyautés radicales. L'Islam et les "mauvais garçons" de la nation.* Paris: La Découverte.

Truong, Fabien and Gérôme Truc. 2025. *Grands ensemble. Violence, solidarité et ressentiment dans les quartiers populaires.* Paris: La Découverte.

Tuğal, Cihan. 2021. "Populism Studies: The Case for Theoretical and Comparative Reconstruction." *Annual Review of Sociology* 47: 327–47.

References

Turner, Bryan S. 1981. "Theodicy: The Career of a Concept." Pp. 142–76 in *For Weber: Essays in the Sociology of Fate*. London: Sage.

Tyler, Tom R. 2023. "Whither Legitimacy? Legal Authority in the Twenty-First Century." *Annual Review of Law & Social Science* 19: 1–17.

Ugelvik, Thomas. 2017. "The Incarceration of Foreigners in European Prisons." Pp. 107–20 in *The Routledge Handbook on Crime and International Migration*. Edited by Sharon Pickering and Julie Ham. Abingdon: Routledge.

Ugelvik, Thomas and Jane Dullum (eds.). 2011. *Penal Exceptionalism? Nordic Prison Policy and Practice*. London: Routledge.

Uhnoo, Sara. 2015. "Within 'The Tin Bubble': The Police and Ethnic Minorities in Sweden. *Policing and Society* 25 (2): 129–49.

Ulmen, Gary L. 1985. "The Sociology of the State: Carl Schmitt and Max Weber." *State, Culture & Society* 1 (2): 3–57.

Ulmer, Jeffery T. 1997. *Social Worlds of Sentencing: Court Communities Under Sentencing Guidelines*. Stony Brook, NY: SUNY Press.

Ulmer, Jeffery T. 2019. "Criminal Courts as Inhabited Institutions: Making Sense of Difference and Similarity in Sentencing." *Crime & Justice* 48: 483–522.

Utz, Pamela J. 1978. *Settling the Facts: Discretion and Negotiation in Criminal Court*. Lexington, KY: Lexington Books.

Van Cleve, Nicole Gonzalez. 2016. *Crook County: Racism and Injustice in America's Largest Criminal Court*. Stanford, CA: Stanford University Press.

Van Cleve, Nicole Gonzalez and Lauren Mayes. 2015. "Criminal Justice through 'Colorblind' Lenses: A Call to Examine the Mutual Constitution of Race and Criminal Justice." *Law & Social Inquiry* 40 (2): 406–32.

van der Linden, Marcel. 2019. "The Social Question in Western Europe: Past and Present." Pp. 23–39 in *The Social Question in the Twenty-First Century: A Global View*. Edited by Jan Breman, Kevan Harris, Ching Kwan Lee, and Marcel van der Linden. Berkeley: University of California Press.

Van Waijenburg, Marlous. 2018. "Financing the African Colonial State: The Revenue Imperative and Forced Labor." *The Journal of Economic History* 78 (1): 40–80.

Varella, Drauzio. 2005. *Estação Carandiru*. São Paulo: Companhia das Letras.

Vernant, Jean-Pierre. 1962. *Les Origines de la pensée grecque*. Paris: PUF.

Vigour, Cécile, Bartolomeo Cappellina, Laurence Dumoulin, and Virginie Gautron. 2022. *La Justice en examen. Attentes et expériences citoyennes*. Paris: PUF.

Villarreal, Ana. 2024. *The Two Faces of Fear: Violence and Inequality in the Mexican Metropolis*. New York: Oxford University Press.

Visher, Christy and Jill Farrell. 2005. *Chicago Communities and Prisoner Reentry*. Washington, DC: Urban Institute.

Vogel, Mary E. 2007. *Coercion to Compromise: Plea Bargaining, the Courts, and the Making of Political Authority*. Oxford: Oxford University Press.

465

References

Volpe, Patrizia Pacini. 2022. *Il carcere, un luogo dimenticato. Una ricerca sociologia tra Italia e Francia*. Pisa: Pisa University Press.

Vom Hau, Matthias. 2015. "State Theory." Pp. 131–51 in *The Oxford Handbook of Transformations of the State*. Edited by Stephan Leibfried, Evelyne Huber, Matthew Lange, Jonah D. Levy, and John D. Stephens. Oxford: Oxford University Press.

von Hirsch, Andrew. 1999. "Penal Theories." Pp. 659–83 in *The Handbook of Crime and Punishment*. Edited by Michael Tonry. New York: Oxford University Press.

von Mahs, Jürgen. 2013. *Down and Out in Los Angeles and Berlin: The Sociospatial Exclusion of Homeless People*. Philadelphia, PA: Temple University Press.

von Schriltz, Karl. 1999. "Foucault on the Prison: Torturing History to Punish Capitalism." *Critical Review* 13 (3–4): 391–411.

Wachsmann, Nikolaus. 2015. *Hitler's Prisons: Legal Terror in Nazi Germany*. New Haven, CT: Yale University Press.

Wacquant, Loïc. [2004] 2022. *Body and Soul: Notebooks of an Apprentice Boxer*. Expanded anniversary edition. New York: Oxford University Press.

Wacquant, Loïc. 2008. *Urban Outcasts: A Comparative Sociology of Advanced Marginality*. Cambridge: Polity Press.

Wacquant, Loïc. 2009a. *Prisons of Poverty*. Minneapolis, MN: University of Minnesota Press.

Wacquant, Loïc. 2009b. *Punishing the Poor: The Neoliberal Government of Social Insecurity*. Durham, NC: Duke University Press.

Wacquant, Loïc. 2010a. "Class, Race and Hyperincarceration in Revanchist America." *Daedalus* 139 (3): 74–90.

Wacquant, Loïc. 2010b. "Crafting the Neoliberal State: Workfare, Prisonfare, and Social Insecurity." *Sociological Forum* 25 (2): 197–220.

Wacquant, Loïc. 2010c. "Designing Urban Seclusion in the Twenty-First Century: The 2009 Roth-Symonds Lecture." *Perspecta: The Yale Architectural Journal* 43: 164–75.

Wacquant, Loïc. 2010d. "Prisoner Reentry as Myth and Ceremony." *Dialectical Anthropology* 34: 605–20.

Wacquant, Loïc. 2011. "Habitus as Topic and Tool: Reflections on Becoming a Prizefighter." *Qualitative Research in Psychology* 8 (1): 81–92.

Wacquant, Loïc. 2012a. "The Wedding of Workfare and Prisonfare in the 21st Century." *Journal of Poverty* 16 (3): 236–49.

Wacquant, Loïc. 2012b. "Three Steps to a Historical Anthropology of Actually Existing Neoliberalism." *Social Anthropology/Anthropologie Sociale* 20 (1): 66–79.

Wacquant, Loïc. 2015. "For a Sociology of Flesh and Blood." *Qualitative Sociology* 38 (1): 1–11.

Wacquant, Loïc. 2016. "A Concise Genealogy and Anatomy of Habitus." *The Sociological Review* 64 (1): 64–72.

References

Wacquant, Loïc. 2022. *The Invention of the "Underclass": A Study in the Politics of Knowledge*. Cambridge: Polity Press.

Wacquant, Loïc. 2023. *Bourdieu in the City: Challenging Urban Theory*. Cambridge: Polity Press.

Wacquant, Loïc. [2023] 2025. *The Poverty of the Ethnography of Poverty*. New York: Oxford University Press.

Wacquant, Loïc. 2024a. *Jim Crow. Le terrorisme de caste en Amérique*. Paris: Raisons d'agir Éditions.

Wacquant, Loïc. 2024b. *Racial Domination*. Cambridge: Polity Press.

Wacquant, Loïc. 2025. "In Praise of 'Thick Construction'." *Qualitative Sociology* 48 (3): 435–45.

Wacquant, Loïc. 2026. "Sealing the Fate of the 'Kid': A Field Note on the Swirl of Plea Bargaining." *Punishment & Society*, https://doi.org/10.1177/14624745251378634.

Wacquant, Loïc. Forthcoming. *The Two Faces of the Ghetto*. Cambridge: Polity Press.

Wacquant, Loïc, Tom Slater and Virgílio Borges Pereira. 2014. "Territorial Stigmatization in Action." *Environment & Planning A* 46 (6): 1270–80.

Wakefield, Sara and Christopher Uggen. 2010. "Incarceration and Stratification." *Annual Review of Sociology* 36: 387–406.

Walker, Michael L. 2016. "Race Making in a Penal Institution." *American Journal of Sociology* 121 (4): 1051–78.

Walker, Michael L. 2022. *Indefinite: Doing Time in Jail*. New York: Oxford University Press.

Wästerfors, David and Veronika Burcar Alm. 2020. "'They are Harsher to Me than to my Friend Who is Blonde'. Police Critique among Ethnic Minority Youth in Sweden." *Journal of Youth Studies* 23 (2): 170–88.

Watkins-Hayes, Celeste. 2009. *The New Welfare Bureaucrats: Entanglements of Race, Class and Policy Reform*. Chicago: University of Chicago Press.

Weaver, Vesla Mae. 2007. *Frontlash: Race and the Politics of Punishment*. Cambridge, MA: Harvard University Press.

Weber, Benjamin D. 2023. *American Purgatory: Prison Imperialism and the Rise of Mass Incarceration*. New York: New Press.

Weber, Max. [1904–1905] 1930. *The Protestant Ethic and the Spirit of Capitalism*. Boston: Unwin Hyman.

Weber, Max. [1917, 1919] 2003. *Le Savant et le politique, une nouvelle traduction*. Translated and introduced by Catherine Colliot-Thélène. Paris: La Découverte.

Weber, Max. [1920] 1978. *Economy and Society: An Outline of Interpretive Sociology*. Berkeley: University of California Press.

Weber, Max. [1920] 1993. *The Sociology of Religion*. Boston, MA: Beacon Press.

Weber, Max. 1948. *From Max Weber: Essays in Sociology*. Edited by Hans Gerth and C. Wright Mills. New York: Oxford University Press.

References

Weber, Max. 1949. *The Methodology of the Social Sciences.* Glencoe, IL: Free Press.

Weber, Max. 1954. *On Law in Economy and Society.* Cambridge, MA: Harvard University Press.

Weed, Frank. 1995. *Certainty of Justice: Reform in the Crime Victim Movement.* New York: De Gruyter.

Werth, Robert. 2012. "I Do What I'm Told, Sort Of: Reformed Subjects, Unruly Citizens, and Parole." *Theoretical Criminology* 16 (3): 329–46.

Western, Bruce. 2006. *Punishment and Inequality in America.* New York: Russell Sage Foundation.

Western, Bruce. 2018. *Homeward: Life in the Year After Prison.* New York: Russell Sage Foundation.

Western, Bruce and David J. Harding. 2022. "Careers in Criminalization: Reentry, Recidivism, and Repeated Incarceration." *Crime & Justice* 51: 435–69.

Whitman, James Q. 2008. *The Origins of Reasonable Doubt: Theological Roots of the Criminal Trial.* New Haven, CT: Yale University Press.

Wice, Paul B. 1978. *Criminal Lawyers: An Endangered Species.* Beverly Hills, CA: Sage.

Wice, Paul B. 2005. *Public Defenders and the American Justice System.* Greenwood, CT: Praeger.

Wiener, Martin Joel. 1994. *Reconstructing the Criminal: Culture, Law, and Policy in England, 1830–1914.* Cambridge: Cambridge University Press.

Wihtol de Wenden, Catherine. 2013. "Le contact des civilisations. Migrations et peur de l'Autre en France." *Anatoli* 4: 153–66.

Wildeman, Christopher and Robert J. Sampson. 2024. "Desistance as an Intergenerational Process." *Annual Review of Criminology* 7: 85–104.

Williamson, Oliver. 1975. *Markets and Hierarchies: Analysis and Antitrust Implications.* New York: Free Press.

Willis, Graham Denyer. 2015. *The Killing Consensus: Police, Organized Crime, and the Regulation of Life and Death in Urban Brazil.* Berkeley: University of California Press.

Willrich, Michael. 2003. *City of Courts: Socializing Justice in Progressive Era Chicago.* New York: Cambridge University Press.

Wilson, Conor. 2024. "Trading Crime for Culture? Activating Territorial Stigma through Cultural Regeneration in Paisley." *Urban Geography* 45 (9): 1661–80.

Wilson, William Julius. [1987] 2012. *The Truly Disadvantaged: The Underclass, the Inner City and Public Policy.* Chicago: University of Chicago Press.

Wimmer, Andreas. 2013. *Ethnic Boundary Making: Institutions, Power, Networks.* New York: Oxford University Press.

Wimmer, Andreas. 2015. "Race-Centrism: A Critique and a Research Agenda." *Ethnic & Racial Studies* 38 (13): 2186–205.

Worrall, John L. 2008. "Prosecutors in Problem-Solving Courts." Pp. 231–44 in *The Changing Role of the American Prosecutor*. Edited by John Worrall and M. Elaine Nugent-Borakove. Stony Brook, NY: SUNY Press.

Wright, Erik Olin. 1997. *Class Counts: Comparative Studies in Class Analysis*. Cambridge: Cambridge University Press.

Wright, Erik Olin. 2013. "Transforming Capitalism through Real Utopias." *American Sociological Review* 78 (1): 1–25.

Wright, Megan S., Shima Baradaran Baughman, and Christopher Robertson. 2022. "Inside the Black Box of Prosecutor Discretion." *UC Davis Law Review* 55: 2133–208.

Wright, Richard T. and Scott H. Decker. 1997. *Armed Robbers in Action: Stick-ups and Street Culture*. Boston, MA: Northeastern University Press.

Wright, Ronald F. 2017. "Reinventing American Prosecution Systems." *Crime & Justice* 46: 395–439.

Wright, Ronald F. and Kay L. Levine. 2014. "The Cure for Young Prosecutors' Syndrome." *Arizona Law Review* 56: 1065–128.

Wright, Ronald F. and Kay L. Levine. 2016. "Place Matters in Prosecution Research." *Ohio State Journal of Criminal Law* 14: 675–703.

Wright, Ronald F. and Kay L. Levine. 2018. "Career Motivations of State Prosecutors." *George Washington Law Review* 86 (6): 1667–710.

Wright, Ronald and Jenny Roberts. 2023. "Expanded Criminal Defense Lawyering." *Annual Review of Criminology* 6: 241–64.

Wright, Ronald F., Kay L. Levine, and Marc L. Miller. 2014. "The Many Faces of Prosecution." *Stanford Journal of Criminal Law & Policy* 1: 27–47.

Wright, Ronald F., Kay L. Levine, and Russell M. Gold (eds.). 2021. *The Oxford Handbook of Prosecutors and Prosecution*. New York: Oxford University Press.

Wu, Jawjeong. 2016. "Racial/Ethnic Discrimination and Prosecution: A Meta-Analysis." *Criminal Justice and Behavior* 43 (4): 437–58.

Yang, Anand A. 2021. *Empire of Convicts: Indian Penal Labor in Colonial Southeast Asia*. Berkeley: University of California Press.

Yllö, Kersti and M. Gabriela Torres (eds.). 2016. *Marital Rape: Consent, Marriage, and Social Change in Global Context*. New York: Oxford University Press.

Young, Crawford. 1994. *The African Colonial State in Comparative Perspective*. New Haven, CT: Yale University Press.

Young, Iris Marion. 1990. *Justice and the Politics of Difference*. Princeton, NJ: Princeton University Press.

Young, Jock. 1999. *The Exclusive Society: Social Exclusion, Crime and Difference in Late Modernity*. London: Sage.

Young, Jock. 2007. *The Vertigo of Late Modernity*. London: Sage.

Zacka, Bernardo. 2017. *When the State Meets the Street: Public Service and Moral Agency*. Cambridge, MA: Harvard University Press.

Zarinebaf, Fariba. 2010. *Crime and Punishment in Istanbul, 1700–1800*. Berkeley: University of California Press.

469

References

Zimring, Franklin E. 2007. *The Great American Crime Decline*. New York: Oxford University Press.

Zimring, Franklin E. 2023. *The Insidious Momentum of American Mass Incarceration*. New York: Oxford University Press.

Zimring, Franklin E., Gordon Hawkins, and Sam Kamin. 2001. *Punishment and Democracy: Three Strikes and You're Out in California*. New York: Oxford University Press.

Zinoman, Peter. 2001. *The Colonial Bastille: A History of Imprisonment in Vietnam, 1862–1940*. Berkeley: University of California Press.

Index of Names

Index of Notions

Page numbers in *italics* refer to figures and tables;
* indicates folk concepts.

481

483

484

493

494

509